THE ADVENTURE ZONE

The Eleventh Hour

THE ADVENTURE ZONE

The Eleventh Hour

Based on the podcast by

Griffin McElroy   Clint McElroy

Travis McElroy   Justin McElroy

Adaptation by

Clint McElroy   Carey Pietsch

Griffin McElroy

Art by

Carey Pietsch

First Second

New York

First Second

Text © 2023 by Clint McElroy, Griffin McElroy, Justin McElroy, Travis McElroy
Illustrations © 2023 by Carey Pietsch

Letterer: Tess Stone
Flatters: Ensley Chau, Leigh Davis, Cassandra Tassoni
Authenticity Reader: Ryan Douglass
Crystal Kingdom Summary Illustration © 2023 by Natalie Riess

Published by First Second
First Second is an imprint of Roaring Brook Press,
a division of Holtzbrinck Publishing Holdings Limited Partnership
120 Broadway, New York, NY 10271

Don't miss your next favorite book from First Second!
For the latest updates go to firstsecondnewsletter.com and sign up for our enewsletter.

Library of Congress Control Number: 2022938139
Hardcover ISBN: 978-1-250-79379-9
Paperback ISBN: 978-1-250-79378-2
Special Edition ISBN: 978-1-250-88237-0
Special Edition ISBN: 978-1-250-88236-3
Special Edition ISBN: 978-1-250-88235-6

Our books may be purchased in bulk for promotional, educational, or business use.
Please contact your local bookseller or the Macmillan Corporate and Premium Sales Department
at (800) 221-7945 ext. 5442 or by email at MacmillanSpecialMarkets@macmillan.com.

First edition, 2023
Edited by Calista Brill and Benjamin A. Wilgus
Cover design by Kirk Benshoff and Carey Pietsch
Series design by Andrew Arnold
Interior book design by Molly Johanson
Production editing by Helen Seachrist

Printed in China

Penciled with a 2B pencil-style tool in Procreate.
Inked with a brush-style digital nib in Clip Studio Paint and colored digitally in Photoshop.

Paperback: 10 9 8 7 6 5 4 3 2 1
Hardcover: 10 9 8 7 6 5 4 3 2 1

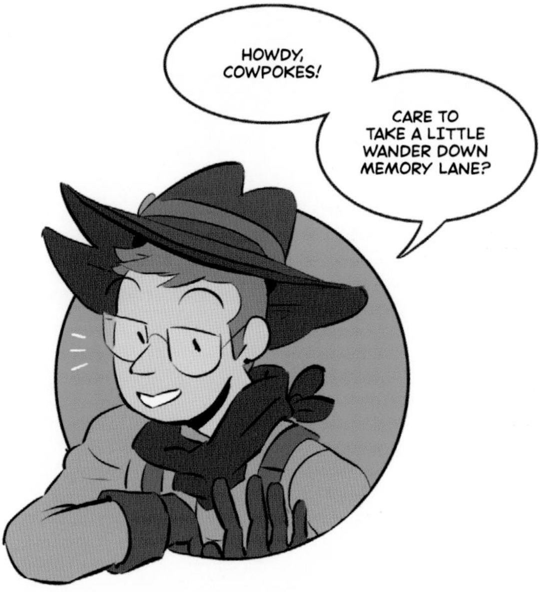
HOWDY, COWPOKES!
CARE TO TAKE A LITTLE WANDER DOWN MEMORY LANE?

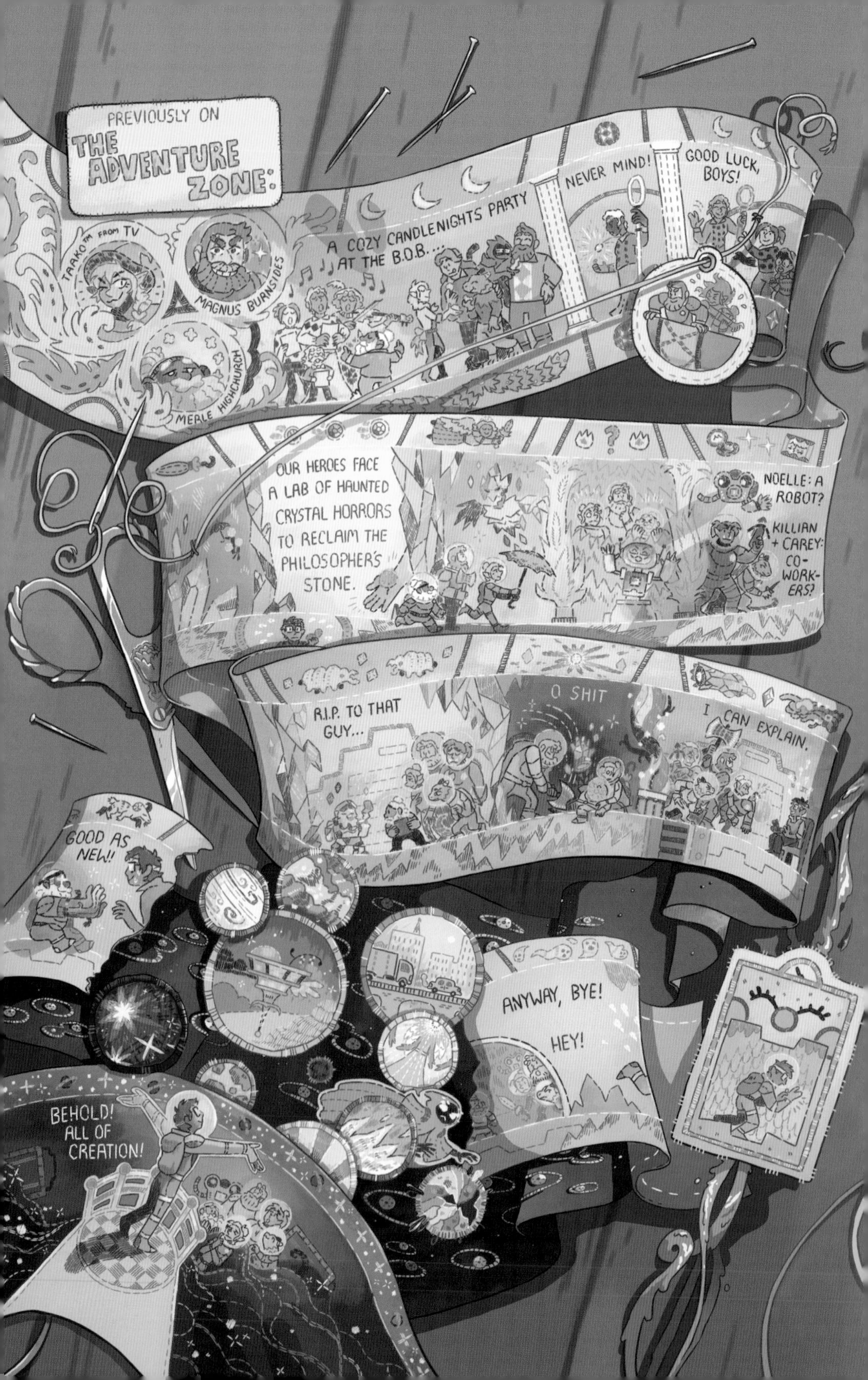
PREVIOUSLY ON
THE ADVENTURE ZONE:
TAAKO™ FROM TV
MAGNUS BURNSIDES
MERLE HIGHCHURCH
A COZY CANDLENIGHTS PARTY AT THE B.O.B. ...
NEVER MIND!
GOOD LUCK, BOYS!
OUR HEROES FACE A LAB OF HAUNTED CRYSTAL HORRORS TO RECLAIM THE PHILOSOPHER'S STONE.
NOELLE: A ROBOT?
KILLIAN + CAREY: CO-WORKERS?
R.I.P. TO THAT GUY...
O SHIT
I CAN EXPLAIN.
GOOD AS NEW!!
ANYWAY, BYE!
HEY!
BEHOLD! ALL OF CREATION!

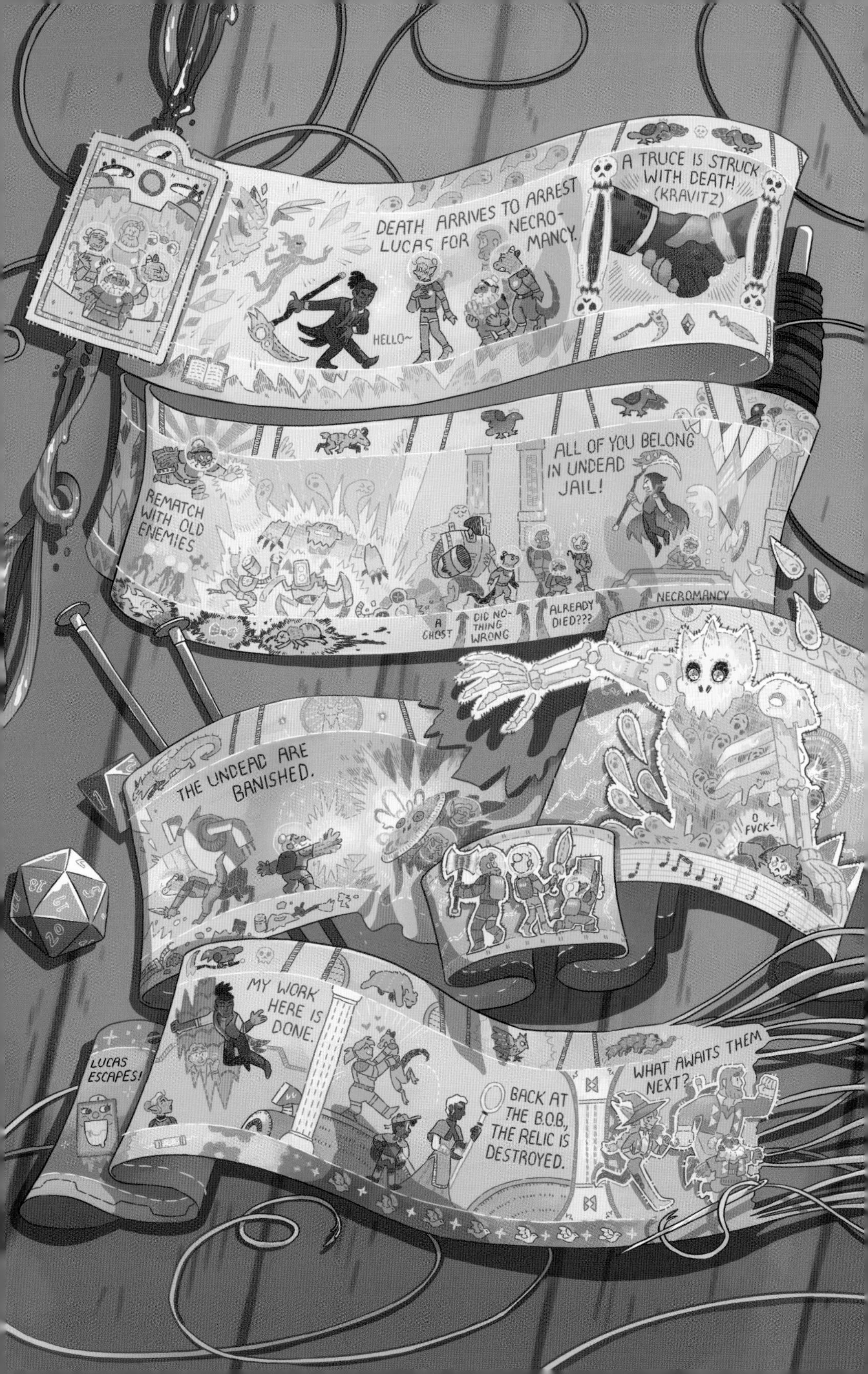

DEATH ARRIVES TO ARREST LUCAS FOR NECRO-MANCY.
HELLO~
A TRUCE IS STRUCK WITH DEATH (KRAVITZ)
REMATCH WITH OLD ENEMIES
ALL OF YOU BELONG IN UNDEAD JAIL!
A GHOST
DID NO-THING WRONG
ALREADY DIED???
NECROMANCY
THE UNDEAD ARE BANISHED.
O FVCK-
MY WORK HERE IS DONE.
LUCAS ESCAPES!
BACK AT THE B.O.B., THE RELIC IS DESTROYED.
WHAT AWAITS THEM NEXT?

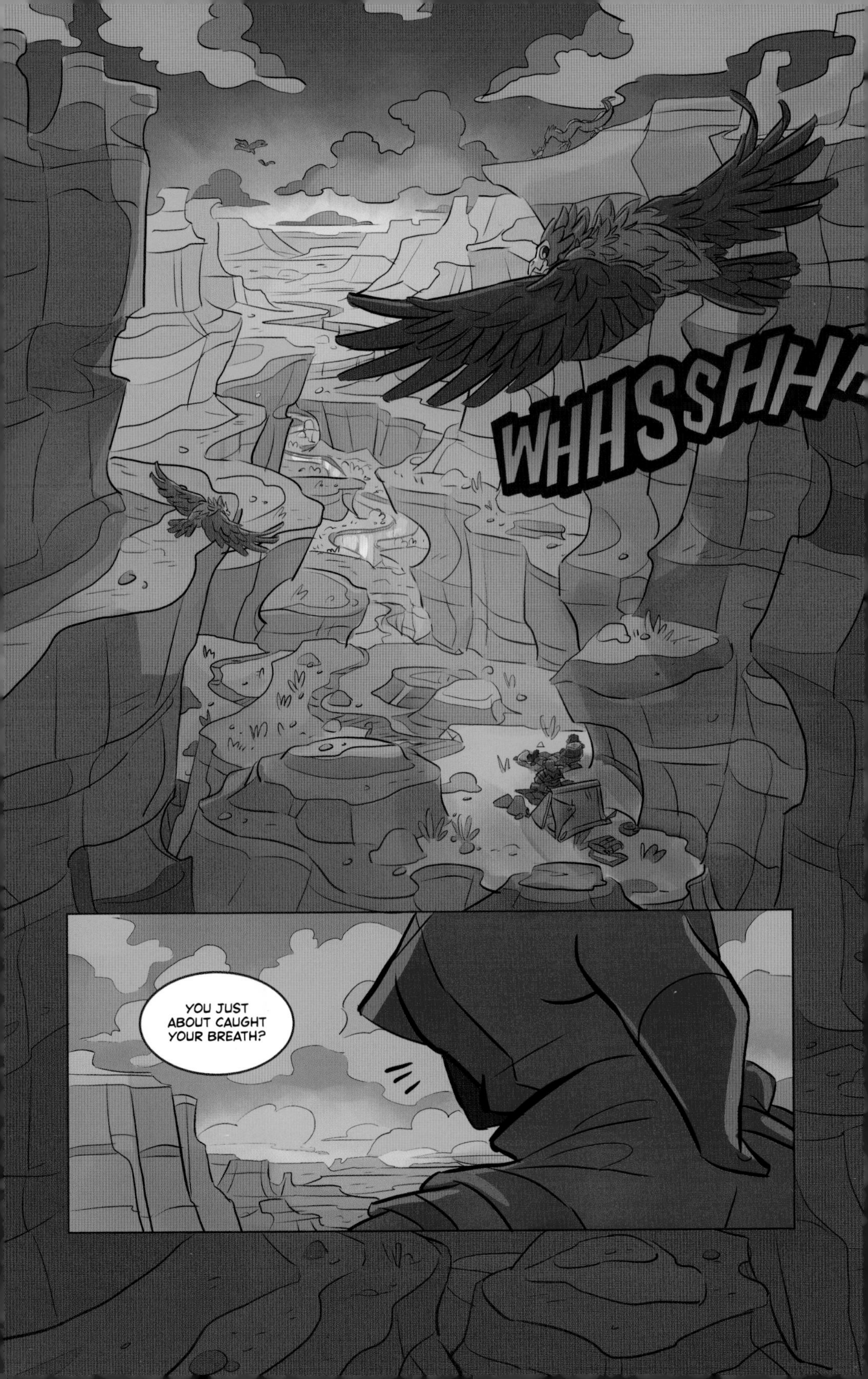
WHHSSHH
YOU JUST ABOUT CAUGHT YOUR BREATH?

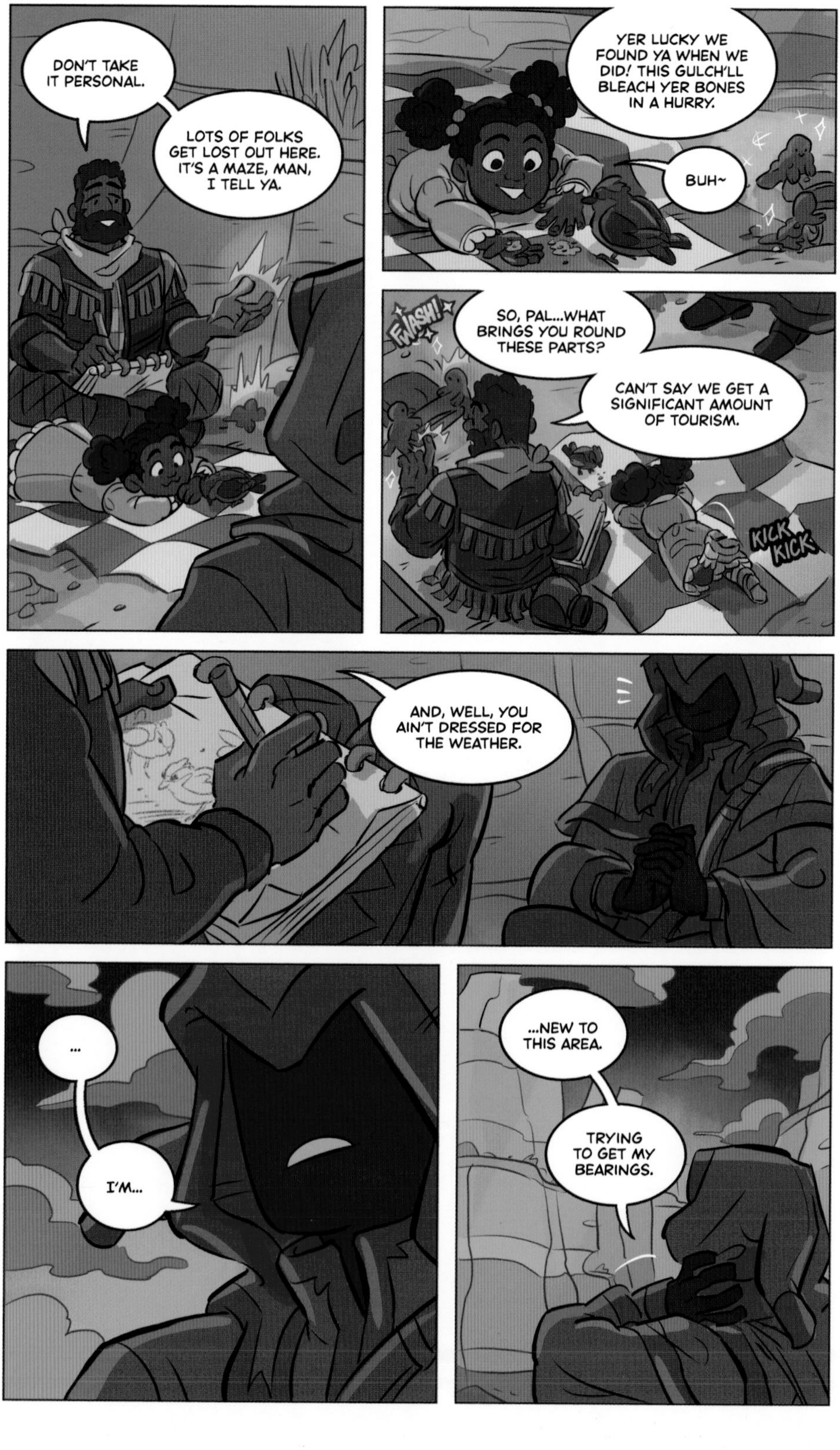
DON'T TAKE IT PERSONAL.
LOTS OF FOLKS GET LOST OUT HERE. IT'S A MAZE, MAN, I TELL YA.
YER LUCKY WE FOUND YA WHEN WE DID! THIS GULCH'LL BLEACH YER BONES IN A HURRY.
BUH~
FWASH!
SO, PAL...WHAT BRINGS YOU ROUND THESE PARTS?
CAN'T SAY WE GET A SIGNIFICANT AMOUNT OF TOURISM.
KICK KICK
AND, WELL, YOU AIN'T DRESSED FOR THE WEATHER.
...
I'M...
...NEW TO THIS AREA.
TRYING TO GET MY BEARINGS.

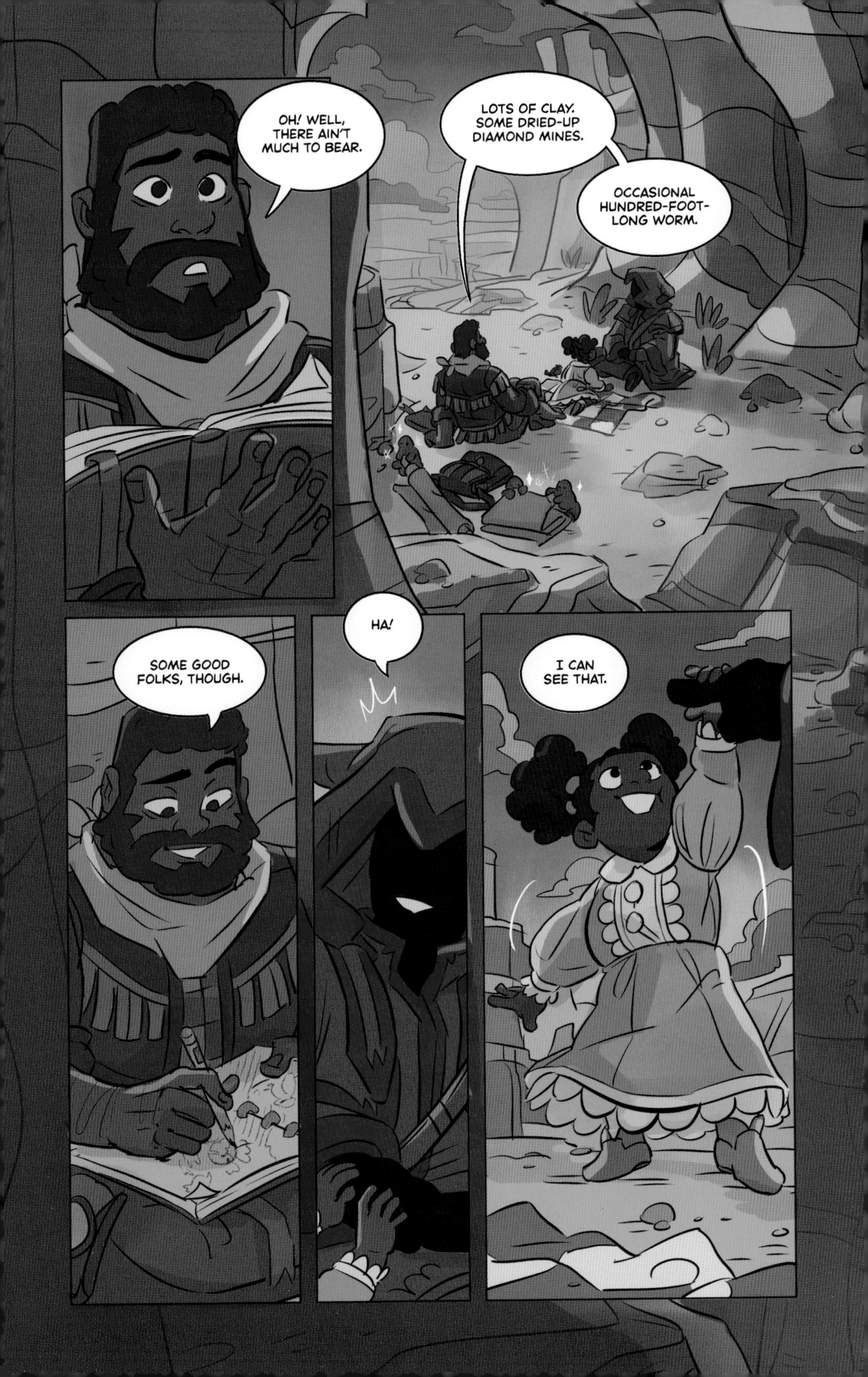
OH! WELL, THERE AIN'T MUCH TO BEAR.
LOTS OF CLAY. SOME DRIED-UP DIAMOND MINES.
OCCASIONAL HUNDRED-FOOT-LONG WORM.
SOME GOOD FOLKS, THOUGH.
HA!
I CAN SEE THAT.

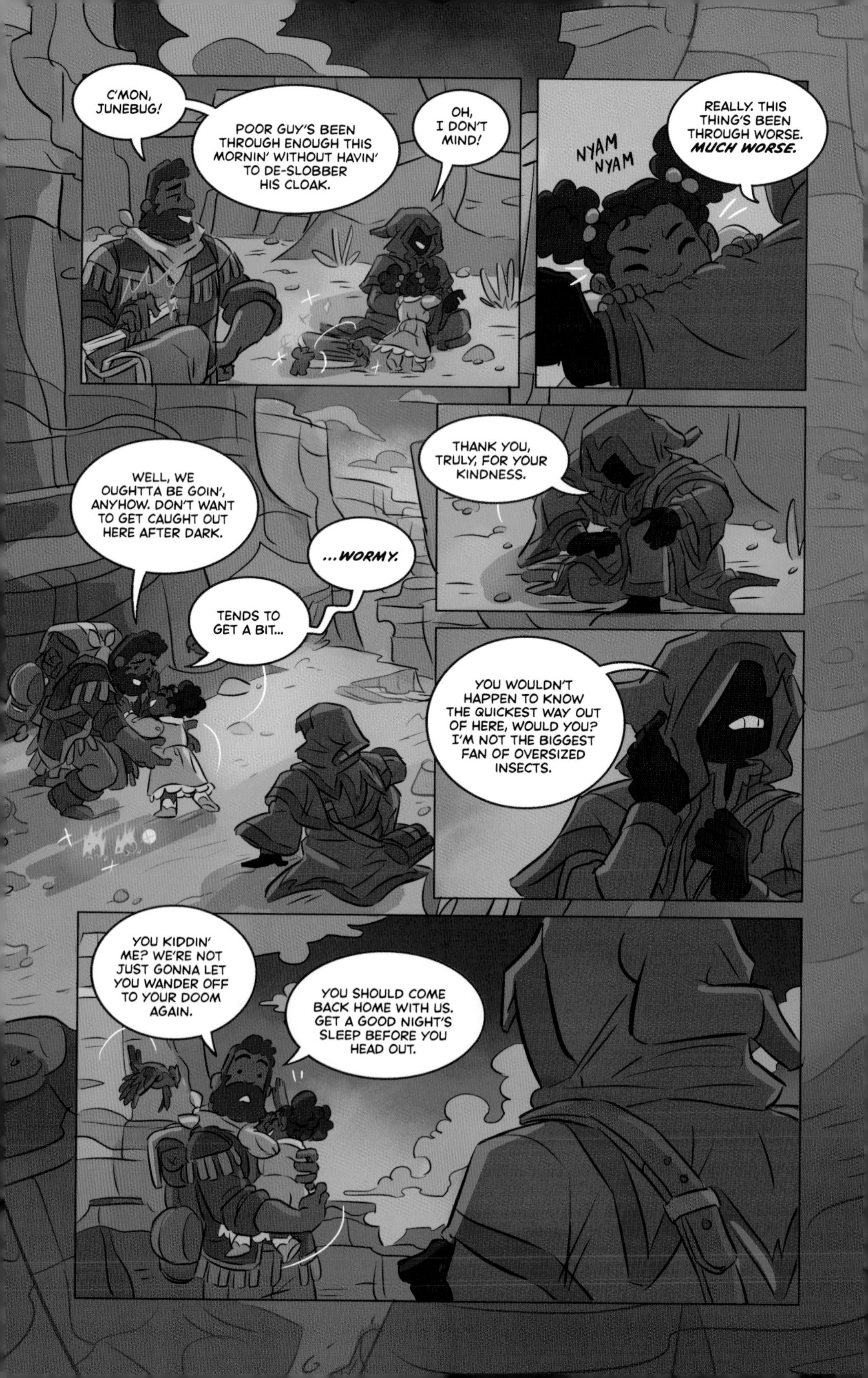
C'MON, JUNEBUG!
POOR GUY'S BEEN THROUGH ENOUGH THIS MORNIN' WITHOUT HAVIN' TO DE-SLOBBER HIS CLOAK.
OH, I DON'T MIND!
NYAM NYAM
REALLY. THIS THING'S BEEN THROUGH WORSE. MUCH WORSE.
WELL, WE OUGHTTA BE GOIN', ANYHOW. DON'T WANT TO GET CAUGHT OUT HERE AFTER DARK.
TENDS TO GET A BIT...
...WORMY.
THANK YOU, TRULY, FOR YOUR KINDNESS.
YOU WOULDN'T HAPPEN TO KNOW THE QUICKEST WAY OUT OF HERE, WOULD YOU? I'M NOT THE BIGGEST FAN OF OVERSIZED INSECTS.
YOU KIDDIN' ME? WE'RE NOT JUST GONNA LET YOU WANDER OFF TO YOUR DOOM AGAIN.
YOU SHOULD COME BACK HOME WITH US. GET A GOOD NIGHT'S SLEEP BEFORE YOU HEAD OUT.

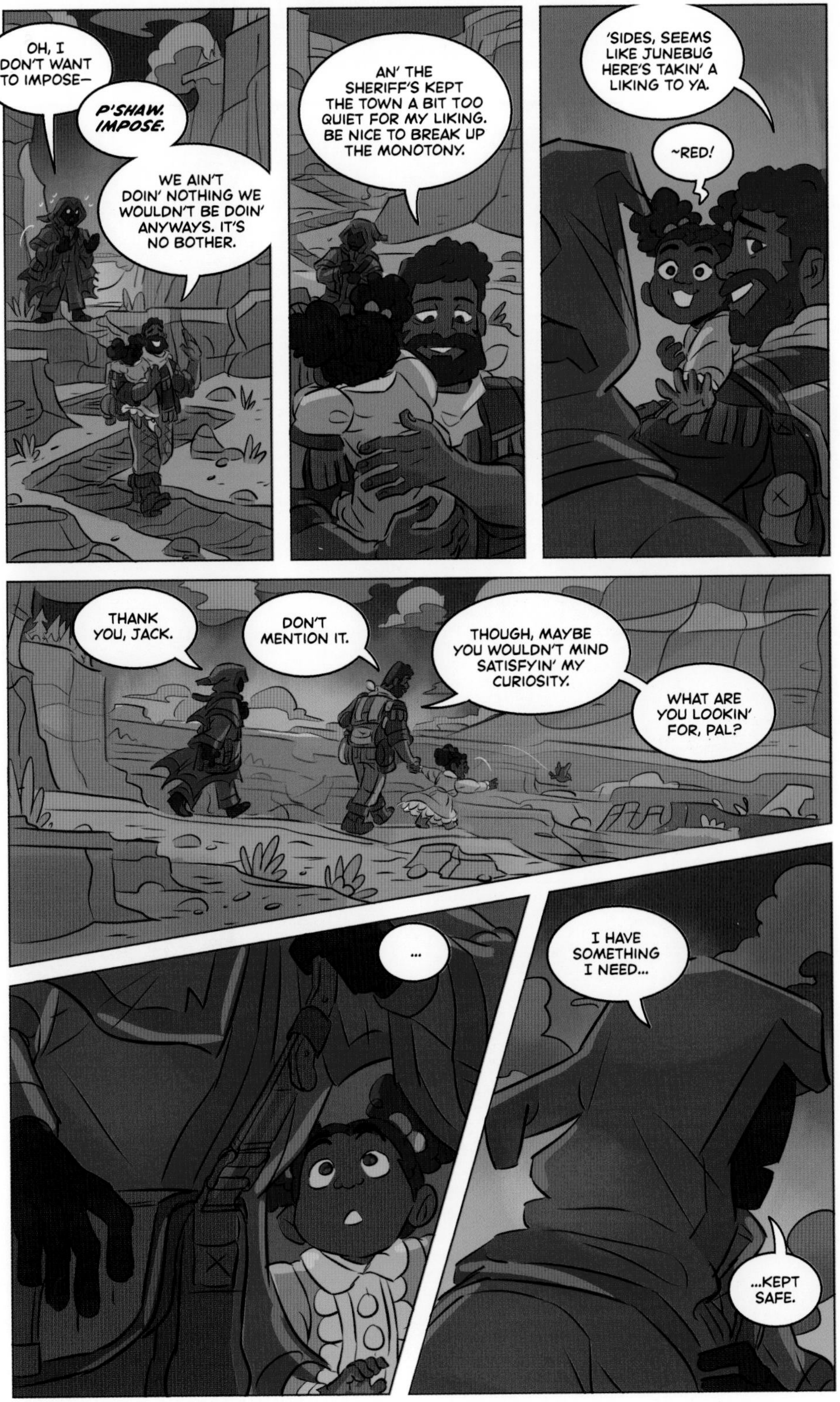

OH, I DON'T WANT TO IMPOSE—
P'SHAW. IMPOSE.
WE AIN'T DOIN' NOTHING WE WOULDN'T BE DOIN' ANYWAYS. IT'S NO BOTHER.
AN' THE SHERIFF'S KEPT THE TOWN A BIT TOO QUIET FOR MY LIKING. BE NICE TO BREAK UP THE MONOTONY.
'SIDES, SEEMS LIKE JUNEBUG HERE'S TAKIN' A LIKING TO YA.
~RED!
THANK YOU, JACK.
DON'T MENTION IT.
THOUGH, MAYBE YOU WOULDN'T MIND SATISFYIN' MY CURIOSITY.
WHAT ARE YOU LOOKIN' FOR, PAL?
...
I HAVE SOMETHING I NEED...
...KEPT SAFE.

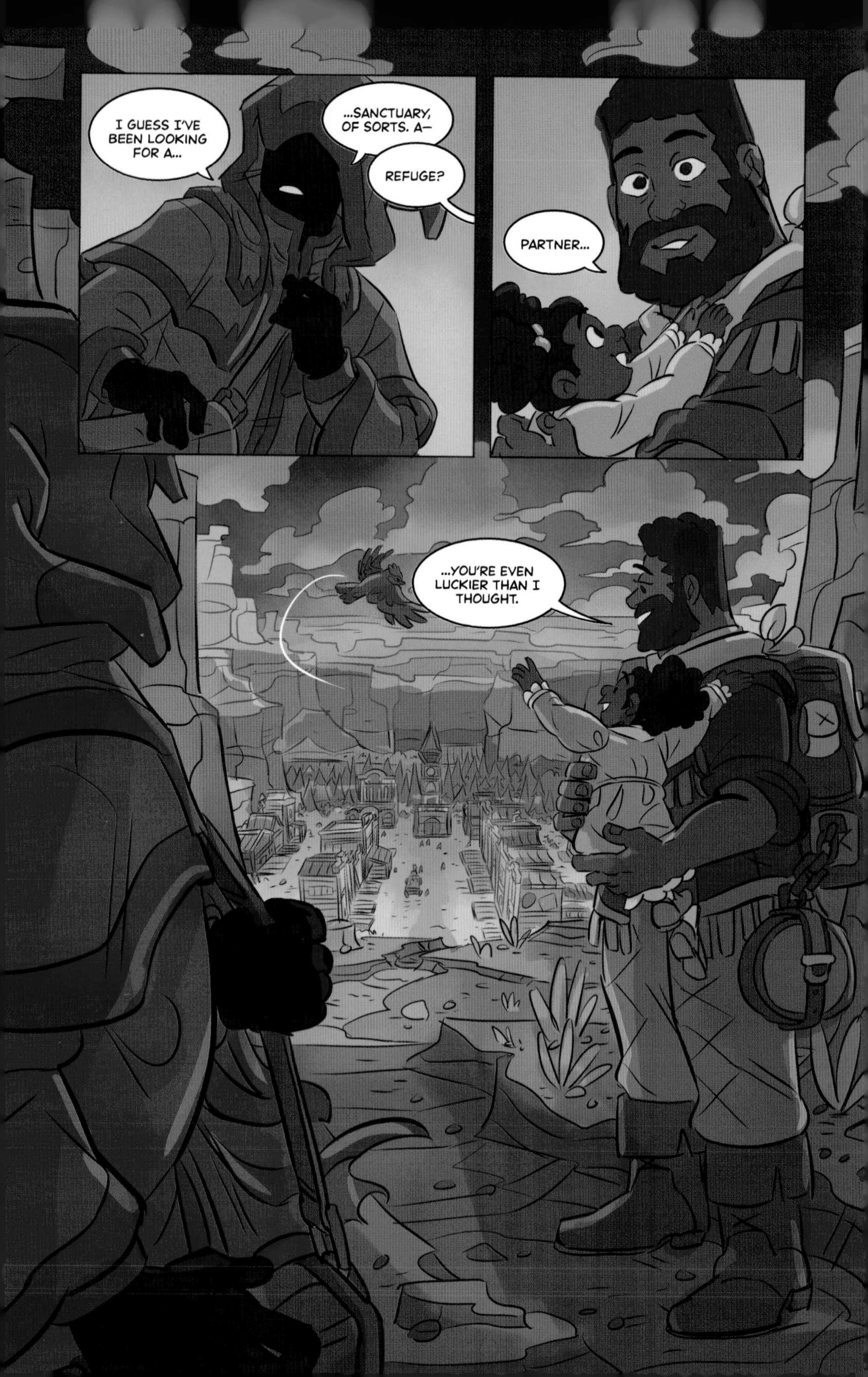
I GUESS I'VE BEEN LOOKING FOR A...
...SANCTUARY, OF SORTS. A—
REFUGE?
PARTNER...
...YOU'RE EVEN LUCKIER THAN I THOUGHT.

Chapter

1

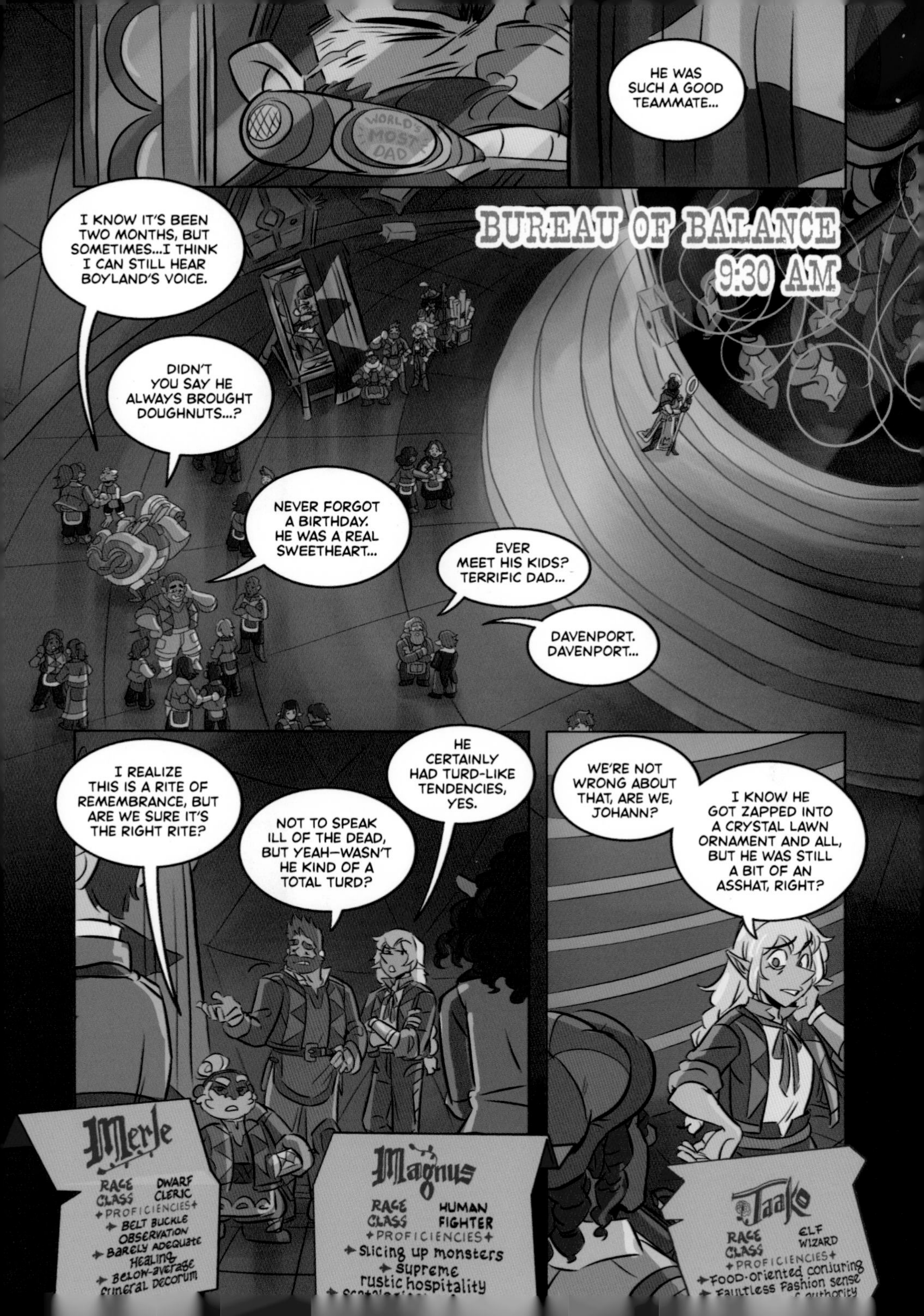
WORLD'S MOST DAD
HE WAS SUCH A GOOD TEAMMATE...
BUREAU OF BALANCE 9:30 AM
I KNOW IT'S BEEN TWO MONTHS, BUT SOMETIMES...I THINK I CAN STILL HEAR BOYLAND'S VOICE.
DIDN'T YOU SAY HE ALWAYS BROUGHT DOUGHNUTS...?
NEVER FORGOT A BIRTHDAY. HE WAS A REAL SWEETHEART...
EVER MEET HIS KIDS? TERRIFIC DAD...
DAVENPORT. DAVENPORT...
I REALIZE THIS IS A RITE OF REMEMBRANCE, BUT ARE WE SURE IT'S THE RIGHT RITE?
NOT TO SPEAK ILL OF THE DEAD, BUT YEAH—WASN'T HE KIND OF A TOTAL TURD?
HE CERTAINLY HAD TURD-LIKE TENDENCIES, YES.
WE'RE NOT WRONG ABOUT THAT, ARE WE, JOHANN?
I KNOW HE GOT ZAPPED INTO A CRYSTAL LAWN ORNAMENT AND ALL, BUT HE WAS STILL A BIT OF AN ASSHAT, RIGHT?
Merle
RACE DWARF
CLASS CLERIC
PROFICIENCIES
Belt buckle observation
Barely adequate healing
Below-average funeral decorum
Magnus
RACE HUMAN
CLASS FIGHTER
PROFICIENCIES
Slicing up monsters
Supreme rustic hospitality
Taako
RACE ELF
CLASS WIZARD
PROFICIENCIES
Food-oriented conjuring
Faultless fashion sense

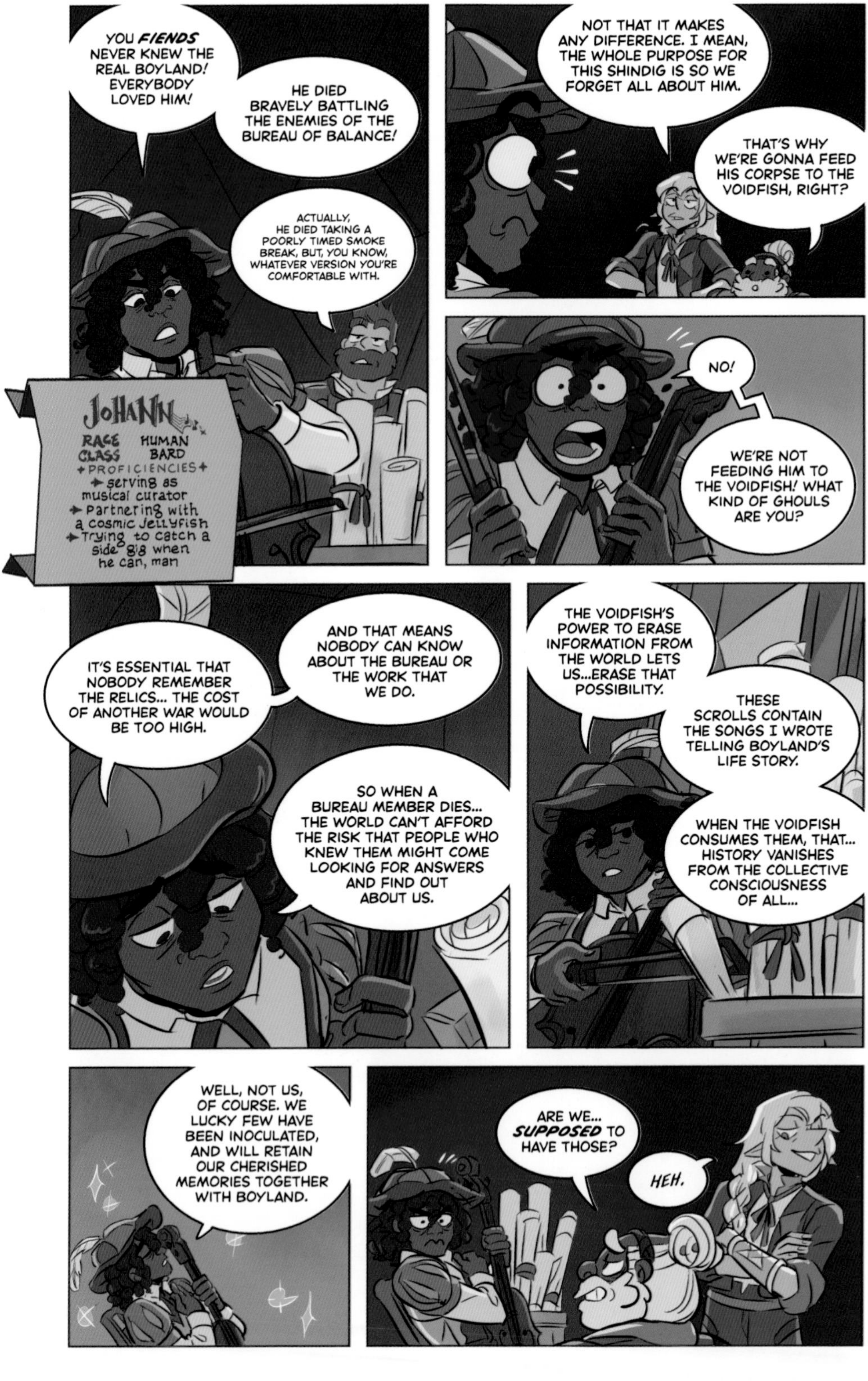
YOU FIENDS NEVER KNEW THE REAL BOYLAND! EVERYBODY LOVED HIM!
HE DIED BRAVELY BATTLING THE ENEMIES OF THE BUREAU OF BALANCE!
ACTUALLY, HE DIED TAKING A POORLY TIMED SMOKE BREAK, BUT, YOU KNOW, WHATEVER VERSION YOU'RE COMFORTABLE WITH.
JOHANN
RACE HUMAN
CLASS BARD
PROFICIENCIES
serving as musical curator
Partnering with a cosmic Jellyfish
Trying to catch a side gig when he can, man
NOT THAT IT MAKES ANY DIFFERENCE. I MEAN, THE WHOLE PURPOSE FOR THIS SHINDIG IS SO WE FORGET ALL ABOUT HIM.
THAT'S WHY WE'RE GONNA FEED HIS CORPSE TO THE VOIDFISH, RIGHT?
NO!
WE'RE NOT FEEDING HIM TO THE VOIDFISH! WHAT KIND OF GHOULS ARE YOU?
IT'S ESSENTIAL THAT NOBODY REMEMBER THE RELICS... THE COST OF ANOTHER WAR WOULD BE TOO HIGH.
AND THAT MEANS NOBODY CAN KNOW ABOUT THE BUREAU OR THE WORK THAT WE DO.
SO WHEN A BUREAU MEMBER DIES... THE WORLD CAN'T AFFORD THE RISK THAT PEOPLE WHO KNEW THEM MIGHT COME LOOKING FOR ANSWERS AND FIND OUT ABOUT US.
THE VOIDFISH'S POWER TO ERASE INFORMATION FROM THE WORLD LETS US...ERASE THAT POSSIBILITY.
THESE SCROLLS CONTAIN THE SONGS I WROTE TELLING BOYLAND'S LIFE STORY.
WHEN THE VOIDFISH CONSUMES THEM, THAT... HISTORY VANISHES FROM THE COLLECTIVE CONSCIOUSNESS OF ALL...
WELL, NOT US, OF COURSE. WE LUCKY FEW HAVE BEEN INOCULATED, AND WILL RETAIN OUR CHERISHED MEMORIES TOGETHER WITH BOYLAND.
ARE WE... SUPPOSED TO HAVE THOSE?
HEH.

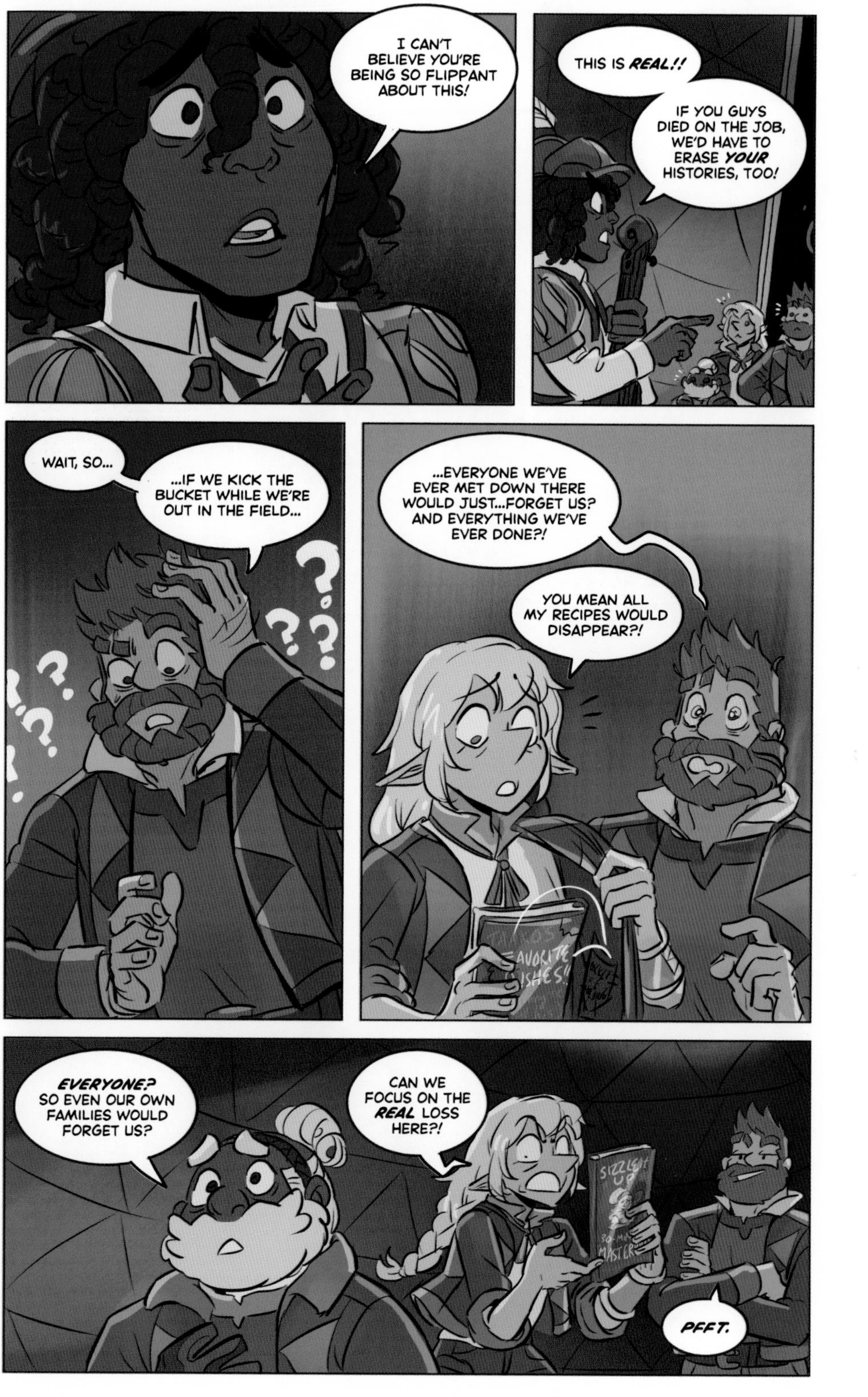
I CAN'T BELIEVE YOU'RE BEING SO FLIPPANT ABOUT THIS!
THIS IS *REAL!!*
IF YOU GUYS DIED ON THE JOB, WE'D HAVE TO ERASE *YOUR* HISTORIES, TOO!
WAIT, SO...
...IF WE KICK THE BUCKET WHILE WE'RE OUT IN THE FIELD...
...EVERYONE WE'VE EVER MET DOWN THERE WOULD JUST...FORGET US? AND EVERYTHING WE'VE EVER DONE?!
YOU MEAN ALL MY RECIPES WOULD DISAPPEAR?!
EVERYONE? SO EVEN OUR OWN FAMILIES WOULD FORGET US?
CAN WE FOCUS ON THE *REAL* LOSS HERE?!
PFFT.

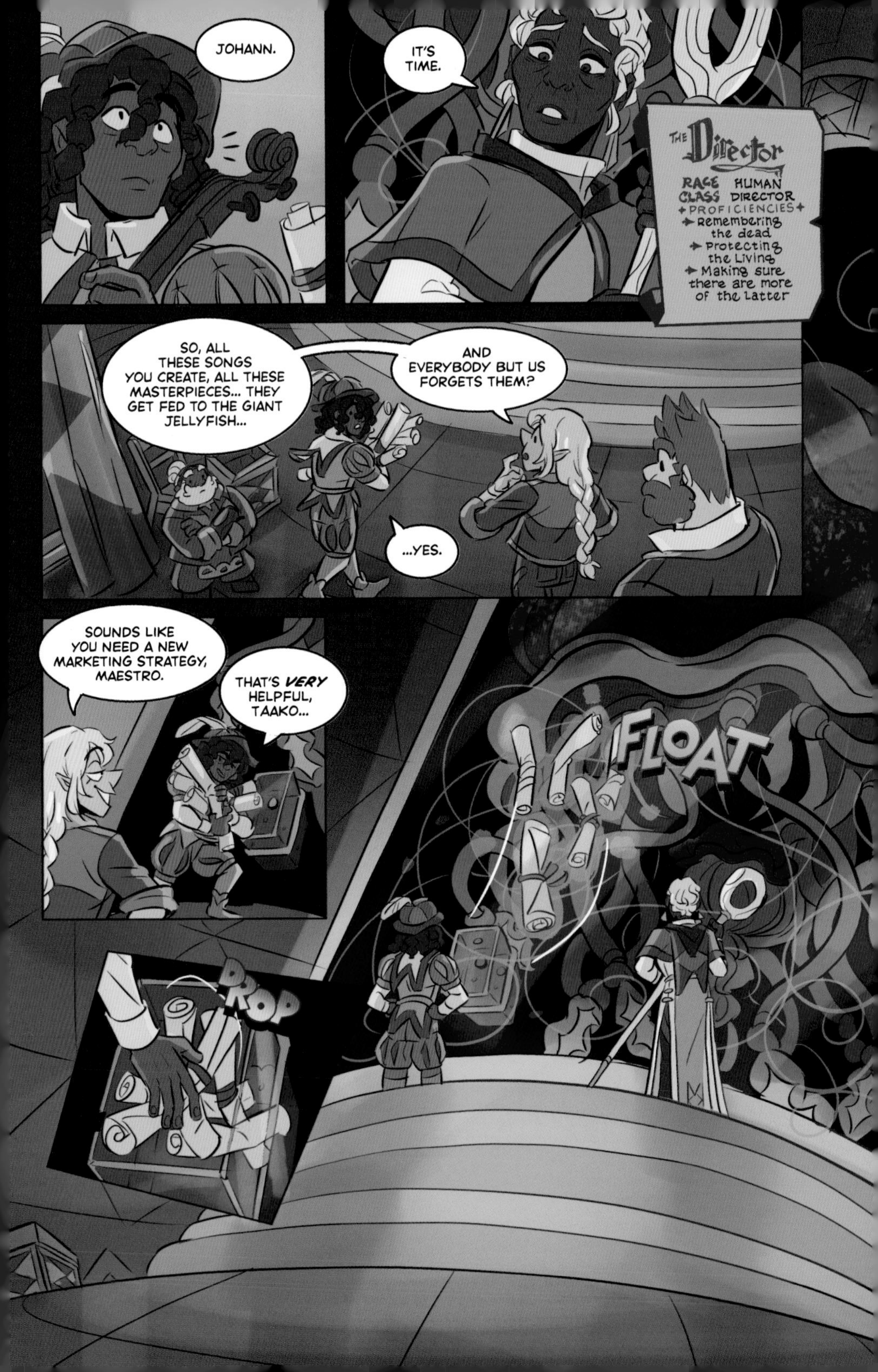

JOHANN.
IT'S TIME.
THE Director
RACE HUMAN
CLASS DIRECTOR
✦PROFICIENCIES✦
✦ Remembering the dead
✦ Protecting the Living
✦ Making sure there are more of the Latter
SO, ALL THESE SONGS YOU CREATE, ALL THESE MASTERPIECES... THEY GET FED TO THE GIANT JELLYFISH...
AND EVERYBODY BUT US FORGETS THEM?
...YES.
SOUNDS LIKE YOU NEED A NEW MARKETING STRATEGY, MAESTRO.
THAT'S *VERY* HELPFUL, TAAKO...
FLOAT
DROP

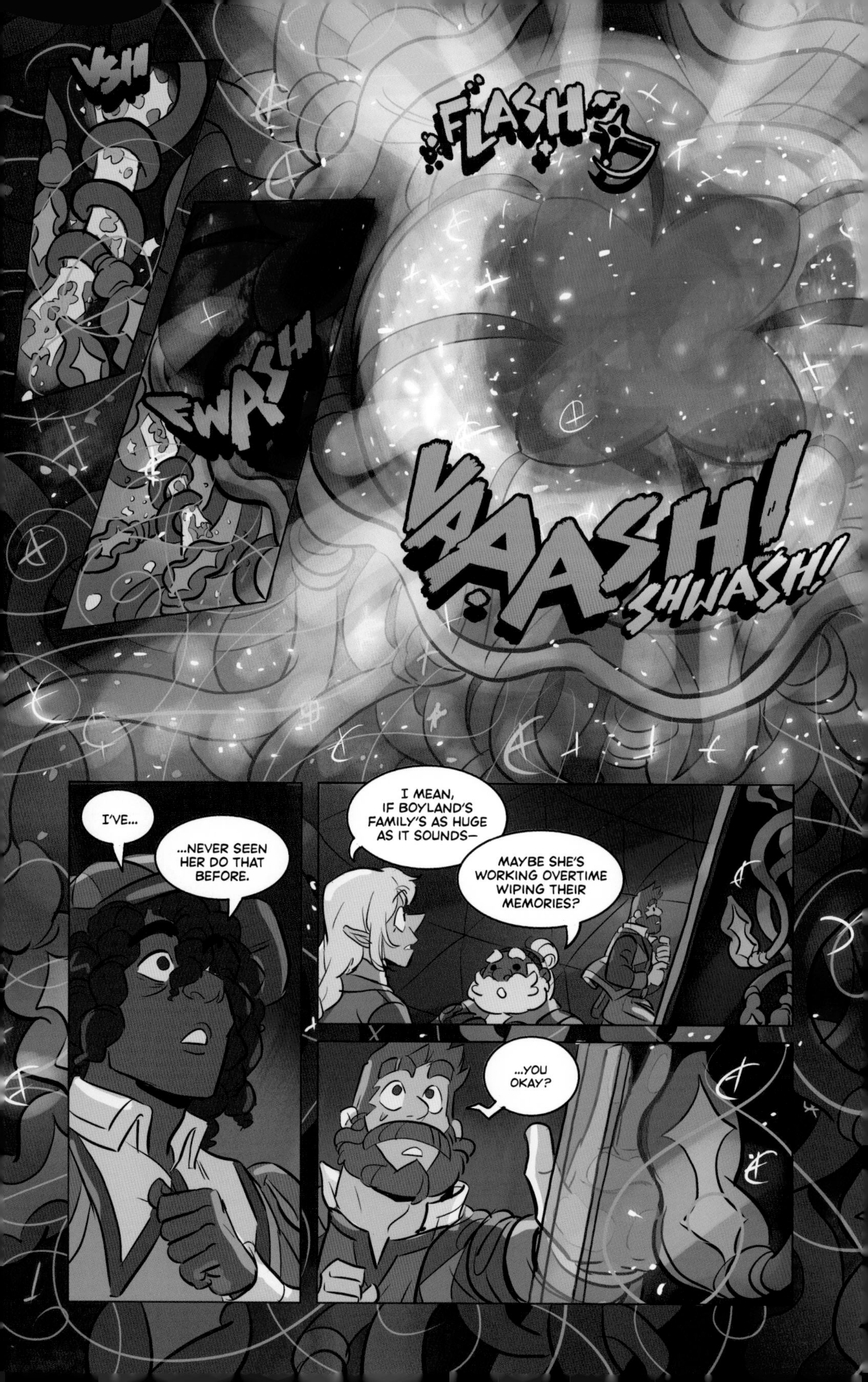
VSH
FLASH
FWASH
VAASH!
SHWASH!
I'VE...
...NEVER SEEN HER DO THAT BEFORE.
I MEAN, IF BOYLAND'S FAMILY'S AS HUGE AS IT SOUNDS—
MAYBE SHE'S WORKING OVERTIME WIPING THEIR MEMORIES?
...YOU OKAY?

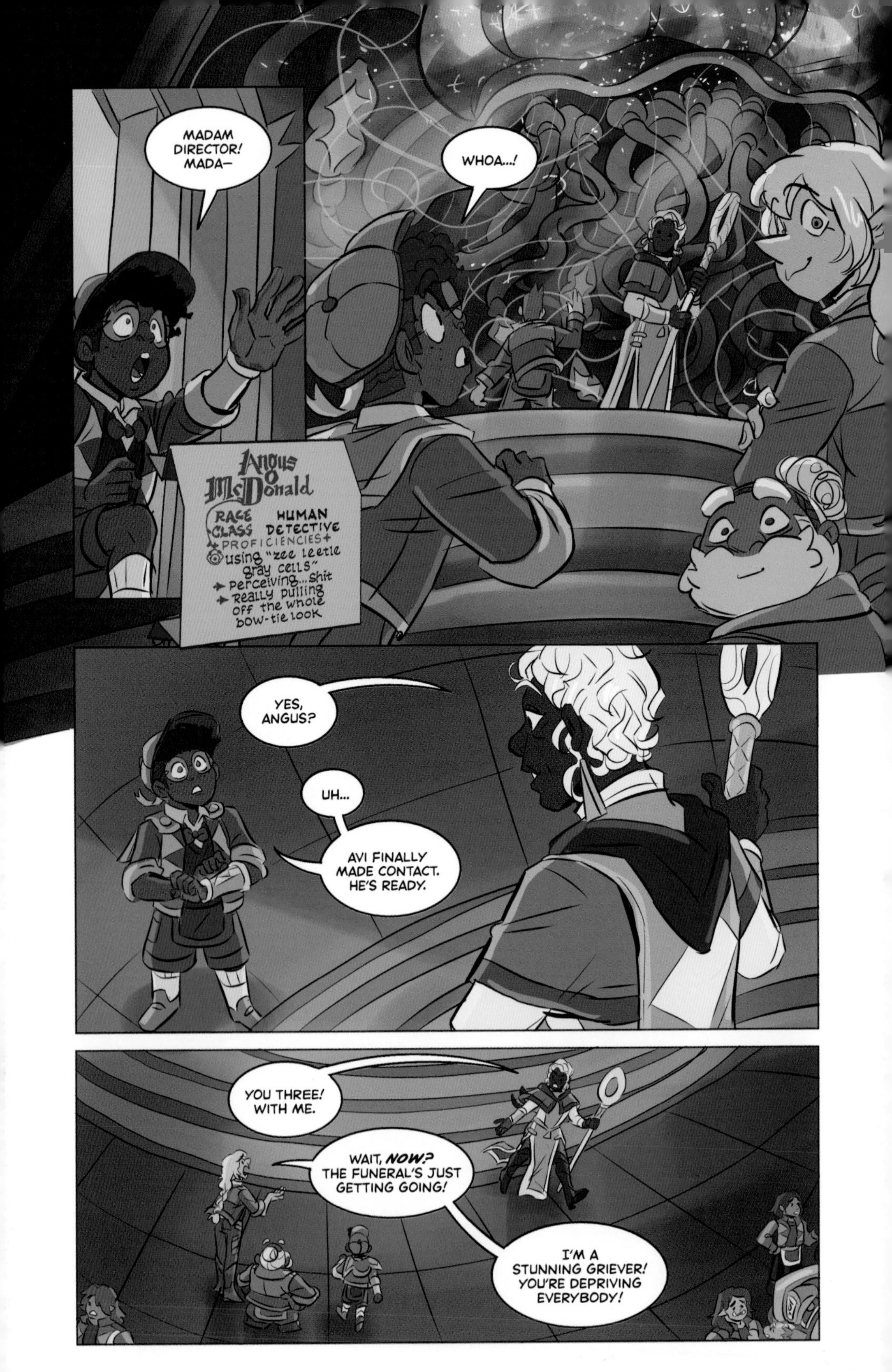
MADAM DIRECTOR! MADA—
WHOA...!
Angus McDonald
RACE HUMAN
CLASS DETECTIVE
PROFICIENCIES
using "zee leetle gray cells"
Perceiving...Shit
Really pulling off the whole bow-tie look
YES, ANGUS?
UH...
AVI FINALLY MADE CONTACT. HE'S READY.
YOU THREE! WITH ME.
WAIT, NOW? THE FUNERAL'S JUST GETTING GOING!
I'M A STUNNING GRIEVER! YOU'RE DEPRIVING EVERYBODY!

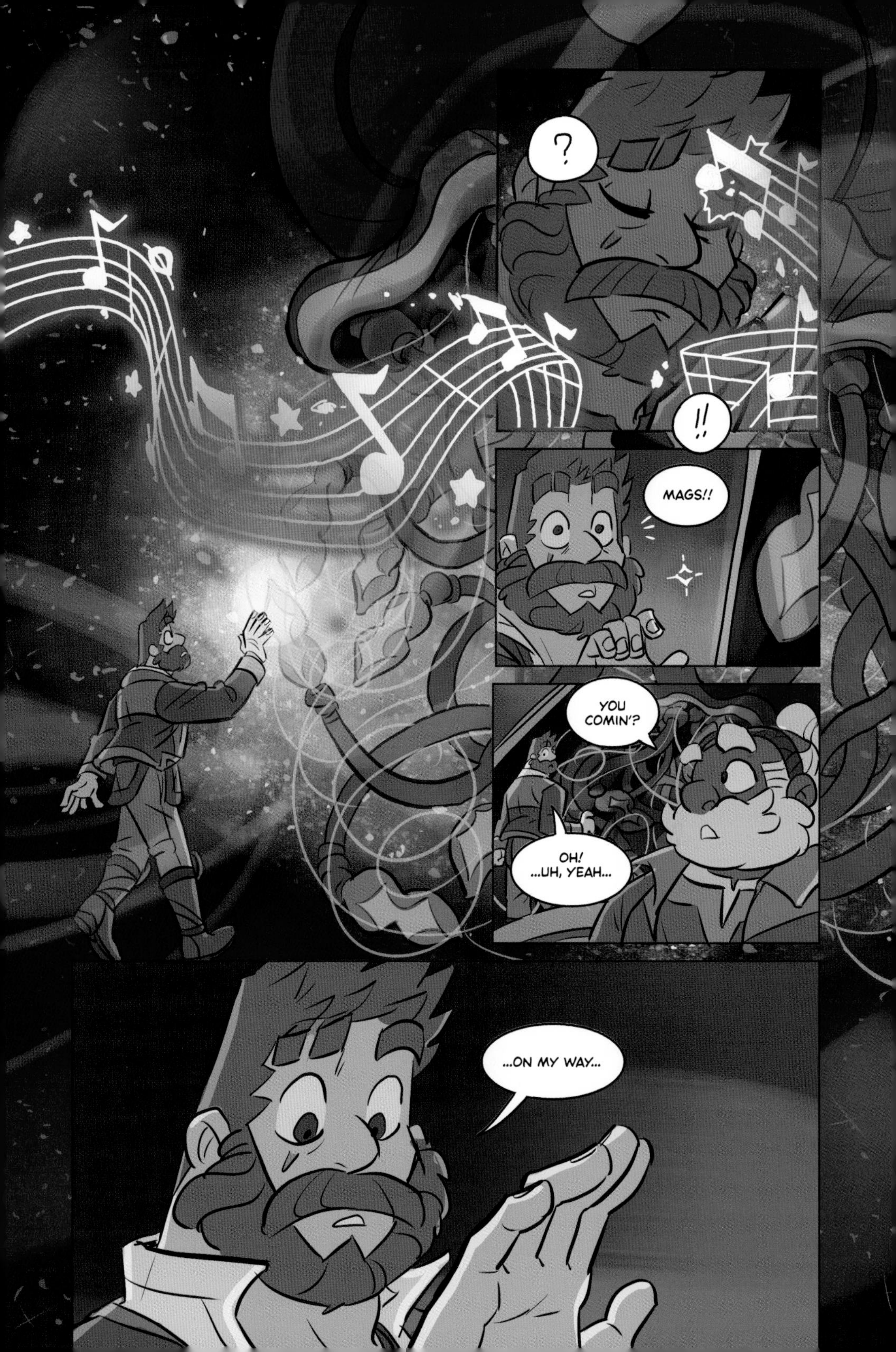
?
!!
MAGS!!
YOU COMIN'?
OH! ...UH, YEAH...
...ON MY WAY...

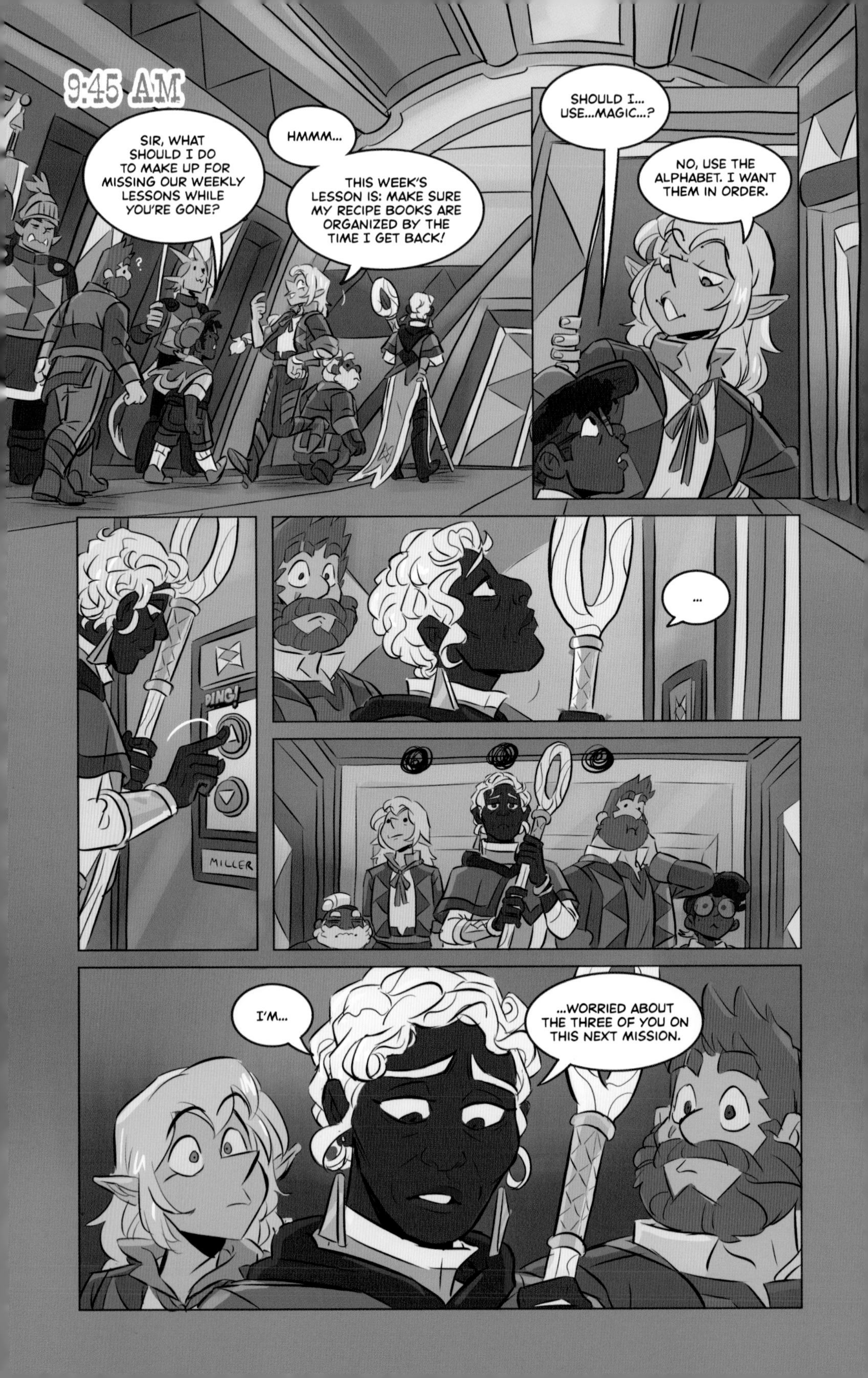
9:45 AM
SIR, WHAT SHOULD I DO TO MAKE UP FOR MISSING OUR WEEKLY LESSONS WHILE YOU'RE GONE?
HMMM...
THIS WEEK'S LESSON IS: MAKE SURE MY RECIPE BOOKS ARE ORGANIZED BY THE TIME I GET BACK!
SHOULD I... USE...MAGIC...?
NO, USE THE ALPHABET. I WANT THEM IN ORDER.
PING!
MILLER
...
I'M...
...WORRIED ABOUT THE THREE OF YOU ON THIS NEXT MISSION.

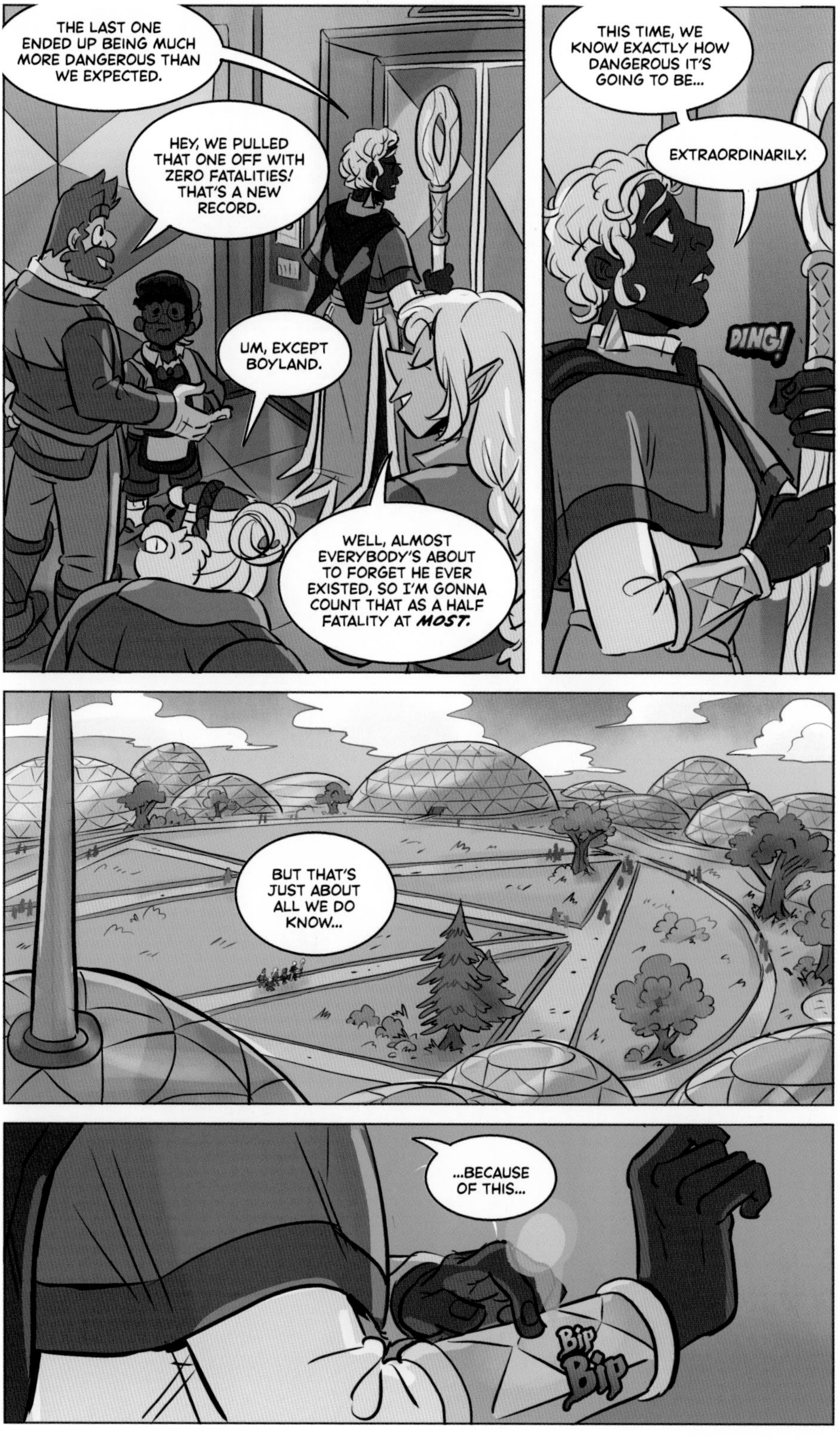
THE LAST ONE ENDED UP BEING MUCH MORE DANGEROUS THAN WE EXPECTED.
HEY, WE PULLED THAT ONE OFF WITH ZERO FATALITIES! THAT'S A NEW RECORD.
UM, EXCEPT BOYLAND.
WELL, ALMOST EVERYBODY'S ABOUT TO FORGET HE EVER EXISTED, SO I'M GONNA COUNT THAT AS A HALF FATALITY AT *MOST.*
THIS TIME, WE KNOW EXACTLY HOW DANGEROUS IT'S GOING TO BE...
EXTRAORDINARILY.
DING!
BUT THAT'S JUST ABOUT ALL WE DO KNOW...
...BECAUSE OF THIS...
Bip
Bip

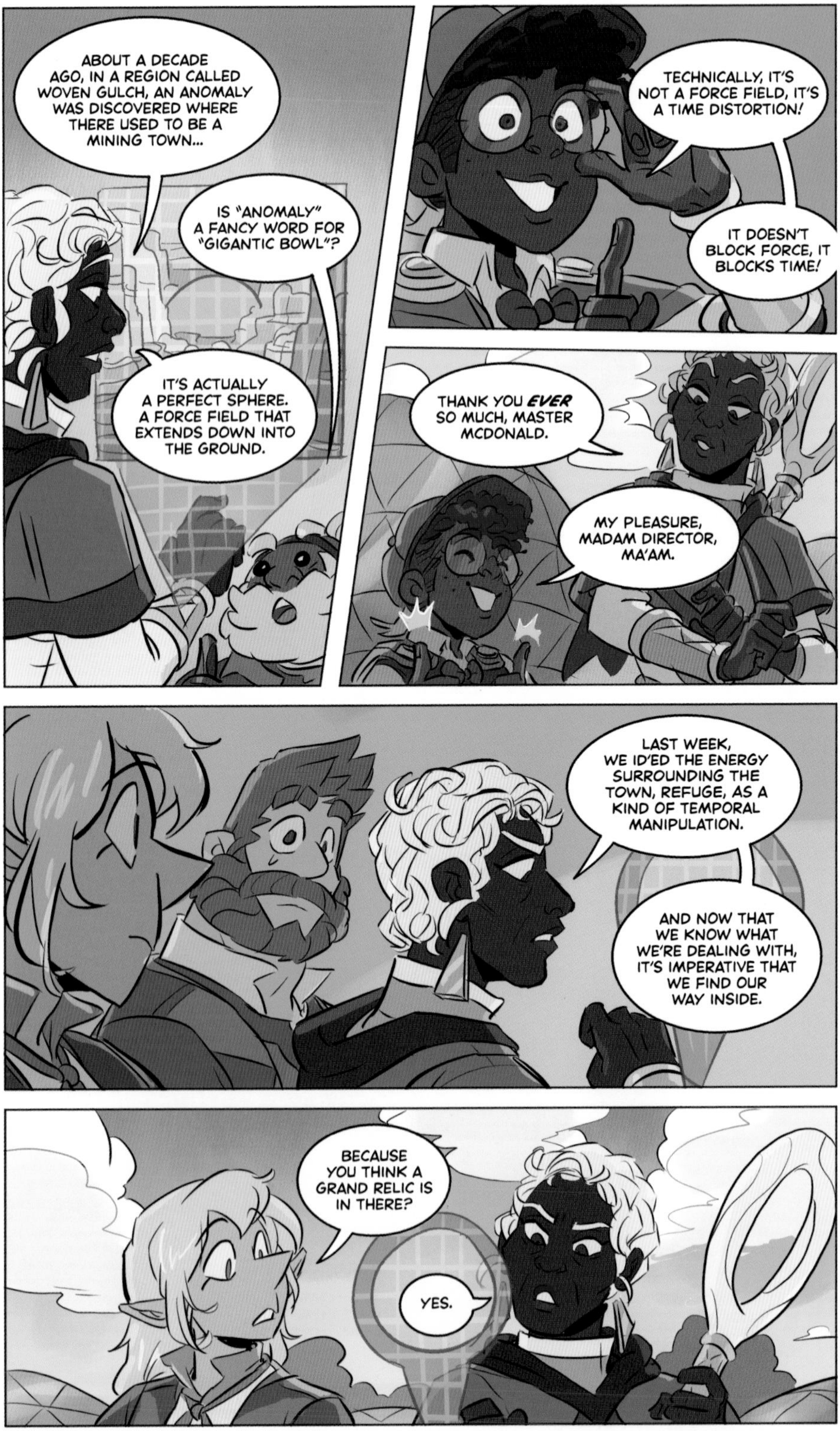
ABOUT A DECADE AGO, IN A REGION CALLED WOVEN GULCH, AN ANOMALY WAS DISCOVERED WHERE THERE USED TO BE A MINING TOWN...
IS "ANOMALY" A FANCY WORD FOR "GIGANTIC BOWL"?
IT'S ACTUALLY A PERFECT SPHERE. A FORCE FIELD THAT EXTENDS DOWN INTO THE GROUND.
TECHNICALLY, IT'S NOT A FORCE FIELD, IT'S A TIME DISTORTION!
IT DOESN'T BLOCK FORCE, IT BLOCKS TIME!
THANK YOU *EVER* SO MUCH, MASTER MCDONALD.
MY PLEASURE, MADAM DIRECTOR, MA'AM.
LAST WEEK, WE ID'ED THE ENERGY SURROUNDING THE TOWN, REFUGE, AS A KIND OF TEMPORAL MANIPULATION.
AND NOW THAT WE KNOW WHAT WE'RE DEALING WITH, IT'S IMPERATIVE THAT WE FIND OUR WAY INSIDE.
BECAUSE YOU THINK A GRAND RELIC IS IN THERE?
YES.

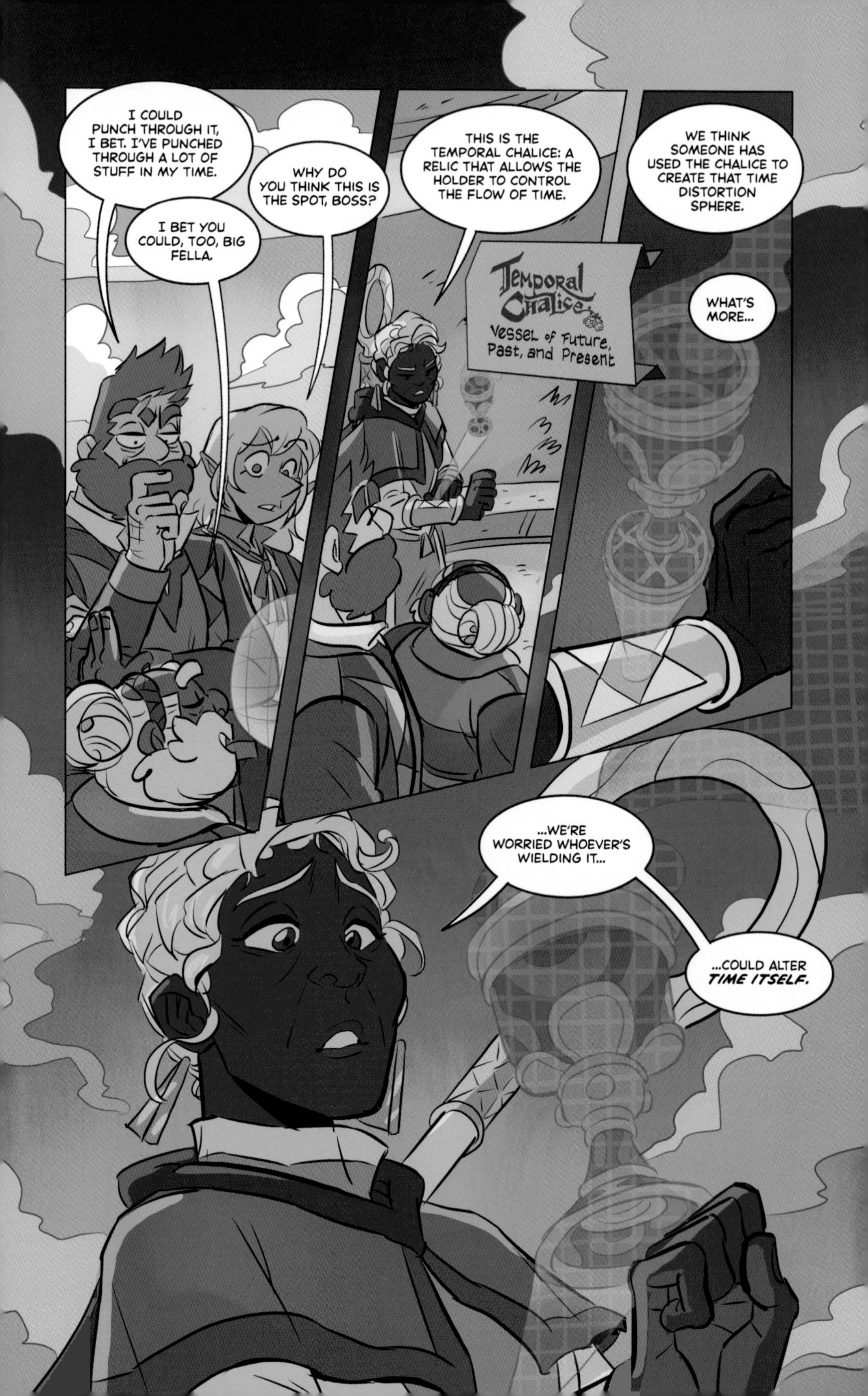
I COULD PUNCH THROUGH IT, I BET. I'VE PUNCHED THROUGH A LOT OF STUFF IN MY TIME.
I BET YOU COULD, TOO, BIG FELLA.
WHY DO YOU THINK THIS IS THE SPOT, BOSS?
THIS IS THE TEMPORAL CHALICE: A RELIC THAT ALLOWS THE HOLDER TO CONTROL THE FLOW OF TIME.
Temporal Chalice
Vessel of Future, Past, and Present
WE THINK SOMEONE HAS USED THE CHALICE TO CREATE THAT TIME DISTORTION SPHERE.
WHAT'S MORE...
...WE'RE WORRIED WHOEVER'S WIELDING IT...
...COULD ALTER *TIME ITSELF.*

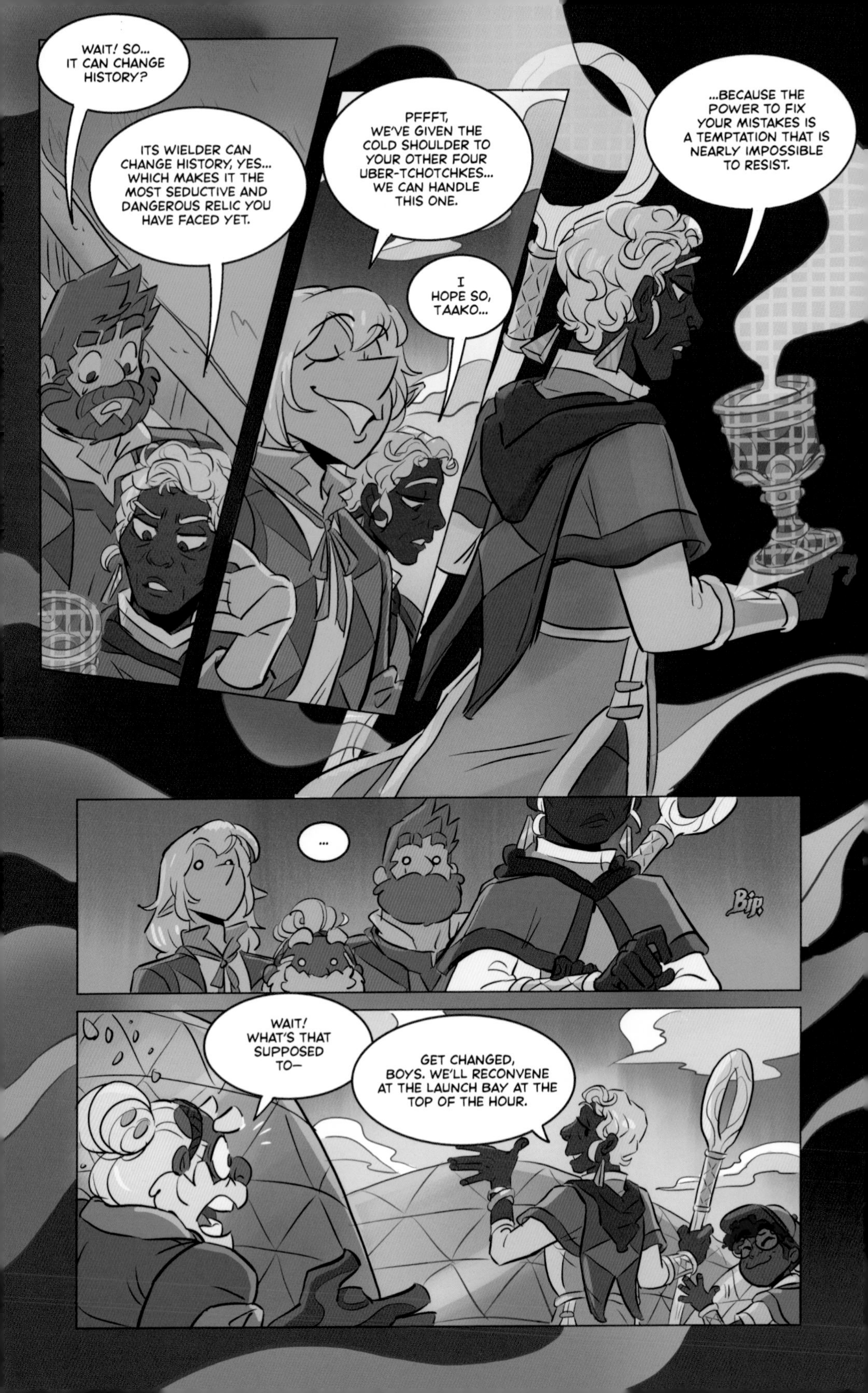
WAIT! SO... IT CAN CHANGE HISTORY?
ITS WIELDER CAN CHANGE HISTORY, YES... WHICH MAKES IT THE MOST SEDUCTIVE AND DANGEROUS RELIC YOU HAVE FACED YET.
PFFFT, WE'VE GIVEN THE COLD SHOULDER TO YOUR OTHER FOUR UBER-TCHOTCHKES... WE CAN HANDLE THIS ONE.
I HOPE SO, TAAKO...
...BECAUSE THE POWER TO FIX YOUR MISTAKES IS A TEMPTATION THAT IS NEARLY IMPOSSIBLE TO RESIST.
...
Bip!
WAIT! WHAT'S THAT SUPPOSED TO—
GET CHANGED, BOYS. WE'LL RECONVENE AT THE LAUNCH BAY AT THE TOP OF THE HOUR.

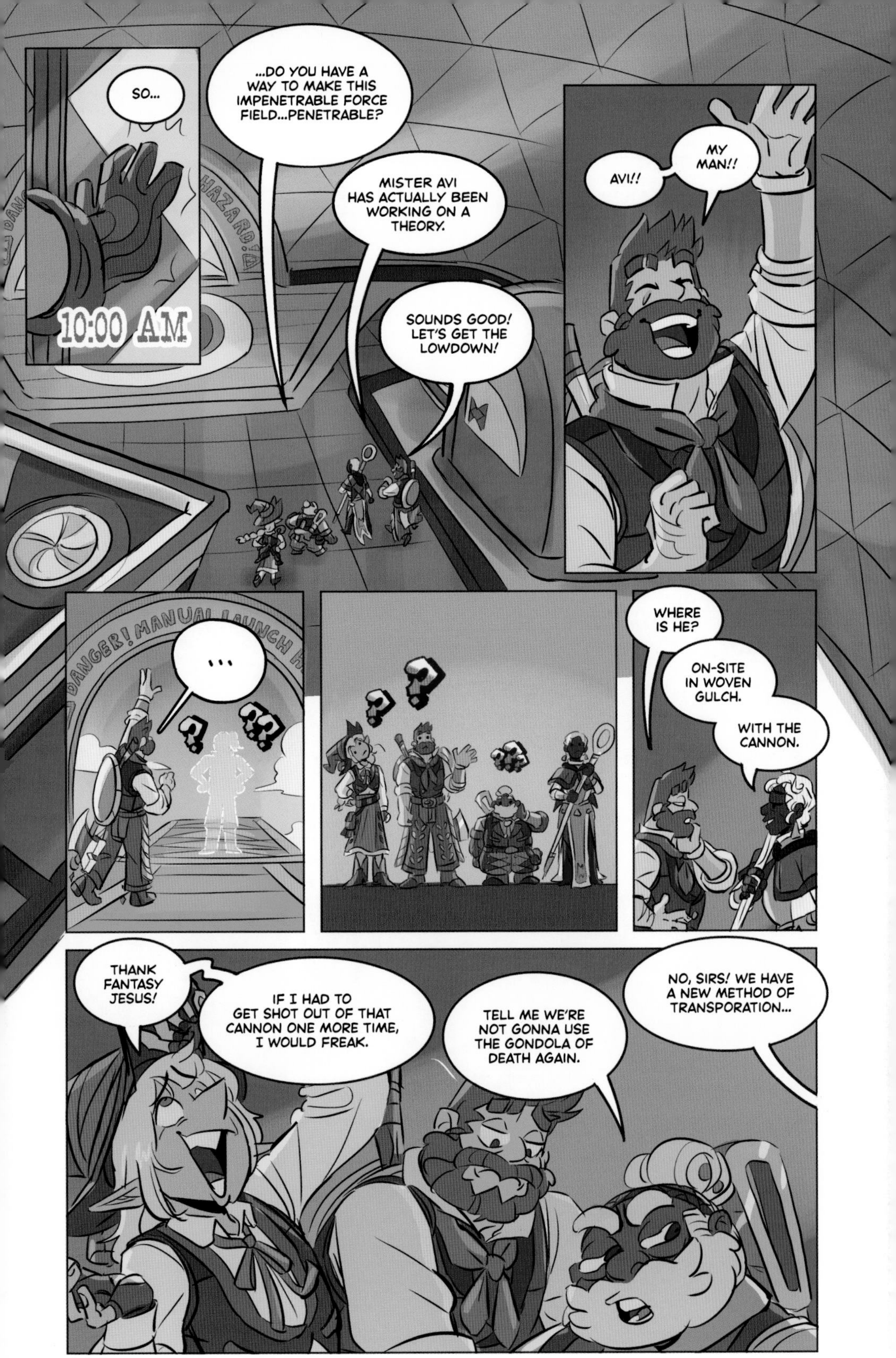
SO...
...DO YOU HAVE A WAY TO MAKE THIS IMPENETRABLE FORCE FIELD...PENETRABLE?
10:00 AM
HAZARD!
MISTER AVI HAS ACTUALLY BEEN WORKING ON A THEORY.
SOUNDS GOOD! LET'S GET THE LOWDOWN!
AVI!!
MY MAN!!
DANGER! MANUAL LAUNCH
...
WHERE IS HE?
ON-SITE IN WOVEN GULCH.
WITH THE CANNON.
THANK FANTASY JESUS!
IF I HAD TO GET SHOT OUT OF THAT CANNON ONE MORE TIME, I WOULD FREAK.
TELL ME WE'RE NOT GONNA USE THE GONDOLA OF DEATH AGAIN.
NO, SIRS! WE HAVE A NEW METHOD OF TRANSPORATION...

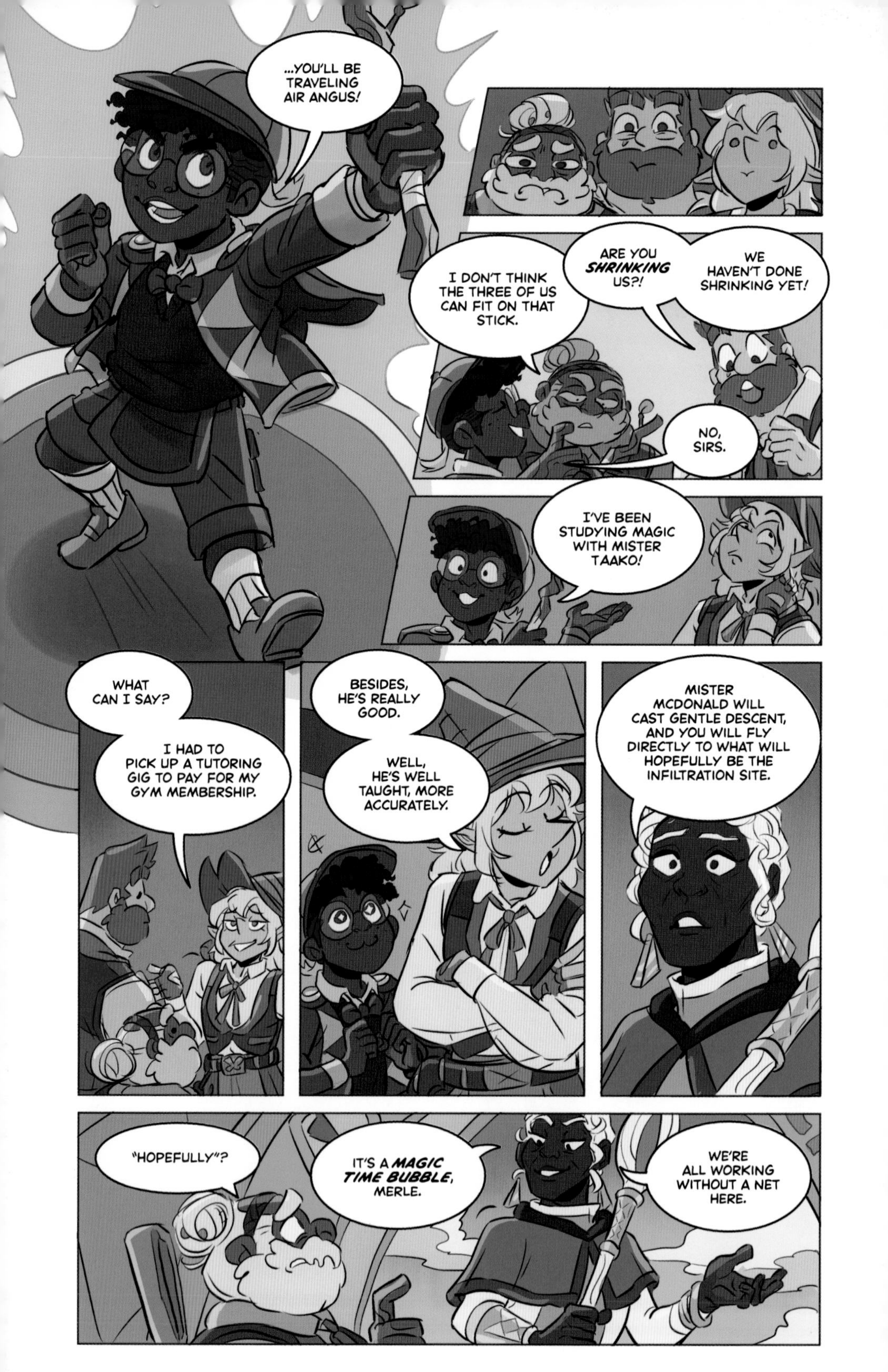
...YOU'LL BE TRAVELING AIR ANGUS!
I DON'T THINK THE THREE OF US CAN FIT ON THAT STICK.
ARE YOU SHRINKING US?!
WE HAVEN'T DONE SHRINKING YET!
NO, SIRS.
I'VE BEEN STUDYING MAGIC WITH MISTER TAAKO!
WHAT CAN I SAY?
I HAD TO PICK UP A TUTORING GIG TO PAY FOR MY GYM MEMBERSHIP.
BESIDES, HE'S REALLY GOOD.
WELL, HE'S WELL TAUGHT, MORE ACCURATELY.
MISTER MCDONALD WILL CAST GENTLE DESCENT, AND YOU WILL FLY DIRECTLY TO WHAT WILL HOPEFULLY BE THE INFILTRATION SITE.
"HOPEFULLY"?
IT'S A MAGIC TIME BUBBLE, MERLE.
WE'RE ALL WORKING WITHOUT A NET HERE.

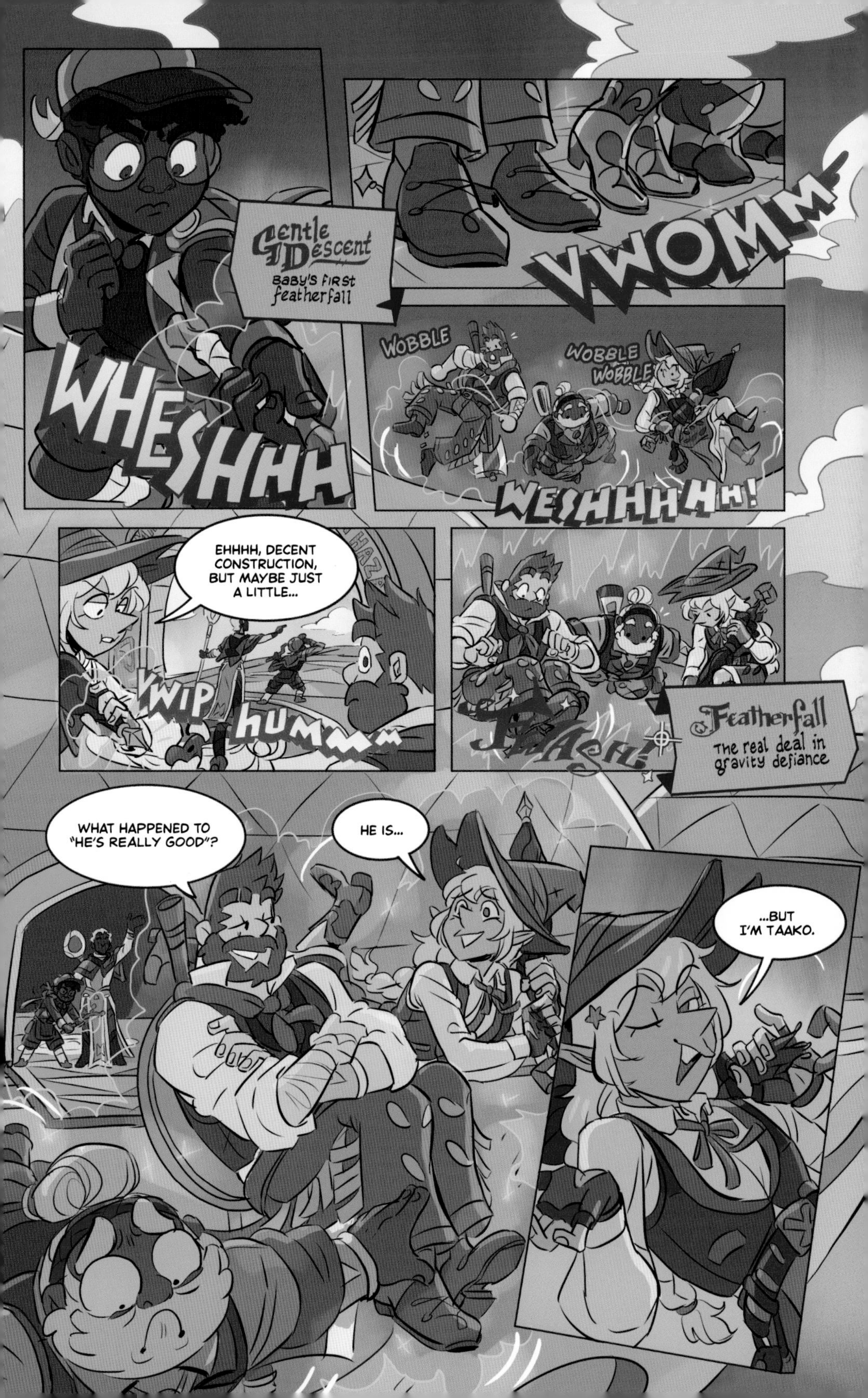
Gentle Descent
Baby's first featherfall
VWOMM
WHESHHH
WOBBLE
WOBBLE WOBBLE
WESHHHHHH!
EHHHH, DECENT CONSTRUCTION, BUT MAYBE JUST A LITTLE...
VWIP
HUMMM
Featherfall
The real deal in gravity defiance
WHAT HAPPENED TO "HE'S REALLY GOOD"?
HE IS...
...BUT I'M TAAKO.

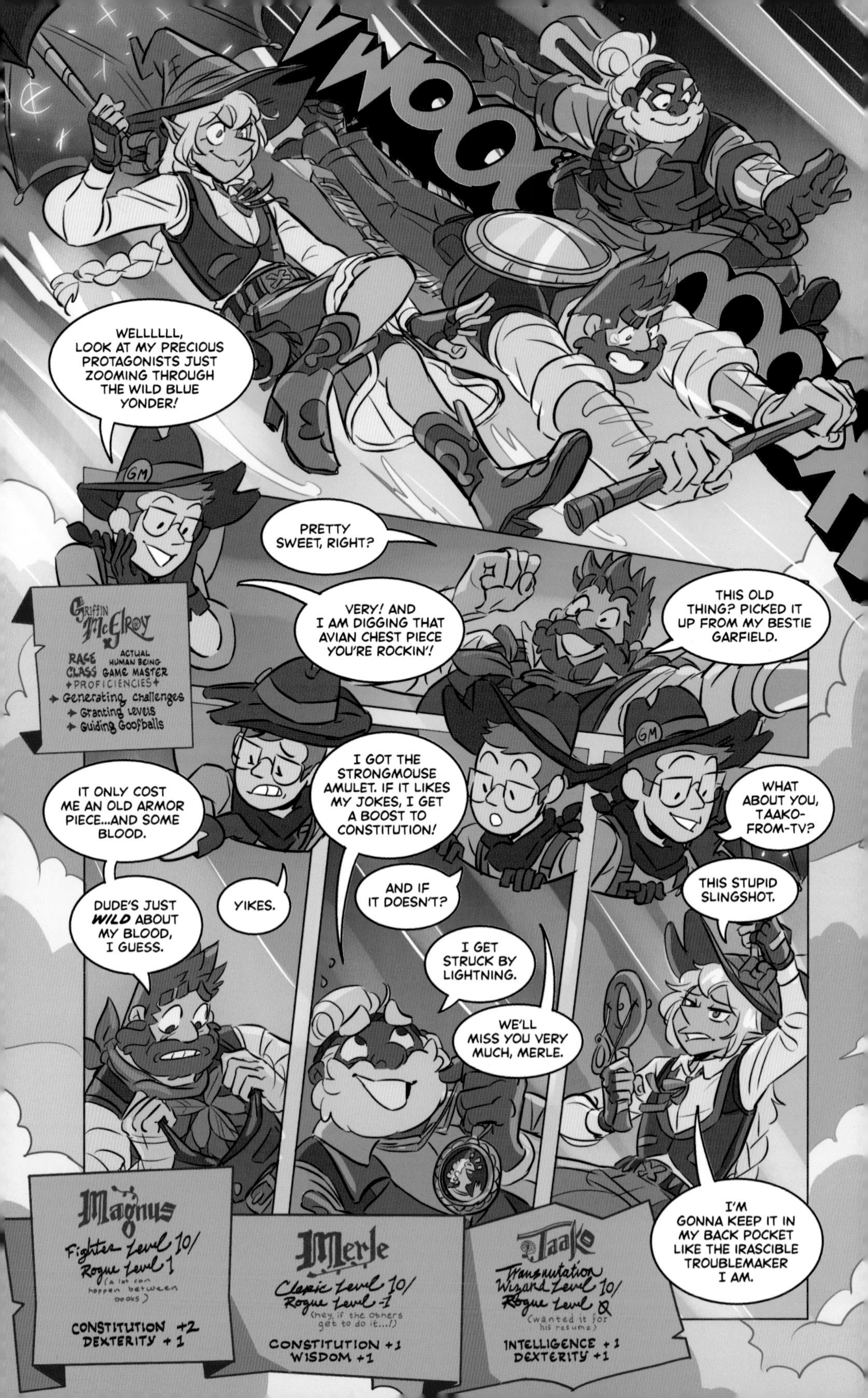
WELLLLLL, LOOK AT MY PRECIOUS PROTAGONISTS JUST ZOOMING THROUGH THE WILD BLUE YONDER!
PRETTY SWEET, RIGHT?
VERY! AND I AM DIGGING THAT AVIAN CHEST PIECE YOU'RE ROCKIN'!
THIS OLD THING? PICKED IT UP FROM MY BESTIE GARFIELD.
Griffin McElroy
RACE ACTUAL HUMAN BEING
CLASS GAME MASTER
PROFICIENCIES
Generating Challenges
Granting Levels
Guiding Goofballs
IT ONLY COST ME AN OLD ARMOR PIECE...AND SOME BLOOD.
I GOT THE STRONGMOUSE AMULET. IF IT LIKES MY JOKES, I GET A BOOST TO CONSTITUTION!
WHAT ABOUT YOU, TAAKO-FROM-TV?
DUDE'S JUST ***WILD*** ABOUT MY BLOOD, I GUESS.
YIKES.
AND IF IT DOESN'T?
THIS STUPID SLINGSHOT.
I GET STRUCK BY LIGHTNING.
WE'LL MISS YOU VERY MUCH, MERLE.
I'M GONNA KEEP IT IN MY BACK POCKET LIKE THE IRASCIBLE TROUBLEMAKER I AM.
Magnus
Fighter Level 10/
Rogue Level 1
(a lot can happen between books)
CONSTITUTION +2
DEXTERITY +1
Merle
Cleric Level 10/
Rogue Level -1
(hey, if the others get to do it...!)
CONSTITUTION +1
WISDOM +1
Taako
Transmutation Wizard Level 10/
Rogue Level X
(wanted it for his resume)
INTELLIGENCE +1
DEXTERITY +1

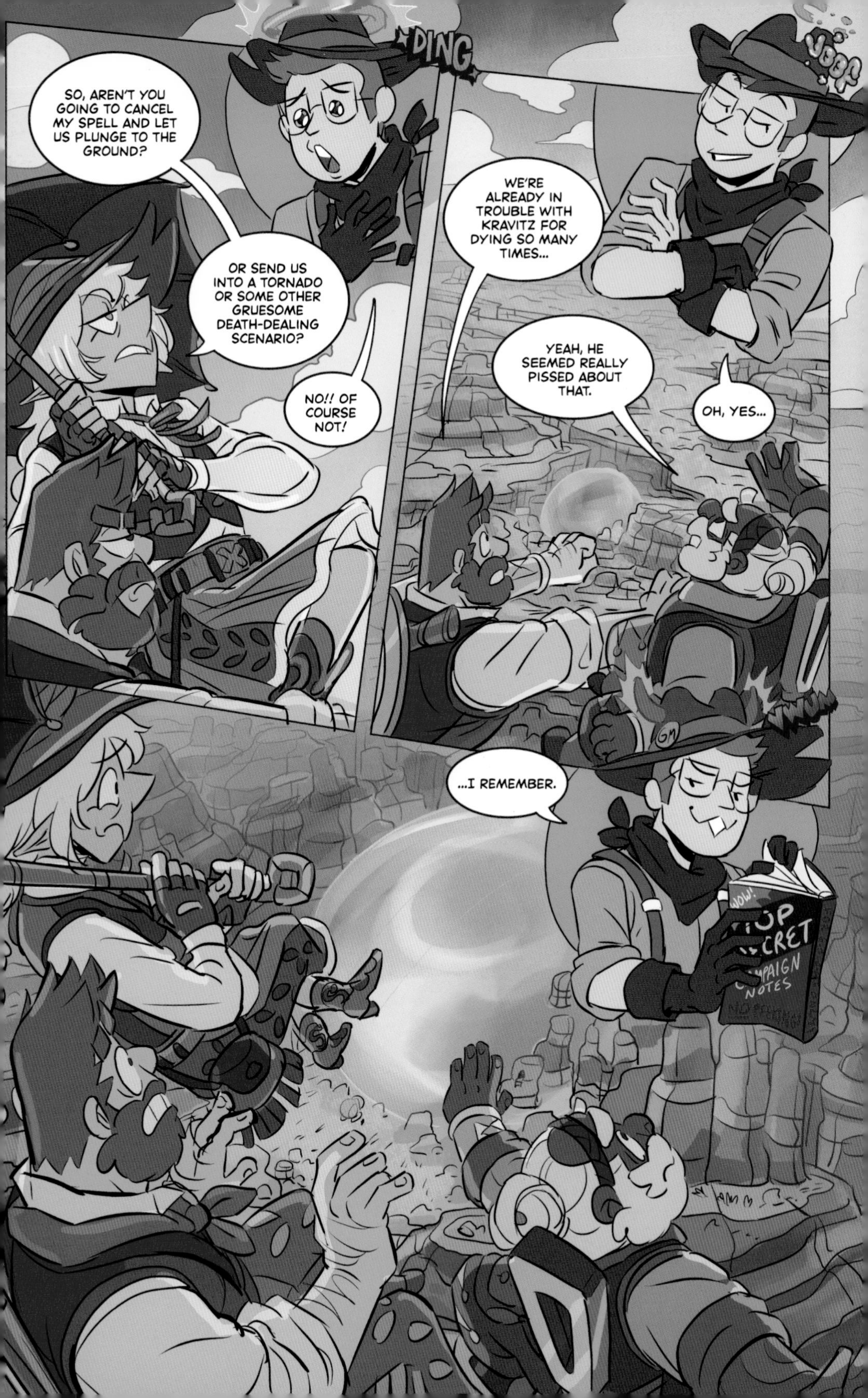
DING
SO, AREN'T YOU GOING TO CANCEL MY SPELL AND LET US PLUNGE TO THE GROUND?
OR SEND US INTO A TORNADO OR SOME OTHER GRUESOME DEATH-DEALING SCENARIO?
NO!! OF COURSE NOT!
OOF
WE'RE ALREADY IN TROUBLE WITH KRAVITZ FOR DYING SO MANY TIMES...
YEAH, HE SEEMED REALLY PISSED ABOUT THAT.
OH, YES...
...I REMEMBER.
WOW!
TOP SECRET CAMPAIGN NOTES

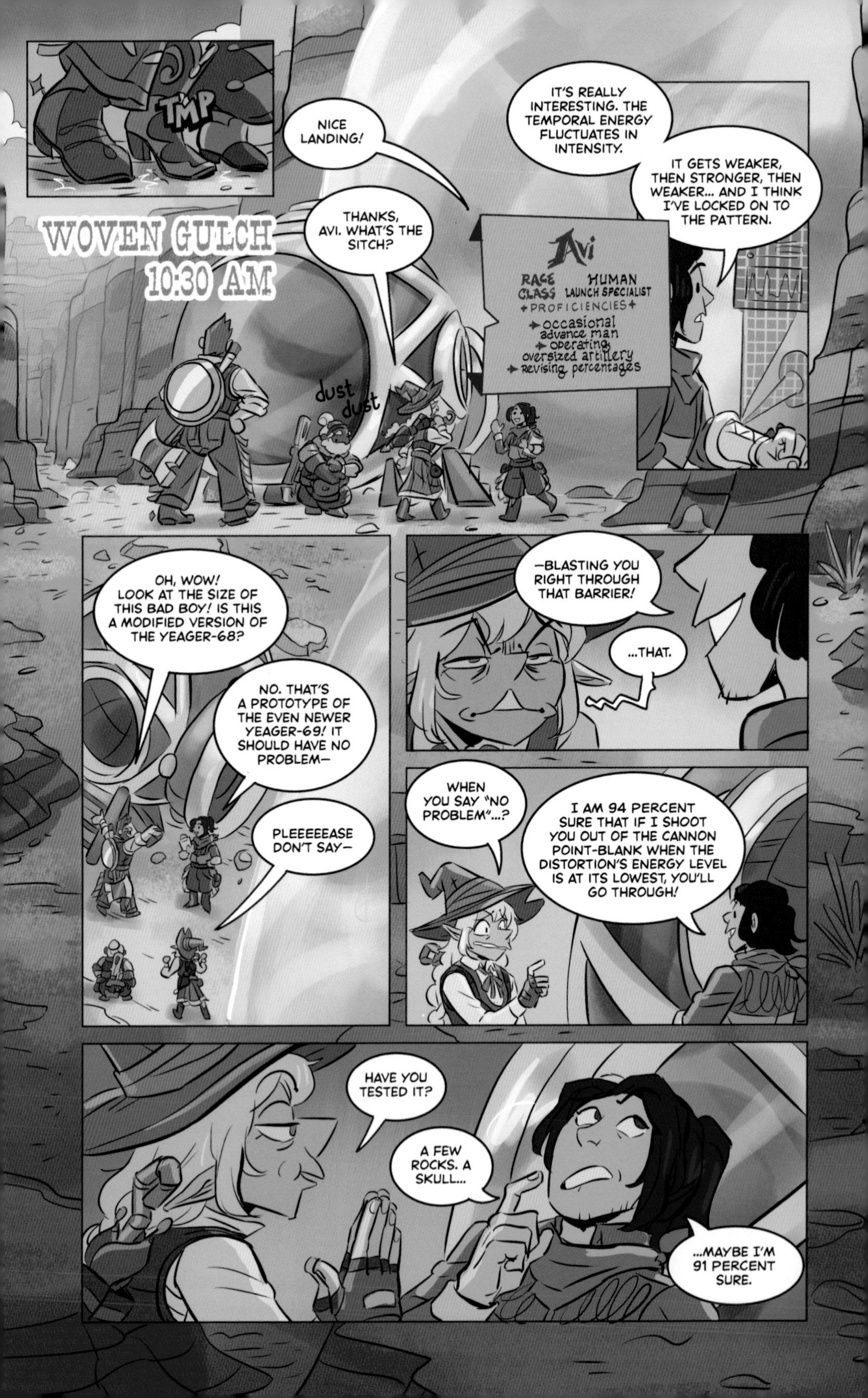
TMP
WOVEN GULCH 10:30 AM
NICE LANDING!
THANKS, AVI. WHAT'S THE SITCH?
dust dust
IT'S REALLY INTERESTING. THE TEMPORAL ENERGY FLUCTUATES IN INTENSITY.
IT GETS WEAKER, THEN STRONGER, THEN WEAKER... AND I THINK I'VE LOCKED ON TO THE PATTERN.
Avi
RACE HUMAN
CLASS LAUNCH SPECIALIST
PROFICIENCIES
occasional advance man
operating oversized artillery
revising percentages
OH, WOW! LOOK AT THE SIZE OF THIS BAD BOY! IS THIS A MODIFIED VERSION OF THE YEAGER-68?
NO. THAT'S A PROTOTYPE OF THE EVEN NEWER YEAGER-69! IT SHOULD HAVE NO PROBLEM—
PLEEEEEASE DON'T SAY—
—BLASTING YOU RIGHT THROUGH THAT BARRIER!
...THAT.
WHEN YOU SAY "NO PROBLEM"...?
I AM 94 PERCENT SURE THAT IF I SHOOT YOU OUT OF THE CANNON POINT-BLANK WHEN THE DISTORTION'S ENERGY LEVEL IS AT ITS LOWEST, YOU'LL GO THROUGH!
HAVE YOU TESTED IT?
A FEW ROCKS. A SKULL...
...MAYBE I'M 91 PERCENT SURE.

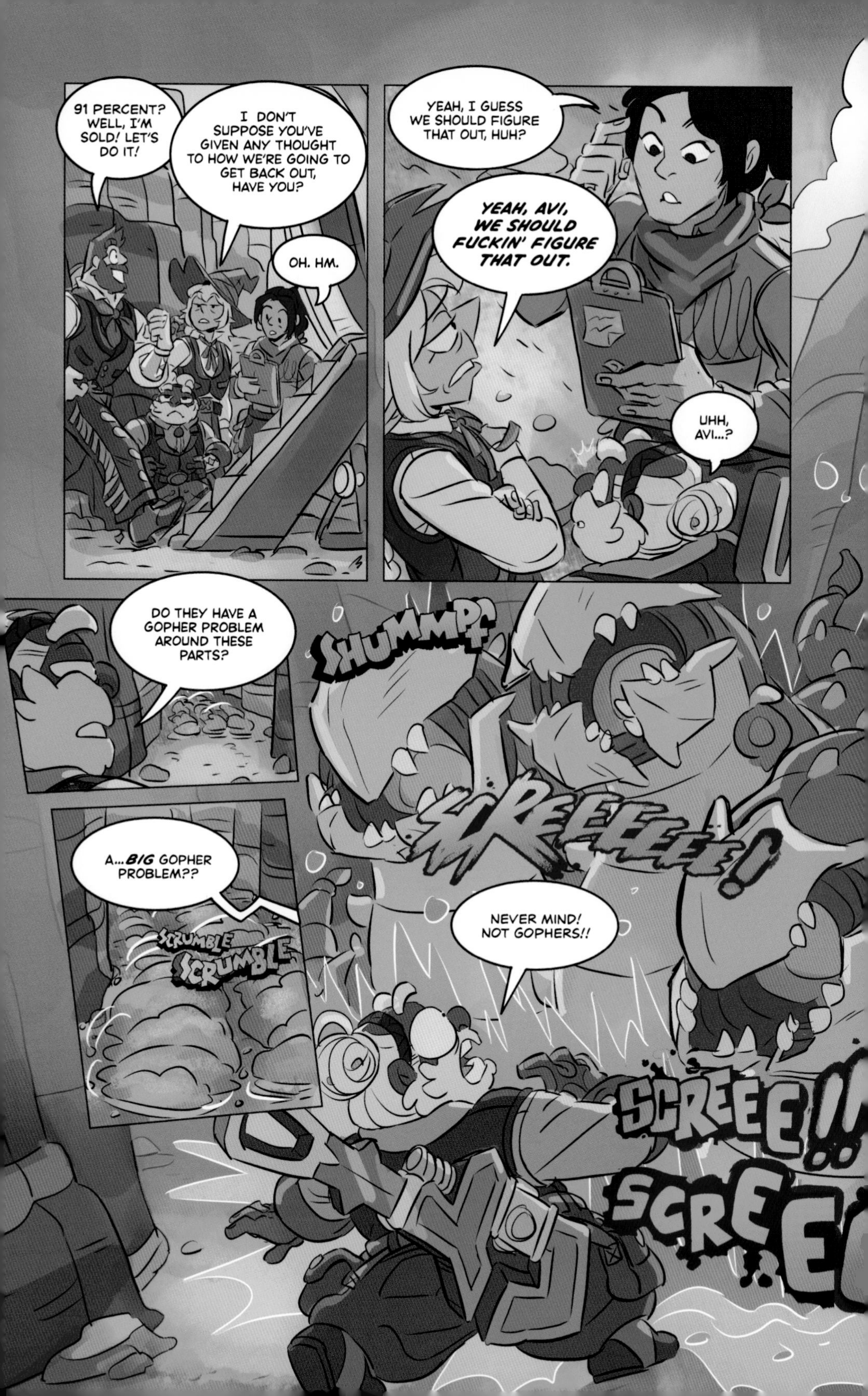
91 PERCENT? WELL, I'M SOLD! LET'S DO IT!
I DON'T SUPPOSE YOU'VE GIVEN ANY THOUGHT TO HOW WE'RE GOING TO GET BACK OUT, HAVE YOU?
OH. HM.
YEAH, I GUESS WE SHOULD FIGURE THAT OUT, HUH?
YEAH, AVI, WE SHOULD FUCKIN' FIGURE THAT OUT.
UHH, AVI...?
DO THEY HAVE A GOPHER PROBLEM AROUND THESE PARTS?
A...*BIG* GOPHER PROBLEM??
SCRUMBLE
SCRUMBLE
SHUMMPF
SCREEEEEE!
NEVER MIND! NOT GOPHERS!!
SCREEE!!

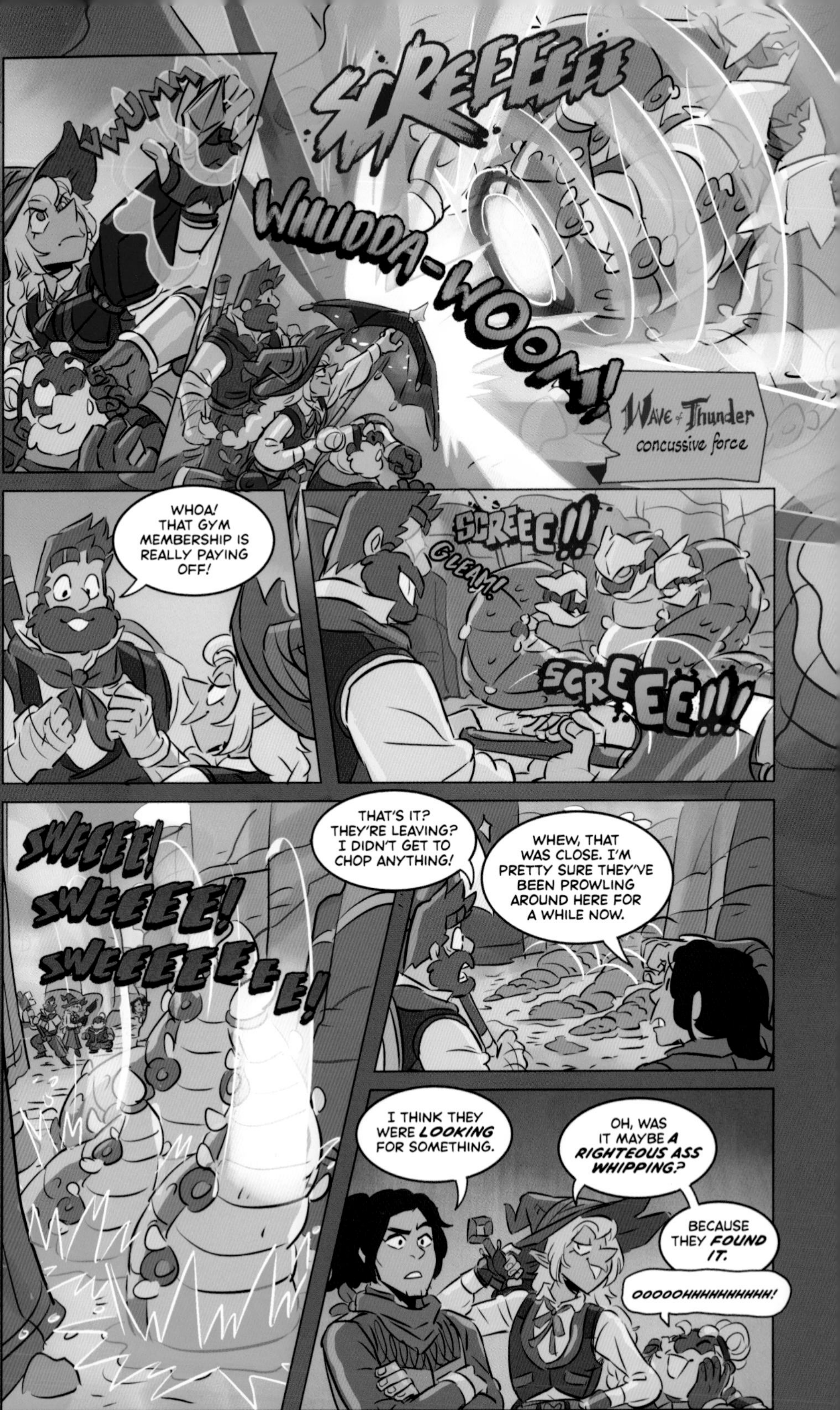
WWUMM
SKREEEEEE
WHUDDA-WOOM!
Wave of Thunder
concussive force
WHOA! THAT GYM MEMBERSHIP IS REALLY PAYING OFF!
SCREEE!!
GLEAM!
SCREEE!!!
SWEEEE!
SWEEEEE!
SWEEEEEEEE!
THAT'S IT? THEY'RE LEAVING? I DIDN'T GET TO CHOP ANYTHING!
WHEW, THAT WAS CLOSE. I'M PRETTY SURE THEY'VE BEEN PROWLING AROUND HERE FOR A WHILE NOW.
I THINK THEY WERE *LOOKING* FOR SOMETHING.
OH, WAS IT MAYBE ***A RIGHTEOUS ASS WHIPPING?***
BECAUSE THEY ***FOUND IT.***
OOOOOHHHHHHHHHH!

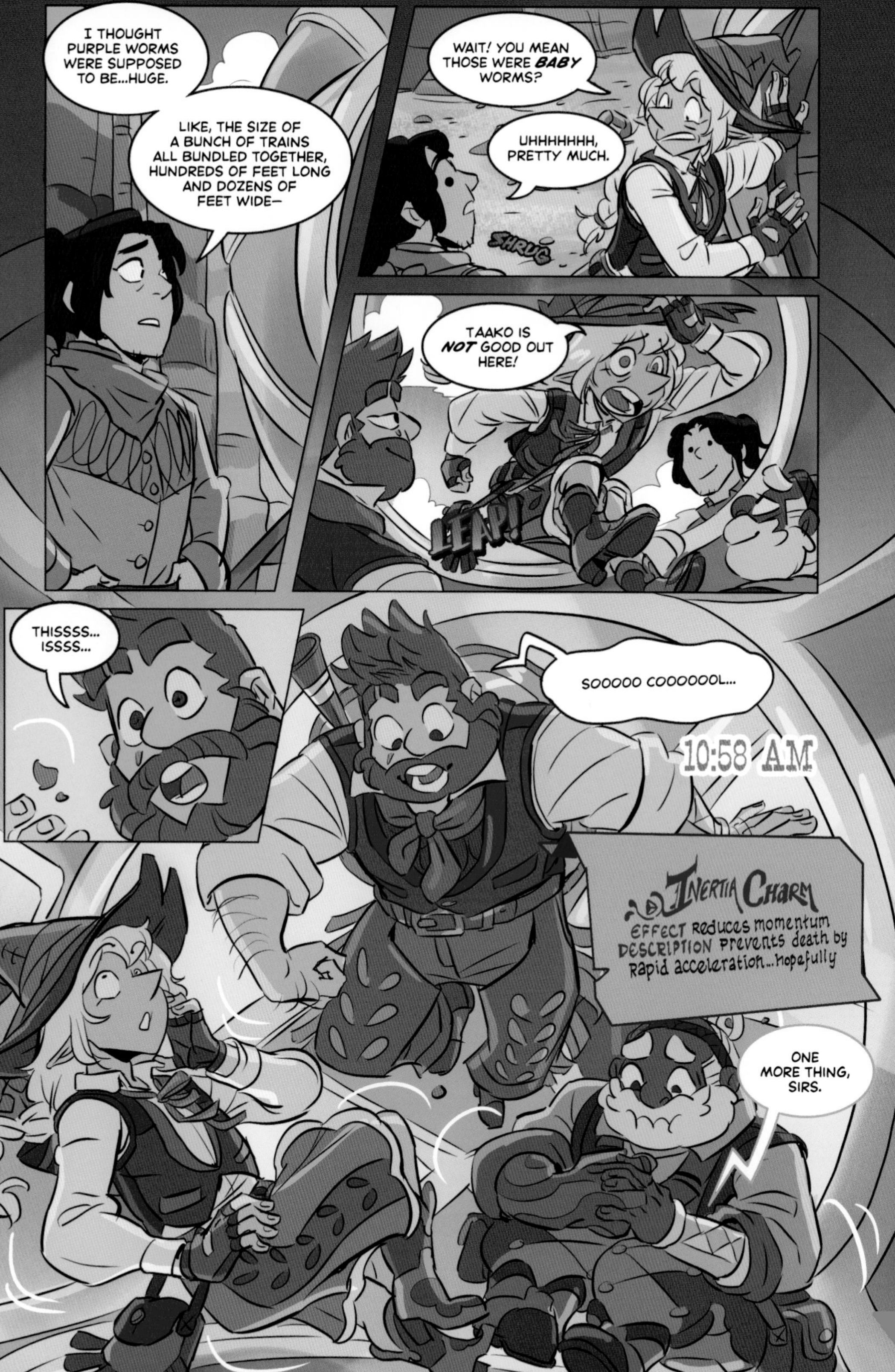
I THOUGHT PURPLE WORMS WERE SUPPOSED TO BE...HUGE.
LIKE, THE SIZE OF A BUNCH OF TRAINS ALL BUNDLED TOGETHER, HUNDREDS OF FEET LONG AND DOZENS OF FEET WIDE—
WAIT! YOU MEAN THOSE WERE BABY WORMS?
UHHHHHHH, PRETTY MUCH.
SHRUG
TAAKO IS NOT GOOD OUT HERE!
LEAP!
THISSSS... ISSSS...
SOOOOO COOOOOOL...
10:58 AM
INERTIA CHARM
EFFECT Reduces momentum
DESCRIPTION Prevents death by Rapid acceleration...hopefully
ONE MORE THING, SIRS.

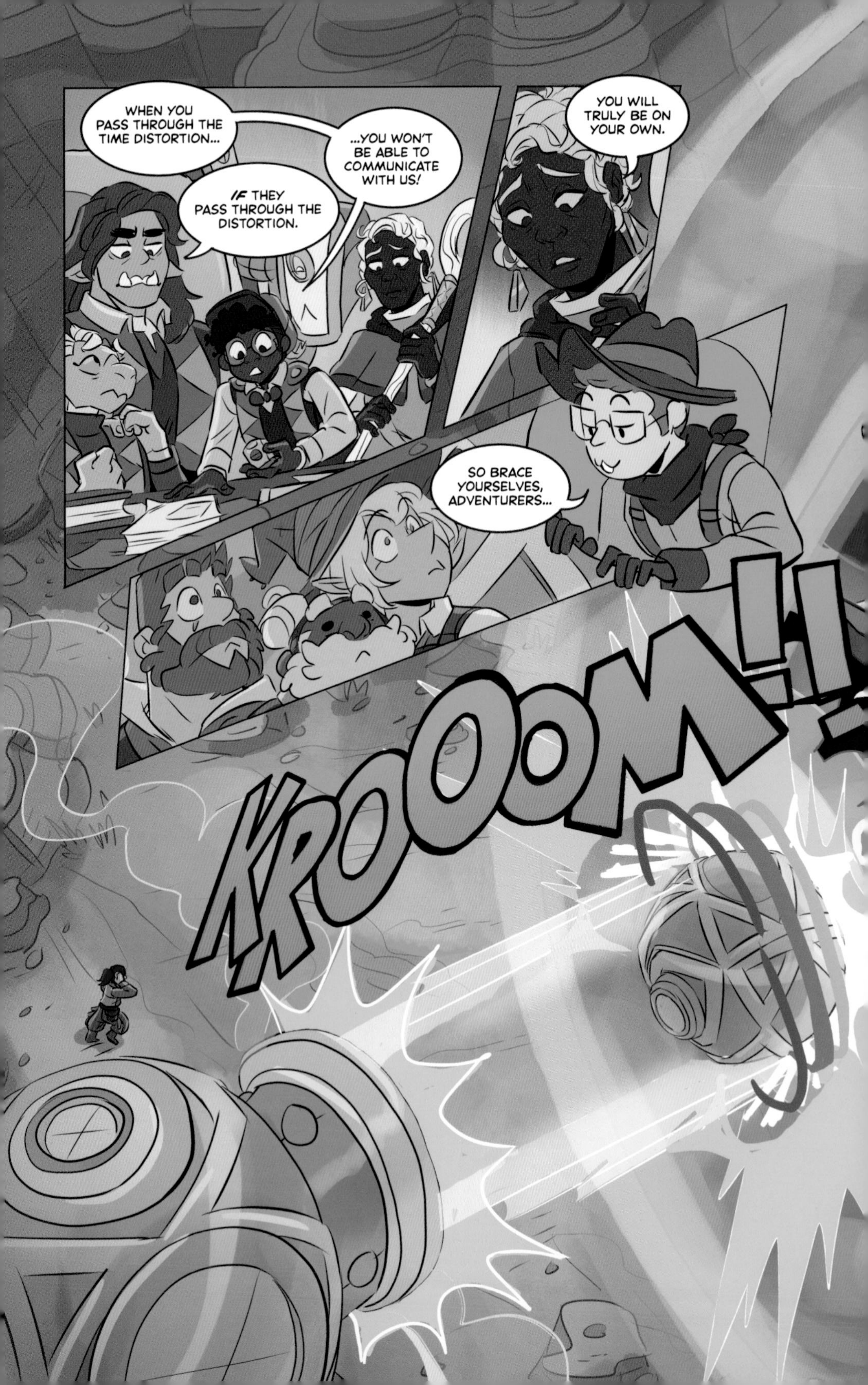

WHEN YOU PASS THROUGH THE TIME DISTORTION...
IF THEY PASS THROUGH THE DISTORTION.
...YOU WON'T BE ABLE TO COMMUNICATE WITH US!
YOU WILL TRULY BE ON YOUR OWN.
SO BRACE YOURSELVES, ADVENTURERS...
KROOOM!!!

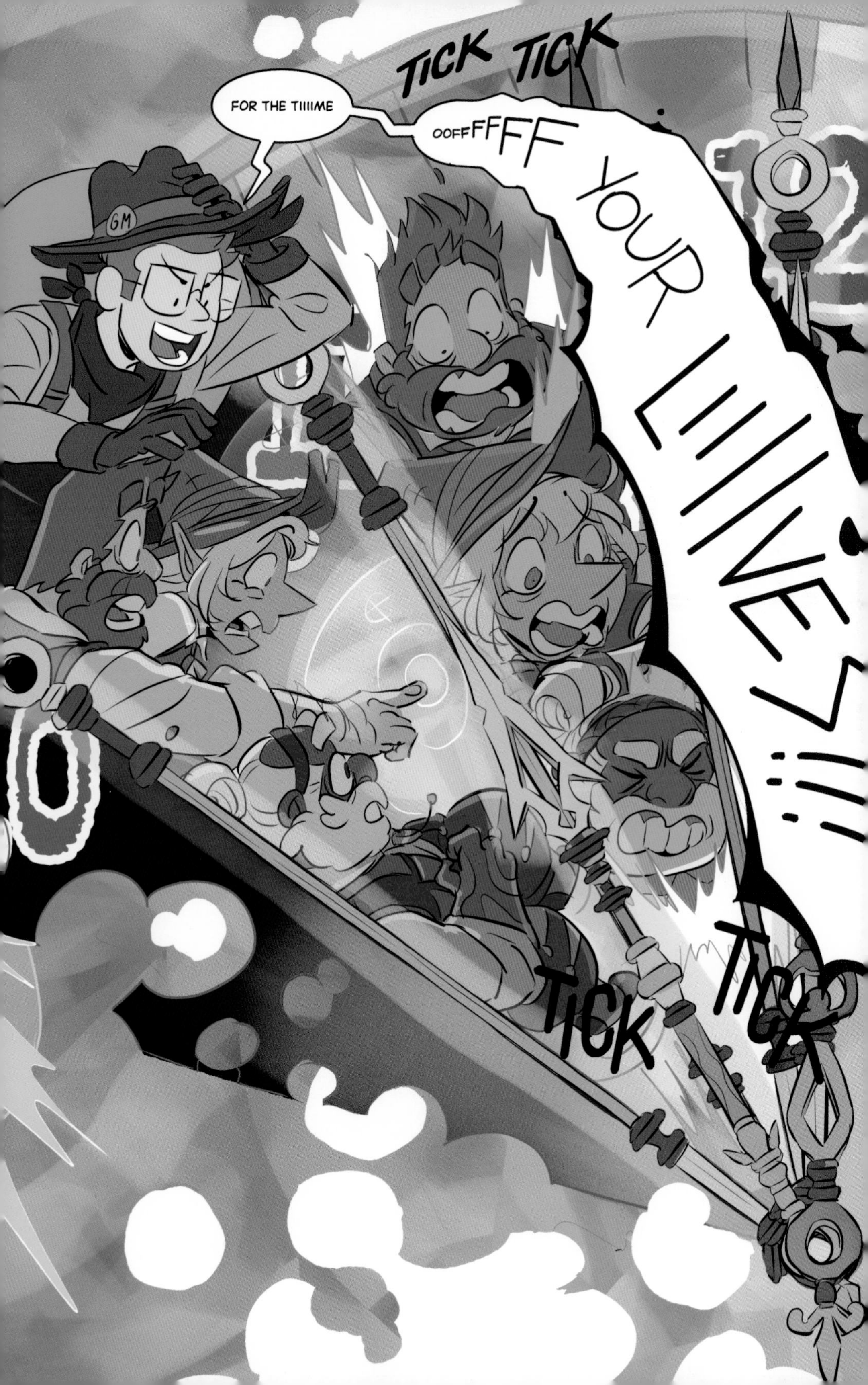

TICK TICK
FOR THE TIIIIME
OOFFFFFF YOUR LIIIIVES!!!
TICK TICK

Chapter

2

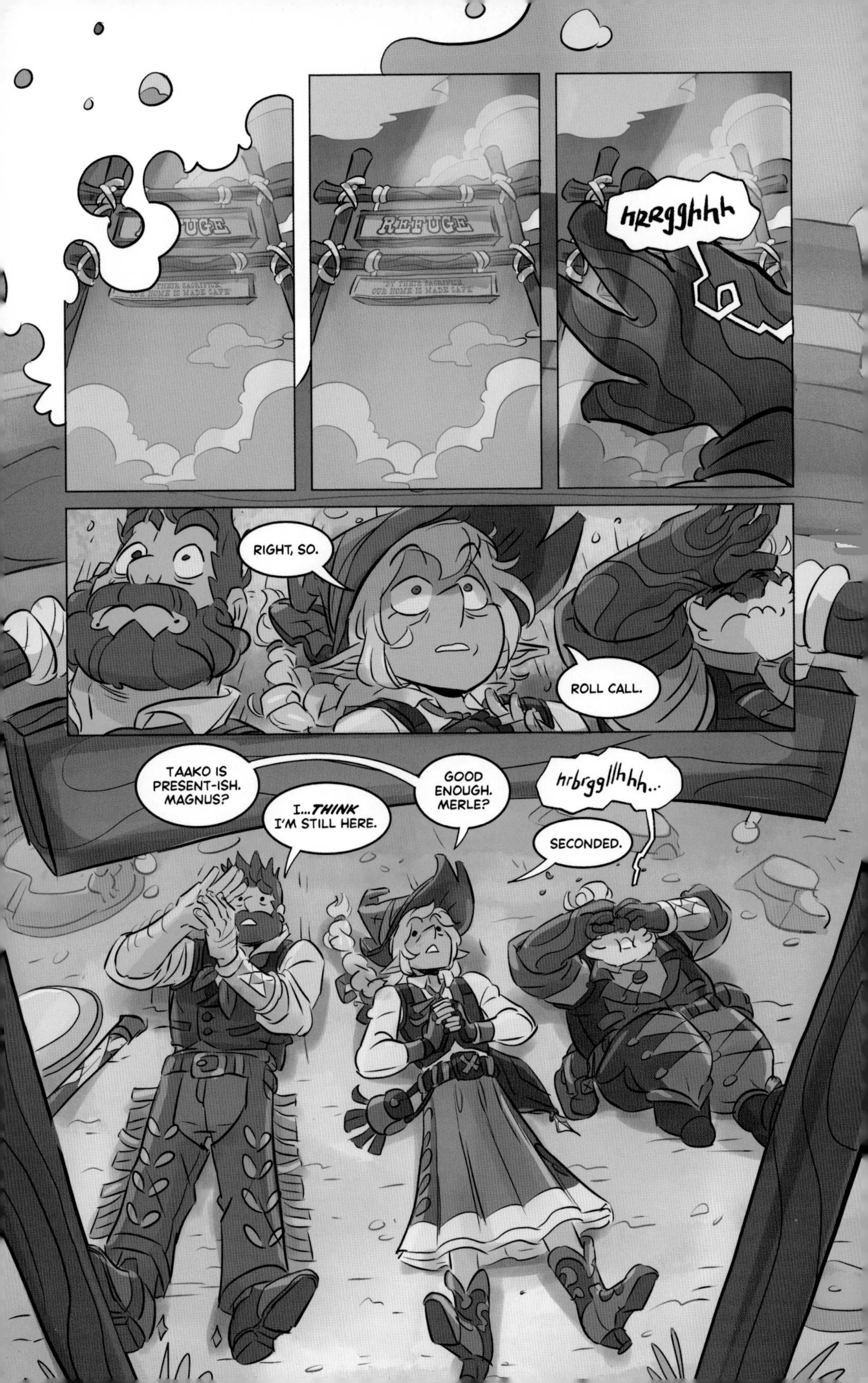
REFUGE
"BY THEIR SACRIFICE, OUR HOME IS MADE SAFE"
hrrgghhh
RIGHT, SO.
ROLL CALL.
TAAKO IS PRESENT-ISH. MAGNUS?
I...*THINK* I'M STILL HERE.
GOOD ENOUGH. MERLE?
hrbrggllhhh...
SECONDED.

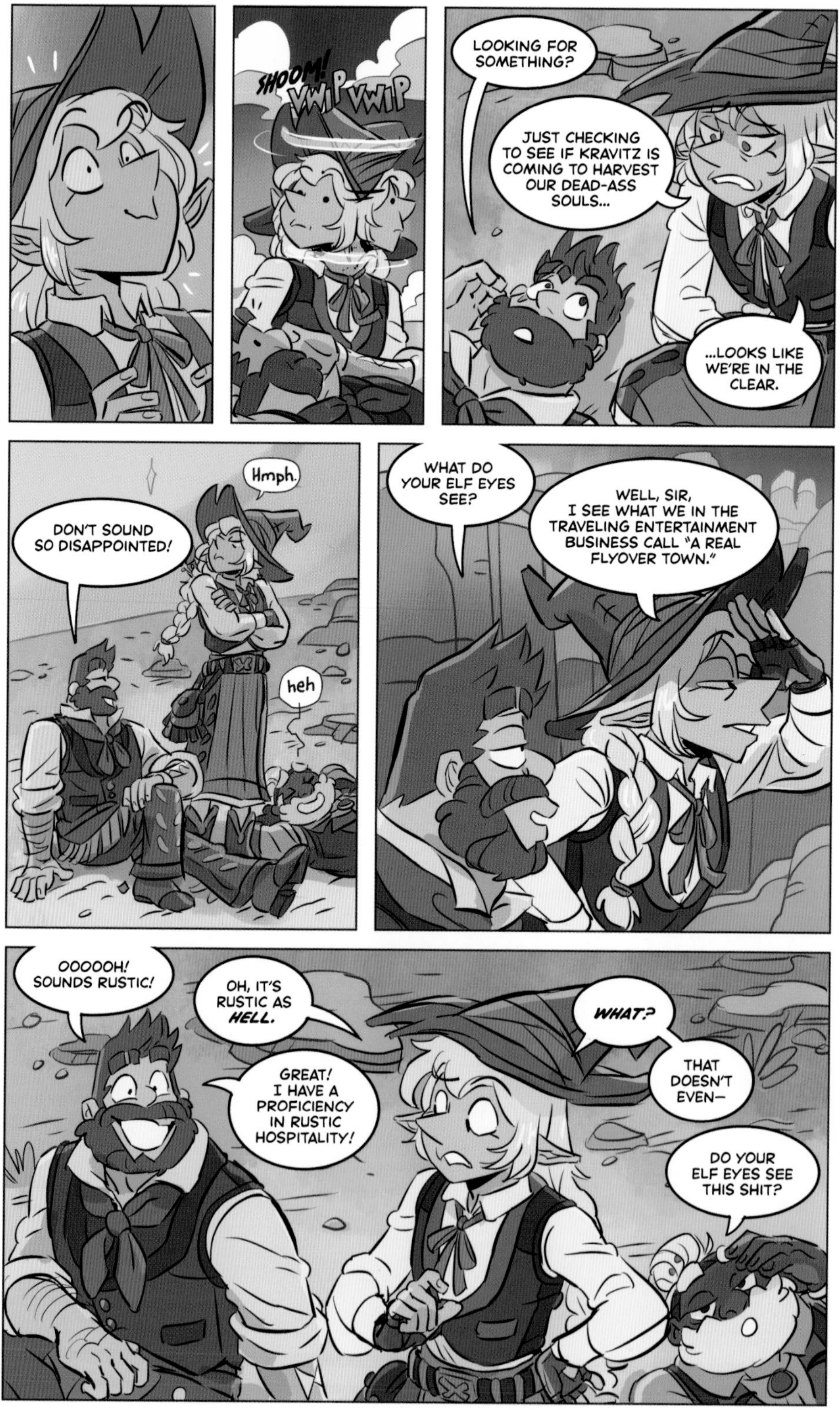
SHOOM!
VWIP VWIP
LOOKING FOR SOMETHING?
JUST CHECKING TO SEE IF KRAVITZ IS COMING TO HARVEST OUR DEAD-ASS SOULS...
...LOOKS LIKE WE'RE IN THE CLEAR.
Hmph.
DON'T SOUND SO DISAPPOINTED!
heh
WHAT DO YOUR ELF EYES SEE?
WELL, SIR, I SEE WHAT WE IN THE TRAVELING ENTERTAINMENT BUSINESS CALL "A REAL FLYOVER TOWN."
OOOOOH! SOUNDS RUSTIC!
OH, IT'S RUSTIC AS HELL.
GREAT! I HAVE A PROFICIENCY IN RUSTIC HOSPITALITY!
WHAT?
THAT DOESN'T EVEN—
DO YOUR ELF EYES SEE THIS SHIT?

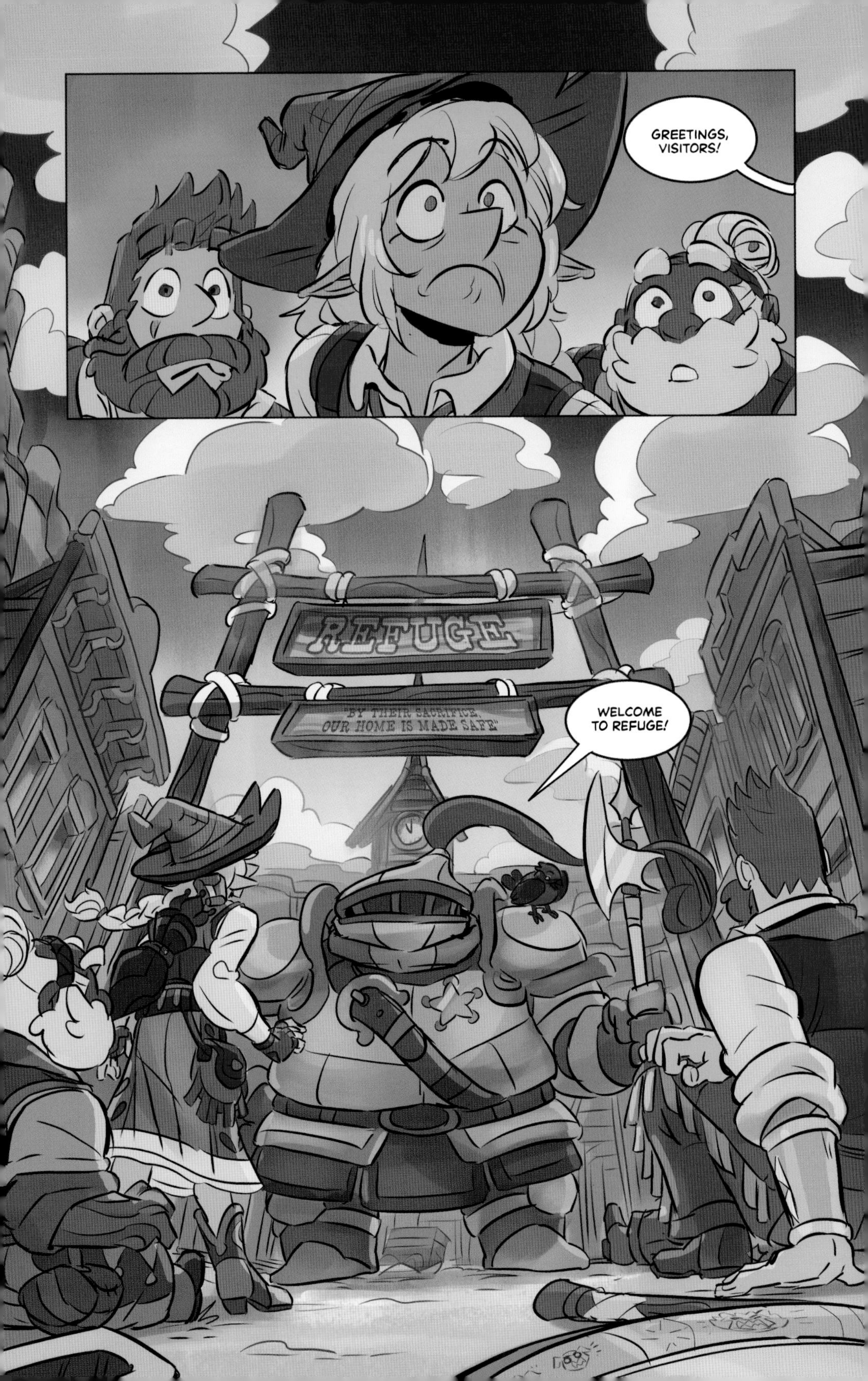
GREETINGS, VISITORS!
REFUGE
"BY THEIR SACRIFICE, OUR HOME IS MADE SAFE"
WELCOME TO REFUGE!

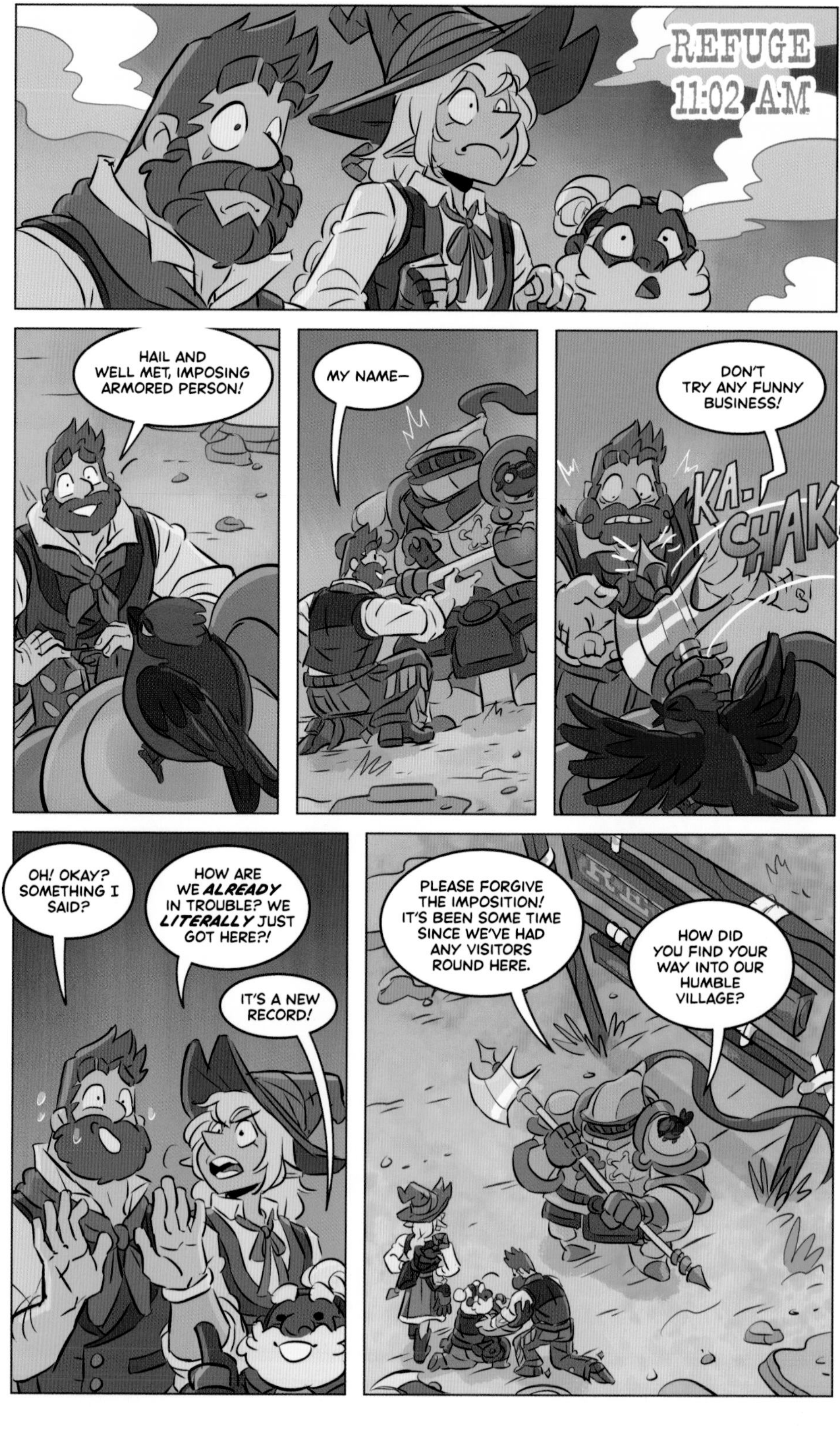
REFUGE
11:02 AM
HAIL AND WELL MET, IMPOSING ARMORED PERSON!
MY NAME—
DON'T TRY ANY FUNNY BUSINESS!
KA-CHAK!
OH! OKAY? SOMETHING I SAID?
HOW ARE WE ALREADY IN TROUBLE? WE LITERALLY JUST GOT HERE?!
IT'S A NEW RECORD!
PLEASE FORGIVE THE IMPOSITION! IT'S BEEN SOME TIME SINCE WE'VE HAD ANY VISITORS ROUND HERE.
HOW DID YOU FIND YOUR WAY INTO OUR HUMBLE VILLAGE?

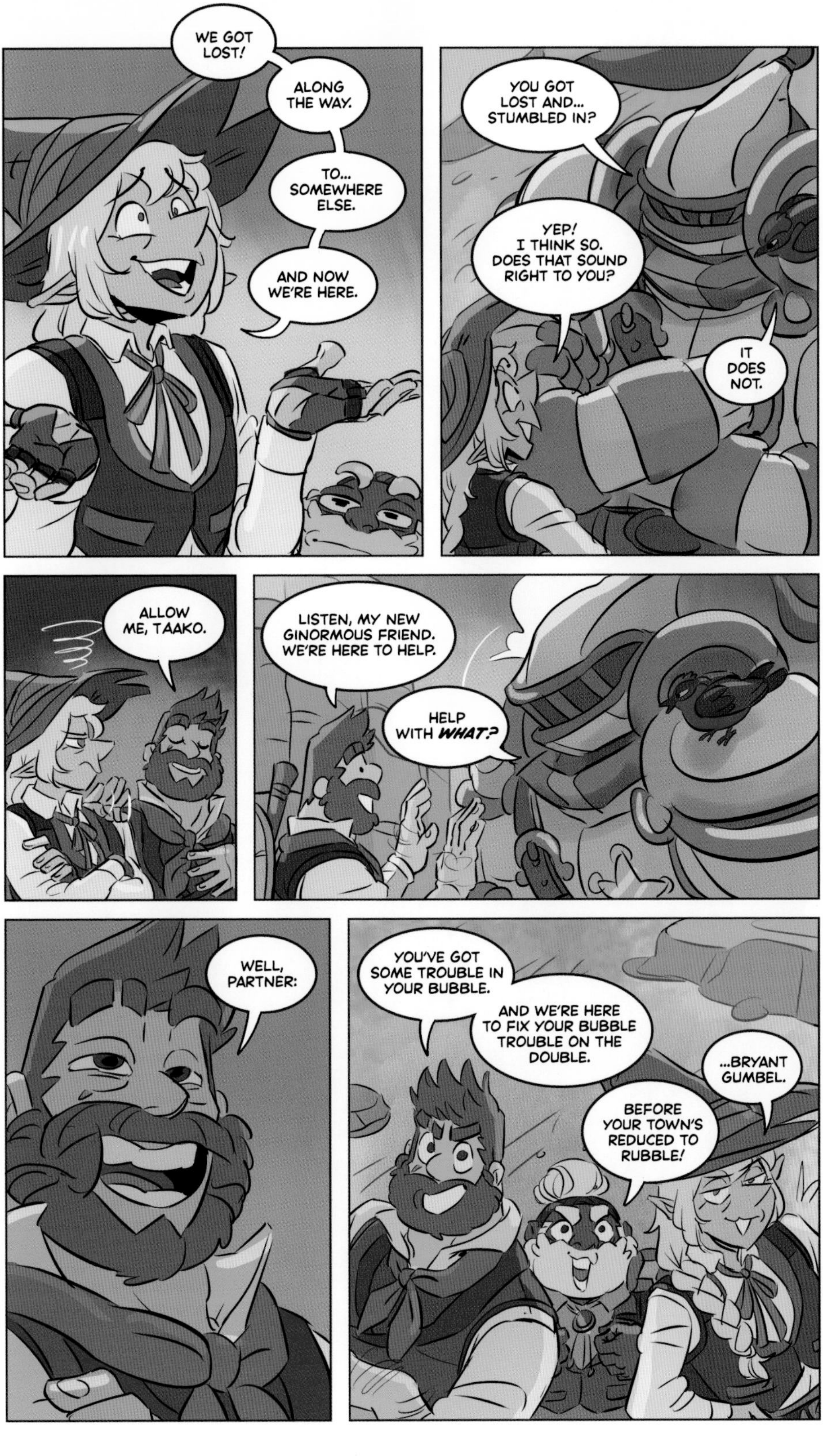
WE GOT LOST!
ALONG THE WAY.
TO... SOMEWHERE ELSE.
AND NOW WE'RE HERE.
YOU GOT LOST AND... STUMBLED IN?
YEP! I THINK SO. DOES THAT SOUND RIGHT TO YOU?
IT DOES NOT.
ALLOW ME, TAAKO.
LISTEN, MY NEW GINORMOUS FRIEND. WE'RE HERE TO HELP.
HELP WITH *WHAT?*
WELL, PARTNER:
YOU'VE GOT SOME TROUBLE IN YOUR BUBBLE.
AND WE'RE HERE TO FIX YOUR BUBBLE TROUBLE ON THE DOUBLE.
BEFORE YOUR TOWN'S REDUCED TO RUBBLE!
...BRYANT GUMBEL.

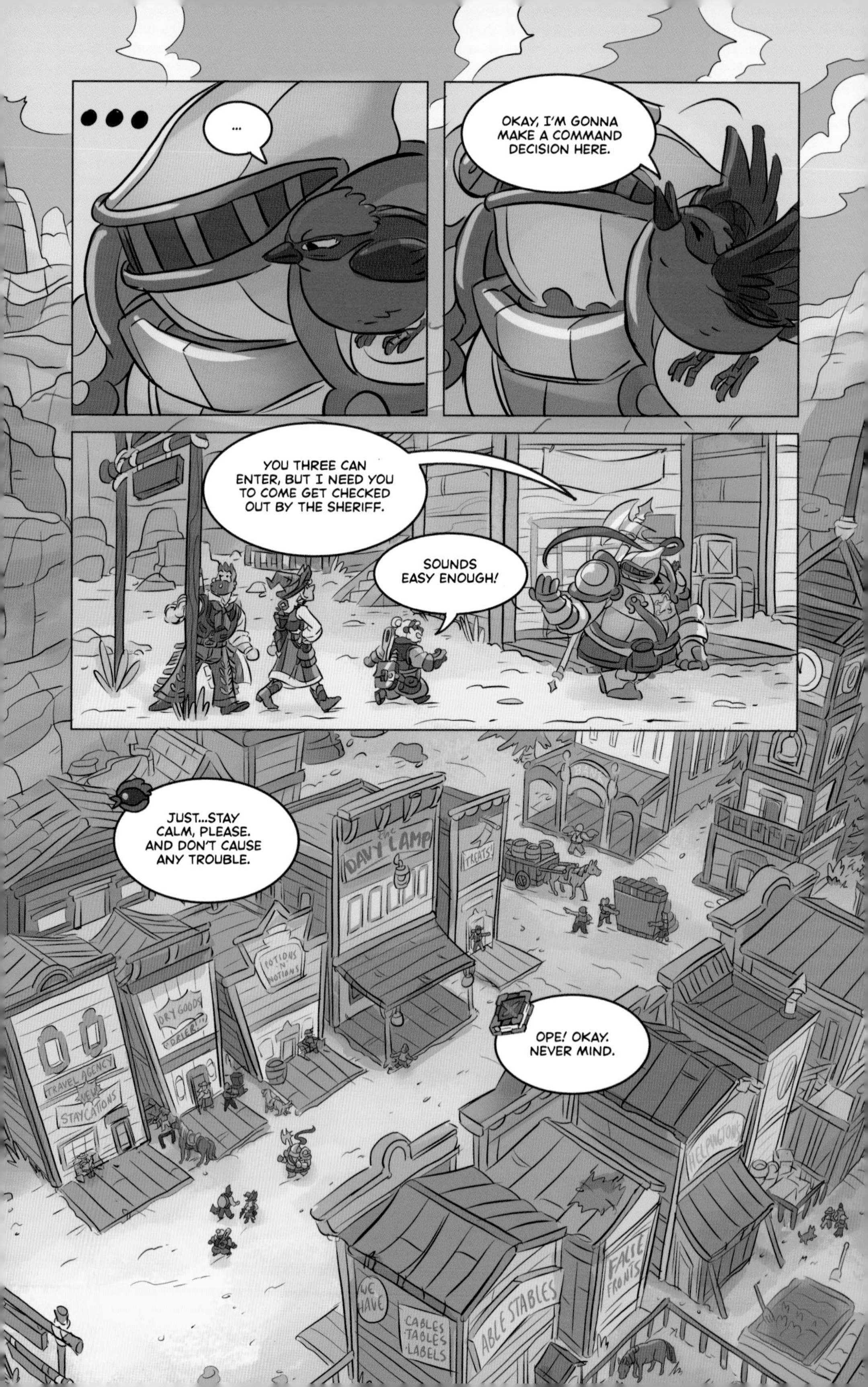

...
OKAY, I'M GONNA MAKE A COMMAND DECISION HERE.
YOU THREE CAN ENTER, BUT I NEED YOU TO COME GET CHECKED OUT BY THE SHERIFF.
SOUNDS EASY ENOUGH!
JUST...STAY CALM, PLEASE. AND DON'T CAUSE ANY TROUBLE.
THE DAVY LAMP
TREATS!
POTIONS 'N' MOTIONS
DRY GOODS
TRAVEL AGENCY
NEW
STAYCATIONS
OPE! OKAY. NEVER MIND.
HELPINGTONS
FALSE FRONTS
ABLE STABLES
WE HAVE
CABLES TABLES LABELS

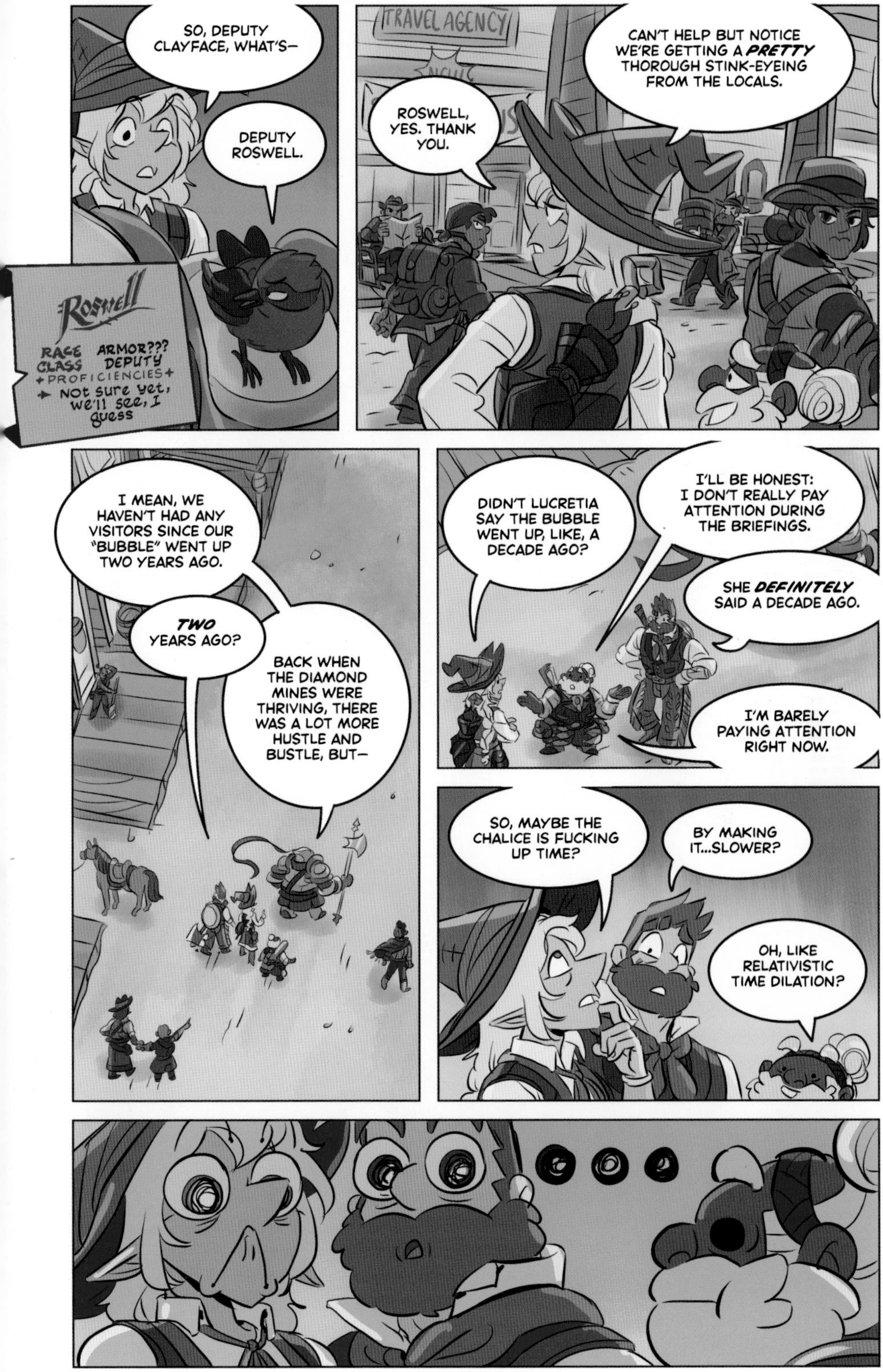
SO, DEPUTY CLAYFACE, WHAT'S—
DEPUTY ROSWELL.
Roswell
RACE ARMOR???
CLASS DEPUTY
✦PROFICIENCIES✦
✦ Not sure yet, we'll see, I guess
TRAVEL AGENCY
ROSWELL, YES. THANK YOU.
CAN'T HELP BUT NOTICE WE'RE GETTING A PRETTY THOROUGH STINK-EYEING FROM THE LOCALS.
I MEAN, WE HAVEN'T HAD ANY VISITORS SINCE OUR "BUBBLE" WENT UP TWO YEARS AGO.
TWO YEARS AGO?
BACK WHEN THE DIAMOND MINES WERE THRIVING, THERE WAS A LOT MORE HUSTLE AND BUSTLE, BUT—
DIDN'T LUCRETIA SAY THE BUBBLE WENT UP, LIKE, A DECADE AGO?
I'LL BE HONEST: I DON'T REALLY PAY ATTENTION DURING THE BRIEFINGS.
SHE DEFINITELY SAID A DECADE AGO.
I'M BARELY PAYING ATTENTION RIGHT NOW.
SO, MAYBE THE CHALICE IS FUCKING UP TIME?
BY MAKING IT...SLOWER?
OH, LIKE RELATIVISTIC TIME DILATION?

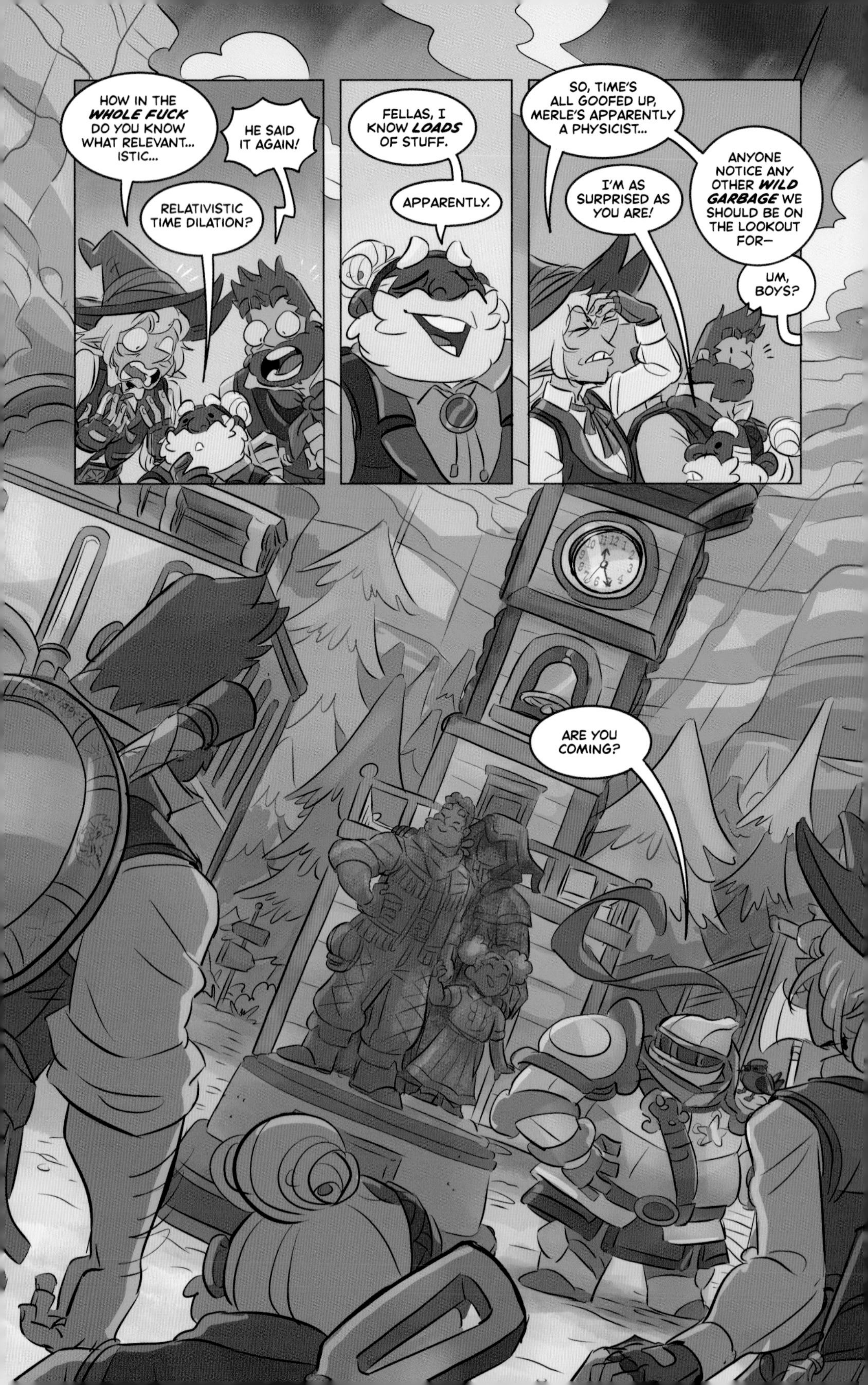
HOW IN THE WHOLE FUCK DO YOU KNOW WHAT RELEVANT... ISTIC...
HE SAID IT AGAIN!
RELATIVISTIC TIME DILATION?
FELLAS, I KNOW LOADS OF STUFF.
APPARENTLY.
SO, TIME'S ALL GOOFED UP, MERLE'S APPARENTLY A PHYSICIST...
I'M AS SURPRISED AS YOU ARE!
ANYONE NOTICE ANY OTHER WILD GARBAGE WE SHOULD BE ON THE LOOKOUT FOR—
UM, BOYS?
ARE YOU COMING?

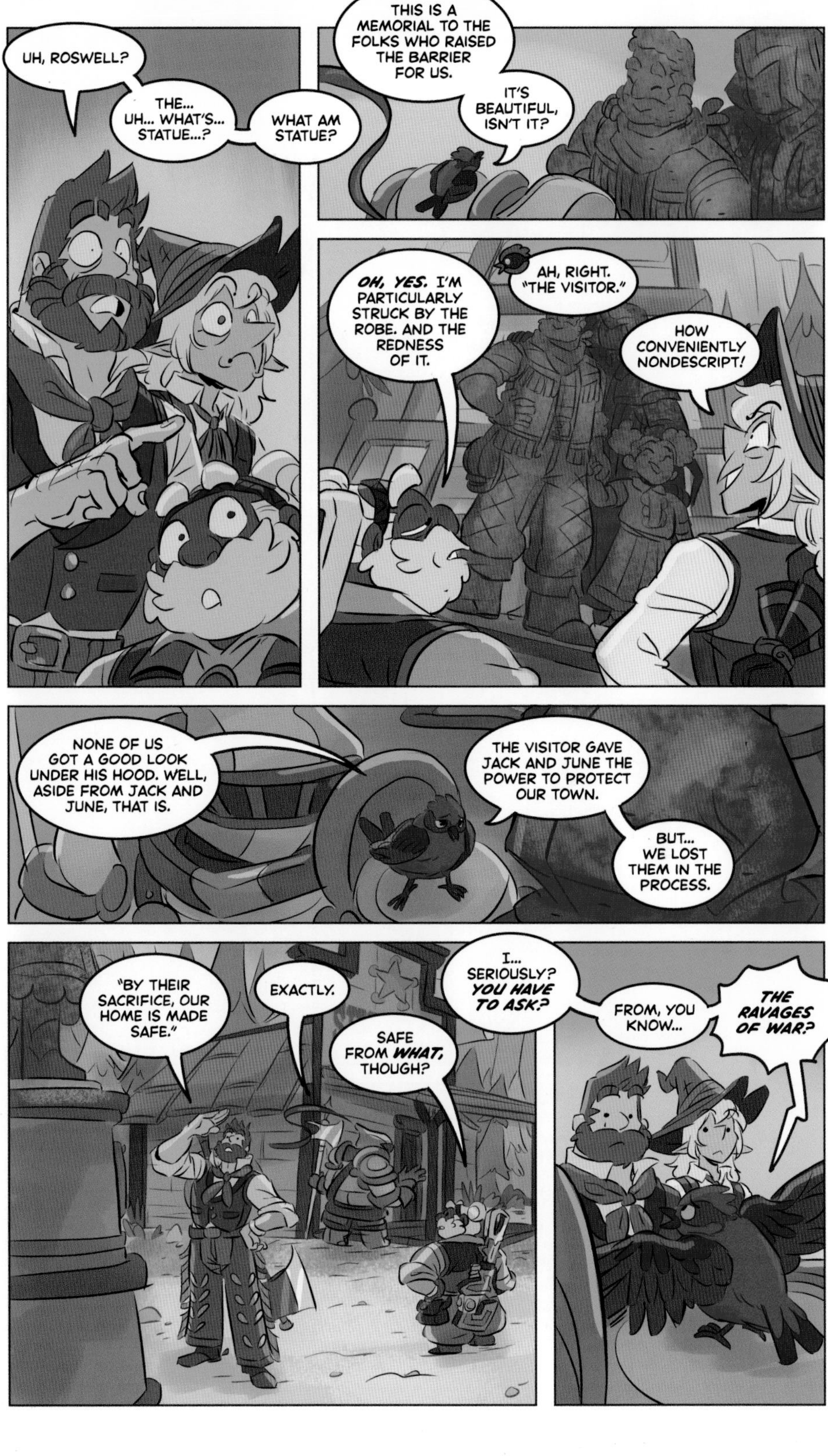
UH, ROSWELL?
THE... UH... WHAT'S... STATUE...?
WHAT AM STATUE?
THIS IS A MEMORIAL TO THE FOLKS WHO RAISED THE BARRIER FOR US.
IT'S BEAUTIFUL, ISN'T IT?
OH, YES. I'M PARTICULARLY STRUCK BY THE ROBE. AND THE REDNESS OF IT.
AH, RIGHT. "THE VISITOR."
HOW CONVENIENTLY NONDESCRIPT!
NONE OF US GOT A GOOD LOOK UNDER HIS HOOD. WELL, ASIDE FROM JACK AND JUNE, THAT IS.
THE VISITOR GAVE JACK AND JUNE THE POWER TO PROTECT OUR TOWN.
BUT... WE LOST THEM IN THE PROCESS.
"BY THEIR SACRIFICE, OUR HOME IS MADE SAFE."
EXACTLY.
SAFE FROM WHAT, THOUGH?
I... SERIOUSLY? YOU HAVE TO ASK?
FROM, YOU KNOW...
THE RAVAGES OF WAR?

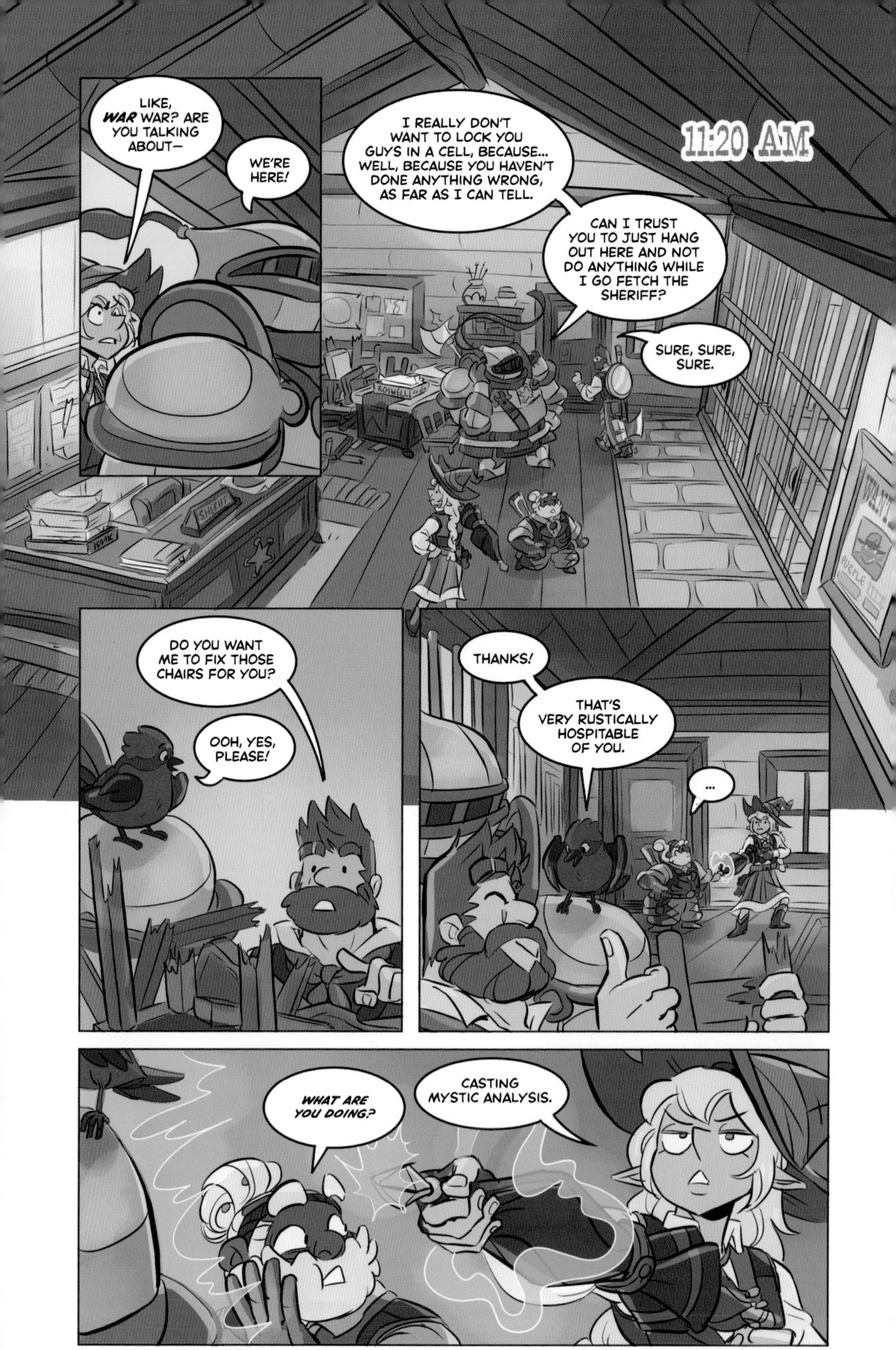
11:20 AM
LIKE, WAR WAR? ARE YOU TALKING ABOUT—
WE'RE HERE!
I REALLY DON'T WANT TO LOCK YOU GUYS IN A CELL, BECAUSE... WELL, BECAUSE YOU HAVEN'T DONE ANYTHING WRONG, AS FAR AS I CAN TELL.
CAN I TRUST YOU TO JUST HANG OUT HERE AND NOT DO ANYTHING WHILE I GO FETCH THE SHERIFF?
SURE, SURE, SURE.
SHERIFF
DO YOU WANT ME TO FIX THOSE CHAIRS FOR YOU?
OOH, YES, PLEASE!
THANKS!
THAT'S VERY RUSTICALLY HOSPITABLE OF YOU.
...
WHAT ARE YOU DOING?
CASTING MYSTIC ANALYSIS.

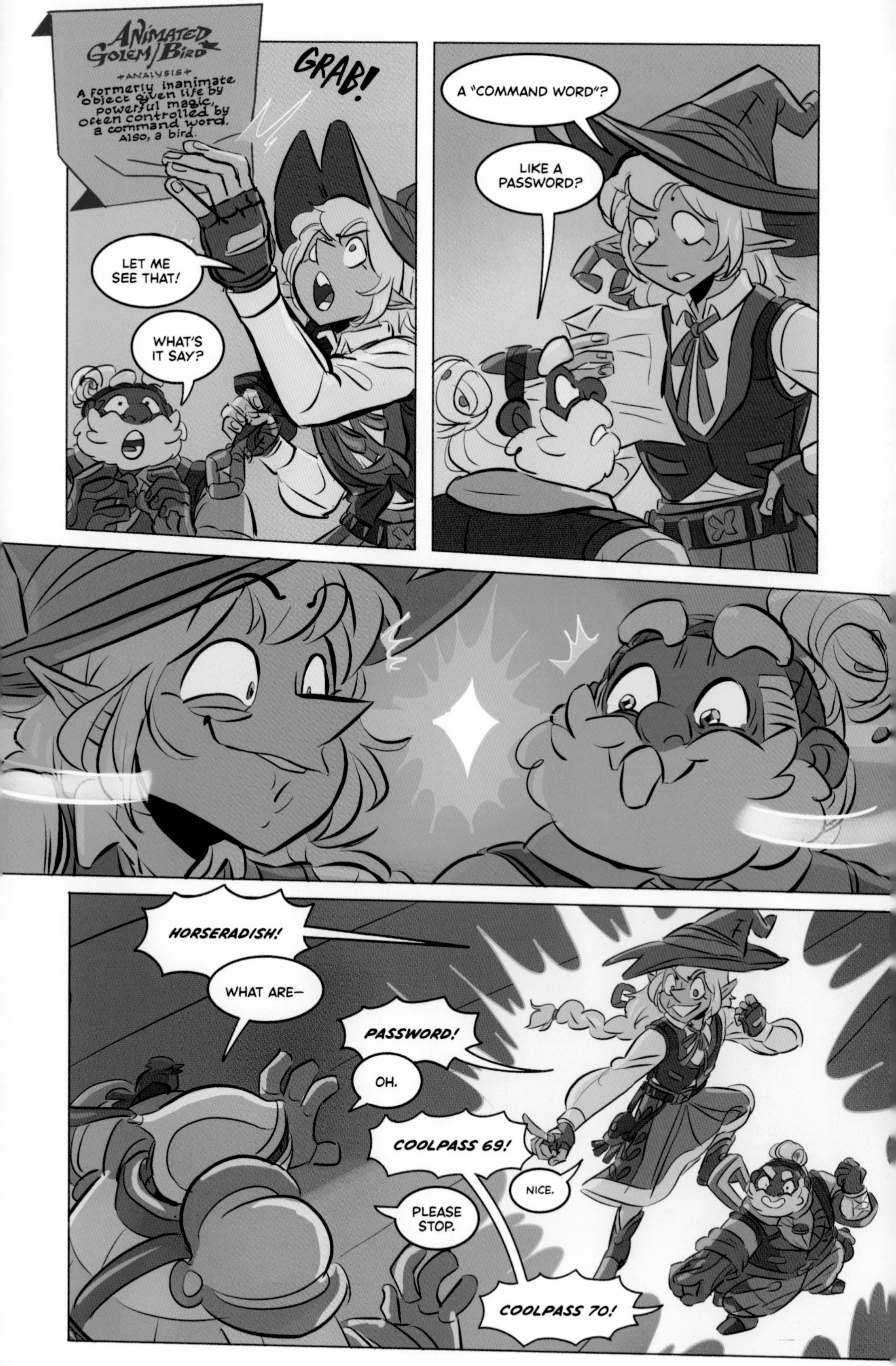
Animated Golem/Bird
+ANALYSIS+
A formerly inanimate object given life by powerful magic, often controlled by a command word. Also, a bird.
GRAB!
LET ME SEE THAT!
WHAT'S IT SAY?
A "COMMAND WORD"?
LIKE A PASSWORD?
HORSERADISH!
WHAT ARE—
PASSWORD!
OH.
COOLPASS 69!
NICE.
PLEASE STOP.
COOLPASS 70!

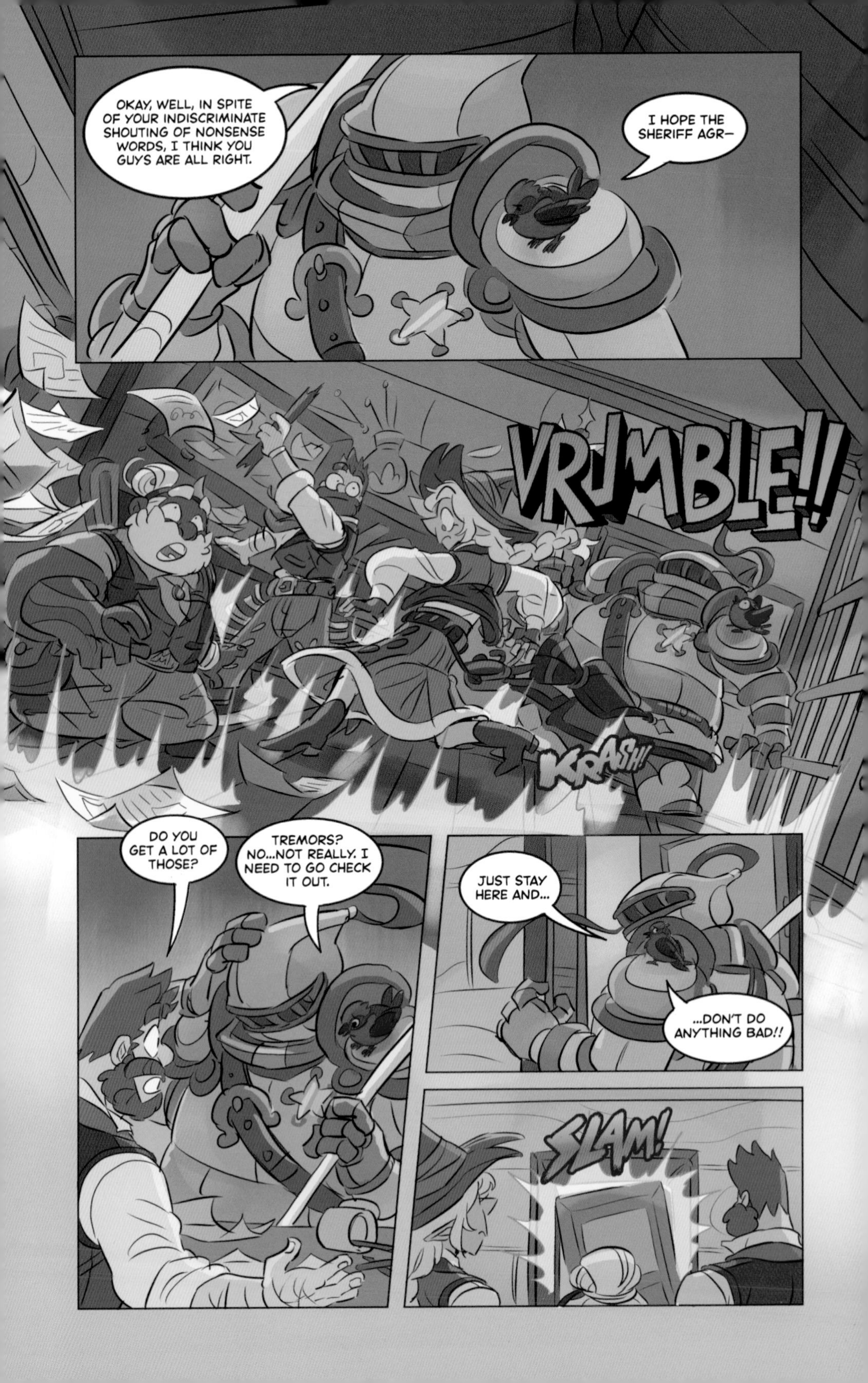
OKAY, WELL, IN SPITE OF YOUR INDISCRIMINATE SHOUTING OF NONSENSE WORDS, I THINK YOU GUYS ARE ALL RIGHT.
I HOPE THE SHERIFF AGR—
VRUMBLE!!
KRASH!
DO YOU GET A LOT OF THOSE?
TREMORS? NO...NOT REALLY. I NEED TO GO CHECK IT OUT.
JUST STAY HERE AND...
...DON'T DO ANYTHING BAD!!
SLAM!

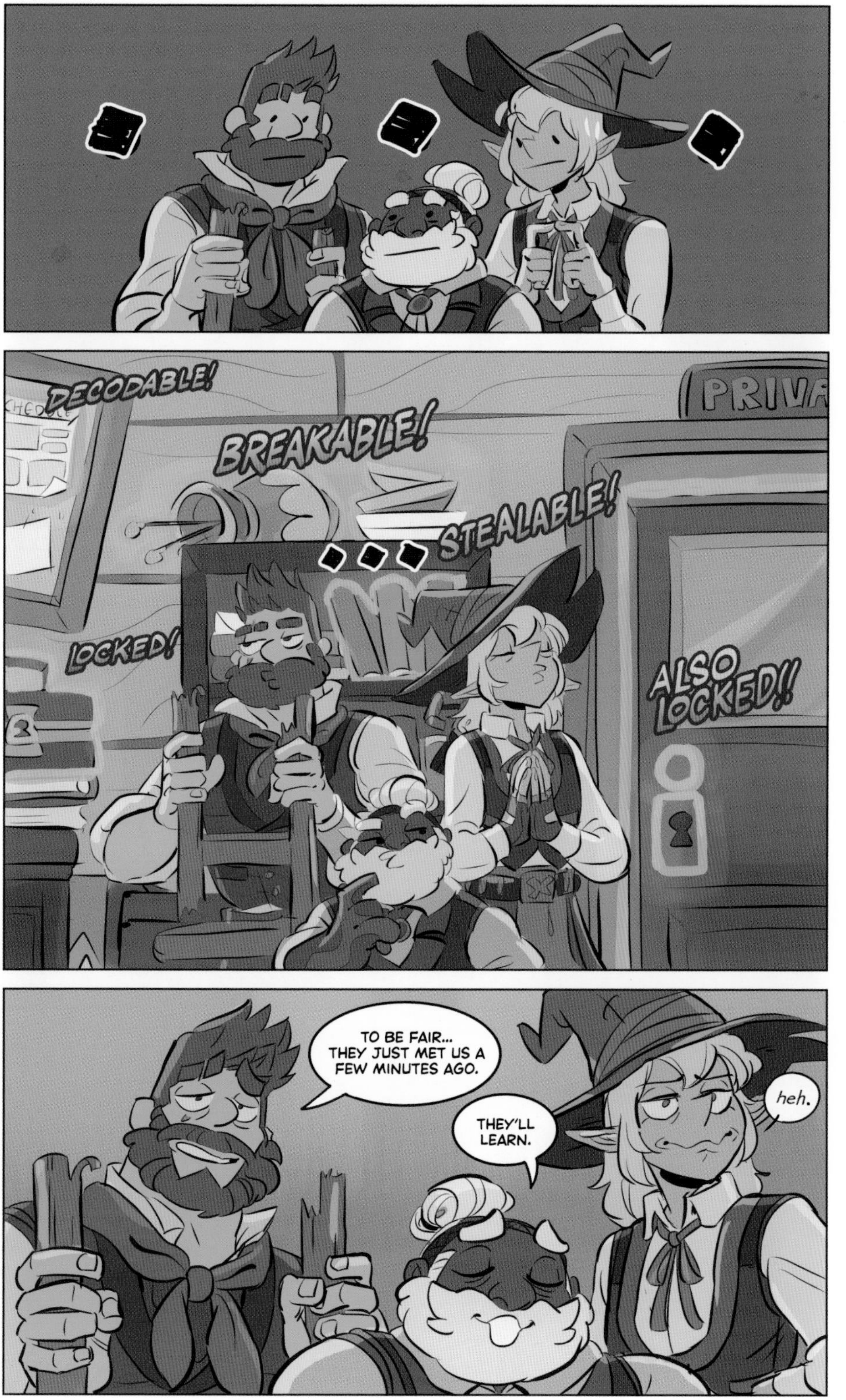
DECODABLE!
SCHEDULE
BREAKABLE!
STEALABLE!
LOCKED!
ALSO LOCKED!!
PRIVA
TO BE FAIR... THEY JUST MET US A FEW MINUTES AGO.
THEY'LL LEARN.
heh.

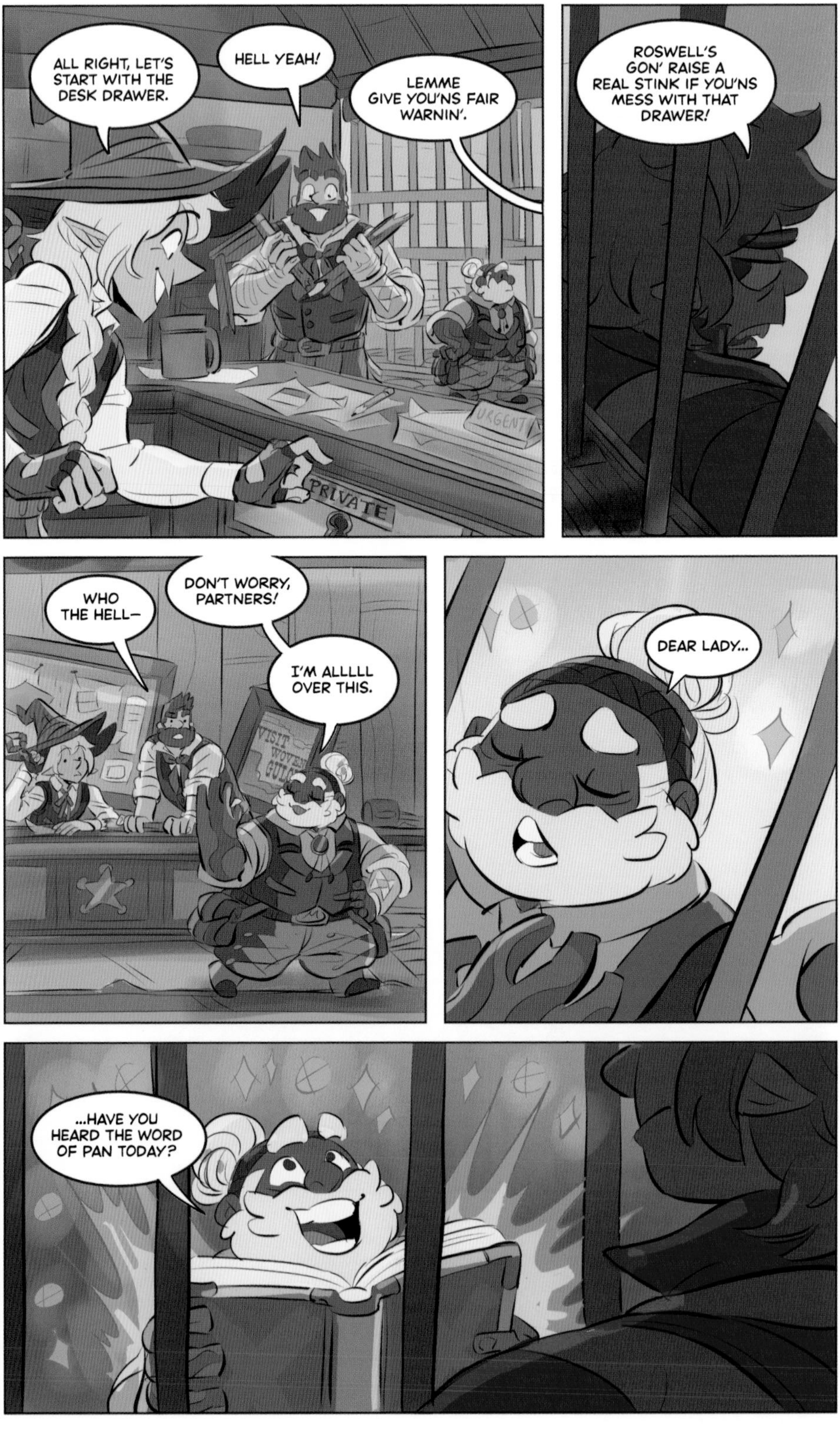
ALL RIGHT, LET'S START WITH THE DESK DRAWER.
HELL YEAH!
LEMME GIVE YOU'NS FAIR WARNIN'.
URGENT
PRIVATE
ROSWELL'S GON' RAISE A REAL STINK IF YOU'NS MESS WITH THAT DRAWER!
WHO THE HELL—
DON'T WORRY, PARTNERS!
I'M ALLLLL OVER THIS.
DEAR LADY...
...HAVE YOU HEARD THE WORD OF PAN TODAY?

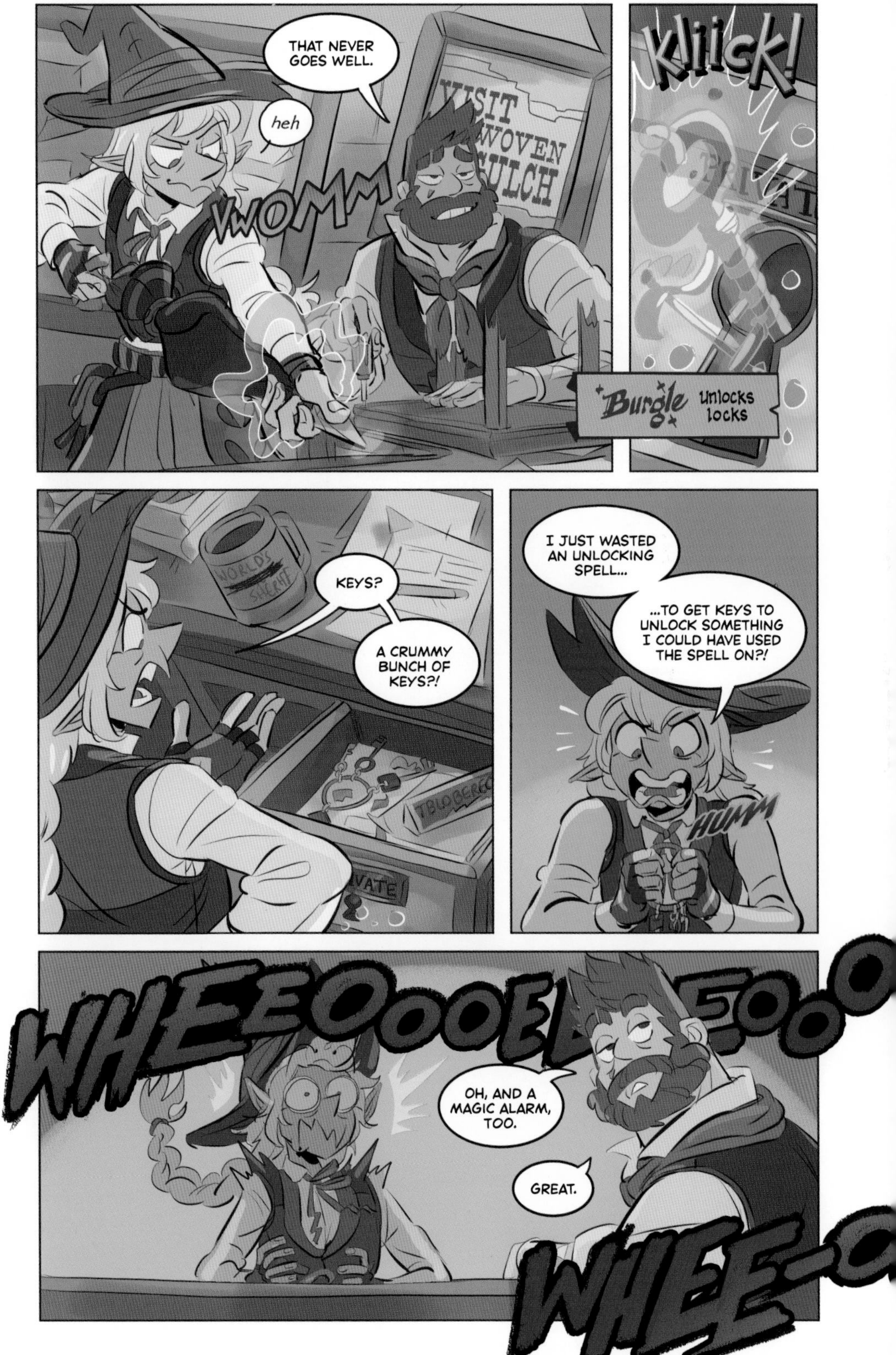
THAT NEVER GOES WELL.
heh
VISIT WOVEN GULCH
WOMM
KLIICK!
Burgle unlocks locks
WORLD'S SHERIFF
KEYS?
A CRUMMY BUNCH OF KEYS?!
I JUST WASTED AN UNLOCKING SPELL...
...TO GET KEYS TO UNLOCK SOMETHING I COULD HAVE USED THE SPELL ON?!
HUMM
WHEEOOOOEE
OH, AND A MAGIC ALARM, TOO.
GREAT.
WHEE-O

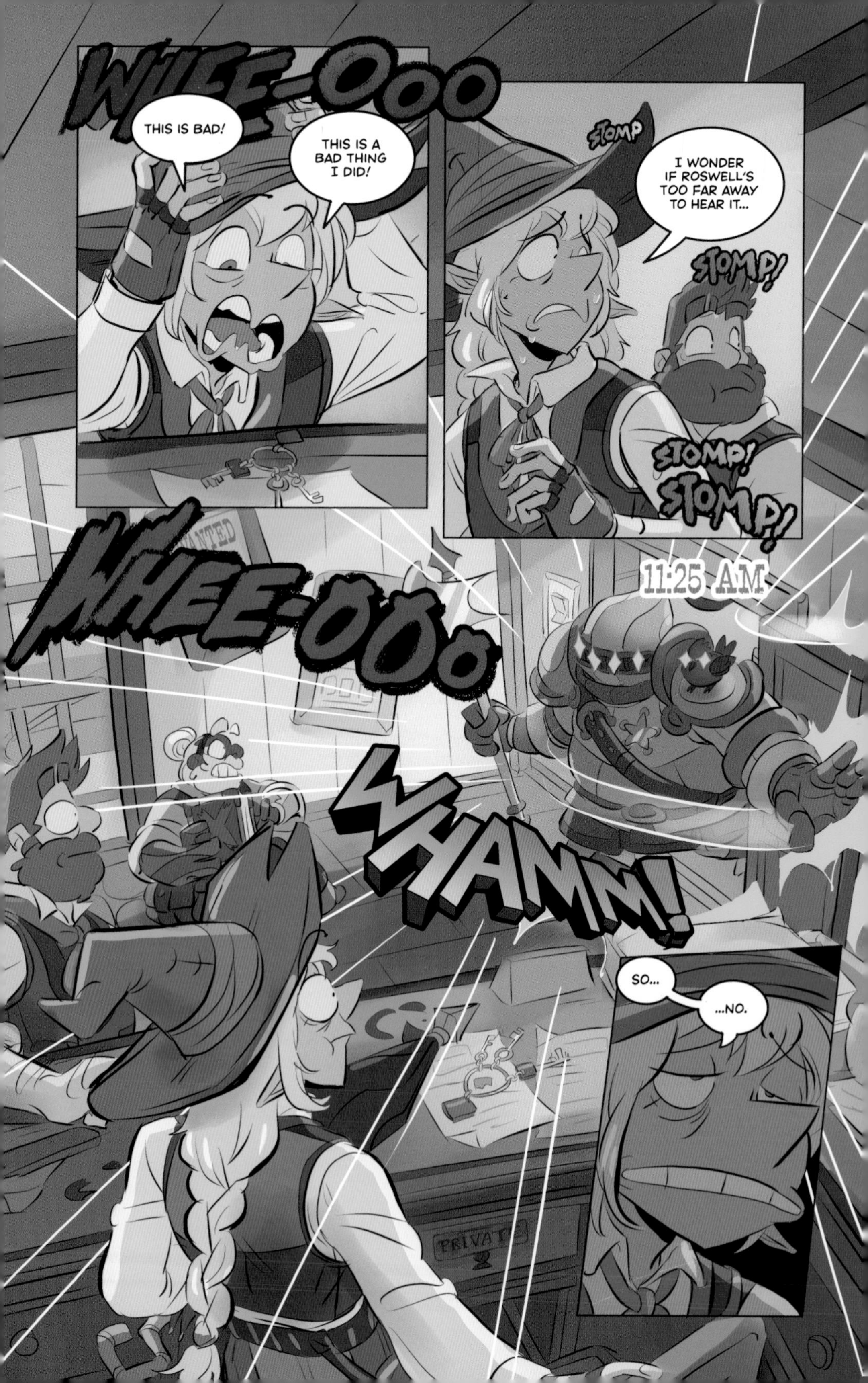
WHEE-OOO
THIS IS BAD!
THIS IS A BAD THING I DID!
STOMP
I WONDER IF ROSWELL'S TOO FAR AWAY TO HEAR IT...
STOMP!
STOMP! STOMP!
WHEE-OOO
11:25 AM
WHAMM!
SO...
...NO.
PRIVATE

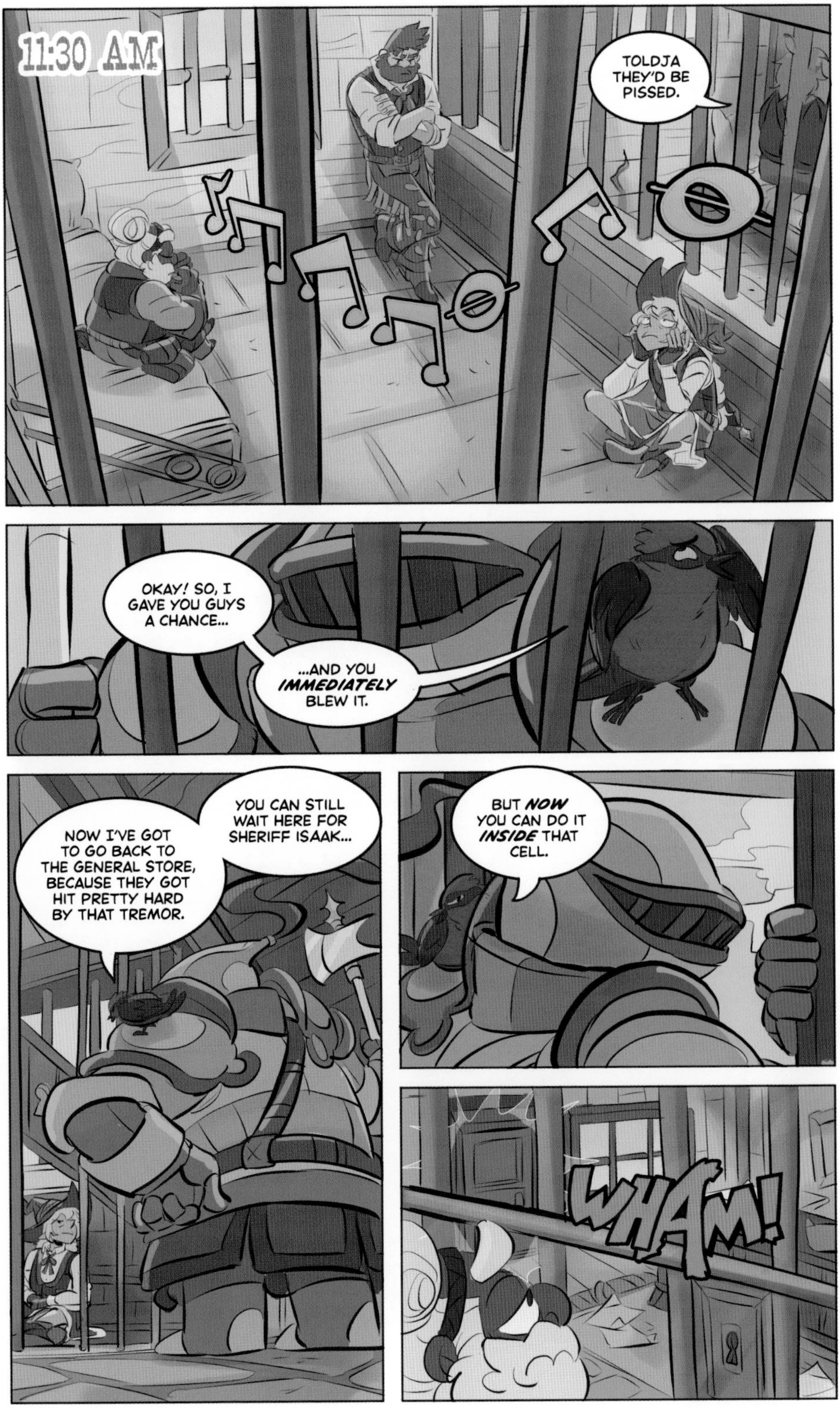
11:30 AM
TOLDJA THEY'D BE PISSED.
OKAY! SO, I GAVE YOU GUYS A CHANCE...
...AND YOU *IMMEDIATELY* BLEW IT.
NOW I'VE GOT TO GO BACK TO THE GENERAL STORE, BECAUSE THEY GOT HIT PRETTY HARD BY THAT TREMOR.
YOU CAN STILL WAIT HERE FOR SHERIFF ISAAK...
BUT *NOW* YOU CAN DO IT *INSIDE* THAT CELL.
WHAM!

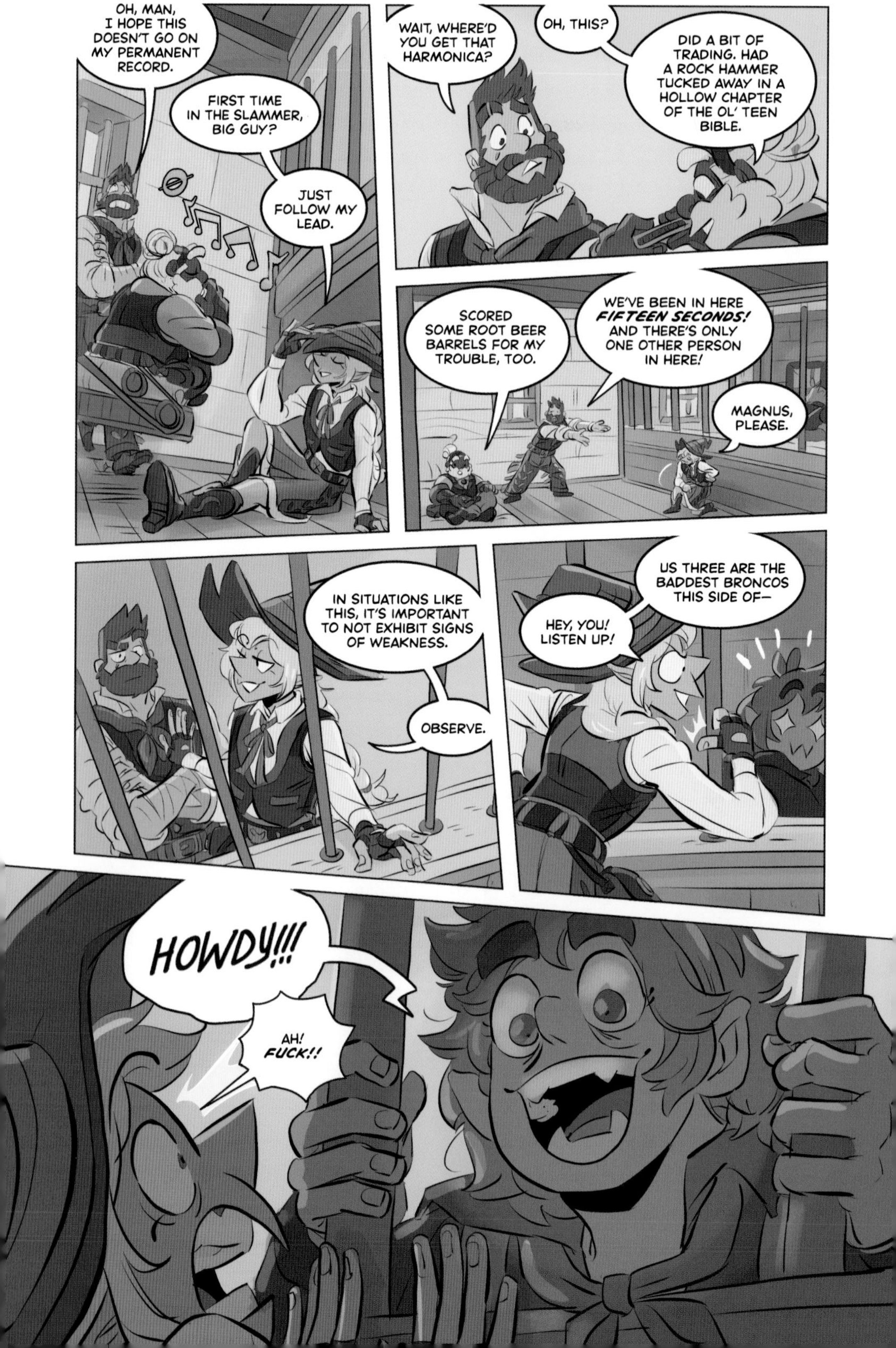
OH, MAN, I HOPE THIS DOESN'T GO ON MY PERMANENT RECORD.
FIRST TIME IN THE SLAMMER, BIG GUY?
JUST FOLLOW MY LEAD.
WAIT, WHERE'D YOU GET THAT HARMONICA?
OH, THIS?
DID A BIT OF TRADING. HAD A ROCK HAMMER TUCKED AWAY IN A HOLLOW CHAPTER OF THE OL' TEEN BIBLE.
SCORED SOME ROOT BEER BARRELS FOR MY TROUBLE, TOO.
WE'VE BEEN IN HERE *FIFTEEN SECONDS!* AND THERE'S ONLY ONE OTHER PERSON IN HERE!
MAGNUS, PLEASE.
IN SITUATIONS LIKE THIS, IT'S IMPORTANT TO NOT EXHIBIT SIGNS OF WEAKNESS.
OBSERVE.
US THREE ARE THE BADDEST BRONCOS THIS SIDE OF—
HEY, YOU! LISTEN UP!
HOWDY!!!
AH! *FUCK!!*

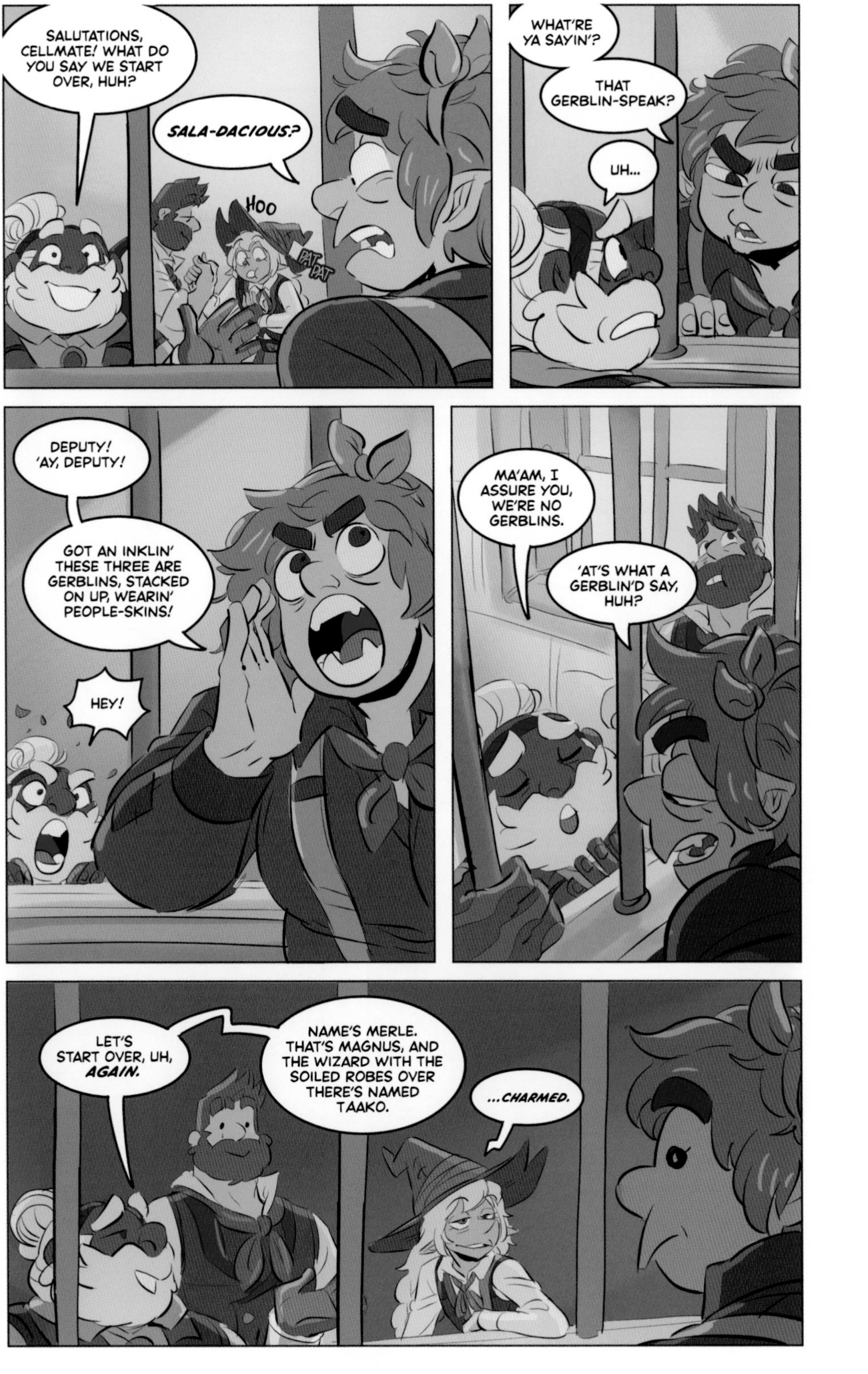
SALUTATIONS, CELLMATE! WHAT DO YOU SAY WE START OVER, HUH?
SALA-DACIOUS?
HOO
PAT PAT
WHAT'RE YA SAYIN'?
THAT GERBLIN-SPEAK?
UH...
DEPUTY! 'AY, DEPUTY!
GOT AN INKLIN' THESE THREE ARE GERBLINS, STACKED ON UP, WEARIN' PEOPLE-SKINS!
HEY!
MA'AM, I ASSURE YOU, WE'RE NO GERBLINS.
'AT'S WHAT A GERBLIN'D SAY, HUH?
LET'S START OVER, UH, AGAIN.
NAME'S MERLE. THAT'S MAGNUS, AND THE WIZARD WITH THE SOILED ROBES OVER THERE'S NAMED TAAKO.
...CHARMED.

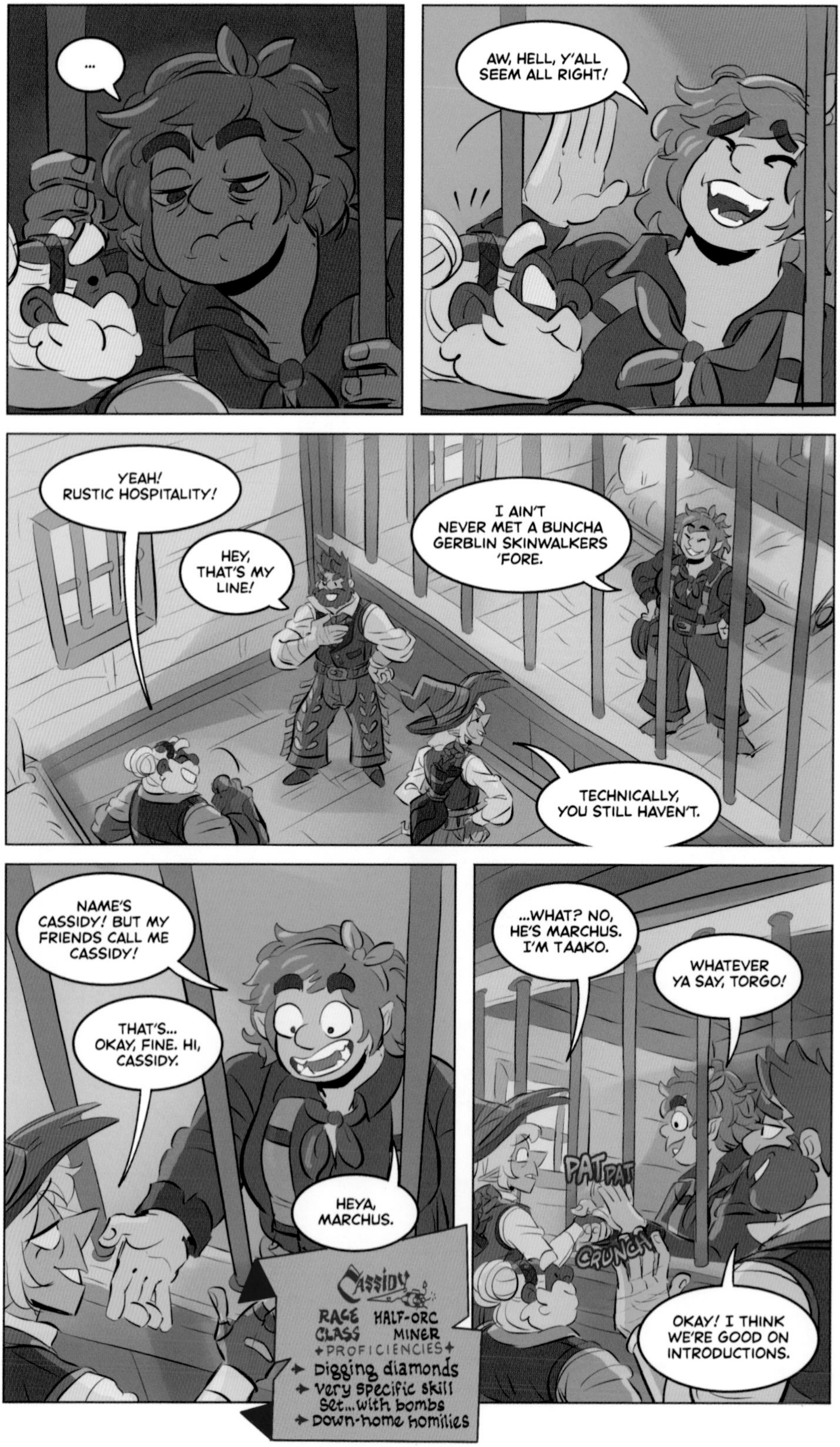

...
AW, HELL, Y'ALL SEEM ALL RIGHT!
YEAH! RUSTIC HOSPITALITY!
HEY, THAT'S MY LINE!
I AIN'T NEVER MET A BUNCHA GERBLIN SKINWALKERS 'FORE.
TECHNICALLY, YOU STILL HAVEN'T.
NAME'S CASSIDY! BUT MY FRIENDS CALL ME CASSIDY!
THAT'S... OKAY, FINE. HI, CASSIDY.
HEYA, MARCHUS.
CASSIDY
RACE HALF-ORC
CLASS MINER
PROFICIENCIES
Digging diamonds
very specific skill set...with bombs
Down-home homilies
...WHAT? NO, HE'S MARCHUS. I'M TAAKO.
WHATEVER YA SAY, TORGO!
PAT PAT
CRUNCH
OKAY! I THINK WE'RE GOOD ON INTRODUCTIONS.

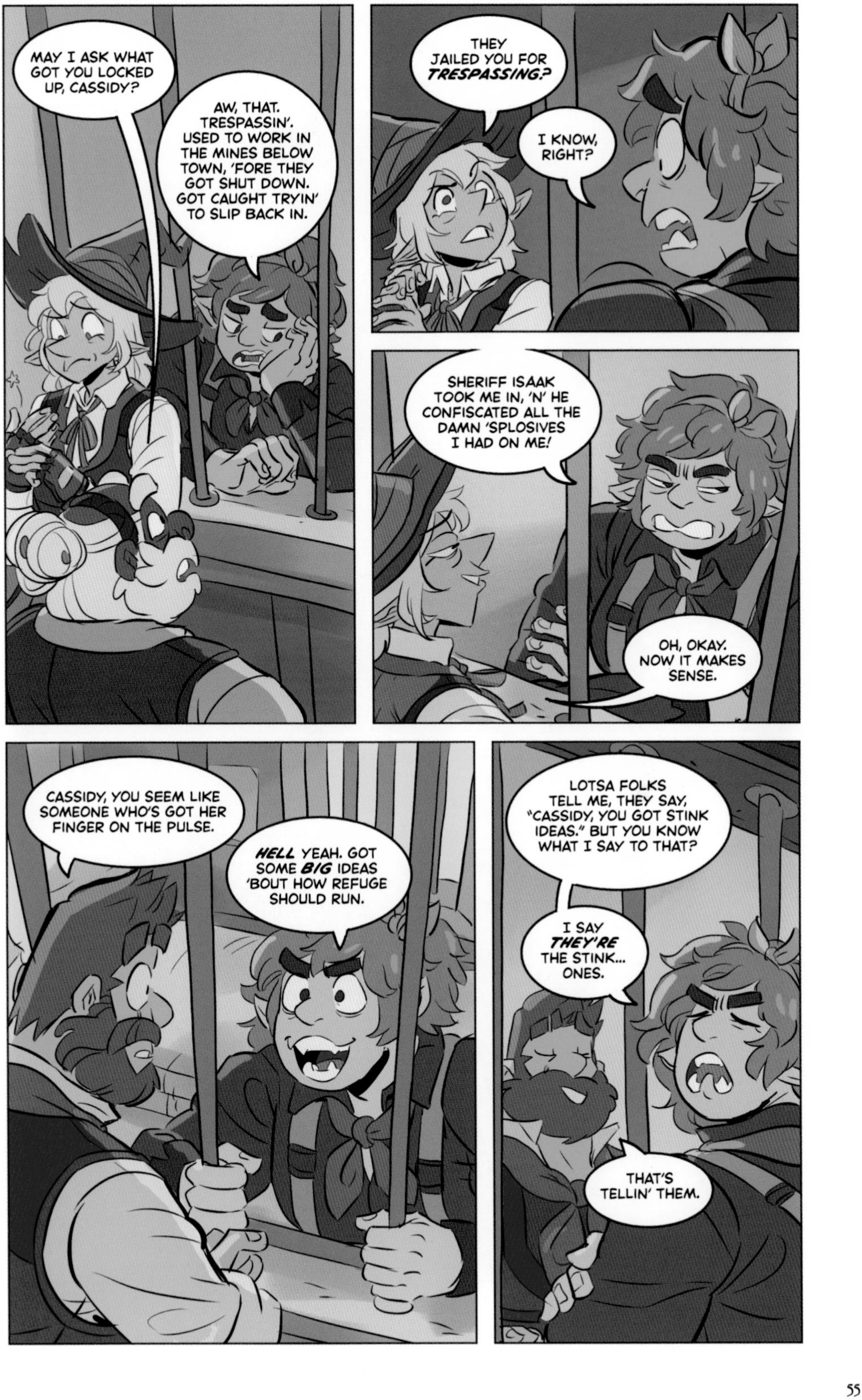
MAY I ASK WHAT GOT YOU LOCKED UP, CASSIDY?
AW, THAT. TRESPASSIN'. USED TO WORK IN THE MINES BELOW TOWN, 'FORE THEY GOT SHUT DOWN. GOT CAUGHT TRYIN' TO SLIP BACK IN.
THEY JAILED YOU FOR *TRESPASSING?*
I KNOW, RIGHT?
SHERIFF ISAAK TOOK ME IN, 'N' HE CONFISCATED ALL THE DAMN 'SPLOSIVES I HAD ON ME!
OH, OKAY. NOW IT MAKES SENSE.
CASSIDY, YOU SEEM LIKE SOMEONE WHO'S GOT HER FINGER ON THE PULSE.
HELL YEAH. GOT SOME *BIG* IDEAS 'BOUT HOW REFUGE SHOULD RUN.
LOTSA FOLKS TELL ME, THEY SAY, "CASSIDY, YOU GOT STINK IDEAS." BUT YOU KNOW WHAT I SAY TO THAT?
I SAY *THEY'RE* THE STINK... ONES.
THAT'S TELLIN' THEM.

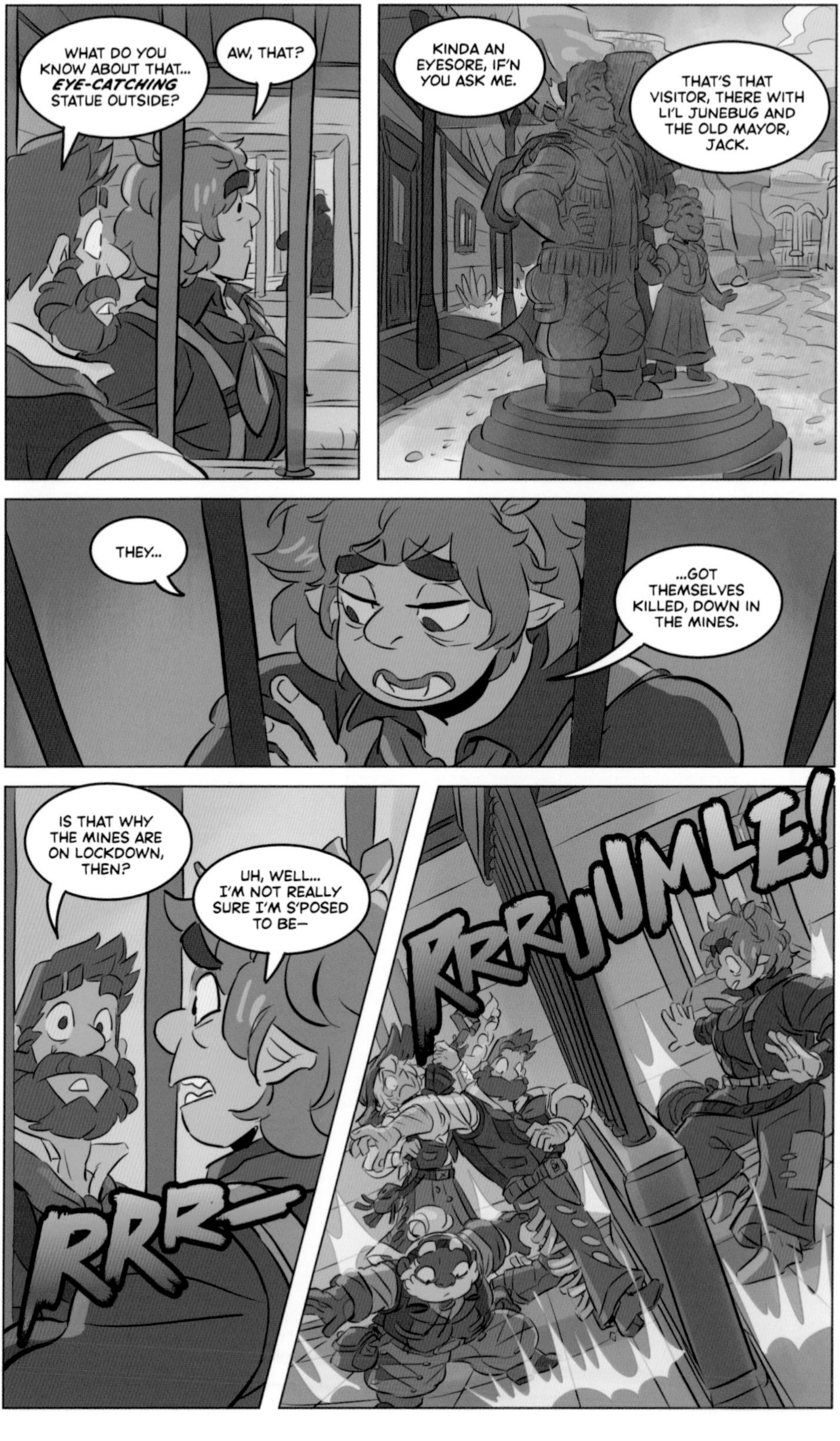
WHAT DO YOU KNOW ABOUT THAT... *EYE-CATCHING* STATUE OUTSIDE?
AW, THAT?
KINDA AN EYESORE, IF'N YOU ASK ME.
THAT'S THAT VISITOR, THERE WITH LI'L JUNEBUG AND THE OLD MAYOR, JACK.
THEY...
...GOT THEMSELVES KILLED, DOWN IN THE MINES.
IS THAT WHY THE MINES ARE ON LOCKDOWN, THEN?
UH, WELL... I'M NOT REALLY SURE I'M S'POSED TO BE—
RRR—
RRRUUMLE!

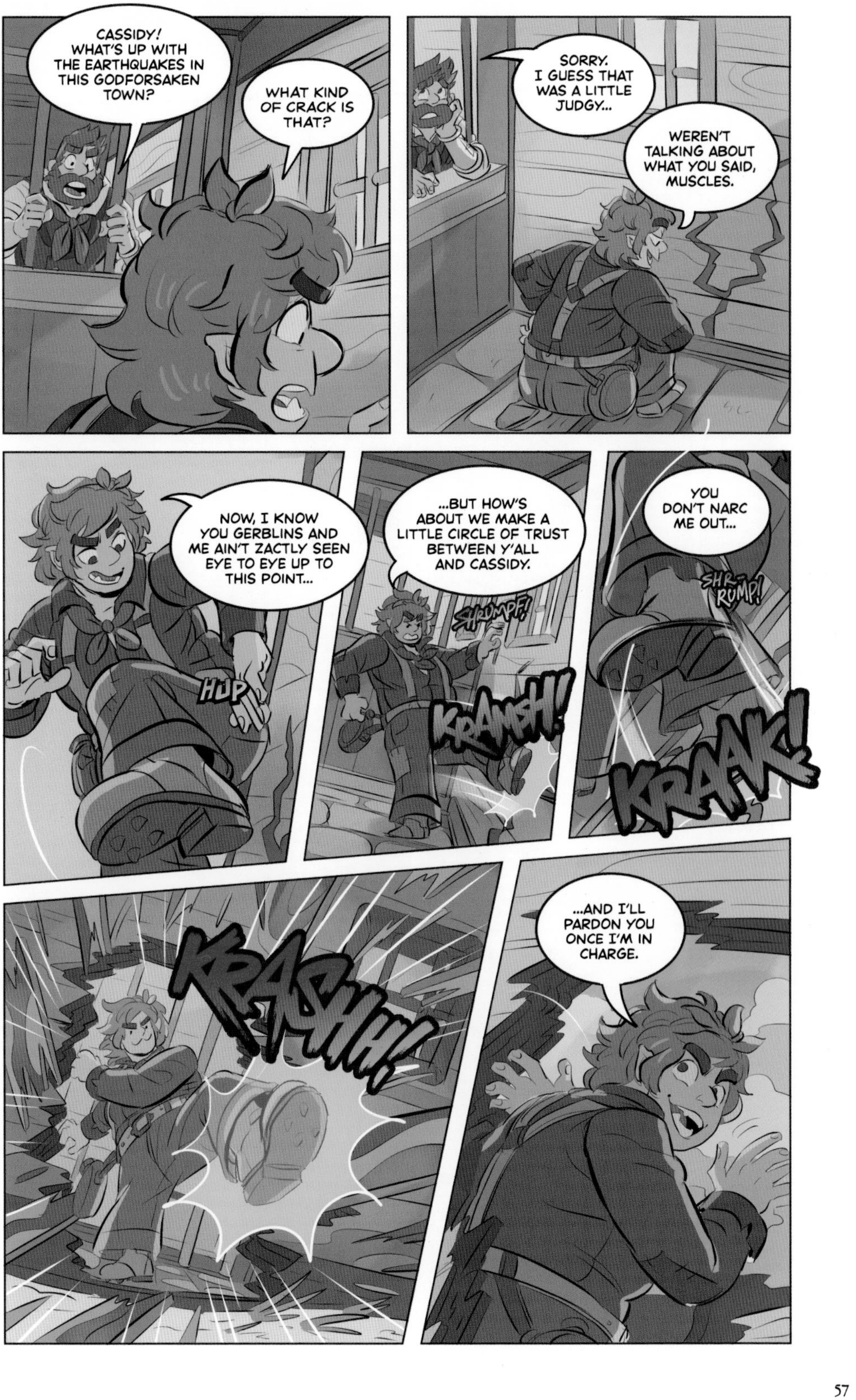
CASSIDY! WHAT'S UP WITH THE EARTHQUAKES IN THIS GODFORSAKEN TOWN?
WHAT KIND OF CRACK IS THAT?
SORRY. I GUESS THAT WAS A LITTLE JUDGY...
WEREN'T TALKING ABOUT WHAT YOU SAID, MUSCLES.
NOW, I KNOW YOU GERBLINS AND ME AIN'T ZACTLY SEEN EYE TO EYE UP TO THIS POINT...
HUP
...BUT HOW'S ABOUT WE MAKE A LITTLE CIRCLE OF TRUST BETWEEN Y'ALL AND CASSIDY.
SHRUMPF!
KRAMSH!
YOU DON'T NARC ME OUT...
SHR-RUMP!
KRAAK!
KRASHH!
...AND I'LL PARDON YOU ONCE I'M IN CHARGE.

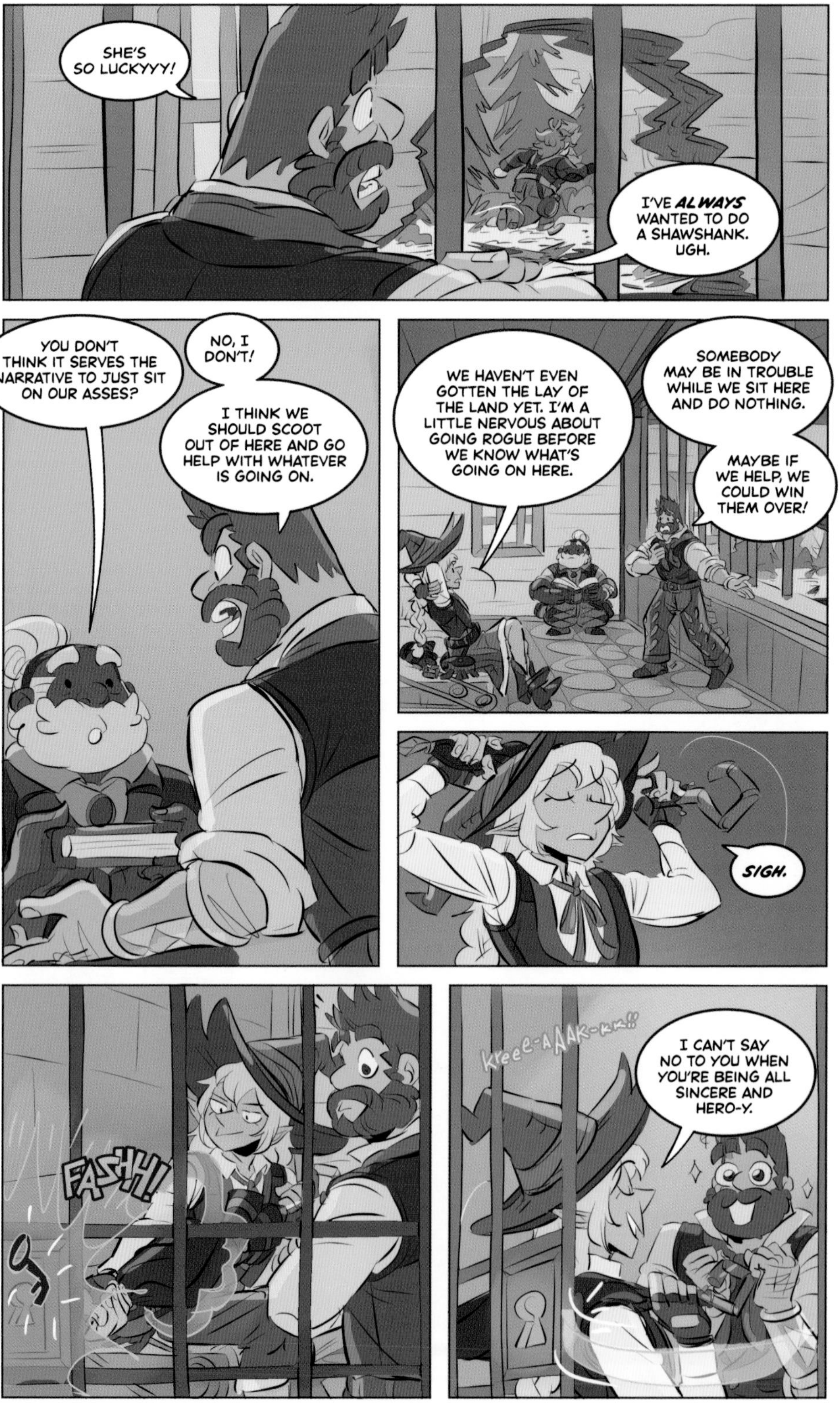
SHE'S SO LUCKYYY!
I'VE *ALWAYS* WANTED TO DO A SHAWSHANK. UGH.
YOU DON'T THINK IT SERVES THE NARRATIVE TO JUST SIT ON OUR ASSES?
NO, I DON'T!
I THINK WE SHOULD SCOOT OUT OF HERE AND GO HELP WITH WHATEVER IS GOING ON.
WE HAVEN'T EVEN GOTTEN THE LAY OF THE LAND YET. I'M A LITTLE NERVOUS ABOUT GOING ROGUE BEFORE WE KNOW WHAT'S GOING ON HERE.
SOMEBODY MAY BE IN TROUBLE WHILE WE SIT HERE AND DO NOTHING.
MAYBE IF WE HELP, WE COULD WIN THEM OVER!
SIGH.
FASHH!
kreeee-AAAK-kk!!
I CAN'T SAY NO TO YOU WHEN YOU'RE BEING ALL SINCERE AND HERO-Y.

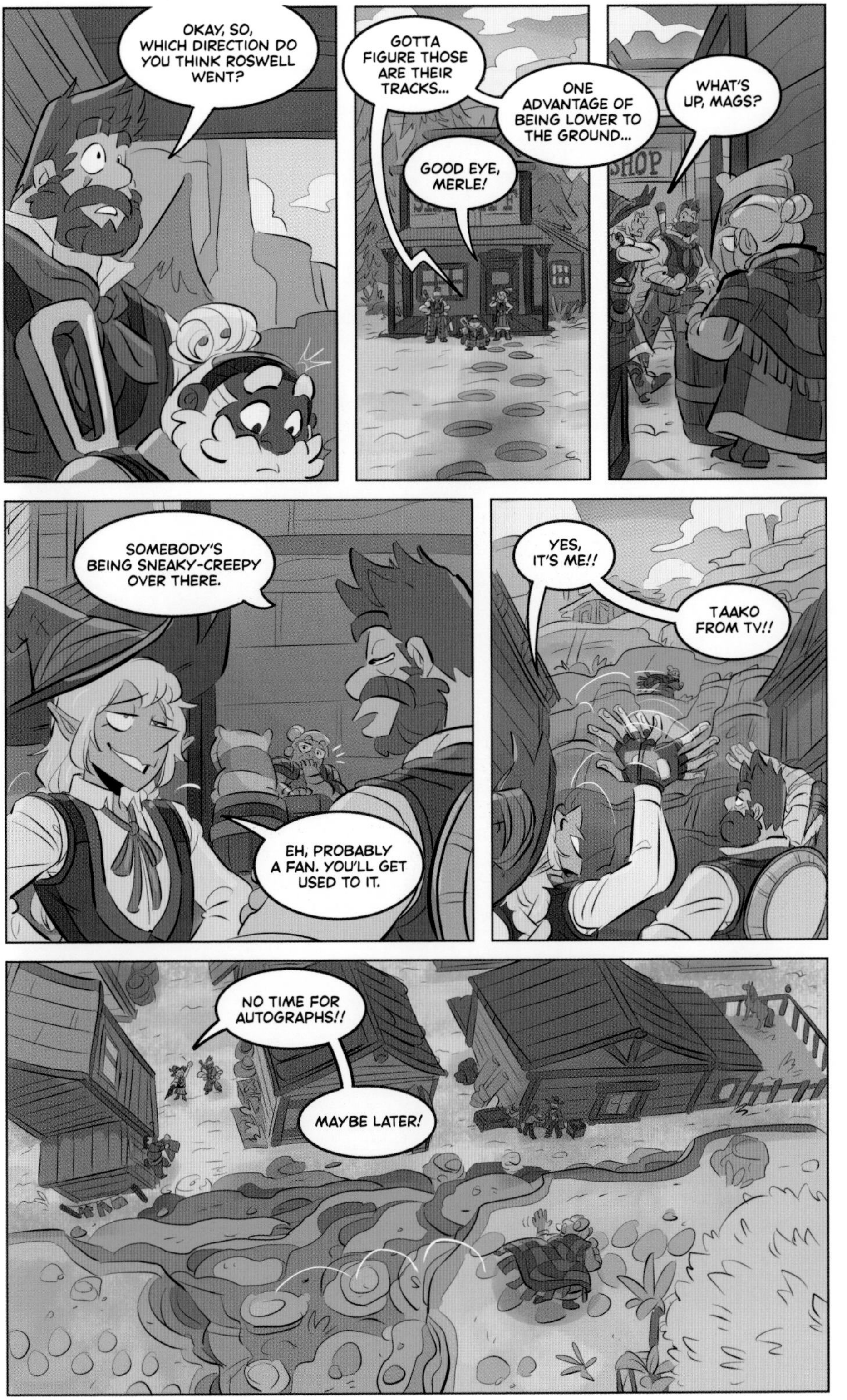
OKAY, SO, WHICH DIRECTION DO YOU THINK ROSWELL WENT?
GOTTA FIGURE THOSE ARE THEIR TRACKS...
ONE ADVANTAGE OF BEING LOWER TO THE GROUND...
GOOD EYE, MERLE!
WHAT'S UP, MAGS?
SHOP
SOMEBODY'S BEING SNEAKY-CREEPY OVER THERE.
EH, PROBABLY A FAN. YOU'LL GET USED TO IT.
YES, IT'S ME!!
TAAKO FROM TV!!
NO TIME FOR AUTOGRAPHS!!
MAYBE LATER!

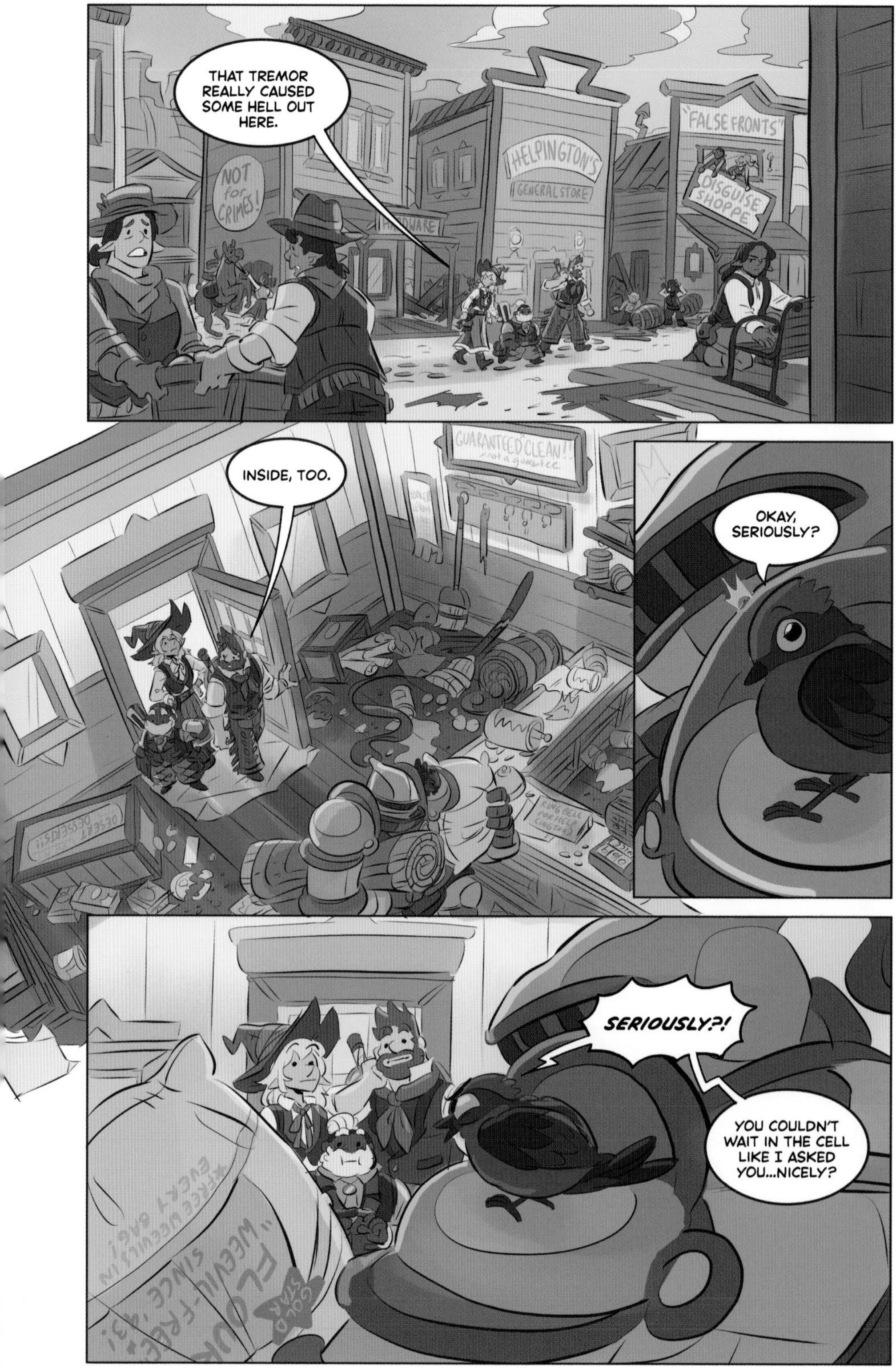
THAT TREMOR REALLY CAUSED SOME HELL OUT HERE.
NOT for CRIMES!
HELPINGTON'S
GENERAL STORE
"FALSE FRONTS"
DISGUISE SHOPPE
INSIDE, TOO.
GUARANTEED CLEAN!
OKAY, SERIOUSLY?
SERIOUSLY?!
YOU COULDN'T WAIT IN THE CELL LIKE I ASKED YOU...NICELY?

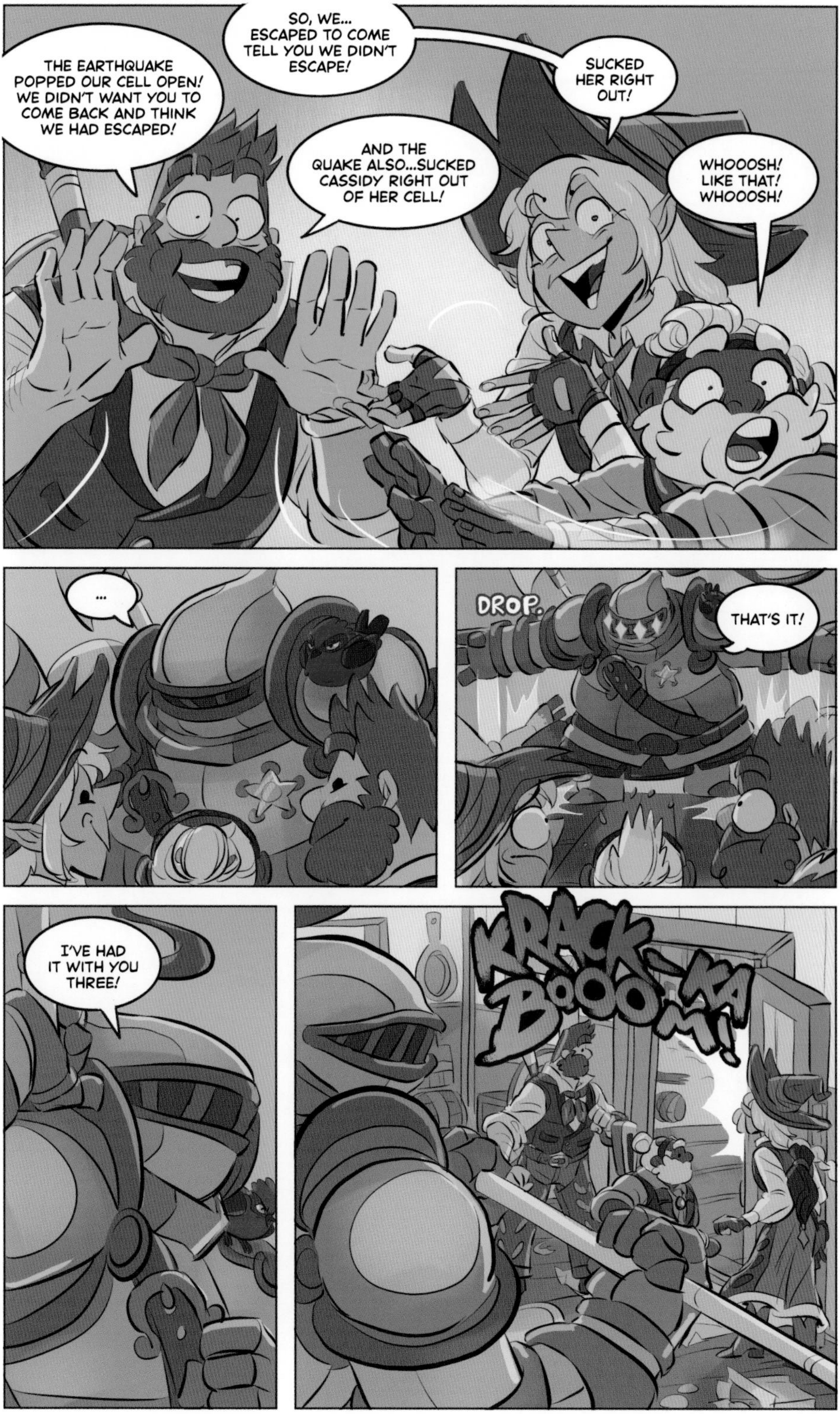
THE EARTHQUAKE POPPED OUR CELL OPEN! WE DIDN'T WANT YOU TO COME BACK AND THINK WE HAD ESCAPED!
SO, WE... ESCAPED TO COME TELL YOU WE DIDN'T ESCAPE!
AND THE QUAKE ALSO...SUCKED CASSIDY RIGHT OUT OF HER CELL!
SUCKED HER RIGHT OUT!
WHOOOSH! LIKE THAT! WHOOOSH!
...
DROP.
THAT'S IT!
I'VE HAD IT WITH YOU THREE!
KRACK-KA BOOOOM!

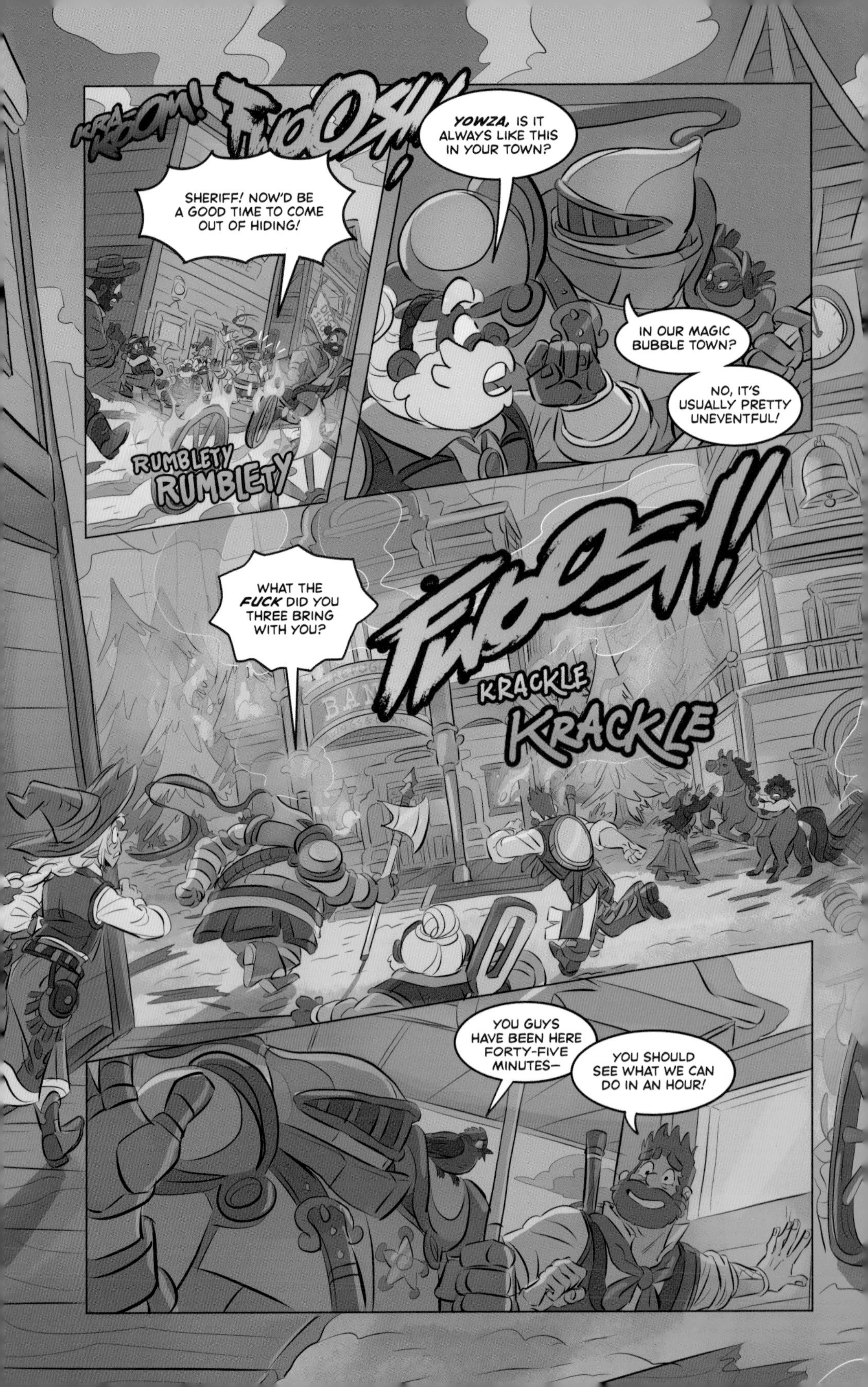
KRA-KOOM! FWOOSH!
SHERIFF! NOW'D BE A GOOD TIME TO COME OUT OF HIDING!
RUMBLETY RUMBLETY
YOWZA, IS IT ALWAYS LIKE THIS IN YOUR TOWN?
IN OUR MAGIC BUBBLE TOWN?
NO, IT'S USUALLY PRETTY UNEVENTFUL!
WHAT THE FUCK DID YOU THREE BRING WITH YOU?
FWOOSH!
KRACKLE KRACKLE
YOU GUYS HAVE BEEN HERE FORTY-FIVE MINUTES—
YOU SHOULD SEE WHAT WE CAN DO IN AN HOUR!

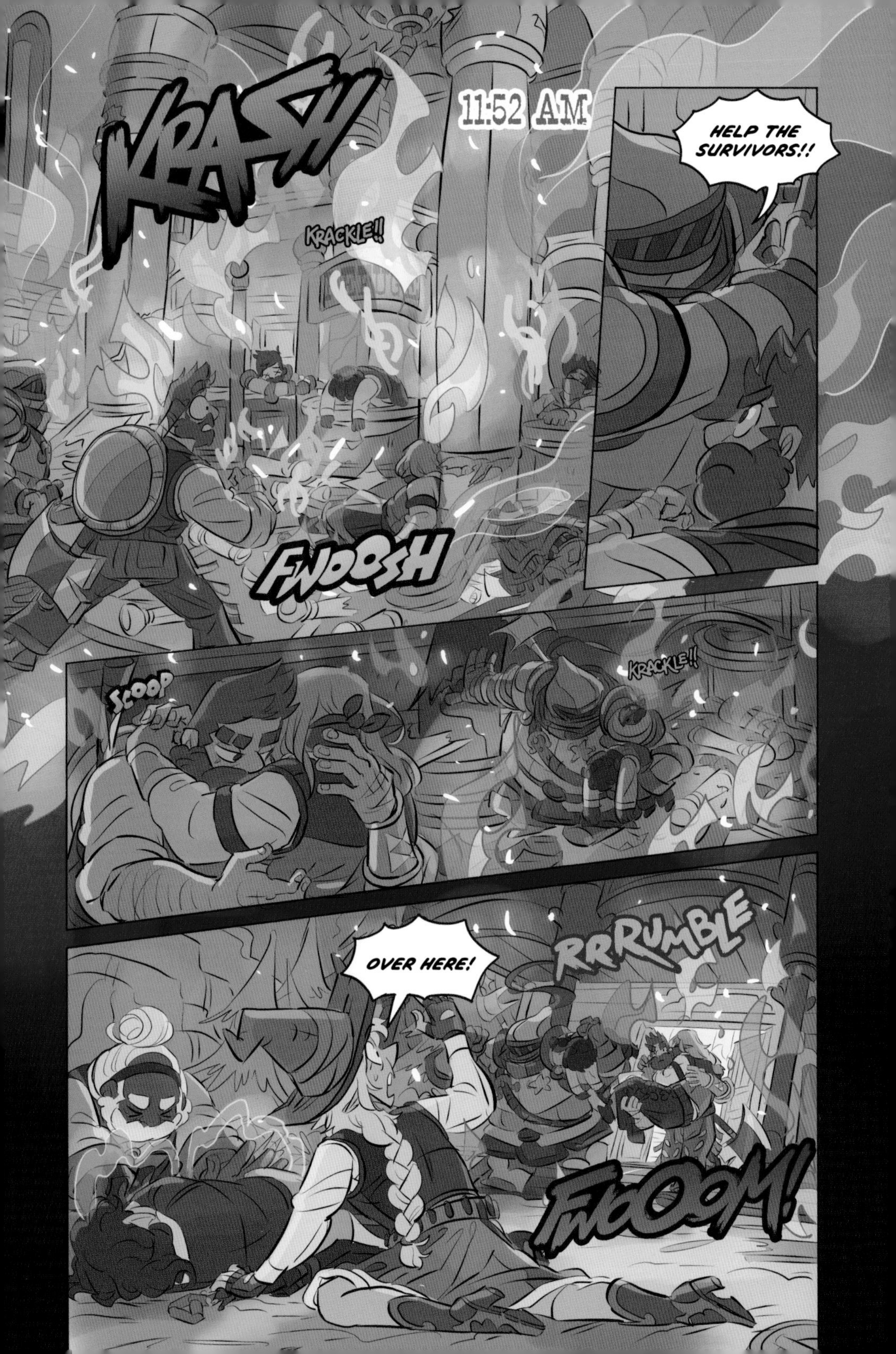
KRASH
11:52 AM
KRACKLE!!
HELP THE SURVIVORS!!
FWOOSH
SCOOP
KRACKLE!!
OVER HERE!
RRRUMBLE
FWOOOM!

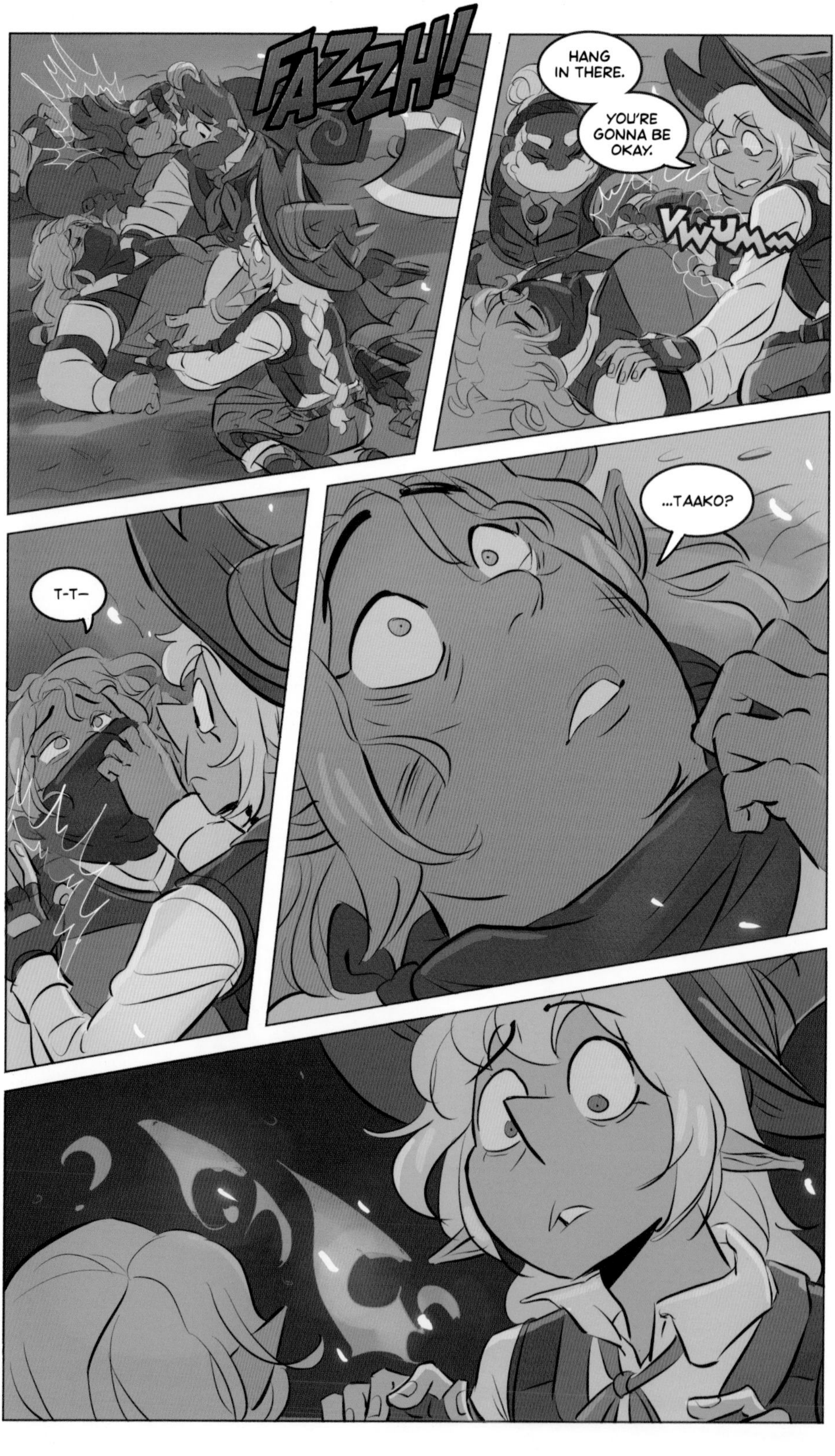
FAZZH!
HANG IN THERE.
YOU'RE GONNA BE OKAY.
VWUM
...TAAKO?
T-T—

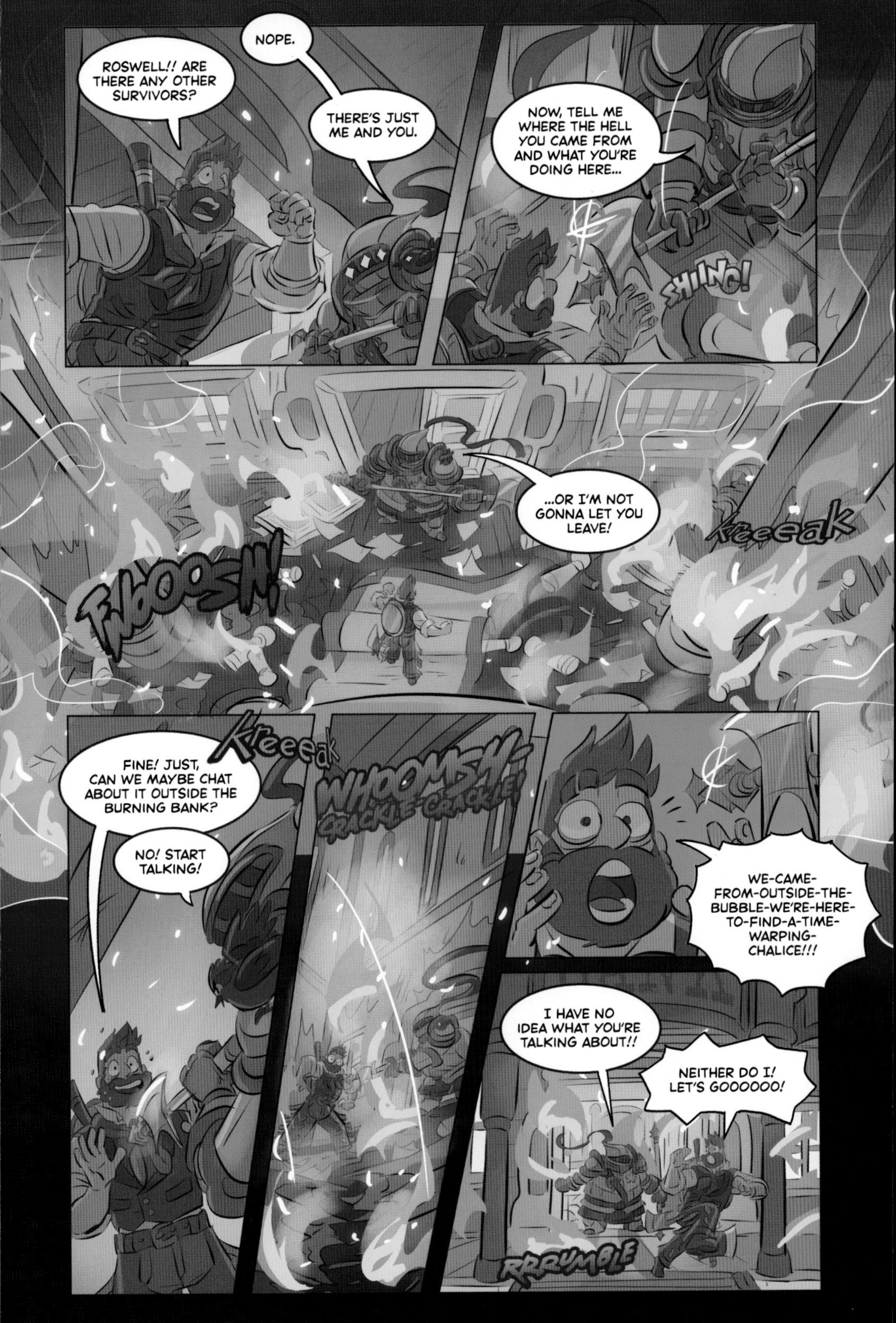
ROSWELL!! ARE THERE ANY OTHER SURVIVORS?
NOPE.
THERE'S JUST ME AND YOU.
NOW, TELL ME WHERE THE HELL YOU CAME FROM AND WHAT YOU'RE DOING HERE...
SHIING!
...OR I'M NOT GONNA LET YOU LEAVE!
FWOOSH!
kreeeak
kreeeak
FINE! JUST, CAN WE MAYBE CHAT ABOUT IT OUTSIDE THE BURNING BANK?
NO! START TALKING!
WHOOMSH
CRACKLE-CRACKLE!
WE-CAME-FROM-OUTSIDE-THE-BUBBLE-WE'RE-HERE-TO-FIND-A-TIME-WARPING-CHALICE!!!
I HAVE NO IDEA WHAT YOU'RE TALKING ABOUT!!
NEITHER DO I! LET'S GOOOOOO!
RRRUMBLE

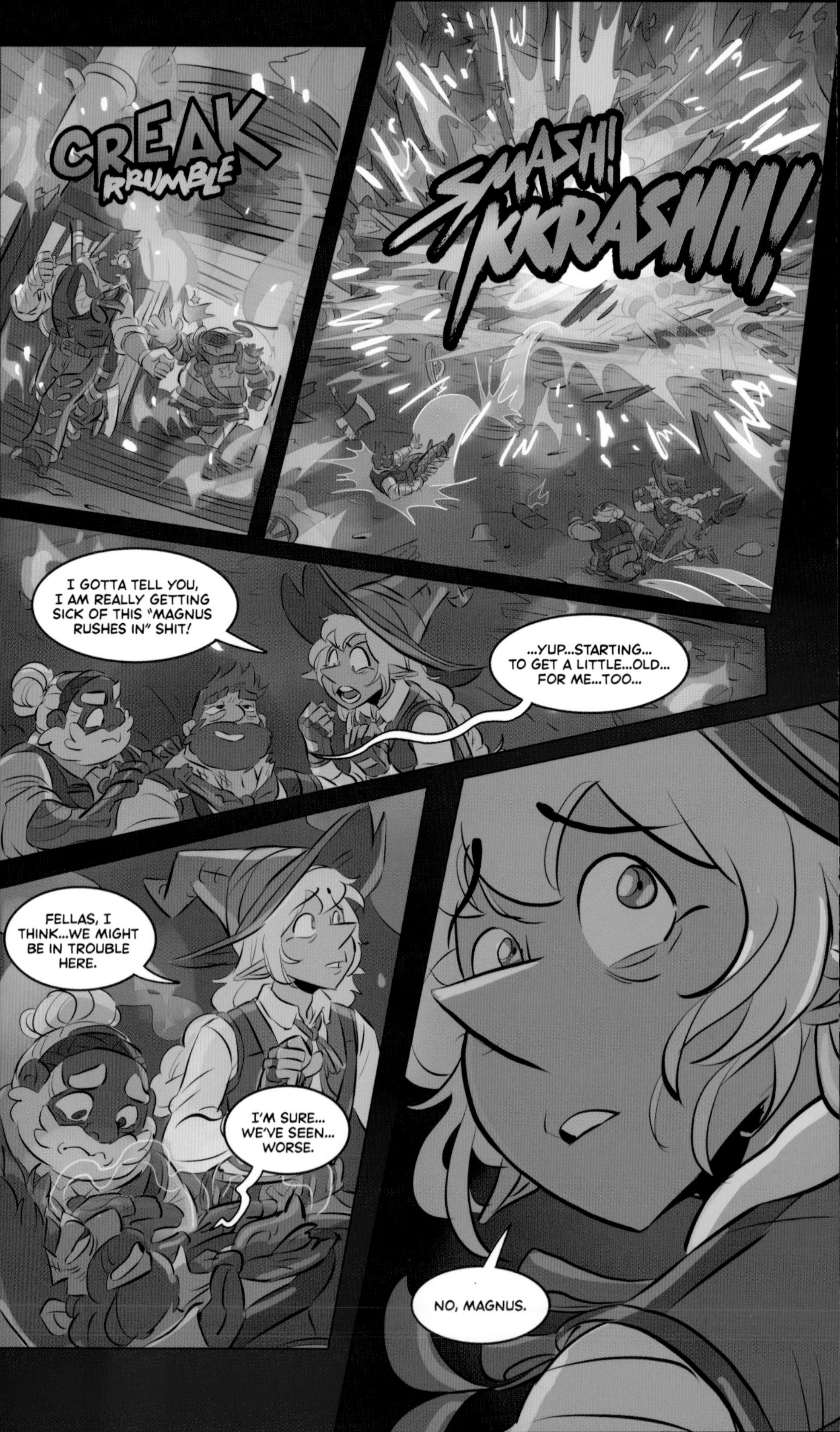
CREAK
RRUMBLE
SMASH!
KKRASHH!
I GOTTA TELL YOU, I AM REALLY GETTING SICK OF THIS "MAGNUS RUSHES IN" SHIT!
...YUP...STARTING... TO GET A LITTLE...OLD... FOR ME...TOO...
FELLAS, I THINK...WE MIGHT BE IN TROUBLE HERE.
I'M SURE... WE'VE SEEN... WORSE.
NO, MAGNUS.

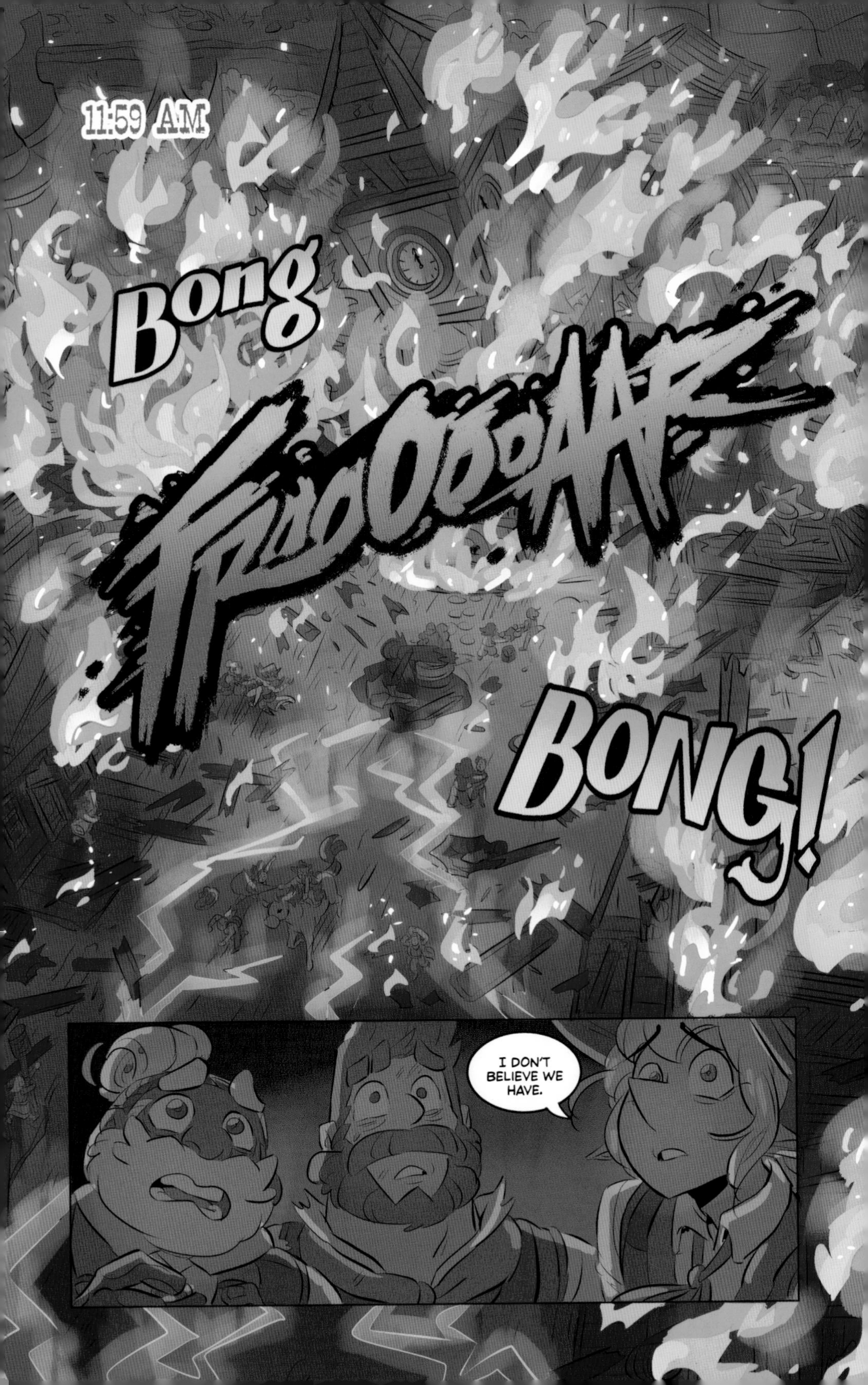
11:59 AM
Bong
BONG!
I DON'T BELIEVE WE HAVE.

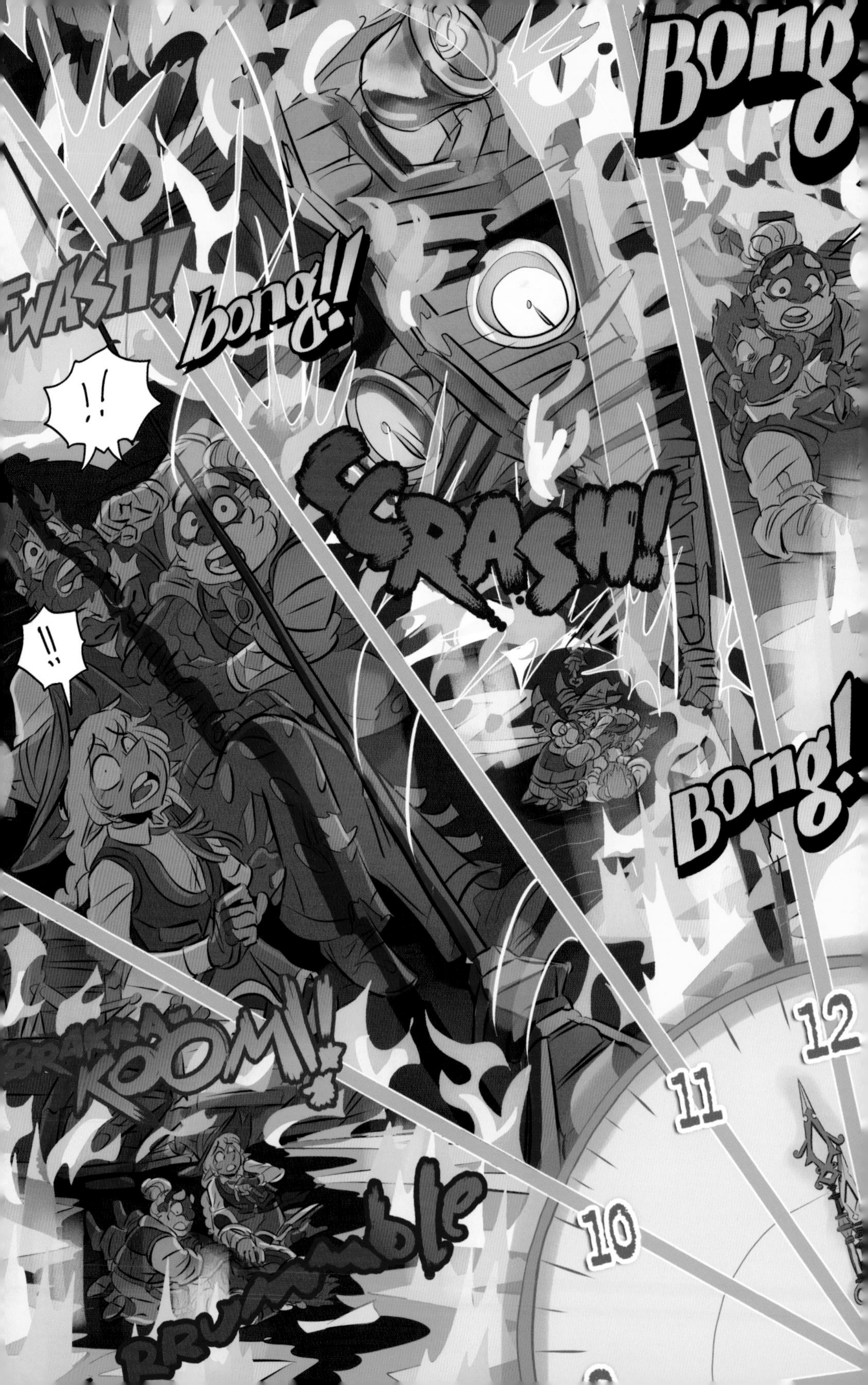

Bong
FWASH!
bong!!
!!
CRASH!
!!
Bong!
KOOM!!
12
11
10
ble

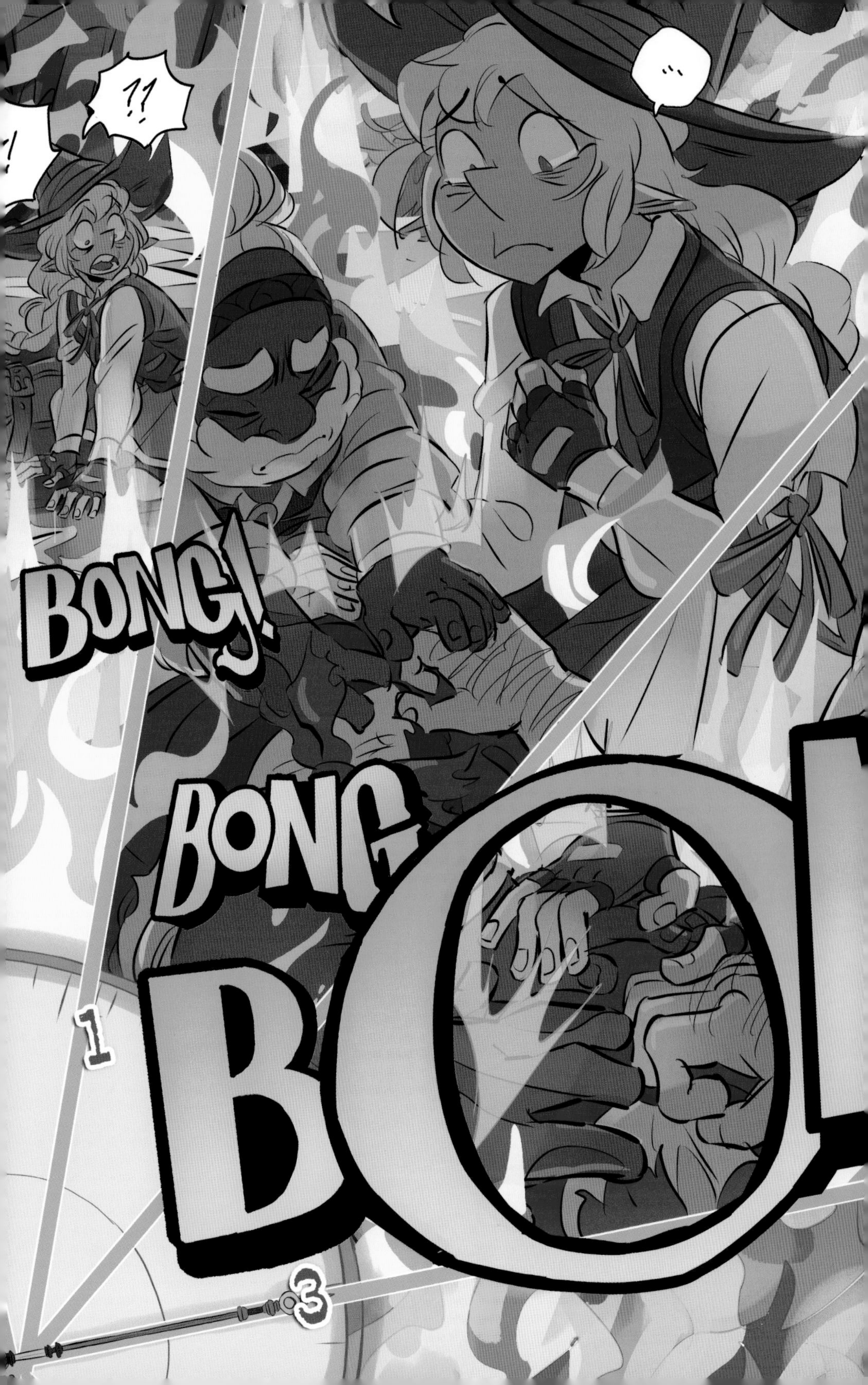

??
...
BONG!
BONG
BO
1
3

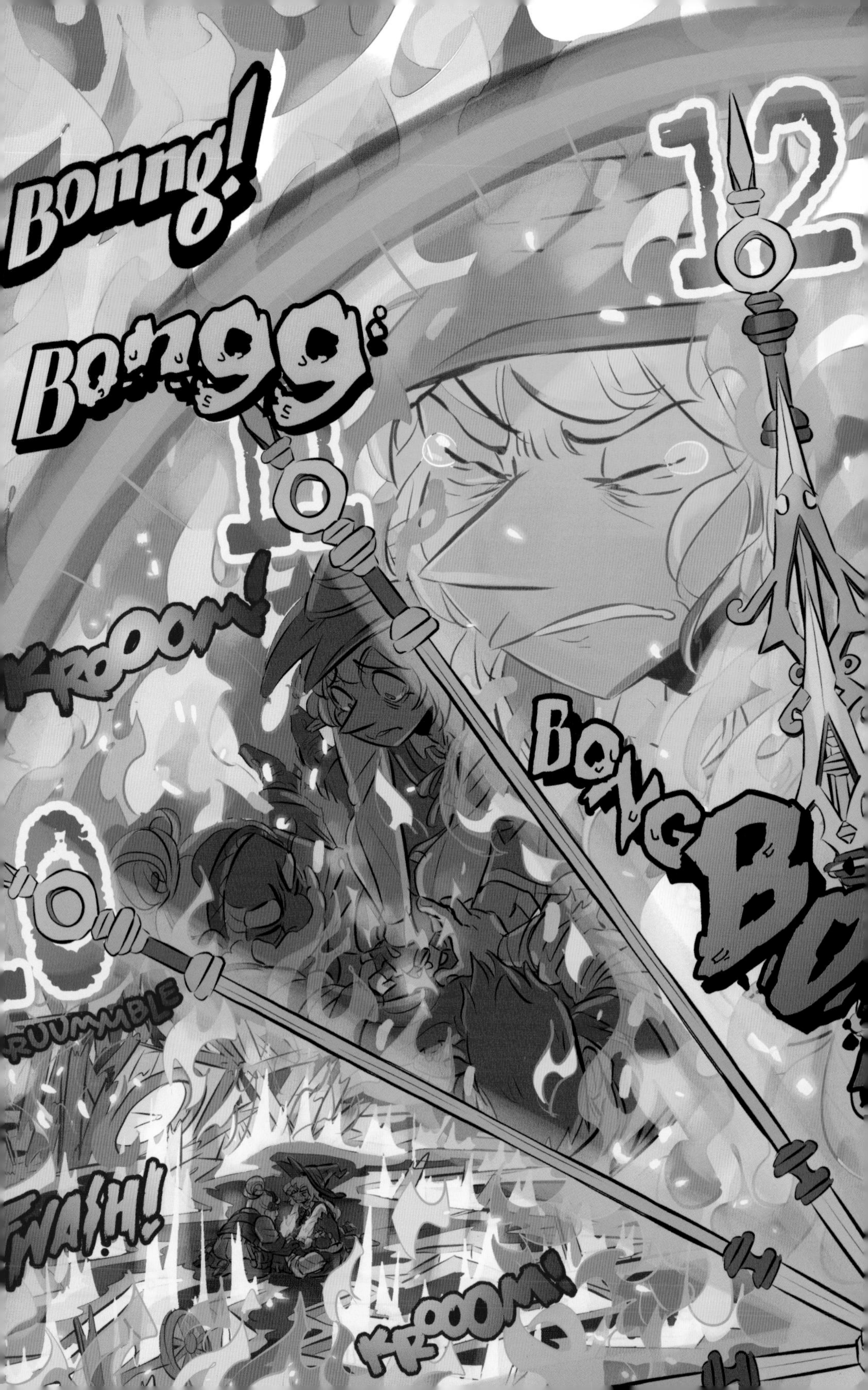
Bonng!
Bonggg!
12
KROOOM!
BONG
10
RUUMMBLE
FWASH!
KROOOM!

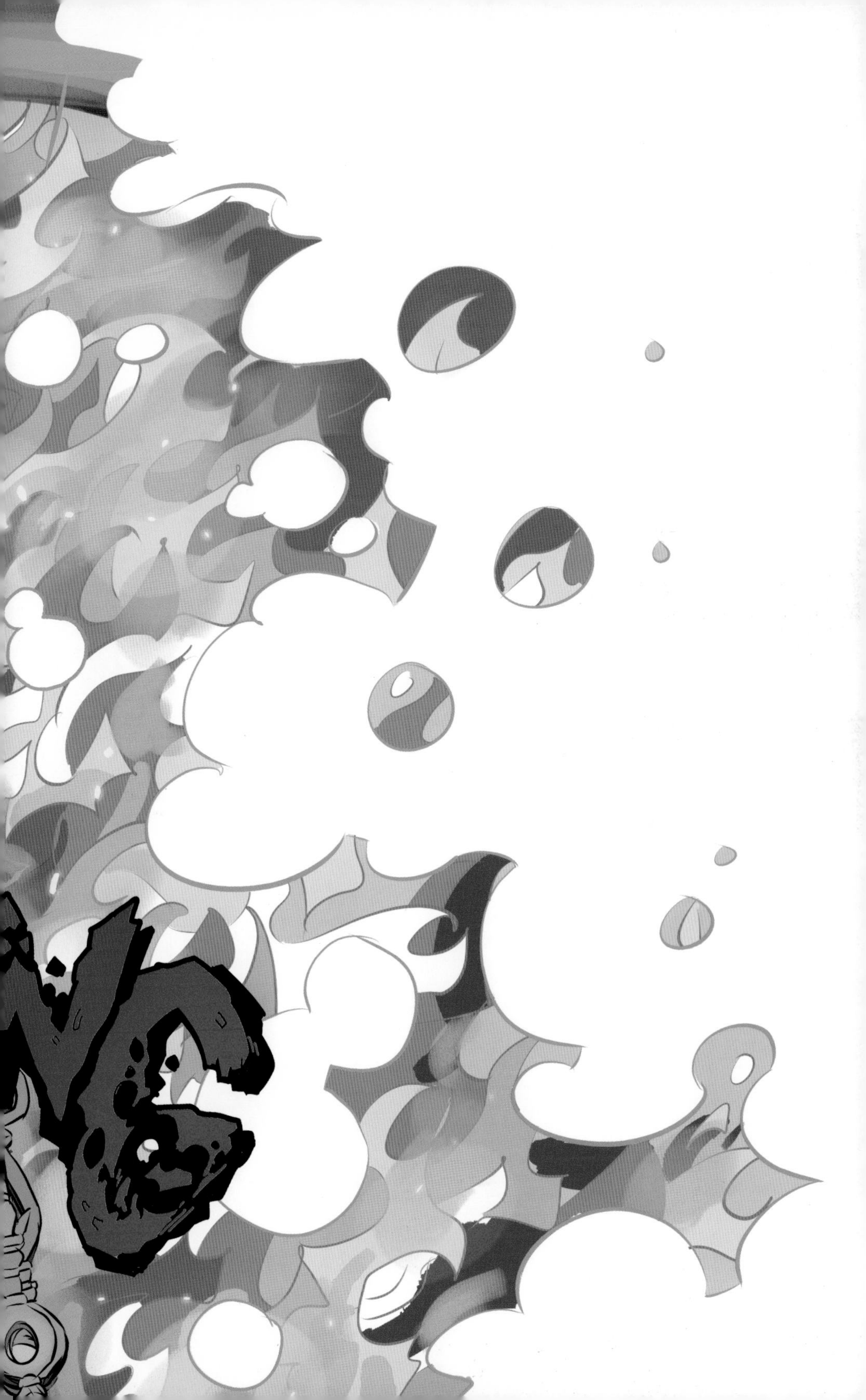

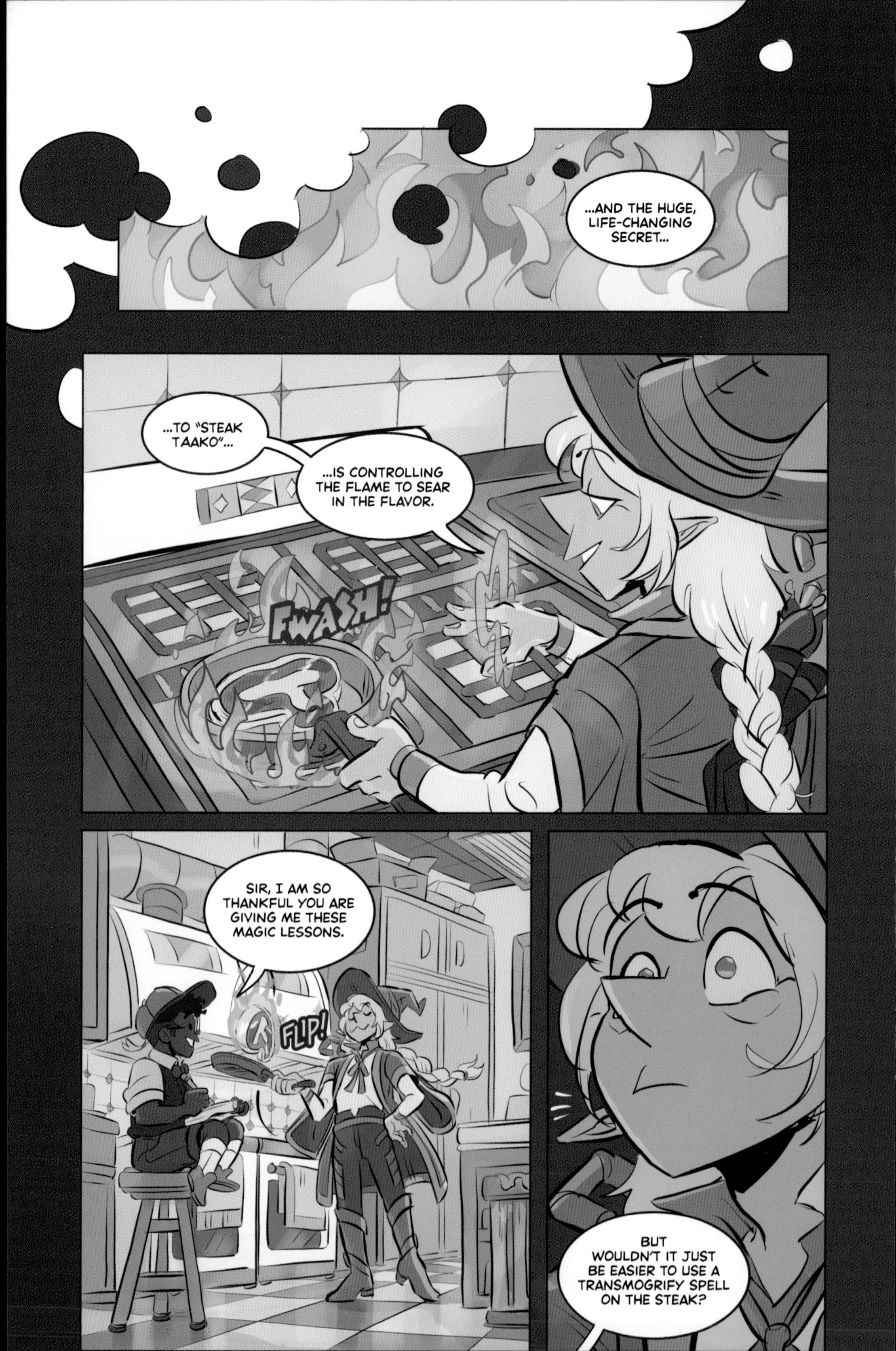

...AND THE HUGE, LIFE-CHANGING SECRET...
...TO "STEAK TAAKO"...
...IS CONTROLLING THE FLAME TO SEAR IN THE FLAVOR.
FWASH!
SIR, I AM SO THANKFUL YOU ARE GIVING ME THESE MAGIC LESSONS.
FLIP!
BUT WOULDN'T IT JUST BE EASIER TO USE A TRANSMOGRIFY SPELL ON THE STEAK?

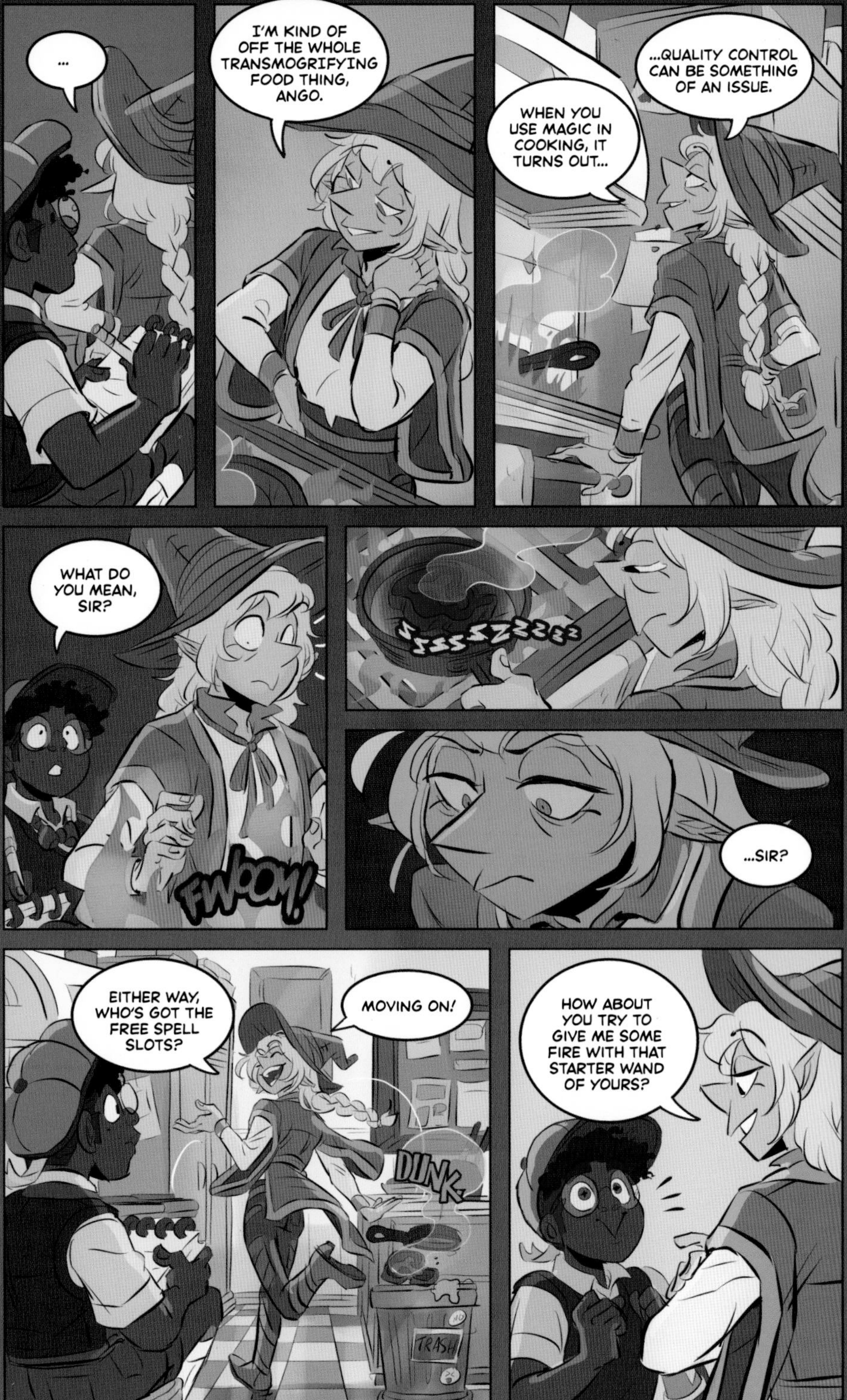
...
I'M KIND OF OFF THE WHOLE TRANSMOGRIFYING FOOD THING, ANGO.
WHEN YOU USE MAGIC IN COOKING, IT TURNS OUT...
...QUALITY CONTROL CAN BE SOMETHING OF AN ISSUE.
WHAT DO YOU MEAN, SIR?
FWOOM!
SSSSSZZZZZ
...SIR?
EITHER WAY, WHO'S GOT THE FREE SPELL SLOTS?
MOVING ON!
DUNK
TRASH
HOW ABOUT YOU TRY TO GIVE ME SOME FIRE WITH THAT STARTER WAND OF YOURS?

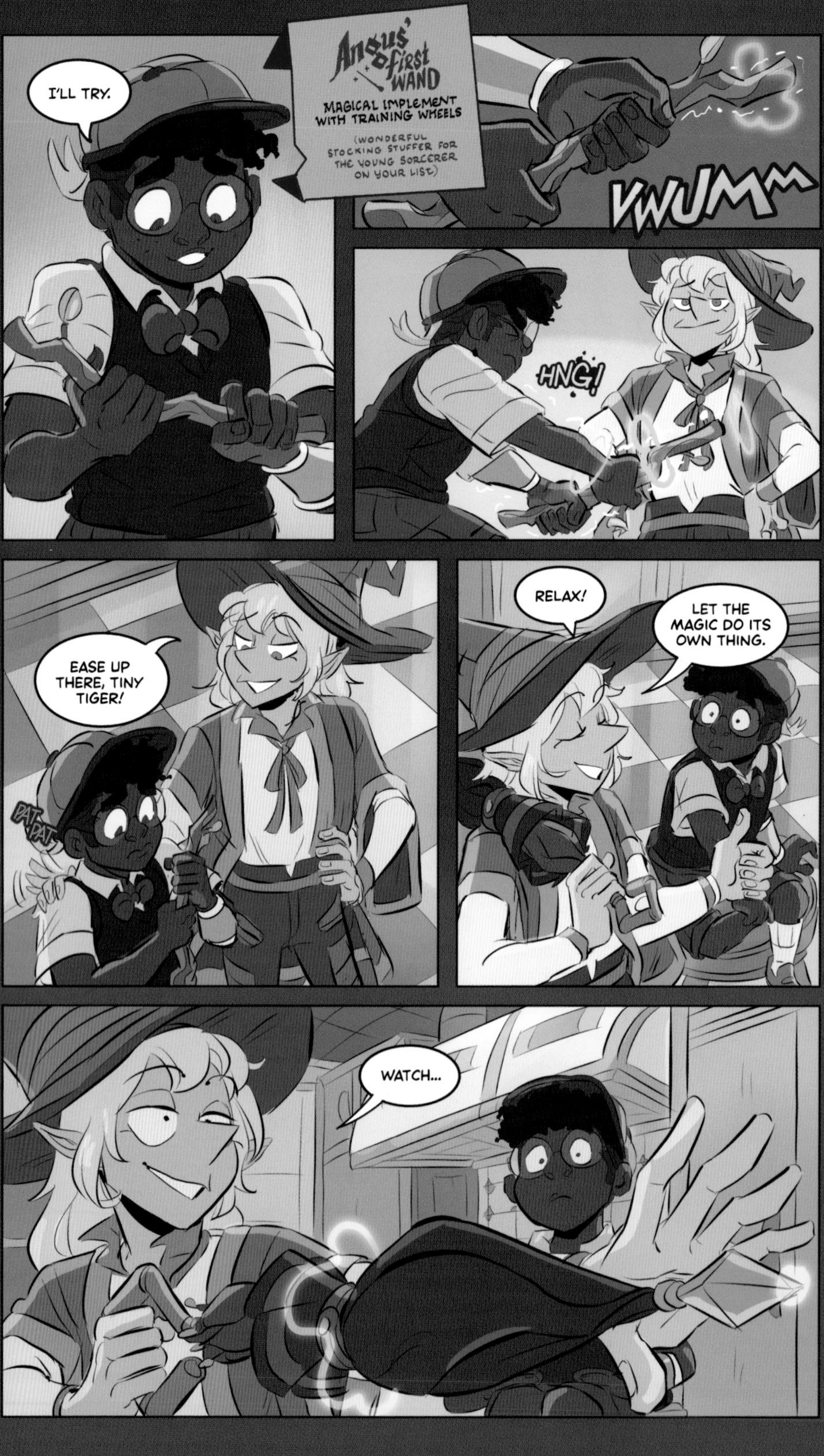
I'LL TRY.
Angus' first WAND
MAGICAL IMPLEMENT WITH TRAINING WHEELS
(WONDERFUL STOCKING STUFFER FOR THE YOUNG SORCERER ON YOUR LIST)
VWUMM
HNG!
EASE UP THERE, TINY TIGER!
PAT PAT
RELAX!
LET THE MAGIC DO ITS OWN THING.
WATCH...

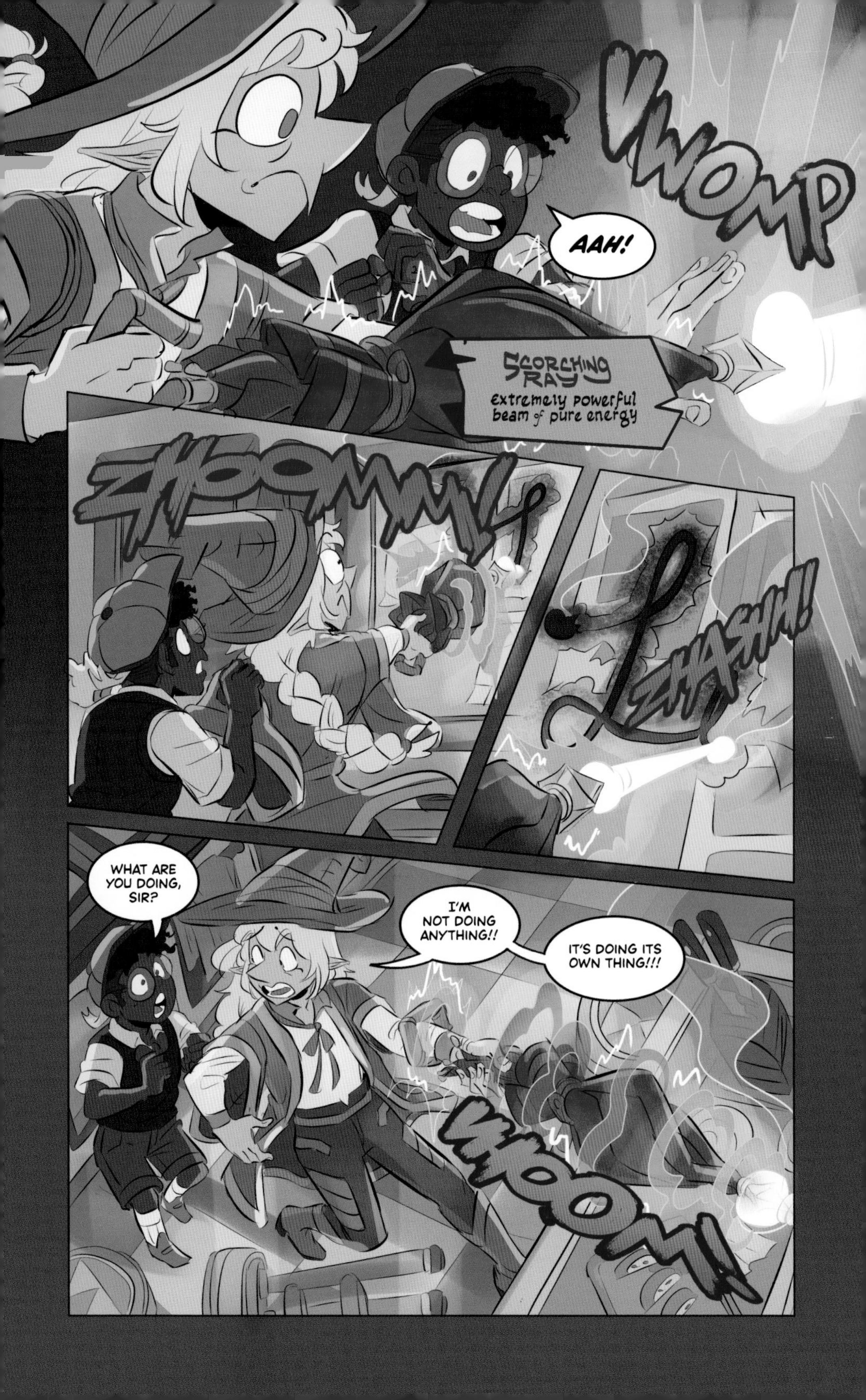
VWOMP
AAH!
SCORCHING RAY
extremely powerful beam of pure energy
ZHOOMMM!
ZHASHH!
WHAT ARE YOU DOING, SIR?
I'M NOT DOING ANYTHING!!
IT'S DOING ITS OWN THING!!!
WHOOOM!

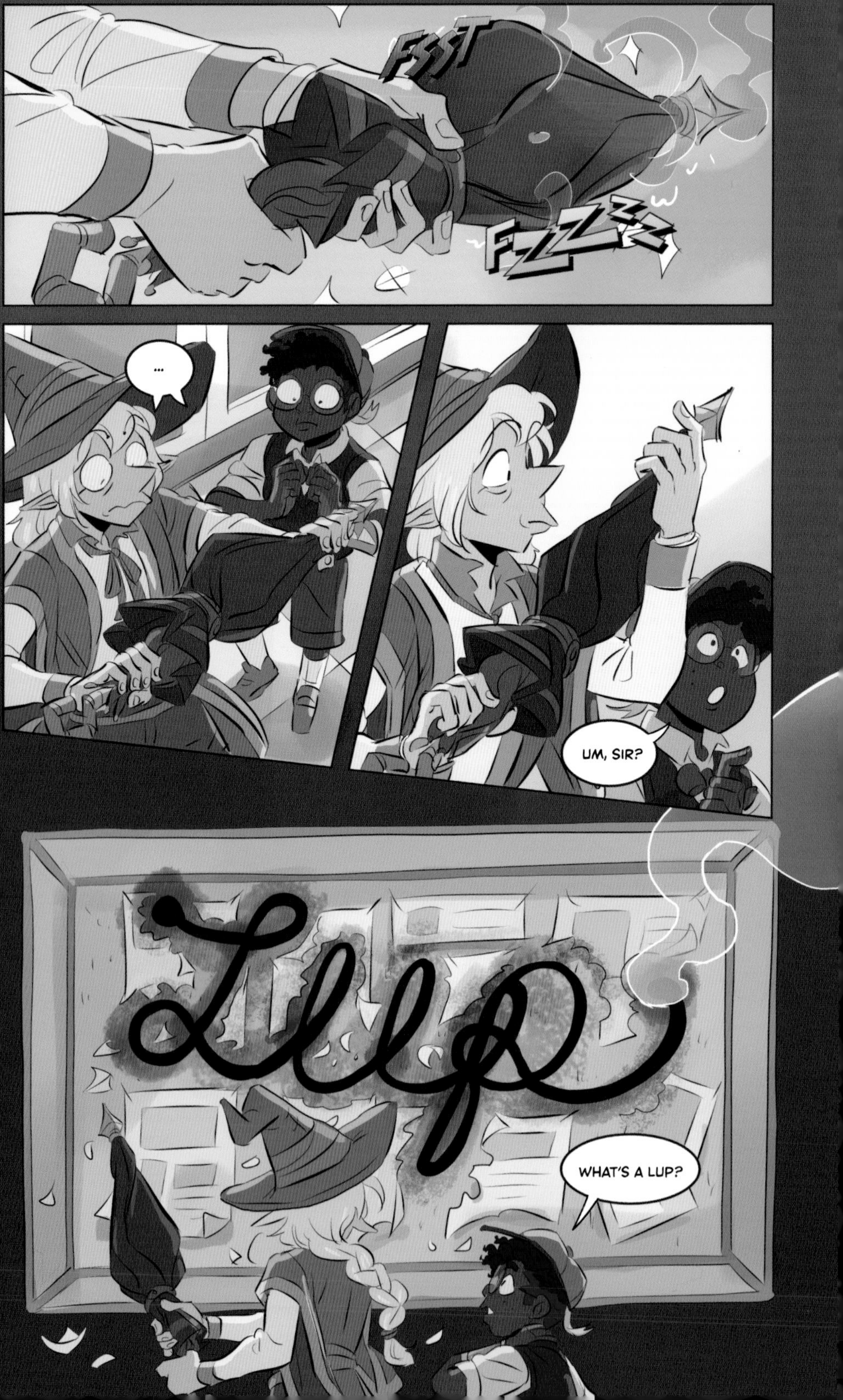
FSST
FZZZZZ
...
UM, SIR?
LUP
WHAT'S A LUP?

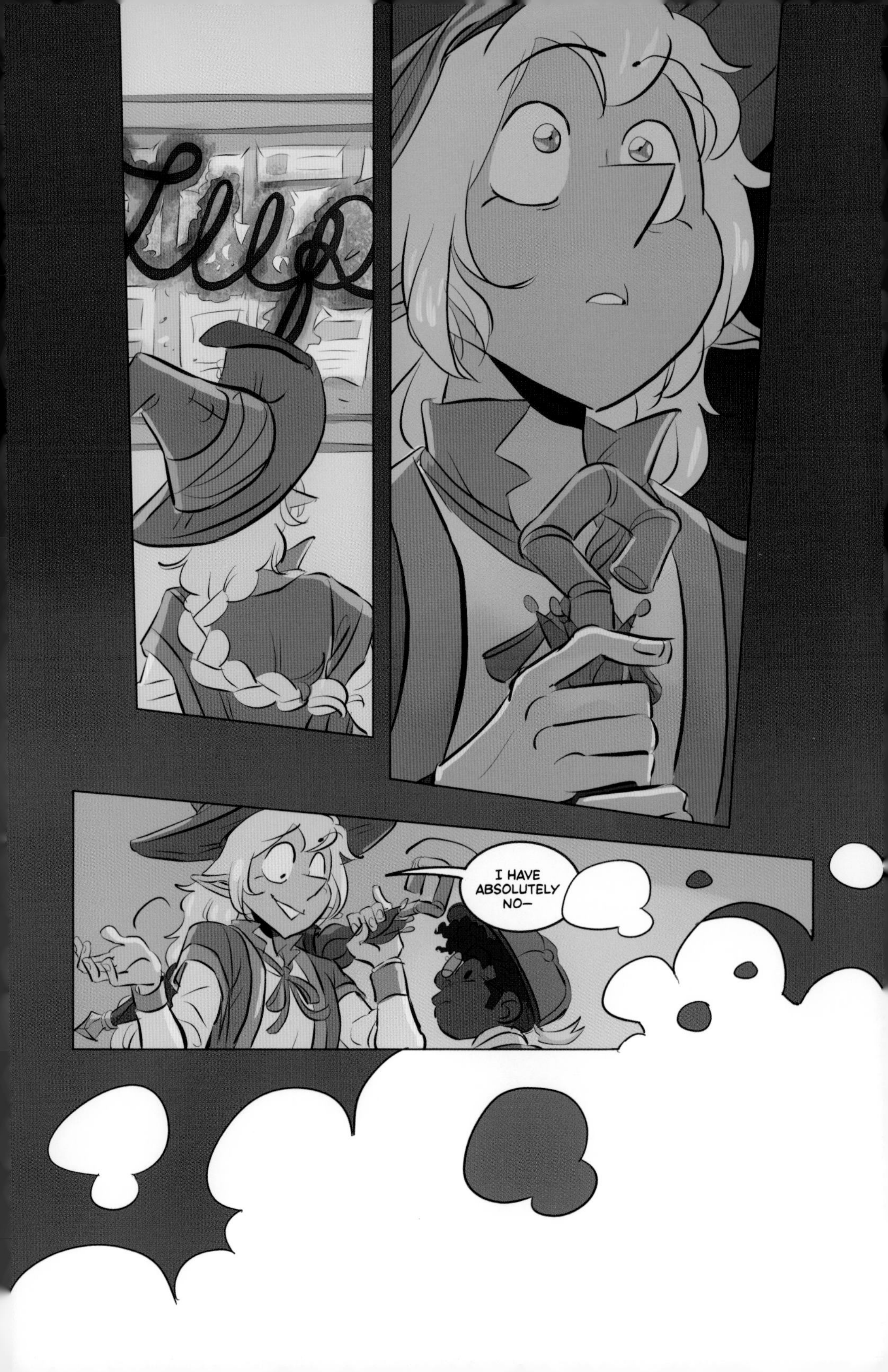
I HAVE ABSOLUTELY NO—

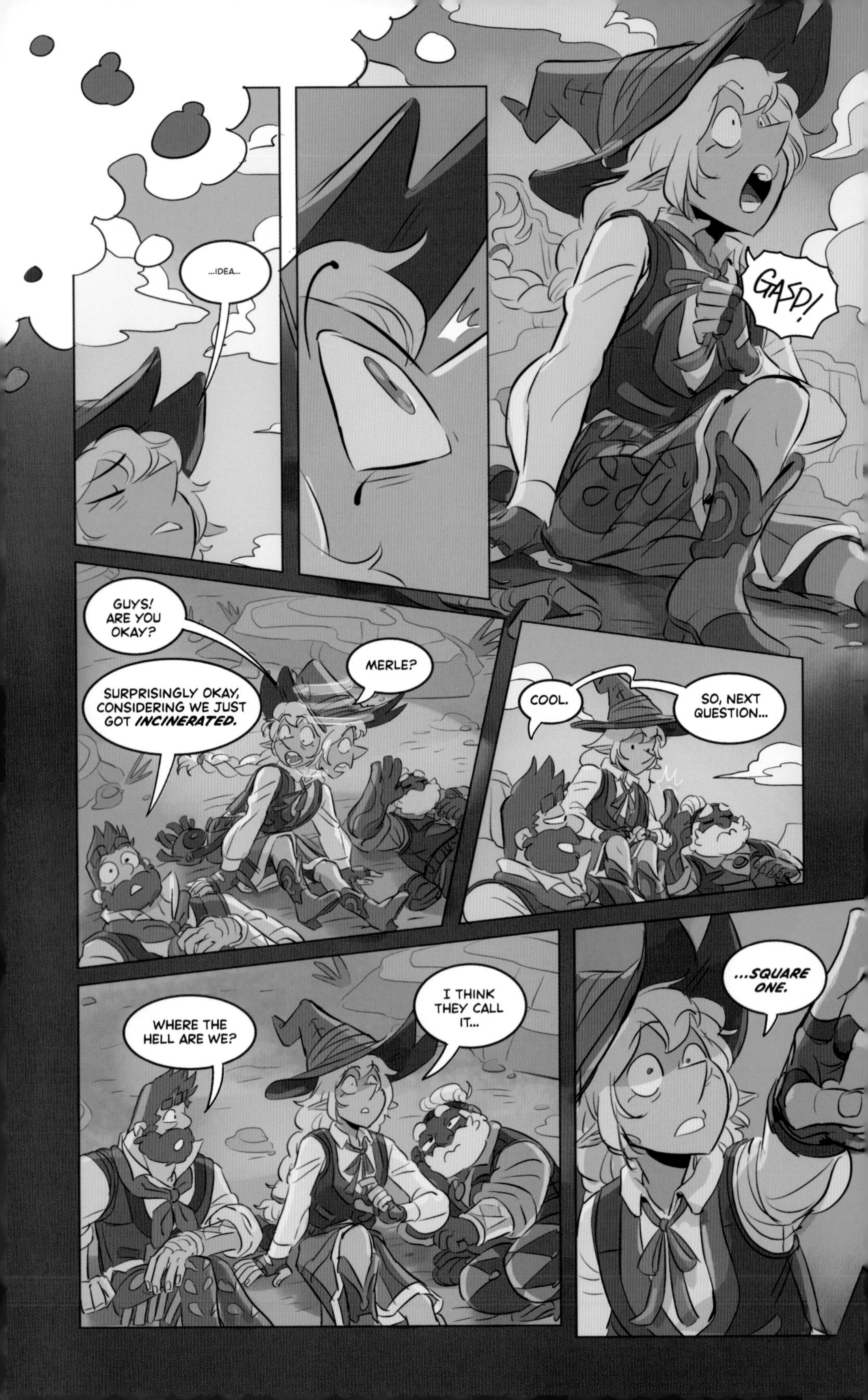
...IDEA...
GASP!
GUYS! ARE YOU OKAY?
MERLE?
SURPRISINGLY OKAY, CONSIDERING WE JUST GOT *INCINERATED.*
COOL.
SO, NEXT QUESTION...
WHERE THE HELL ARE WE?
I THINK THEY CALL IT...
...SQUARE ONE.

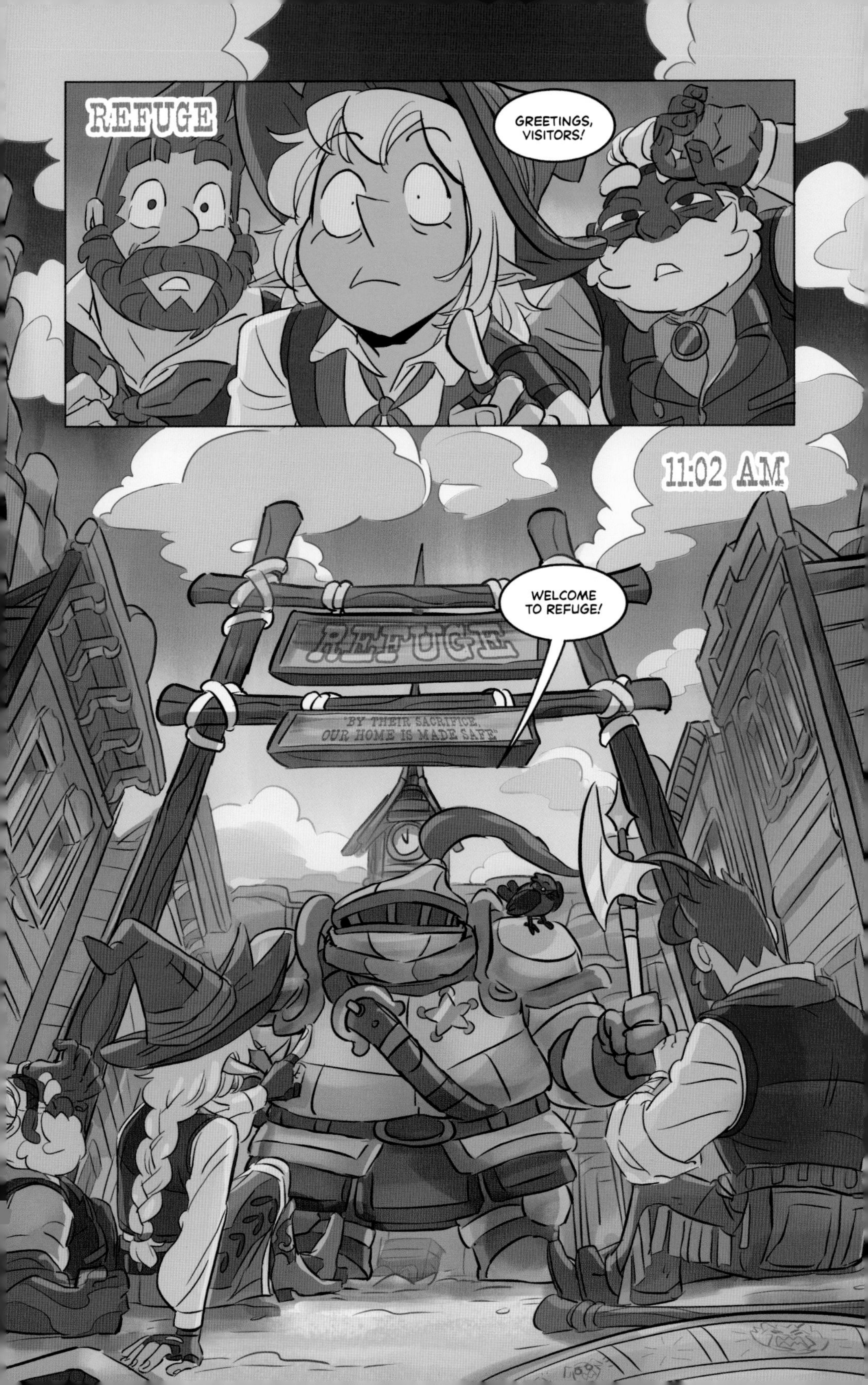
REFUGE
GREETINGS, VISITORS!
11:02 AM
REFUGE
"BY THEIR SACRIFICE, OUR HOME IS MADE SAFE"
WELCOME TO REFUGE!

Chapter
3

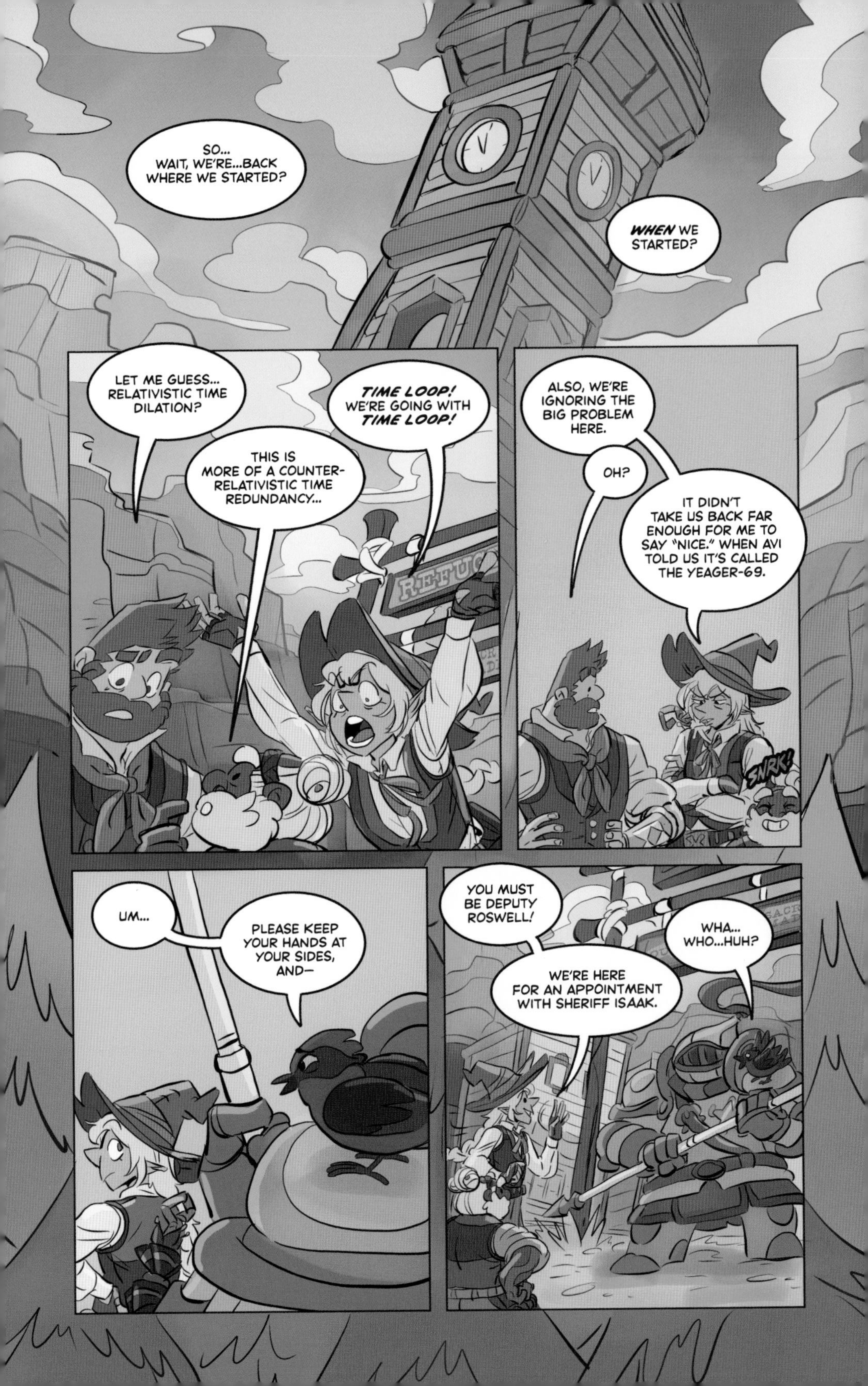
SO... WAIT, WE'RE...BACK WHERE WE STARTED?
WHEN WE STARTED?
LET ME GUESS... RELATIVISTIC TIME DILATION?
TIME LOOP! WE'RE GOING WITH *TIME LOOP!*
THIS IS MORE OF A COUNTER-RELATIVISTIC TIME REDUNDANCY...
ALSO, WE'RE IGNORING THE BIG PROBLEM HERE.
OH?
IT DIDN'T TAKE US BACK FAR ENOUGH FOR ME TO SAY "NICE." WHEN AVI TOLD US IT'S CALLED THE YEAGER-69.
SNRK!
UM...
PLEASE KEEP YOUR HANDS AT YOUR SIDES, AND—
YOU MUST BE DEPUTY ROSWELL!
WE'RE HERE FOR AN APPOINTMENT WITH SHERIFF ISAAK.
WHA... WHO...HUH?

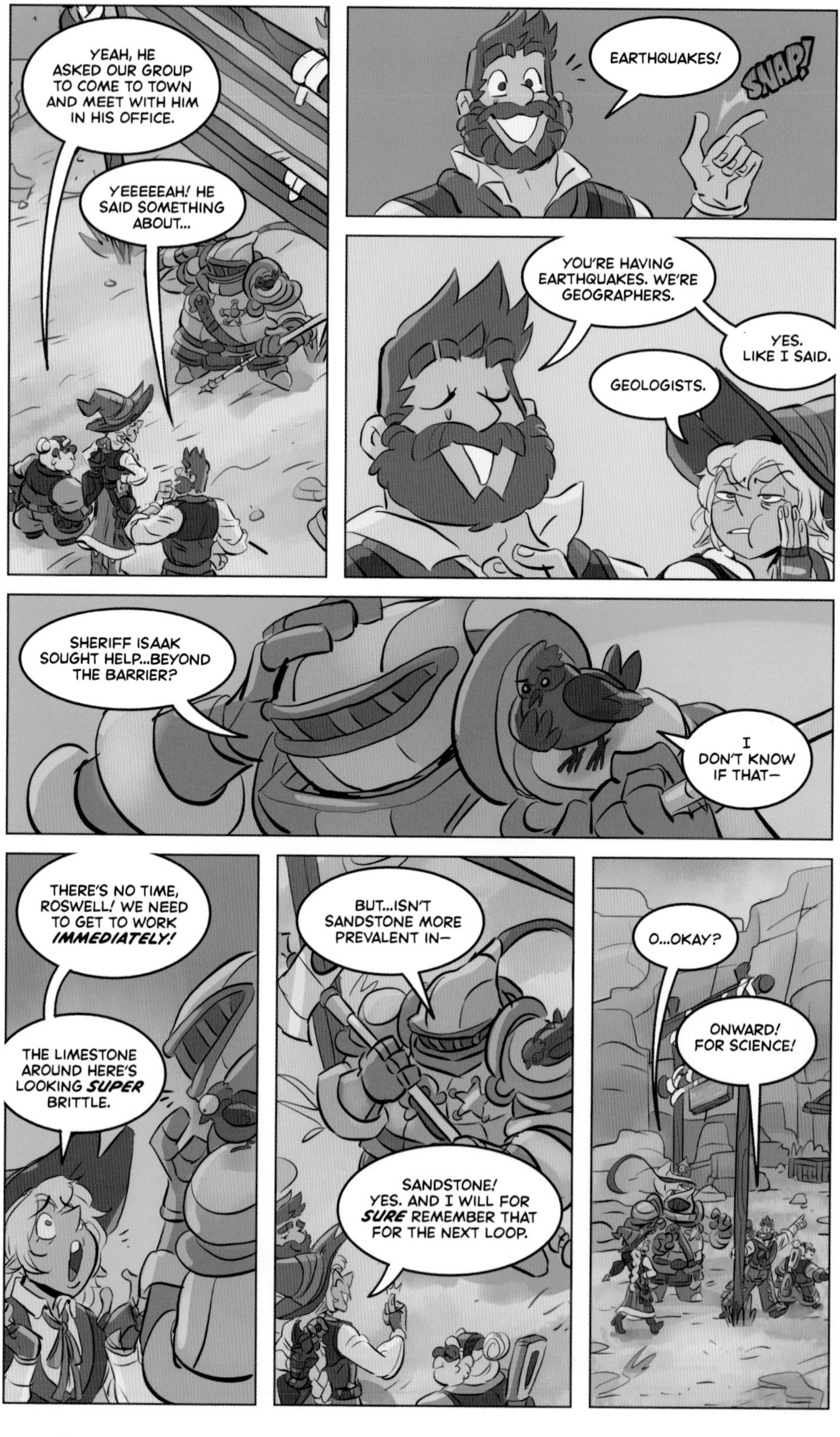
YEAH, HE ASKED OUR GROUP TO COME TO TOWN AND MEET WITH HIM IN HIS OFFICE.
YEEEEEAH! HE SAID SOMETHING ABOUT...
EARTHQUAKES!
SNAP!
YOU'RE HAVING EARTHQUAKES. WE'RE GEOGRAPHERS.
GEOLOGISTS.
YES. LIKE I SAID.
SHERIFF ISAAK SOUGHT HELP...BEYOND THE BARRIER?
I DON'T KNOW IF THAT—
THERE'S NO TIME, ROSWELL! WE NEED TO GET TO WORK IMMEDIATELY!
THE LIMESTONE AROUND HERE'S LOOKING SUPER BRITTLE.
BUT...ISN'T SANDSTONE MORE PREVALENT IN—
SANDSTONE! YES. AND I WILL FOR SURE REMEMBER THAT FOR THE NEXT LOOP.
O...OKAY?
ONWARD! FOR SCIENCE!

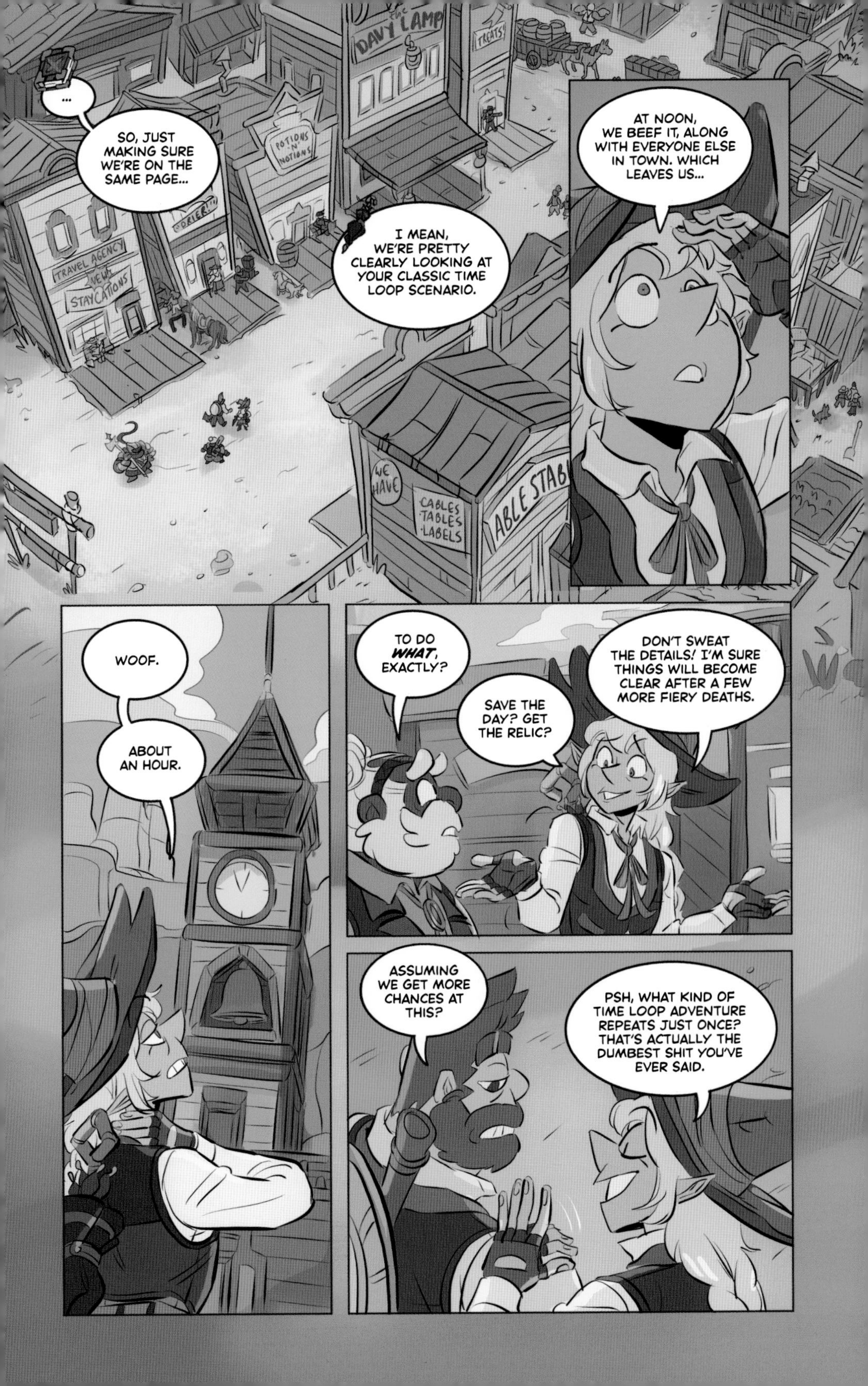
THE DAVY LAMP
TREATS!
POTIONS 'N' NOTIONS
DRIER
TRAVEL AGENCY
NEW STAYCATIONS
...
SO, JUST MAKING SURE WE'RE ON THE SAME PAGE...
I MEAN, WE'RE PRETTY CLEARLY LOOKING AT YOUR CLASSIC TIME LOOP SCENARIO.
WE HAVE
CABLES TABLES LABELS
ABLE STAB
AT NOON, WE BEEF IT, ALONG WITH EVERYONE ELSE IN TOWN. WHICH LEAVES US...
WOOF.
ABOUT AN HOUR.
TO DO *WHAT*, EXACTLY?
SAVE THE DAY? GET THE RELIC?
DON'T SWEAT THE DETAILS! I'M SURE THINGS WILL BECOME CLEAR AFTER A FEW MORE FIERY DEATHS.
ASSUMING WE GET MORE CHANCES AT THIS?
PSH, WHAT KIND OF TIME LOOP ADVENTURE REPEATS JUST ONCE? THAT'S ACTUALLY THE DUMBEST SHIT YOU'VE EVER SAID.

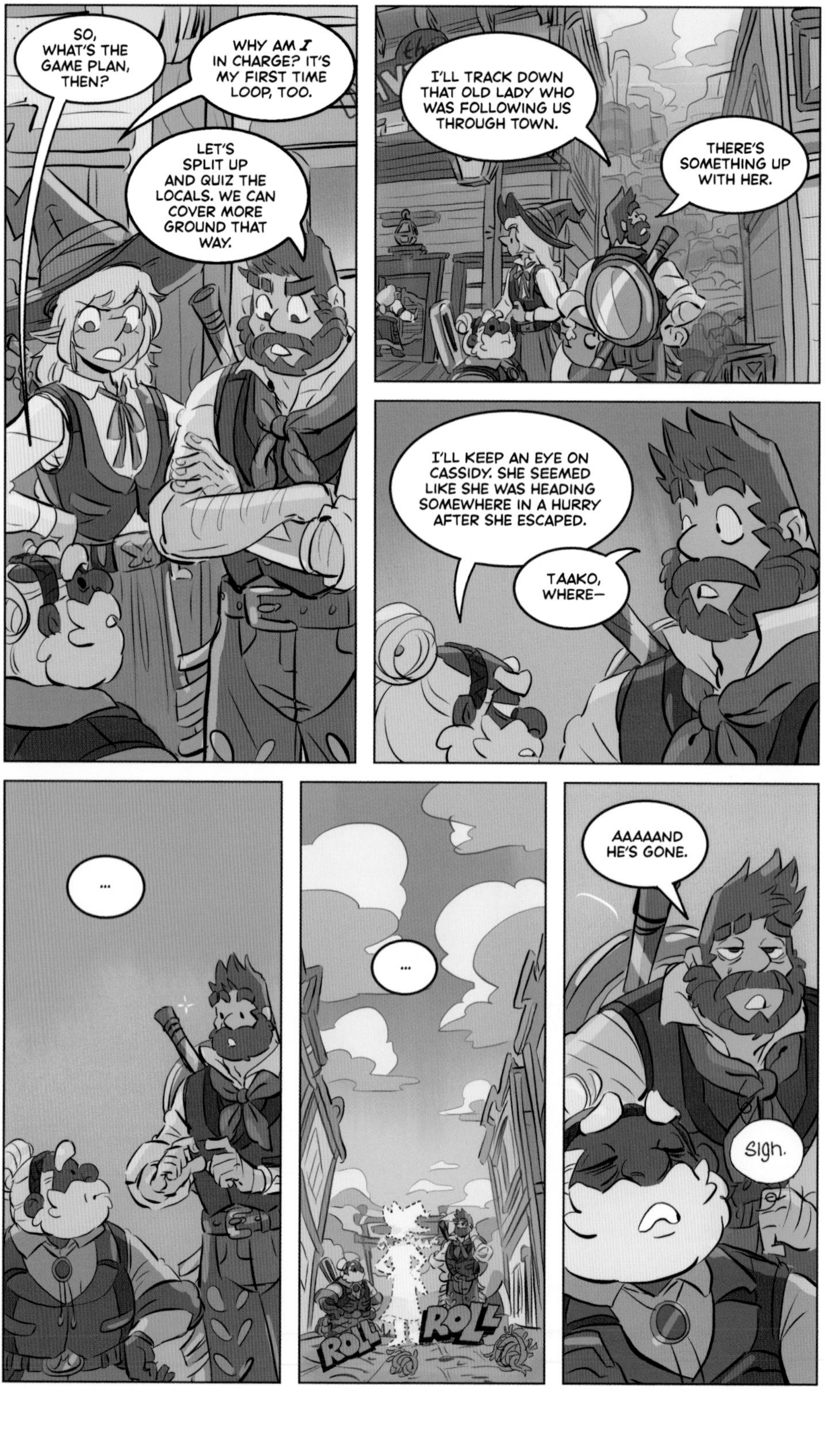
SO, WHAT'S THE GAME PLAN, THEN?
WHY AM I IN CHARGE? IT'S MY FIRST TIME LOOP, TOO.
LET'S SPLIT UP AND QUIZ THE LOCALS. WE CAN COVER MORE GROUND THAT WAY.
I'LL TRACK DOWN THAT OLD LADY WHO WAS FOLLOWING US THROUGH TOWN.
THERE'S SOMETHING UP WITH HER.
I'LL KEEP AN EYE ON CASSIDY. SHE SEEMED LIKE SHE WAS HEADING SOMEWHERE IN A HURRY AFTER SHE ESCAPED.
TAAKO, WHERE—
...
...
ROLL
ROLL
AAAAAND HE'S GONE.
Sigh.

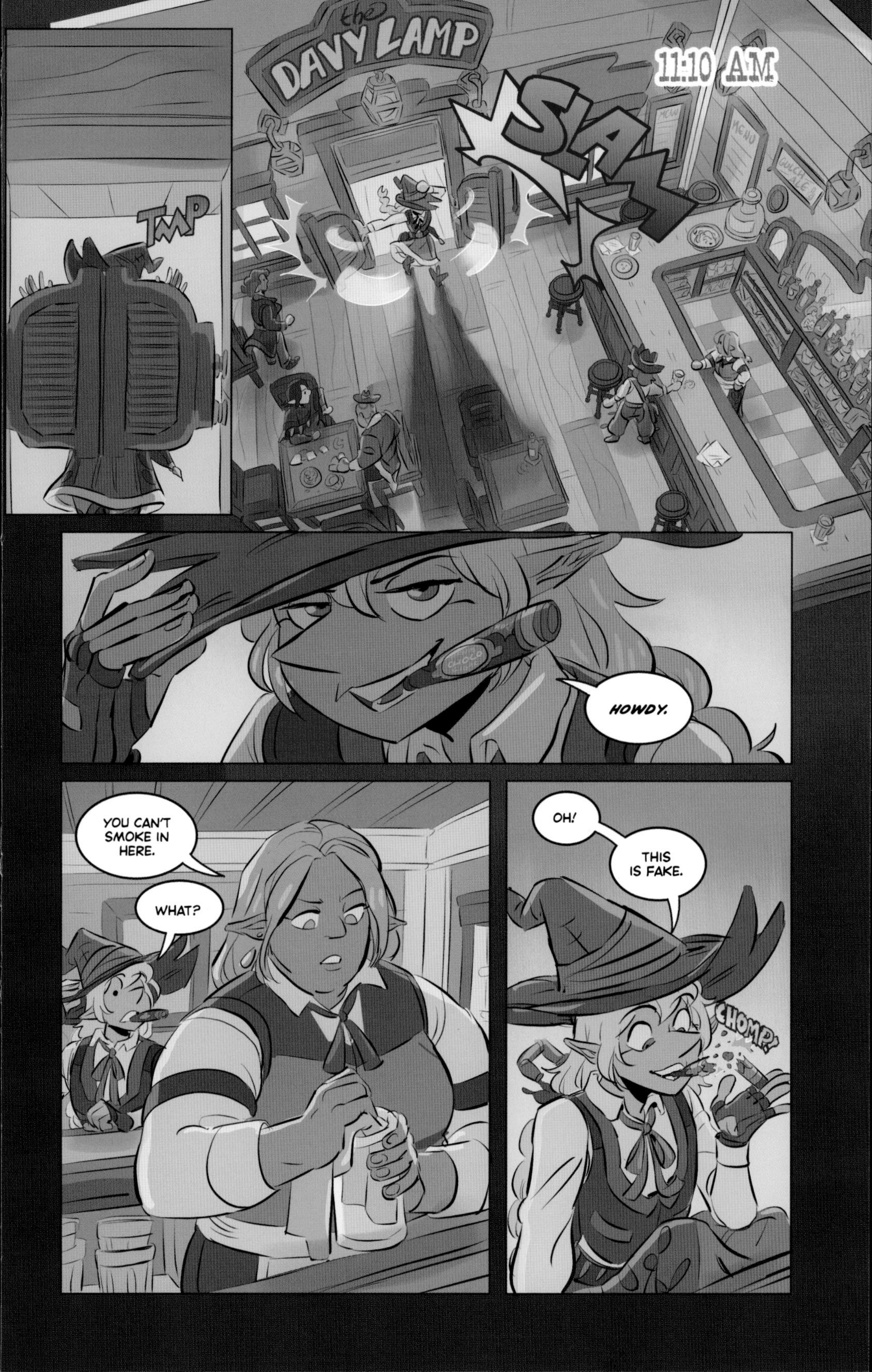
TMP
the DAVY LAMP
11:10 AM
SLAM
MENU
MENU
GULCH ALE
CHOCO
HOWDY.
YOU CAN'T SMOKE IN HERE.
WHAT?
OH!
THIS IS FAKE.
CHOMP!

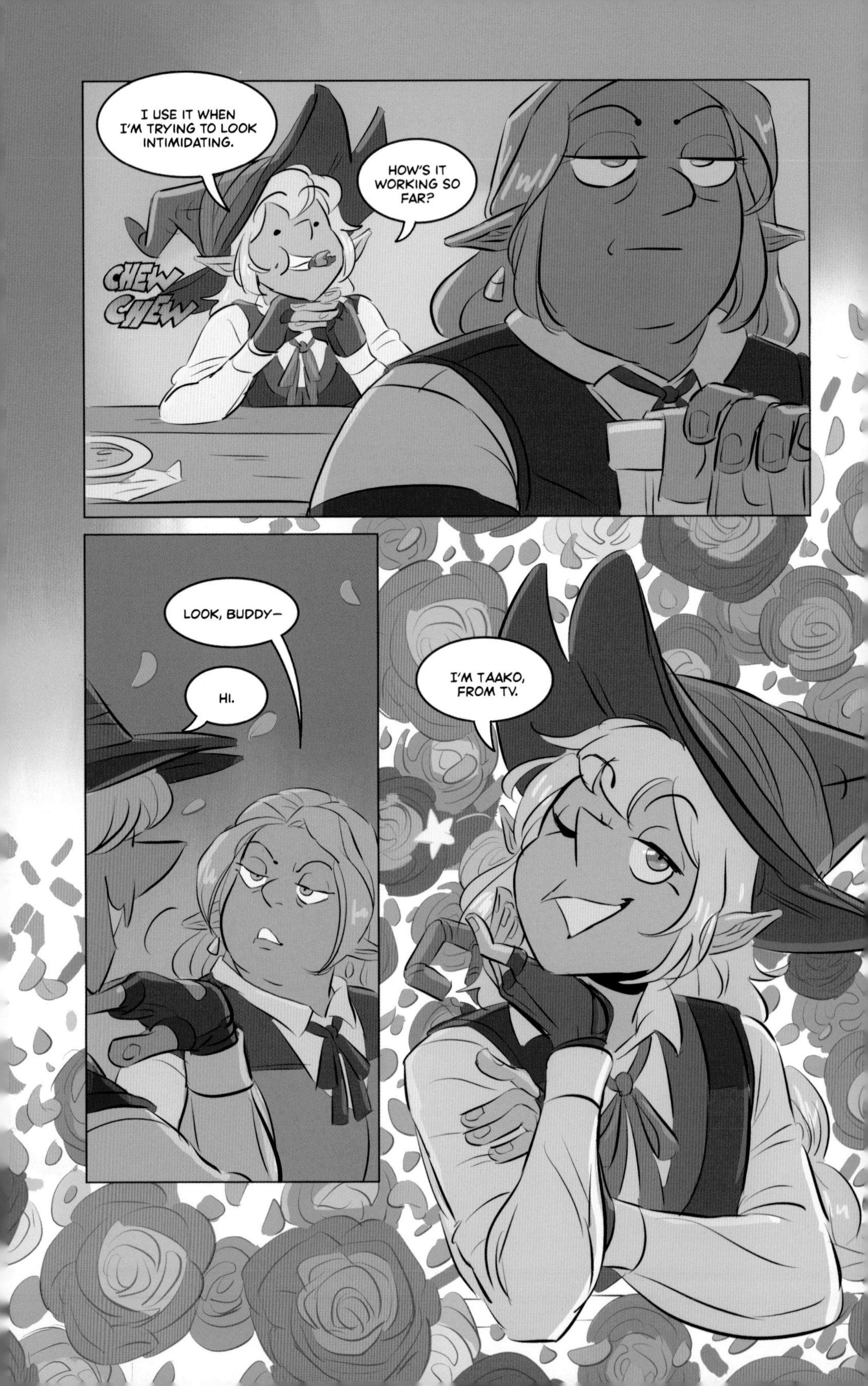
I USE IT WHEN I'M TRYING TO LOOK INTIMIDATING.
HOW'S IT WORKING SO FAR?
CHEW CHEW
LOOK, BUDDY—
HI.
I'M TAAKO, FROM TV.

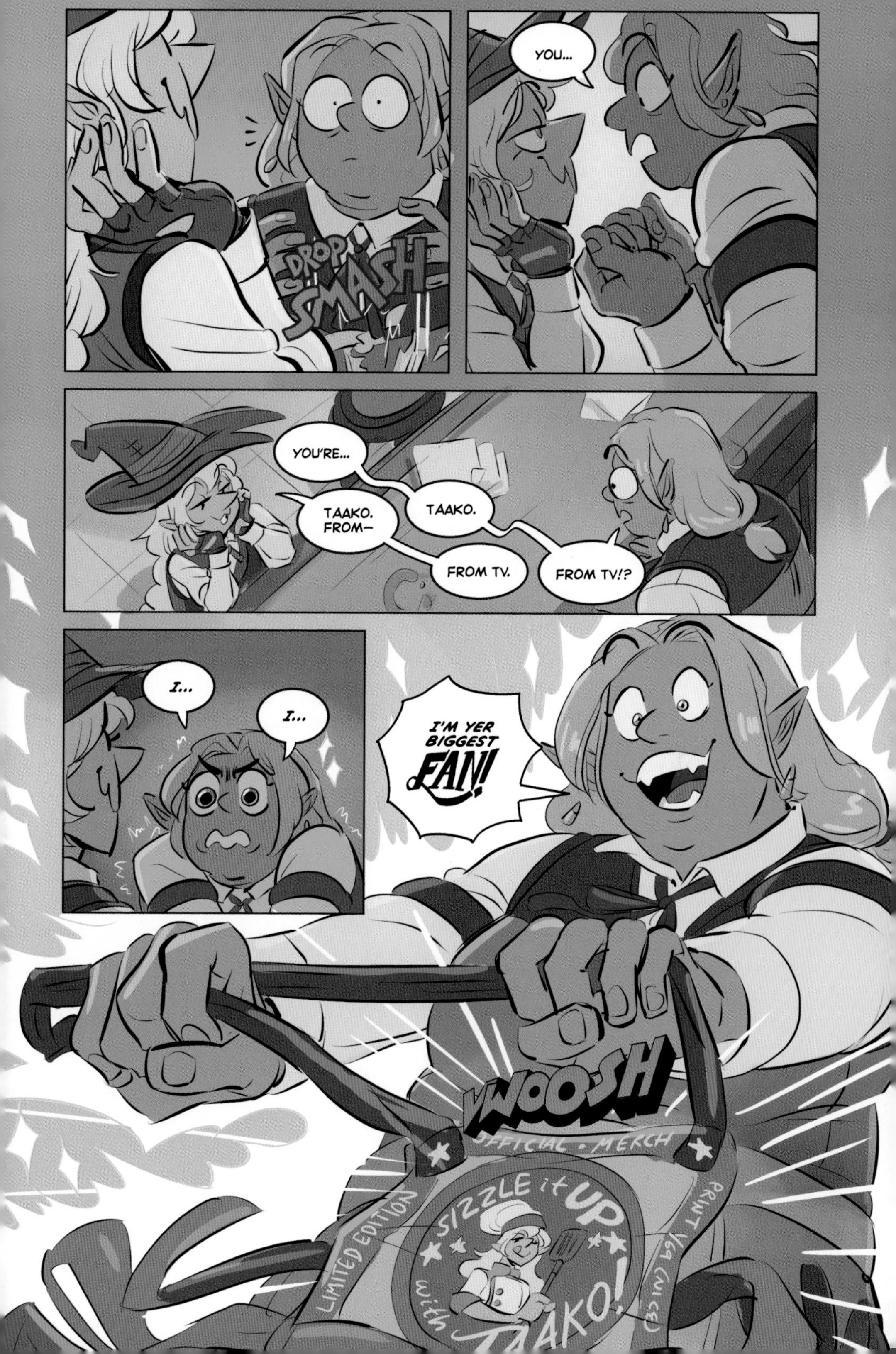
DROP
SMASH
YOU...
YOU'RE...
TAAKO. FROM—
TAAKO.
FROM TV.
FROM TV!?
I...
I...
I'M YER BIGGEST FAN!
WOOSH
OFFICIAL • MERCH
LIMITED EDITION
SIZZLE it UP with TAAKO!
PRINT V69 (NICE)

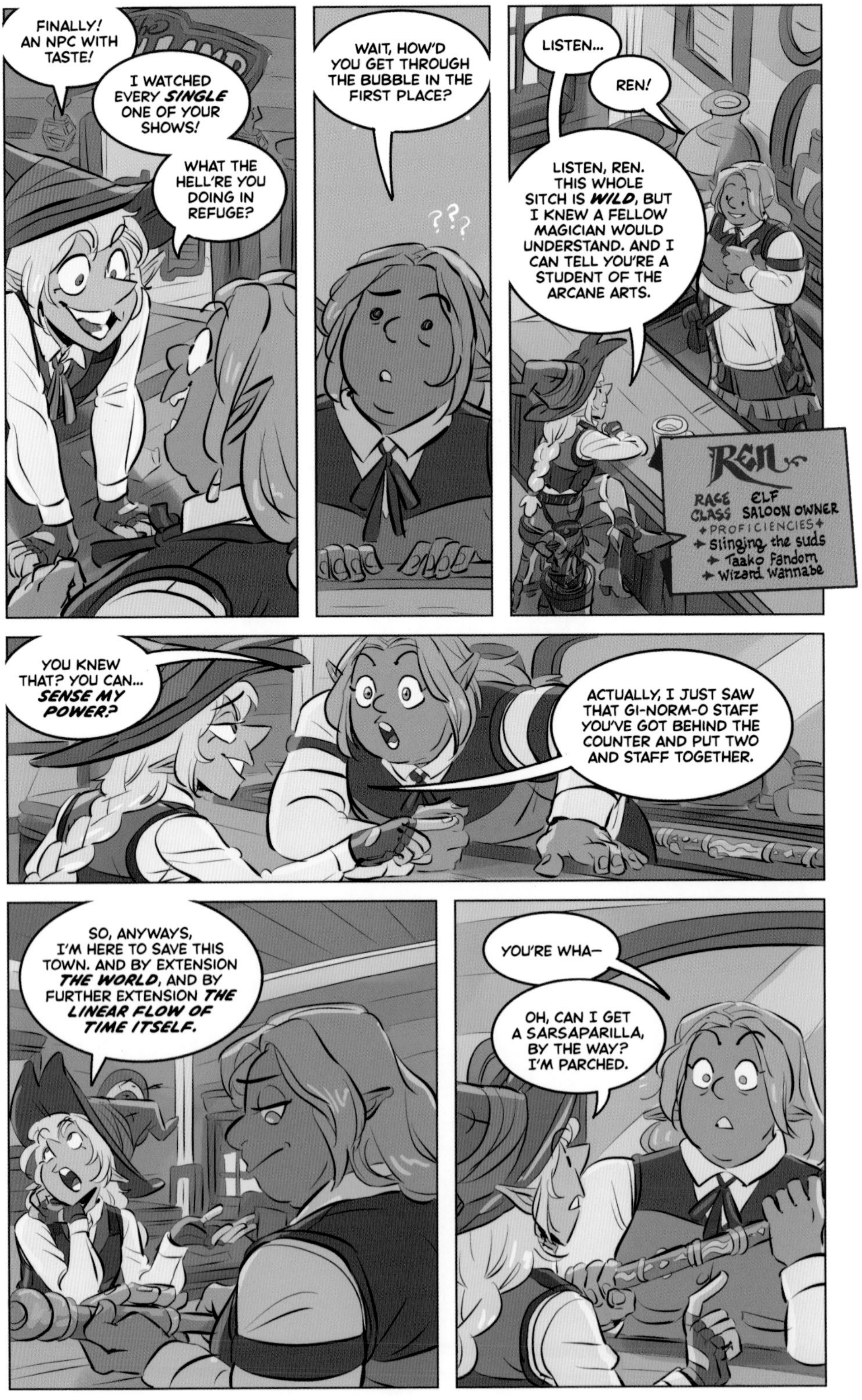
FINALLY! AN NPC WITH TASTE!
I WATCHED EVERY SINGLE ONE OF YOUR SHOWS!
WHAT THE HELL'RE YOU DOING IN REFUGE?
WAIT, HOW'D YOU GET THROUGH THE BUBBLE IN THE FIRST PLACE?
??
LISTEN...
REN!
LISTEN, REN. THIS WHOLE SITCH IS WILD, BUT I KNEW A FELLOW MAGICIAN WOULD UNDERSTAND. AND I CAN TELL YOU'RE A STUDENT OF THE ARCANE ARTS.
REN
RACE ELF
CLASS SALOON OWNER
PROFICIENCIES
Slinging the suds
Taako fandom
Wizard wannabe
YOU KNEW THAT? YOU CAN... SENSE MY POWER?
ACTUALLY, I JUST SAW THAT GI-NORM-O STAFF YOU'VE GOT BEHIND THE COUNTER AND PUT TWO AND STAFF TOGETHER.
SO, ANYWAYS, I'M HERE TO SAVE THIS TOWN. AND BY EXTENSION THE WORLD, AND BY FURTHER EXTENSION THE LINEAR FLOW OF TIME ITSELF.
YOU'RE WHA—
OH, CAN I GET A SARSAPARILLA, BY THE WAY? I'M PARCHED.

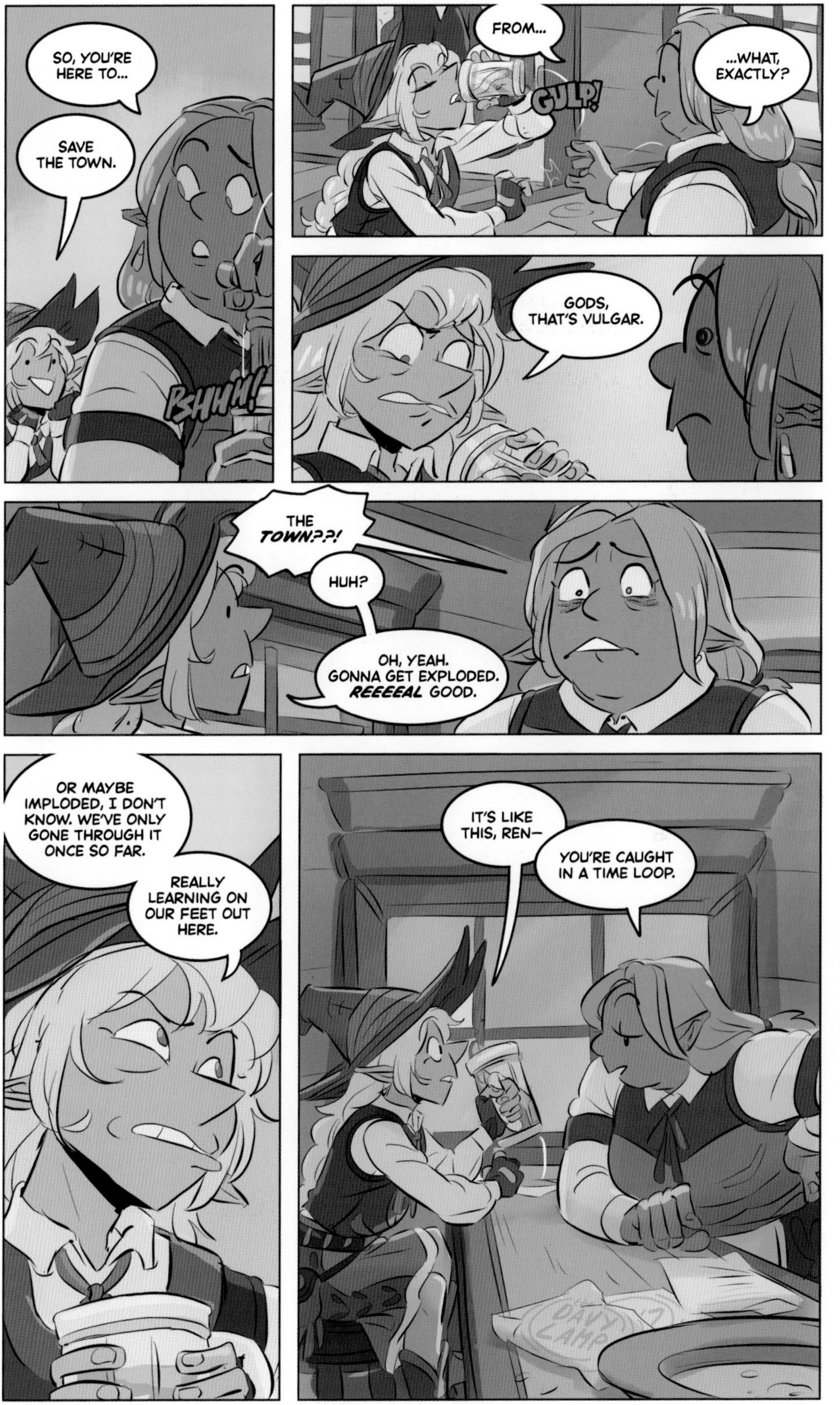
SO, YOU'RE HERE TO...
SAVE THE TOWN.
PSHHH!
FROM...
GULP!
...WHAT, EXACTLY?
GODS, THAT'S VULGAR.
THE TOWN??!
HUH?
OH, YEAH. GONNA GET EXPLODED. REEEEAL GOOD.
OR MAYBE IMPLODED, I DON'T KNOW. WE'VE ONLY GONE THROUGH IT ONCE SO FAR.
REALLY LEARNING ON OUR FEET OUT HERE.
IT'S LIKE THIS, REN—
YOU'RE CAUGHT IN A TIME LOOP.
DAVY LAMP

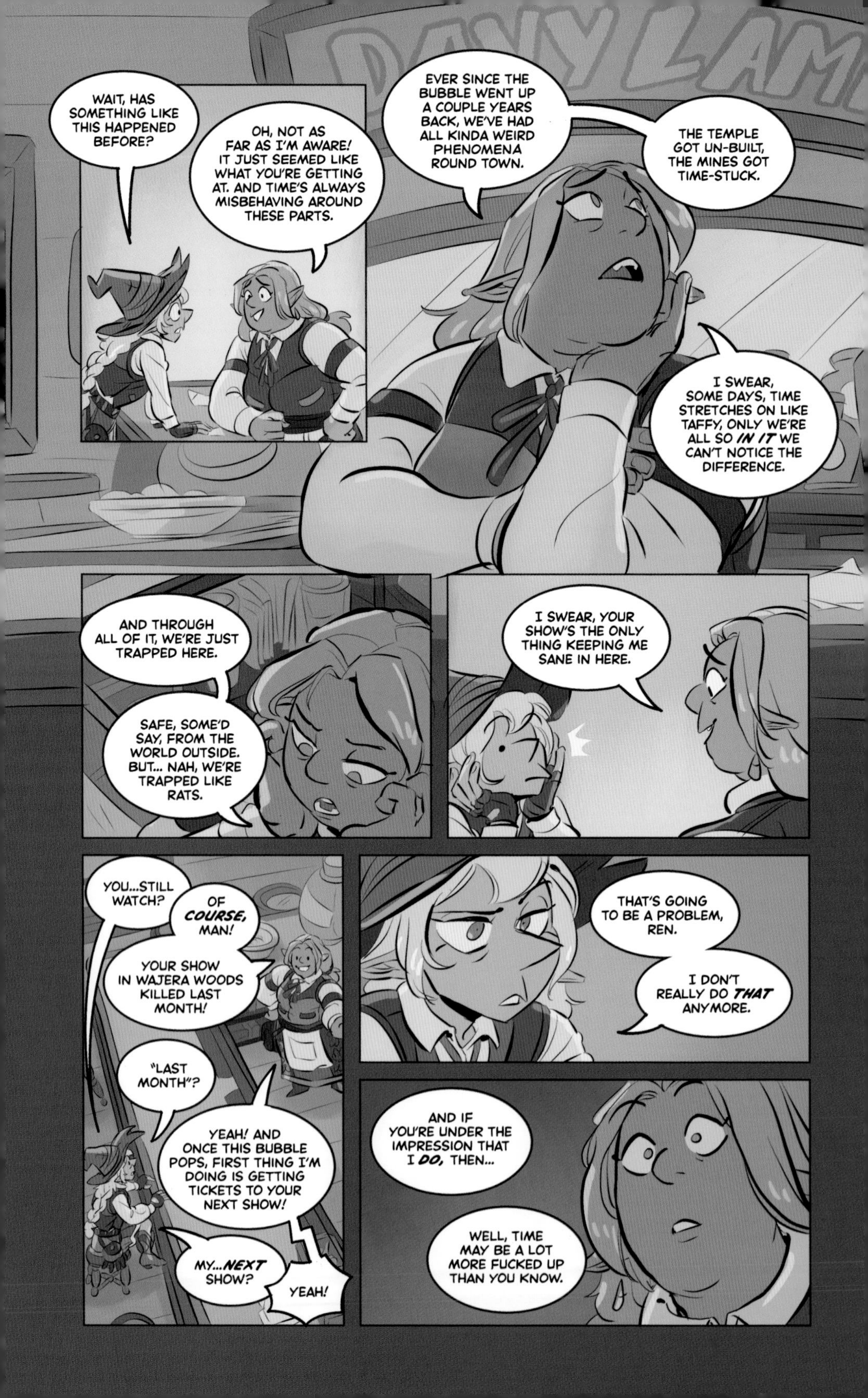
DAVY LAM
WAIT, HAS SOMETHING LIKE THIS HAPPENED BEFORE?
OH, NOT AS FAR AS I'M AWARE! IT JUST SEEMED LIKE WHAT YOU'RE GETTING AT. AND TIME'S ALWAYS MISBEHAVING AROUND THESE PARTS.
EVER SINCE THE BUBBLE WENT UP A COUPLE YEARS BACK, WE'VE HAD ALL KINDA WEIRD PHENOMENA ROUND TOWN.
THE TEMPLE GOT UN-BUILT, THE MINES GOT TIME-STUCK.
I SWEAR, SOME DAYS, TIME STRETCHES ON LIKE TAFFY, ONLY WE'RE ALL SO ***IN IT*** WE CAN'T NOTICE THE DIFFERENCE.
AND THROUGH ALL OF IT, WE'RE JUST TRAPPED HERE.
SAFE, SOME'D SAY, FROM THE WORLD OUTSIDE. BUT... NAH, WE'RE TRAPPED LIKE RATS.
I SWEAR, YOUR SHOW'S THE ONLY THING KEEPING ME SANE IN HERE.
YOU...STILL WATCH?
OF ***COURSE,*** MAN!
YOUR SHOW IN WAJERA WOODS KILLED LAST MONTH!
"LAST MONTH"?
YEAH! AND ONCE THIS BUBBLE POPS, FIRST THING I'M DOING IS GETTING TICKETS TO YOUR NEXT SHOW!
MY...***NEXT*** SHOW?
YEAH!
THAT'S GOING TO BE A PROBLEM, REN.
I DON'T REALLY DO ***THAT*** ANYMORE.
AND IF YOU'RE UNDER THE IMPRESSION THAT I ***DO,*** THEN...
WELL, TIME MAY BE A LOT MORE FUCKED UP THAN YOU KNOW.

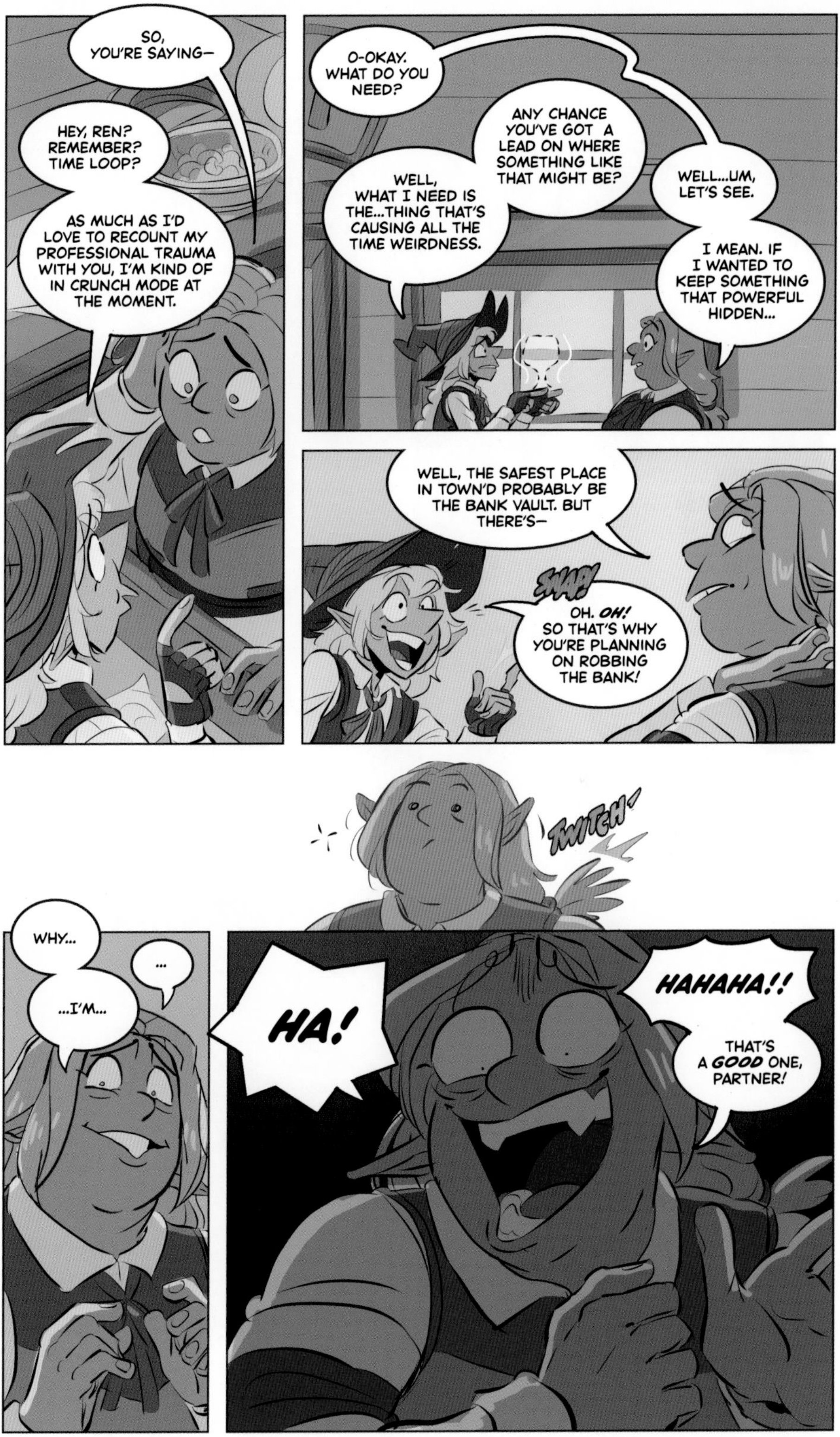
SO, YOU'RE SAYING—
HEY, REN? REMEMBER? TIME LOOP?
AS MUCH AS I'D LOVE TO RECOUNT MY PROFESSIONAL TRAUMA WITH YOU, I'M KIND OF IN CRUNCH MODE AT THE MOMENT.
O-OKAY. WHAT DO YOU NEED?
WELL, WHAT I NEED IS THE...THING THAT'S CAUSING ALL THE TIME WEIRDNESS.
ANY CHANCE YOU'VE GOT A LEAD ON WHERE SOMETHING LIKE THAT MIGHT BE?
WELL...UM, LET'S SEE.
I MEAN. IF I WANTED TO KEEP SOMETHING THAT POWERFUL HIDDEN...
WELL, THE SAFEST PLACE IN TOWN'D PROBABLY BE THE BANK VAULT. BUT THERE'S—
SNAP!
OH. OH! SO THAT'S WHY YOU'RE PLANNING ON ROBBING THE BANK!
TWITCH
WHY...
...
...I'M...
HA!
HAHAHA!!
THAT'S A GOOD ONE, PARTNER!

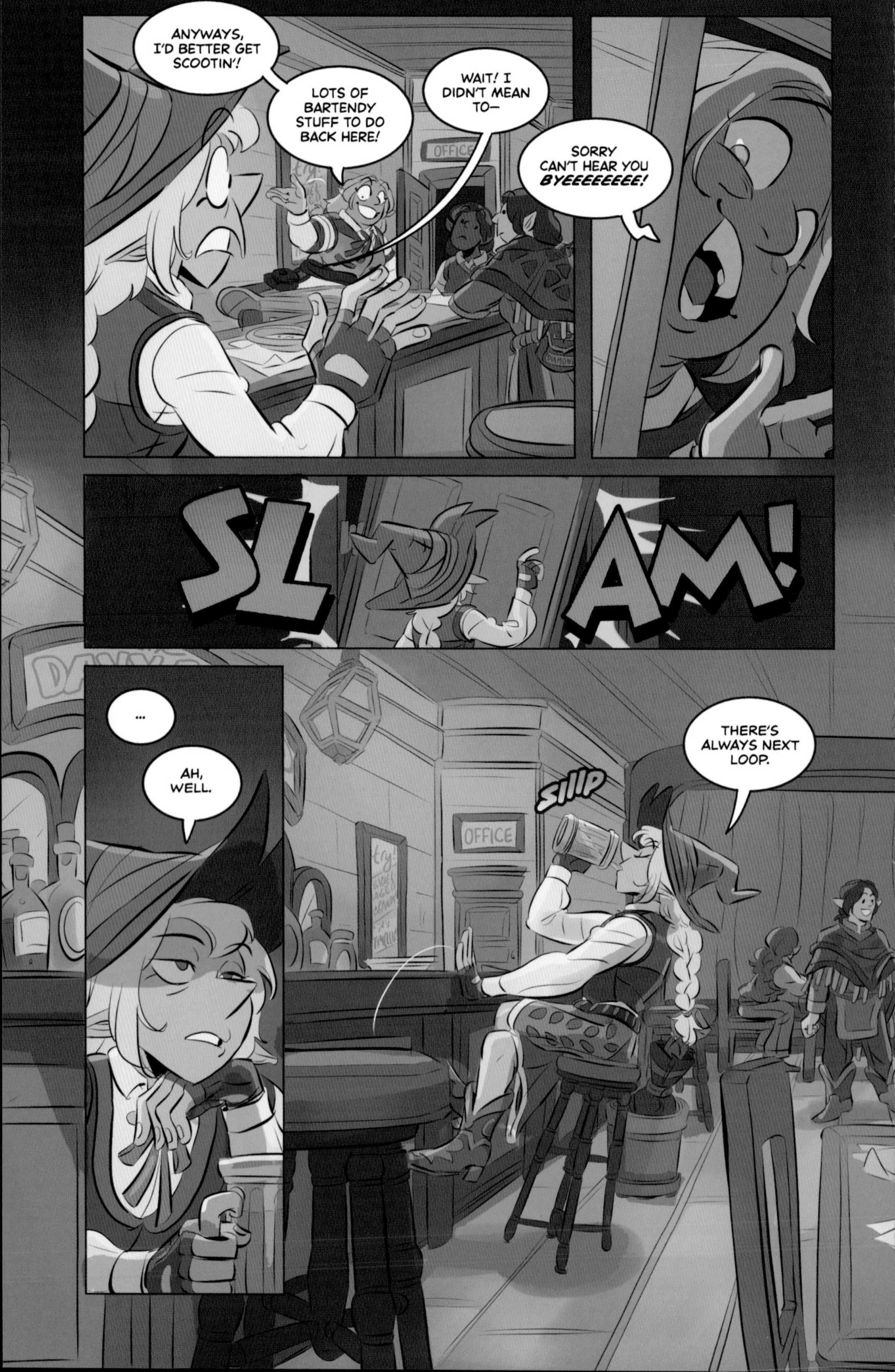
ANYWAYS, I'D BETTER GET SCOOTIN'!
LOTS OF BARTENDY STUFF TO DO BACK HERE!
WAIT! I DIDN'T MEAN TO—
OFFICE
SORRY CAN'T HEAR YOU *BYEEEEEEEE!*
SL AM!
...
AH, WELL.
SIIIP
OFFICE
THERE'S ALWAYS NEXT LOOP.

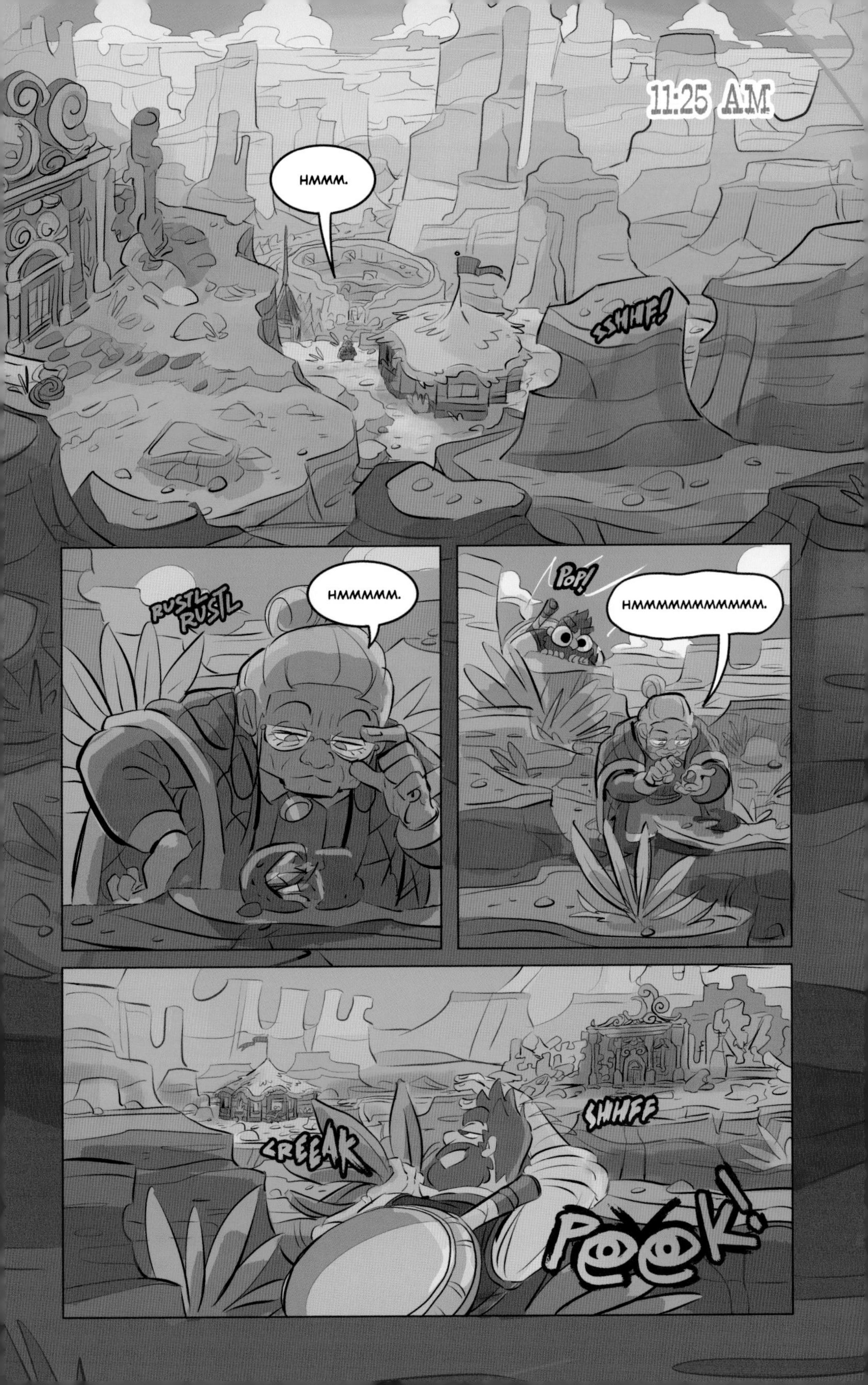
11:25 AM
HMMM.
SSHHF!
RUSTL RUSTL
HMMMMM.
POP!
HMMMMMMMMMMMM.
CREEAK
SHHFF
PEEK!

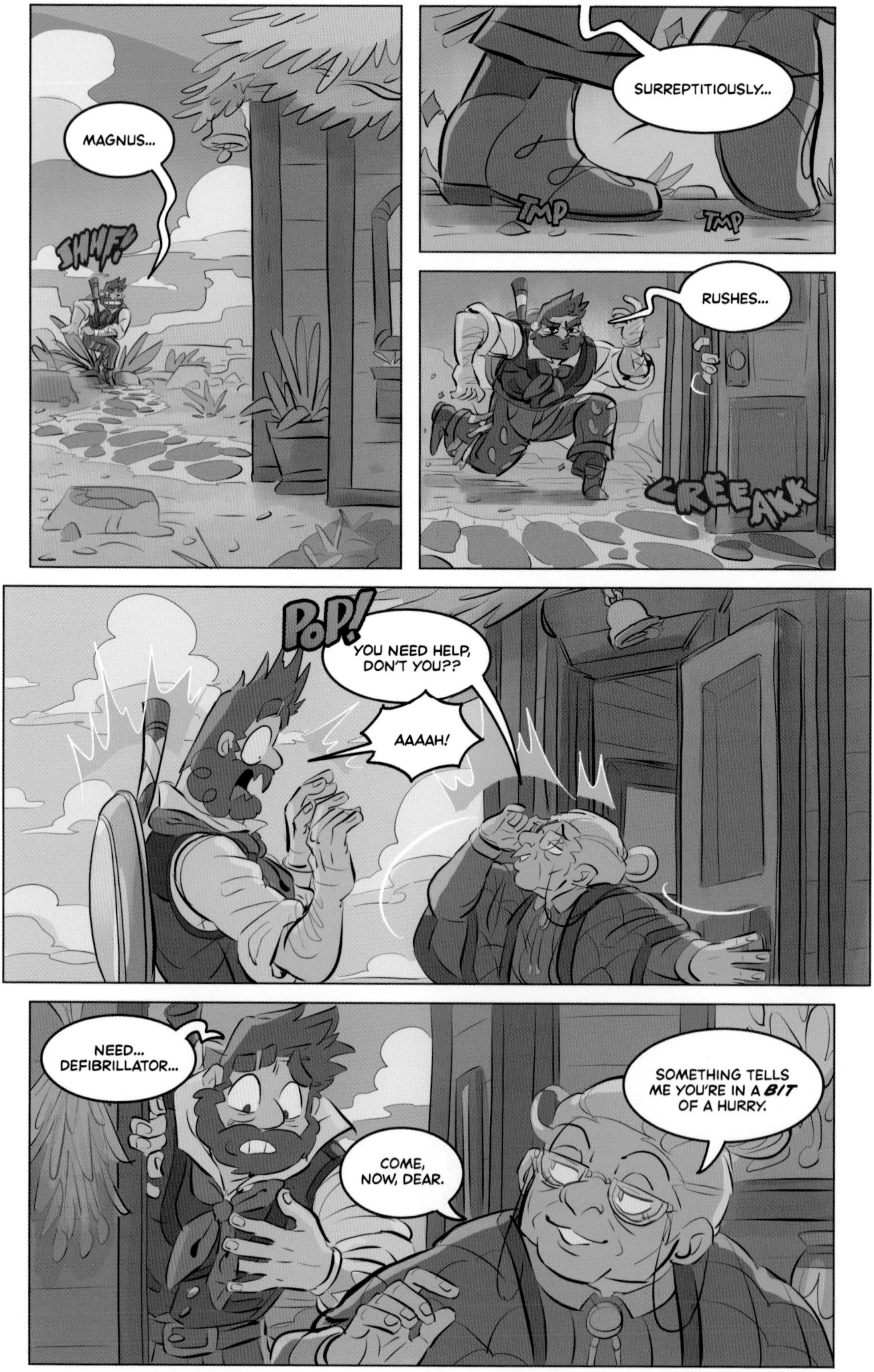
MAGNUS...
SHHF!
SURREPTITIOUSLY...
TMP
TMP
RUSHES...
CREEAKK
POP!
YOU NEED HELP, DON'T YOU??
AAAAH!
NEED... DEFIBRILLATOR...
SOMETHING TELLS ME YOU'RE IN A *BIT* OF A HURRY.
COME, NOW, DEAR.

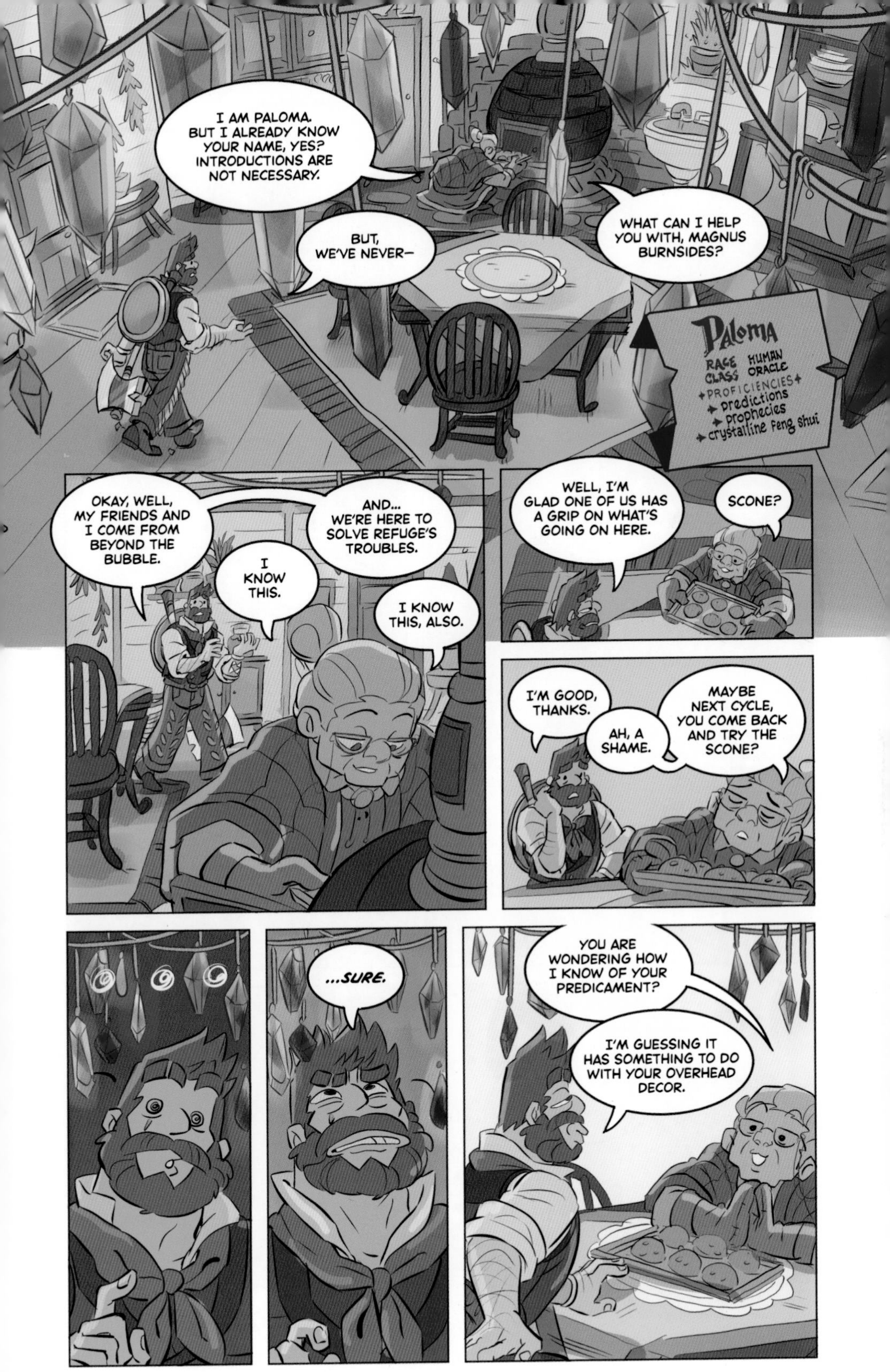
I AM PALOMA. BUT I ALREADY KNOW YOUR NAME, YES? INTRODUCTIONS ARE NOT NECESSARY.
BUT, WE'VE NEVER—
WHAT CAN I HELP YOU WITH, MAGNUS BURNSIDES?
Paloma
RACE HUMAN
CLASS ORACLE
PROFICIENCIES
predictions
prophecies
crystalline feng shui
OKAY, WELL, MY FRIENDS AND I COME FROM BEYOND THE BUBBLE.
I KNOW THIS.
AND... WE'RE HERE TO SOLVE REFUGE'S TROUBLES.
I KNOW THIS, ALSO.
WELL, I'M GLAD ONE OF US HAS A GRIP ON WHAT'S GOING ON HERE.
SCONE?
I'M GOOD, THANKS.
AH, A SHAME.
MAYBE NEXT CYCLE, YOU COME BACK AND TRY THE SCONE?
...SURE.
YOU ARE WONDERING HOW I KNOW OF YOUR PREDICAMENT?
I'M GUESSING IT HAS SOMETHING TO DO WITH YOUR OVERHEAD DECOR.

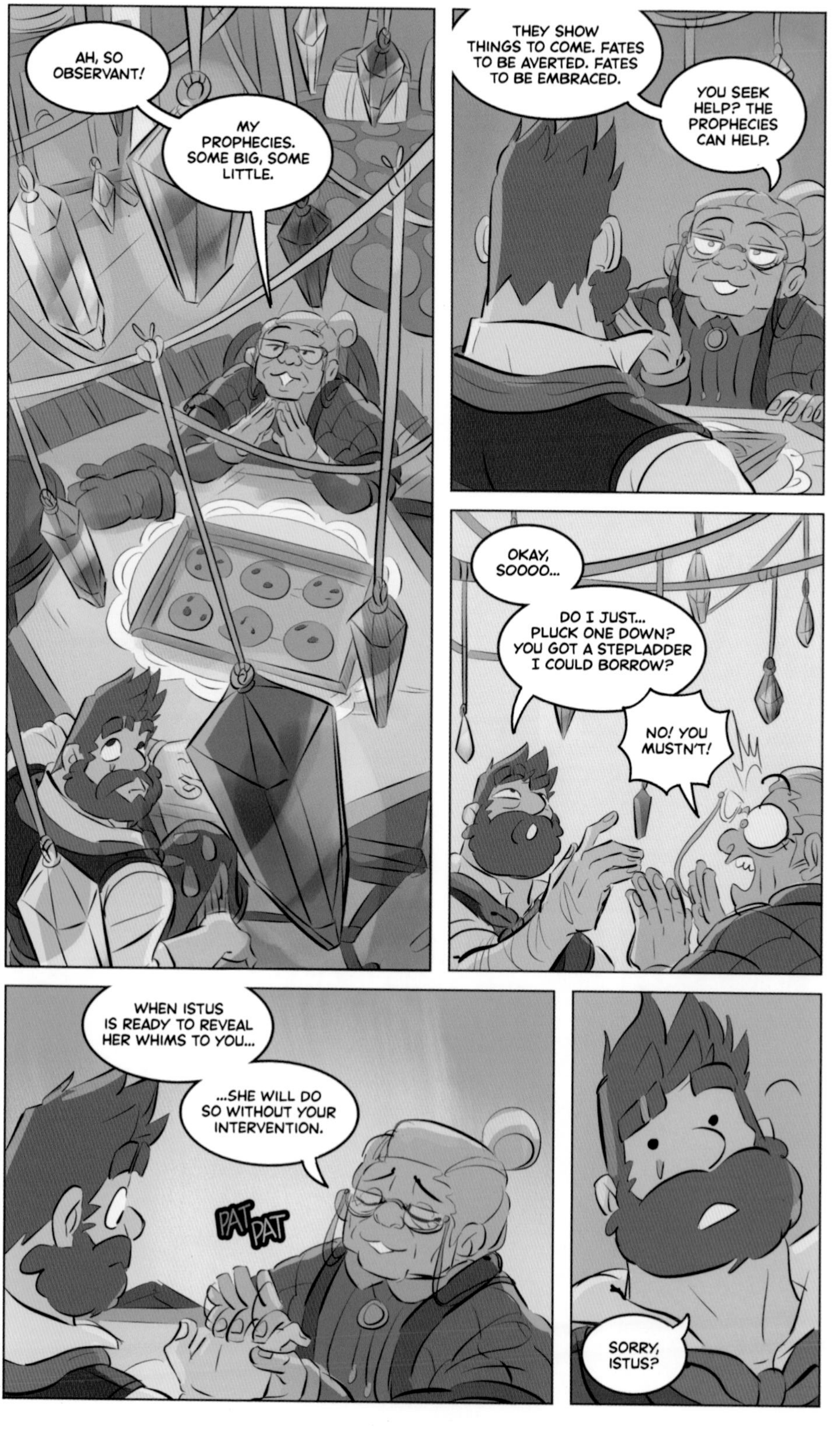
AH, SO OBSERVANT!
MY PROPHECIES. SOME BIG, SOME LITTLE.
THEY SHOW THINGS TO COME. FATES TO BE AVERTED. FATES TO BE EMBRACED.
YOU SEEK HELP? THE PROPHECIES CAN HELP.
OKAY, SOOOO...
DO I JUST... PLUCK ONE DOWN? YOU GOT A STEPLADDER I COULD BORROW?
NO! YOU MUSTN'T!
WHEN ISTUS IS READY TO REVEAL HER WHIMS TO YOU...
...SHE WILL DO SO WITHOUT YOUR INTERVENTION.
PAT PAT
SORRY, ISTUS?

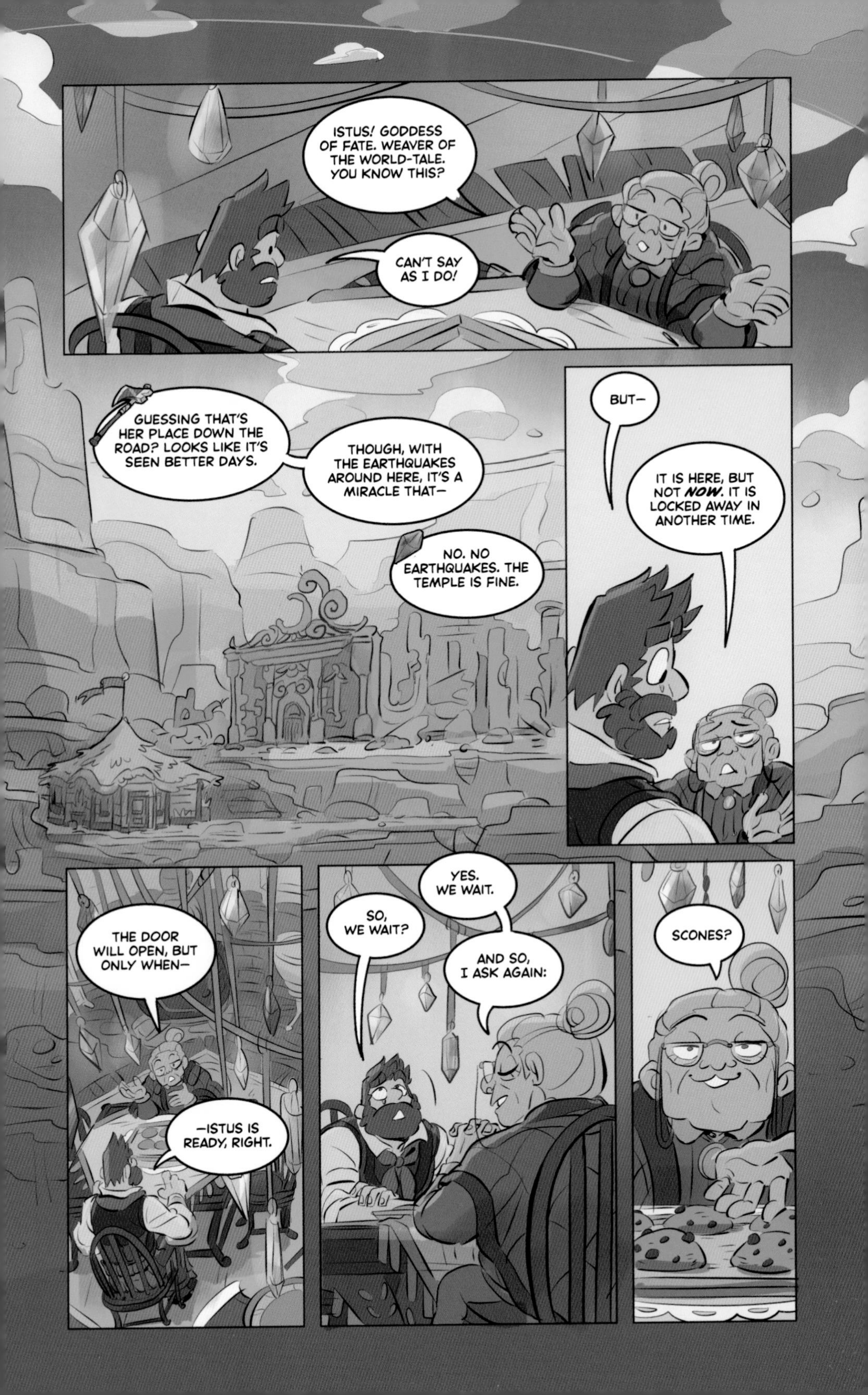
ISTUS! GODDESS OF FATE. WEAVER OF THE WORLD-TALE. YOU KNOW THIS?
CAN'T SAY AS I DO!
GUESSING THAT'S HER PLACE DOWN THE ROAD? LOOKS LIKE IT'S SEEN BETTER DAYS.
THOUGH, WITH THE EARTHQUAKES AROUND HERE, IT'S A MIRACLE THAT—
NO. NO EARTHQUAKES. THE TEMPLE IS FINE.
BUT—
IT IS HERE, BUT NOT ***NOW***. IT IS LOCKED AWAY IN ANOTHER TIME.
THE DOOR WILL OPEN, BUT ONLY WHEN—
—ISTUS IS READY, RIGHT.
SO, WE WAIT?
YES. WE WAIT.
AND SO, I ASK AGAIN:
SCONES?

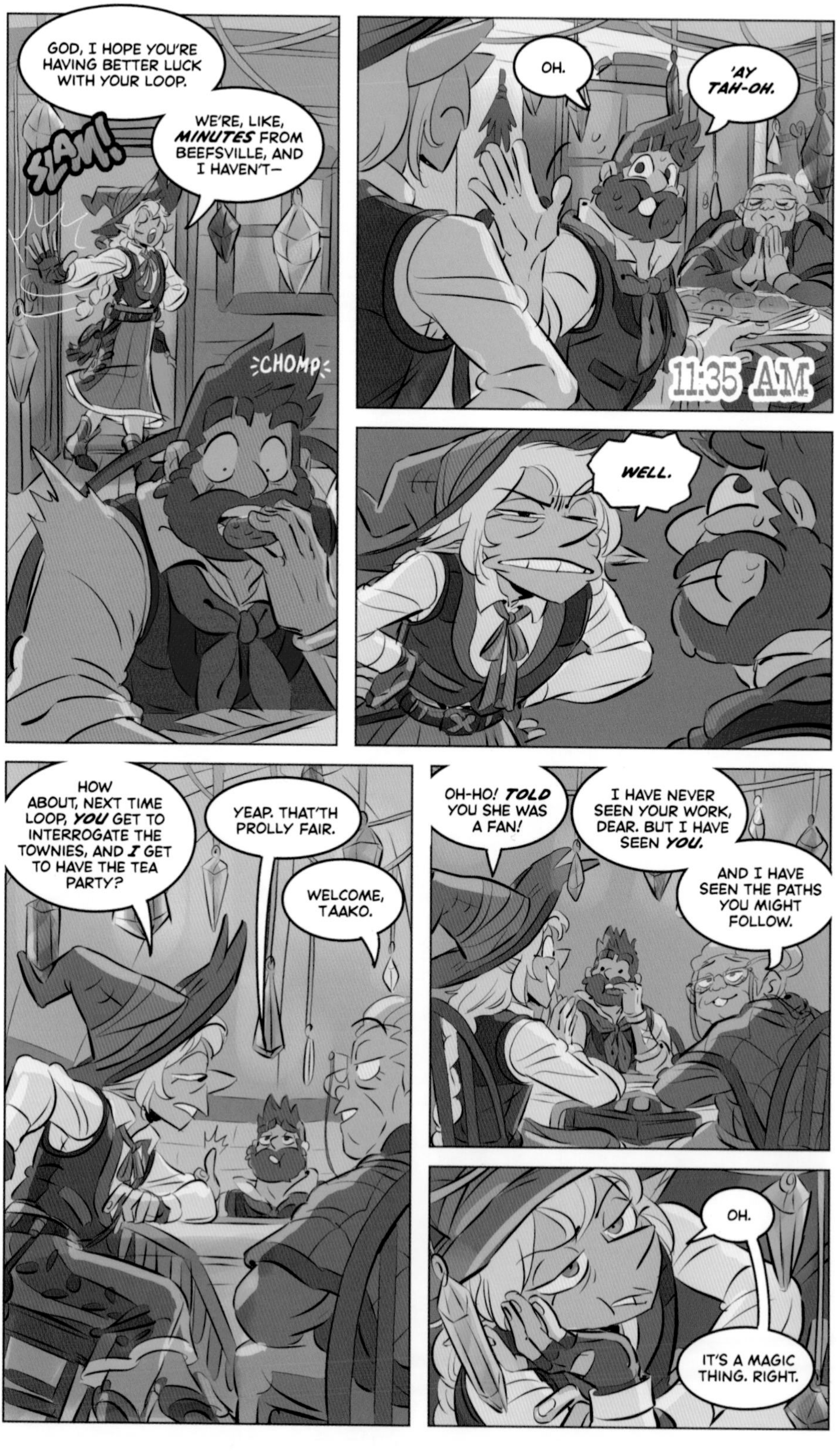
GOD, I HOPE YOU'RE HAVING BETTER LUCK WITH YOUR LOOP.
WE'RE, LIKE, MINUTES FROM BEEFSVILLE, AND I HAVEN'T—
SLAM!
CHOMP
OH.
'AY TAH-OH.
11:35 AM
WELL.
HOW ABOUT, NEXT TIME LOOP, YOU GET TO INTERROGATE THE TOWNIES, AND I GET TO HAVE THE TEA PARTY?
YEAP. THAT'TH PROLLY FAIR.
WELCOME, TAAKO.
OH-HO! TOLD YOU SHE WAS A FAN!
I HAVE NEVER SEEN YOUR WORK, DEAR. BUT I HAVE SEEN YOU.
AND I HAVE SEEN THE PATHS YOU MIGHT FOLLOW.
OH.
IT'S A MAGIC THING. RIGHT.

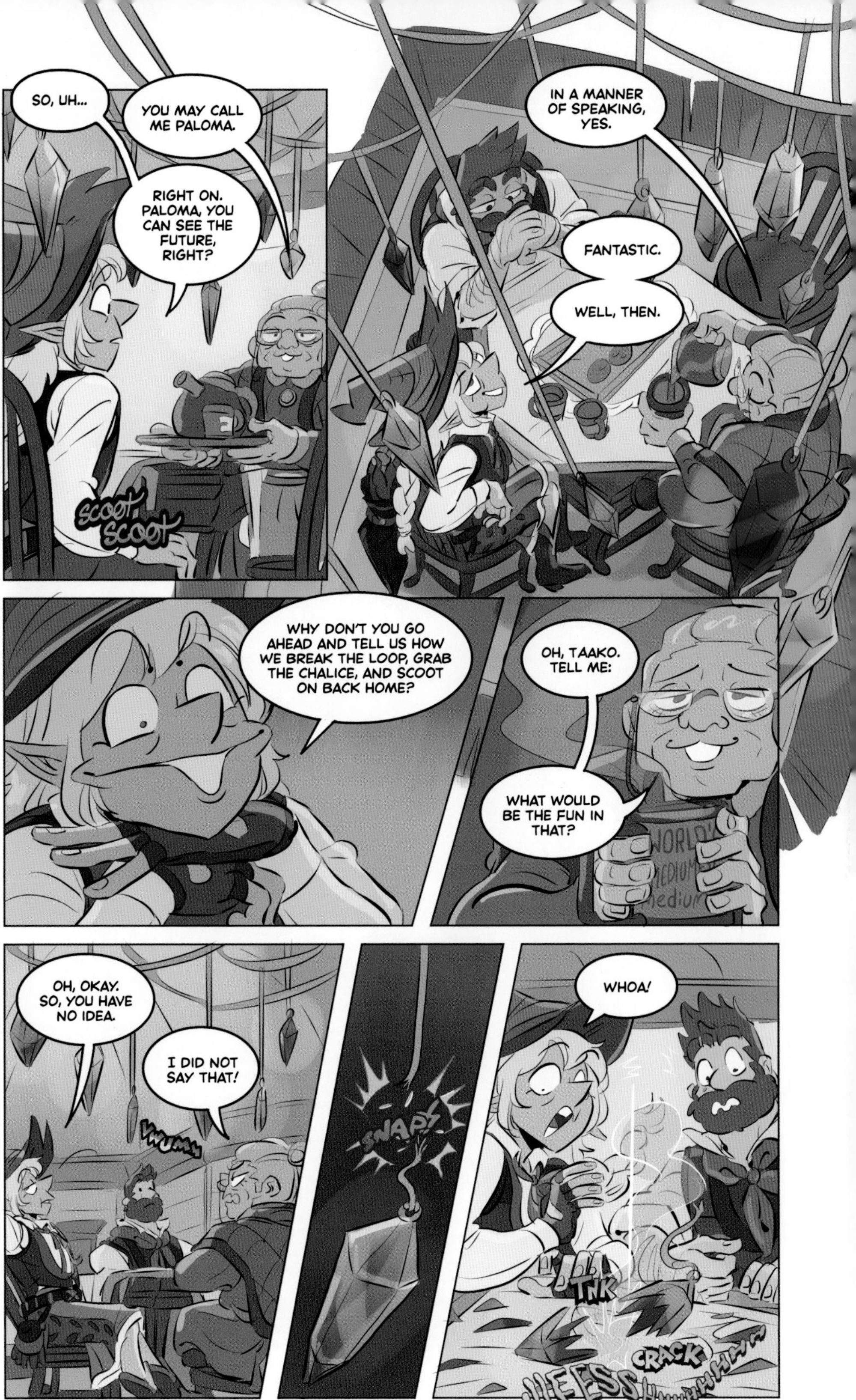
SO, UH...
YOU MAY CALL ME PALOMA.
RIGHT ON. PALOMA, YOU CAN SEE THE FUTURE, RIGHT?
scoot scoot
IN A MANNER OF SPEAKING, YES.
FANTASTIC.
WELL, THEN.
WHY DON'T YOU GO AHEAD AND TELL US HOW WE BREAK THE LOOP, GRAB THE CHALICE, AND SCOOT ON BACK HOME?
OH, TAAKO. TELL ME:
WHAT WOULD BE THE FUN IN THAT?
WORLD'S MEDIUM medium
OH, OKAY. SO, YOU HAVE NO IDEA.
I DID NOT SAY THAT!
VWUM
SNAP
WHOA!
TNK
CRACK
WHEESSHHHHHHHH

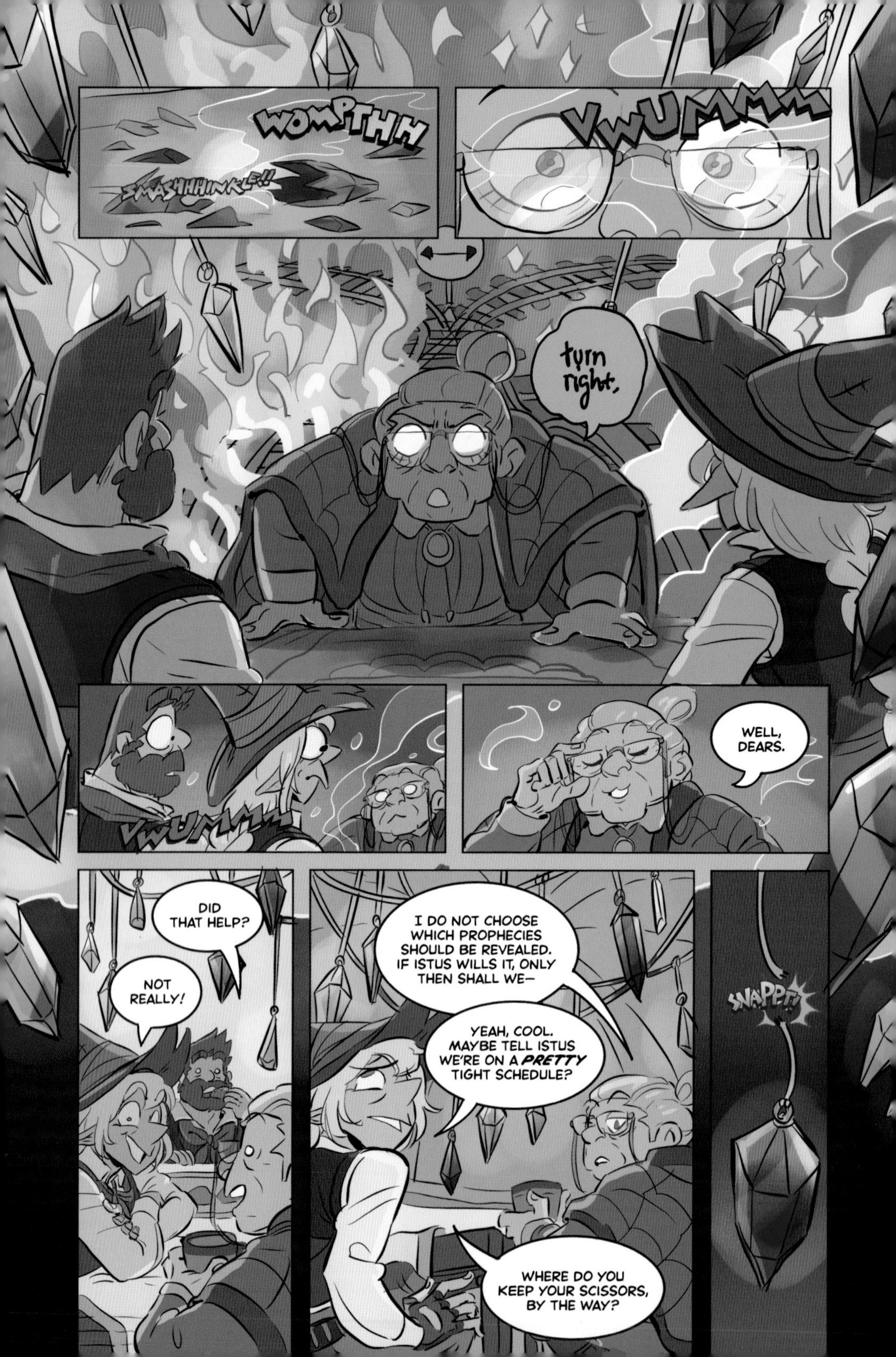
WOMPTHH
SMASHHHINKLE!!
VWUMMM
turn right.
VWUMMM
WELL, DEARS.
DID THAT HELP?
NOT REALLY!
I DO NOT CHOOSE WHICH PROPHECIES SHOULD BE REVEALED. IF ISTUS WILLS IT, ONLY THEN SHALL WE—
YEAH, COOL. MAYBE TELL ISTUS WE'RE ON A *PRETTY* TIGHT SCHEDULE?
WHERE DO YOU KEEP YOUR SCISSORS, BY THE WAY?
SNAPPT!!

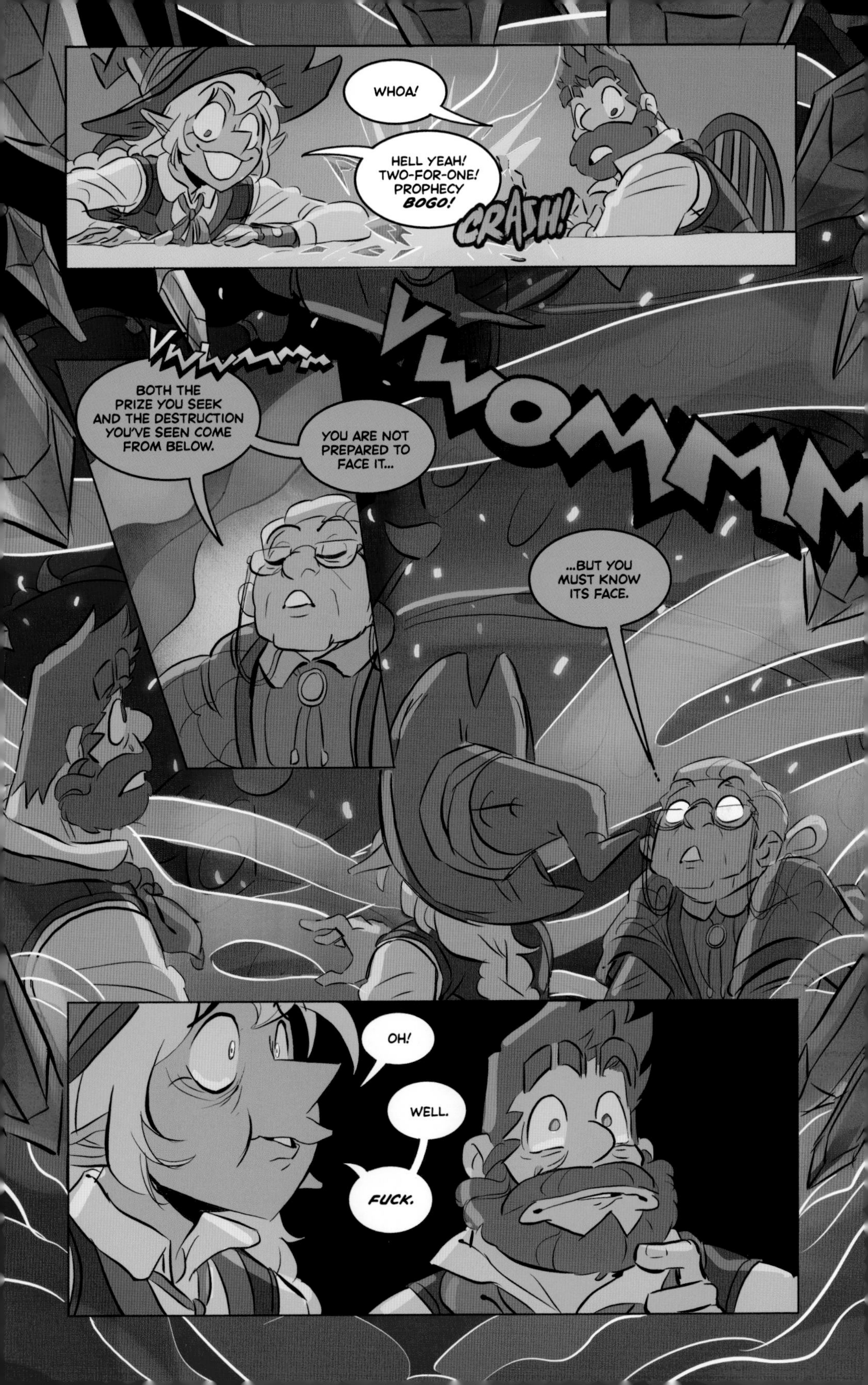
WHOA!
HELL YEAH! TWO-FOR-ONE! PROPHECY BOGO!
CRASH!
VWWMM
VWOMMM
BOTH THE PRIZE YOU SEEK AND THE DESTRUCTION YOU'VE SEEN COME FROM BELOW.
YOU ARE NOT PREPARED TO FACE IT...
...BUT YOU MUST KNOW ITS FACE.
OH!
WELL.
FUCK.

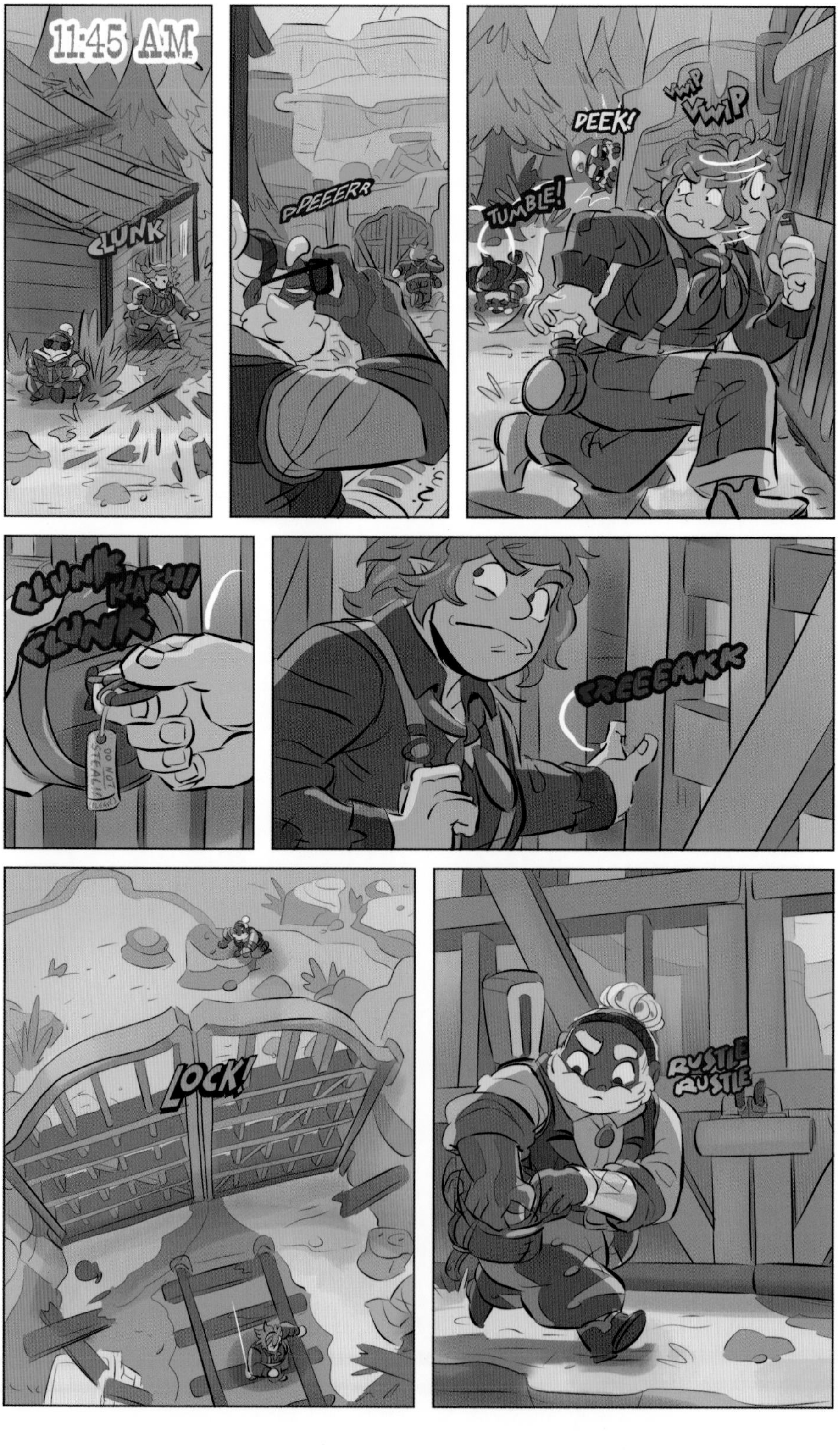
11:45 AM
CLUNK
PPEEERR
DEEK!
VWIP VWIP
TUMBLE!
KLUNK KLATCH! CLUNK
DO NOT STEAL!! PLEASE
CREEEAKK
LOCK!
RUSTLE RUSTLE

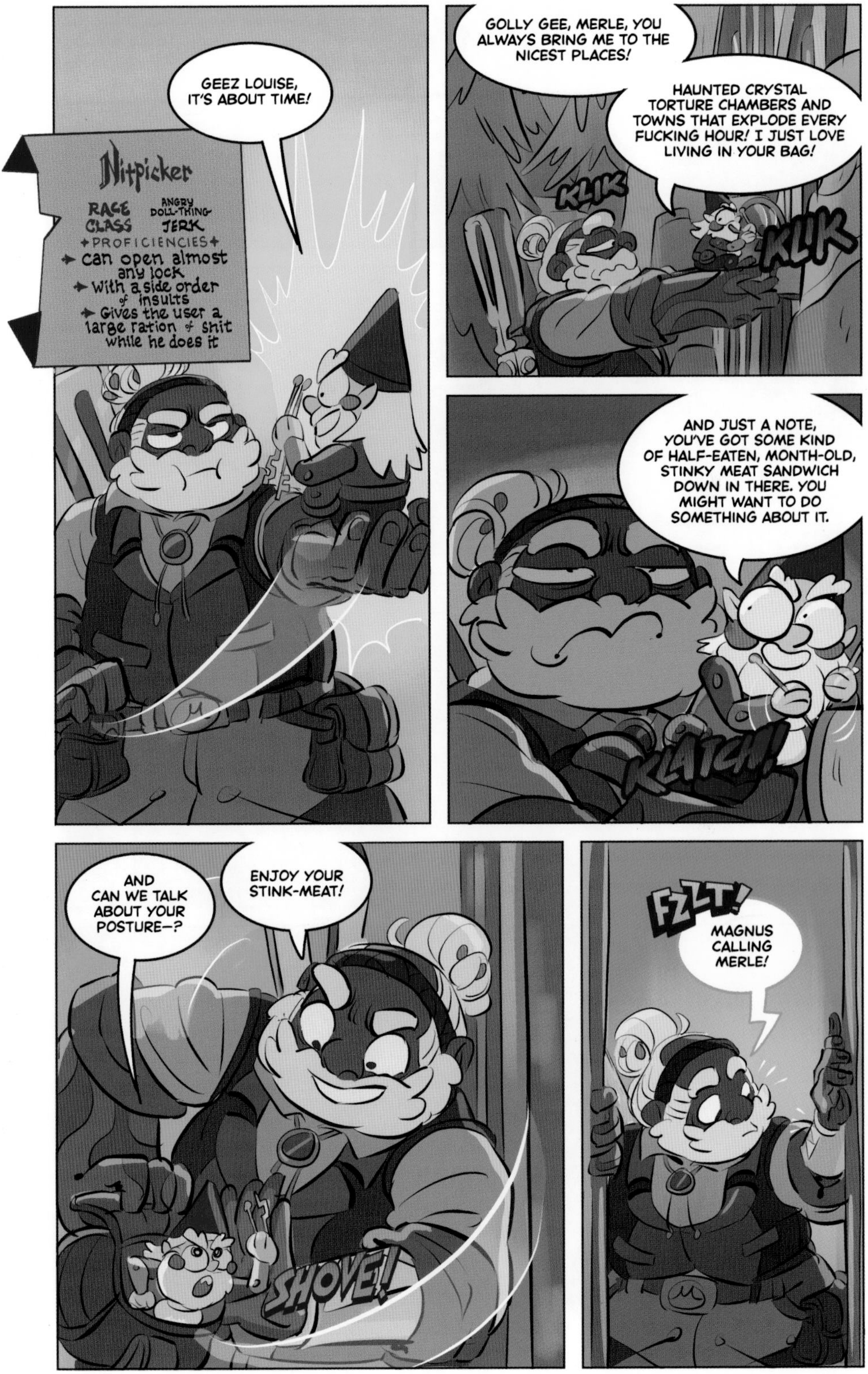
GEEZ LOUISE, IT'S ABOUT TIME!
Nitpicker
RACE ANGRY DOLL-THING
CLASS JERK
PROFICIENCIES
can open almost any lock
With a side order of insults
Gives the user a large ration of shit while he does it
GOLLY GEE, MERLE, YOU ALWAYS BRING ME TO THE NICEST PLACES!
HAUNTED CRYSTAL TORTURE CHAMBERS AND TOWNS THAT EXPLODE EVERY FUCKING HOUR! I JUST LOVE LIVING IN YOUR BAG!
KLIK
KLIK
AND JUST A NOTE, YOU'VE GOT SOME KIND OF HALF-EATEN, MONTH-OLD, STINKY MEAT SANDWICH DOWN IN THERE. YOU MIGHT WANT TO DO SOMETHING ABOUT IT.
KLATCH!
AND CAN WE TALK ABOUT YOUR POSTURE—?
ENJOY YOUR STINK-MEAT!
SHOVE!
FZZT!
MAGNUS CALLING MERLE!

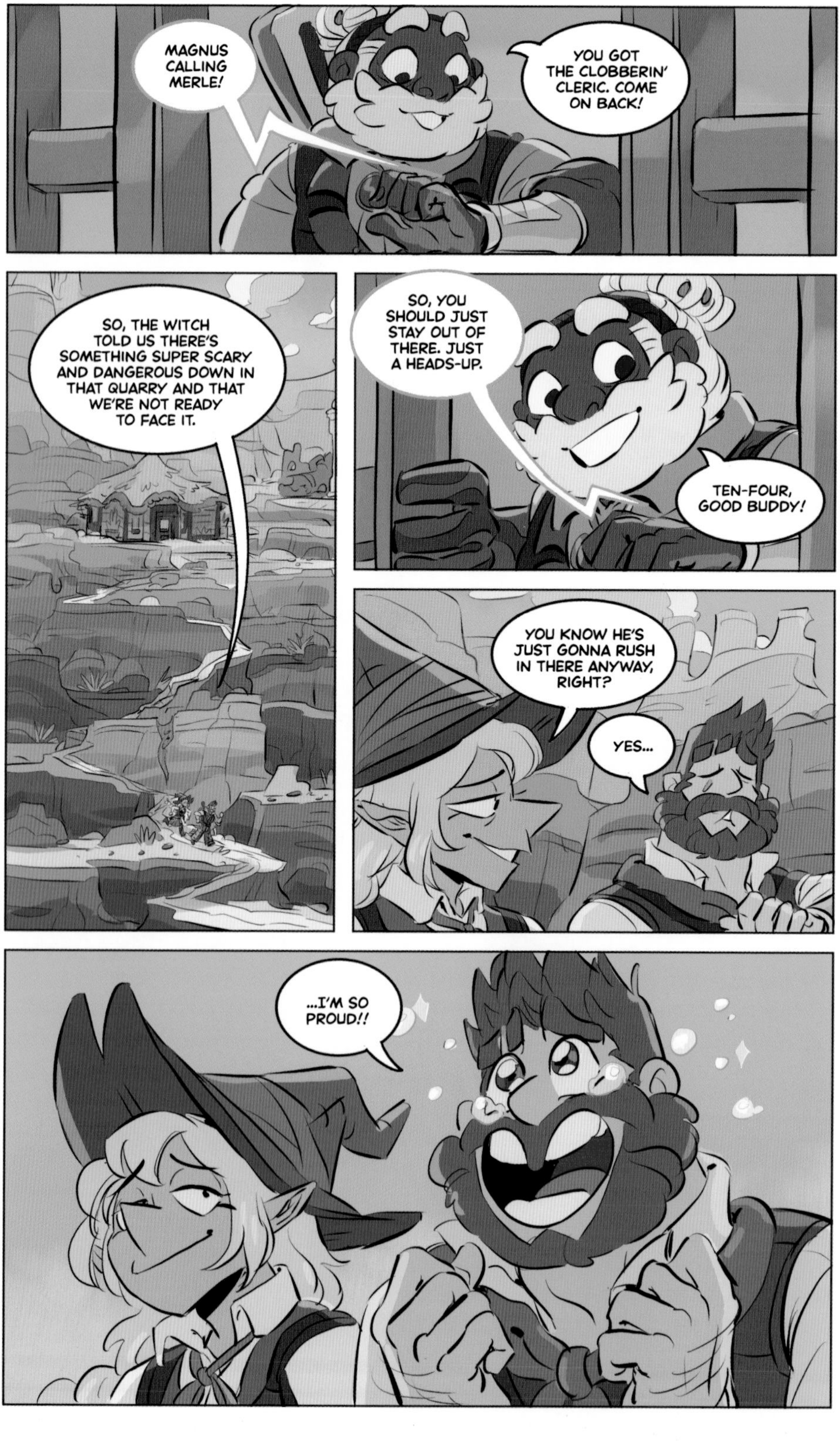
MAGNUS CALLING MERLE!
YOU GOT THE CLOBBERIN' CLERIC. COME ON BACK!
SO, THE WITCH TOLD US THERE'S SOMETHING SUPER SCARY AND DANGEROUS DOWN IN THAT QUARRY AND THAT WE'RE NOT READY TO FACE IT.
SO, YOU SHOULD JUST STAY OUT OF THERE. JUST A HEADS-UP.
TEN-FOUR, GOOD BUDDY!
YOU KNOW HE'S JUST GONNA RUSH IN THERE ANYWAY, RIGHT?
YES...
...I'M SO PROUD!!

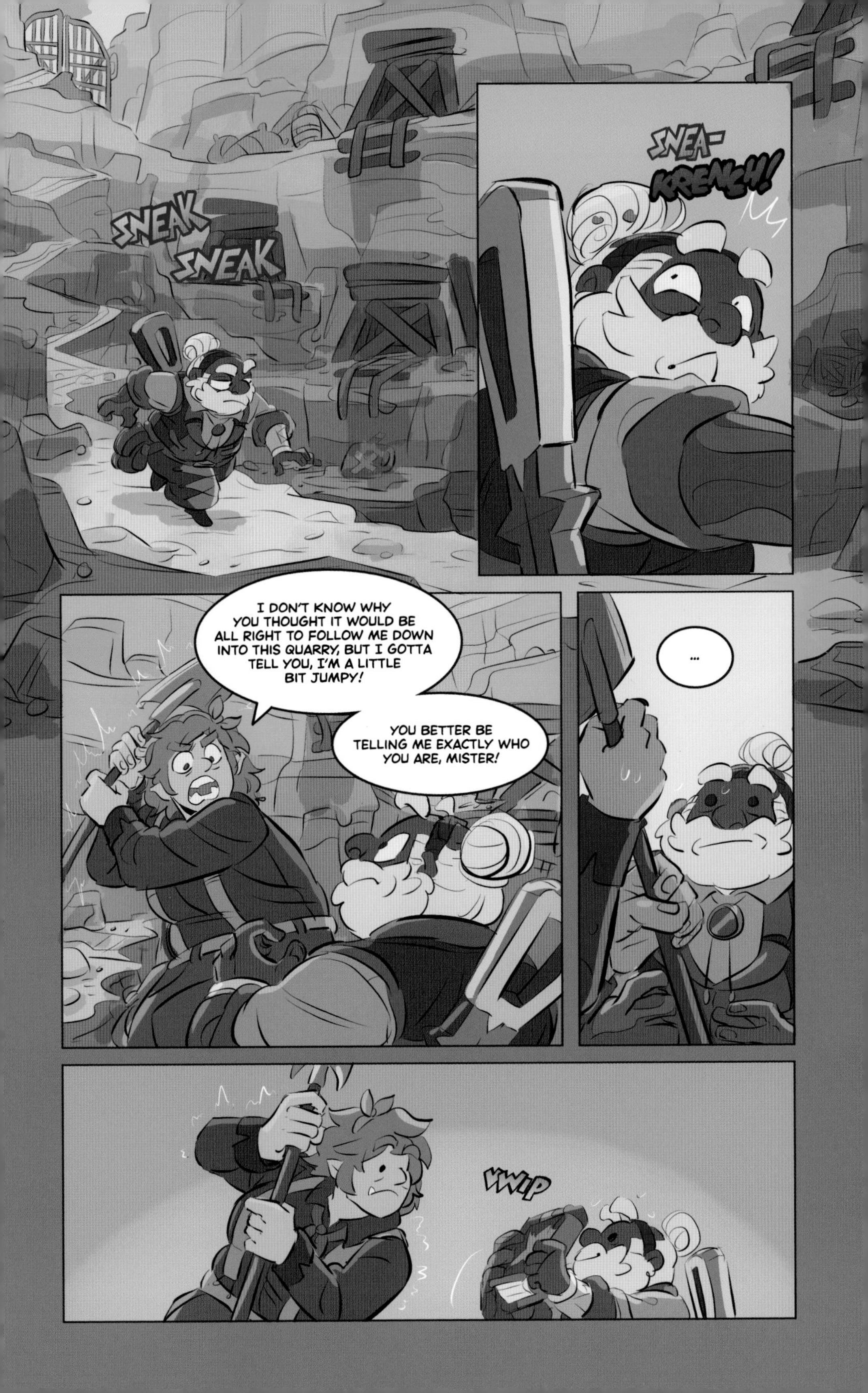
SNEAK
SNEAK
SNEA-
KRENCH!
I DON'T KNOW WHY YOU THOUGHT IT WOULD BE ALL RIGHT TO FOLLOW ME DOWN INTO THIS QUARRY, BUT I GOTTA TELL YOU, I'M A LITTLE BIT JUMPY!
YOU BETTER BE TELLING ME EXACTLY WHO YOU ARE, MISTER!
...
VWIP

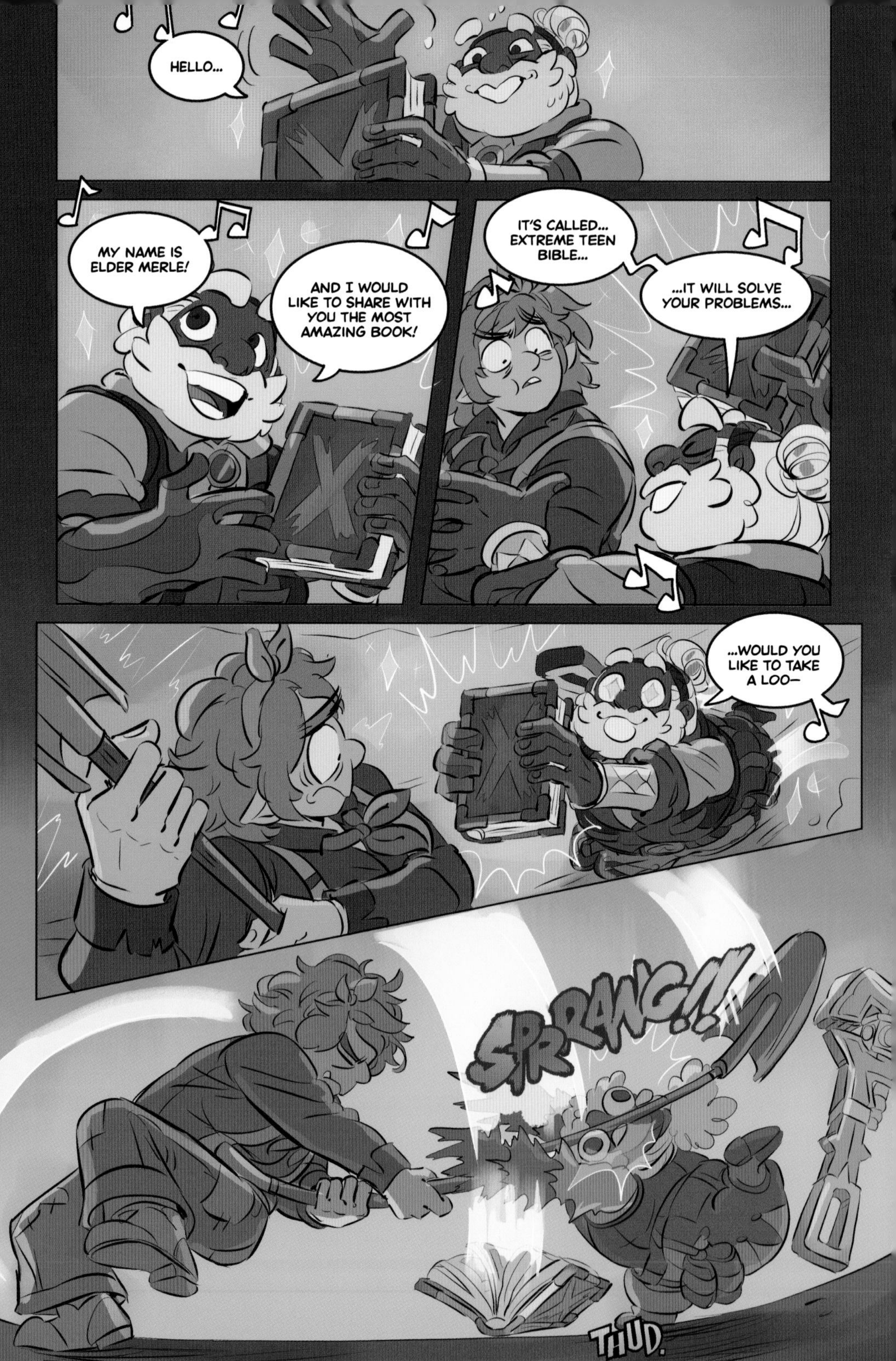
HELLO...
MY NAME IS ELDER MERLE!
AND I WOULD LIKE TO SHARE WITH YOU THE MOST AMAZING BOOK!
IT'S CALLED... EXTREME TEEN BIBLE...
...IT WILL SOLVE YOUR PROBLEMS...
...WOULD YOU LIKE TO TAKE A LOO—
SPRRANG!!
THUD.

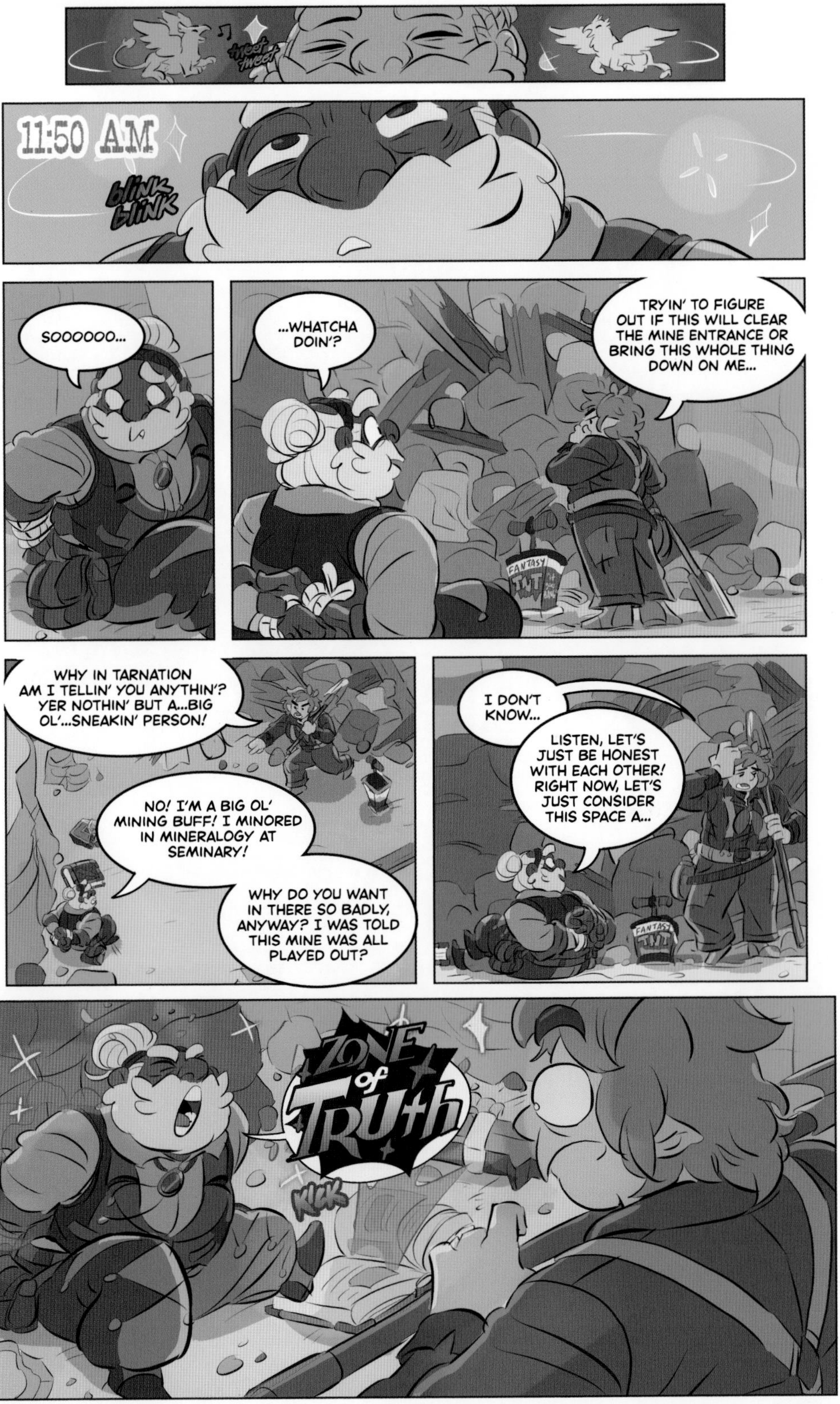
tweet tweet
11:50 AM
blink blink
SOOOOOO...
...WHATCHA DOIN'?
TRYIN' TO FIGURE OUT IF THIS WILL CLEAR THE MINE ENTRANCE OR BRING THIS WHOLE THING DOWN ON ME...
FANTASY TNT
WHY IN TARNATION AM I TELLIN' YOU ANYTHIN'? YER NOTHIN' BUT A...BIG OL'...SNEAKIN' PERSON!
NO! I'M A BIG OL' MINING BUFF! I MINORED IN MINERALOGY AT SEMINARY!
WHY DO YOU WANT IN THERE SO BADLY, ANYWAY? I WAS TOLD THIS MINE WAS ALL PLAYED OUT?
I DON'T KNOW...
LISTEN, LET'S JUST BE HONEST WITH EACH OTHER! RIGHT NOW, LET'S JUST CONSIDER THIS SPACE A...
FANTASY TNT
ZONE of TRUTH
KLICK

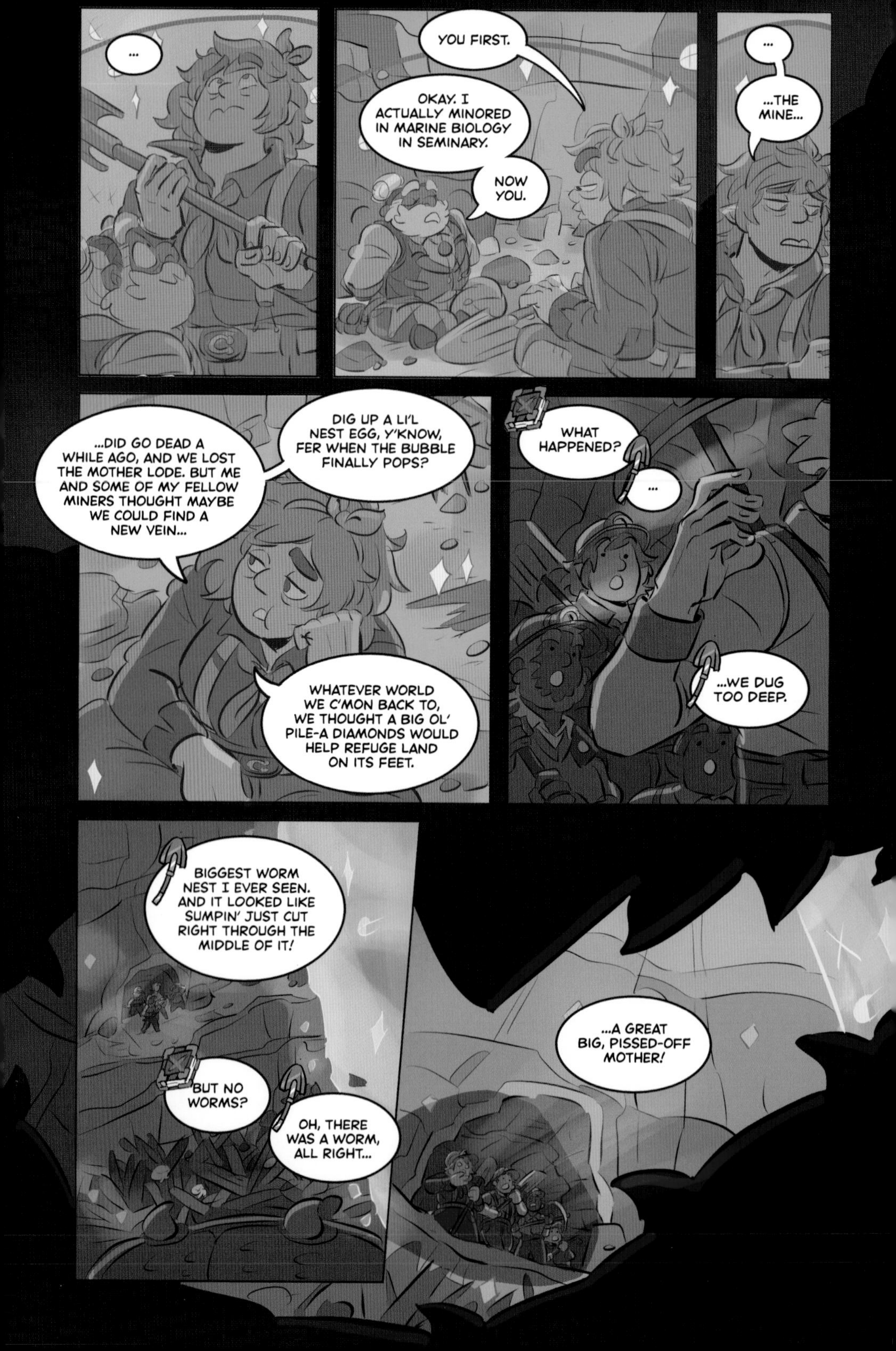
...
YOU FIRST.
OKAY. I ACTUALLY MINORED IN MARINE BIOLOGY IN SEMINARY.
NOW YOU.
...
...THE MINE...
...DID GO DEAD A WHILE AGO, AND WE LOST THE MOTHER LODE. BUT ME AND SOME OF MY FELLOW MINERS THOUGHT MAYBE WE COULD FIND A NEW VEIN...
DIG UP A LI'L NEST EGG, Y'KNOW, FER WHEN THE BUBBLE FINALLY POPS?
WHATEVER WORLD WE C'MON BACK TO, WE THOUGHT A BIG OL' PILE-A DIAMONDS WOULD HELP REFUGE LAND ON ITS FEET.
WHAT HAPPENED?
...
...WE DUG TOO DEEP.
BIGGEST WORM NEST I EVER SEEN. AND IT LOOKED LIKE SUMPIN' JUST CUT RIGHT THROUGH THE MIDDLE OF IT!
BUT NO WORMS?
OH, THERE WAS A WORM, ALL RIGHT...
...A GREAT BIG, PISSED-OFF MOTHER!

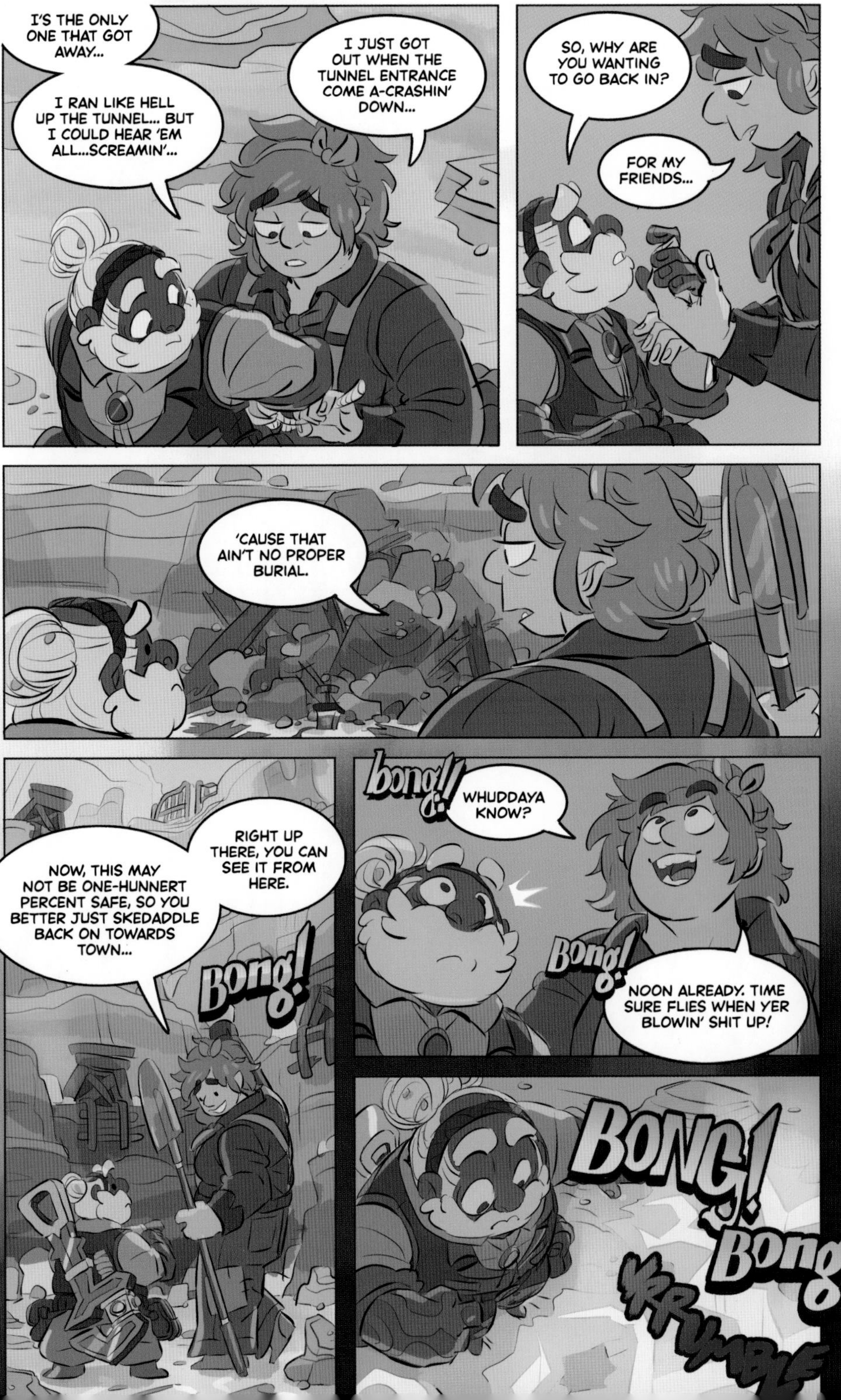
I'S THE ONLY ONE THAT GOT AWAY...
I RAN LIKE HELL UP THE TUNNEL... BUT I COULD HEAR 'EM ALL...SCREAMIN'...
I JUST GOT OUT WHEN THE TUNNEL ENTRANCE COME A-CRASHIN' DOWN...
SO, WHY ARE YOU WANTING TO GO BACK IN?
FOR MY FRIENDS...
'CAUSE THAT AIN'T NO PROPER BURIAL.
NOW, THIS MAY NOT BE ONE-HUNNERT PERCENT SAFE, SO YOU BETTER JUST SKEDADDLE BACK ON TOWARDS TOWN...
RIGHT UP THERE, YOU CAN SEE IT FROM HERE.
Bong!
bong!!
WHUDDAYA KNOW?
Bong!
NOON ALREADY. TIME SURE FLIES WHEN YER BLOWIN' SHIT UP!
BONG!
Bong!
KRUMBLE

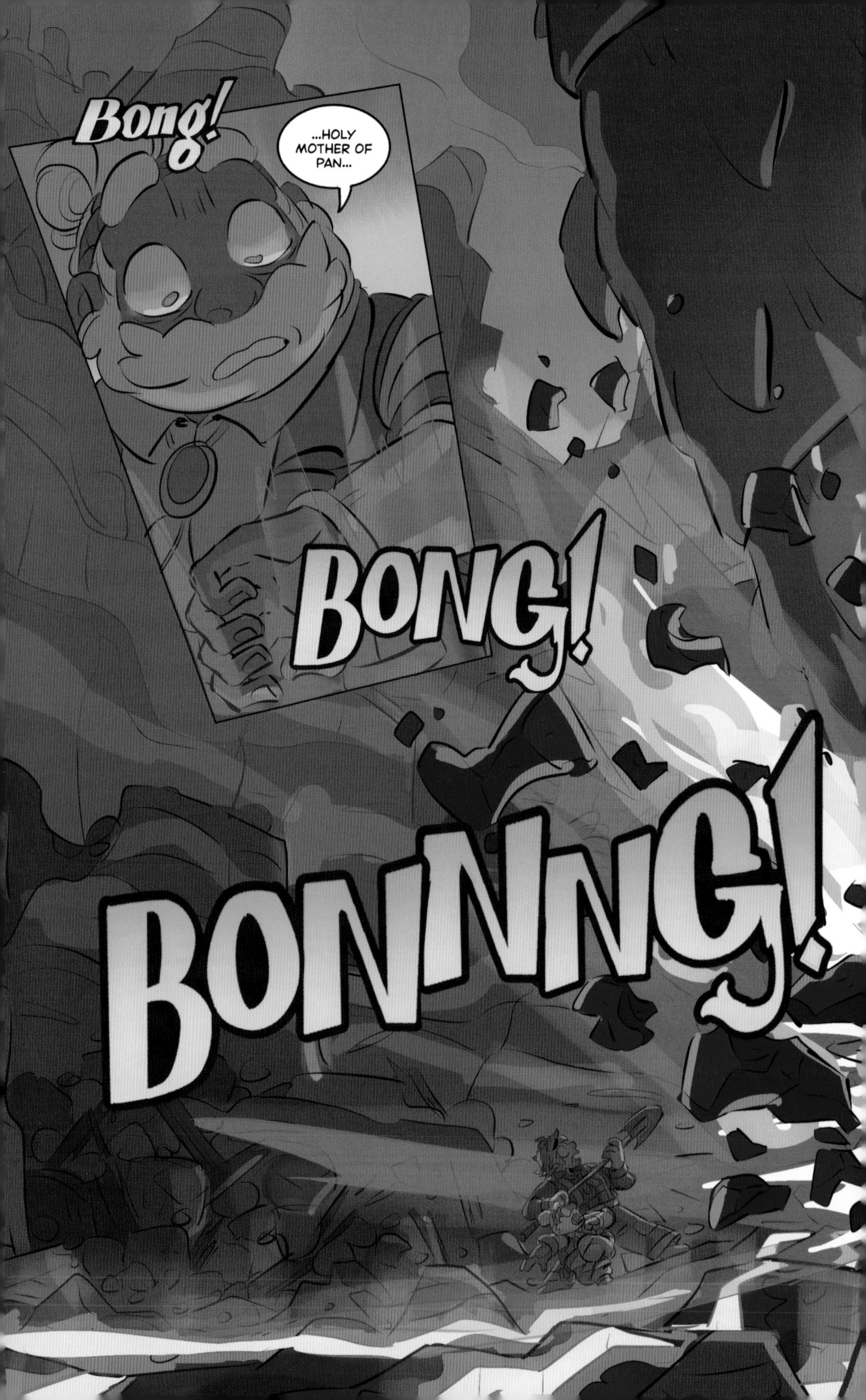
Bong!
...HOLY MOTHER OF PAN...
BONG!
BONNNG!

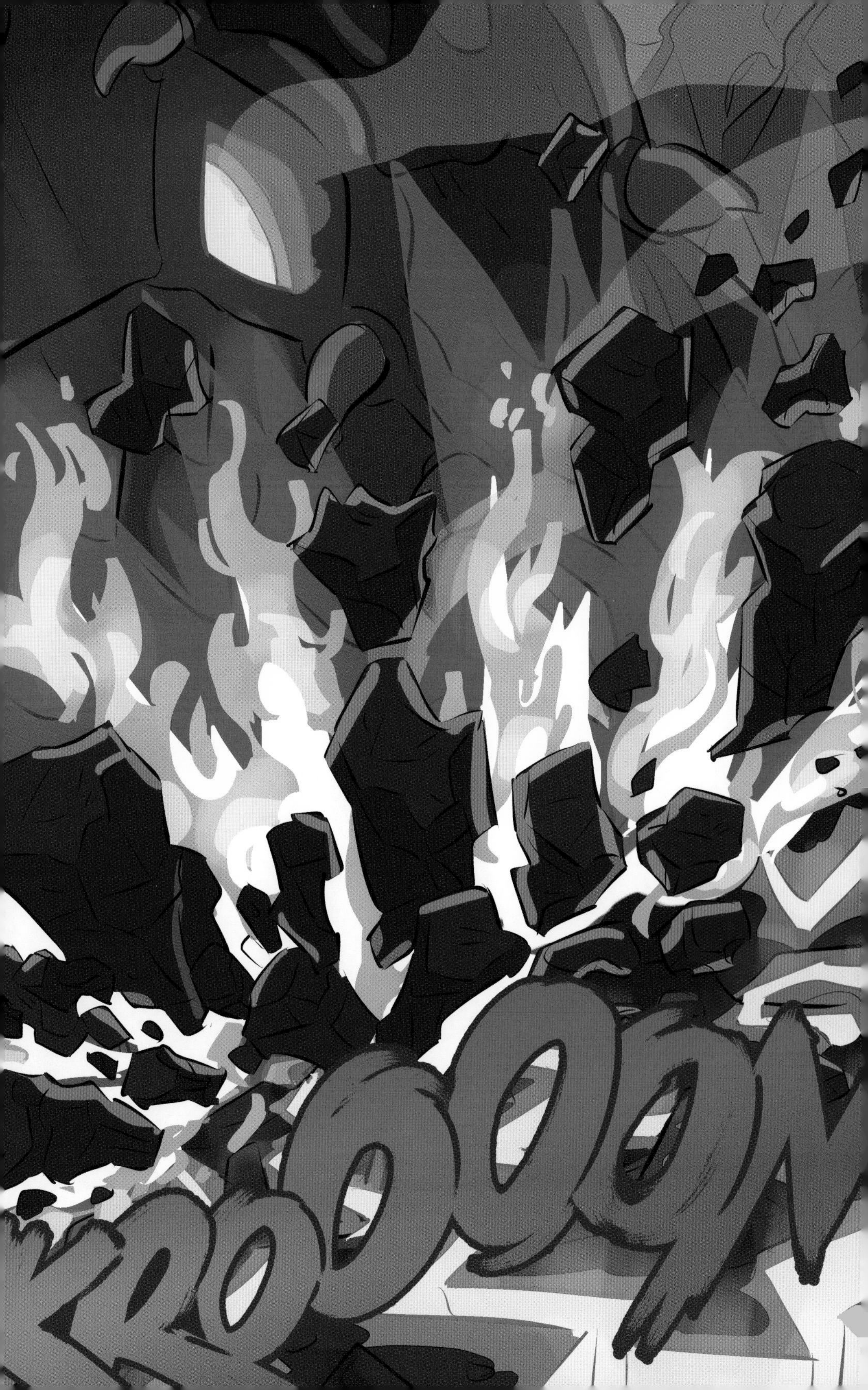

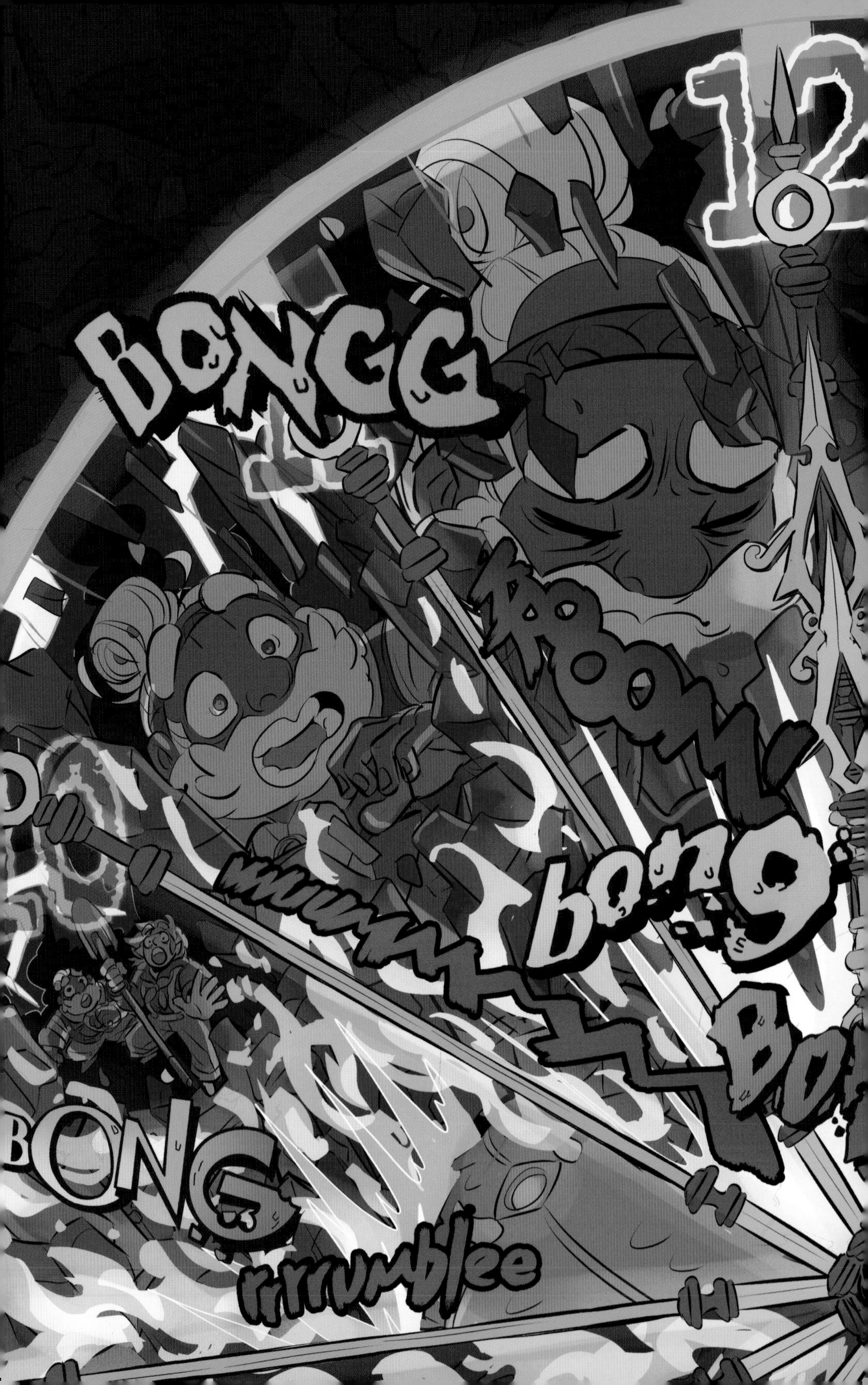

12
BONGG
KRROOOM
WUUUUUMM
bong
BO
BONG
rrrrumblee

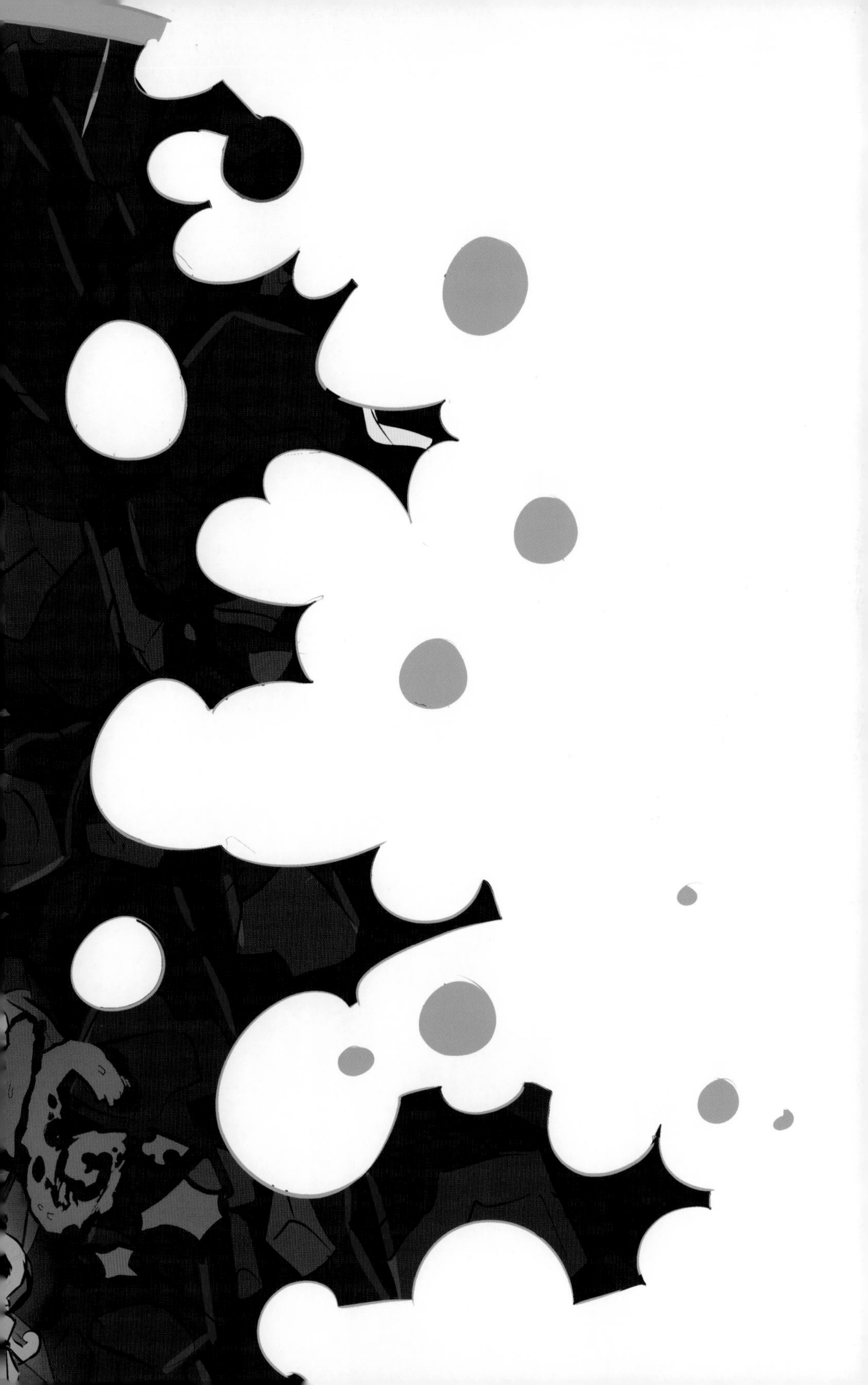

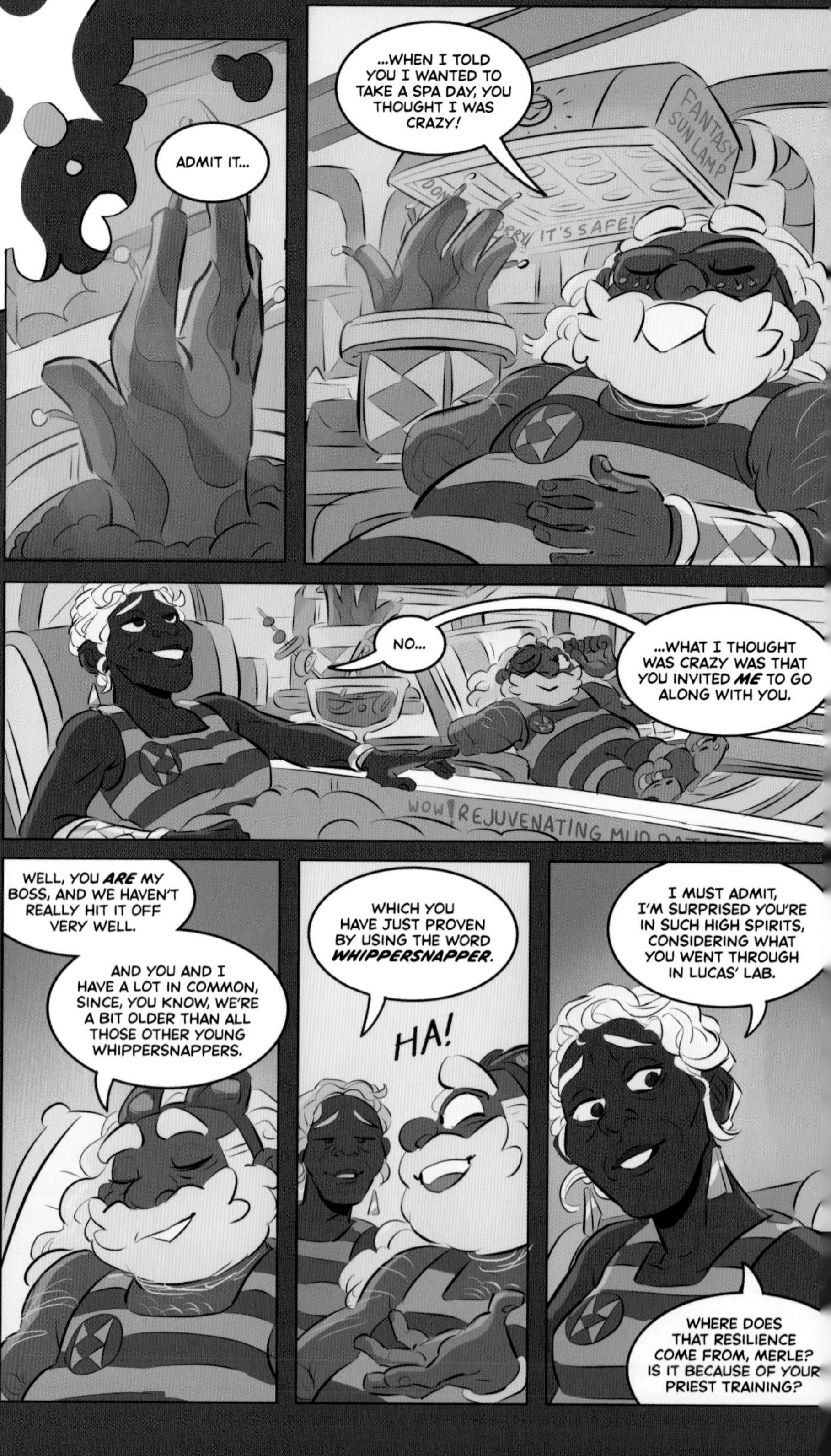
ADMIT IT...
...WHEN I TOLD YOU I WANTED TO TAKE A SPA DAY, YOU THOUGHT I WAS CRAZY!
FANTASY SUN LAMP
IT'S SAFE!
NO...
...WHAT I THOUGHT WAS CRAZY WAS THAT YOU INVITED ME TO GO ALONG WITH YOU.
WOW! REJUVENATING
WELL, YOU ARE MY BOSS, AND WE HAVEN'T REALLY HIT IT OFF VERY WELL.
AND YOU AND I HAVE A LOT IN COMMON, SINCE, YOU KNOW, WE'RE A BIT OLDER THAN ALL THOSE OTHER YOUNG WHIPPERSNAPPERS.
WHICH YOU HAVE JUST PROVEN BY USING THE WORD WHIPPERSNAPPER.
HA!
I MUST ADMIT, I'M SURPRISED YOU'RE IN SUCH HIGH SPIRITS, CONSIDERING WHAT YOU WENT THROUGH IN LUCAS' LAB.
WHERE DOES THAT RESILIENCE COME FROM, MERLE? IS IT BECAUSE OF YOUR PRIEST TRAINING?

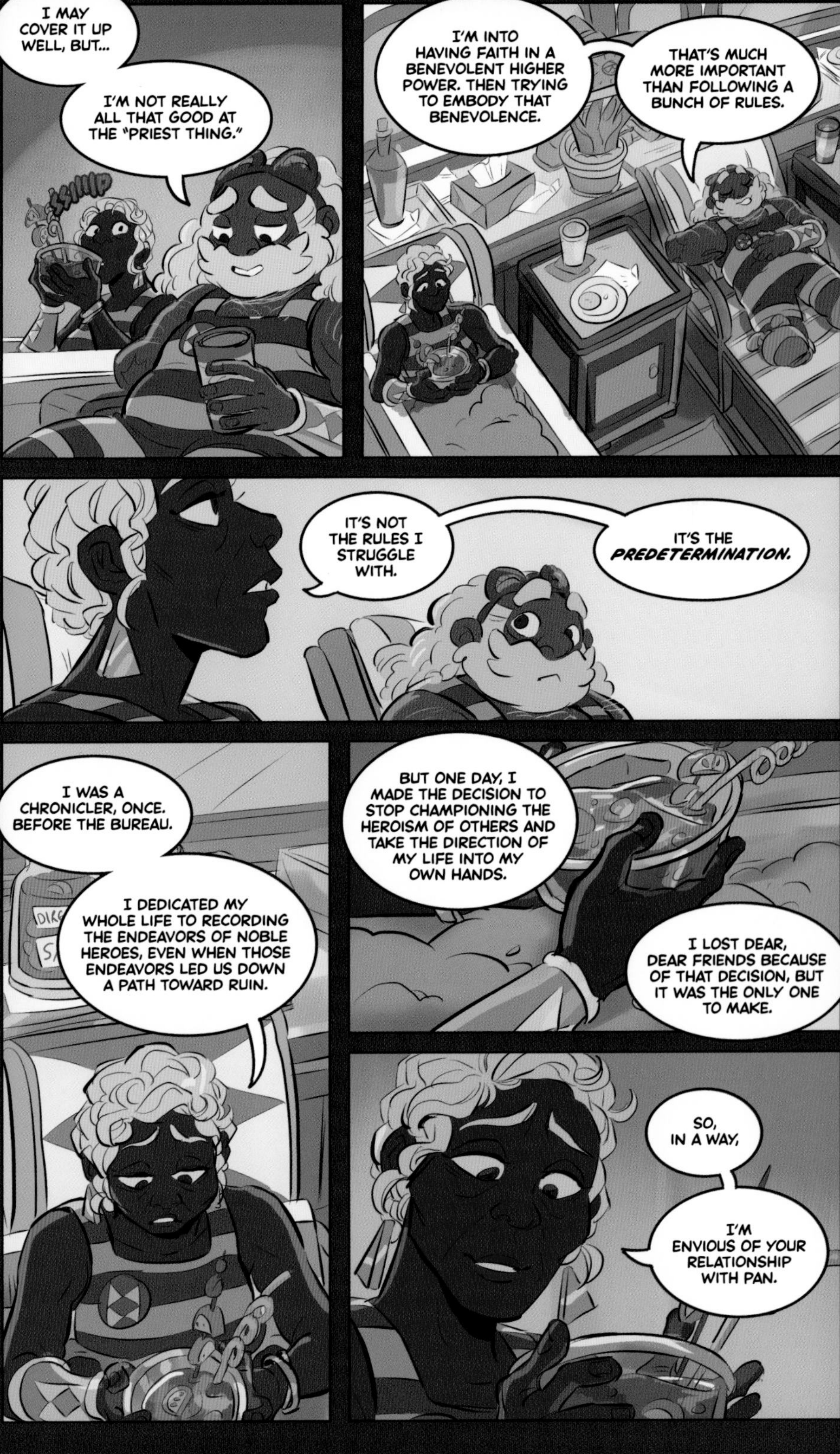

I MAY COVER IT UP WELL, BUT...
I'M NOT REALLY ALL THAT GOOD AT THE "PRIEST THING."
SSHHHP
I'M INTO HAVING FAITH IN A BENEVOLENT HIGHER POWER. THEN TRYING TO EMBODY THAT BENEVOLENCE.
THAT'S MUCH MORE IMPORTANT THAN FOLLOWING A BUNCH OF RULES.
IT'S NOT THE RULES I STRUGGLE WITH.
IT'S THE *PREDETERMINATION.*
I WAS A CHRONICLER, ONCE. BEFORE THE BUREAU.
I DEDICATED MY WHOLE LIFE TO RECORDING THE ENDEAVORS OF NOBLE HEROES, EVEN WHEN THOSE ENDEAVORS LED US DOWN A PATH TOWARD RUIN.
BUT ONE DAY, I MADE THE DECISION TO STOP CHAMPIONING THE HEROISM OF OTHERS AND TAKE THE DIRECTION OF MY LIFE INTO MY OWN HANDS.
I LOST DEAR, DEAR FRIENDS BECAUSE OF THAT DECISION, BUT IT WAS THE ONLY ONE TO MAKE.
SO, IN A WAY,
I'M ENVIOUS OF YOUR RELATIONSHIP WITH PAN.

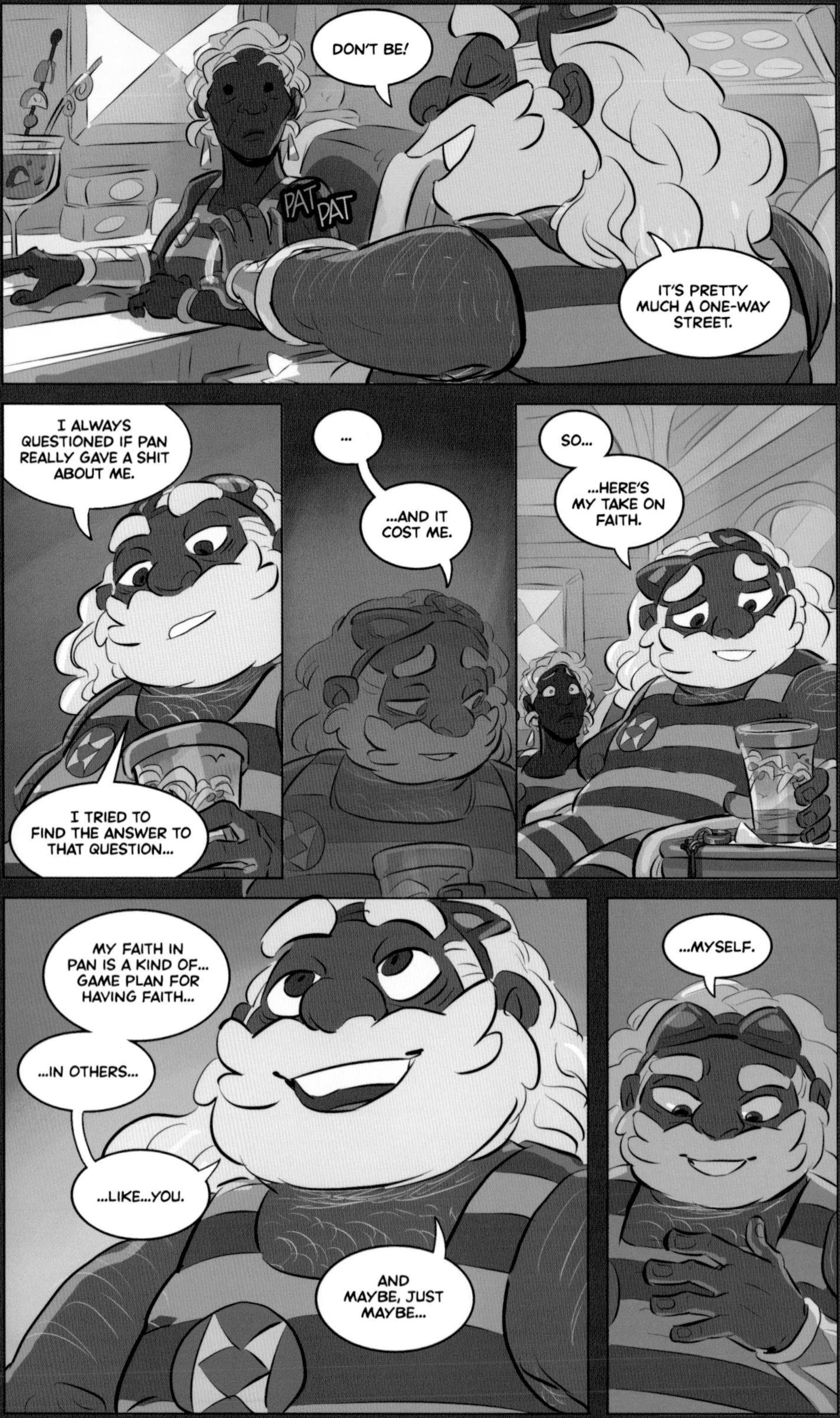
DON'T BE!
PAT PAT
IT'S PRETTY MUCH A ONE-WAY STREET.
I ALWAYS QUESTIONED IF PAN REALLY GAVE A SHIT ABOUT ME.
I TRIED TO FIND THE ANSWER TO THAT QUESTION...
...
...AND IT COST ME.
SO...
...HERE'S MY TAKE ON FAITH.
MY FAITH IN PAN IS A KIND OF... GAME PLAN FOR HAVING FAITH...
...IN OTHERS...
...LIKE...YOU.
AND MAYBE, JUST MAYBE...
...MYSELF.

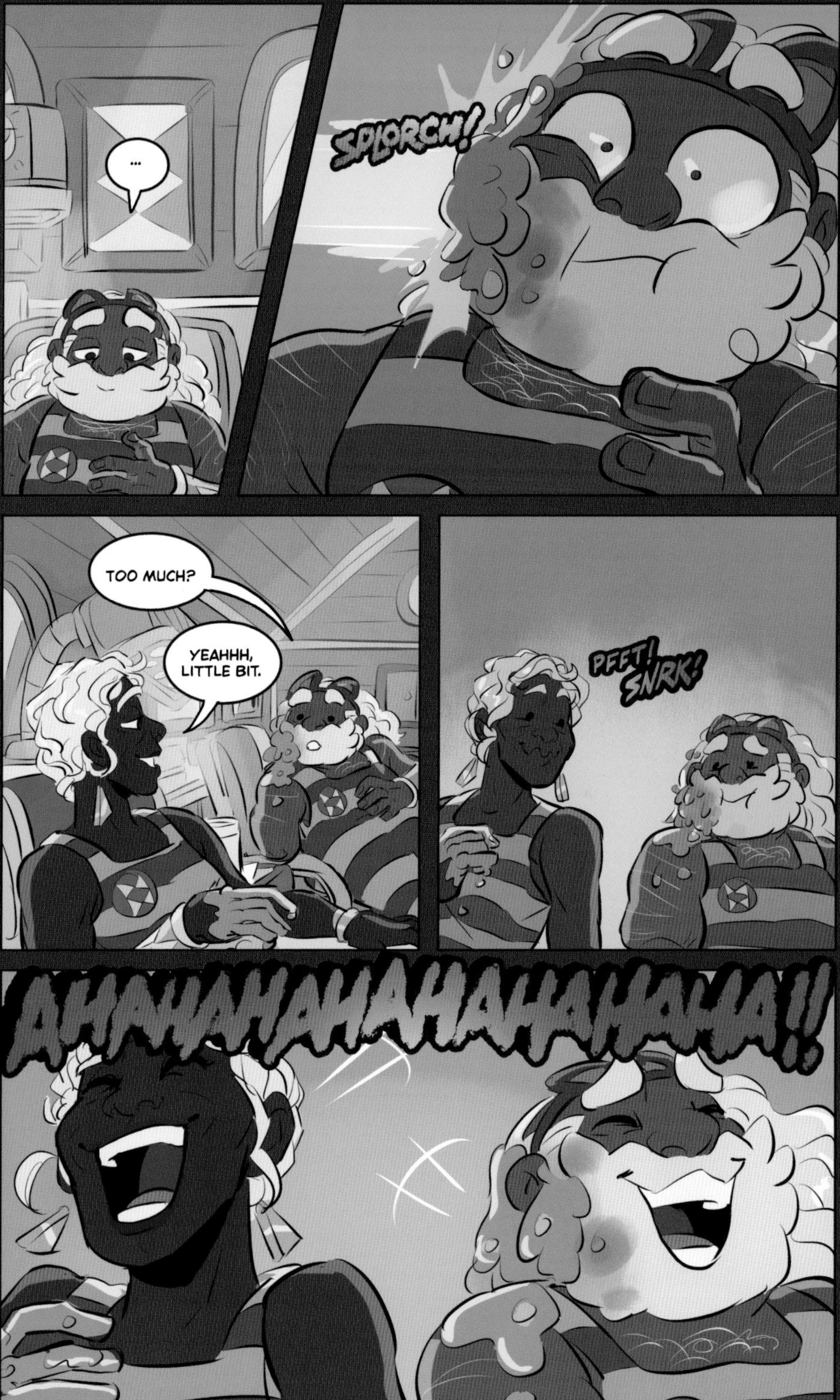
...
SPLORCH!
TOO MUCH?
YEAHHH, LITTLE BIT.
PFFT! SNRK!
AHAHAHAHAHAHAHAHAHA!!

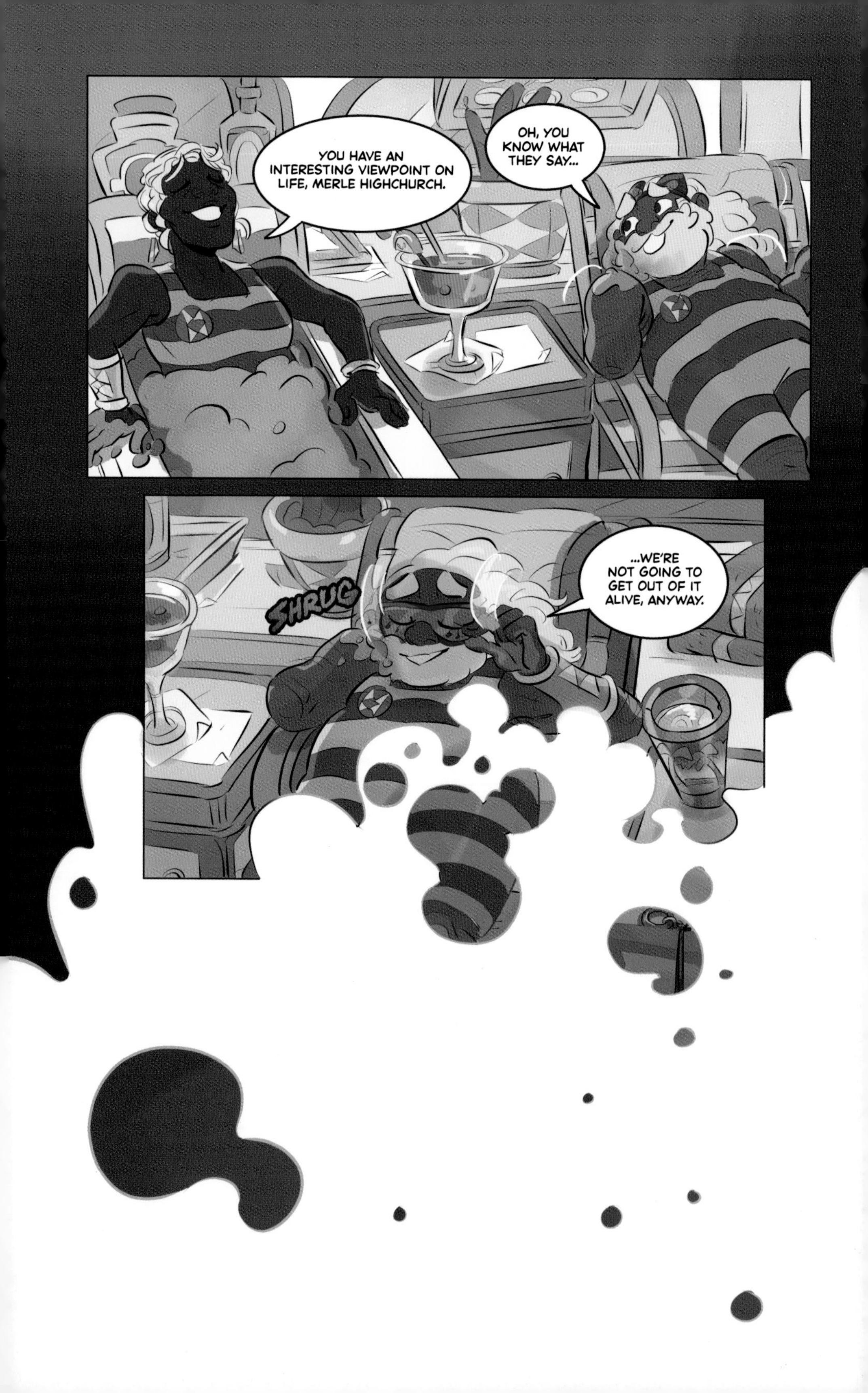
YOU HAVE AN INTERESTING VIEWPOINT ON LIFE, MERLE HIGHCHURCH.
OH, YOU KNOW WHAT THEY SAY...
SHRUG
...WE'RE NOT GOING TO GET OUT OF IT ALIVE, ANYWAY.

Chapter
4

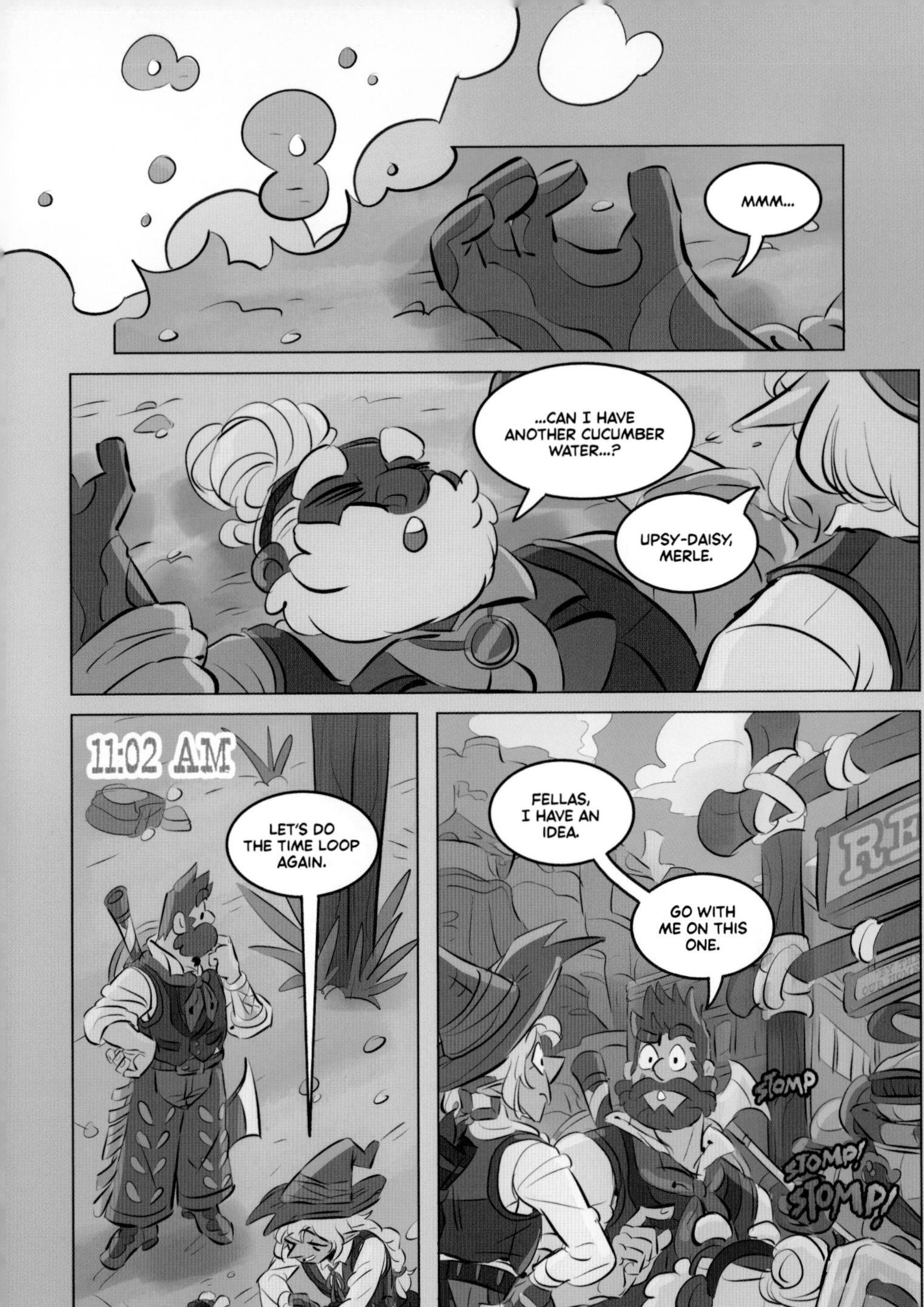
MMM...
...CAN I HAVE ANOTHER CUCUMBER WATER...?
UPSY-DAISY, MERLE.
11:02 AM
LET'S DO THE TIME LOOP AGAIN.
FELLAS, I HAVE AN IDEA.
GO WITH ME ON THIS ONE.
STOMP
STOMP! STOMP!

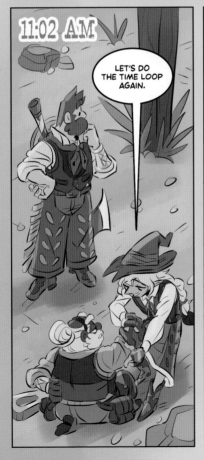

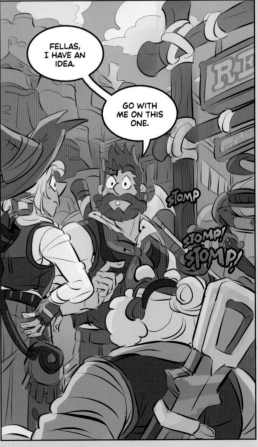

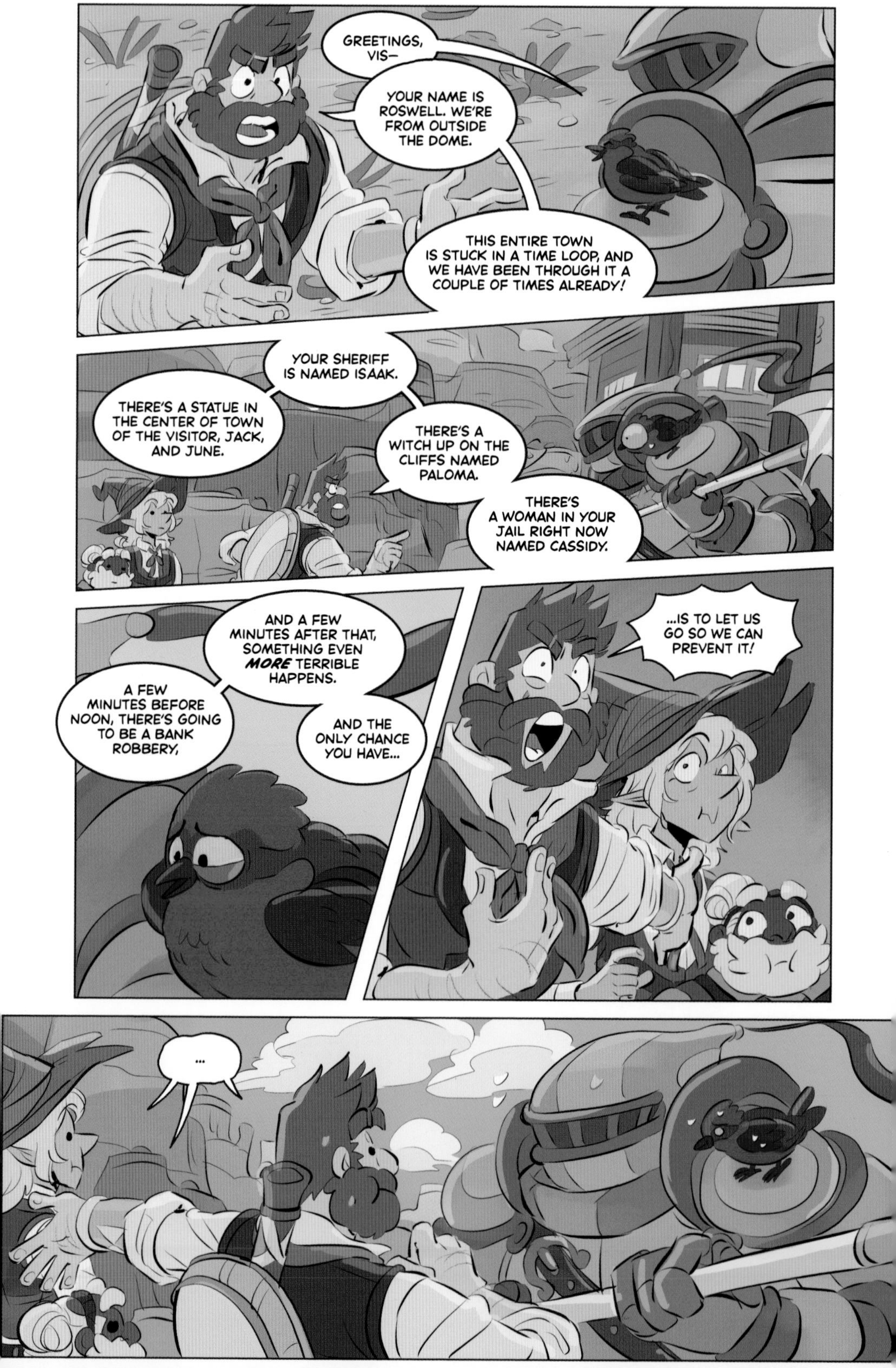
GREETINGS, VIS—
YOUR NAME IS ROSWELL. WE'RE FROM OUTSIDE THE DOME.
THIS ENTIRE TOWN IS STUCK IN A TIME LOOP, AND WE HAVE BEEN THROUGH IT A COUPLE OF TIMES ALREADY!
YOUR SHERIFF IS NAMED ISAAK.
THERE'S A STATUE IN THE CENTER OF TOWN OF THE VISITOR, JACK, AND JUNE.
THERE'S A WITCH UP ON THE CLIFFS NAMED PALOMA.
THERE'S A WOMAN IN YOUR JAIL RIGHT NOW NAMED CASSIDY.
A FEW MINUTES BEFORE NOON, THERE'S GOING TO BE A BANK ROBBERY,
AND A FEW MINUTES AFTER THAT, SOMETHING EVEN *MORE* TERRIBLE HAPPENS.
AND THE ONLY CHANCE YOU HAVE...
...IS TO LET US GO SO WE CAN PREVENT IT!
...

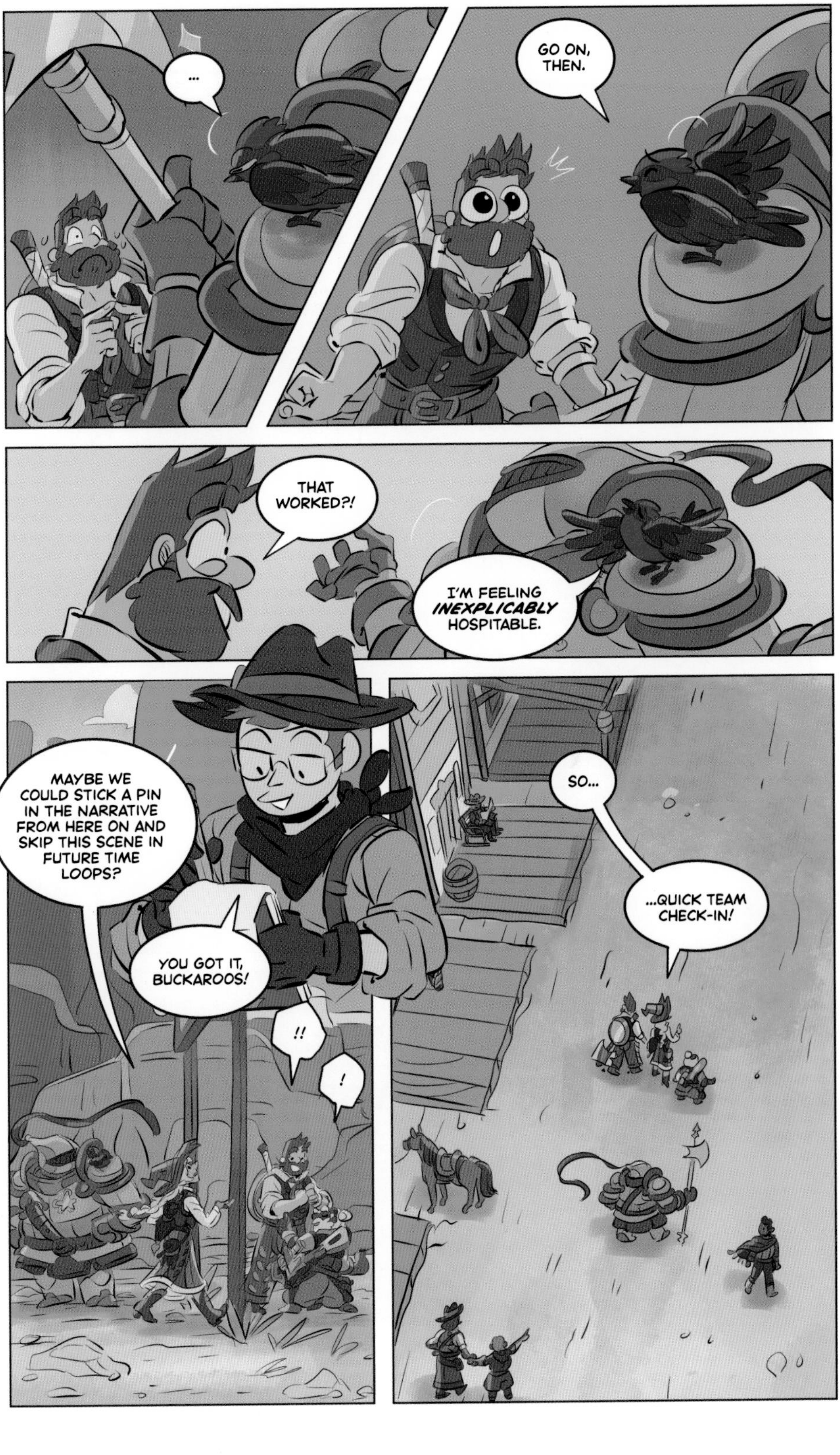
...
GO ON, THEN.
THAT WORKED?!
I'M FEELING INEXPLICABLY HOSPITABLE.
MAYBE WE COULD STICK A PIN IN THE NARRATIVE FROM HERE ON AND SKIP THIS SCENE IN FUTURE TIME LOOPS?
YOU GOT IT, BUCKAROOS!
!!
!
SO...
...QUICK TEAM CHECK-IN!

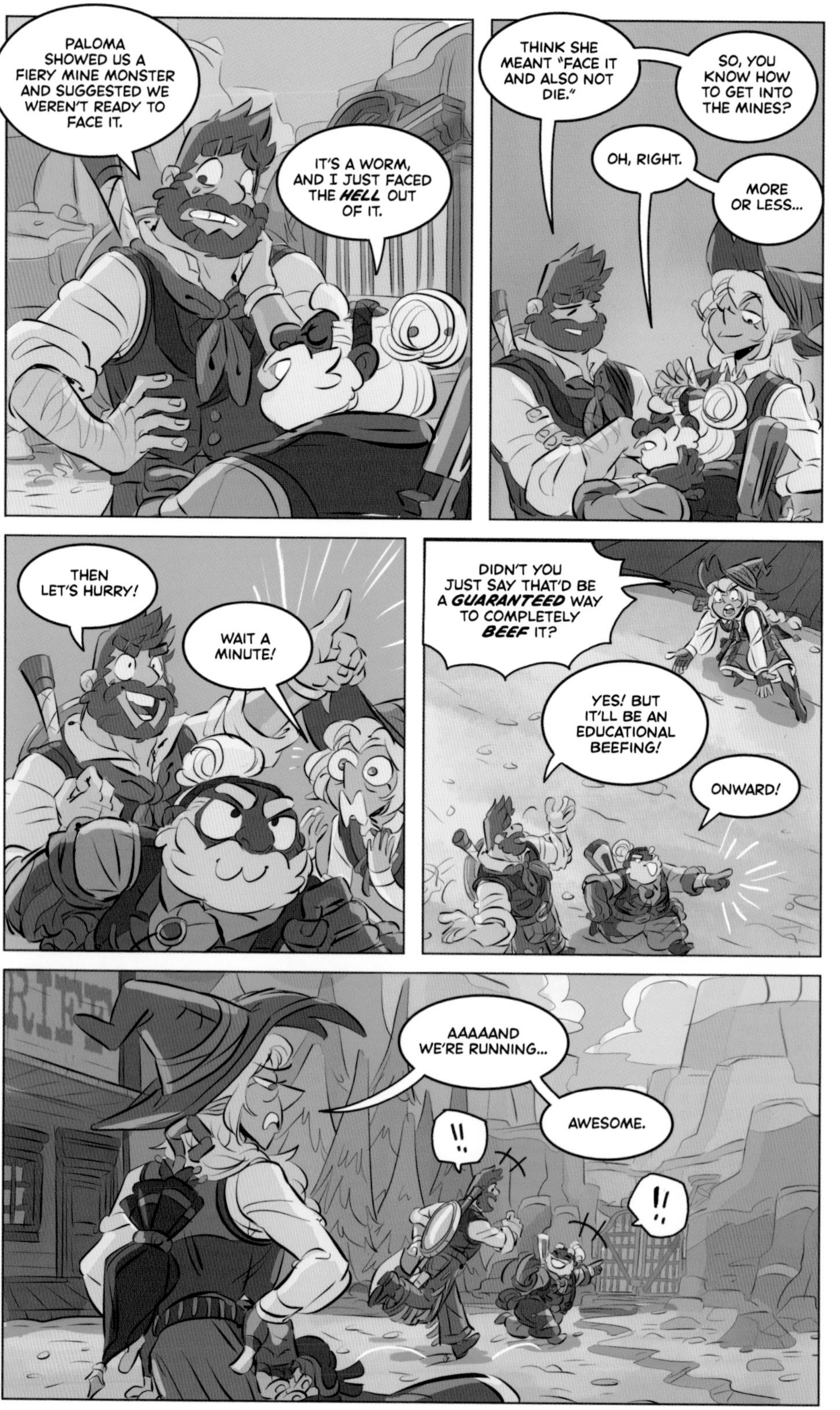
PALOMA SHOWED US A FIERY MINE MONSTER AND SUGGESTED WE WEREN'T READY TO FACE IT.
IT'S A WORM, AND I JUST FACED THE HELL OUT OF IT.
THINK SHE MEANT "FACE IT AND ALSO NOT DIE."
SO, YOU KNOW HOW TO GET INTO THE MINES?
OH, RIGHT.
MORE OR LESS...
THEN LET'S HURRY!
WAIT A MINUTE!
DIDN'T YOU JUST SAY THAT'D BE A GUARANTEED WAY TO COMPLETELY BEEF IT?
YES! BUT IT'LL BE AN EDUCATIONAL BEEFING!
ONWARD!
AAAAAND WE'RE RUNNING...
AWESOME.
!!
!!

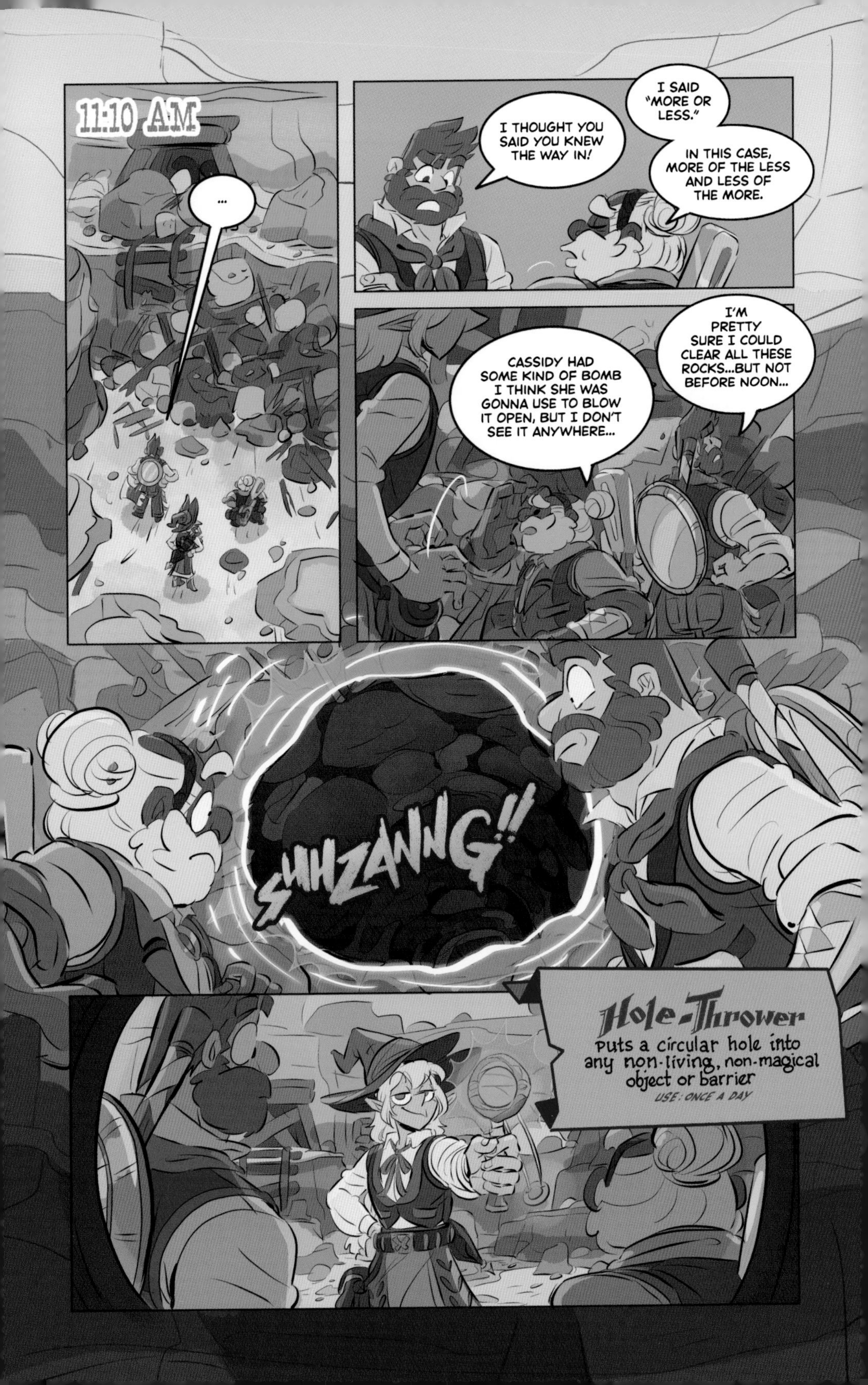
11:10 AM
...
I THOUGHT YOU SAID YOU KNEW THE WAY IN!
I SAID "MORE OR LESS."
IN THIS CASE, MORE OF THE LESS AND LESS OF THE MORE.
CASSIDY HAD SOME KIND OF BOMB I THINK SHE WAS GONNA USE TO BLOW IT OPEN, BUT I DON'T SEE IT ANYWHERE...
I'M PRETTY SURE I COULD CLEAR ALL THESE ROCKS...BUT NOT BEFORE NOON...
SHHZANNG!!
Hole-Thrower
Puts a circular hole into any non-living, non-magical object or barrier
USE: ONCE A DAY

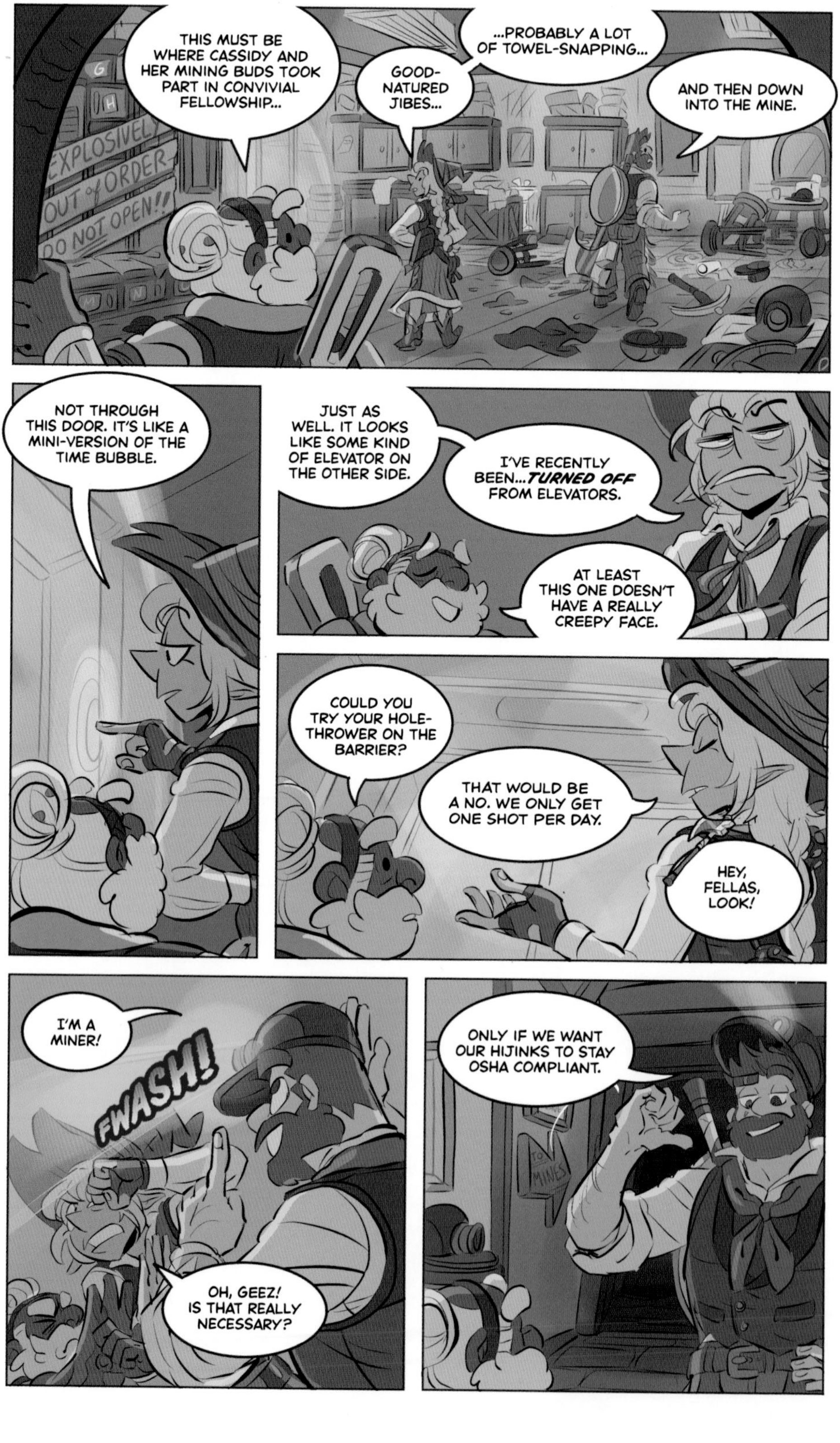
THIS MUST BE WHERE CASSIDY AND HER MINING BUDS TOOK PART IN CONVIVIAL FELLOWSHIP...
GOOD-NATURED JIBES...
...PROBABLY A LOT OF TOWEL-SNAPPING...
AND THEN DOWN INTO THE MINE.
EXPLOSIVELY OUT of ORDER DO NOT OPEN!!
NOT THROUGH THIS DOOR. IT'S LIKE A MINI-VERSION OF THE TIME BUBBLE.
JUST AS WELL. IT LOOKS LIKE SOME KIND OF ELEVATOR ON THE OTHER SIDE.
I'VE RECENTLY BEEN...*TURNED OFF* FROM ELEVATORS.
AT LEAST THIS ONE DOESN'T HAVE A REALLY CREEPY FACE.
COULD YOU TRY YOUR HOLE-THROWER ON THE BARRIER?
THAT WOULD BE A NO. WE ONLY GET ONE SHOT PER DAY.
HEY, FELLAS, LOOK!
I'M A MINER!
FWASH!
OH, GEEZ! IS THAT REALLY NECESSARY?
ONLY IF WE WANT OUR HIJINKS TO STAY OSHA COMPLIANT.
TO MINES

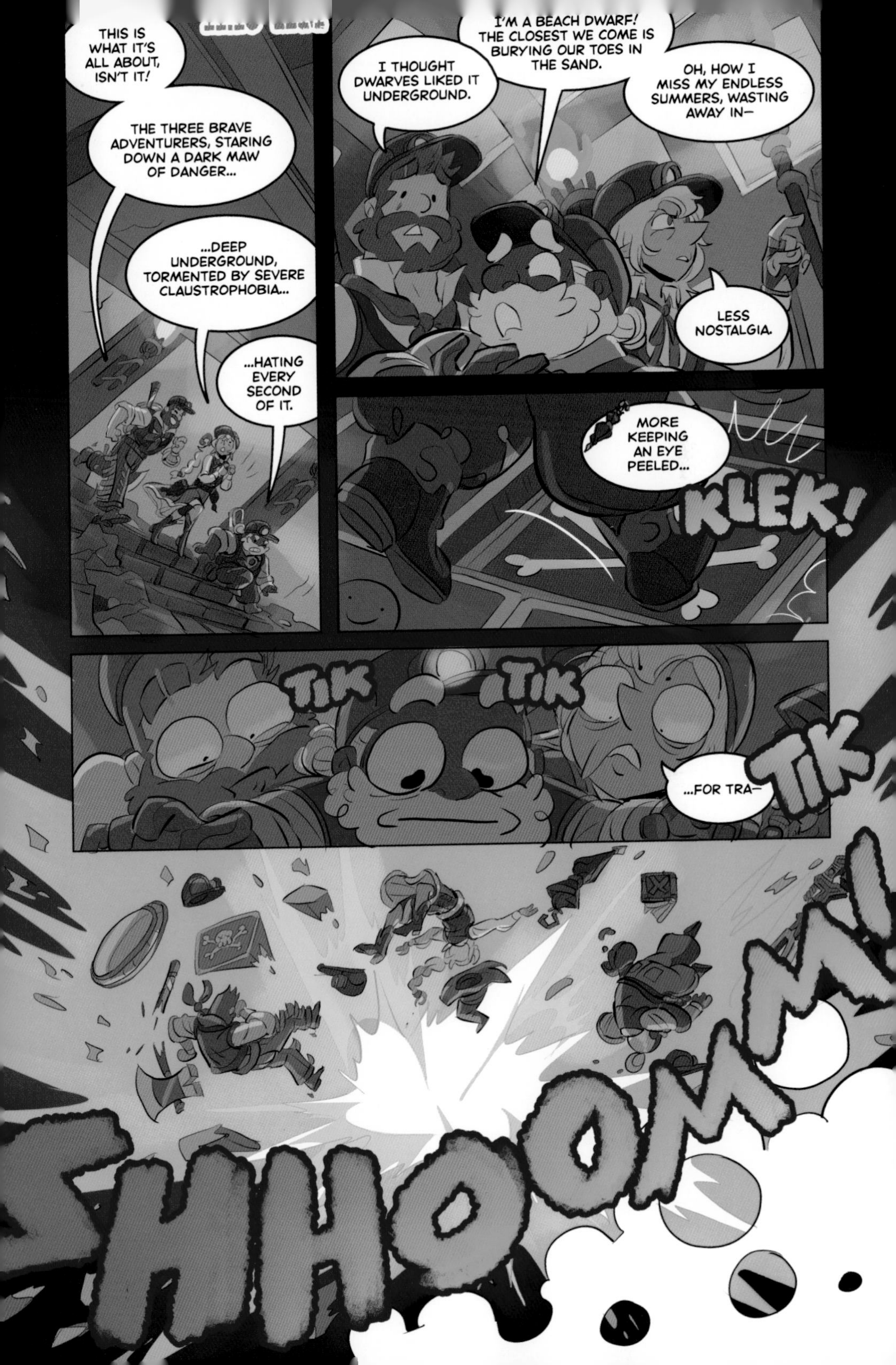
THIS IS WHAT IT'S ALL ABOUT, ISN'T IT!
THE THREE BRAVE ADVENTURERS, STARING DOWN A DARK MAW OF DANGER...
...DEEP UNDERGROUND, TORMENTED BY SEVERE CLAUSTROPHOBIA...
...HATING EVERY SECOND OF IT.
I THOUGHT DWARVES LIKED IT UNDERGROUND.
I'M A BEACH DWARF! THE CLOSEST WE COME IS BURYING OUR TOES IN THE SAND.
OH, HOW I MISS MY ENDLESS SUMMERS, WASTING AWAY IN—
LESS NOSTALGIA.
MORE KEEPING AN EYE PEELED...
KLEK!
TIK
TIK
...FOR TRA—
TIK
SHHOOM!

Chapter

5

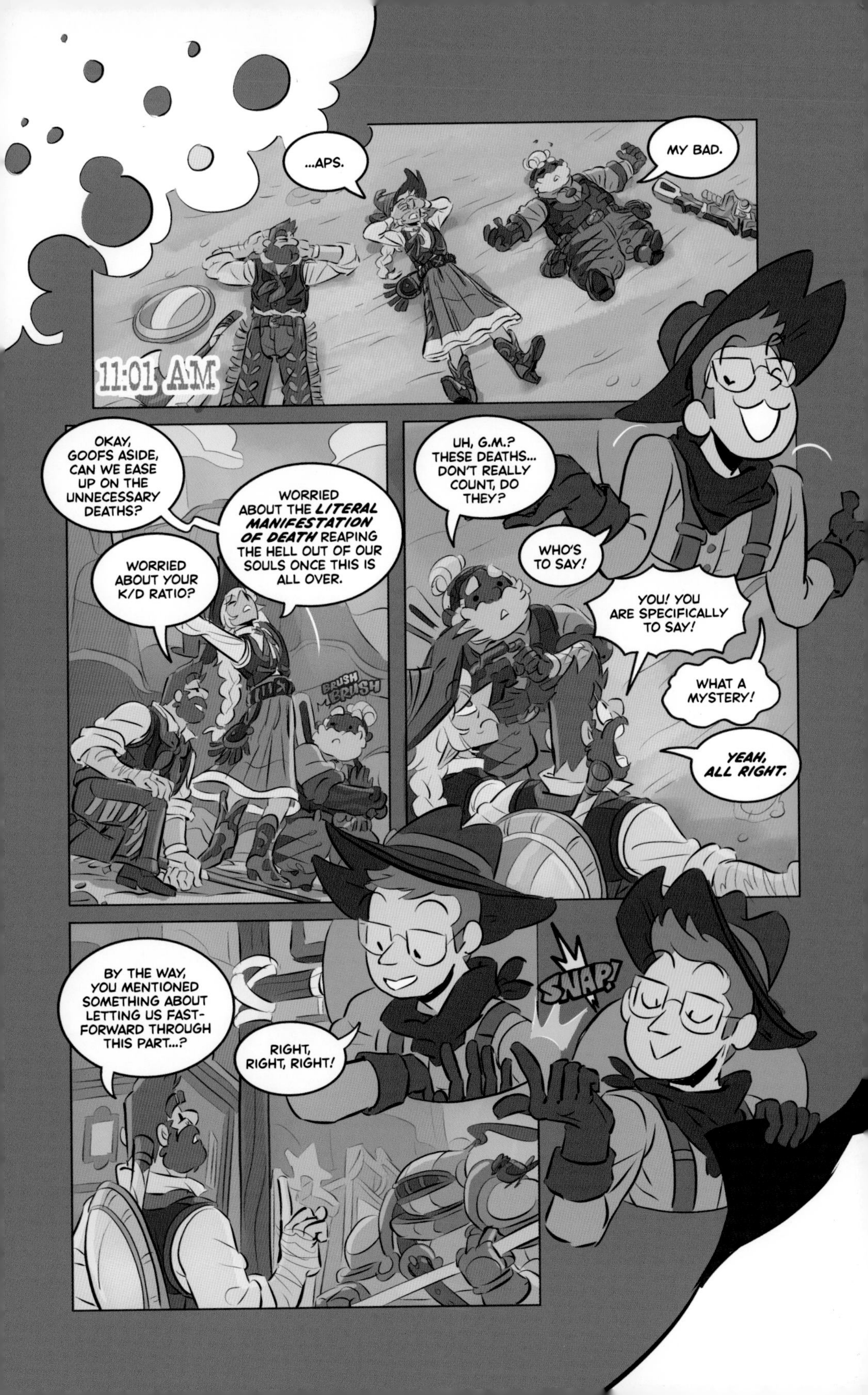
...APS.
MY BAD.
11:01 AM
OKAY, GOOFS ASIDE, CAN WE EASE UP ON THE UNNECESSARY DEATHS?
WORRIED ABOUT YOUR K/D RATIO?
WORRIED ABOUT THE *LITERAL MANIFESTATION OF DEATH* REAPING THE HELL OUT OF OUR SOULS ONCE THIS IS ALL OVER.
BRUSH BRUSH
UH, G.M.? THESE DEATHS... DON'T REALLY COUNT, DO THEY?
WHO'S TO SAY!
YOU! YOU ARE SPECIFICALLY TO SAY!
WHAT A MYSTERY!
YEAH, ALL RIGHT.
BY THE WAY, YOU MENTIONED SOMETHING ABOUT LETTING US FAST-FORWARD THROUGH THIS PART...?
RIGHT, RIGHT, RIGHT!
SNAP!

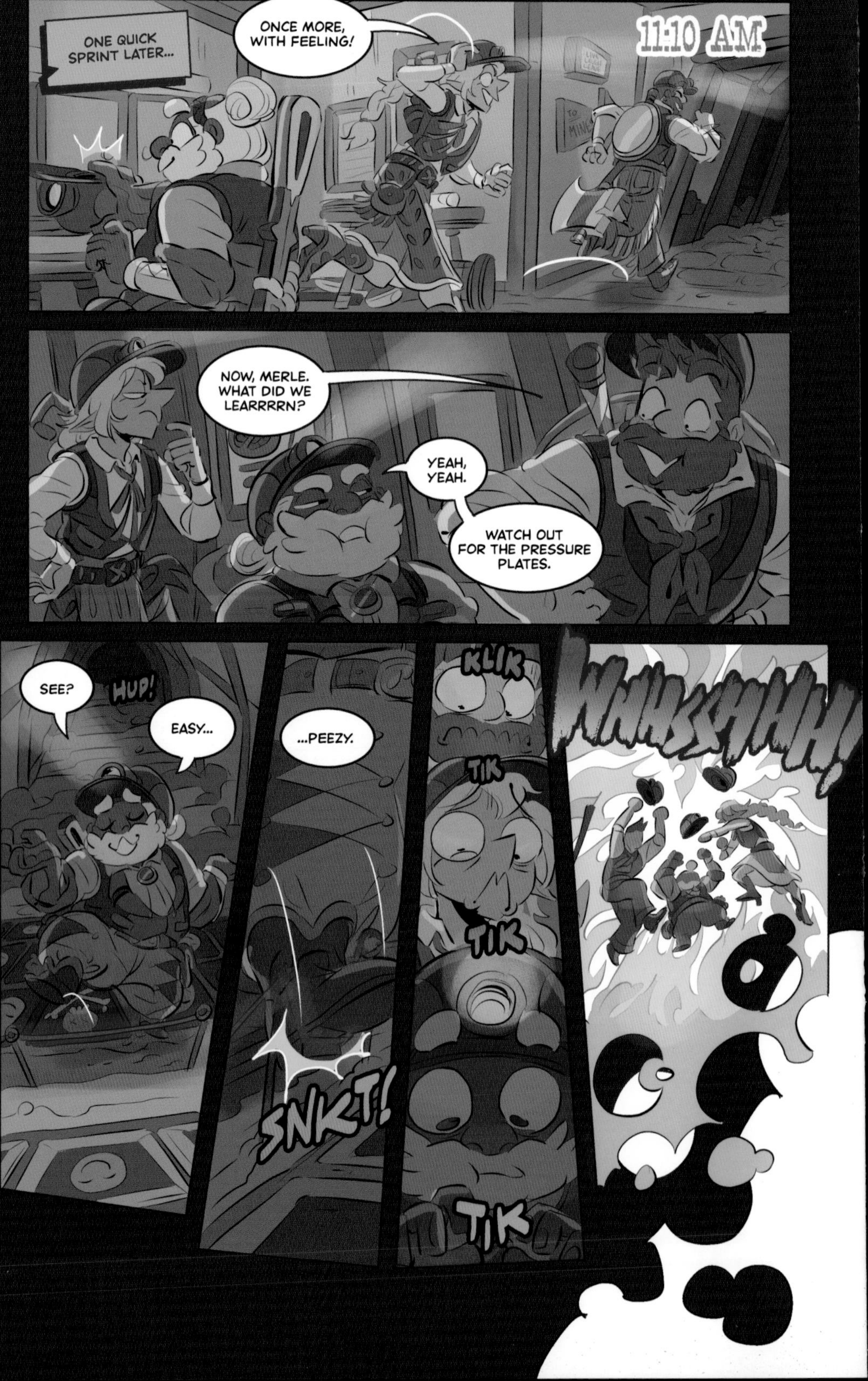
ONE QUICK SPRINT LATER...
ONCE MORE, WITH FEELING!
11:10 AM
NOW, MERLE. WHAT DID WE LEARRRRN?
YEAH, YEAH.
WATCH OUT FOR THE PRESSURE PLATES.
SEE?
HUP!
EASY...
...PEEZY.
SNKT!
KLIK
TIK
TIK
TIK
WHHSHHH!

Chapter
6

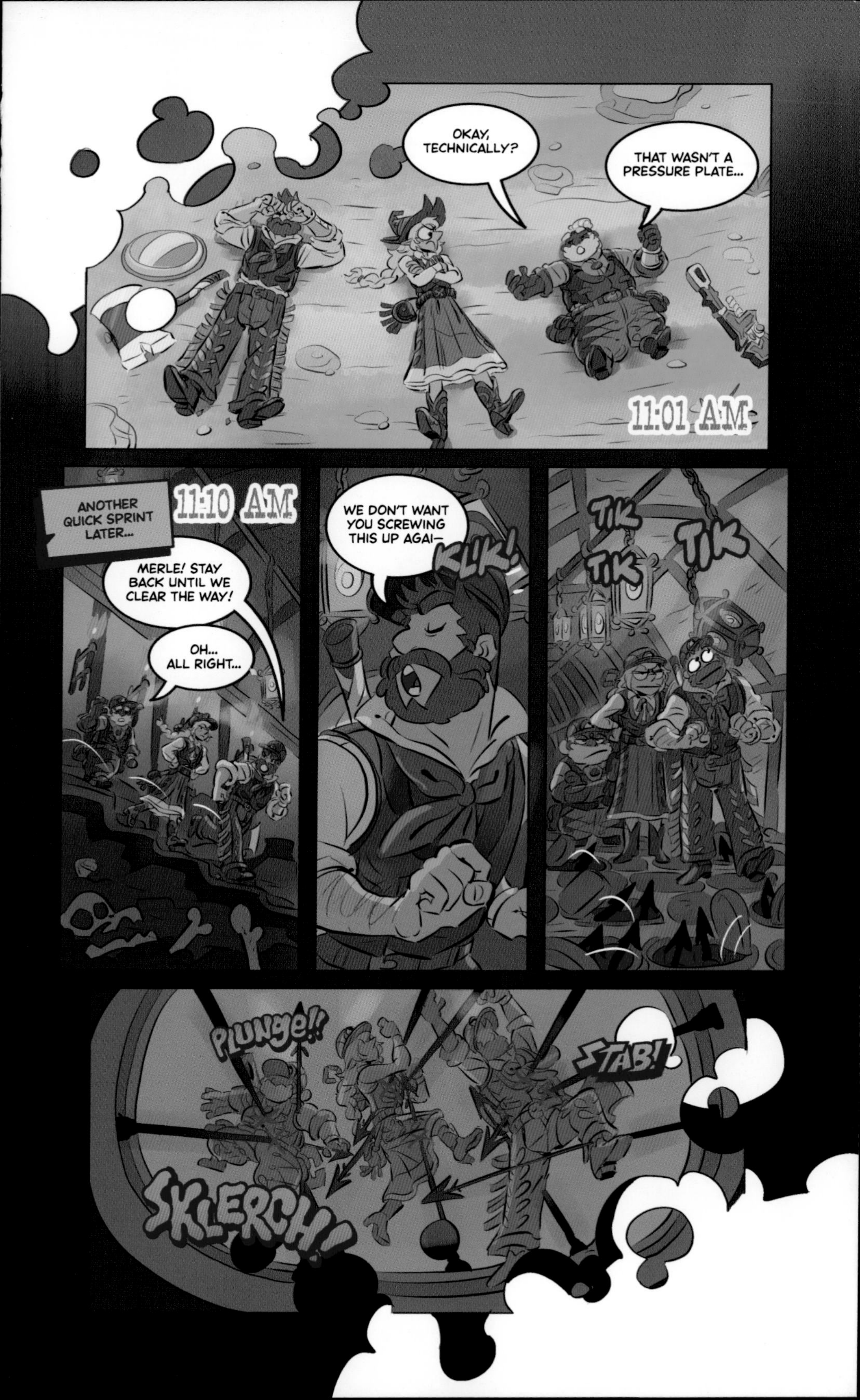
OKAY, TECHNICALLY?
THAT WASN'T A PRESSURE PLATE...
11:01 AM
ANOTHER QUICK SPRINT LATER...
11:10 AM
MERLE! STAY BACK UNTIL WE CLEAR THE WAY!
OH... ALL RIGHT...
WE DON'T WANT YOU SCREWING THIS UP AGAI—
KLIK!
TIK
TIK
TIK
PLUNGE!!
STAB!
SKLERCH!

Chapter
7

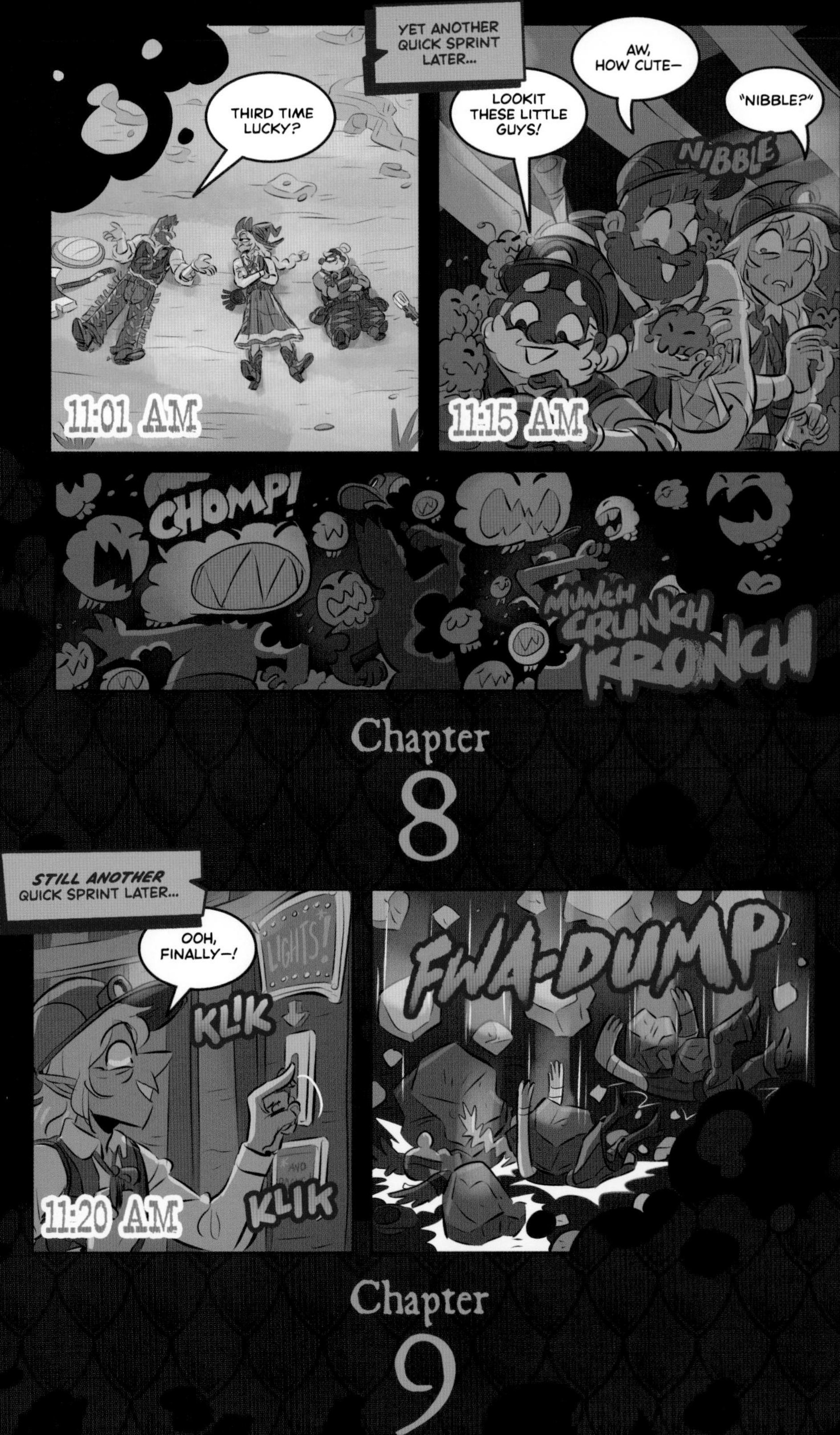
YET ANOTHER QUICK SPRINT LATER...
THIRD TIME LUCKY?
11:01 AM
LOOKIT THESE LITTLE GUYS!
AW, HOW CUTE—
NIBBLE
"NIBBLE?"
11:15 AM
CHOMP!
MUNCH
CRUNCH
KRONCH
Chapter
8
STILL ANOTHER QUICK SPRINT LATER...
OOH, FINALLY—!
LIGHTS!
KLIK
KLIK
11:20 AM
FWA-DUMP
Chapter
9

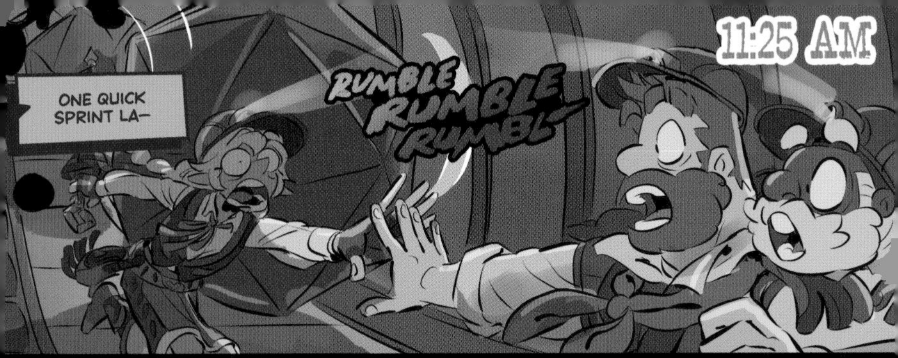
11:25 AM
ONE QUICK SPRINT LA—
RUMBLE RUMBLE RUMBL—

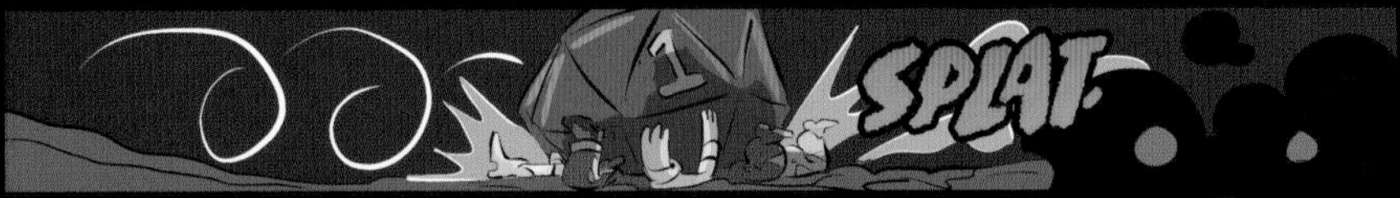
SPLAT

Chapter 10

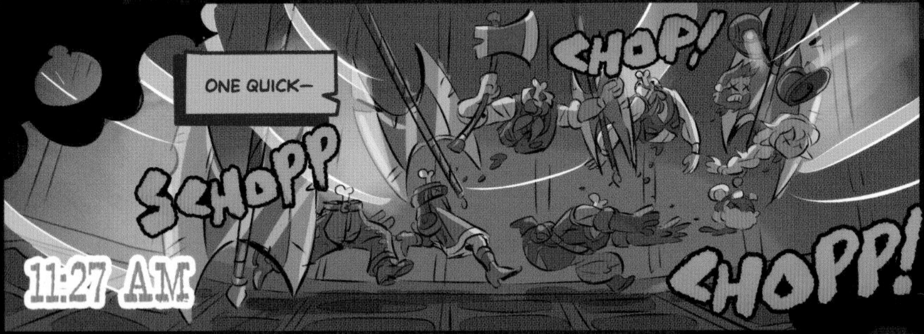
ONE QUICK—
CHOP!
SCHOPP
11:27 AM
CHOPP!

Chapter 11

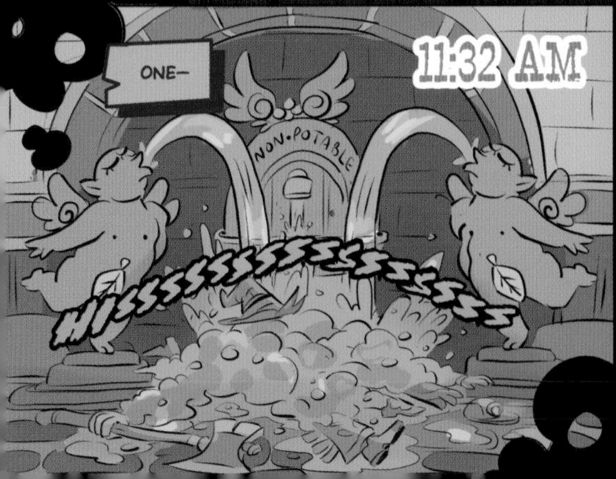
ONE—
11:32 AM
NON-POTABLE
HISSSSSSSSSSSSSSSSSSSS

Chapter 12

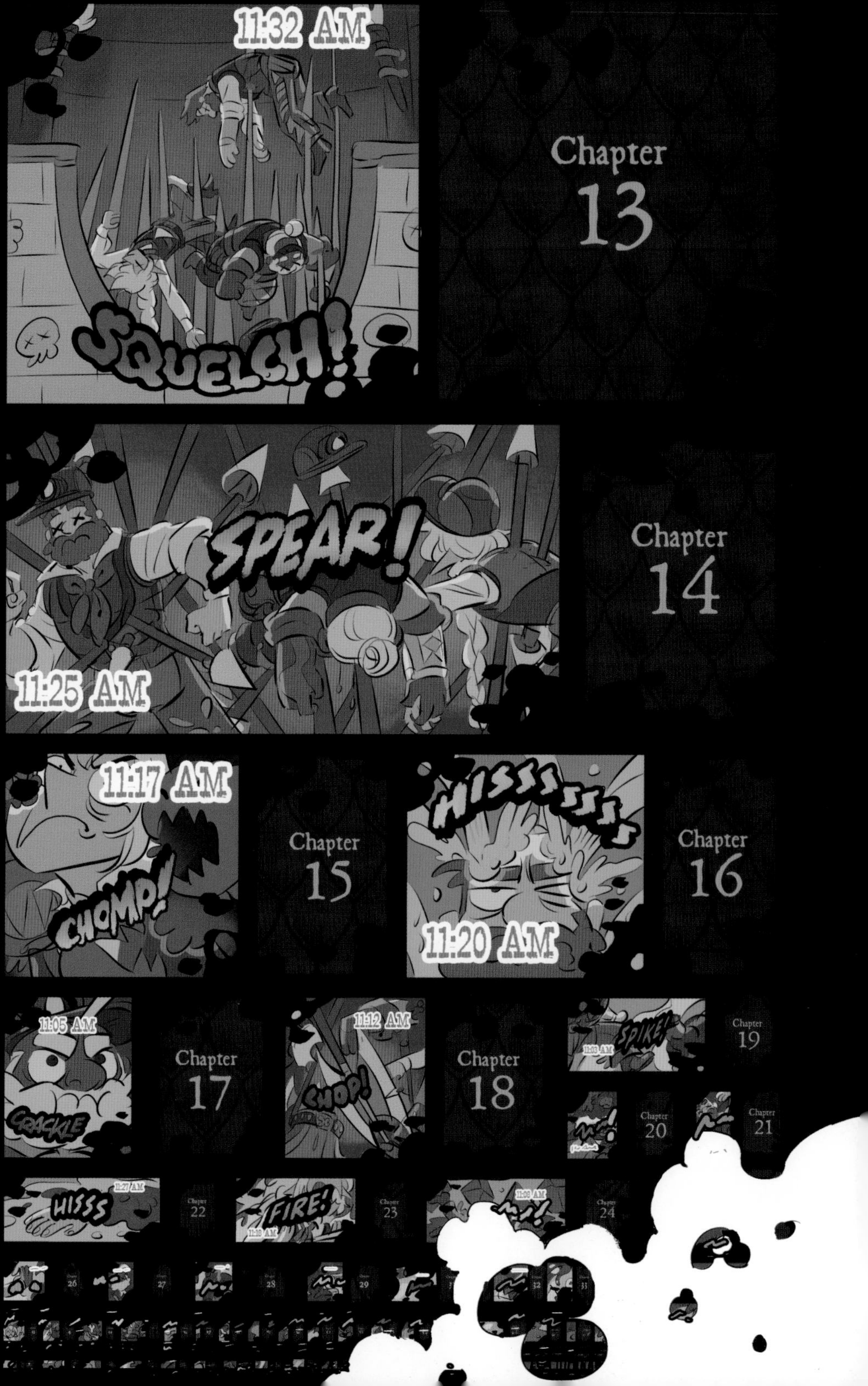

11:32 AM
SQUELCH!
Chapter 13
SPEAR!
11:25 AM
Chapter 14
11:17 AM
CHOMP!
Chapter 15
11:20 AM
Chapter 16
11:05 AM
CRACKLE
Chapter 17
11:12 AM
CHOP!
Chapter 18
SPIKE!
Chapter 19
Chapter 20
Chapter 21
11:27 AM
HISSS
Chapter 22
FIRE!
Chapter 23
Chapter 24

Chapter
108

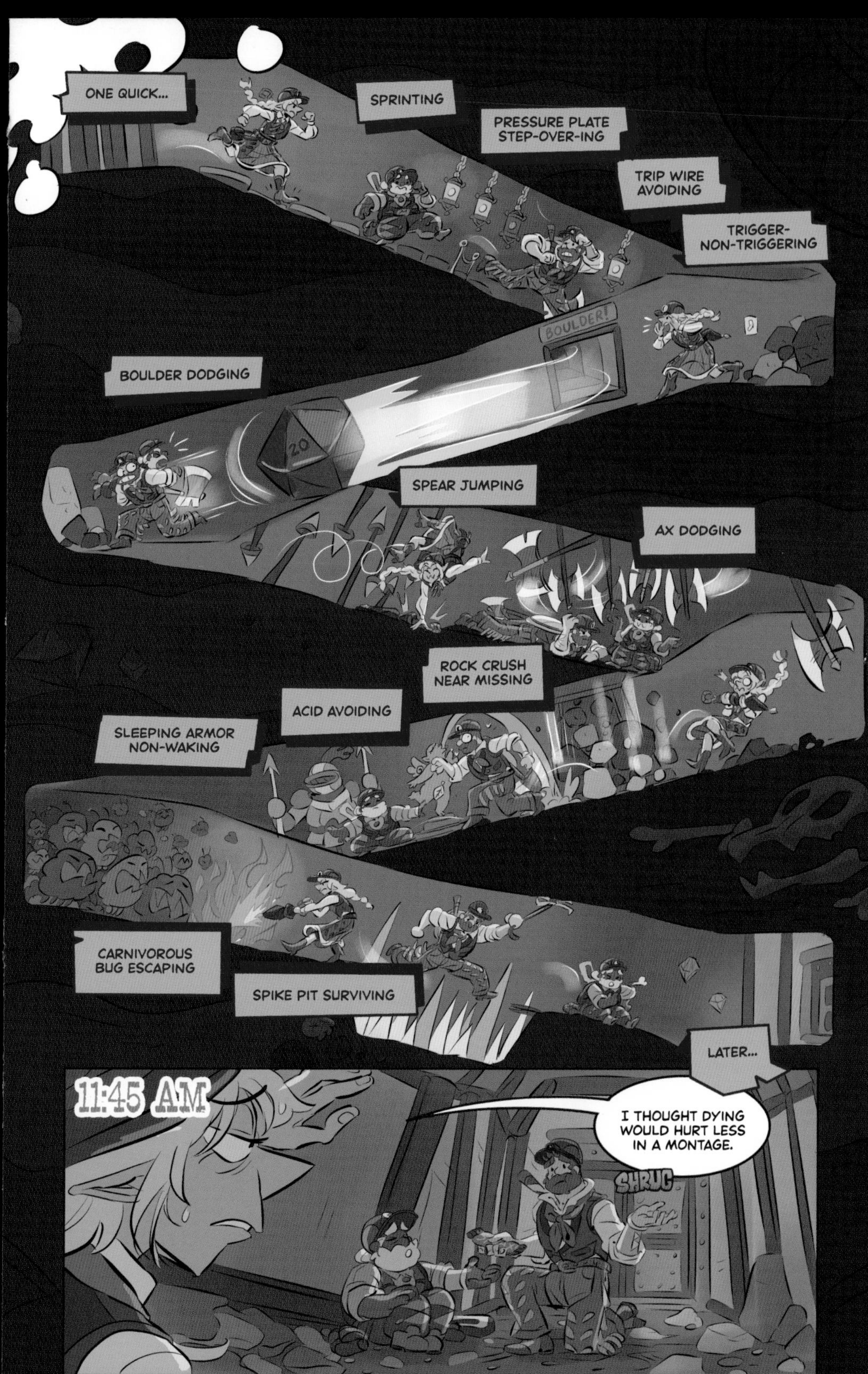
ONE QUICK...
SPRINTING
PRESSURE PLATE STEP-OVER-ING
TRIP WIRE AVOIDING
TRIGGER-NON-TRIGGERING
BOULDER!
BOULDER DODGING
20
SPEAR JUMPING
AX DODGING
ROCK CRUSH NEAR MISSING
ACID AVOIDING
SLEEPING ARMOR NON-WAKING
CARNIVOROUS BUG ESCAPING
SPIKE PIT SURVIVING
LATER...
11:45 AM
I THOUGHT DYING WOULD HURT LESS IN A MONTAGE.
SHRUG

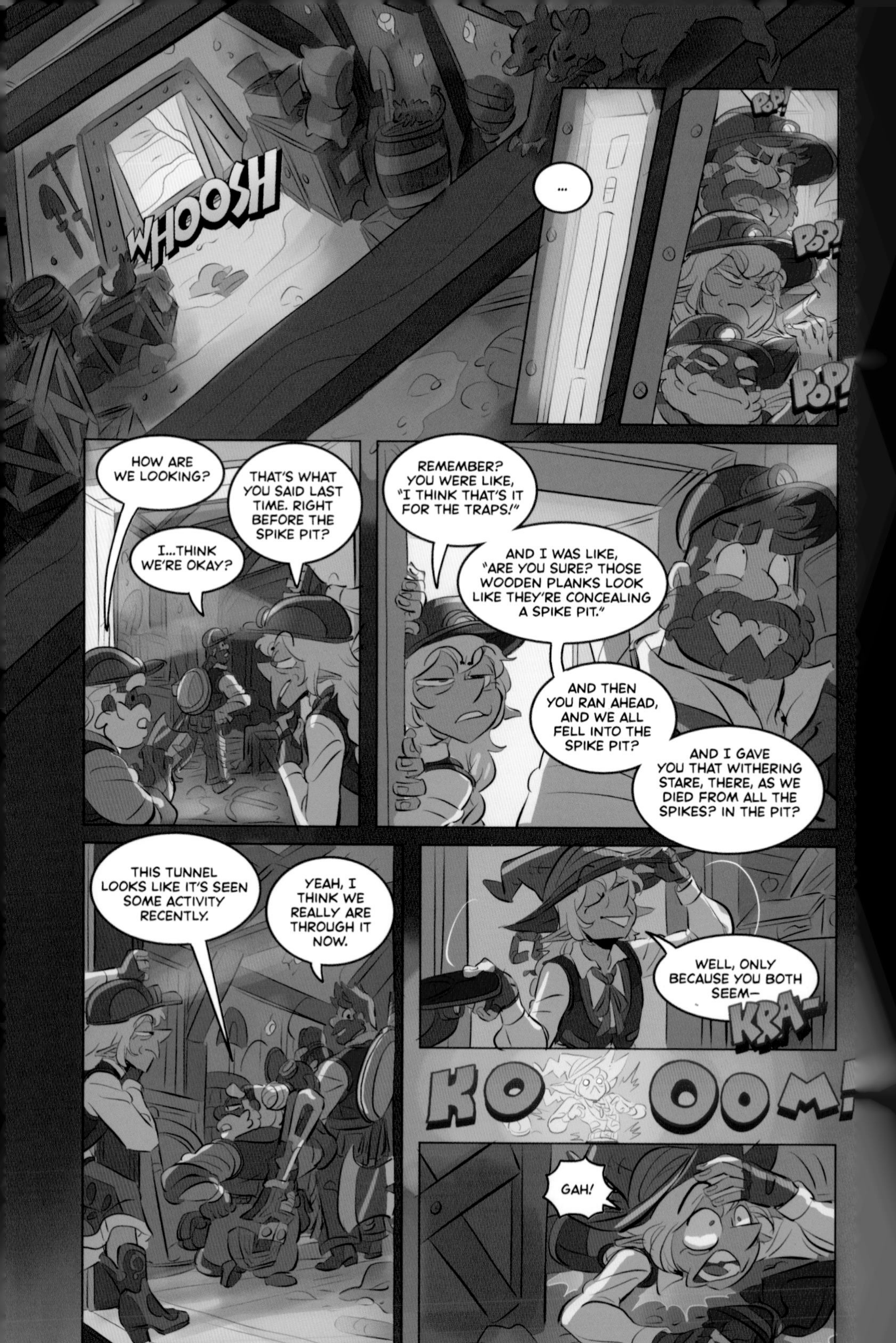
WHOOSH
...
POP!
POP!
POP!
HOW ARE WE LOOKING?
I...THINK WE'RE OKAY?
THAT'S WHAT YOU SAID LAST TIME. RIGHT BEFORE THE SPIKE PIT?
REMEMBER? YOU WERE LIKE, "I THINK THAT'S IT FOR THE TRAPS!"
AND I WAS LIKE, "ARE YOU SURE? THOSE WOODEN PLANKS LOOK LIKE THEY'RE CONCEALING A SPIKE PIT."
AND THEN YOU RAN AHEAD, AND WE ALL FELL INTO THE SPIKE PIT?
AND I GAVE YOU THAT WITHERING STARE, THERE, AS WE DIED FROM ALL THE SPIKES? IN THE PIT?
THIS TUNNEL LOOKS LIKE IT'S SEEN SOME ACTIVITY RECENTLY.
YEAH, I THINK WE REALLY ARE THROUGH IT NOW.
WELL, ONLY BECAUSE YOU BOTH SEEM—
KRA-
KOOOM!
GAH!

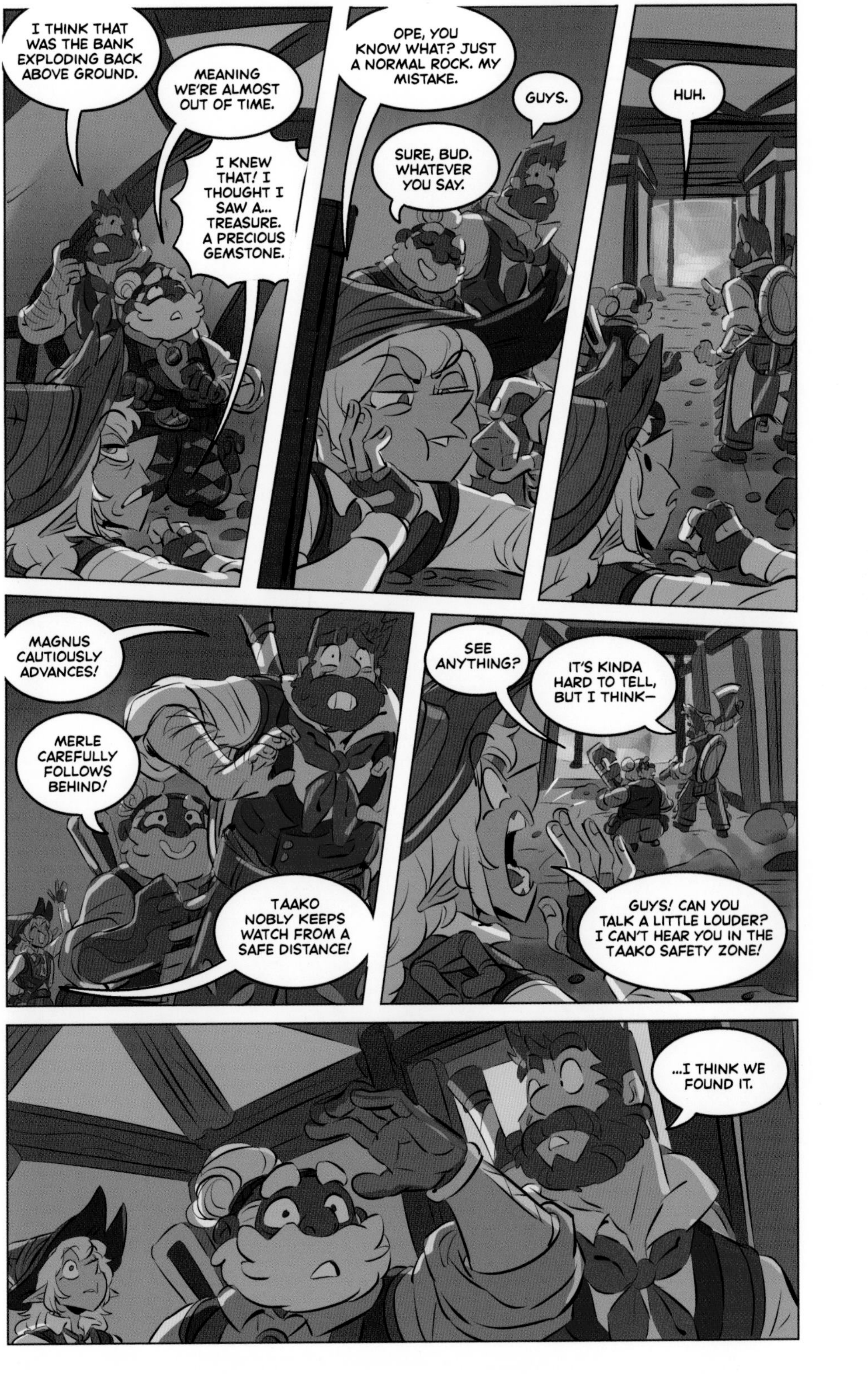

I THINK THAT WAS THE BANK EXPLODING BACK ABOVE GROUND.
MEANING WE'RE ALMOST OUT OF TIME.
I KNEW THAT! I THOUGHT I SAW A... TREASURE. A PRECIOUS GEMSTONE.
OPE, YOU KNOW WHAT? JUST A NORMAL ROCK. MY MISTAKE.
SURE, BUD. WHATEVER YOU SAY.
GUYS.
HUH.
MAGNUS CAUTIOUSLY ADVANCES!
MERLE CAREFULLY FOLLOWS BEHIND!
TAAKO NOBLY KEEPS WATCH FROM A SAFE DISTANCE!
SEE ANYTHING?
IT'S KINDA HARD TO TELL, BUT I THINK—
GUYS! CAN YOU TALK A LITTLE LOUDER? I CAN'T HEAR YOU IN THE TAAKO SAFETY ZONE!
...I THINK WE FOUND IT.

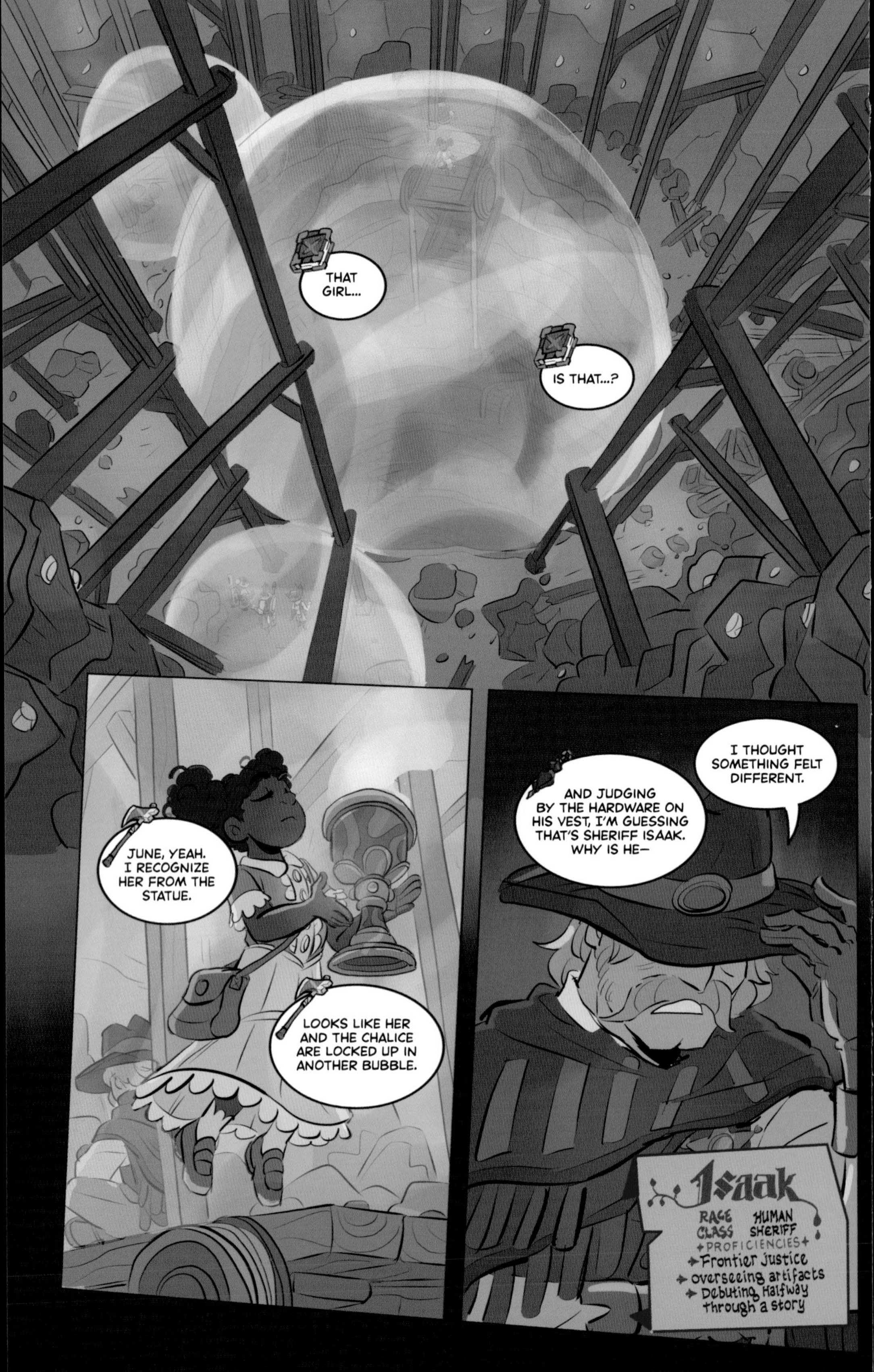
THAT GIRL...
IS THAT...?
JUNE, YEAH. I RECOGNIZE HER FROM THE STATUE.
LOOKS LIKE HER AND THE CHALICE ARE LOCKED UP IN ANOTHER BUBBLE.
I THOUGHT SOMETHING FELT DIFFERENT.
AND JUDGING BY THE HARDWARE ON HIS VEST, I'M GUESSING THAT'S SHERIFF ISAAK. WHY IS HE—
Isaak
RACE HUMAN
CLASS SHERIFF
PROFICIENCIES
Frontier Justice
overseeing artifacts
Debuting Halfway through a story

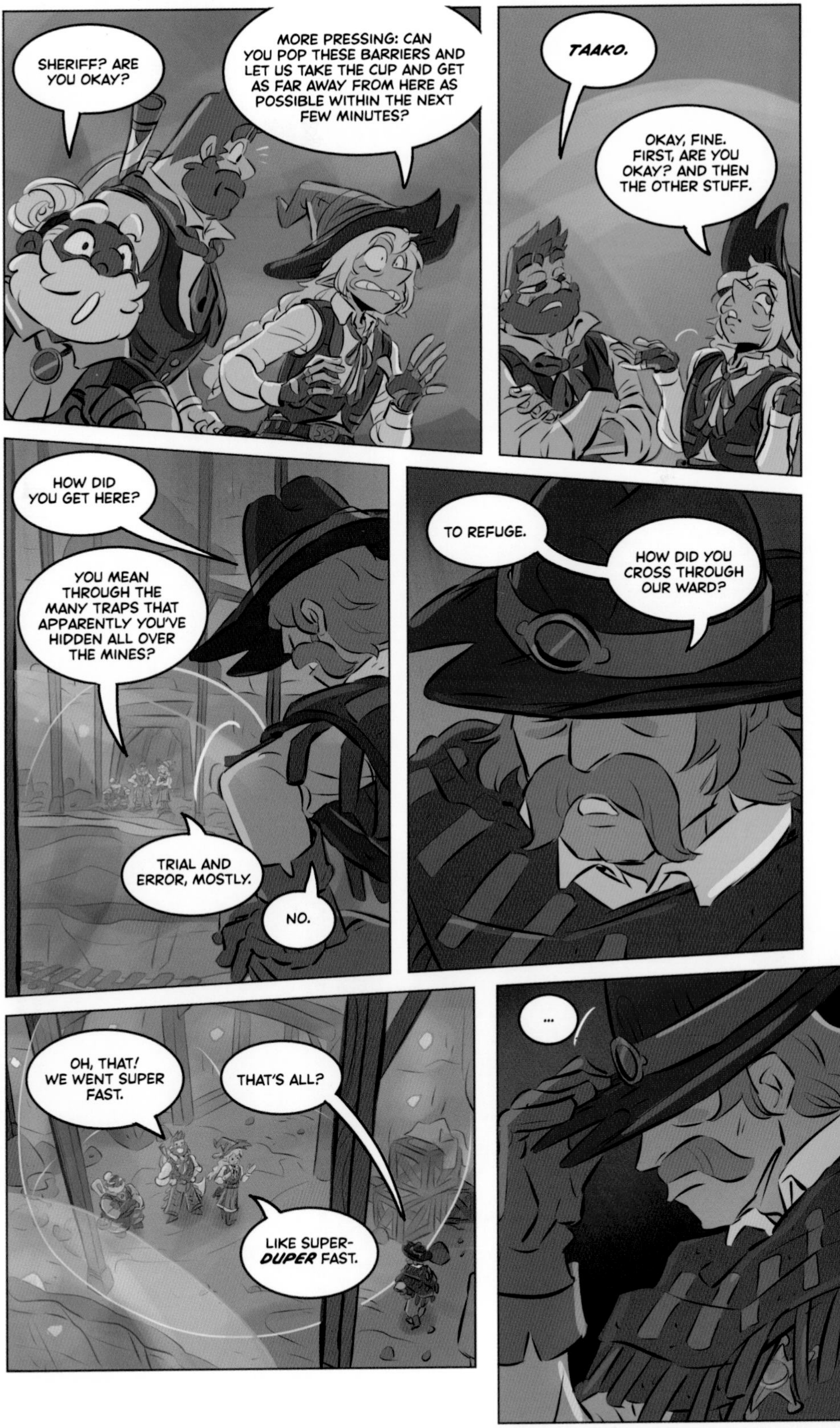
SHERIFF? ARE YOU OKAY?
MORE PRESSING: CAN YOU POP THESE BARRIERS AND LET US TAKE THE CUP AND GET AS FAR AWAY FROM HERE AS POSSIBLE WITHIN THE NEXT FEW MINUTES?
TAAKO.
OKAY, FINE. FIRST, ARE YOU OKAY? AND THEN THE OTHER STUFF.
HOW DID YOU GET HERE?
YOU MEAN THROUGH THE MANY TRAPS THAT APPARENTLY YOU'VE HIDDEN ALL OVER THE MINES?
TRIAL AND ERROR, MOSTLY.
NO.
TO REFUGE.
HOW DID YOU CROSS THROUGH OUR WARD?
OH, THAT! WE WENT SUPER FAST.
THAT'S ALL?
LIKE SUPER-*DUPER* FAST.
...

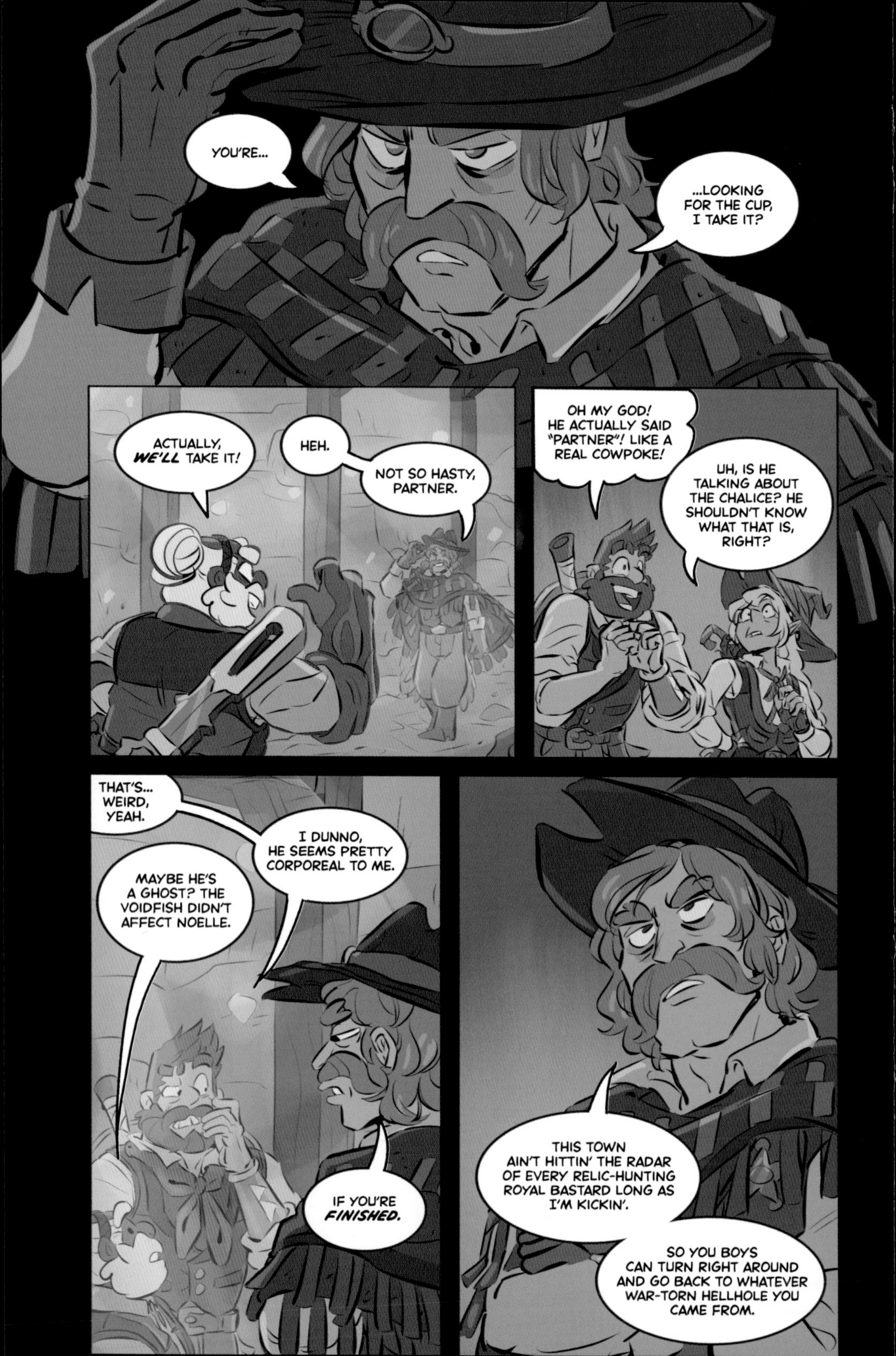

YOU'RE...
...LOOKING FOR THE CUP, I TAKE IT?
ACTUALLY, ***WE'LL*** TAKE IT!
HEH.
NOT SO HASTY, PARTNER.
OH MY GOD! HE ACTUALLY SAID "PARTNER"! LIKE A REAL COWPOKE!
UH, IS HE TALKING ABOUT THE CHALICE? HE SHOULDN'T KNOW WHAT THAT IS, RIGHT?
THAT'S... WEIRD, YEAH.
I DUNNO, HE SEEMS PRETTY CORPOREAL TO ME.
MAYBE HE'S A GHOST? THE VOIDFISH DIDN'T AFFECT NOELLE.
IF YOU'RE ***FINISHED.***
THIS TOWN AIN'T HITTIN' THE RADAR OF EVERY RELIC-HUNTING ROYAL BASTARD LONG AS I'M KICKIN'.
SO YOU BOYS CAN TURN RIGHT AROUND AND GO BACK TO WHATEVER WAR-TORN HELLHOLE YOU CAME FROM.

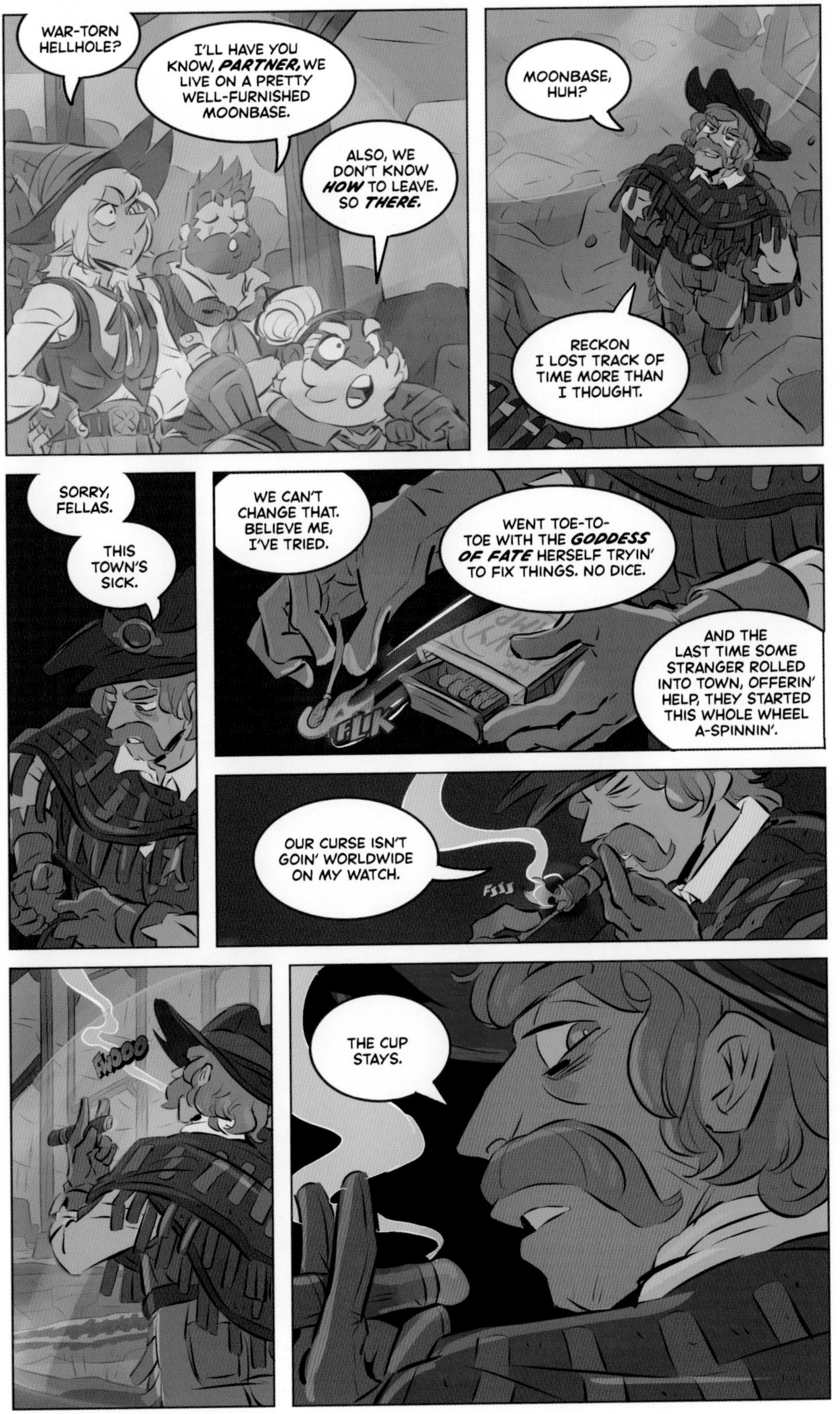
WAR-TORN HELLHOLE?
I'LL HAVE YOU KNOW, PARTNER, WE LIVE ON A PRETTY WELL-FURNISHED MOONBASE.
ALSO, WE DON'T KNOW HOW TO LEAVE. SO THERE.
MOONBASE, HUH?
RECKON I LOST TRACK OF TIME MORE THAN I THOUGHT.
SORRY, FELLAS.
THIS TOWN'S SICK.
WE CAN'T CHANGE THAT. BELIEVE ME, I'VE TRIED.
WENT TOE-TO-TOE WITH THE GODDESS OF FATE HERSELF TRYIN' TO FIX THINGS. NO DICE.
FLIK
AND THE LAST TIME SOME STRANGER ROLLED INTO TOWN, OFFERIN' HELP, THEY STARTED THIS WHOLE WHEEL A-SPINNIN'.
OUR CURSE ISN'T GOIN' WORLDWIDE ON MY WATCH.
FSSS
FWOOO
THE CUP STAYS.

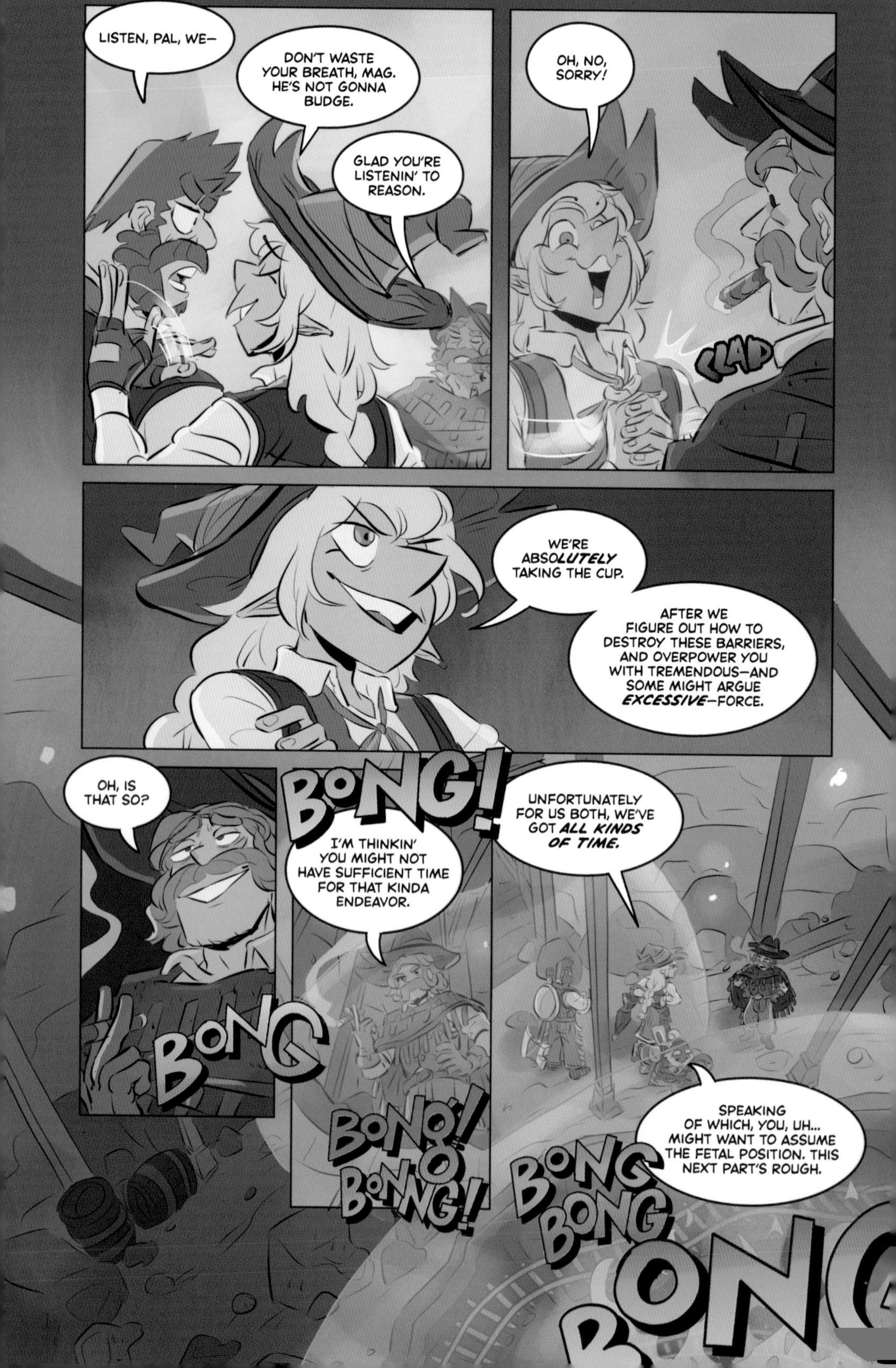
LISTEN, PAL, WE—
DON'T WASTE YOUR BREATH, MAG. HE'S NOT GONNA BUDGE.
GLAD YOU'RE LISTENIN' TO REASON.
OH, NO, SORRY!
CLAP
WE'RE ABSO*LUTELY* TAKING THE CUP.
AFTER WE FIGURE OUT HOW TO DESTROY THESE BARRIERS, AND OVERPOWER YOU WITH TREMENDOUS—AND SOME MIGHT ARGUE ***EXCESSIVE***—FORCE.
OH, IS THAT SO?
BONG!
I'M THINKIN' YOU MIGHT NOT HAVE SUFFICIENT TIME FOR THAT KINDA ENDEAVOR.
BONG
UNFORTUNATELY FOR US BOTH, WE'VE GOT ***ALL KINDS OF TIME.***
BONG! BONG BONNG!
BONG BONG BONG
SPEAKING OF WHICH, YOU, UH... MIGHT WANT TO ASSUME THE FETAL POSITION. THIS NEXT PART'S ROUGH.
BONG

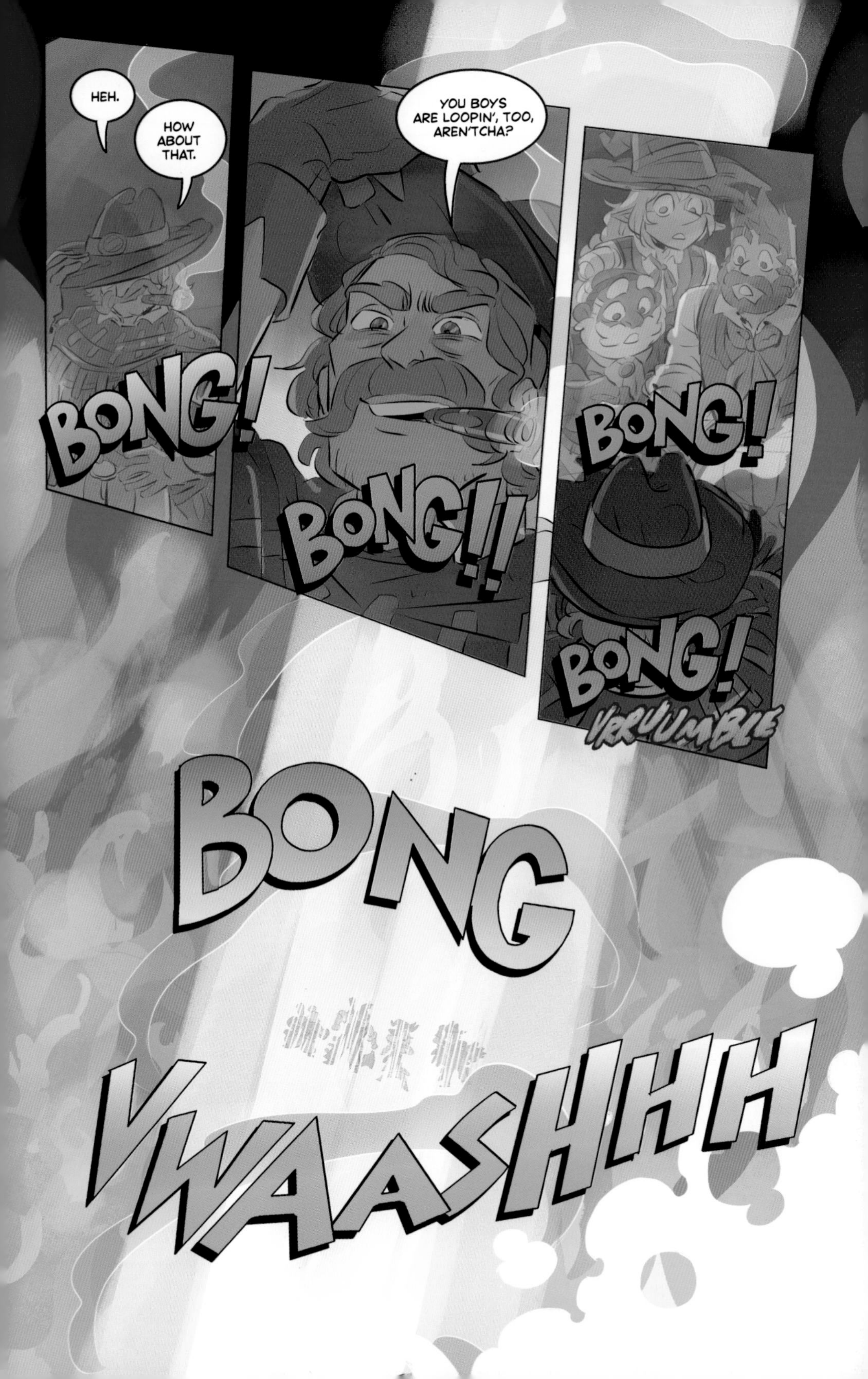
HEH.
HOW ABOUT THAT.
YOU BOYS ARE LOOPIN', TOO, AREN'TCHA?
BONG!
BONG!!
BONG!
BONG!
VRRUMBLE
BONG
VWAASHHH

Chapter
109

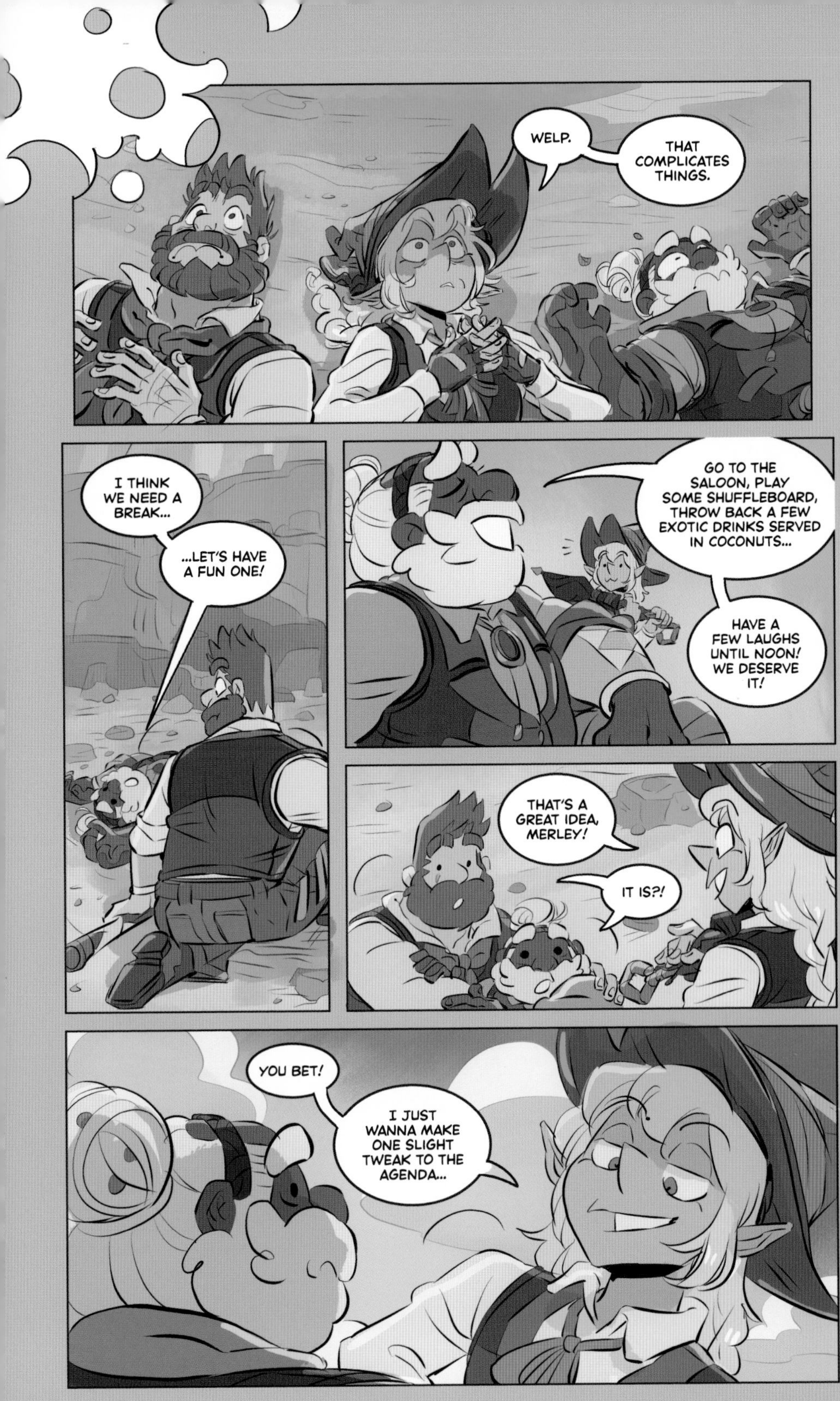
WELP.
THAT COMPLICATES THINGS.
I THINK WE NEED A BREAK...
...LET'S HAVE A FUN ONE!
GO TO THE SALOON, PLAY SOME SHUFFLEBOARD, THROW BACK A FEW EXOTIC DRINKS SERVED IN COCONUTS...
HAVE A FEW LAUGHS UNTIL NOON! WE DESERVE IT!
THAT'S A GREAT IDEA, MERLEY!
IT IS?!
YOU BET!
I JUST WANNA MAKE ONE SLIGHT TWEAK TO THE AGENDA...

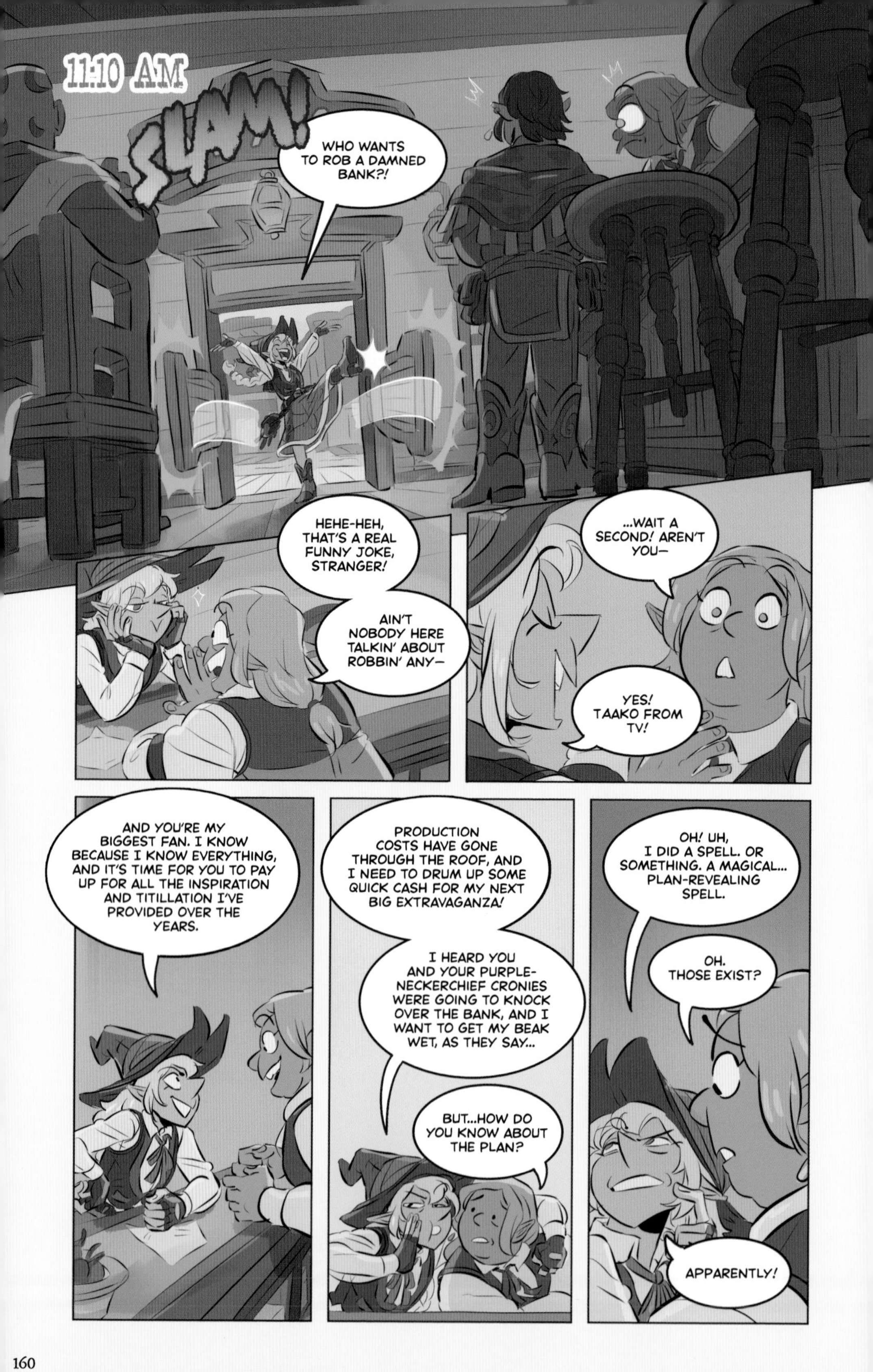
11:10 AM
SLAM!
WHO WANTS TO ROB A DAMNED BANK?!
HEHE-HEH, THAT'S A REAL FUNNY JOKE, STRANGER!
AIN'T NOBODY HERE TALKIN' ABOUT ROBBIN' ANY—
...WAIT A SECOND! AREN'T YOU—
YES! TAAKO FROM TV!
AND YOU'RE MY BIGGEST FAN. I KNOW BECAUSE I KNOW EVERYTHING, AND IT'S TIME FOR YOU TO PAY UP FOR ALL THE INSPIRATION AND TITILLATION I'VE PROVIDED OVER THE YEARS.
PRODUCTION COSTS HAVE GONE THROUGH THE ROOF, AND I NEED TO DRUM UP SOME QUICK CASH FOR MY NEXT BIG EXTRAVAGANZA!
I HEARD YOU AND YOUR PURPLE-NECKERCHIEF CRONIES WERE GOING TO KNOCK OVER THE BANK, AND I WANT TO GET MY BEAK WET, AS THEY SAY...
BUT...HOW DO YOU KNOW ABOUT THE PLAN?
OH! UH, I DID A SPELL. OR SOMETHING. A MAGICAL... PLAN-REVEALING SPELL.
OH. THOSE EXIST?
APPARENTLY!

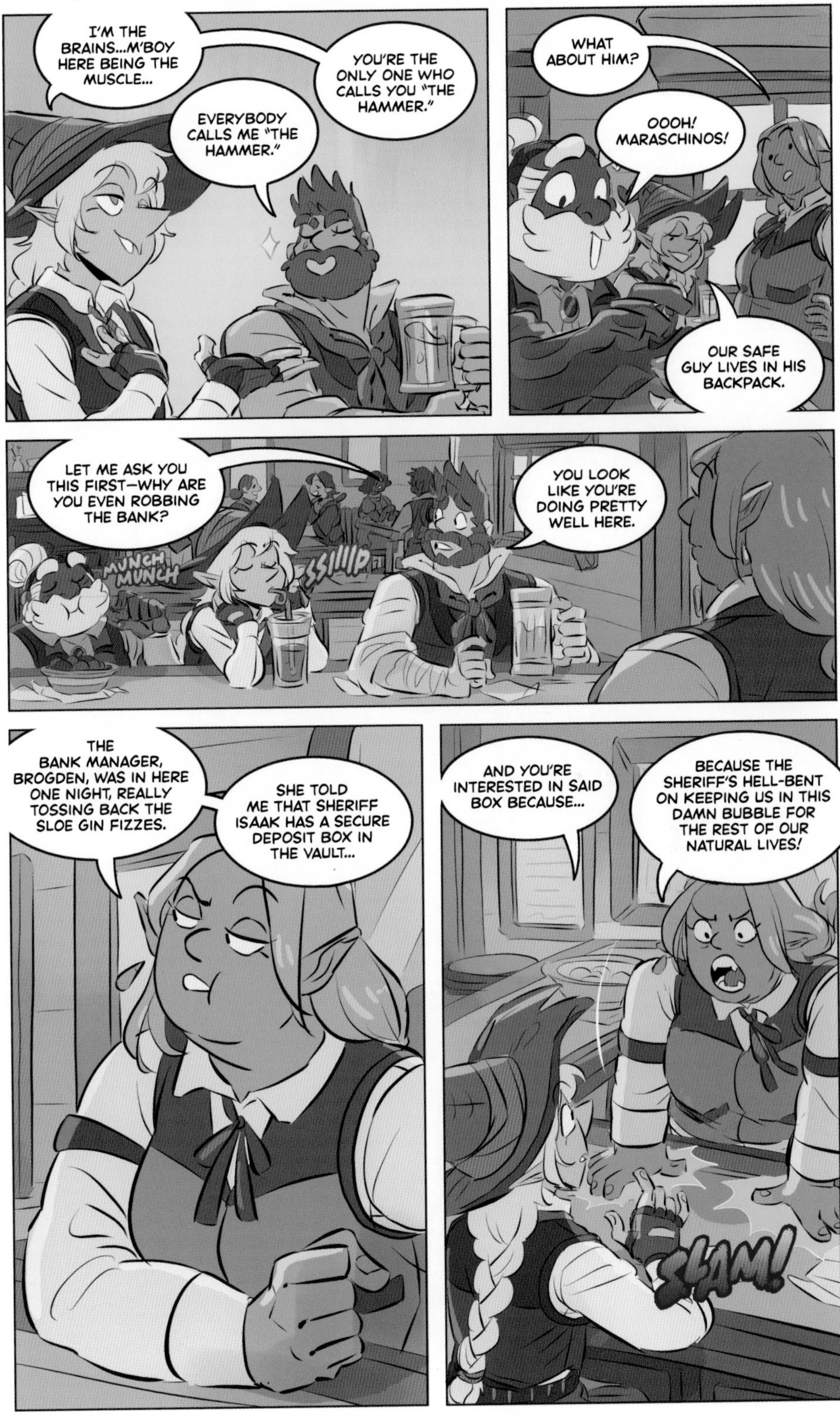
I'M THE BRAINS...M'BOY HERE BEING THE MUSCLE...
EVERYBODY CALLS ME "THE HAMMER."
YOU'RE THE ONLY ONE WHO CALLS YOU "THE HAMMER."
WHAT ABOUT HIM?
OOOH! MARASCHINOS!
OUR SAFE GUY LIVES IN HIS BACKPACK.
LET ME ASK YOU THIS FIRST—WHY ARE YOU EVEN ROBBING THE BANK?
MUNCH MUNCH
SSIIIIP
YOU LOOK LIKE YOU'RE DOING PRETTY WELL HERE.
THE BANK MANAGER, BROGDEN, WAS IN HERE ONE NIGHT, REALLY TOSSING BACK THE SLOE GIN FIZZES.
SHE TOLD ME THAT SHERIFF ISAAK HAS A SECURE DEPOSIT BOX IN THE VAULT...
AND YOU'RE INTERESTED IN SAID BOX BECAUSE...
BECAUSE THE SHERIFF'S HELL-BENT ON KEEPING US IN THIS DAMN BUBBLE FOR THE REST OF OUR NATURAL LIVES!
SLAM!

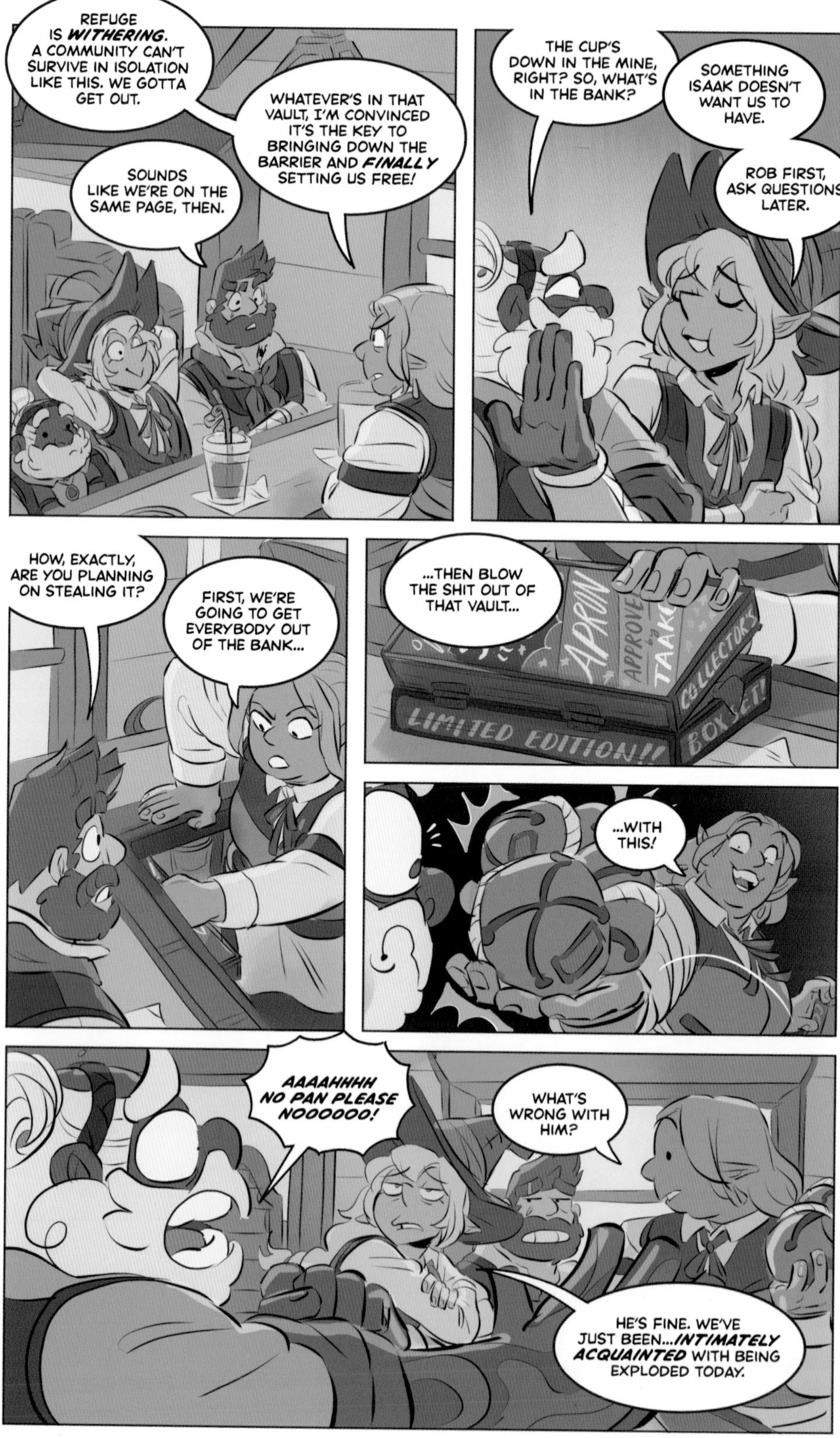
REFUGE IS WITHERING. A COMMUNITY CAN'T SURVIVE IN ISOLATION LIKE THIS. WE GOTTA GET OUT.
WHATEVER'S IN THAT VAULT, I'M CONVINCED IT'S THE KEY TO BRINGING DOWN THE BARRIER AND FINALLY SETTING US FREE!
SOUNDS LIKE WE'RE ON THE SAME PAGE, THEN.
THE CUP'S DOWN IN THE MINE, RIGHT? SO, WHAT'S IN THE BANK?
SOMETHING ISAAK DOESN'T WANT US TO HAVE.
ROB FIRST, ASK QUESTIONS LATER.
HOW, EXACTLY, ARE YOU PLANNING ON STEALING IT?
FIRST, WE'RE GOING TO GET EVERYBODY OUT OF THE BANK...
...THEN BLOW THE SHIT OUT OF THAT VAULT...
APRON
APPROVED
COLLECTOR'S BOX SET!
LIMITED EDITION!!
...WITH THIS!
AAAAHHHH NO PAN PLEASE NOOOOOO!
WHAT'S WRONG WITH HIM?
HE'S FINE. WE'VE JUST BEEN...INTIMATELY ACQUAINTED WITH BEING EXPLODED TODAY.

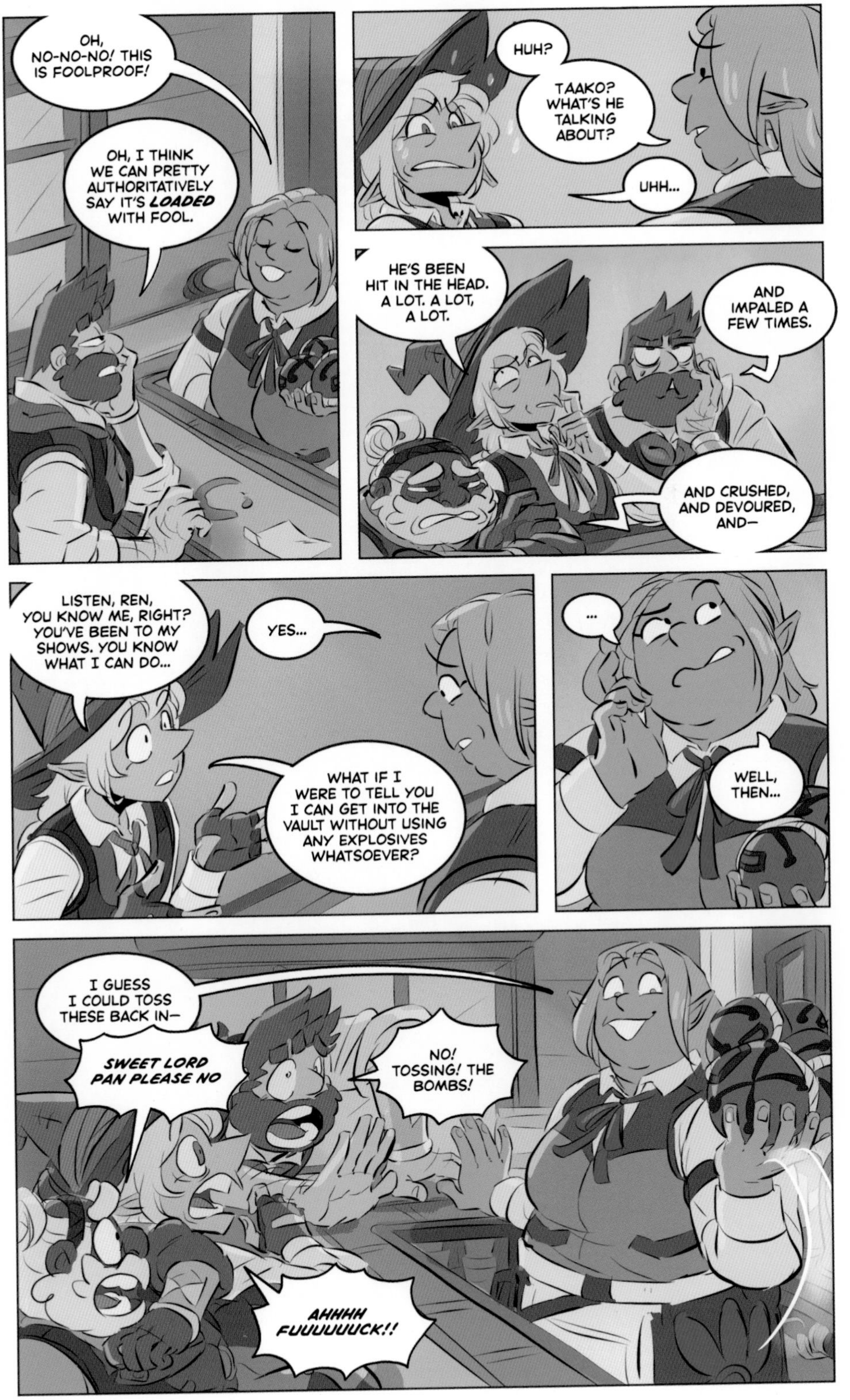
OH, NO-NO-NO! THIS IS FOOLPROOF!
OH, I THINK WE CAN PRETTY AUTHORITATIVELY SAY IT'S LOADED WITH FOOL.
HUH?
TAAKO? WHAT'S HE TALKING ABOUT?
UHH...
HE'S BEEN HIT IN THE HEAD. A LOT. A LOT, A LOT.
AND IMPALED A FEW TIMES.
AND CRUSHED, AND DEVOURED, AND—
LISTEN, REN, YOU KNOW ME, RIGHT? YOU'VE BEEN TO MY SHOWS. YOU KNOW WHAT I CAN DO...
YES...
WHAT IF I WERE TO TELL YOU I CAN GET INTO THE VAULT WITHOUT USING ANY EXPLOSIVES WHATSOEVER?
...
WELL, THEN...
I GUESS I COULD TOSS THESE BACK IN—
SWEET LORD PAN PLEASE NO
NO! TOSSING! THE BOMBS!
AHHHH FUUUUUUCK!!

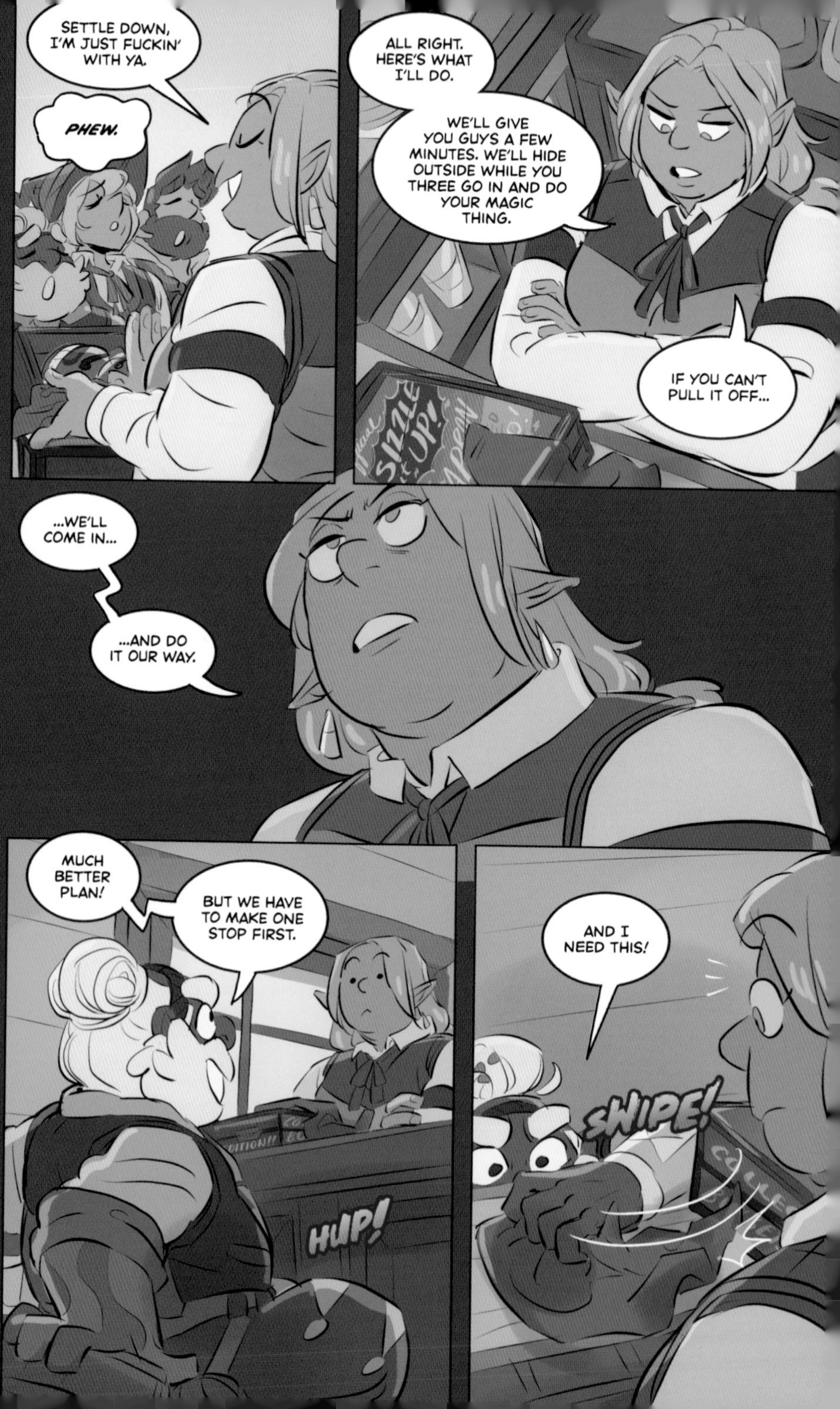
SETTLE DOWN, I'M JUST FUCKIN' WITH YA.
PHEW.
ALL RIGHT. HERE'S WHAT I'LL DO.
WE'LL GIVE YOU GUYS A FEW MINUTES. WE'LL HIDE OUTSIDE WHILE YOU THREE GO IN AND DO YOUR MAGIC THING.
IF YOU CAN'T PULL IT OFF...
...WE'LL COME IN...
...AND DO IT OUR WAY.
MUCH BETTER PLAN!
BUT WE HAVE TO MAKE ONE STOP FIRST.
HUP!
AND I NEED THIS!
SWIPE!

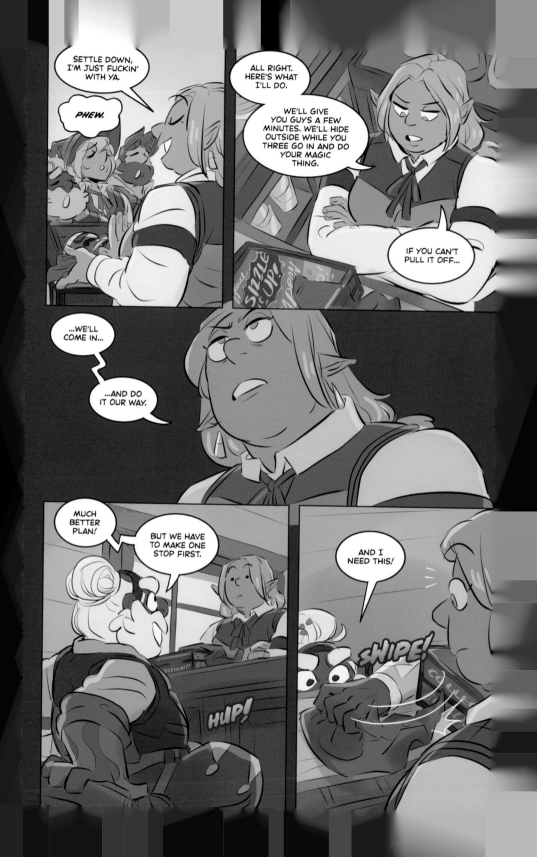

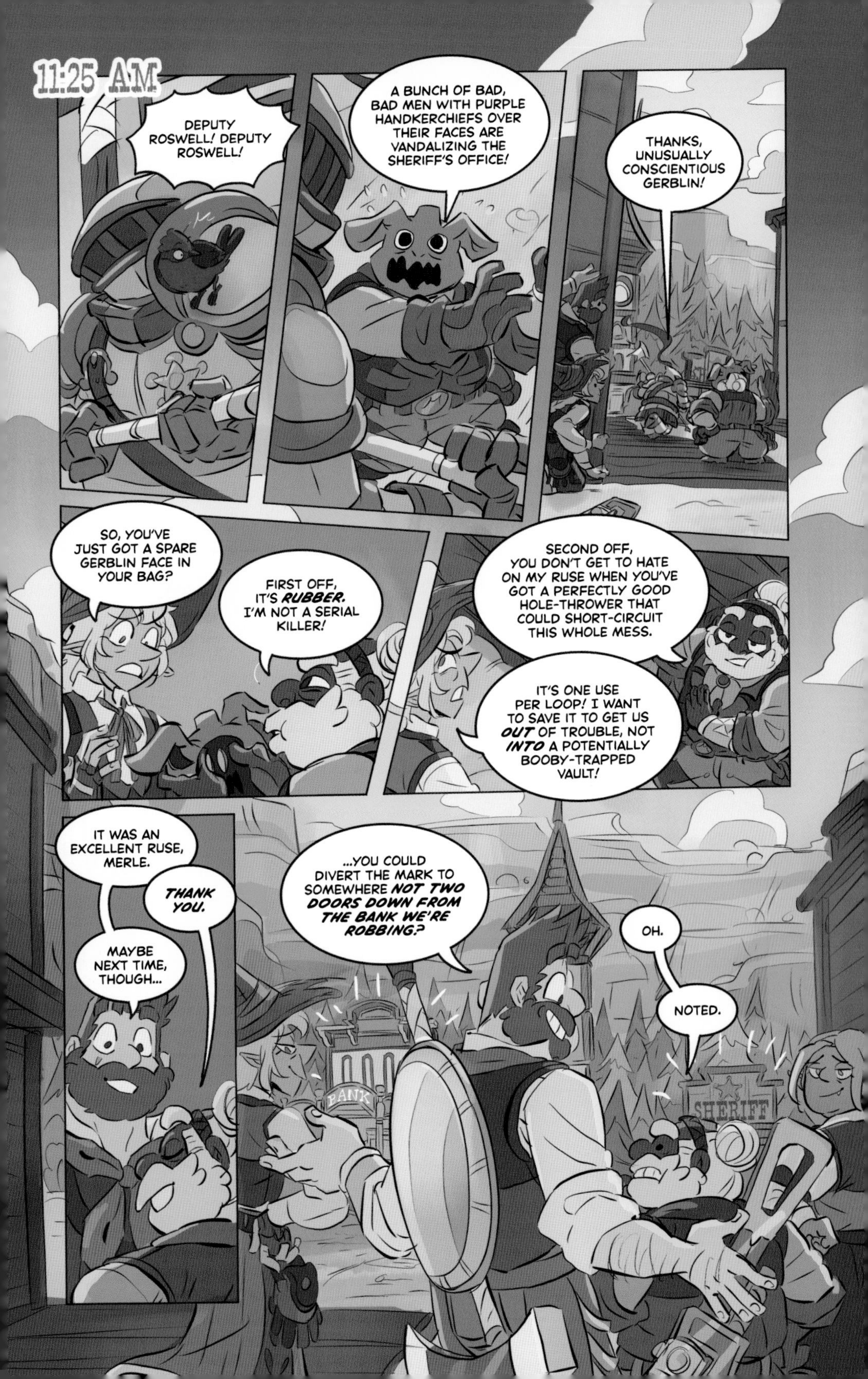
11:25 AM
DEPUTY ROSWELL! DEPUTY ROSWELL!
A BUNCH OF BAD, BAD MEN WITH PURPLE HANDKERCHIEFS OVER THEIR FACES ARE VANDALIZING THE SHERIFF'S OFFICE!
THANKS, UNUSUALLY CONSCIENTIOUS GERBLIN!
SO, YOU'VE JUST GOT A SPARE GERBLIN FACE IN YOUR BAG?
FIRST OFF, IT'S *RUBBER.* I'M NOT A SERIAL KILLER!
SECOND OFF, YOU DON'T GET TO HATE ON MY RUSE WHEN YOU'VE GOT A PERFECTLY GOOD HOLE-THROWER THAT COULD SHORT-CIRCUIT THIS WHOLE MESS.
IT'S ONE USE PER LOOP! I WANT TO SAVE IT TO GET US *OUT* OF TROUBLE, NOT *INTO* A POTENTIALLY BOOBY-TRAPPED VAULT!
IT WAS AN EXCELLENT RUSE, MERLE.
THANK YOU.
MAYBE NEXT TIME, THOUGH...
...YOU COULD DIVERT THE MARK TO SOMEWHERE *NOT TWO DOORS DOWN FROM THE BANK WE'RE ROBBING?*
OH.
NOTED.
BANK
SHERIFF

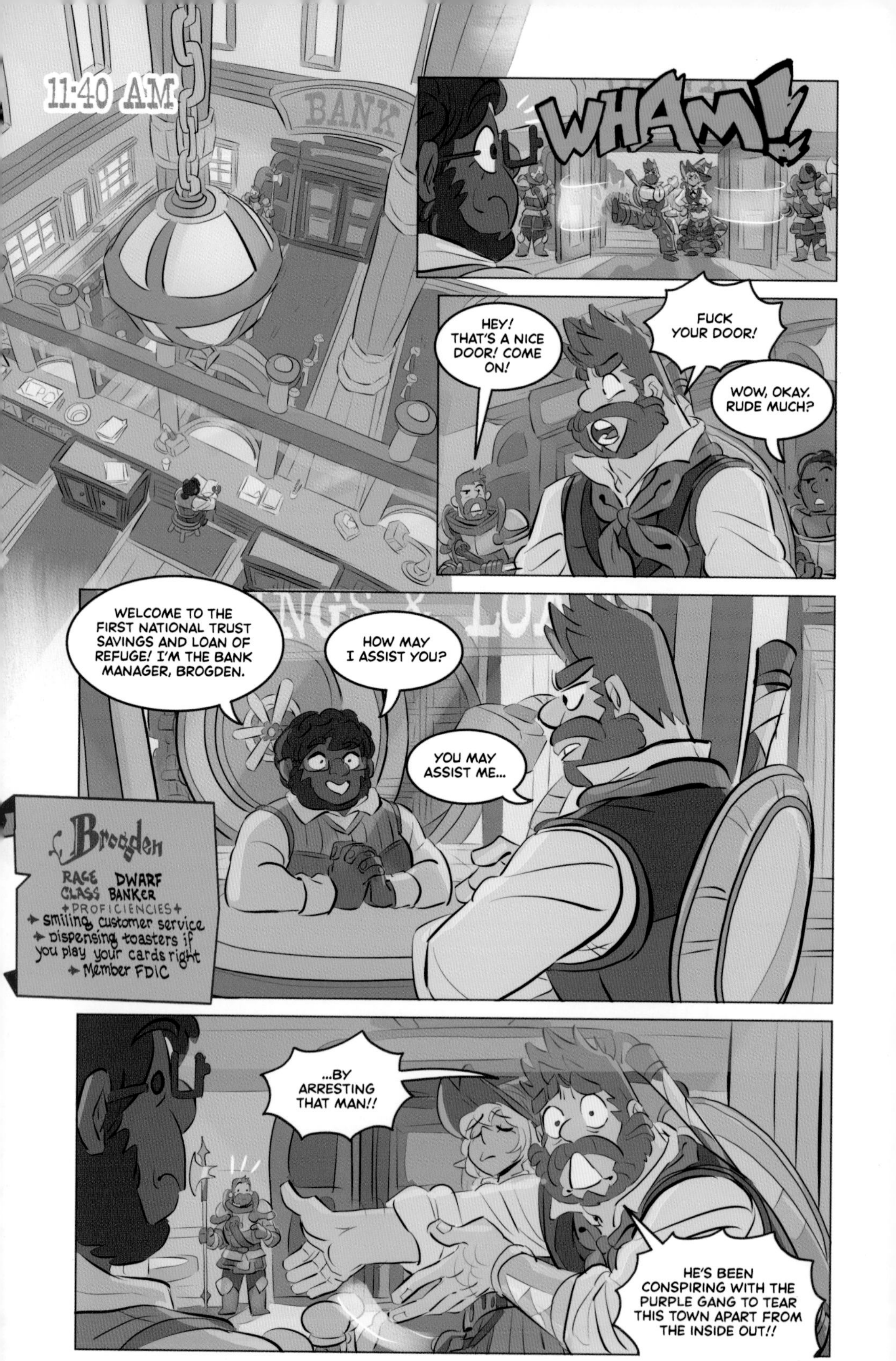
11:40 AM
BANK
WHAM!
HEY! THAT'S A NICE DOOR! COME ON!
FUCK YOUR DOOR!
WOW, OKAY. RUDE MUCH?
WELCOME TO THE FIRST NATIONAL TRUST SAVINGS AND LOAN OF REFUGE! I'M THE BANK MANAGER, BROGDEN.
HOW MAY I ASSIST YOU?
YOU MAY ASSIST ME...
Brogden
RACE DWARF
CLASS BANKER
PROFICIENCIES
smiling customer service
dispensing toasters if you play your cards right
Member FDIC
...BY ARRESTING THAT MAN!!
HE'S BEEN CONSPIRING WITH THE PURPLE GANG TO TEAR THIS TOWN APART FROM THE INSIDE OUT!!

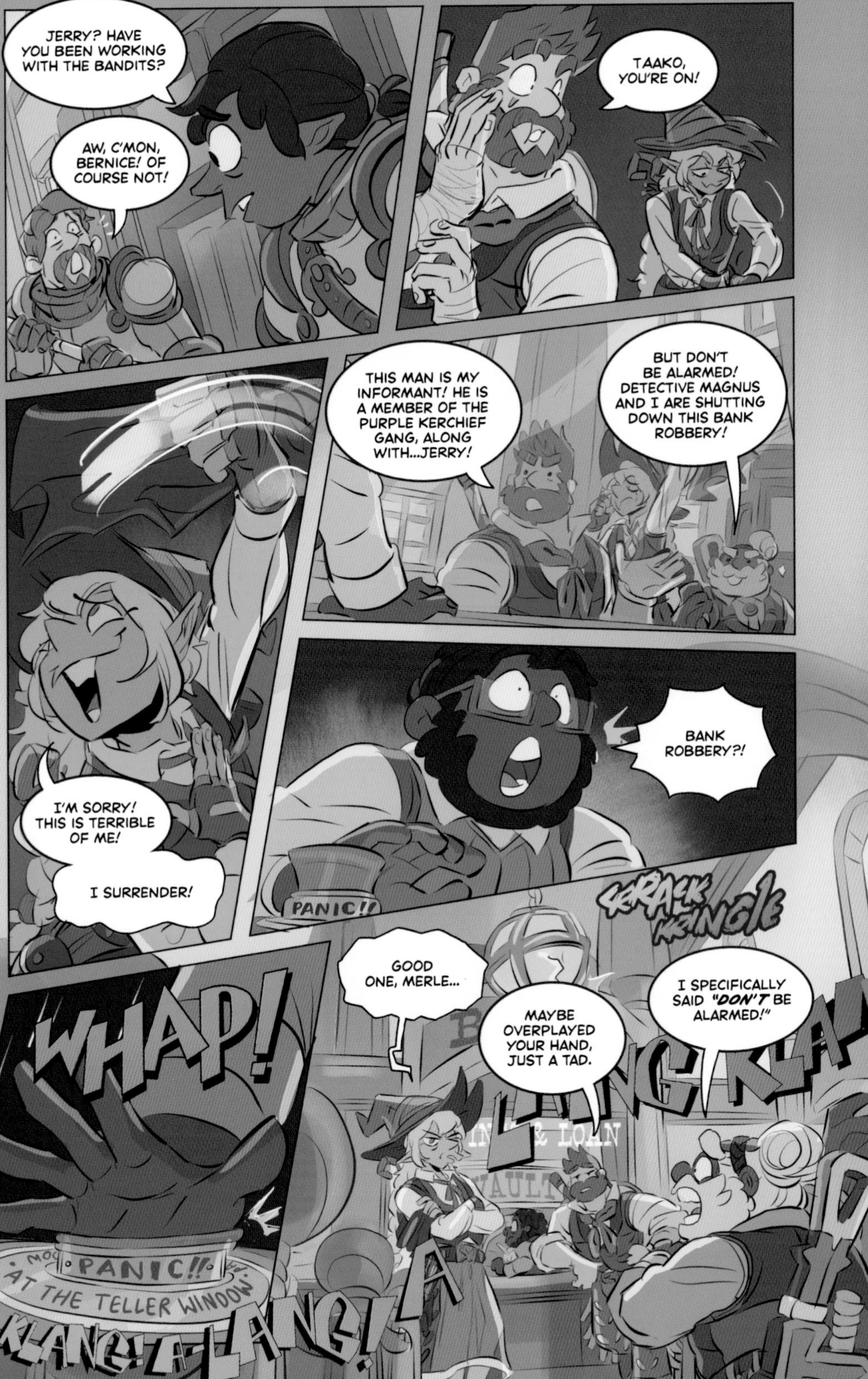
JERRY? HAVE YOU BEEN WORKING WITH THE BANDITS?
AW, C'MON, BERNICE! OF COURSE NOT!
TAAKO, YOU'RE ON!
THIS MAN IS MY INFORMANT! HE IS A MEMBER OF THE PURPLE KERCHIEF GANG, ALONG WITH...JERRY!
BUT DON'T BE ALARMED! DETECTIVE MAGNUS AND I ARE SHUTTING DOWN THIS BANK ROBBERY!
I'M SORRY! THIS IS TERRIBLE OF ME!
I SURRENDER!
BANK ROBBERY?!
PANIC!!
WHAP!
PANIC!!
AT THE TELLER WINDOW
KLANG!-A-LANG!
GOOD ONE, MERLE...
MAYBE OVERPLAYED YOUR HAND, JUST A TAD.
I SPECIFICALLY SAID "*DON'T* BE ALARMED!"
VAULT

11:47 AM

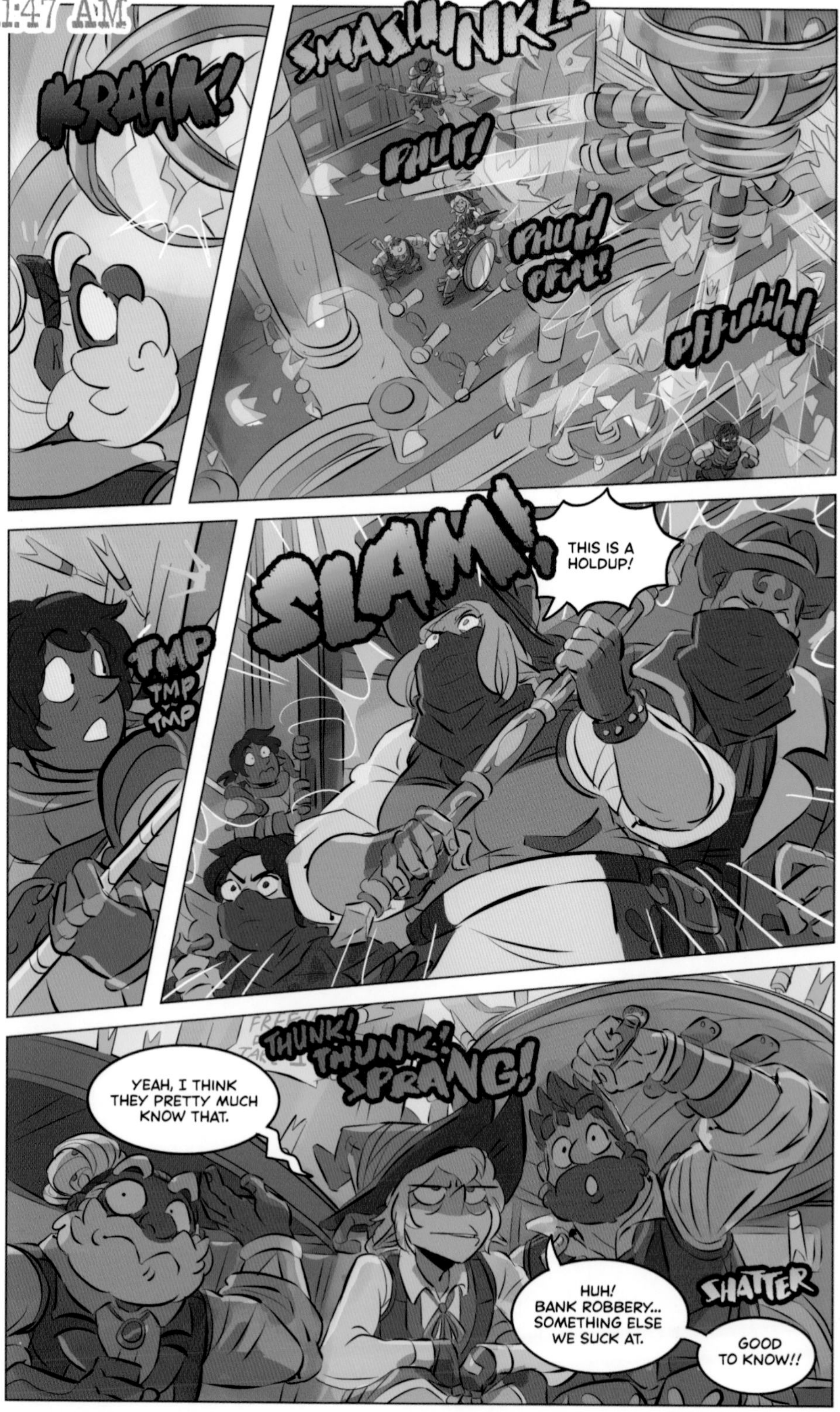
KRAAK!
SMASHINKLE
PHUT!
PHUT! PFUT!
PFFUHH!
TMP TMP TMP
SLAM!
THIS IS A HOLDUP!
YEAH, I THINK THEY PRETTY MUCH KNOW THAT.
THUNK! THUNK! SPRANG!
SHATTER
HUH! BANK ROBBERY... SOMETHING ELSE WE SUCK AT.
GOOD TO KNOW!!

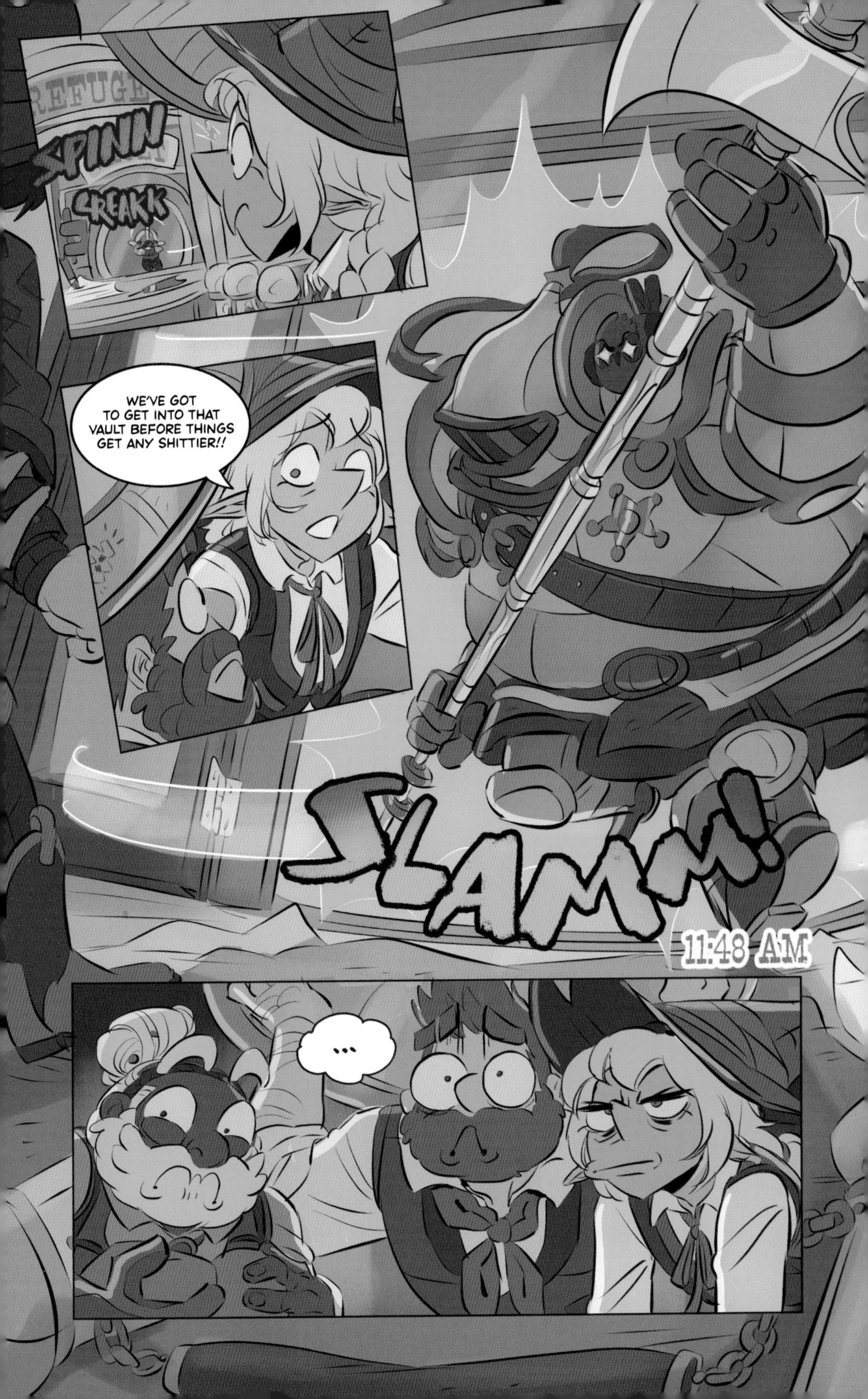
REFUGE
SPINN
CREAKK
WE'VE GOT TO GET INTO THAT VAULT BEFORE THINGS GET ANY SHITTIER!!
SLAMM!
11:48 AM
...

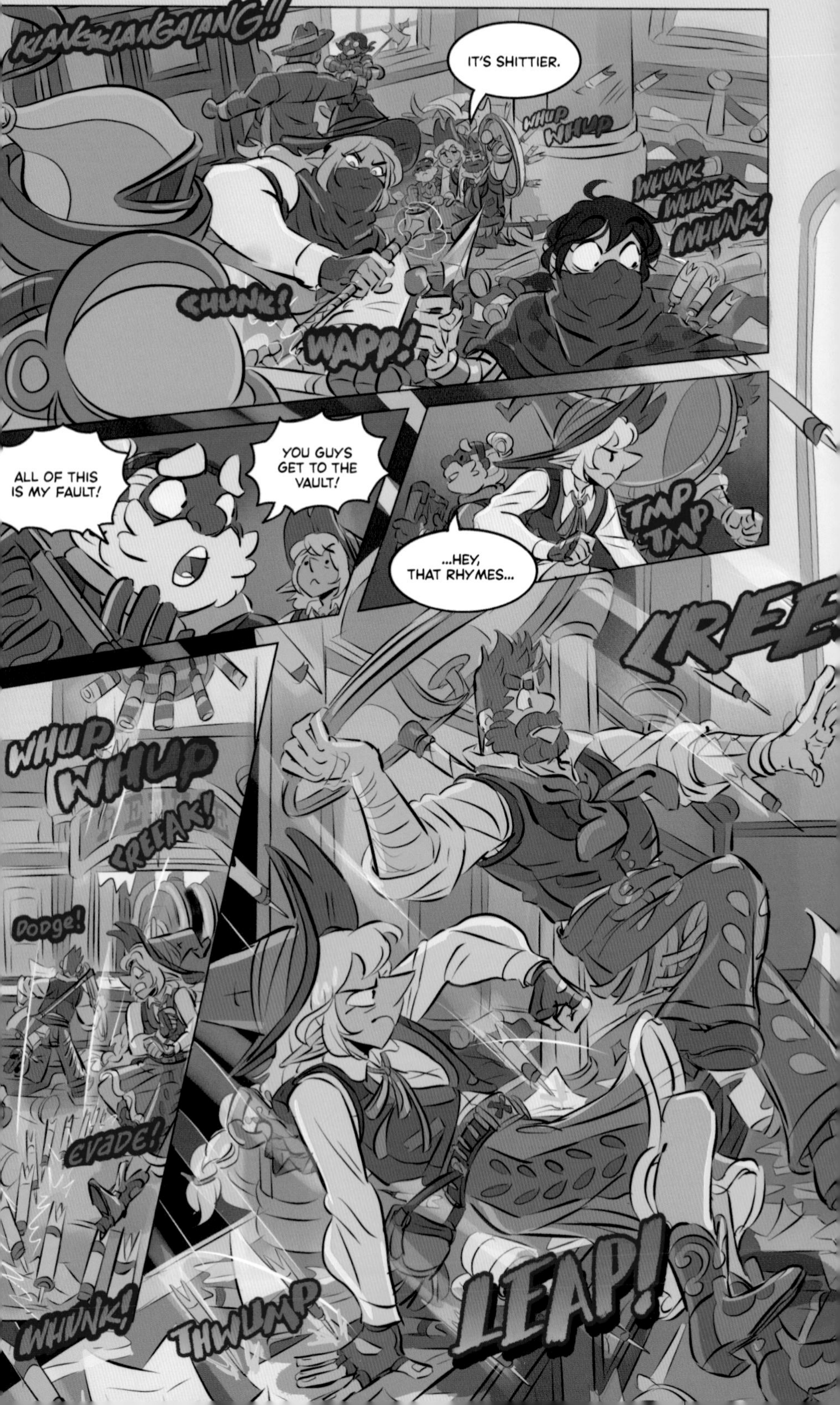
KLANGKLANGALANG!!
IT'S SHITTIER.
WHUP WHUP
WHUNK WHUNK WHUNK!
CHUNK!
WAPP!
ALL OF THIS IS MY FAULT!
YOU GUYS GET TO THE VAULT!
...HEY, THAT RHYMES...
TMP TMP
KREE
WHUP WHUP
KREEAK!
Dodge!
EVADE!
WHUNK!
THWUMP
LEAP!

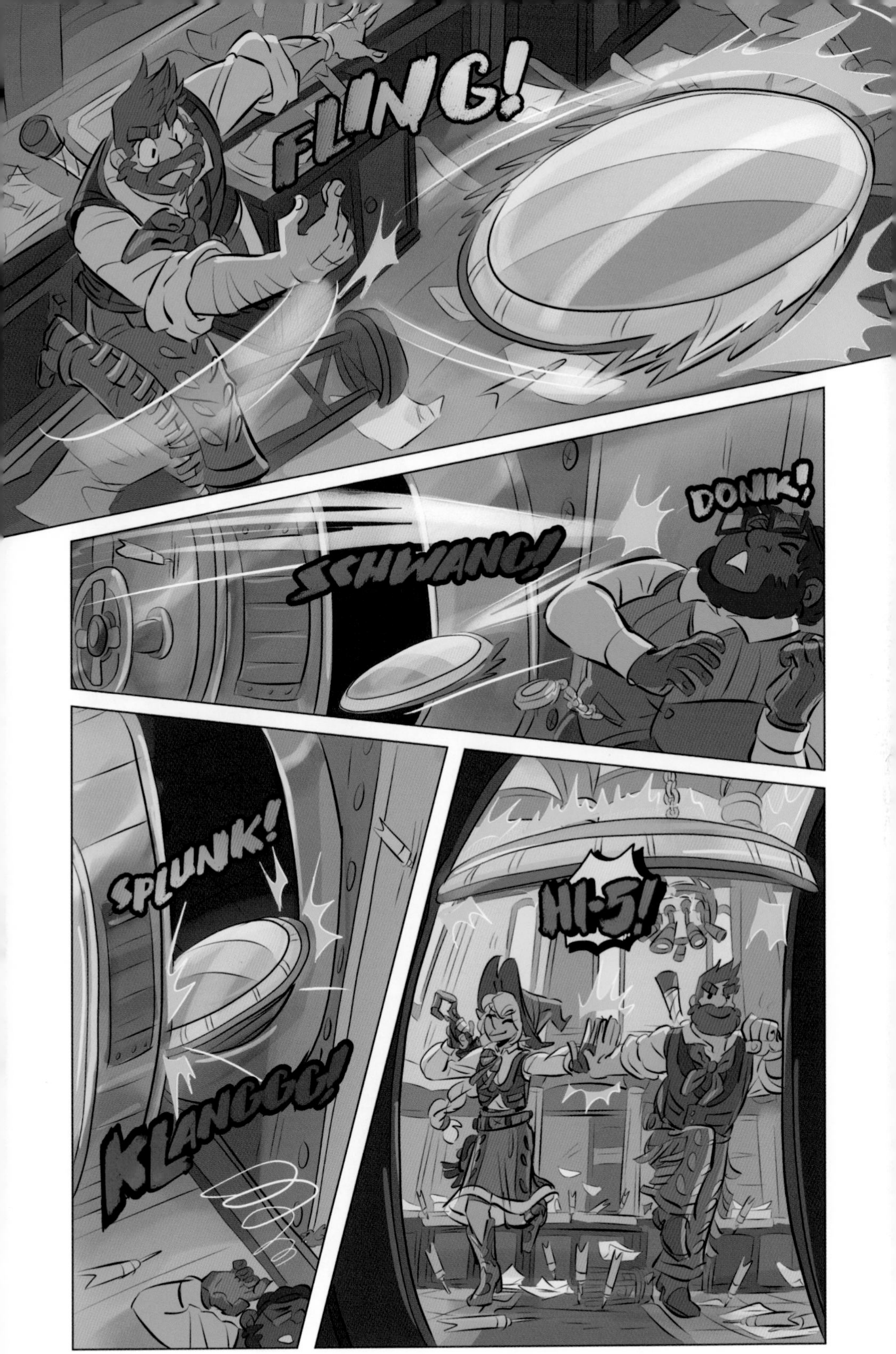
FLING!
SSHWANG!
DONK!
SPLUNK!
KLANGGG!
HI-5!

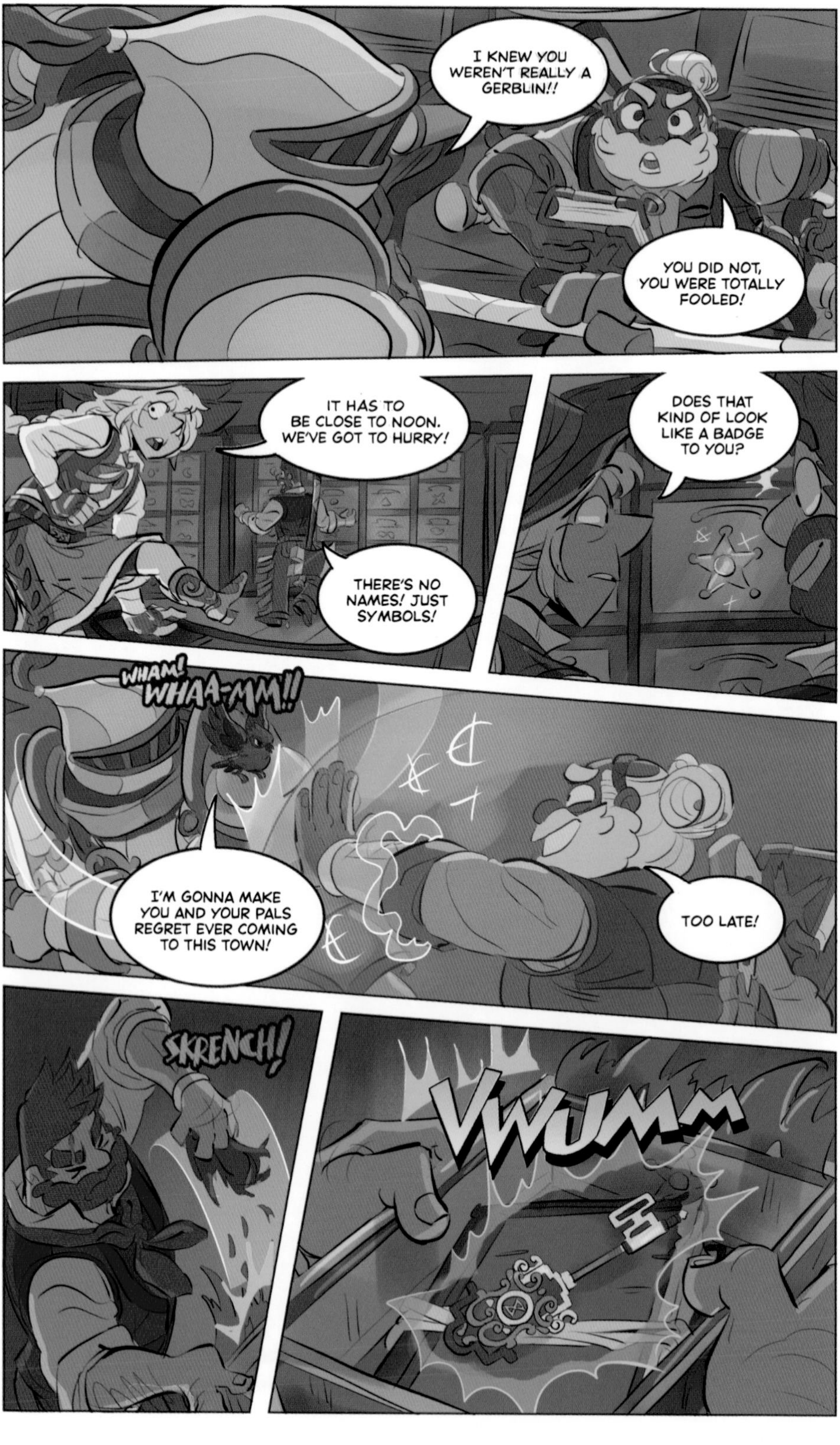
I KNEW YOU WEREN'T REALLY A GERBLIN!!
YOU DID NOT, YOU WERE TOTALLY FOOLED!
IT HAS TO BE CLOSE TO NOON. WE'VE GOT TO HURRY!
THERE'S NO NAMES! JUST SYMBOLS!
DOES THAT KIND OF LOOK LIKE A BADGE TO YOU?
WHAM! WHAA-MM!!
I'M GONNA MAKE YOU AND YOUR PALS REGRET EVER COMING TO THIS TOWN!
TOO LATE!
SKRENCH!
VWUMM

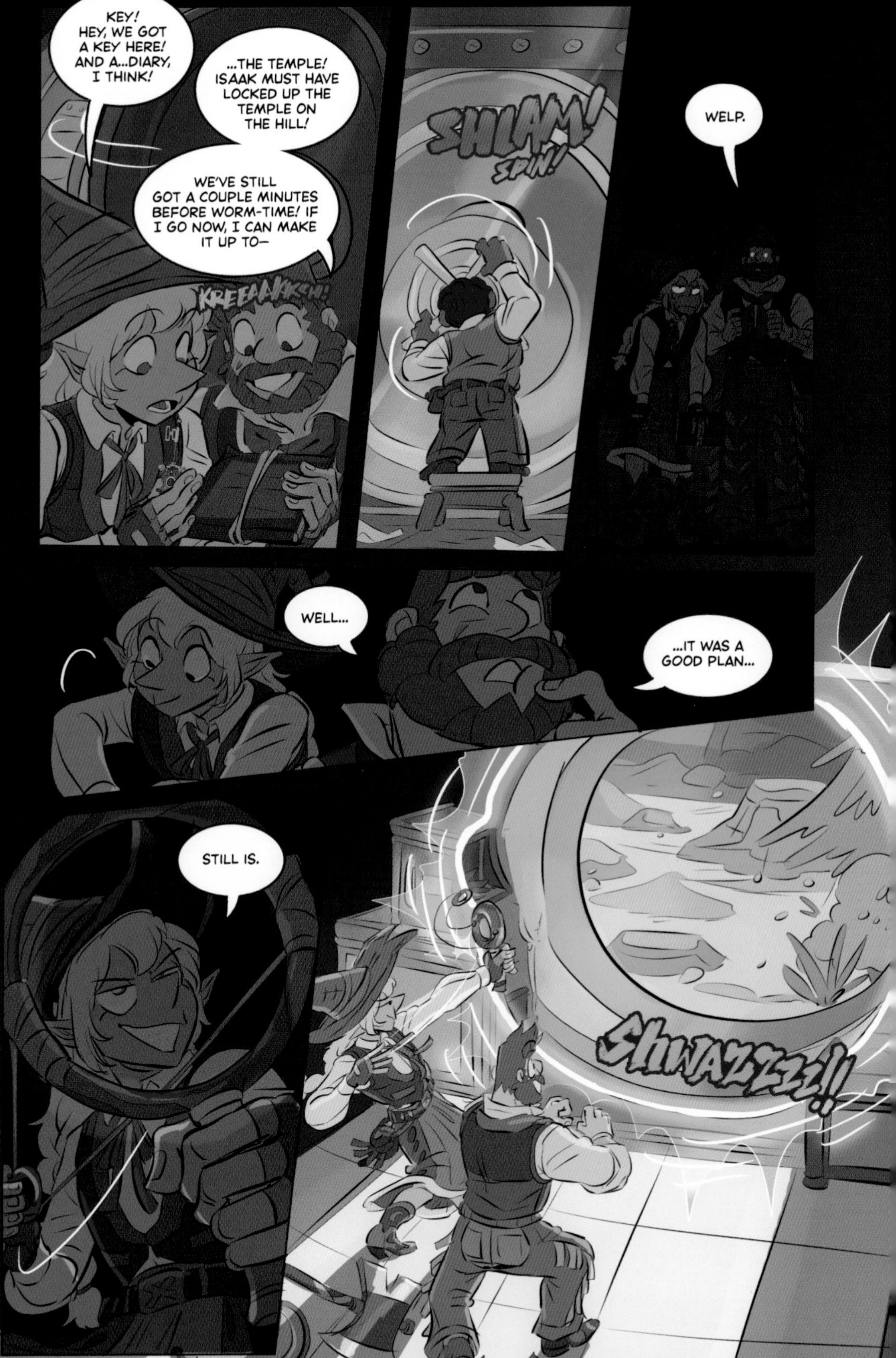
KEY! HEY, WE GOT A KEY HERE! AND A...DIARY, I THINK!
...THE TEMPLE! ISAAK MUST HAVE LOCKED UP THE TEMPLE ON THE HILL!
WE'VE STILL GOT A COUPLE MINUTES BEFORE WORM-TIME! IF I GO NOW, I CAN MAKE IT UP TO—
KREEAAKKSH!
SHLAM!
SPIN!
WELP.
WELL...
...IT WAS A GOOD PLAN...
STILL IS.
SHWAZZZZ!!

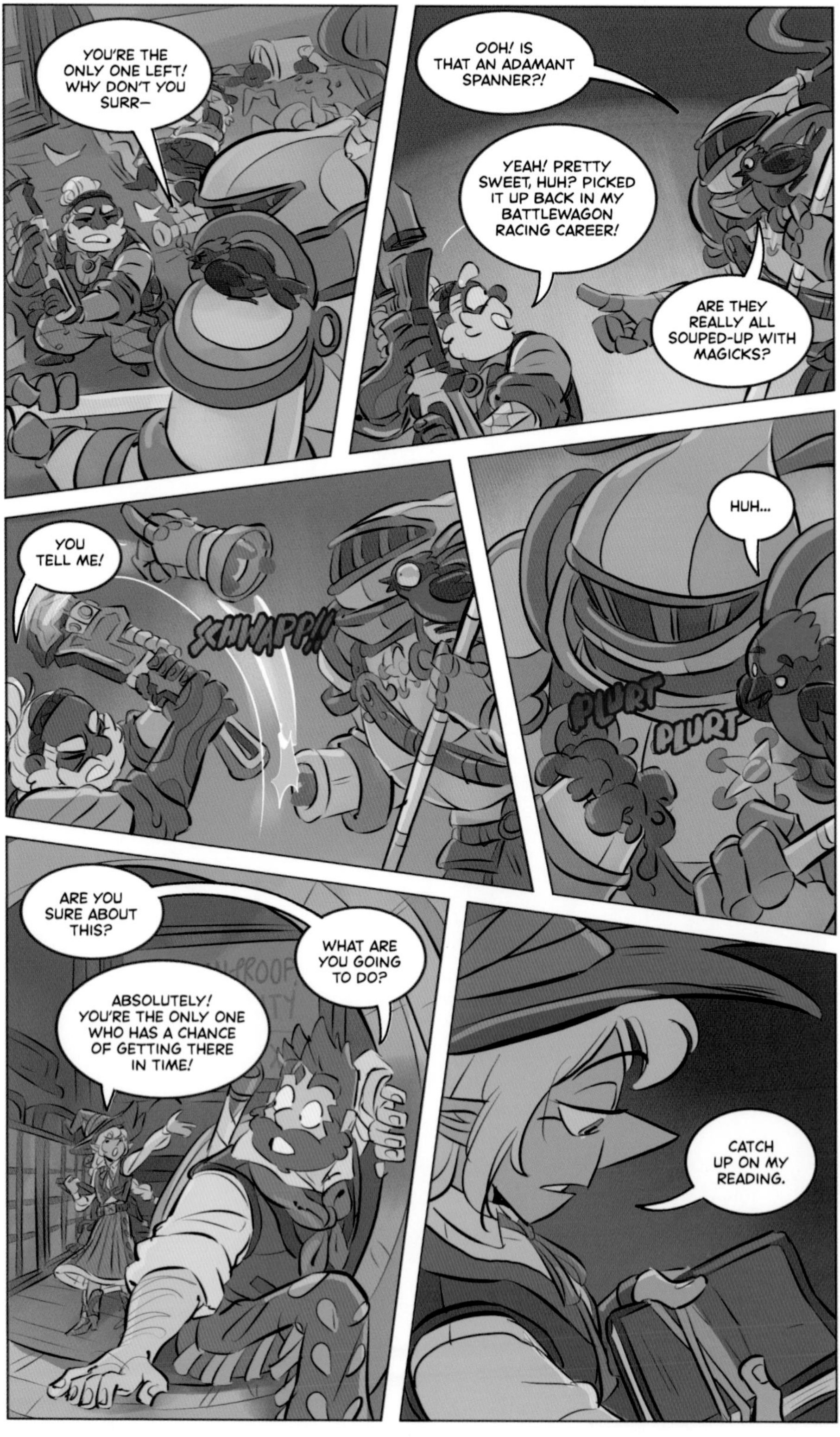
YOU'RE THE ONLY ONE LEFT! WHY DON'T YOU SURR—
OOH! IS THAT AN ADAMANT SPANNER?!
YEAH! PRETTY SWEET, HUH? PICKED IT UP BACK IN MY BATTLEWAGON RACING CAREER!
ARE THEY REALLY ALL SOUPED-UP WITH MAGICKS?
YOU TELL ME!
SCHWAPP!!
HUH...
PLURT
PLURT
ARE YOU SURE ABOUT THIS?
WHAT ARE YOU GOING TO DO?
ABSOLUTELY! YOU'RE THE ONLY ONE WHO HAS A CHANCE OF GETTING THERE IN TIME!
CATCH UP ON MY READING.

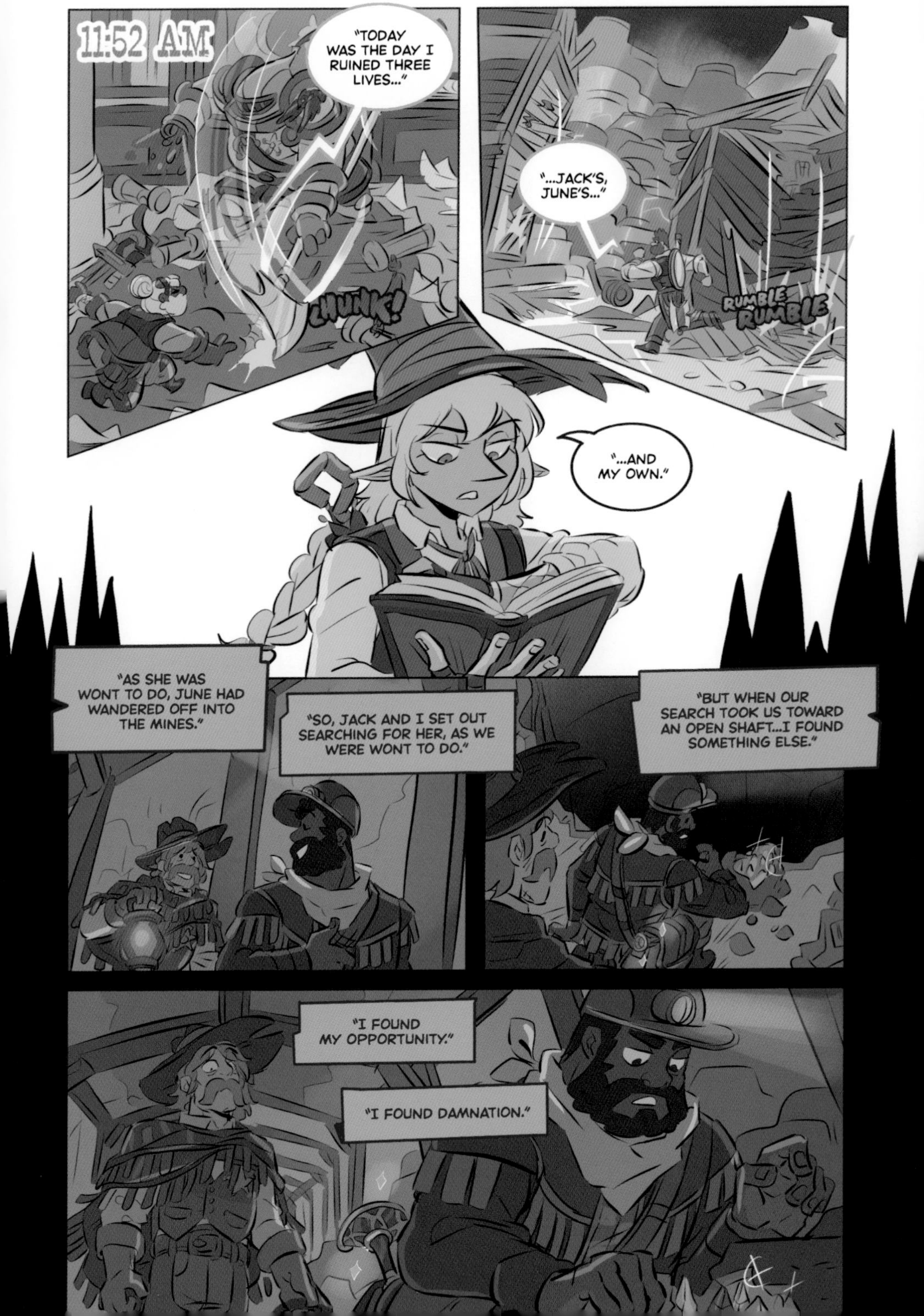
11:52 AM
"TODAY WAS THE DAY I RUINED THREE LIVES..."
CHUNK!
"...JACK'S, JUNE'S..."
RUMBLE RUMBLE
"...AND MY OWN."
"AS SHE WAS WONT TO DO, JUNE HAD WANDERED OFF INTO THE MINES."
"SO, JACK AND I SET OUT SEARCHING FOR HER, AS WE WERE WONT TO DO."
"BUT WHEN OUR SEARCH TOOK US TOWARD AN OPEN SHAFT...I FOUND SOMETHING ELSE."
"I FOUND MY OPPORTUNITY."
"I FOUND DAMNATION."

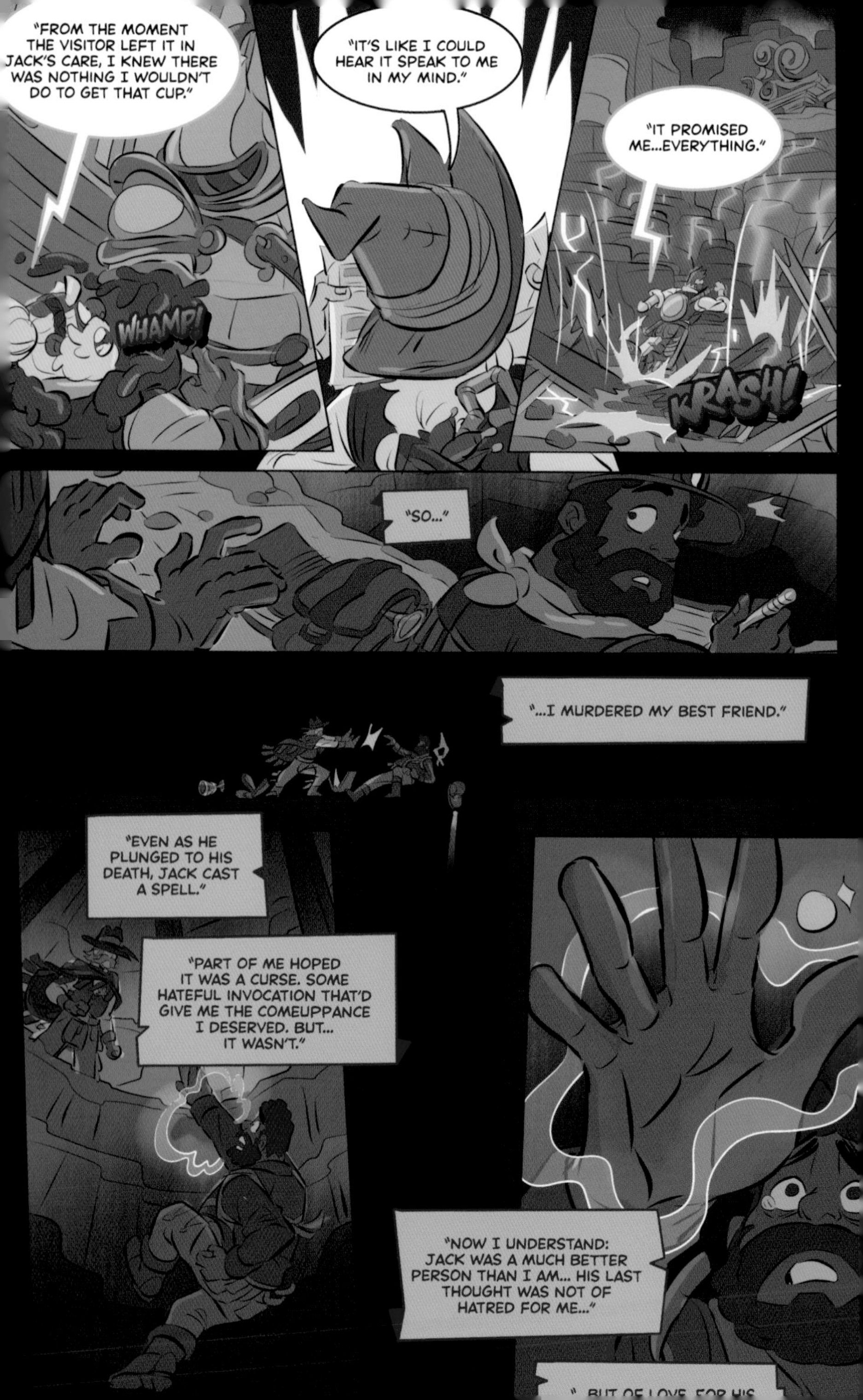
"FROM THE MOMENT THE VISITOR LEFT IT IN JACK'S CARE, I KNEW THERE WAS NOTHING I WOULDN'T DO TO GET THAT CUP."
WHAMP!
"IT'S LIKE I COULD HEAR IT SPEAK TO ME IN MY MIND."
"IT PROMISED ME...EVERYTHING."
KRASH!
"SO..."
"...I MURDERED MY BEST FRIEND."
"EVEN AS HE PLUNGED TO HIS DEATH, JACK CAST A SPELL."
"PART OF ME HOPED IT WAS A CURSE. SOME HATEFUL INVOCATION THAT'D GIVE ME THE COMEUPPANCE I DESERVED. BUT... IT WASN'T."
"NOW I UNDERSTAND: JACK WAS A MUCH BETTER PERSON THAN I AM... HIS LAST THOUGHT WAS NOT OF HATRED FOR ME..."
"...BUT OF LOVE FOR HIS

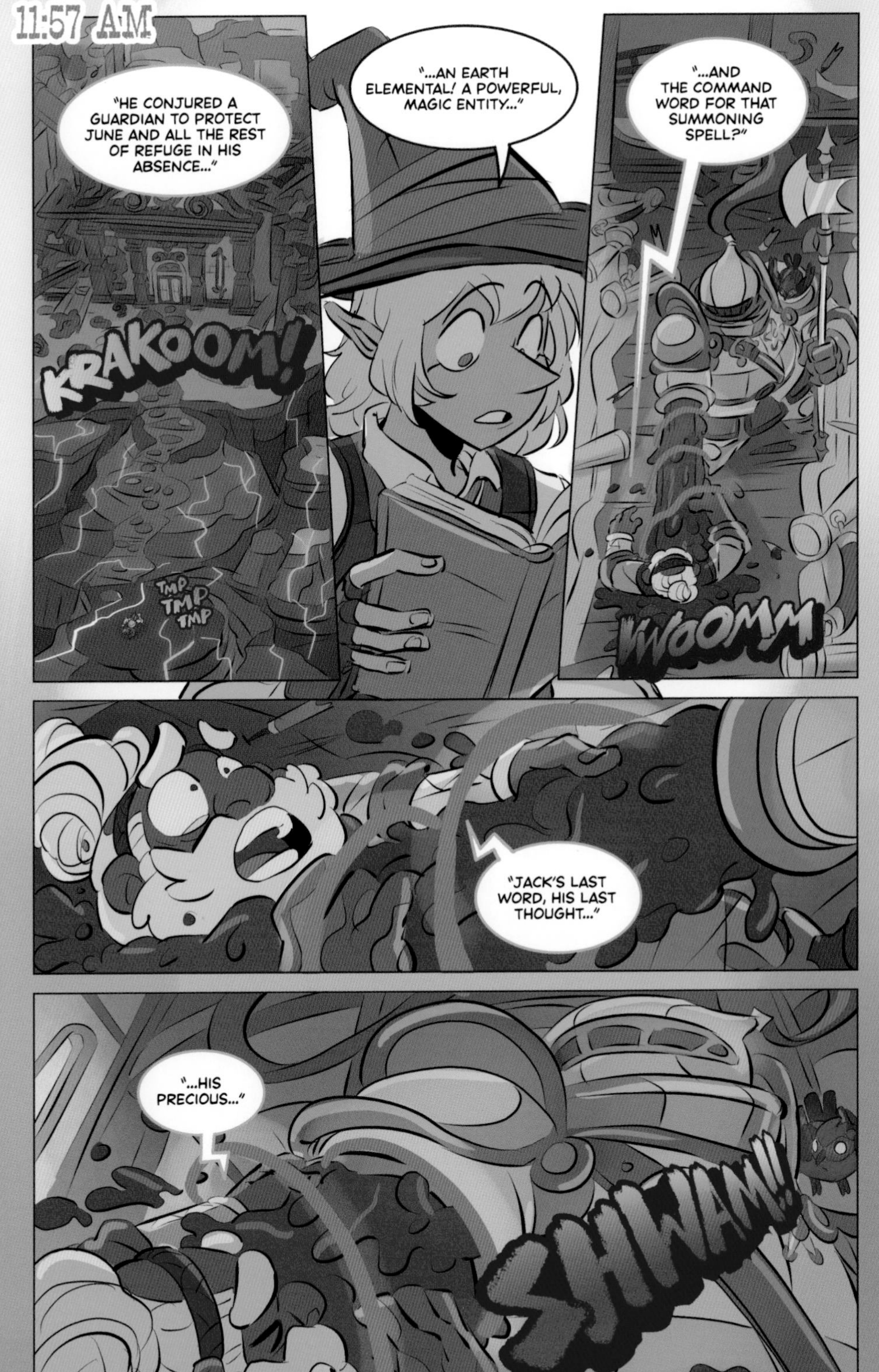
11:57 AM
"HE CONJURED A GUARDIAN TO PROTECT JUNE AND ALL THE REST OF REFUGE IN HIS ABSENCE..."
KRAKOOM!
TMP TMP TMP
"...AN EARTH ELEMENTAL! A POWERFUL, MAGIC ENTITY..."
"...AND THE COMMAND WORD FOR THAT SUMMONING SPELL?"
WOOMM
"JACK'S LAST WORD, HIS LAST THOUGHT..."
"...HIS PRECIOUS..."
SHWAM!

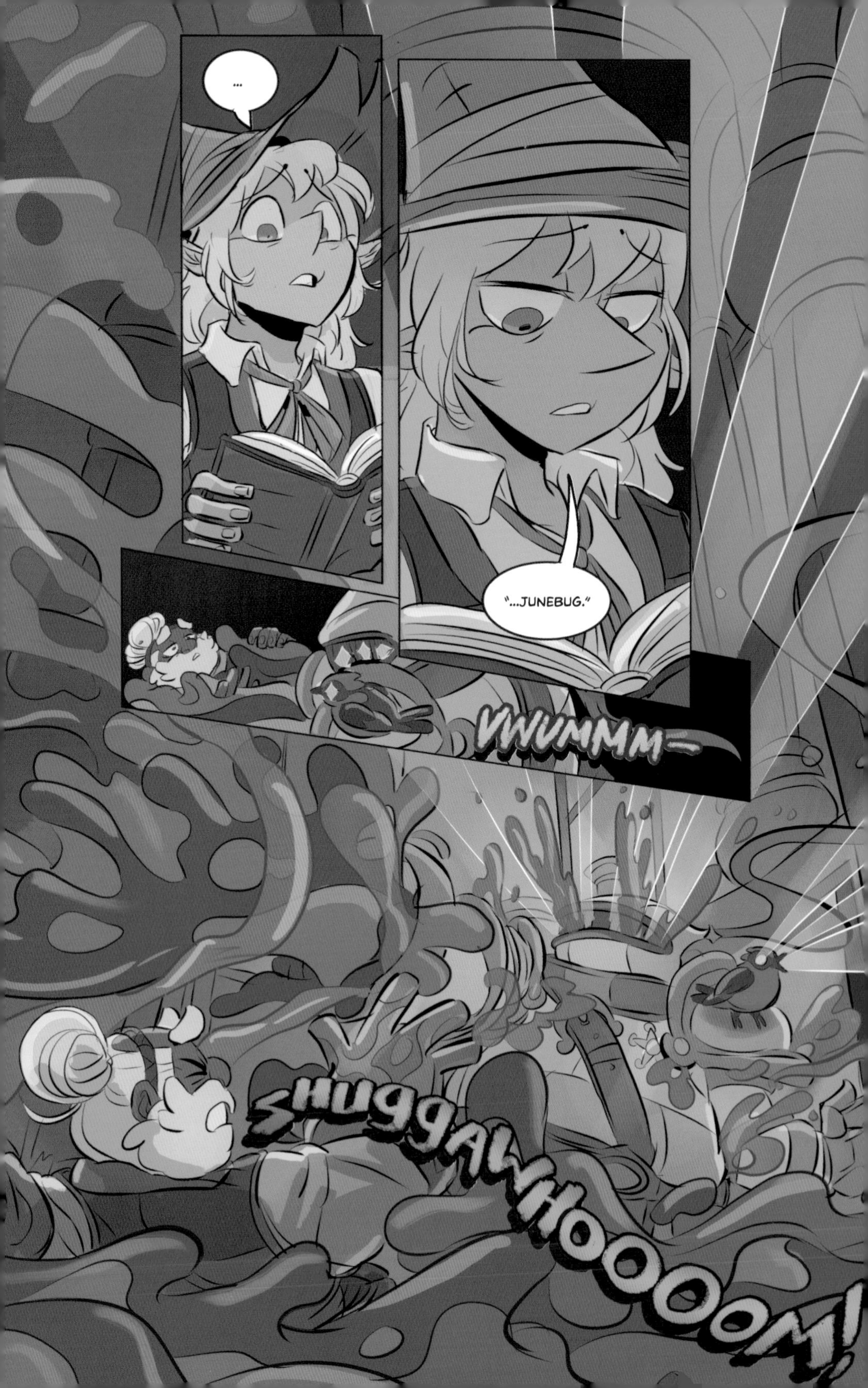
...
"...JUNEBUG."
VWUMMM—
SHUGGAWHOOOOOM!

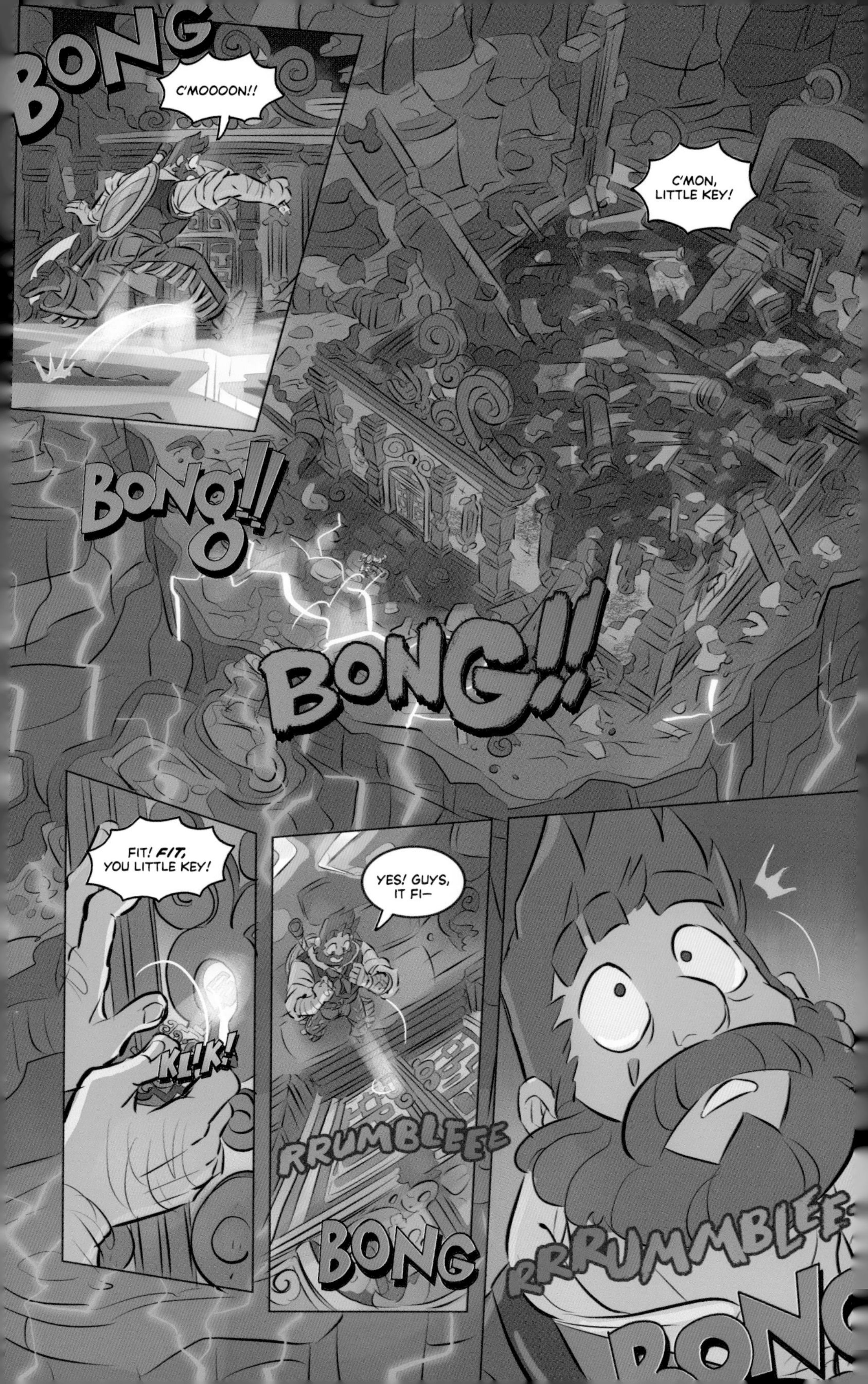
BONG
C'MOOOON!!
C'MON, LITTLE KEY!
BONG!!
BONG!!
FIT! FIT, YOU LITTLE KEY!
KL!K!
YES! GUYS, IT FI—
RRUMBLEEE
BONG
RRRUMMBLEE

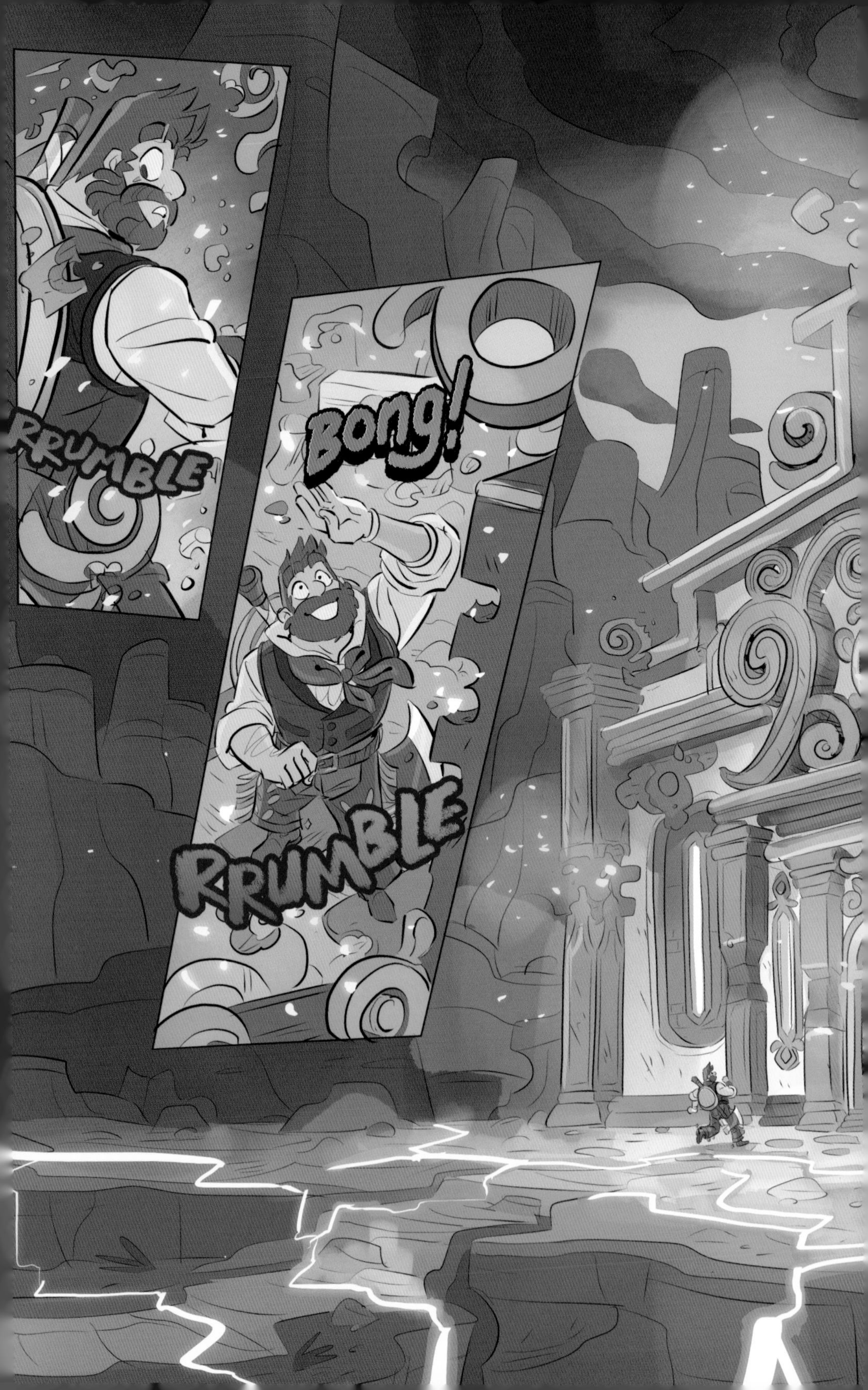
RRUMBLE
BONG!
RRUMBLE

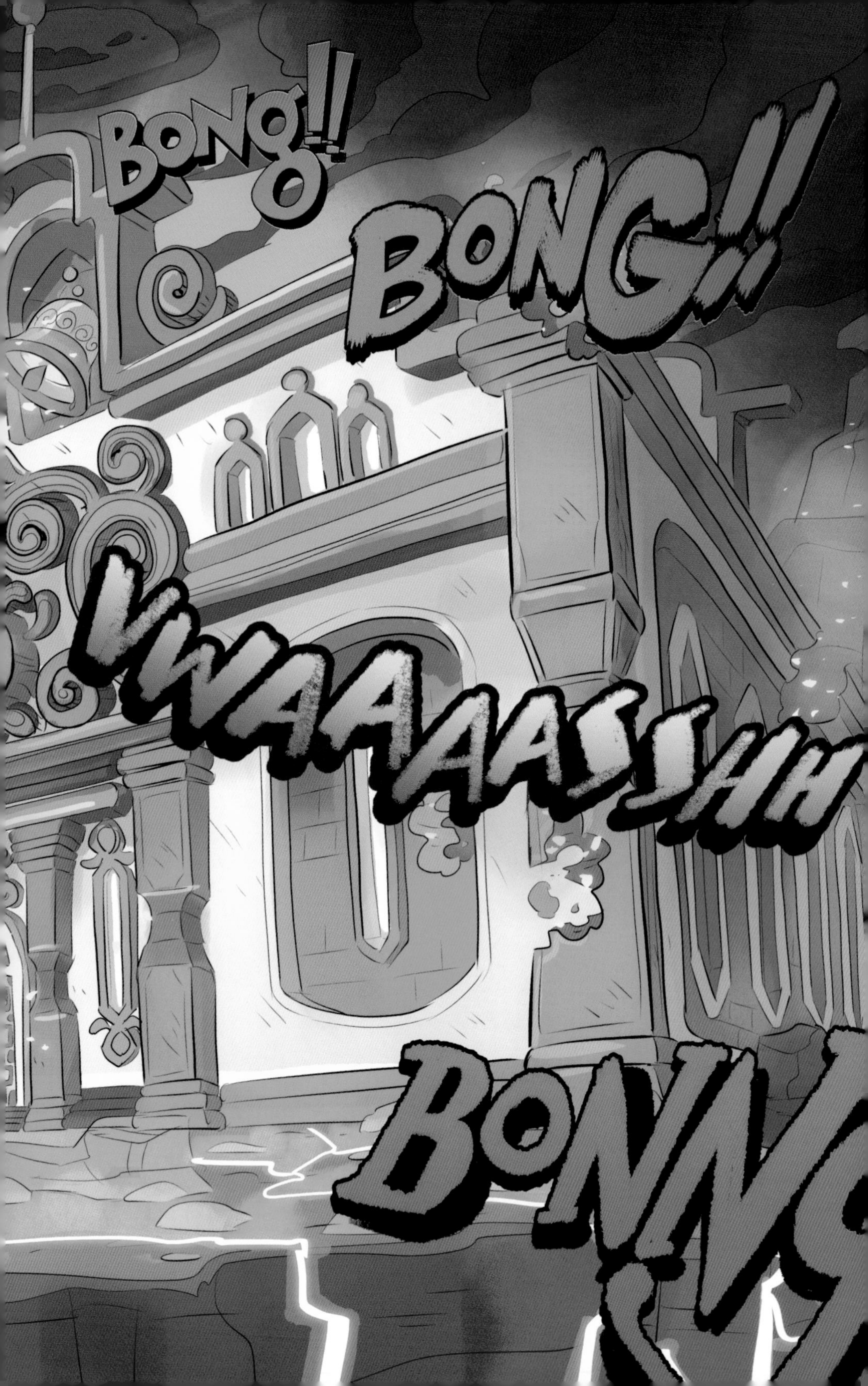
BONG!!
BONG!!
VWAAAASHH
BONN

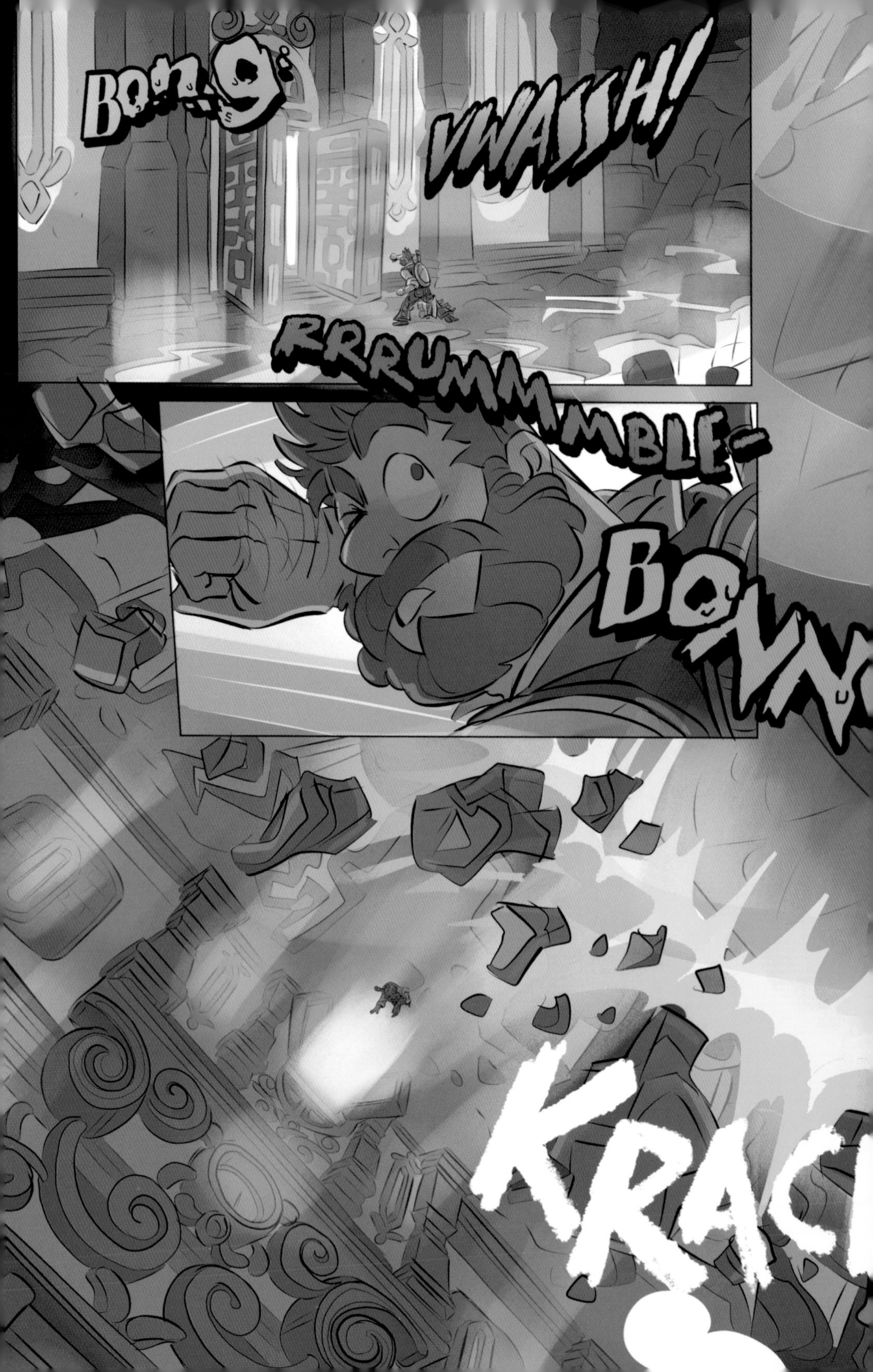
BONG
VWASSH!
RRRUMMMMBLE-
BO
KRAC

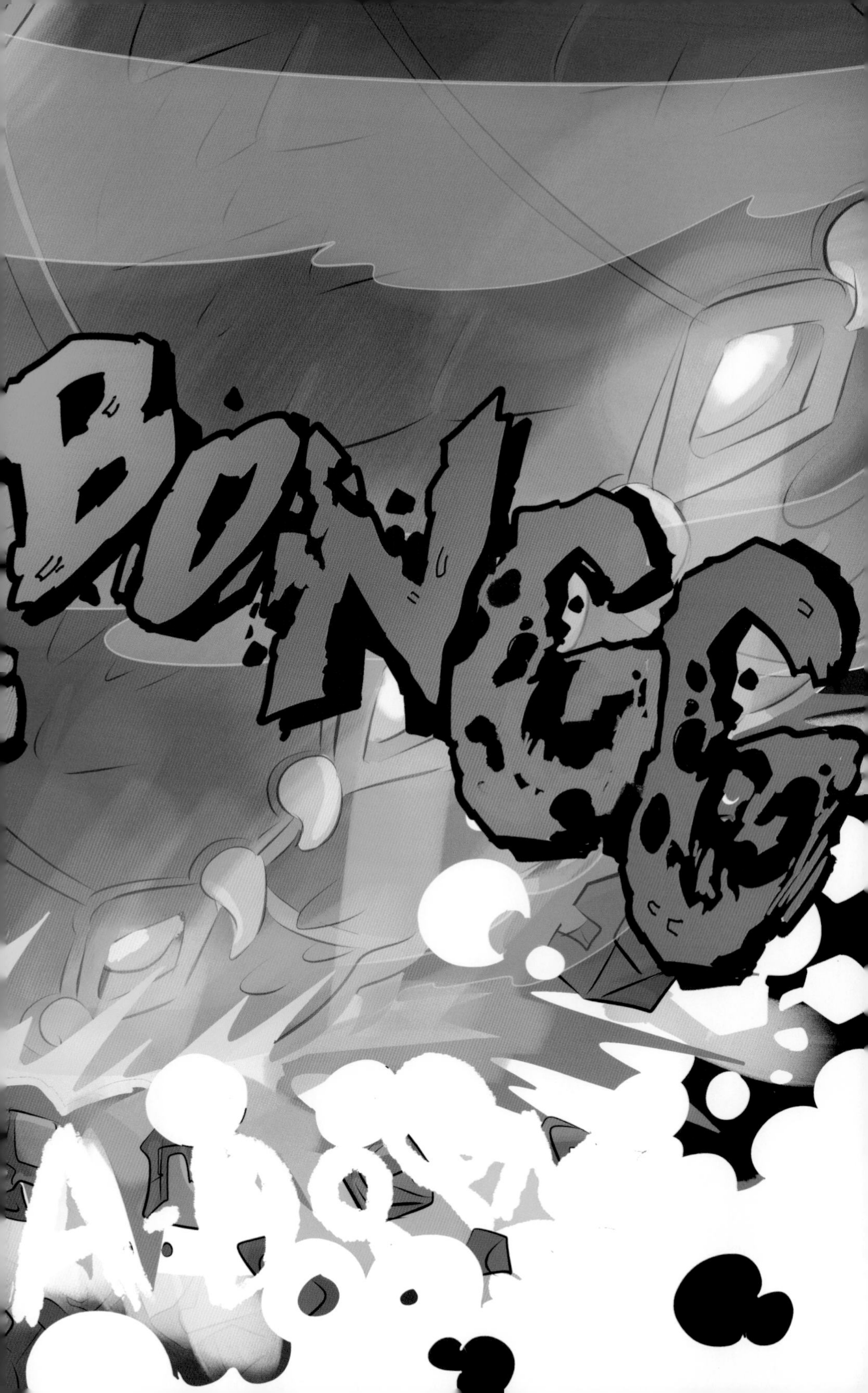
BONGG

Chapter
110

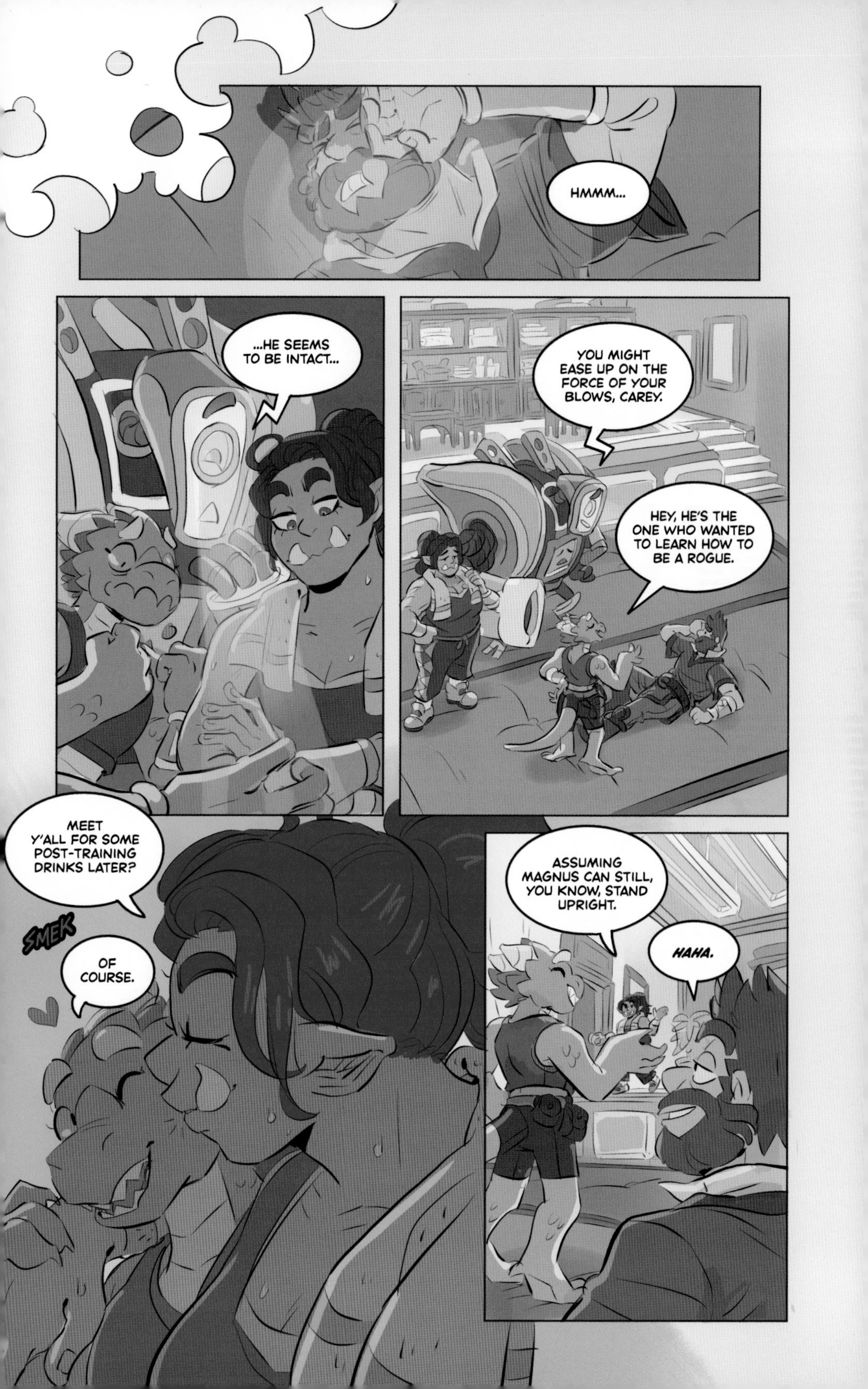
HMMM...
...HE SEEMS TO BE INTACT...
YOU MIGHT EASE UP ON THE FORCE OF YOUR BLOWS, CAREY.
HEY, HE'S THE ONE WHO WANTED TO LEARN HOW TO BE A ROGUE.
MEET Y'ALL FOR SOME POST-TRAINING DRINKS LATER?
SMEK
OF COURSE.
ASSUMING MAGNUS CAN STILL, YOU KNOW, STAND UPRIGHT.
HAHA.

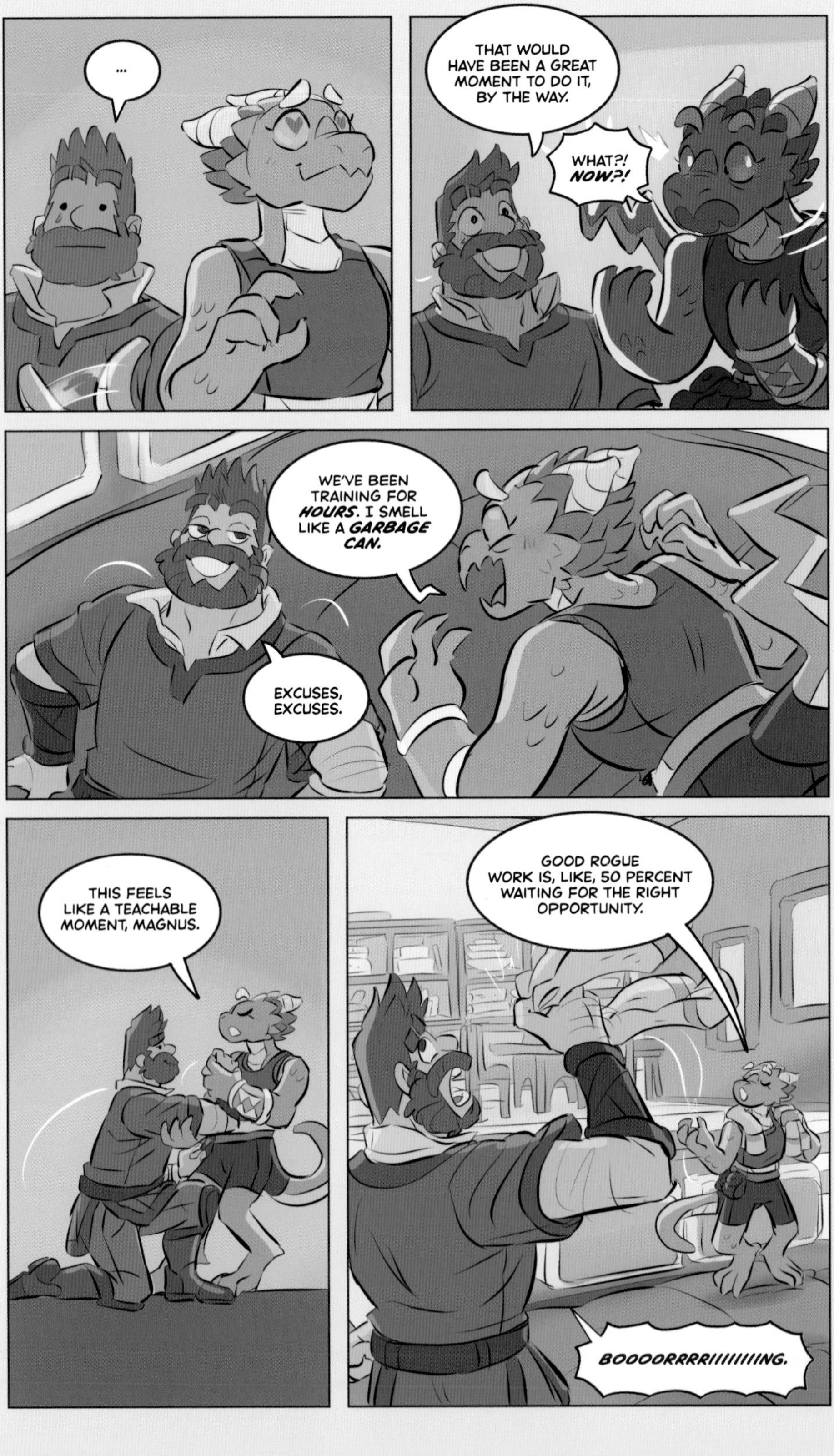
...
THAT WOULD HAVE BEEN A GREAT MOMENT TO DO IT, BY THE WAY.
WHAT?! **NOW?!**
WE'VE BEEN TRAINING FOR ***HOURS***. I SMELL LIKE A ***GARBAGE CAN.***
EXCUSES, EXCUSES.
THIS FEELS LIKE A TEACHABLE MOMENT, MAGNUS.
GOOD ROGUE WORK IS, LIKE, 50 PERCENT WAITING FOR THE RIGHT OPPORTUNITY.
BOOOORRRRIIIIIIIING.

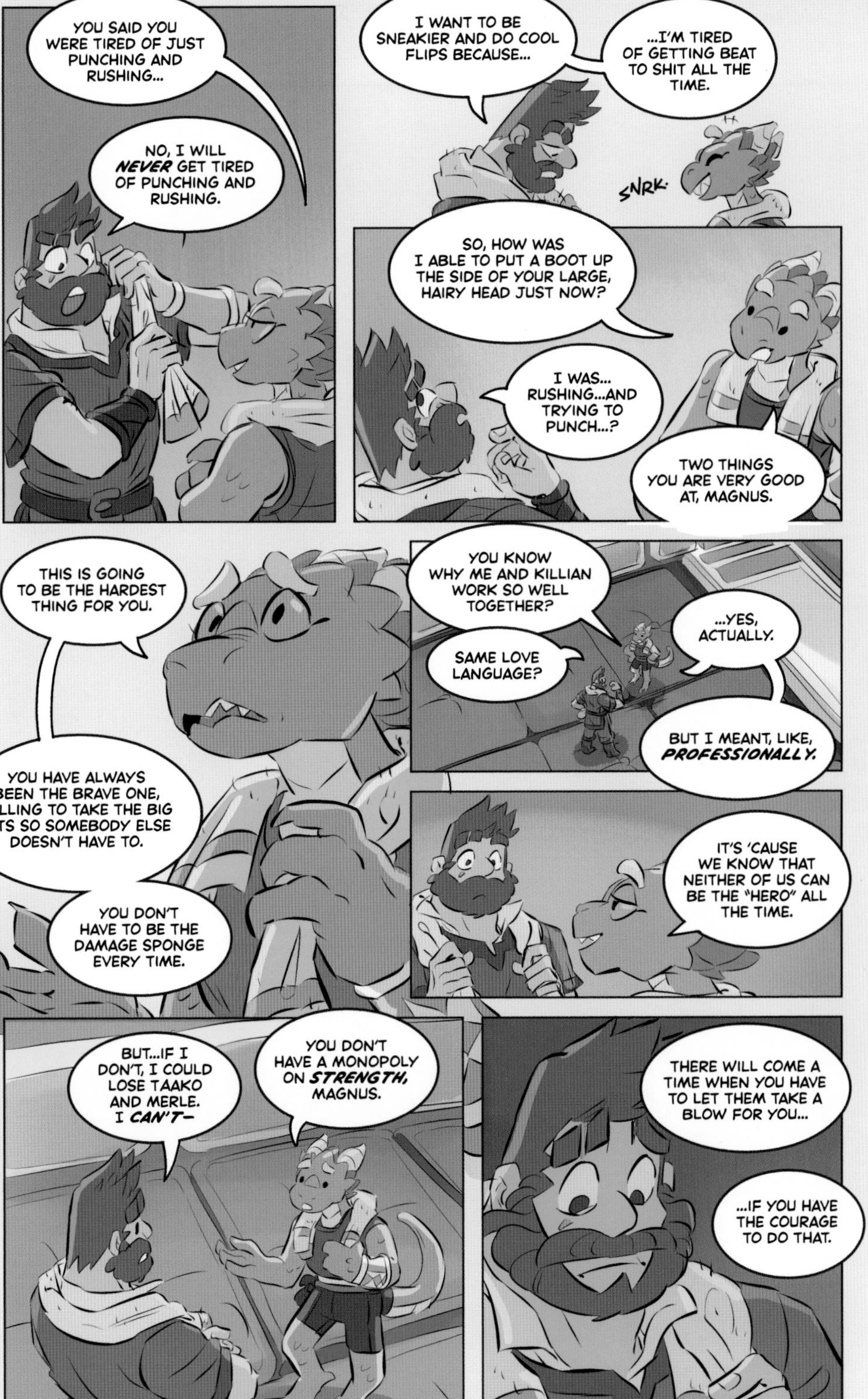
YOU SAID YOU WERE TIRED OF JUST PUNCHING AND RUSHING...
NO, I WILL *NEVER* GET TIRED OF PUNCHING AND RUSHING.
I WANT TO BE SNEAKIER AND DO COOL FLIPS BECAUSE...
...I'M TIRED OF GETTING BEAT TO SHIT ALL THE TIME.
SNRK
SO, HOW WAS I ABLE TO PUT A BOOT UP THE SIDE OF YOUR LARGE, HAIRY HEAD JUST NOW?
I WAS... RUSHING...AND TRYING TO PUNCH...?
TWO THINGS YOU ARE VERY GOOD AT, MAGNUS.
THIS IS GOING TO BE THE HARDEST THING FOR YOU.
YOU HAVE ALWAYS BEEN THE BRAVE ONE, WILLING TO TAKE THE BIG HITS SO SOMEBODY ELSE DOESN'T HAVE TO.
YOU DON'T HAVE TO BE THE DAMAGE SPONGE EVERY TIME.
YOU KNOW WHY ME AND KILLIAN WORK SO WELL TOGETHER?
SAME LOVE LANGUAGE?
...YES, ACTUALLY.
BUT I MEANT, LIKE, ***PROFESSIONALLY.***
IT'S 'CAUSE WE KNOW THAT NEITHER OF US CAN BE THE "HERO" ALL THE TIME.
BUT...IF I DON'T, I COULD LOSE TAAKO AND MERLE. I *CAN'T—*
YOU DON'T HAVE A MONOPOLY ON *STRENGTH,* MAGNUS.
THERE WILL COME A TIME WHEN YOU HAVE TO LET THEM TAKE A BLOW FOR YOU...
...IF YOU HAVE THE COURAGE TO DO THAT.

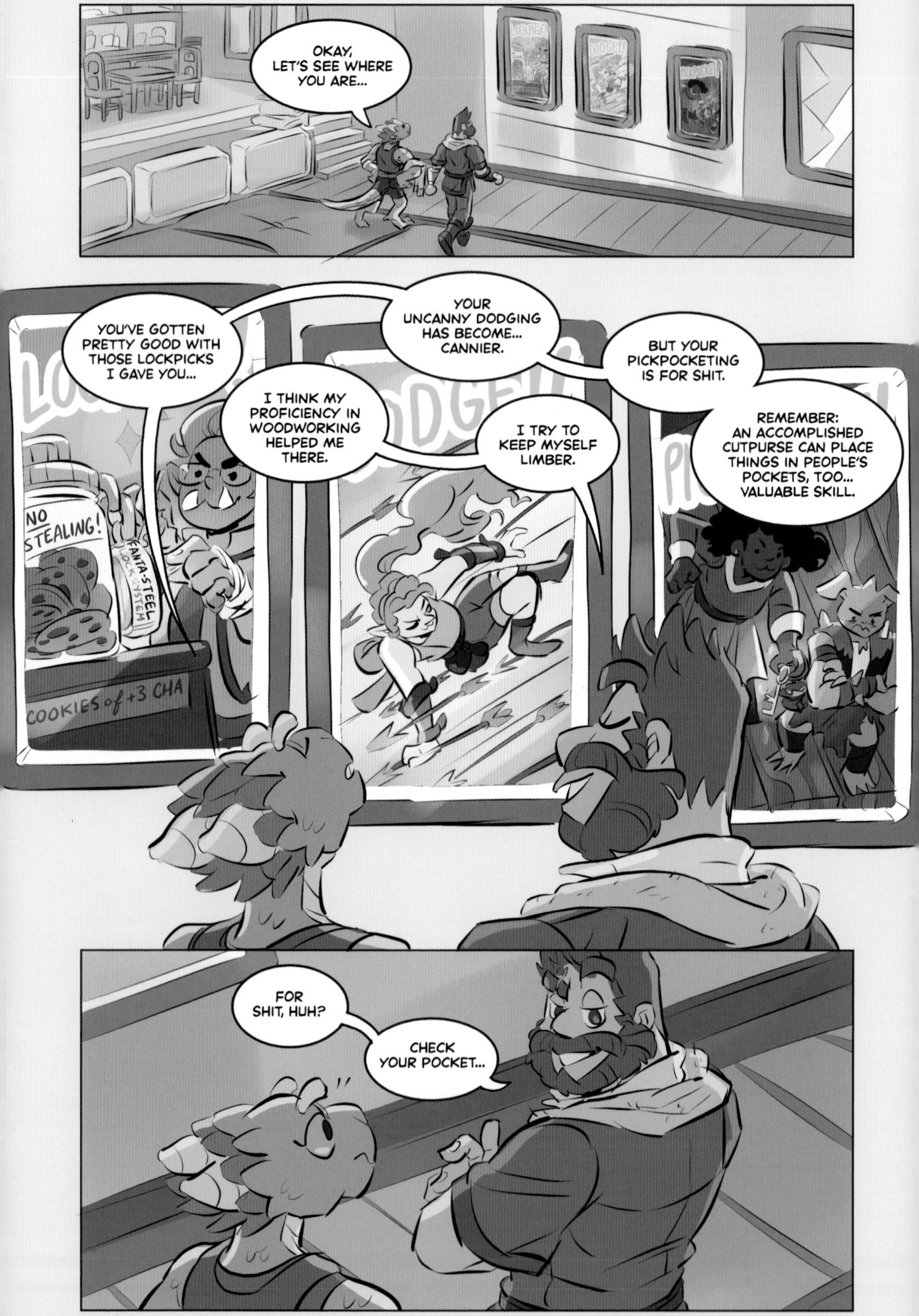
OKAY, LET'S SEE WHERE YOU ARE...
LOCKPICK!
DODGE!!
PICKPOCKET!
YOU'VE GOTTEN PRETTY GOOD WITH THOSE LOCKPICKS I GAVE YOU...
I THINK MY PROFICIENCY IN WOODWORKING HELPED ME THERE.
YOUR UNCANNY DODGING HAS BECOME... CANNIER.
I TRY TO KEEP MYSELF LIMBER.
BUT YOUR PICKPOCKETING IS FOR SHIT.
REMEMBER: AN ACCOMPLISHED CUTPURSE CAN PLACE THINGS IN PEOPLE'S POCKETS, TOO... VALUABLE SKILL.
NO STEALING!
FANTA-STEEL LOCK SYSTEM
COOKIES of +3 CHA
FOR SHIT, HUH?
CHECK YOUR POCKET...

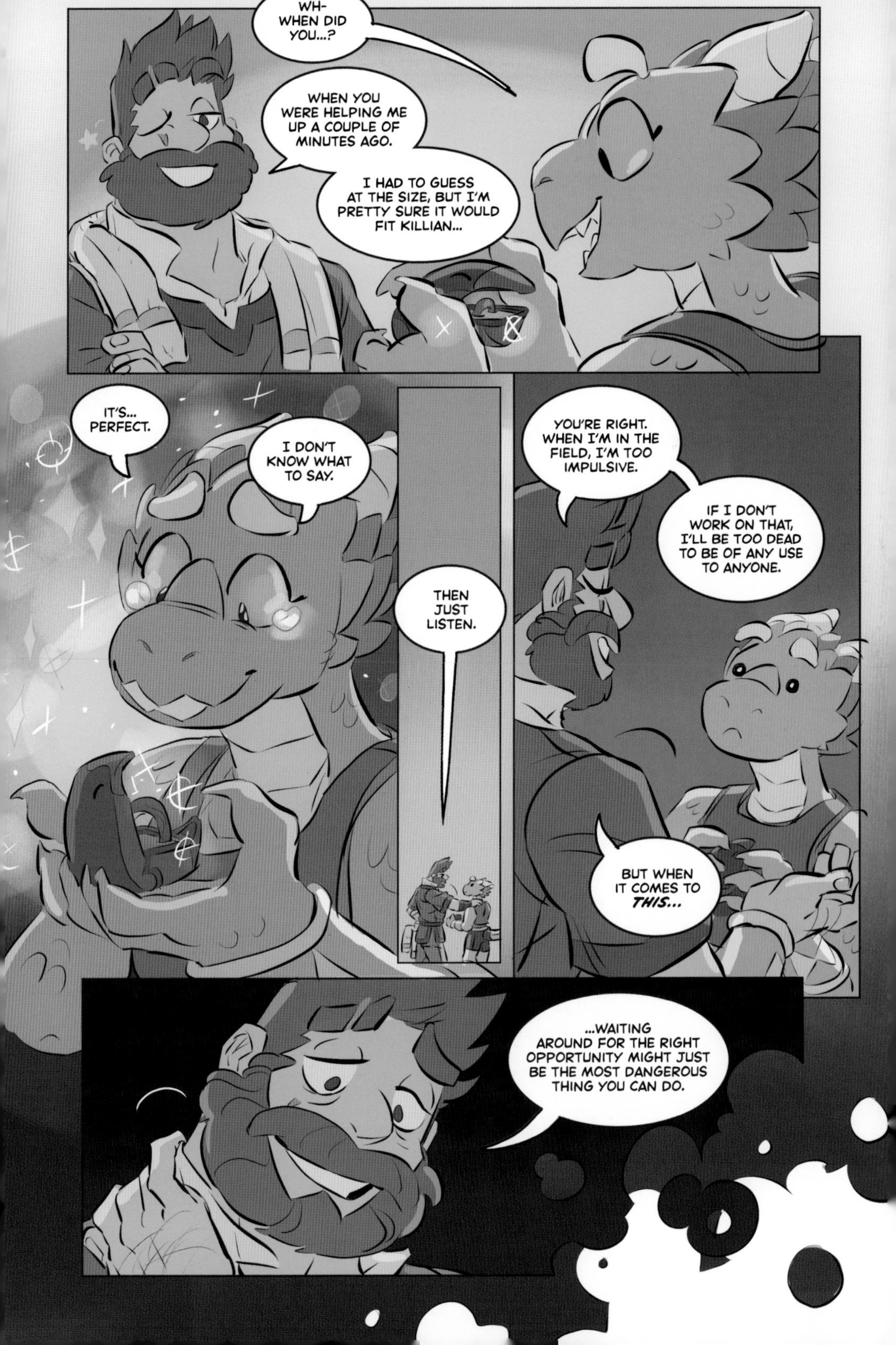
WH- WHEN DID YOU...?
WHEN YOU WERE HELPING ME UP A COUPLE OF MINUTES AGO.
I HAD TO GUESS AT THE SIZE, BUT I'M PRETTY SURE IT WOULD FIT KILLIAN...
IT'S... PERFECT.
I DON'T KNOW WHAT TO SAY.
THEN JUST LISTEN.
YOU'RE RIGHT. WHEN I'M IN THE FIELD, I'M TOO IMPULSIVE.
IF I DON'T WORK ON THAT, I'LL BE TOO DEAD TO BE OF ANY USE TO ANYONE.
BUT WHEN IT COMES TO *THIS...*
...WAITING AROUND FOR THE RIGHT OPPORTUNITY MIGHT JUST BE THE MOST DANGEROUS THING YOU CAN DO.

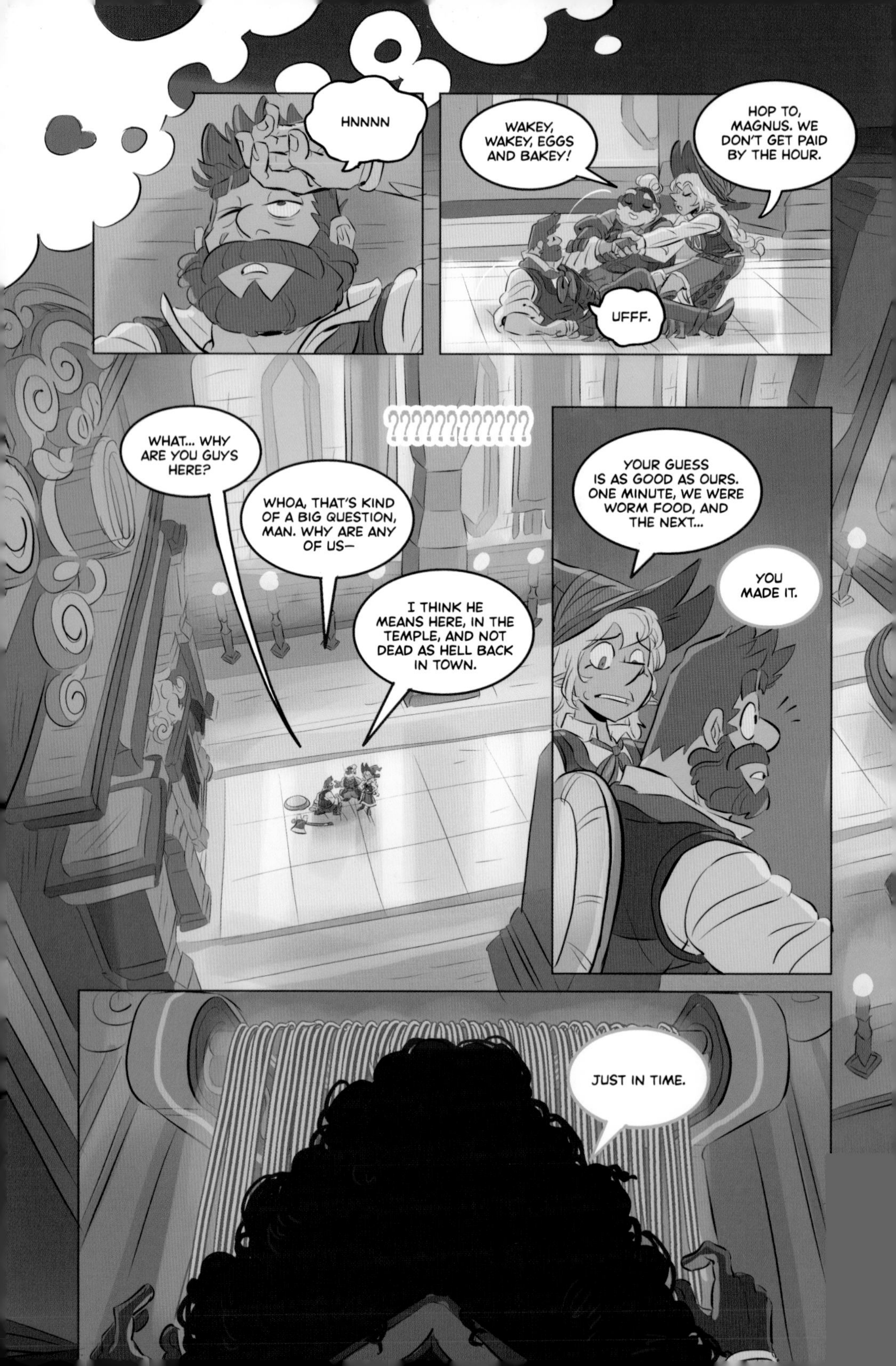
HNNNN
WAKEY, WAKEY, EGGS AND BAKEY!
HOP TO, MAGNUS. WE DON'T GET PAID BY THE HOUR.
UFFF.
??????????????
WHAT... WHY ARE YOU GUYS HERE?
WHOA, THAT'S KIND OF A BIG QUESTION, MAN. WHY ARE ANY OF US—
I THINK HE MEANS HERE, IN THE TEMPLE, AND NOT DEAD AS HELL BACK IN TOWN.
YOUR GUESS IS AS GOOD AS OURS. ONE MINUTE, WE WERE WORM FOOD, AND THE NEXT...
YOU MADE IT.
JUST IN TIME.

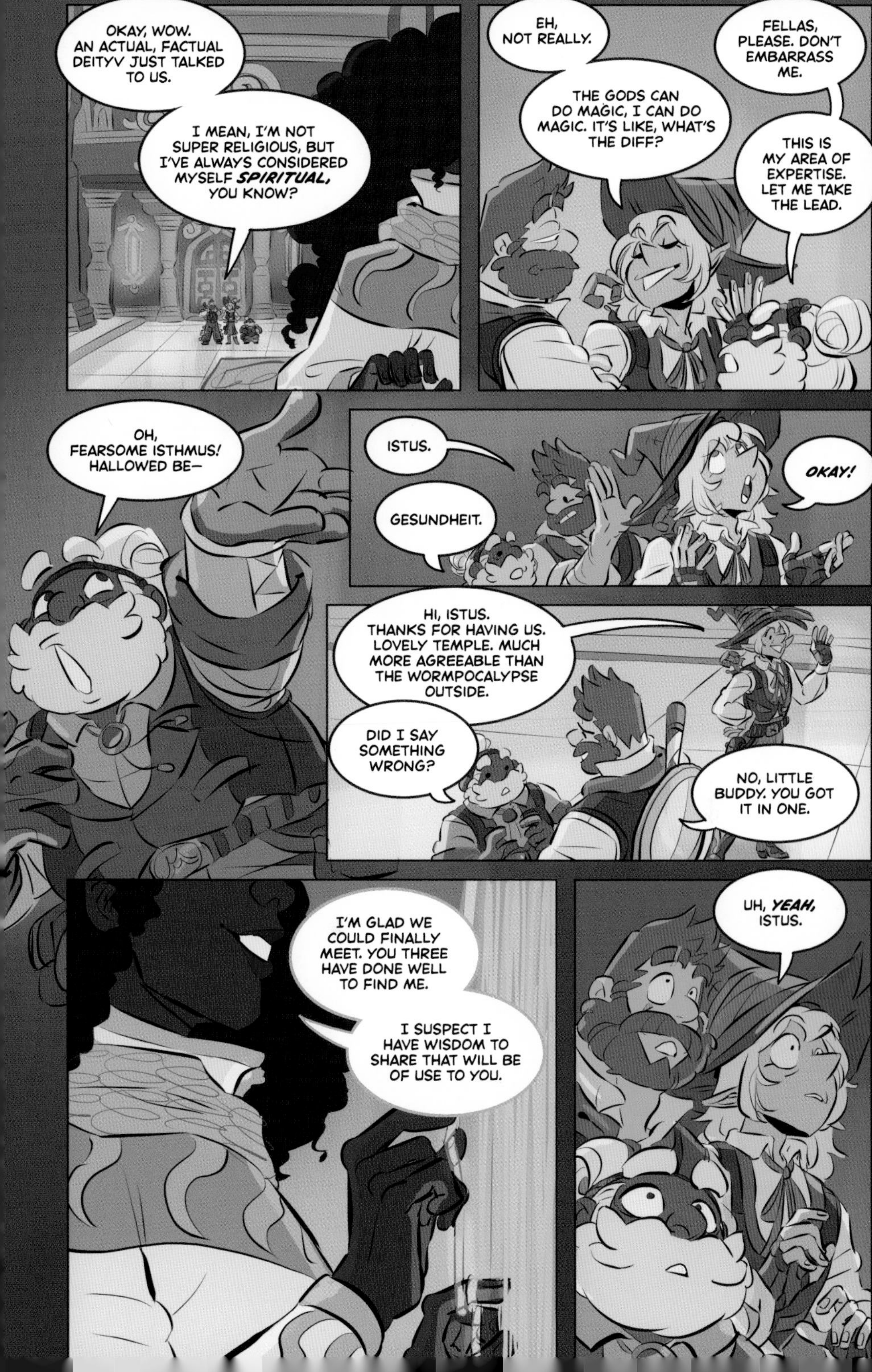
OKAY, WOW. AN ACTUAL, FACTUAL DEITYV JUST TALKED TO US.
I MEAN, I'M NOT SUPER RELIGIOUS, BUT I'VE ALWAYS CONSIDERED MYSELF *SPIRITUAL,* YOU KNOW?
EH, NOT REALLY.
THE GODS CAN DO MAGIC, I CAN DO MAGIC. IT'S LIKE, WHAT'S THE DIFF?
FELLAS, PLEASE. DON'T EMBARRASS ME.
THIS IS MY AREA OF EXPERTISE. LET ME TAKE THE LEAD.
OH, FEARSOME ISTHMUS! HALLOWED BE—
ISTUS.
GESUNDHEIT.
OKAY!
HI, ISTUS. THANKS FOR HAVING US. LOVELY TEMPLE. MUCH MORE AGREEABLE THAN THE WORMPOCALYPSE OUTSIDE.
DID I SAY SOMETHING WRONG?
NO, LITTLE BUDDY. YOU GOT IT IN ONE.
I'M GLAD WE COULD FINALLY MEET. YOU THREE HAVE DONE WELL TO FIND ME.
I SUSPECT I HAVE WISDOM TO SHARE THAT WILL BE OF USE TO YOU.
UH, *YEAH,* ISTUS.

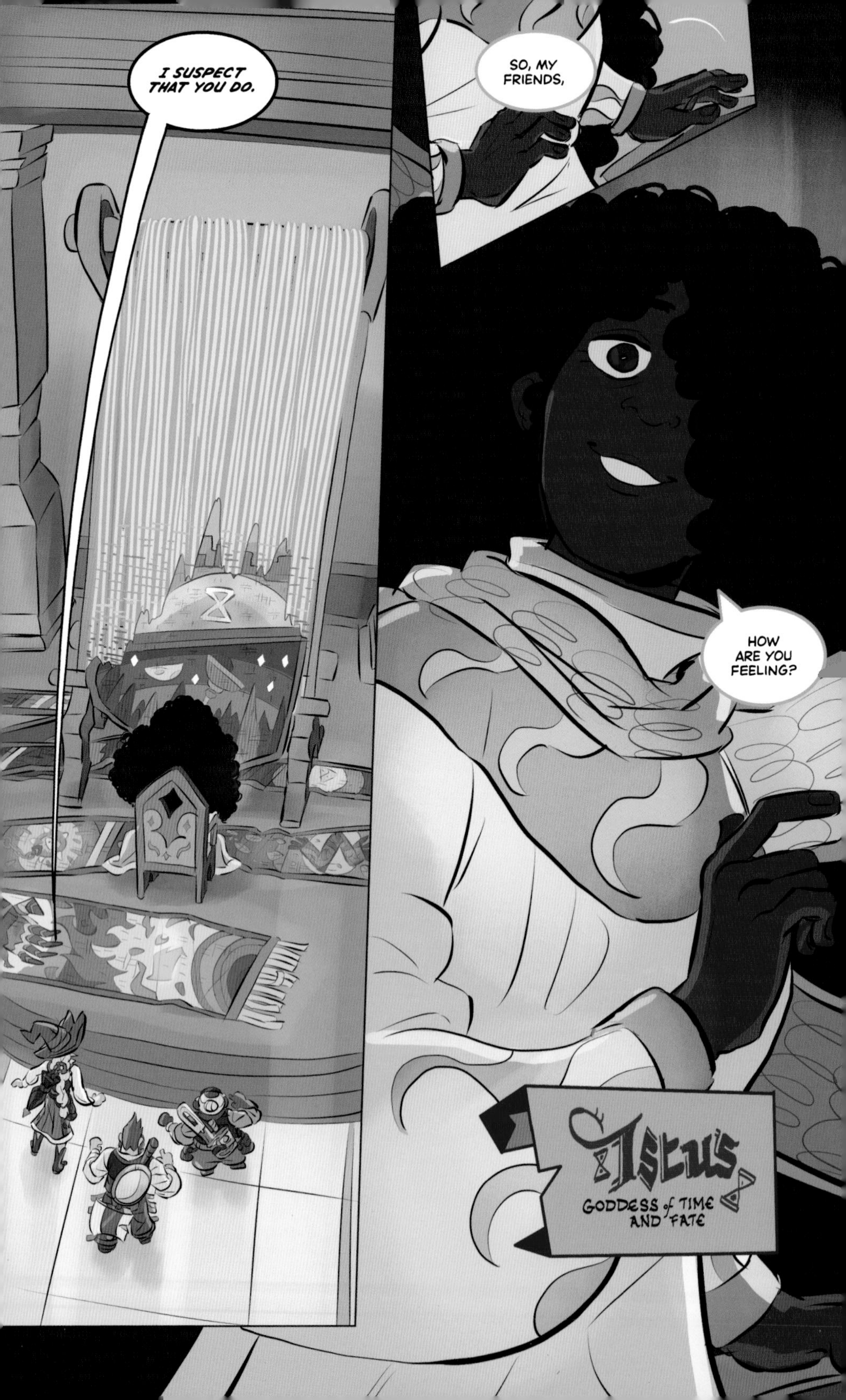
I SUSPECT THAT YOU DO.
SO, MY FRIENDS,
HOW ARE YOU FEELING?
ISTUS
GODDESS of TIME AND FATE

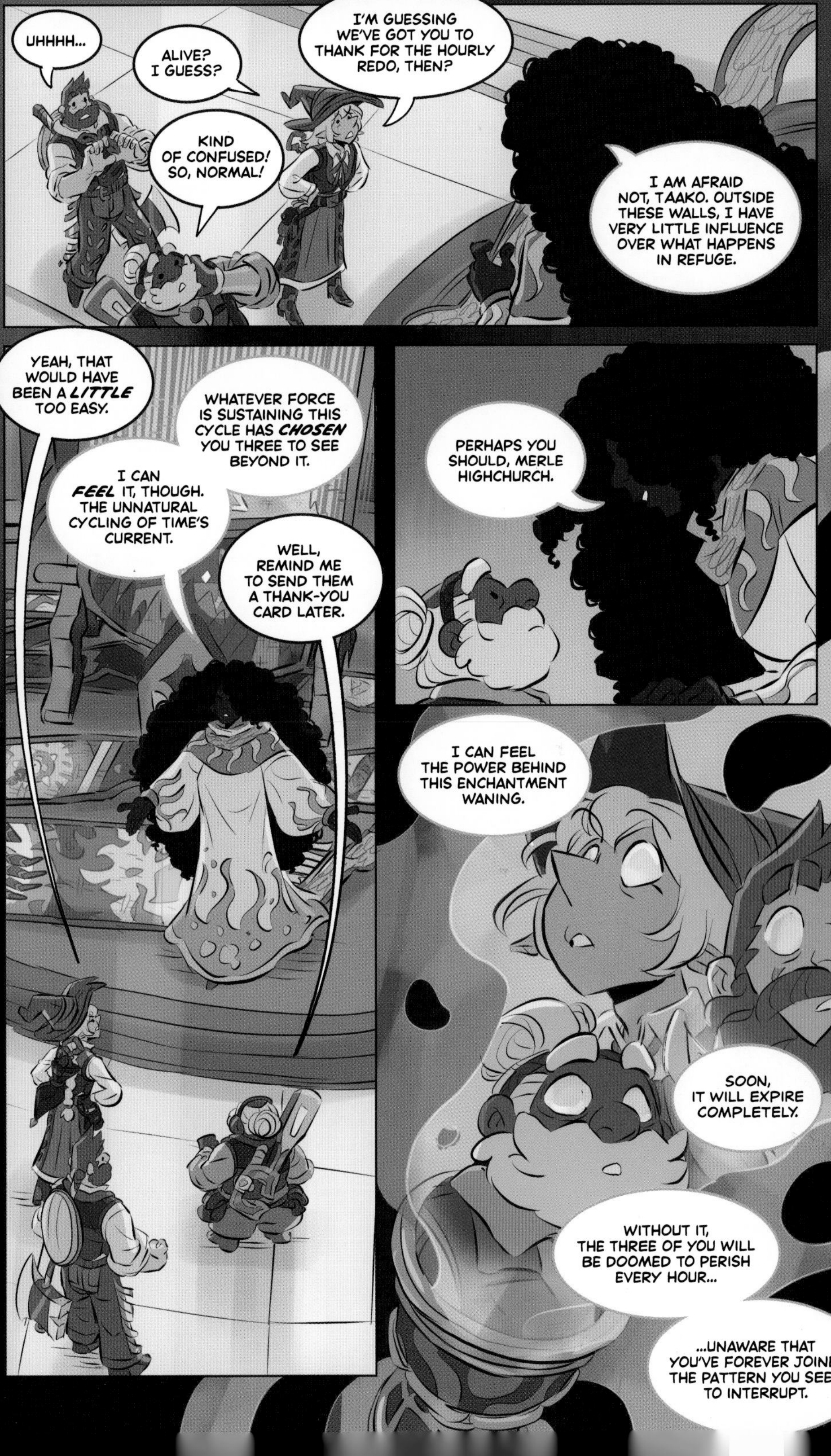
UHHHH...
ALIVE? I GUESS?
I'M GUESSING WE'VE GOT YOU TO THANK FOR THE HOURLY REDO, THEN?
KIND OF CONFUSED! SO, NORMAL!
I AM AFRAID NOT, TAAKO. OUTSIDE THESE WALLS, I HAVE VERY LITTLE INFLUENCE OVER WHAT HAPPENS IN REFUGE.
YEAH, THAT WOULD HAVE BEEN A LITTLE TOO EASY.
WHATEVER FORCE IS SUSTAINING THIS CYCLE HAS CHOSEN YOU THREE TO SEE BEYOND IT.
I CAN FEEL IT, THOUGH. THE UNNATURAL CYCLING OF TIME'S CURRENT.
WELL, REMIND ME TO SEND THEM A THANK-YOU CARD LATER.
PERHAPS YOU SHOULD, MERLE HIGHCHURCH.
I CAN FEEL THE POWER BEHIND THIS ENCHANTMENT WANING.
SOON, IT WILL EXPIRE COMPLETELY.
WITHOUT IT, THE THREE OF YOU WILL BE DOOMED TO PERISH EVERY HOUR...
...UNAWARE THAT YOU'VE FOREVER JOINED THE PATTERN YOU SEEK TO INTERRUPT.

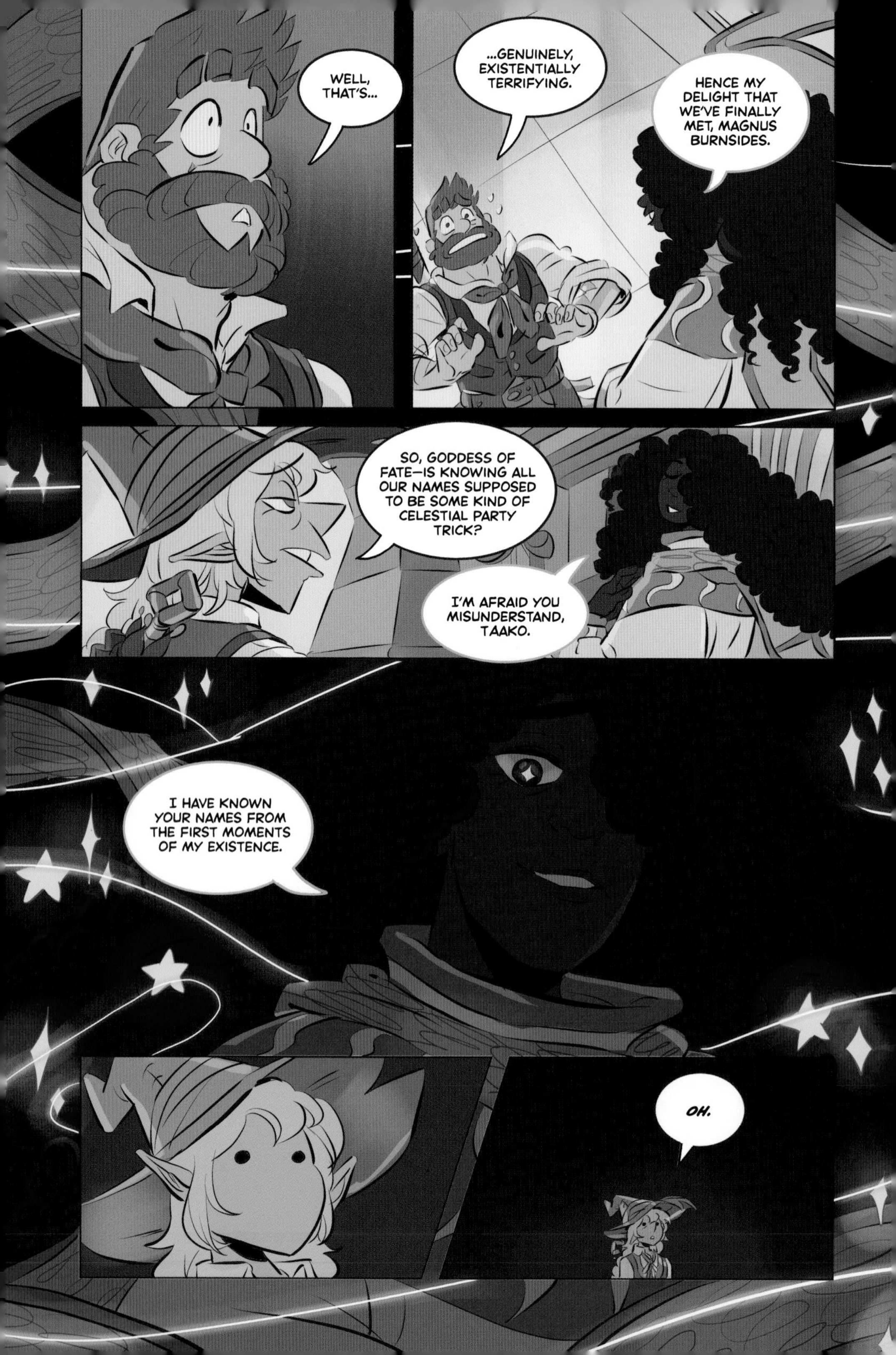
WELL, THAT'S...
...GENUINELY, EXISTENTIALLY TERRIFYING.
HENCE MY DELIGHT THAT WE'VE FINALLY MET, MAGNUS BURNSIDES.
SO, GODDESS OF FATE—IS KNOWING ALL OUR NAMES SUPPOSED TO BE SOME KIND OF CELESTIAL PARTY TRICK?
I'M AFRAID YOU MISUNDERSTAND, TAAKO.
I HAVE KNOWN YOUR NAMES FROM THE FIRST MOMENTS OF MY EXISTENCE.
OH.

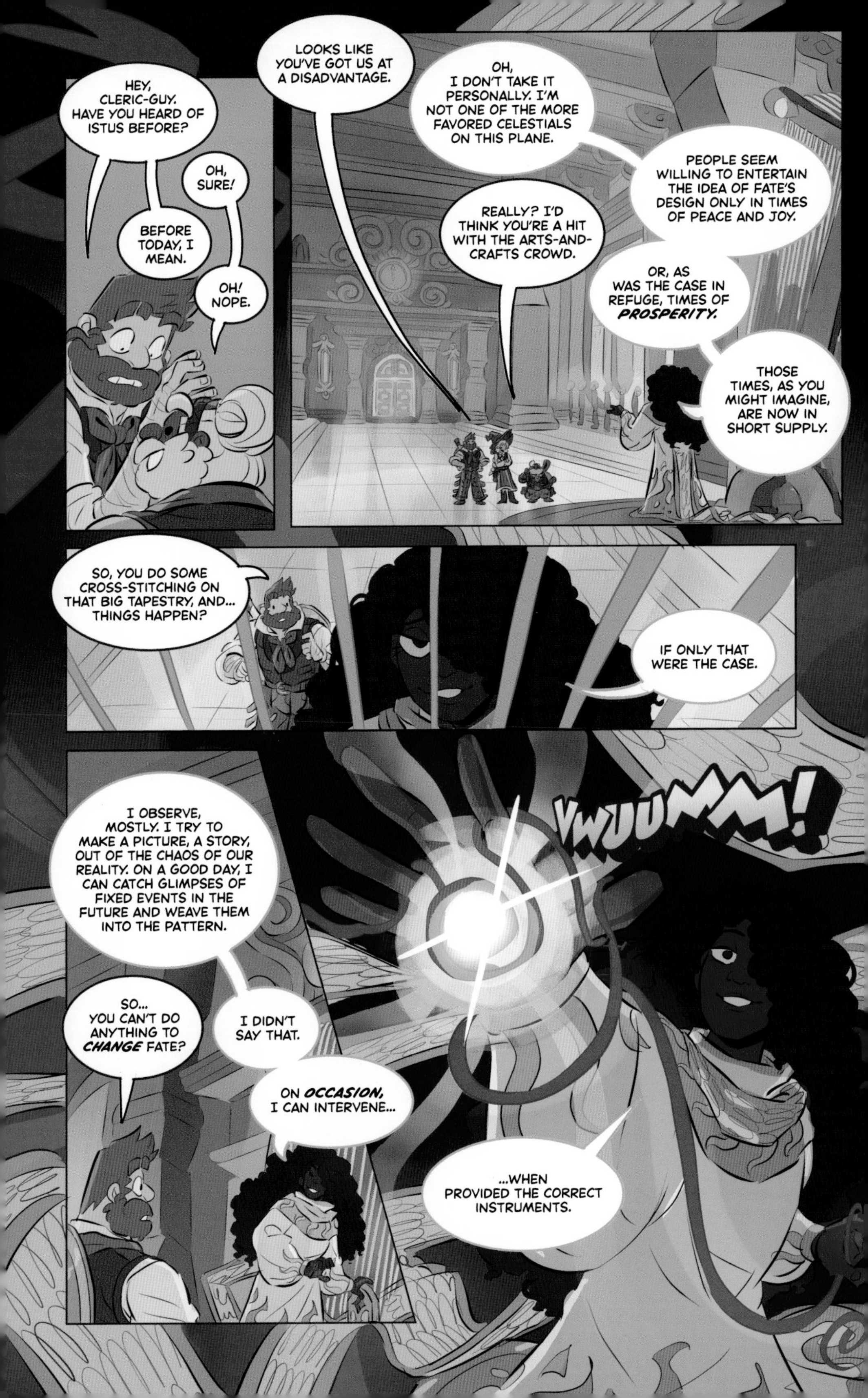
HEY, CLERIC-GUY. HAVE YOU HEARD OF ISTUS BEFORE?
OH, SURE!
BEFORE TODAY, I MEAN.
OH! NOPE.
LOOKS LIKE YOU'VE GOT US AT A DISADVANTAGE.
OH, I DON'T TAKE IT PERSONALLY. I'M NOT ONE OF THE MORE FAVORED CELESTIALS ON THIS PLANE.
REALLY? I'D THINK YOU'RE A HIT WITH THE ARTS-AND-CRAFTS CROWD.
PEOPLE SEEM WILLING TO ENTERTAIN THE IDEA OF FATE'S DESIGN ONLY IN TIMES OF PEACE AND JOY.
OR, AS WAS THE CASE IN REFUGE, TIMES OF ***PROSPERITY.***
THOSE TIMES, AS YOU MIGHT IMAGINE, ARE NOW IN SHORT SUPPLY.
SO, YOU DO SOME CROSS-STITCHING ON THAT BIG TAPESTRY, AND... THINGS HAPPEN?
IF ONLY THAT WERE THE CASE.
I OBSERVE, MOSTLY. I TRY TO MAKE A PICTURE, A STORY, OUT OF THE CHAOS OF OUR REALITY. ON A GOOD DAY, I CAN CATCH GLIMPSES OF FIXED EVENTS IN THE FUTURE AND WEAVE THEM INTO THE PATTERN.
VWUUMM!
SO... YOU CAN'T DO ANYTHING TO ***CHANGE*** FATE?
I DIDN'T SAY THAT.
ON *OCCASION,* I CAN INTERVENE...
...WHEN PROVIDED THE CORRECT INSTRUMENTS.

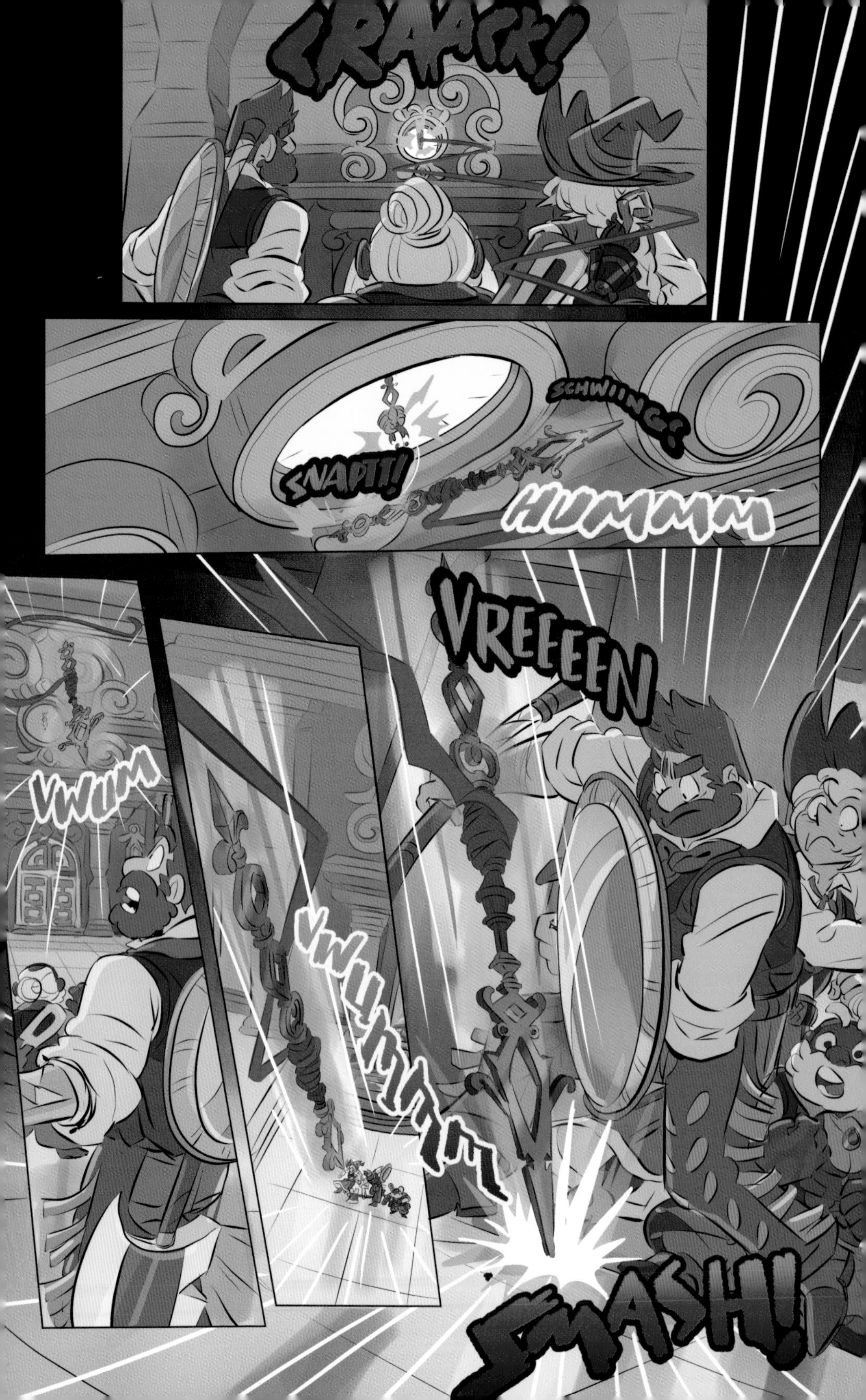
CRAAACK!
SCHWIING!
SNAPTT!
HUMMMM
VWUM
VWUMMMMMM
VREEEEN
SMASH!

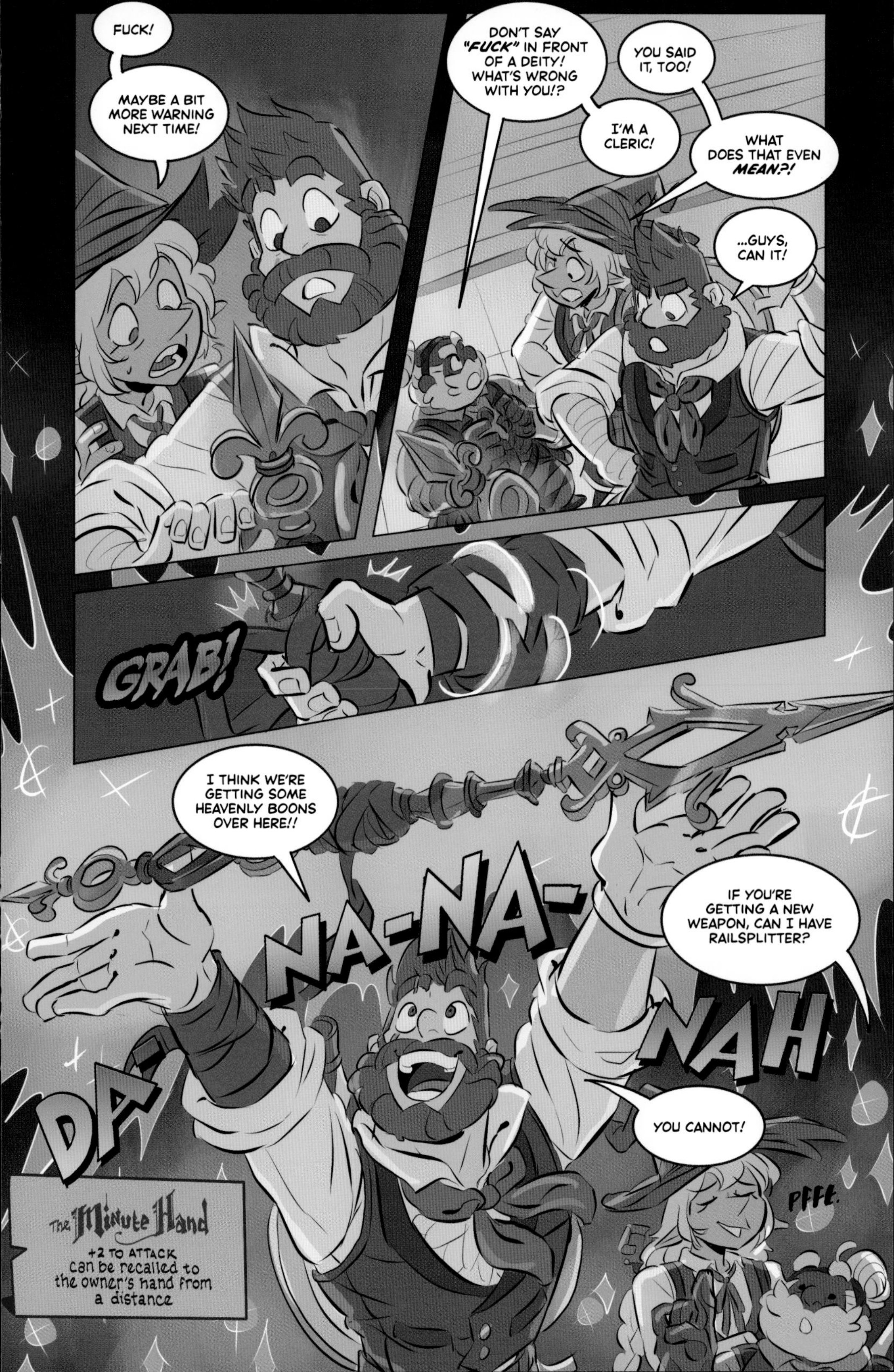
FUCK!
MAYBE A BIT MORE WARNING NEXT TIME!
DON'T SAY "FUCK" IN FRONT OF A DEITY! WHAT'S WRONG WITH YOU!?
I'M A CLERIC!
YOU SAID IT, TOO!
WHAT DOES THAT EVEN MEAN?!
...GUYS, CAN IT!
GRAB!
I THINK WE'RE GETTING SOME HEAVENLY BOONS OVER HERE!!
DA-
NA-NA-
NAH
IF YOU'RE GETTING A NEW WEAPON, CAN I HAVE RAILSPLITTER?
YOU CANNOT!
PFFT.
The Minute Hand
+2 TO ATTACK
can be recalled to the owner's hand from a distance

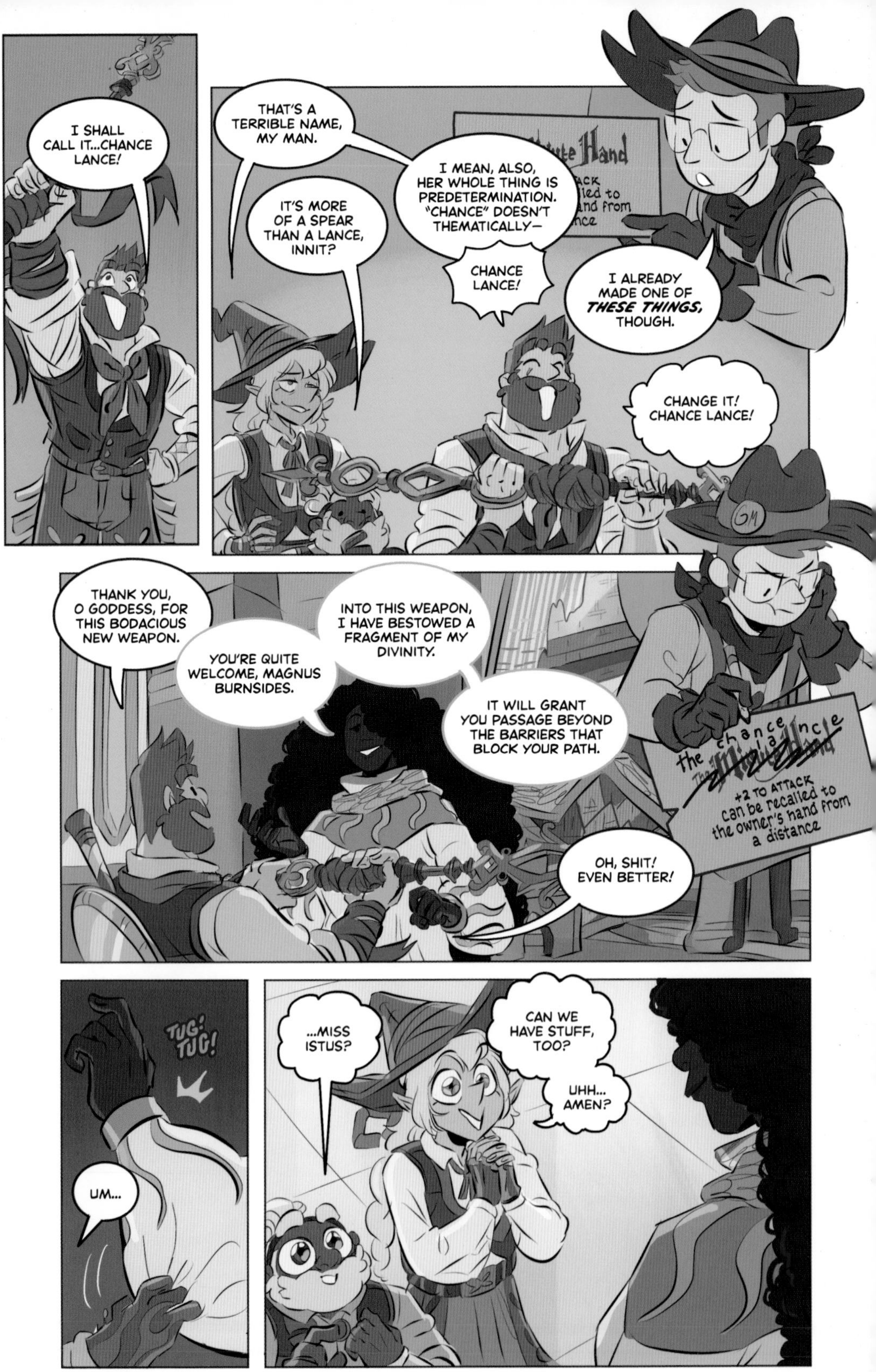

I SHALL CALL IT...CHANCE LANCE!
THAT'S A TERRIBLE NAME, MY MAN.
IT'S MORE OF A SPEAR THAN A LANCE, INNIT?
I MEAN, ALSO, HER WHOLE THING IS PREDETERMINATION. "CHANCE" DOESN'T THEMATICALLY—
CHANCE LANCE!
I ALREADY MADE ONE OF ***THESE THINGS,*** THOUGH.
CHANGE IT! CHANCE LANCE!
THANK YOU, O GODDESS, FOR THIS BODACIOUS NEW WEAPON.
YOU'RE QUITE WELCOME, MAGNUS BURNSIDES.
INTO THIS WEAPON, I HAVE BESTOWED A FRAGMENT OF MY DIVINITY.
IT WILL GRANT YOU PASSAGE BEYOND THE BARRIERS THAT BLOCK YOUR PATH.
+2 TO ATTACK
can be recalled to the owner's hand from a distance
OH, SHIT! EVEN BETTER!
TUG! TUG!
UM...
...MISS ISTUS?
CAN WE HAVE STUFF, TOO?
UHH... AMEN?

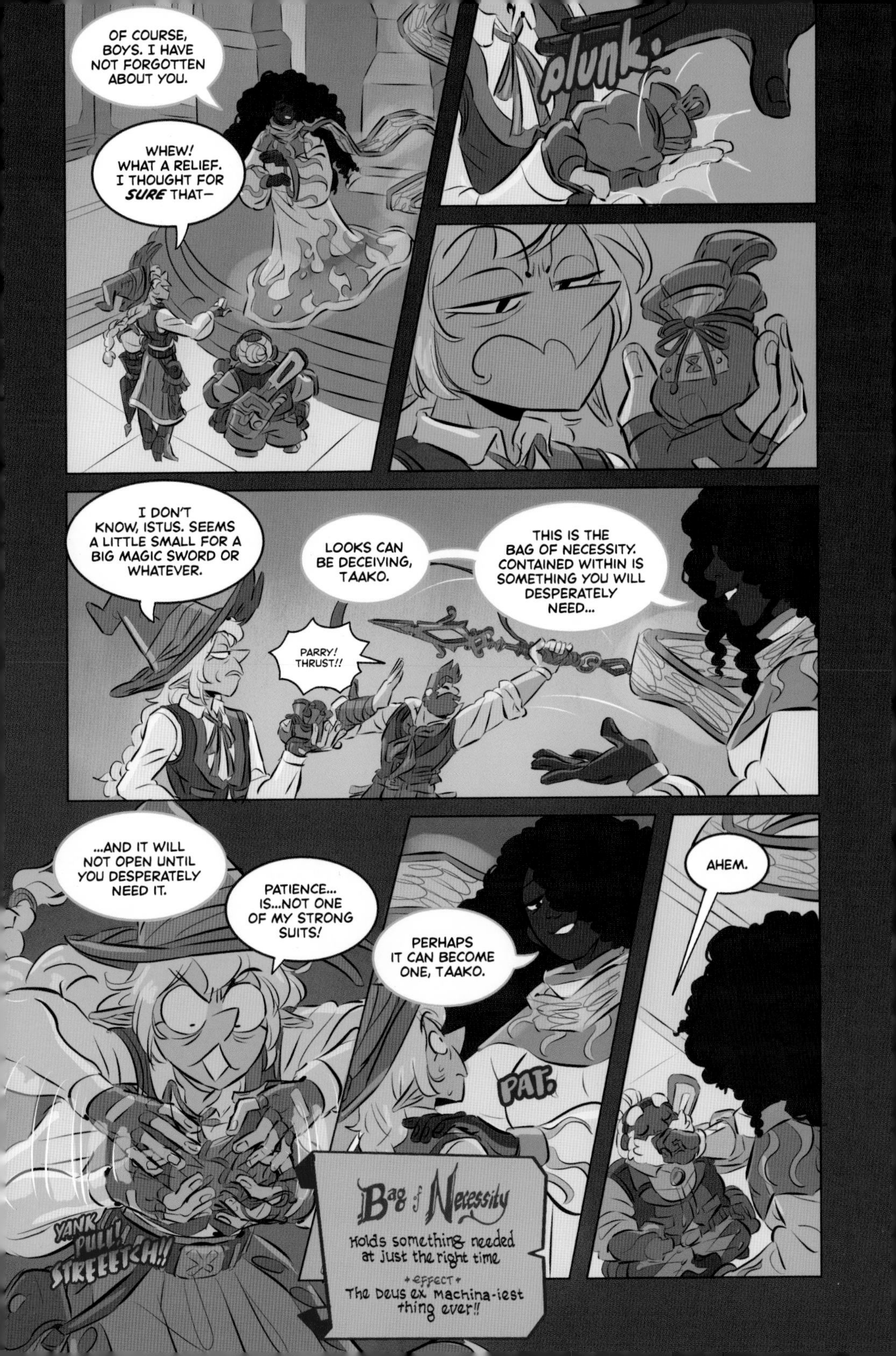
OF COURSE, BOYS. I HAVE NOT FORGOTTEN ABOUT YOU.
WHEW! WHAT A RELIEF. I THOUGHT FOR SURE THAT—
plunk.
I DON'T KNOW, ISTUS. SEEMS A LITTLE SMALL FOR A BIG MAGIC SWORD OR WHATEVER.
LOOKS CAN BE DECEIVING, TAAKO.
THIS IS THE BAG OF NECESSITY. CONTAINED WITHIN IS SOMETHING YOU WILL DESPERATELY NEED...
PARRY! THRUST!!
...AND IT WILL NOT OPEN UNTIL YOU DESPERATELY NEED IT.
PATIENCE... IS...NOT ONE OF MY STRONG SUITS!
PERHAPS IT CAN BECOME ONE, TAAKO.
AHEM.
PAT.
YANK!! PULL!! STREEETCH!!
Bag of Necessity
Holds something needed at just the right time
EFFECT
The Deus ex Machina-iest thing ever!!

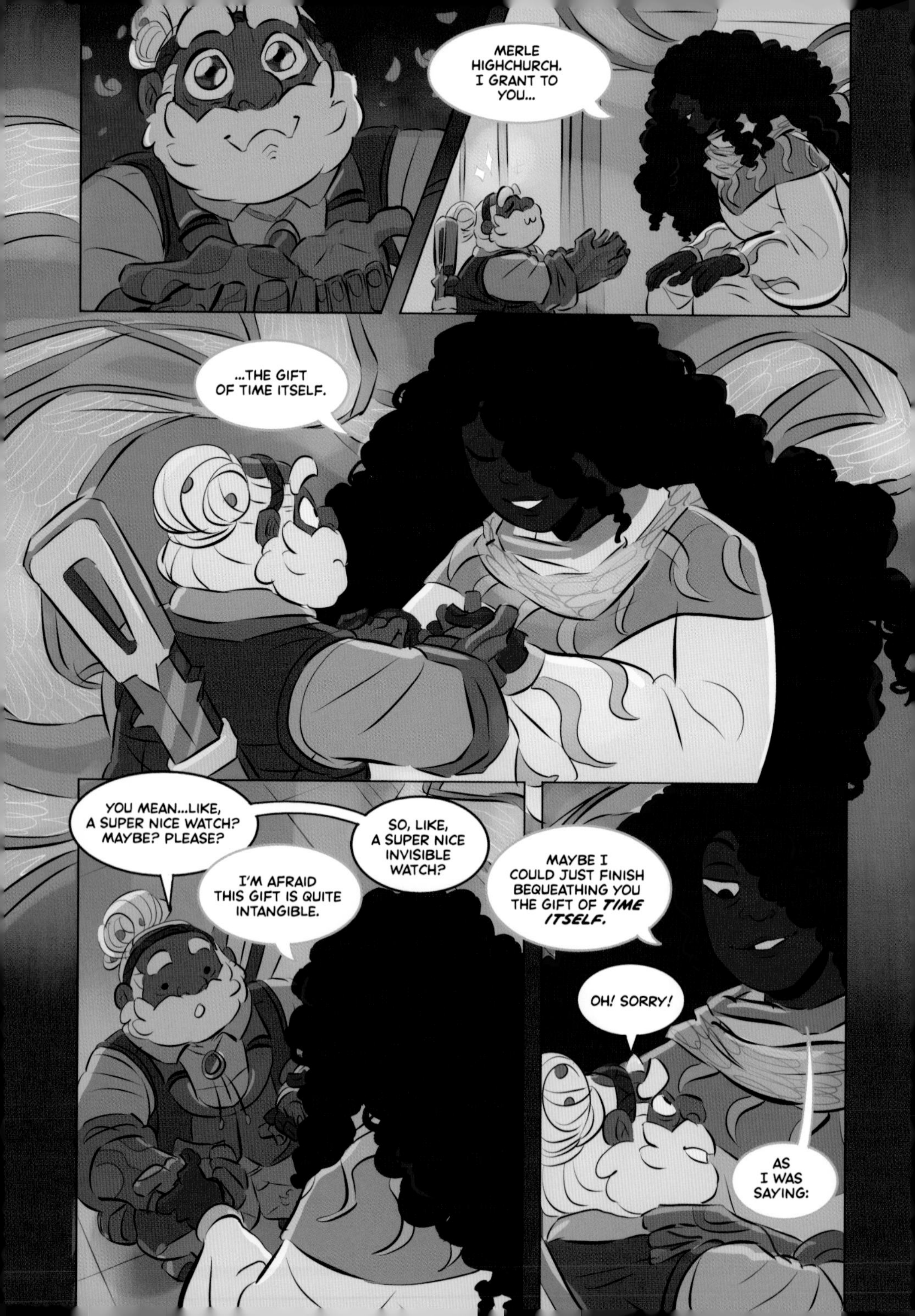
MERLE HIGHCHURCH. I GRANT TO YOU...
...THE GIFT OF TIME ITSELF.
YOU MEAN...LIKE, A SUPER NICE WATCH? MAYBE? PLEASE?
I'M AFRAID THIS GIFT IS QUITE INTANGIBLE.
SO, LIKE, A SUPER NICE INVISIBLE WATCH?
MAYBE I COULD JUST FINISH BEQUEATHING YOU THE GIFT OF *TIME ITSELF.*
OH! SORRY!
AS I WAS SAYING:

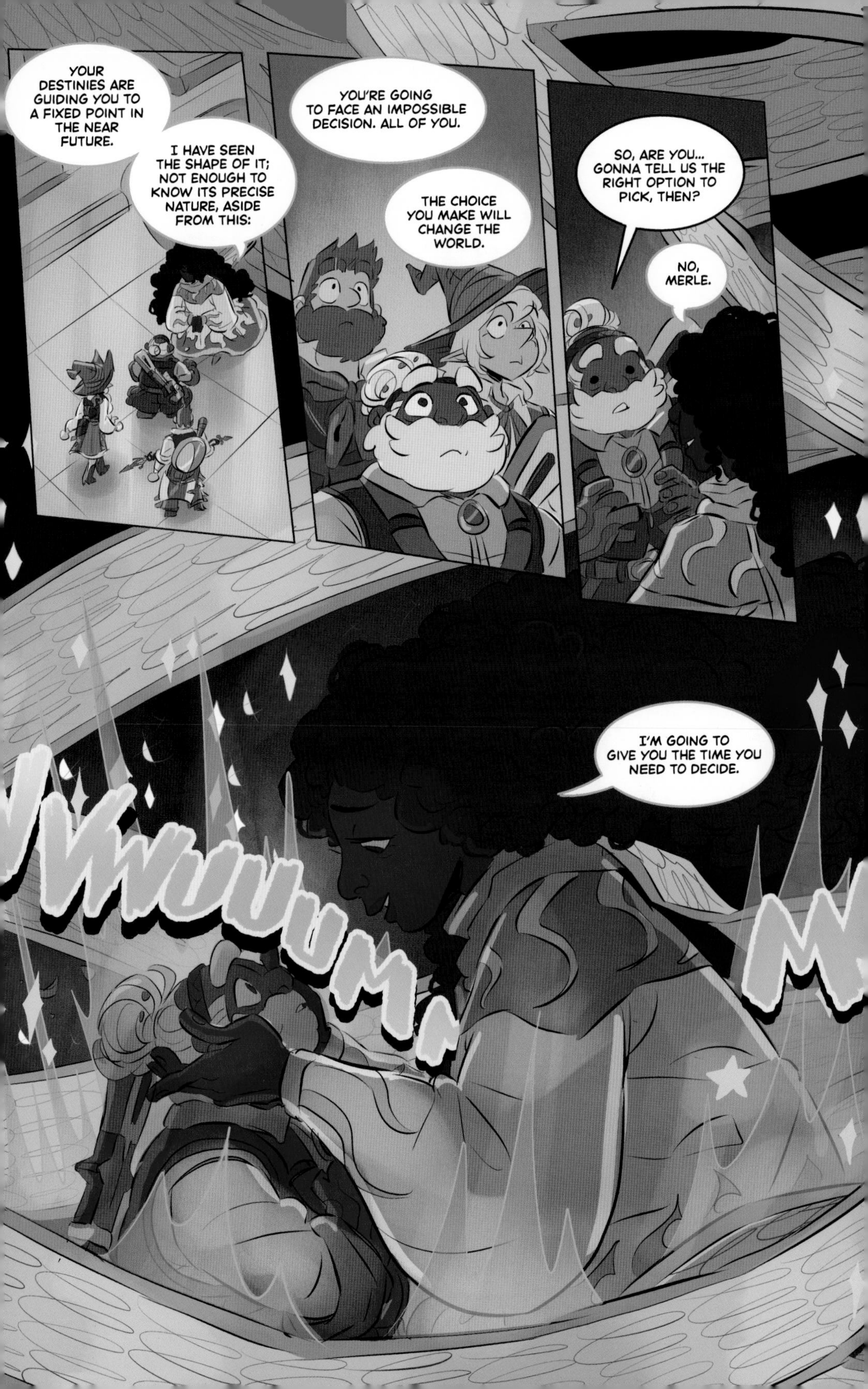
YOUR DESTINIES ARE GUIDING YOU TO A FIXED POINT IN THE NEAR FUTURE.
I HAVE SEEN THE SHAPE OF IT; NOT ENOUGH TO KNOW ITS PRECISE NATURE, ASIDE FROM THIS:
YOU'RE GOING TO FACE AN IMPOSSIBLE DECISION. ALL OF YOU.
THE CHOICE YOU MAKE WILL CHANGE THE WORLD.
SO, ARE YOU... GONNA TELL US THE RIGHT OPTION TO PICK, THEN?
NO, MERLE.
I'M GOING TO GIVE YOU THE TIME YOU NEED TO DECIDE.
VVVVUUUUMMM

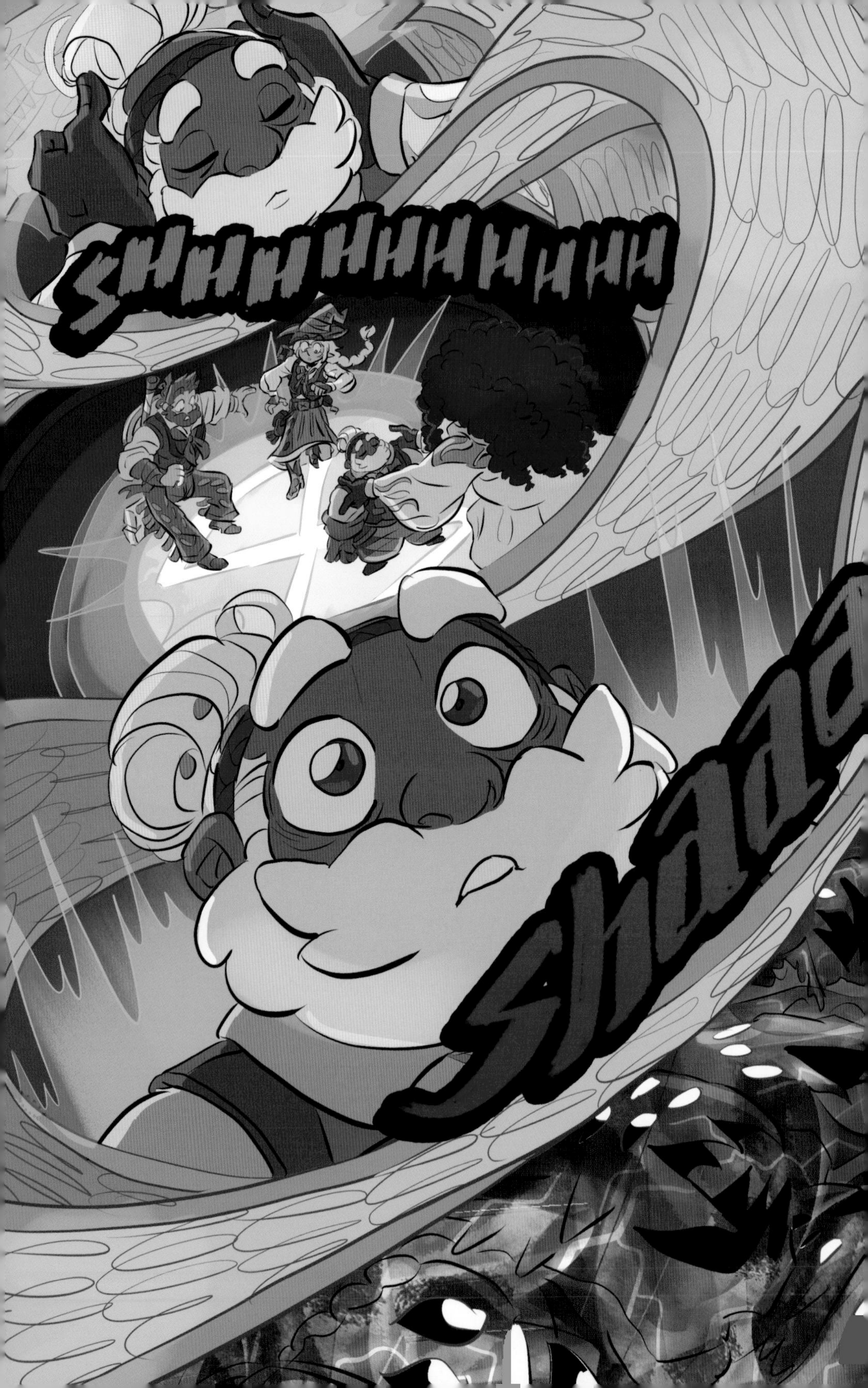
SHHHHHHHHHH
SHAA

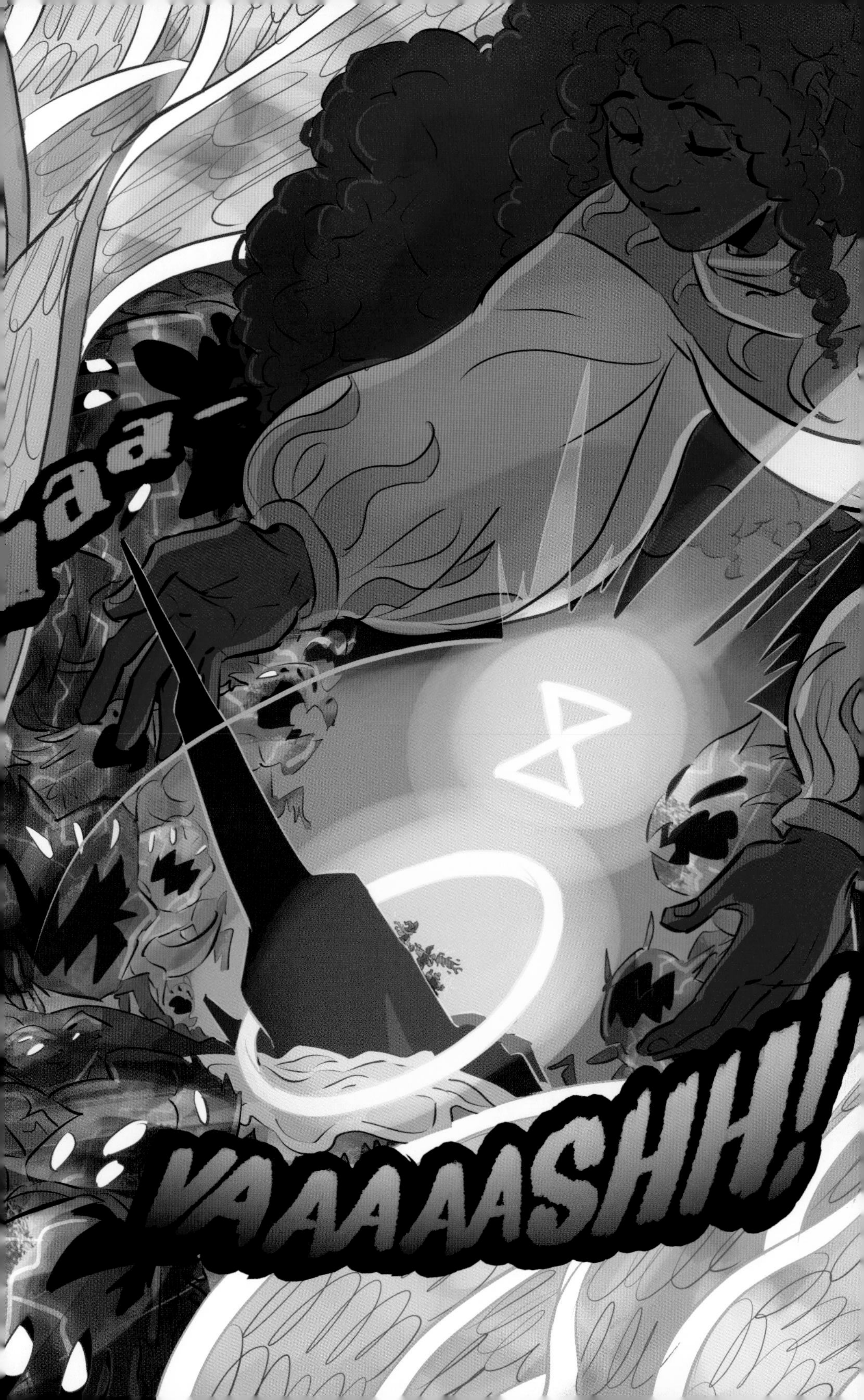
aa
KAAAAASHH!

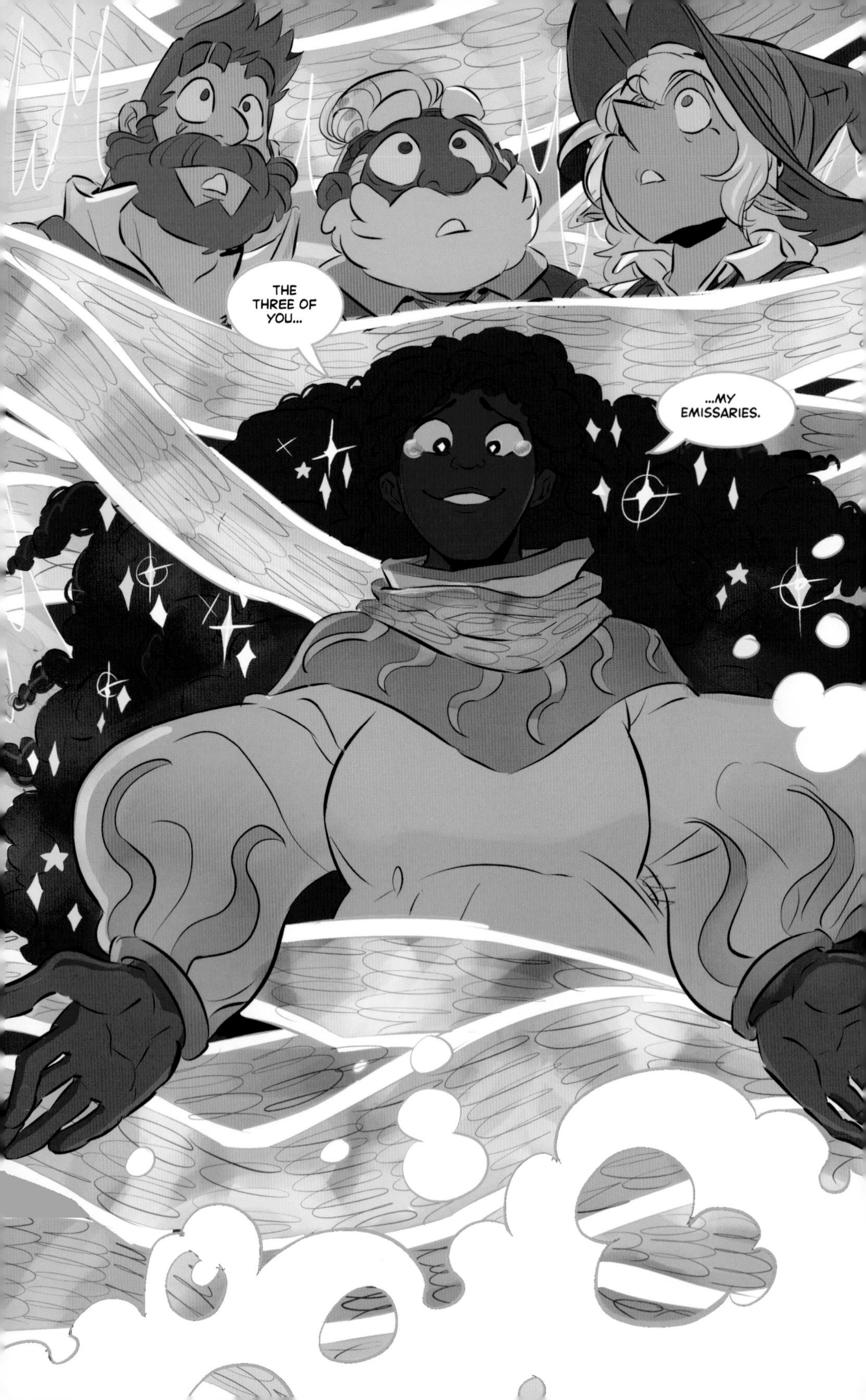
THE THREE OF YOU...
...MY EMISSARIES.

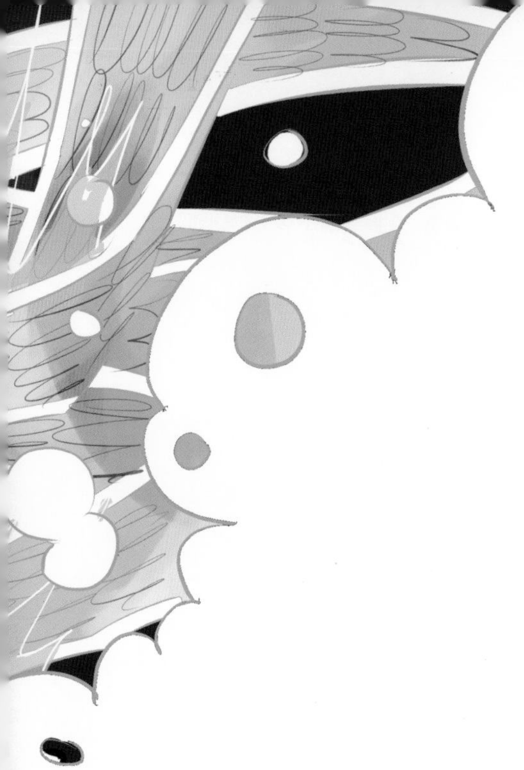

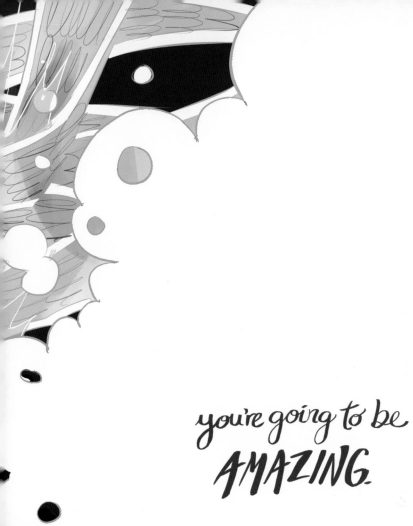

you're going to be

AMAZING.

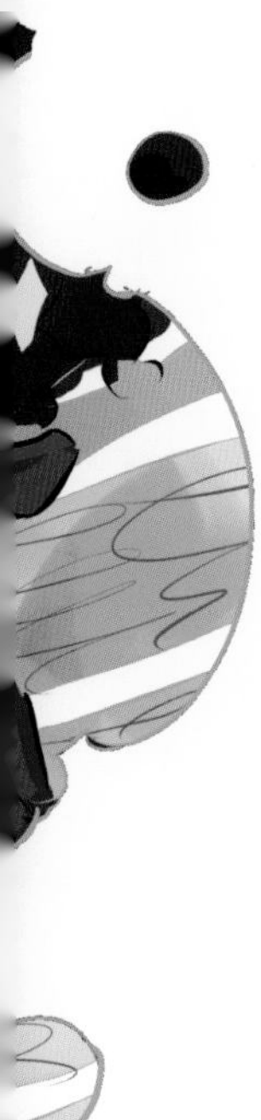

Chapter
111

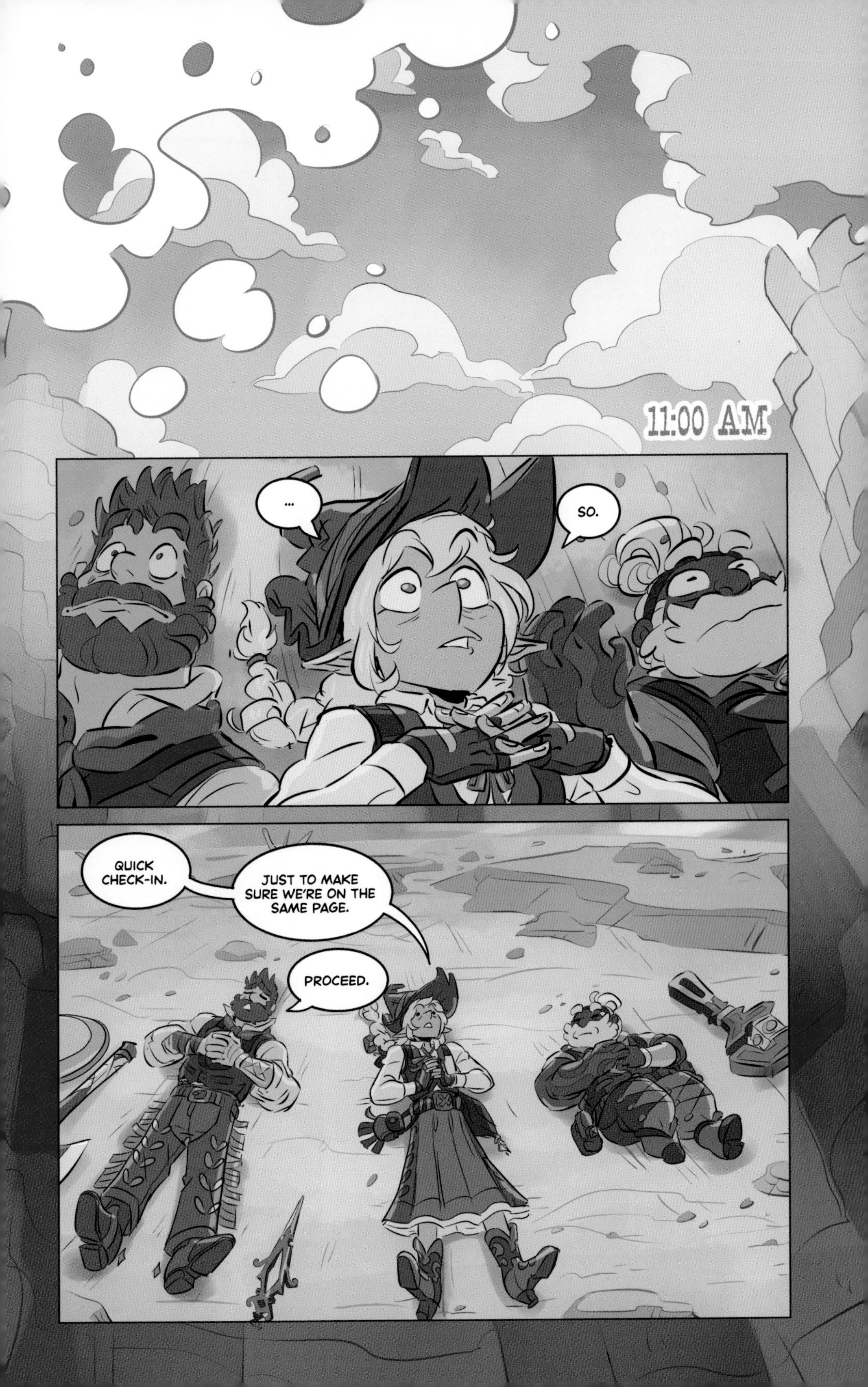
11:00 AM
...
SO.
QUICK CHECK-IN.
JUST TO MAKE SURE WE'RE ON THE SAME PAGE.
PROCEED.

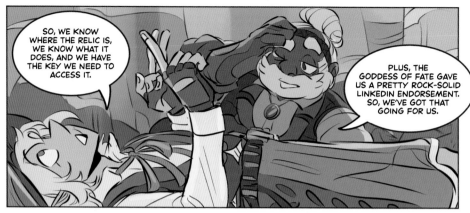

SO, WE KNOW WHERE THE RELIC IS, WE KNOW WHAT IT DOES, AND WE HAVE THE KEY WE NEED TO ACCESS IT.

PLUS, THE GODDESS OF FATE GAVE US A PRETTY ROCK-SOLID LINKEDIN ENDORSEMENT. SO, WE'VE GOT THAT GOING FOR US.

ANYONE GOT ANY OTHER CONSEQUENCE-FREE GOOF-EM-UPS THEY WANT TO DO BEFORE WE BREAK THE CYCLE?

NOPE!

I WOULD LIKE TO NOT GET BLOWN UP ANYMORE.

OR IMPALED, OR DEVOURED, OR STUCK UNKNOWINGLY IN AN ETERNAL DEATH LOOP, OR—

YEAH, ALL THAT JAZZ.

...YEAH.

I'M ALL ABOUT FLIRTING WITH DEATH, BUT...LIKE, *LITERALLY.*

HEH.

SOUNDS LIKE WE'RE IN AGREEMENT, THEN.

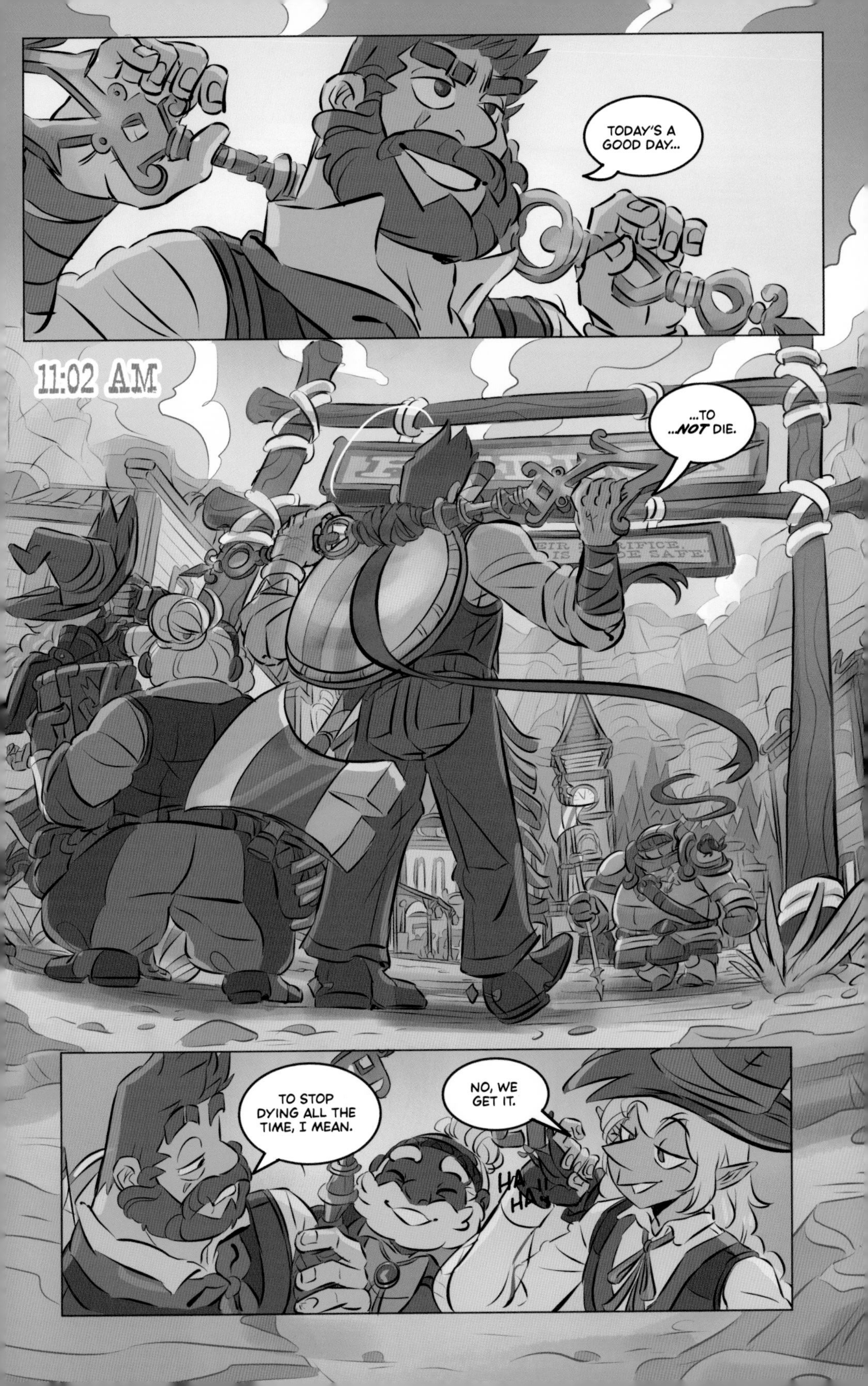
TODAY'S A GOOD DAY...
11:02 AM
...TO ...NOT DIE.
TO STOP DYING ALL THE TIME, I MEAN.
NO, WE GET IT.
HA! HA!

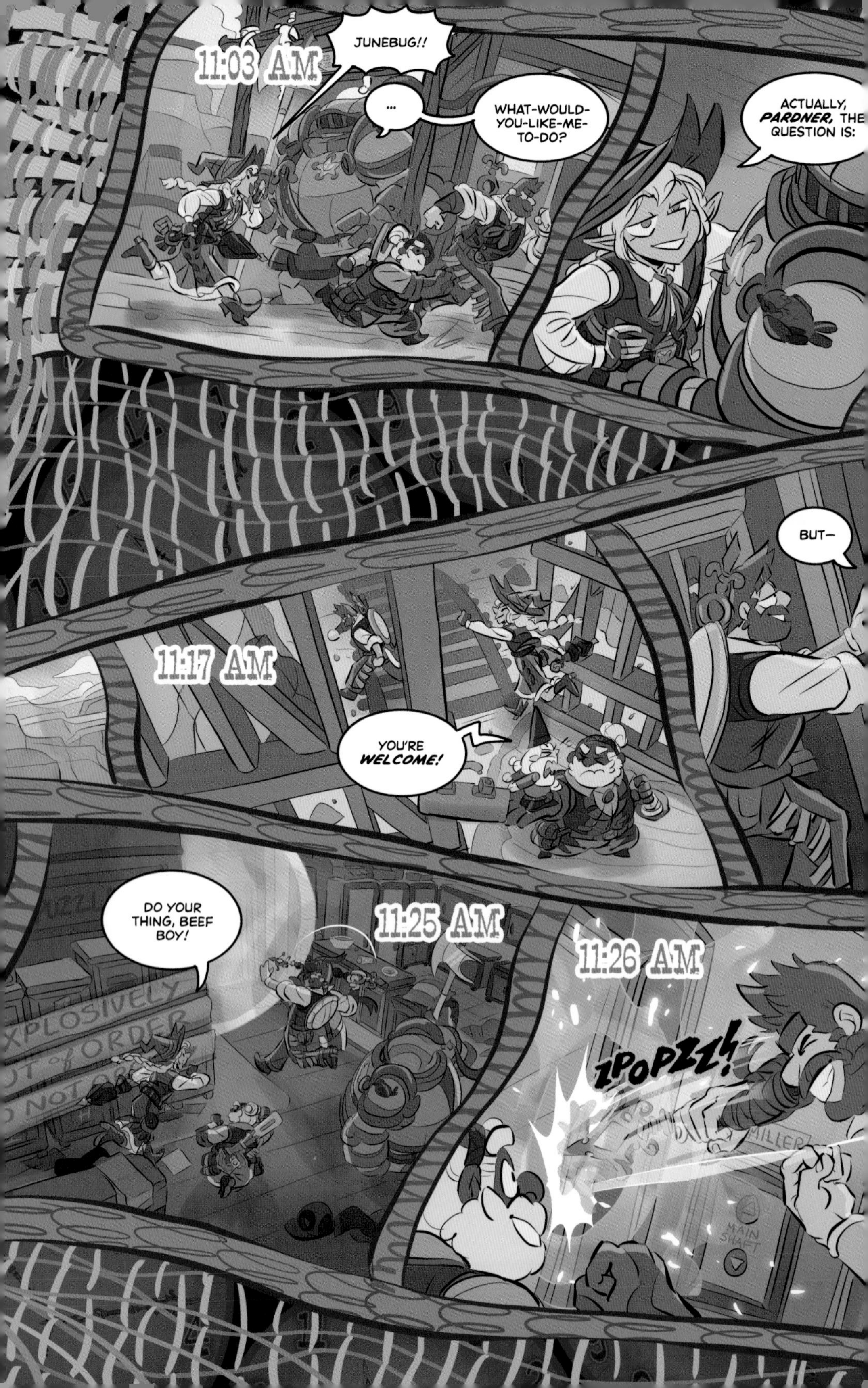
11:03 AM
JUNEBUG!!
...
WHAT-WOULD-YOU-LIKE-ME-TO-DO?
ACTUALLY, PARDNER, THE QUESTION IS:
BUT—
11:17 AM
YOU'RE WELCOME!
DO YOUR THING, BEEF BOY!
11:25 AM
EXPLOSIVELY OUT of ORDER
DO NOT
11:26 AM
ZPOPZZ!
MILLER
MAIN SHAFT

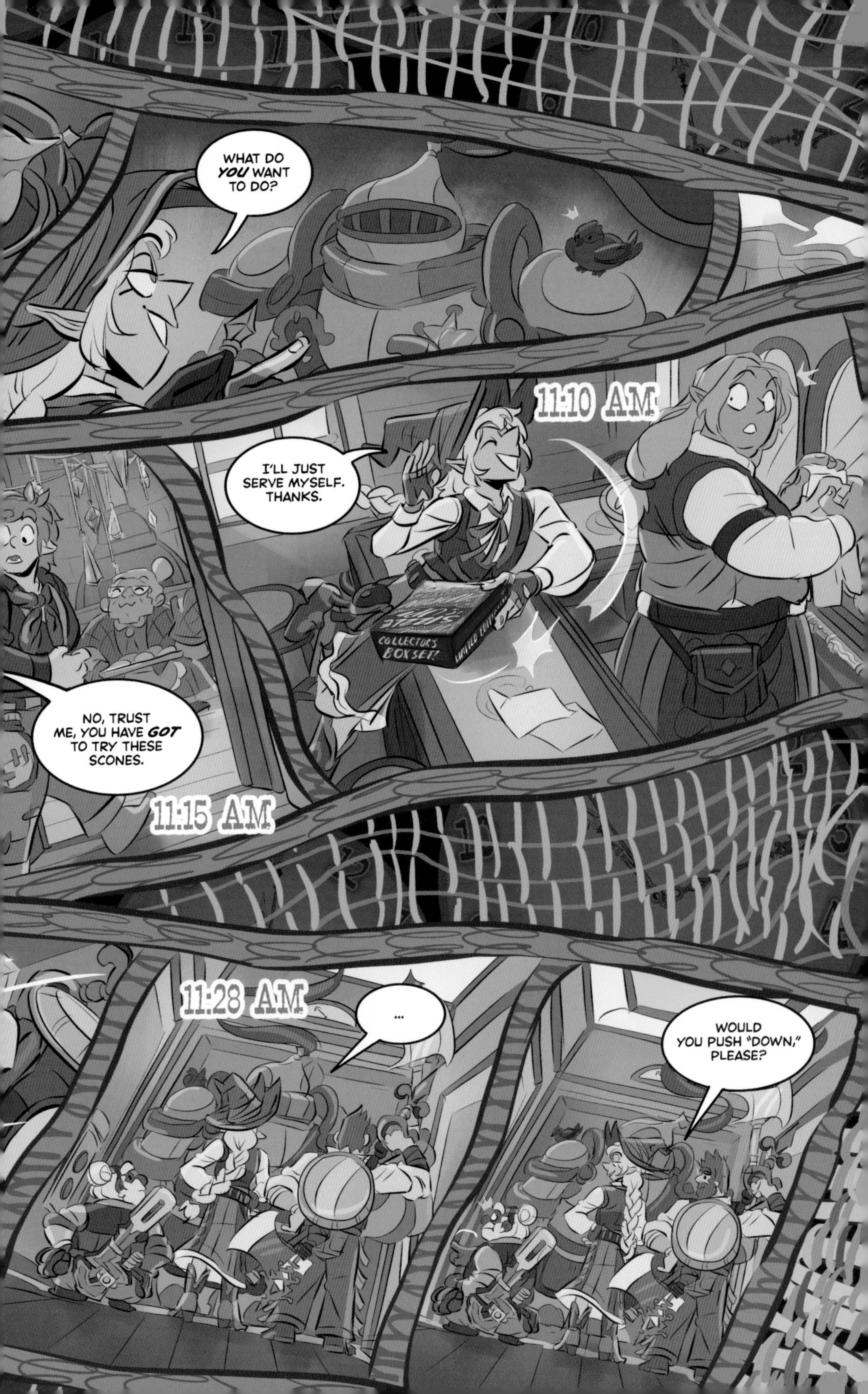
WHAT DO *YOU* WANT TO DO?
11:10 AM
I'LL JUST SERVE MYSELF. THANKS.
COLLECTOR'S BOX SET!
NO, TRUST ME, YOU HAVE *GOT* TO TRY THESE SCONES.
11:15 AM
11:28 AM
...
WOULD YOU PUSH "DOWN," PLEASE?

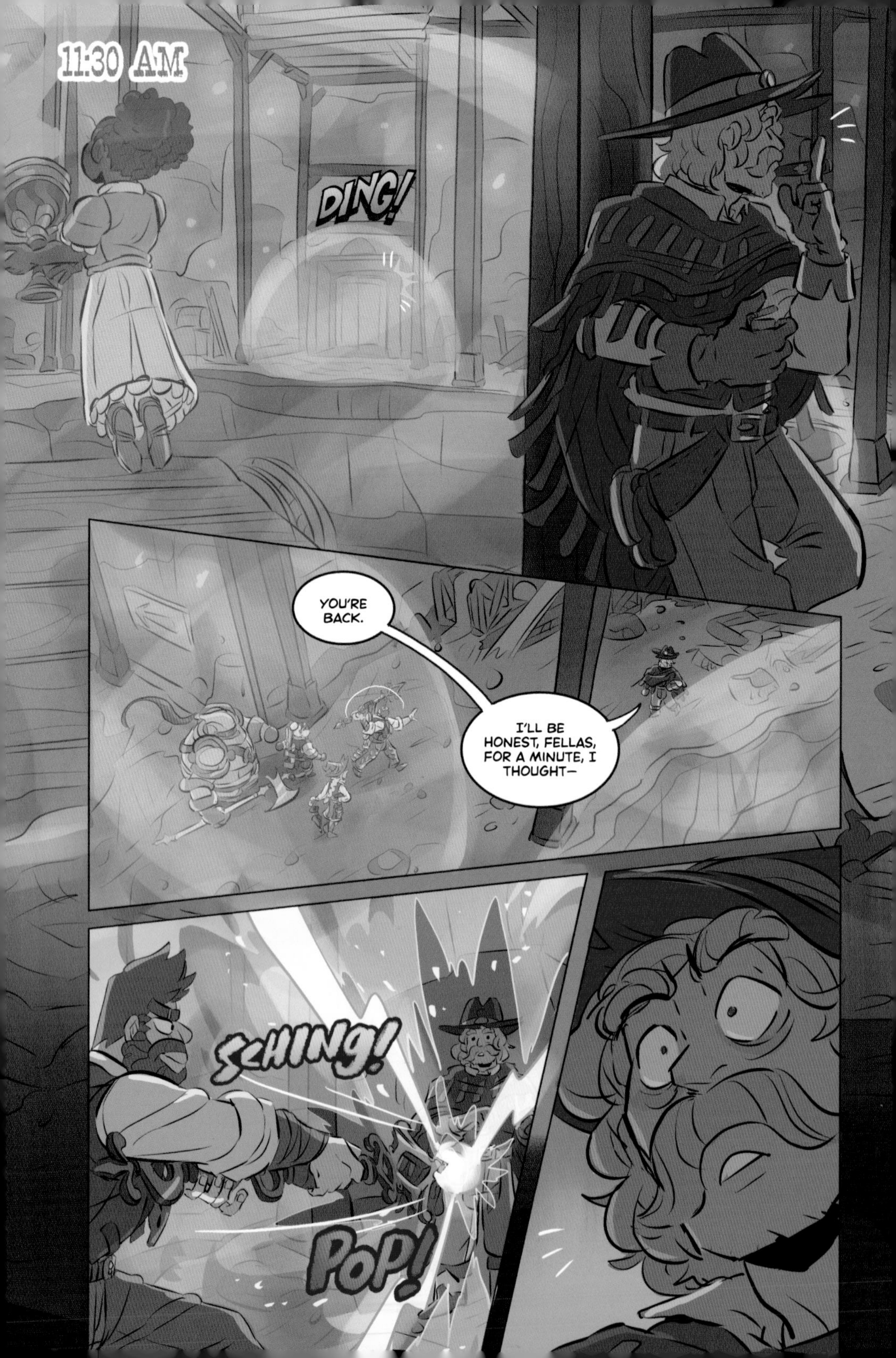
11:30 AM
DING!
YOU'RE BACK.
I'LL BE HONEST, FELLAS, FOR A MINUTE, I THOUGHT—
SCHING!
POP!

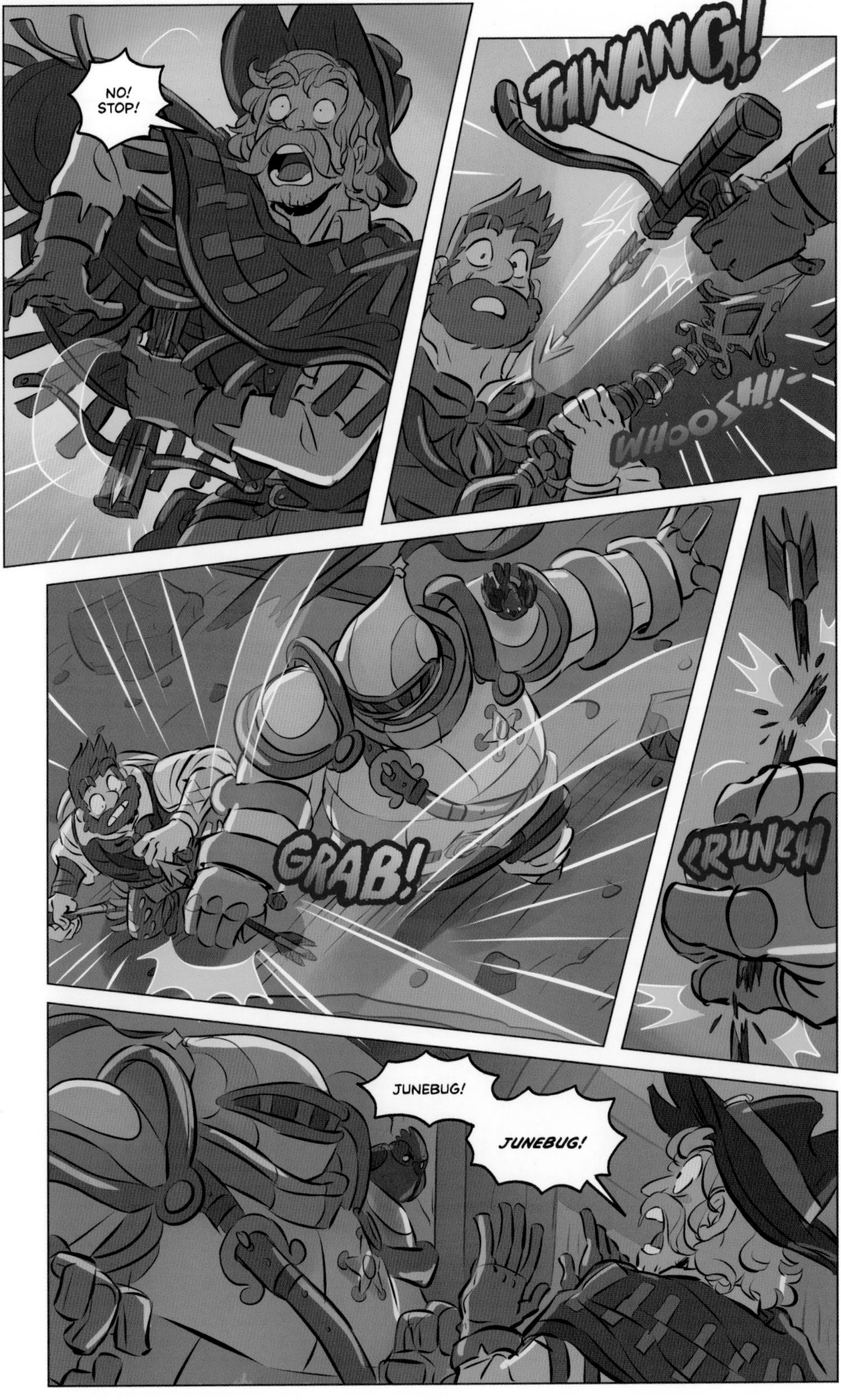
NO! STOP!
THWANG!
WHOOSH!
GRAB!
CRUNCH
JUNEBUG!
JUNEBUG!

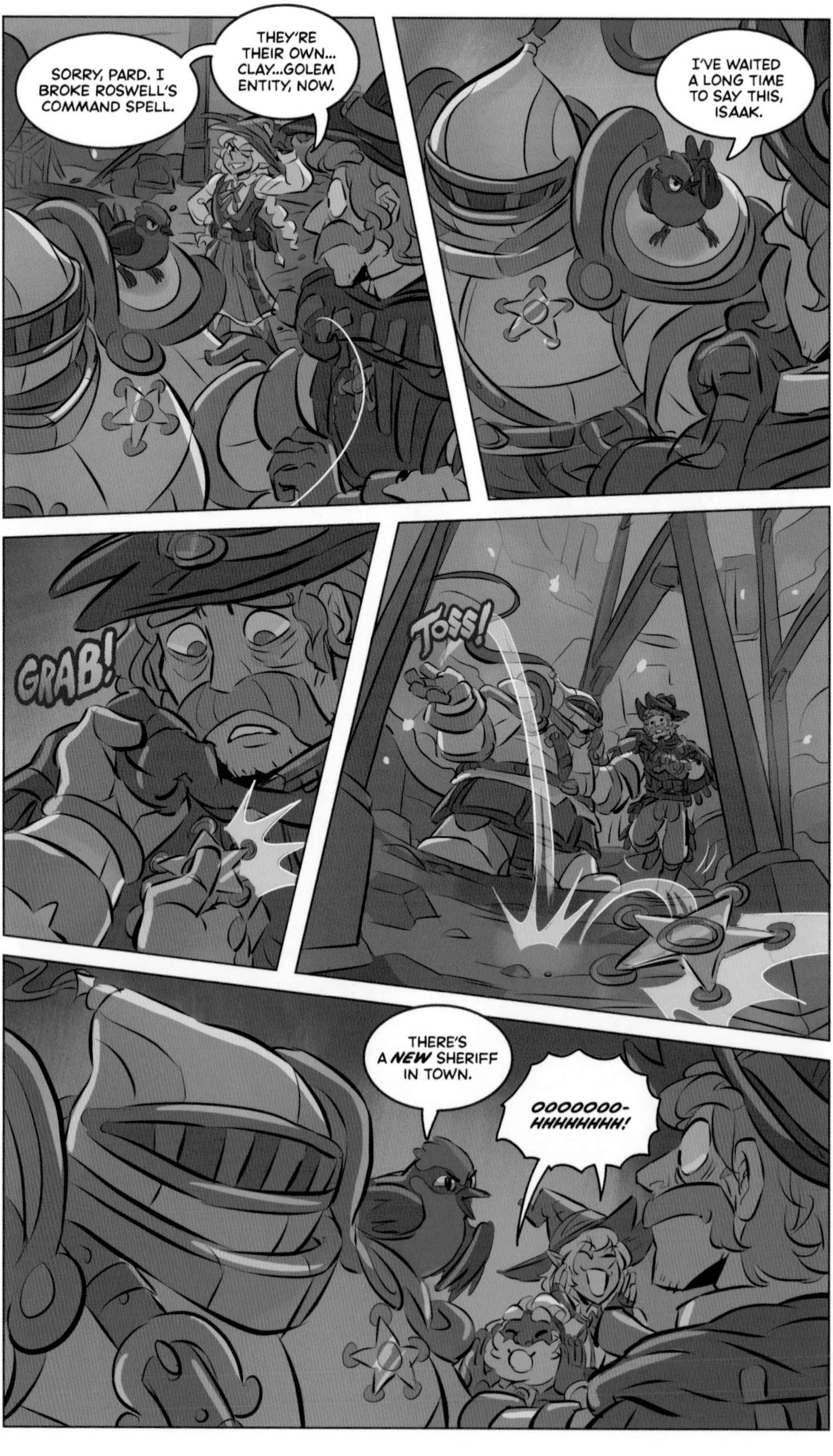
SORRY, PARD. I BROKE ROSWELL'S COMMAND SPELL.
THEY'RE THEIR OWN... CLAY...GOLEM ENTITY, NOW.
I'VE WAITED A LONG TIME TO SAY THIS, ISAAK.
GRAB!
TOSS!
THERE'S A NEW SHERIFF IN TOWN.
OOOOOOO-HHHHHHHH!

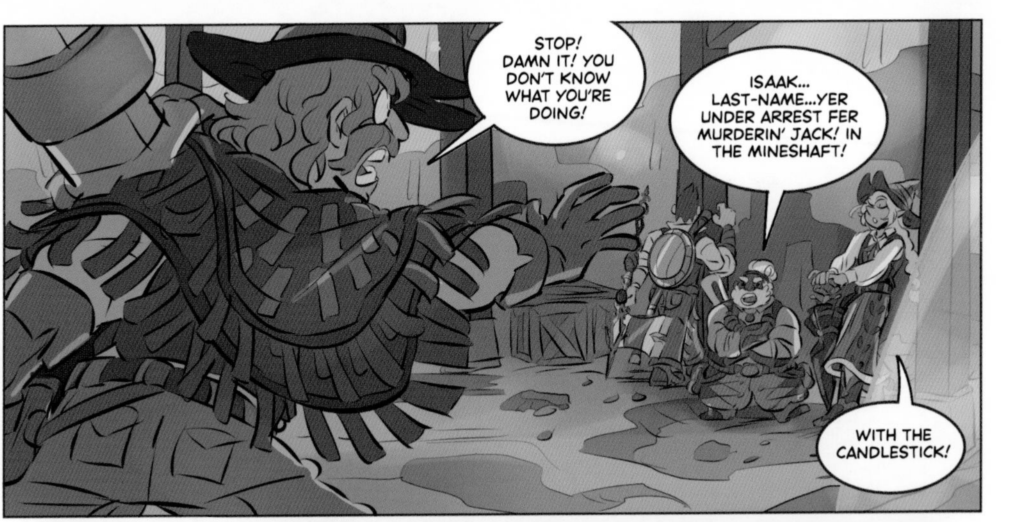
STOP! DAMN IT! YOU DON'T KNOW WHAT YOU'RE DOING!
ISAAK... LAST-NAME...YER UNDER ARREST FER MURDERIN' JACK! IN THE MINESHAFT!
WITH THE CANDLESTICK!

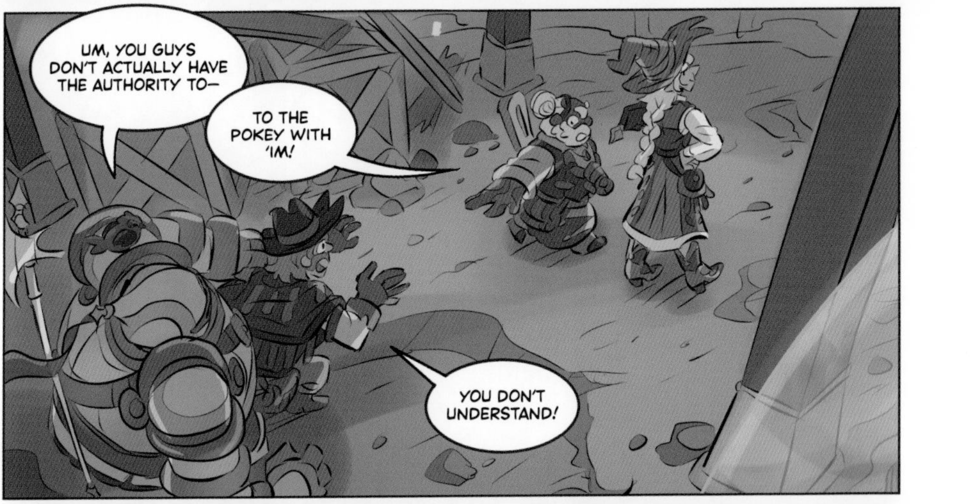
UM, YOU GUYS DON'T ACTUALLY HAVE THE AUTHORITY TO—
TO THE POKEY WITH 'IM!
YOU DON'T UNDERSTAND!

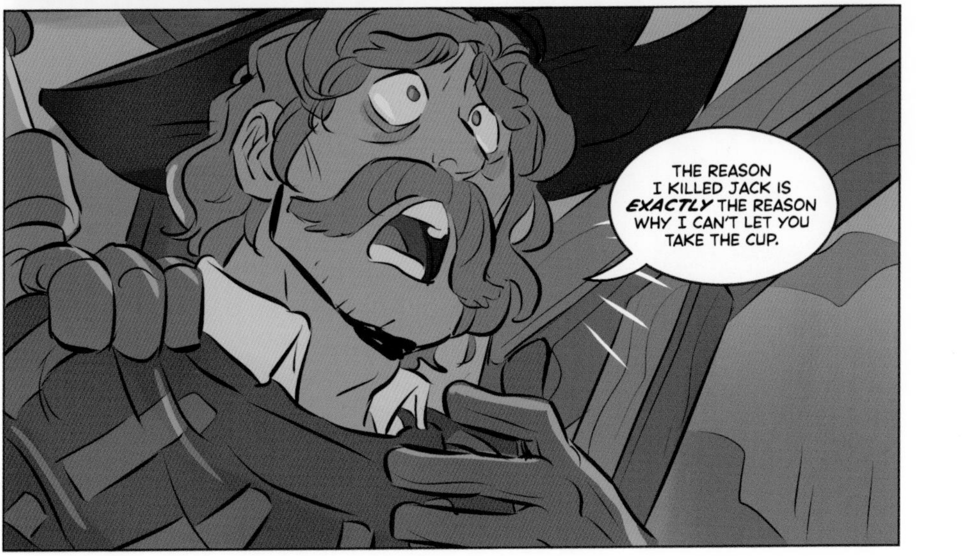
THE REASON I KILLED JACK IS **EXACTLY** THE REASON WHY I CAN'T LET YOU TAKE THE CUP.

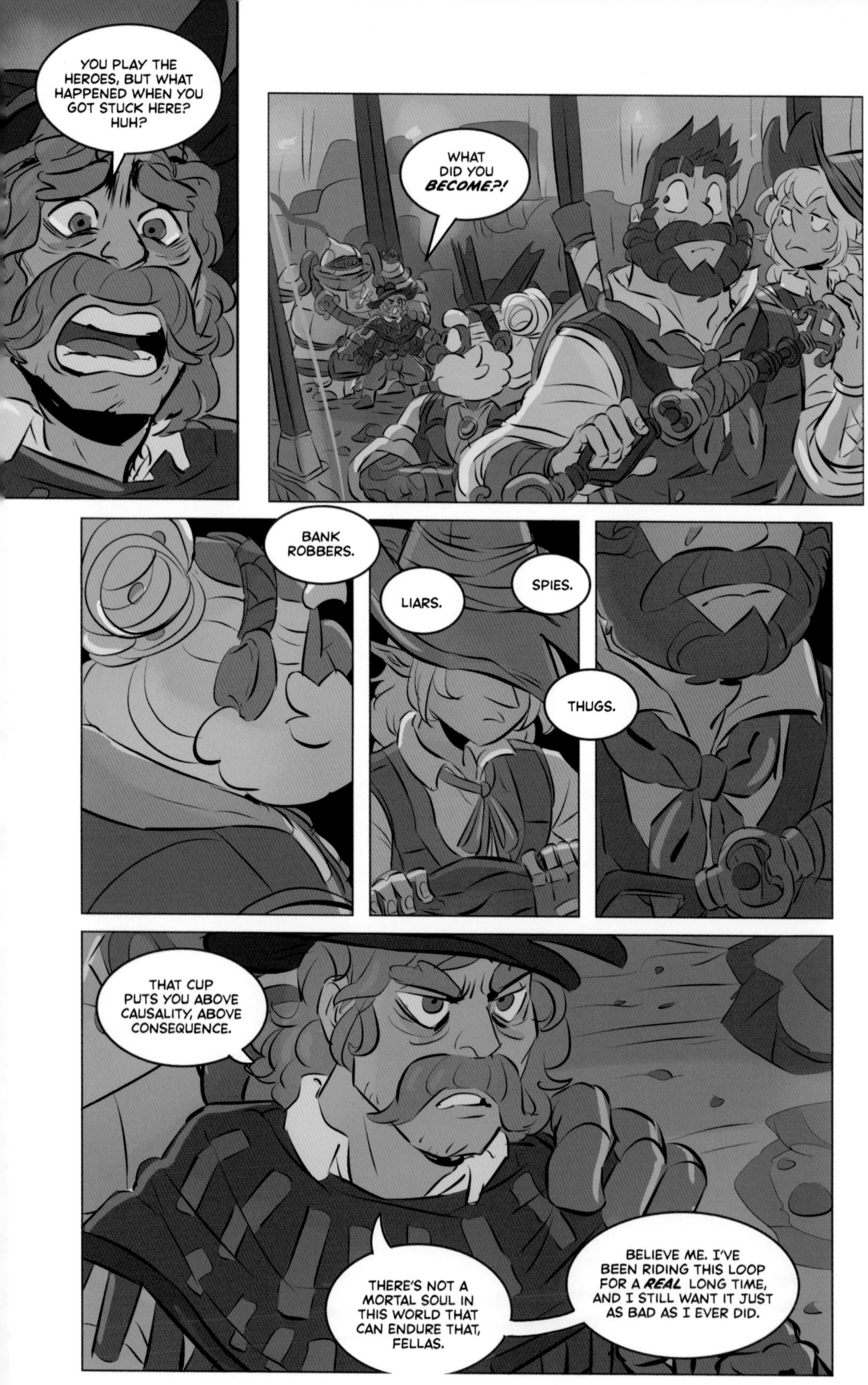
YOU PLAY THE HEROES, BUT WHAT HAPPENED WHEN YOU GOT STUCK HERE? HUH?
WHAT DID YOU *BECOME?!*
BANK ROBBERS.
LIARS.
SPIES.
THUGS.
THAT CUP PUTS YOU ABOVE CAUSALITY, ABOVE CONSEQUENCE.
THERE'S NOT A MORTAL SOUL IN THIS WORLD THAT CAN ENDURE THAT, FELLAS.
BELIEVE ME. I'VE BEEN RIDING THIS LOOP FOR A *REAL* LONG TIME, AND I STILL WANT IT JUST AS BAD AS I EVER DID.

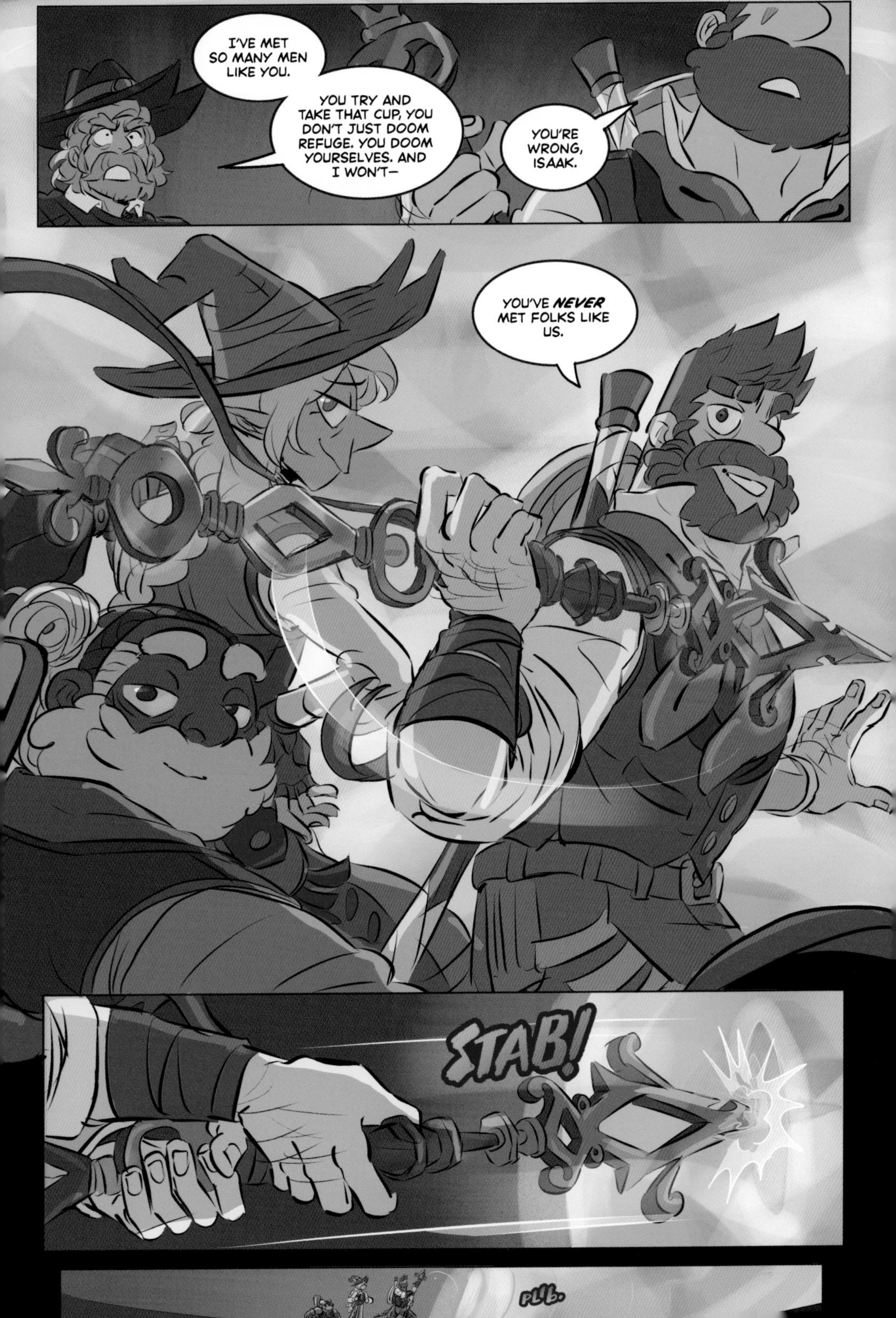
I'VE MET SO MANY MEN LIKE YOU.
YOU TRY AND TAKE THAT CUP, YOU DON'T JUST DOOM REFUGE. YOU DOOM YOURSELVES. AND I WON'T—
YOU'RE WRONG, ISAAK.
YOU'VE ***NEVER*** MET FOLKS LIKE US.
STAB!
plib.

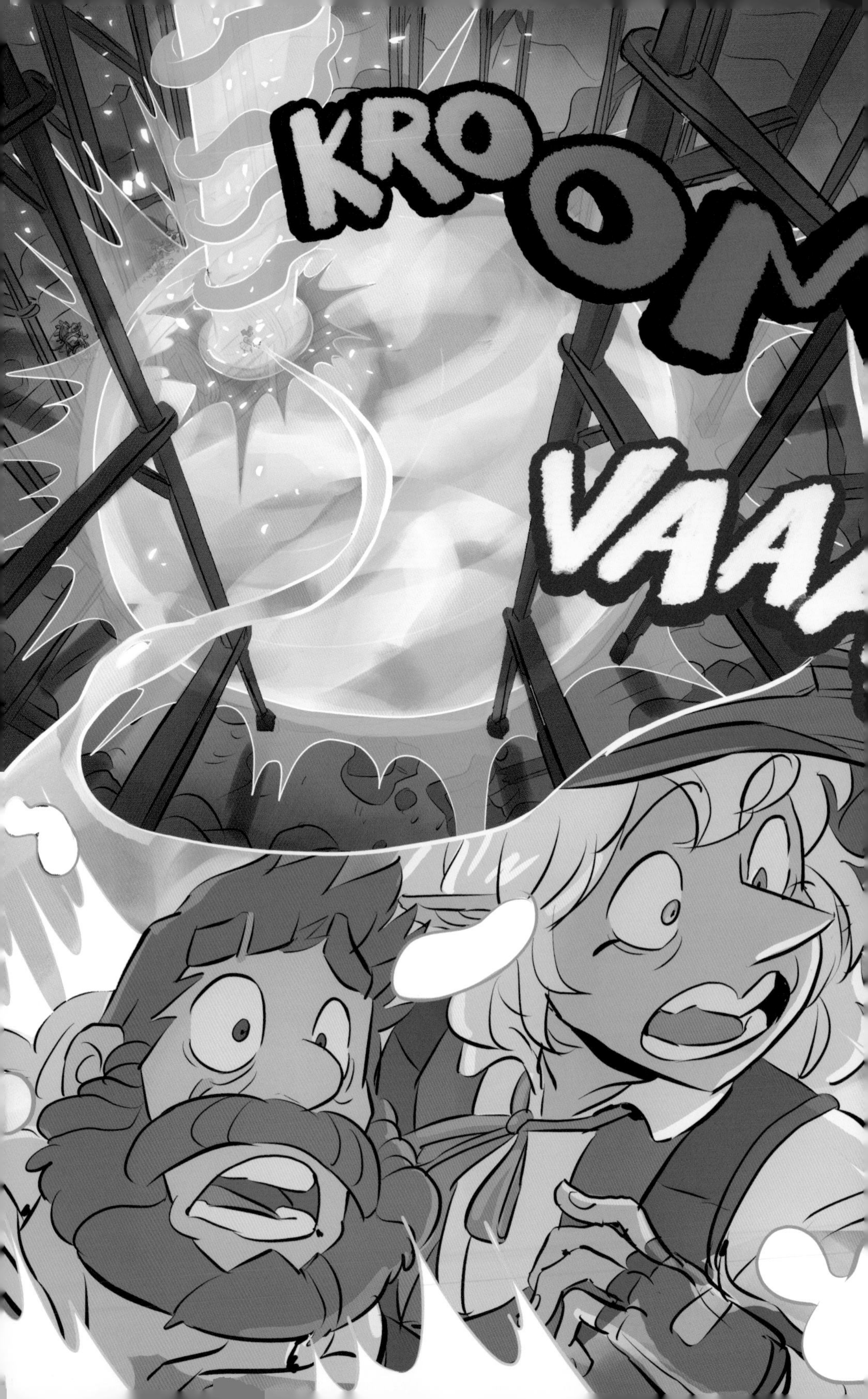
KROOM
VAA

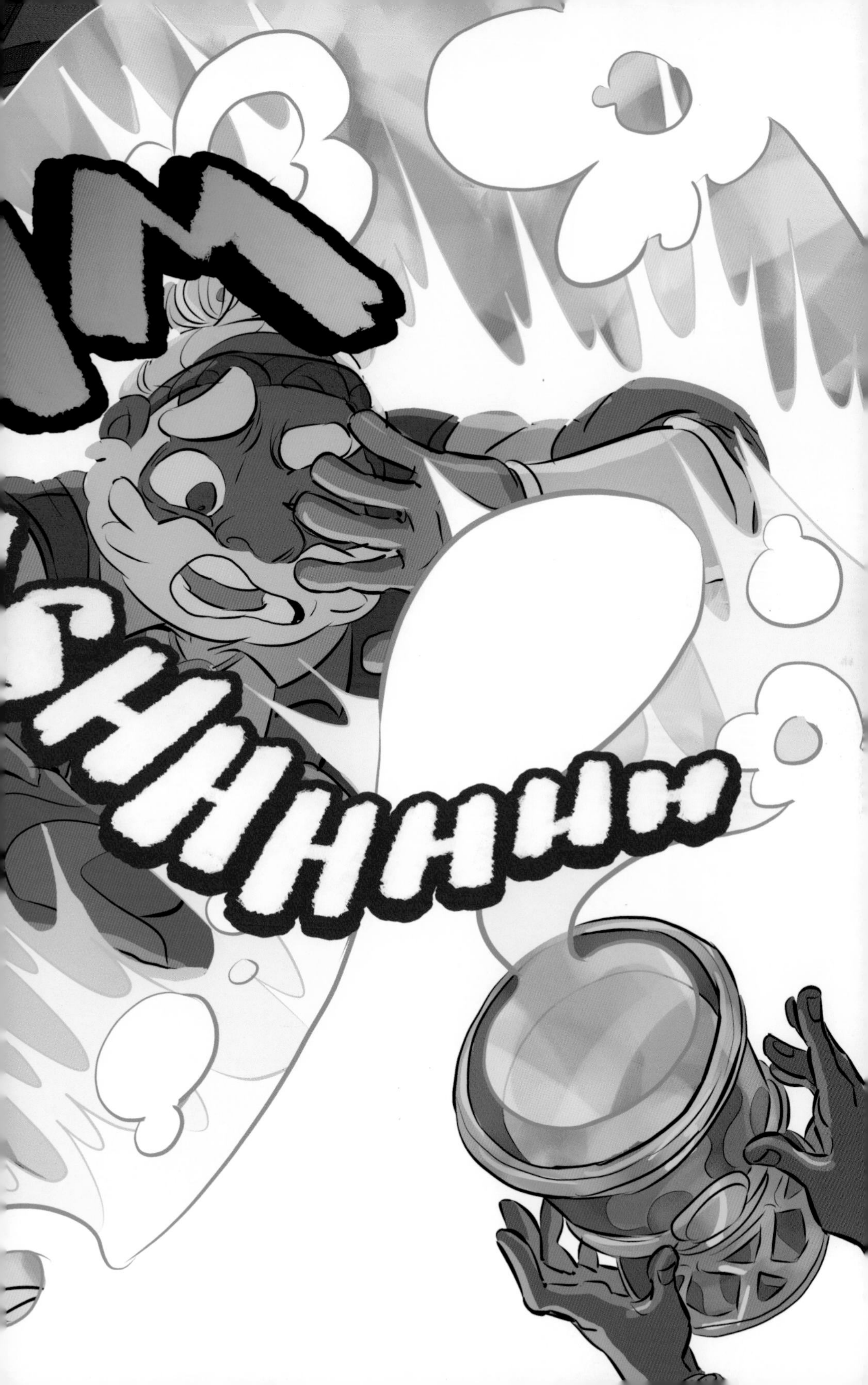
SHHHHHHH

Chapter
112

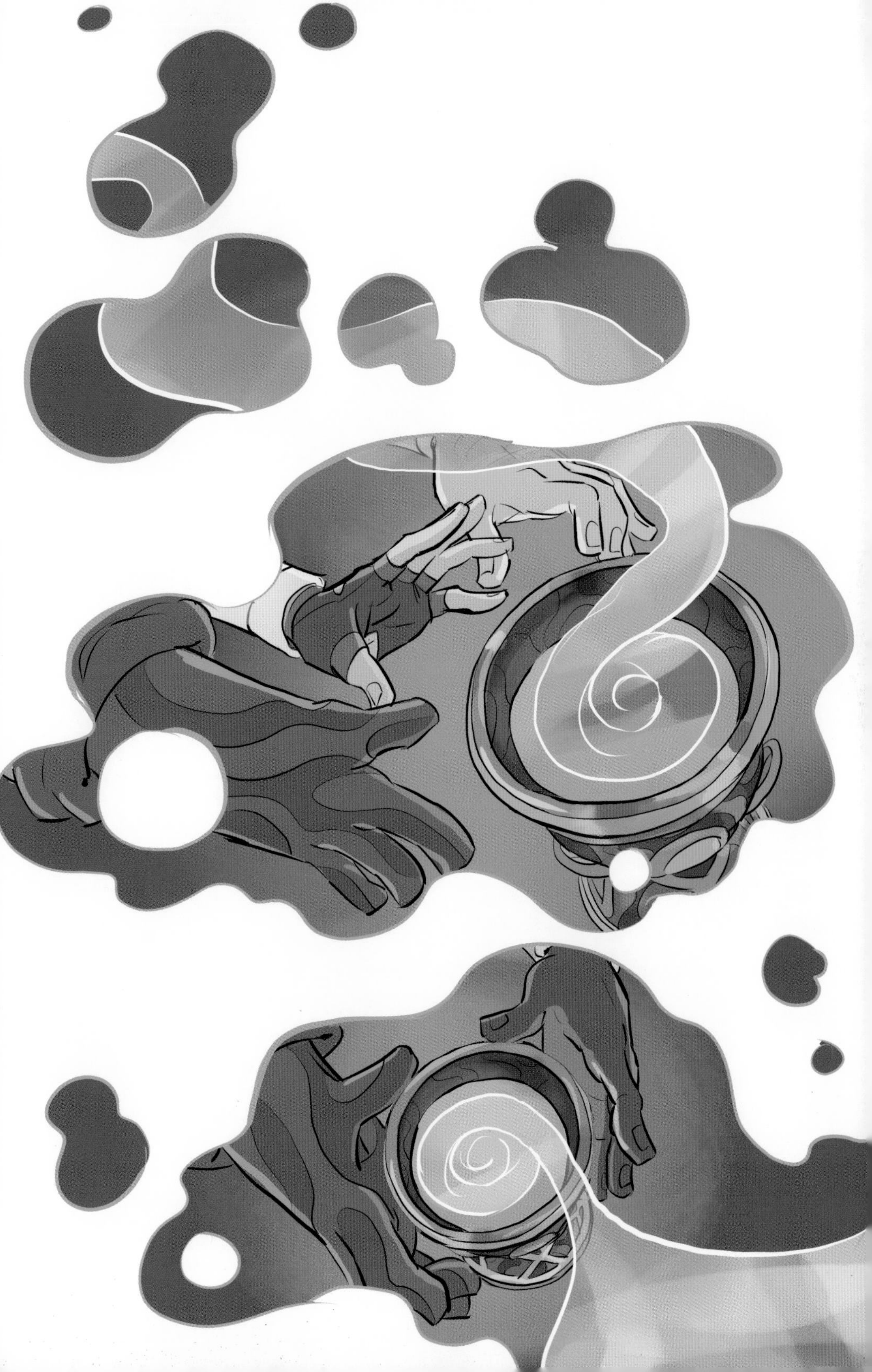

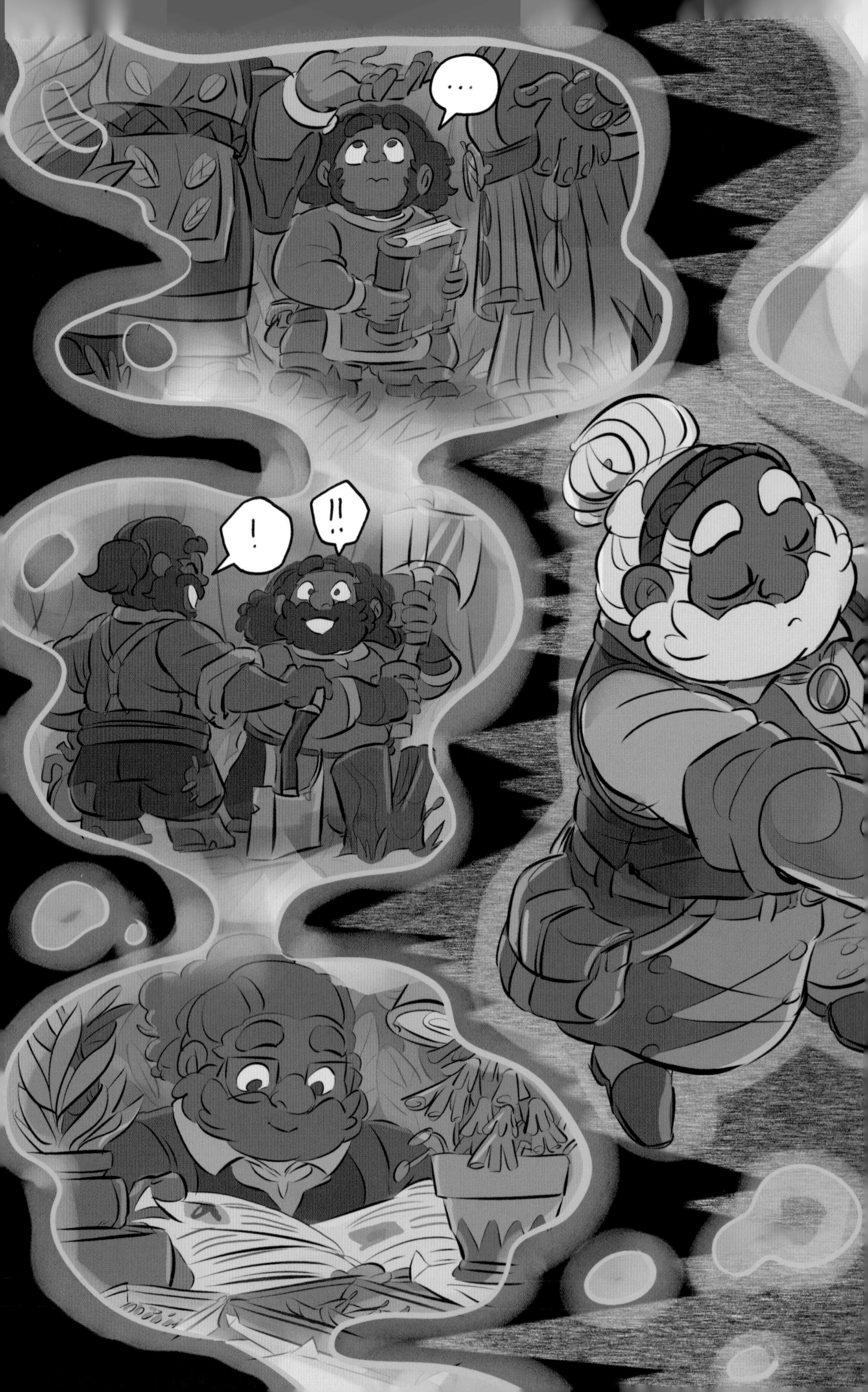
...
!
!!

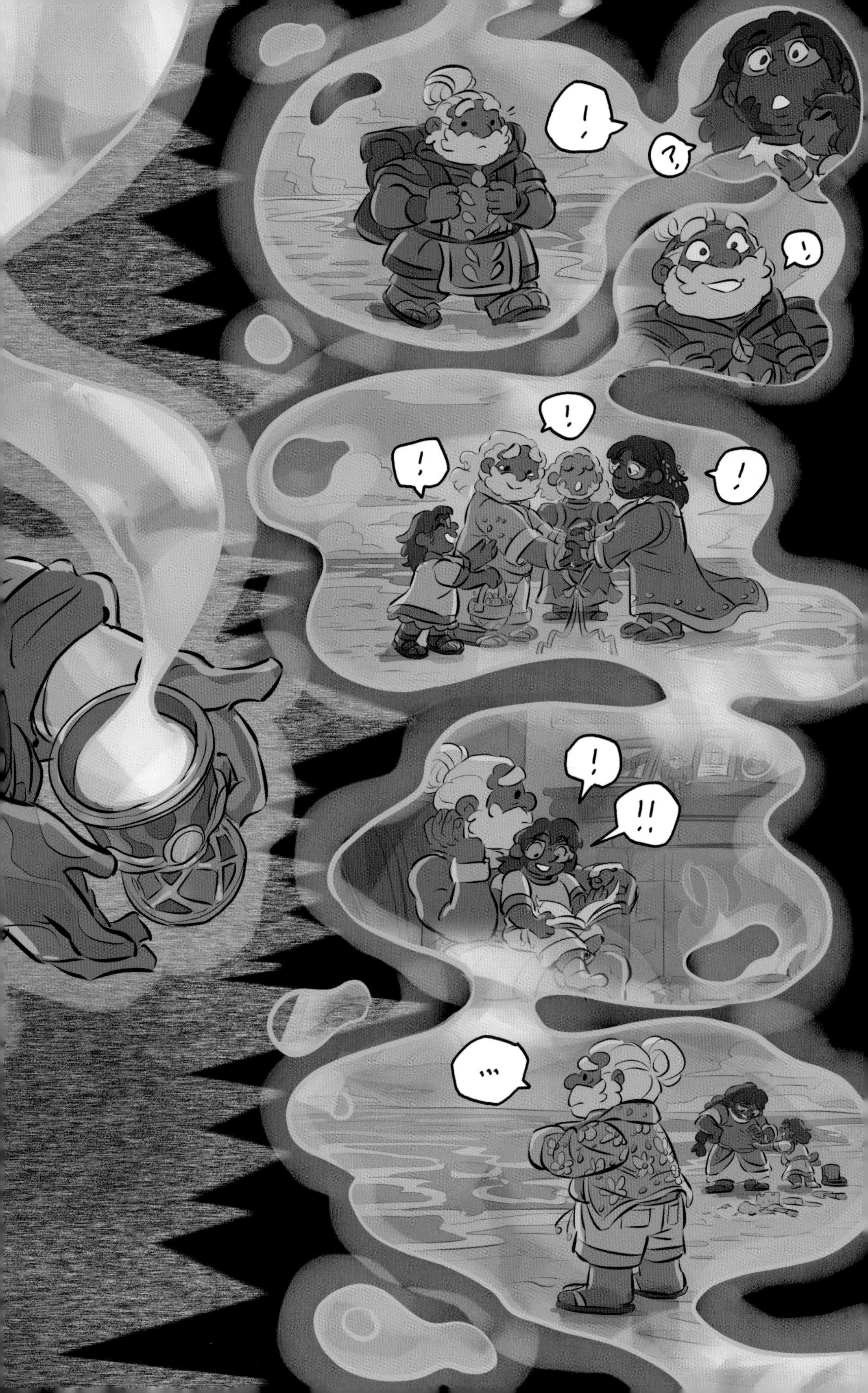
!
?
!
!
!
!
!
!
!!
...

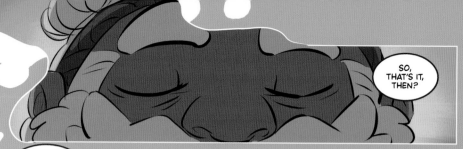

SO, THAT'S IT, THEN?

DAMN IT, *LOOK AT ME!*

MERLE!

AFTER *EVERYTHING* WE'VE GONE THROUGH, YOU'RE JUST *DISAPPEARING?* YOU'RE JUST GONNA—

I DON'T KNOW, HECUBA!

I DON'T KNOW WHAT I'M DOING!

LET ME CLEAR IT UP FOR YOU, THEN, MERLE.

YOU'RE *RUNNING.* YOU'RE DESTROYING THE ONLY GOOD THING IN YOUR GODS-DAMNED *PITIFUL* LIFE. BECAUSE RAISING YOUR CHILDREN IS *HARD.*

YOU'RE RIGHT! I'M A SHITTY DAD!

MAVIS AND MOOKIE ARE THE ONLY GOOD THINGS IN MY LIFE.

BUT THAT LIFE IS...WRONG. SOMETHING IS MISSING.

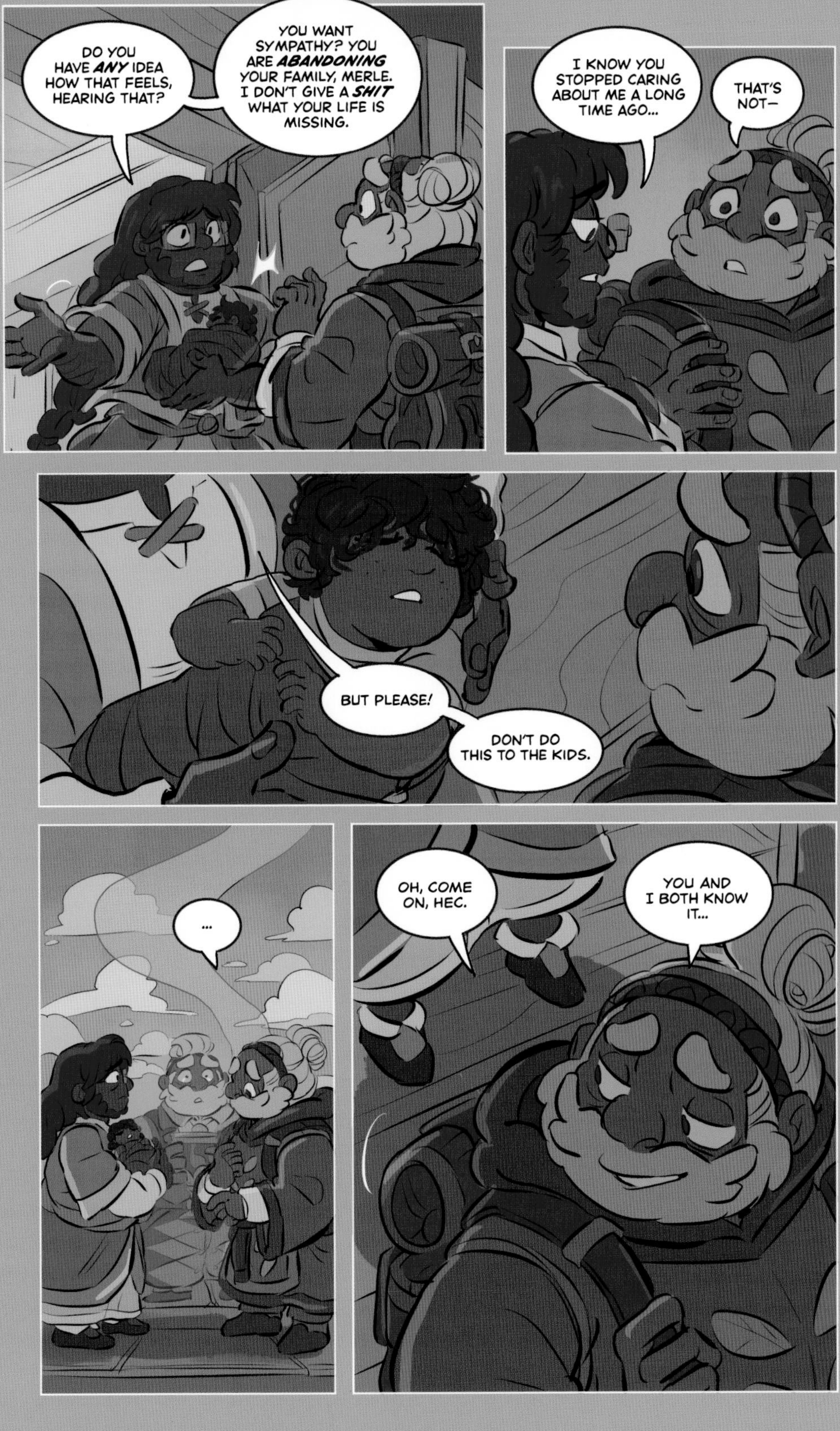
DO YOU HAVE ANY IDEA HOW THAT FEELS, HEARING THAT?
YOU WANT SYMPATHY? YOU ARE ABANDONING YOUR FAMILY, MERLE. I DON'T GIVE A SHIT WHAT YOUR LIFE IS MISSING.
I KNOW YOU STOPPED CARING ABOUT ME A LONG TIME AGO...
THAT'S NOT—
BUT PLEASE!
DON'T DO THIS TO THE KIDS.
...
OH, COME ON, HEC.
YOU AND I BOTH KNOW IT...

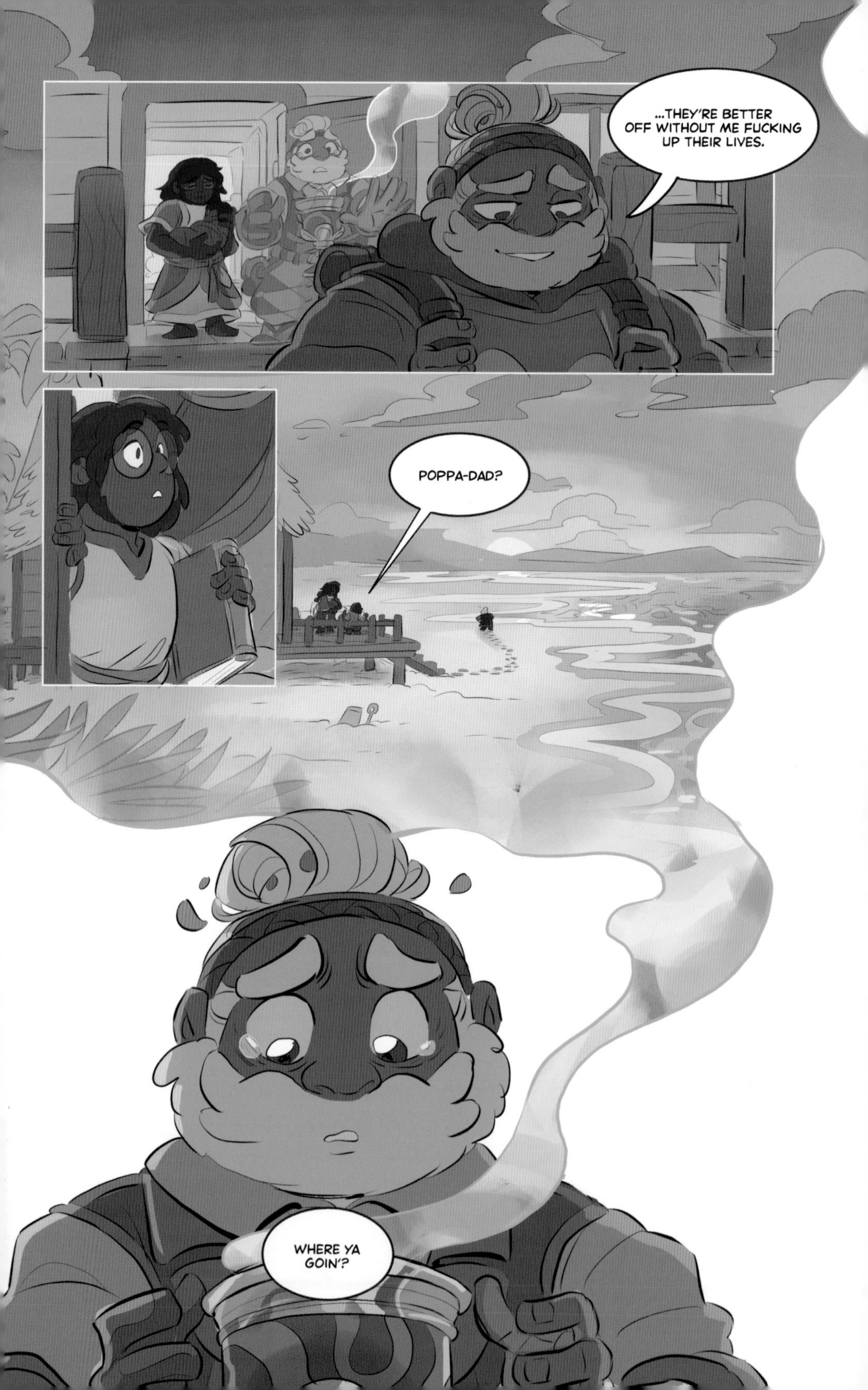
...THEY'RE BETTER OFF WITHOUT ME FUCKING UP THEIR LIVES.
POPPA-DAD?
WHERE YA GOIN'?

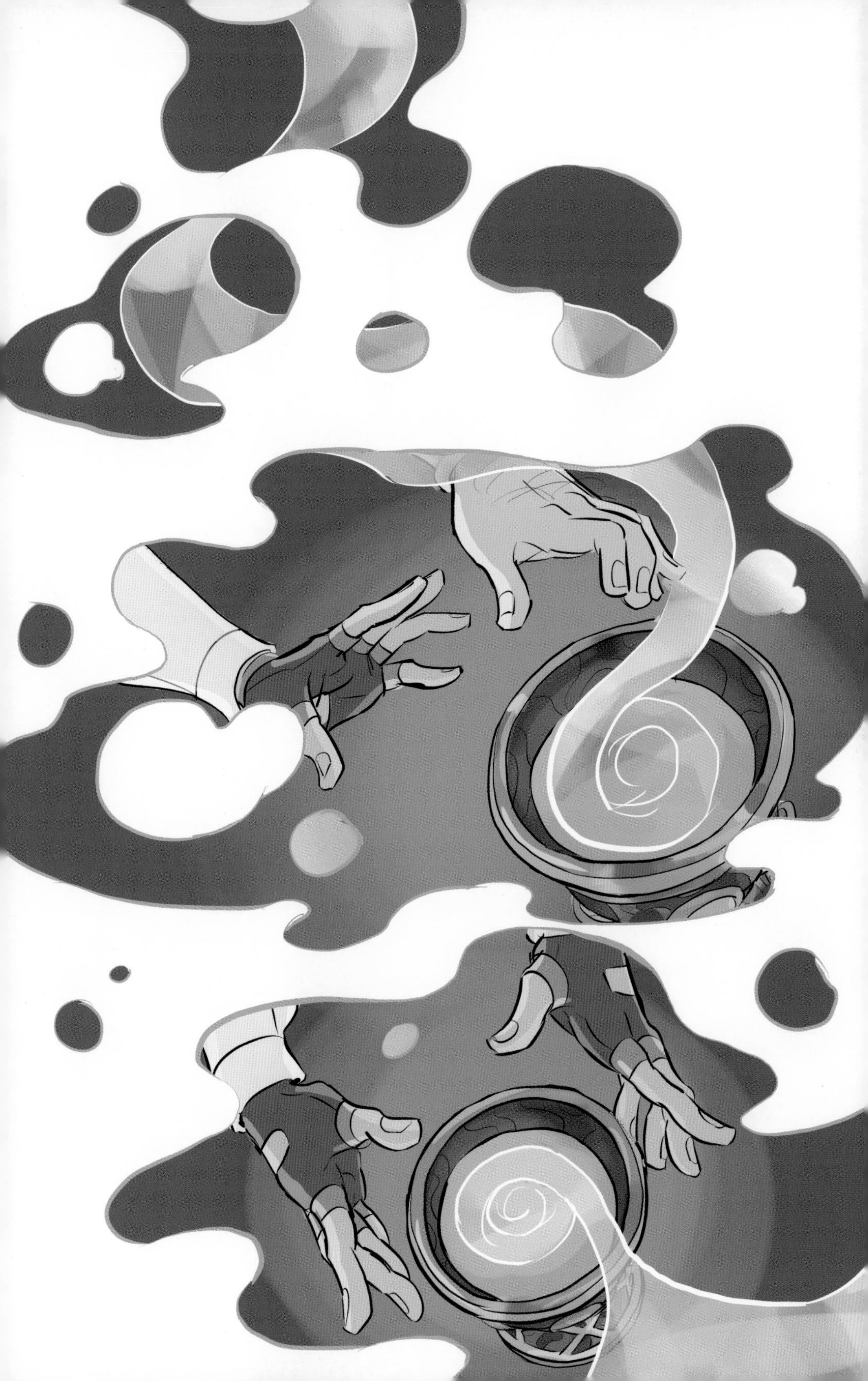

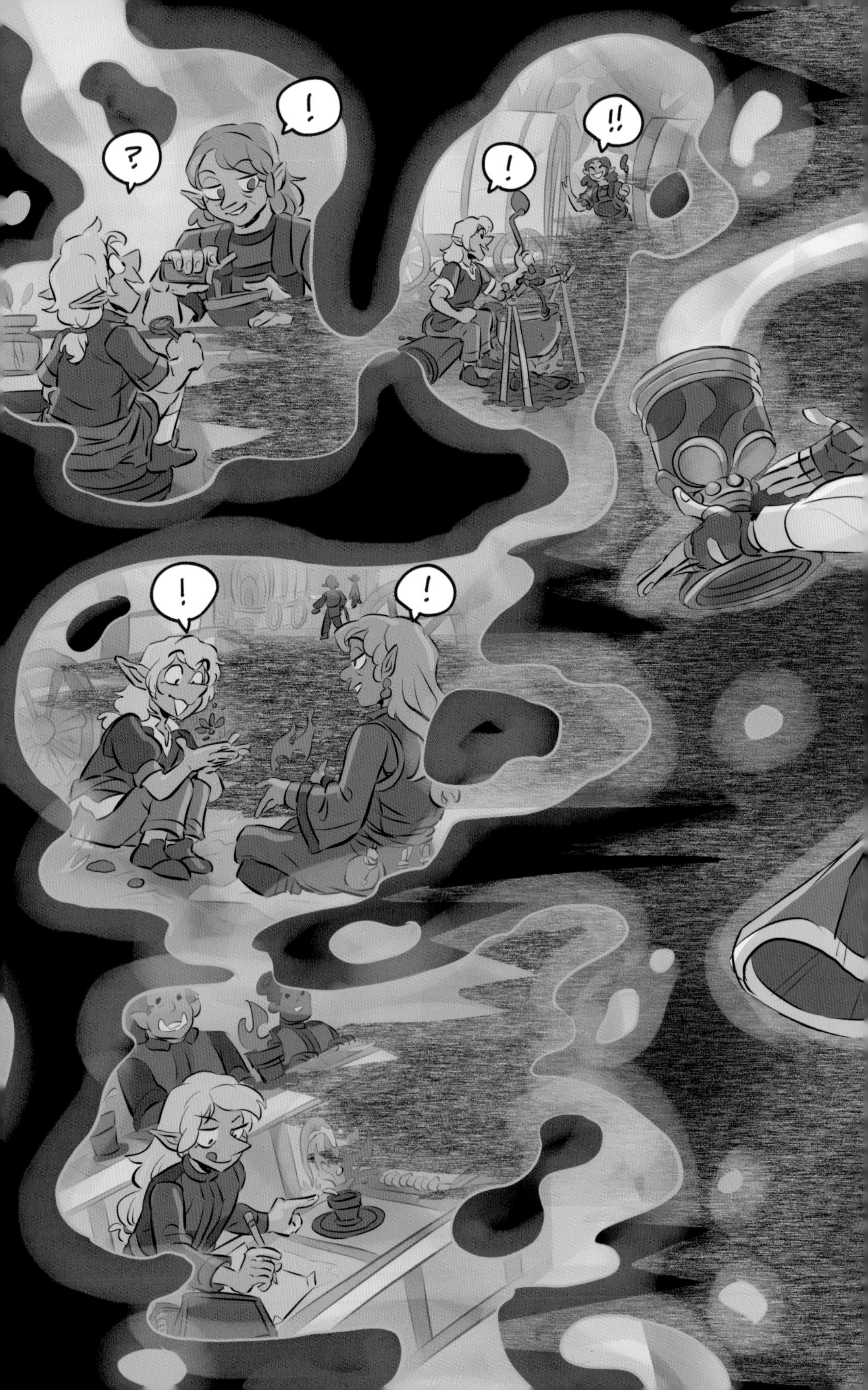
?
!
!
!!
!
!

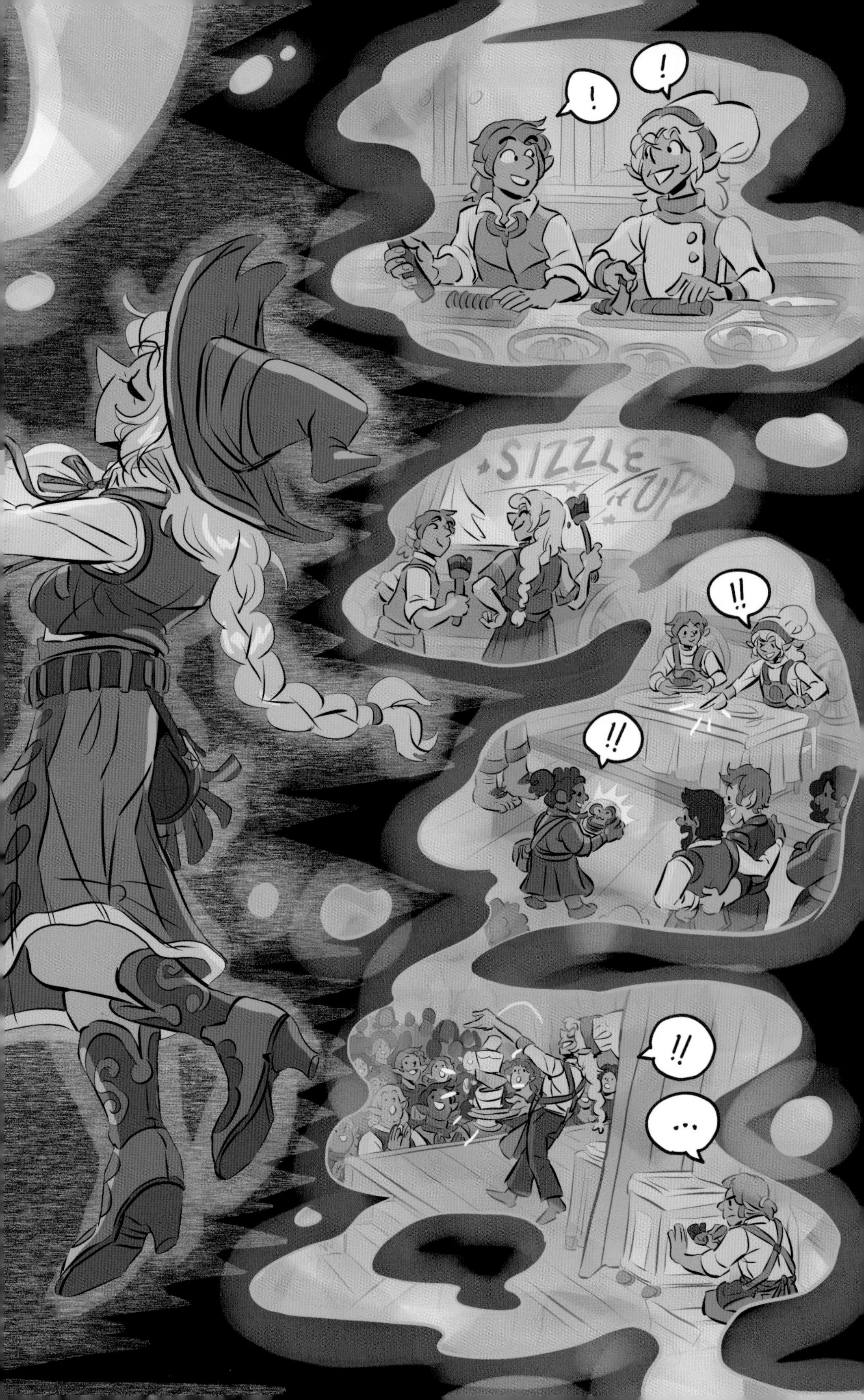
!
!
SIZZLE IT UP
!!
!!
!!
...

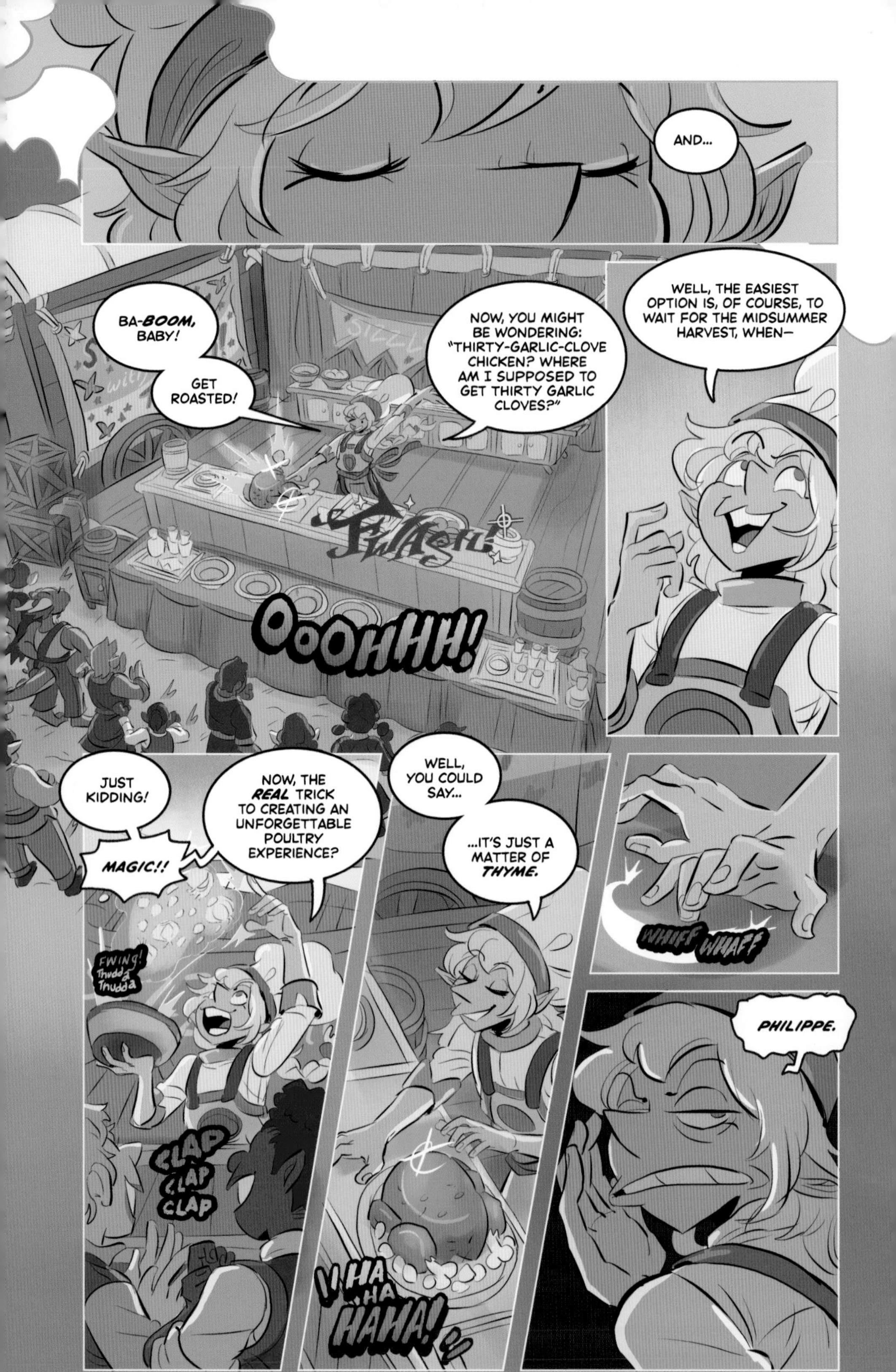
AND...
BA-BOOM, BABY!
GET ROASTED!
NOW, YOU MIGHT BE WONDERING: "THIRTY-GARLIC-CLOVE CHICKEN? WHERE AM I SUPPOSED TO GET THIRTY GARLIC CLOVES?"
SWASH!
OOOHHHH!
WELL, THE EASIEST OPTION IS, OF COURSE, TO WAIT FOR THE MIDSUMMER HARVEST, WHEN—
JUST KIDDING!
MAGIC!!
NOW, THE REAL TRICK TO CREATING AN UNFORGETTABLE POULTRY EXPERIENCE?
FWING! Thudda Thudda
CLAP CLAP CLAP
WELL, YOU COULD SAY...
...IT'S JUST A MATTER OF THYME.
HA HA HAHA!
WHIFF WHAFF
PHILIPPE.

HERE!

SORRY.

THIS IS WHY, PHILIPPE.

YOU ASKED WHY YOU'RE NOT ON STAGE WITH ME ANYMORE?

THIS IS WHY.

WELL, THEN, FOLKS! NOW THAT THE HELP HAS BEEN DEALT WITH—

WHO'S HUNGRY?

GLAMOUR SPRINGS, I TELL YA, YOU GUYS FORM THE MOST ORDERLY LINES.

EVERSUMMER? IT'S LIKE SERVING FOOD TO A PACK OF WILD JACKALS. YOU ALL, THOUGH—

WHOA, WHAT'S WRONG?

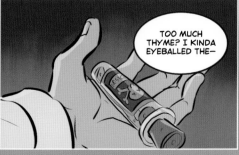

TOO MUCH THYME? I KINDA EYEBALLED THE—

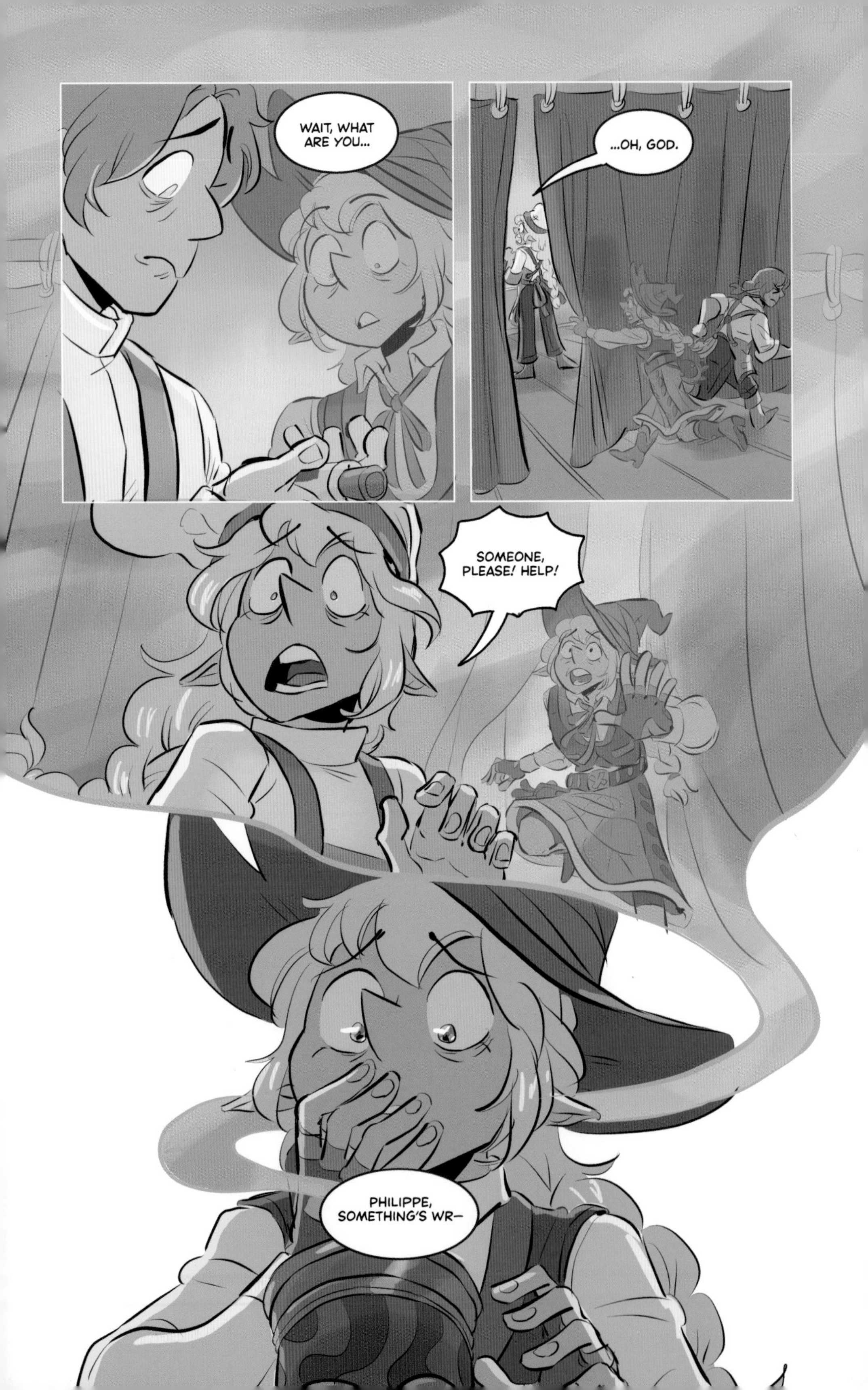
WAIT, WHAT ARE YOU...
...OH, GOD.
SOMEONE, PLEASE! HELP!
PHILIPPE, SOMETHING'S WR—

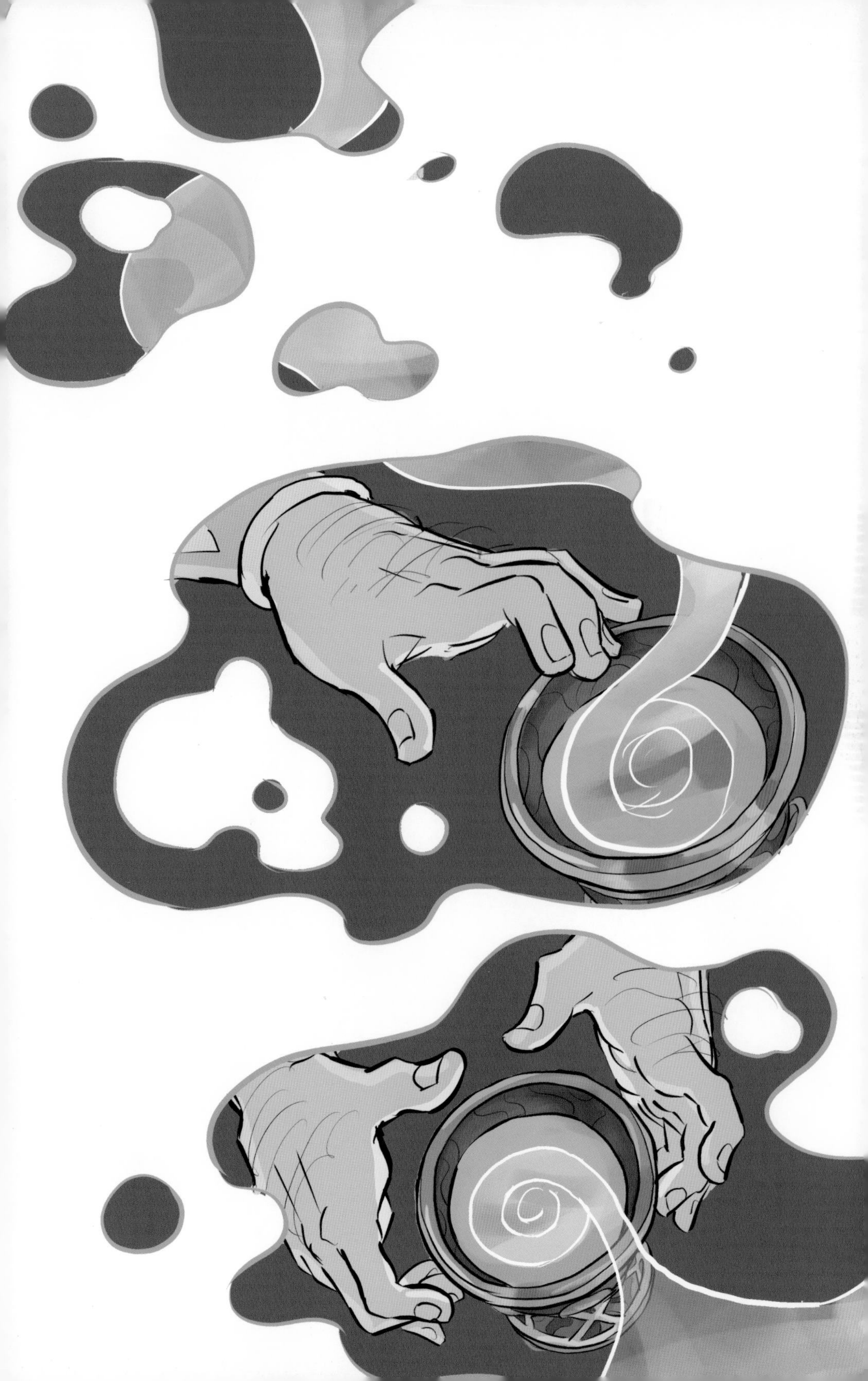

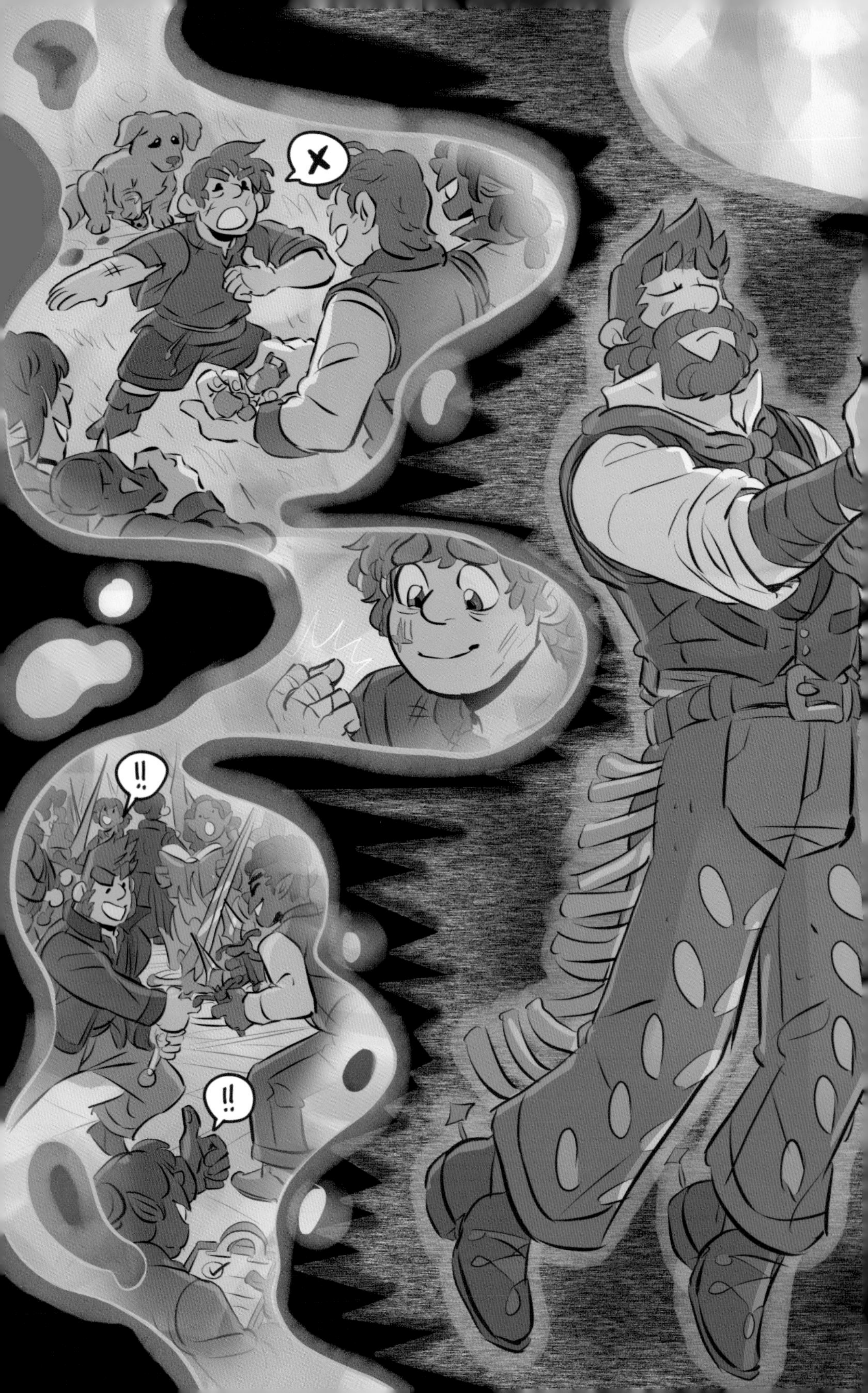
X
!!
!!

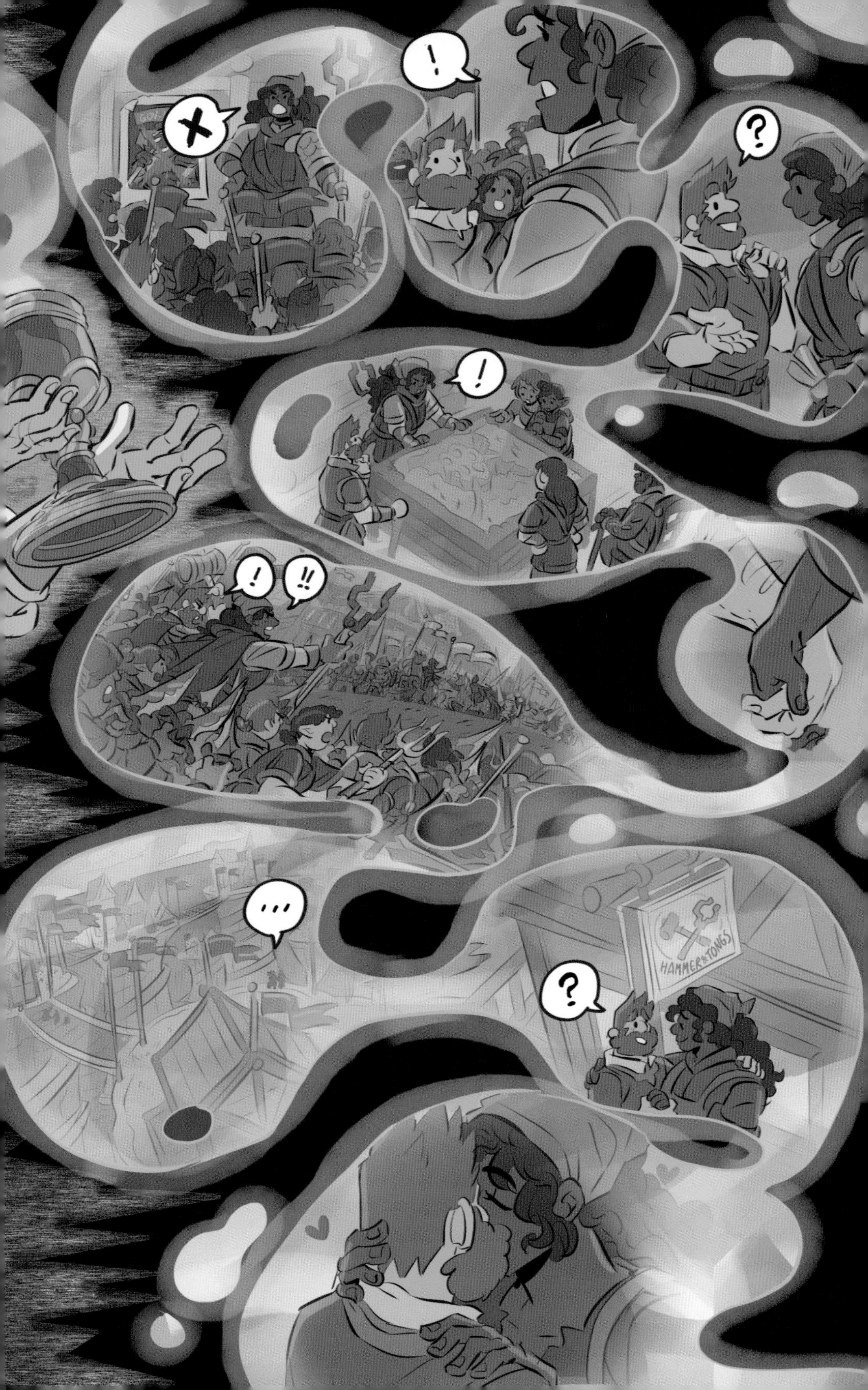
!
?
!
!
!!
...
HAMMER & TONGS
?

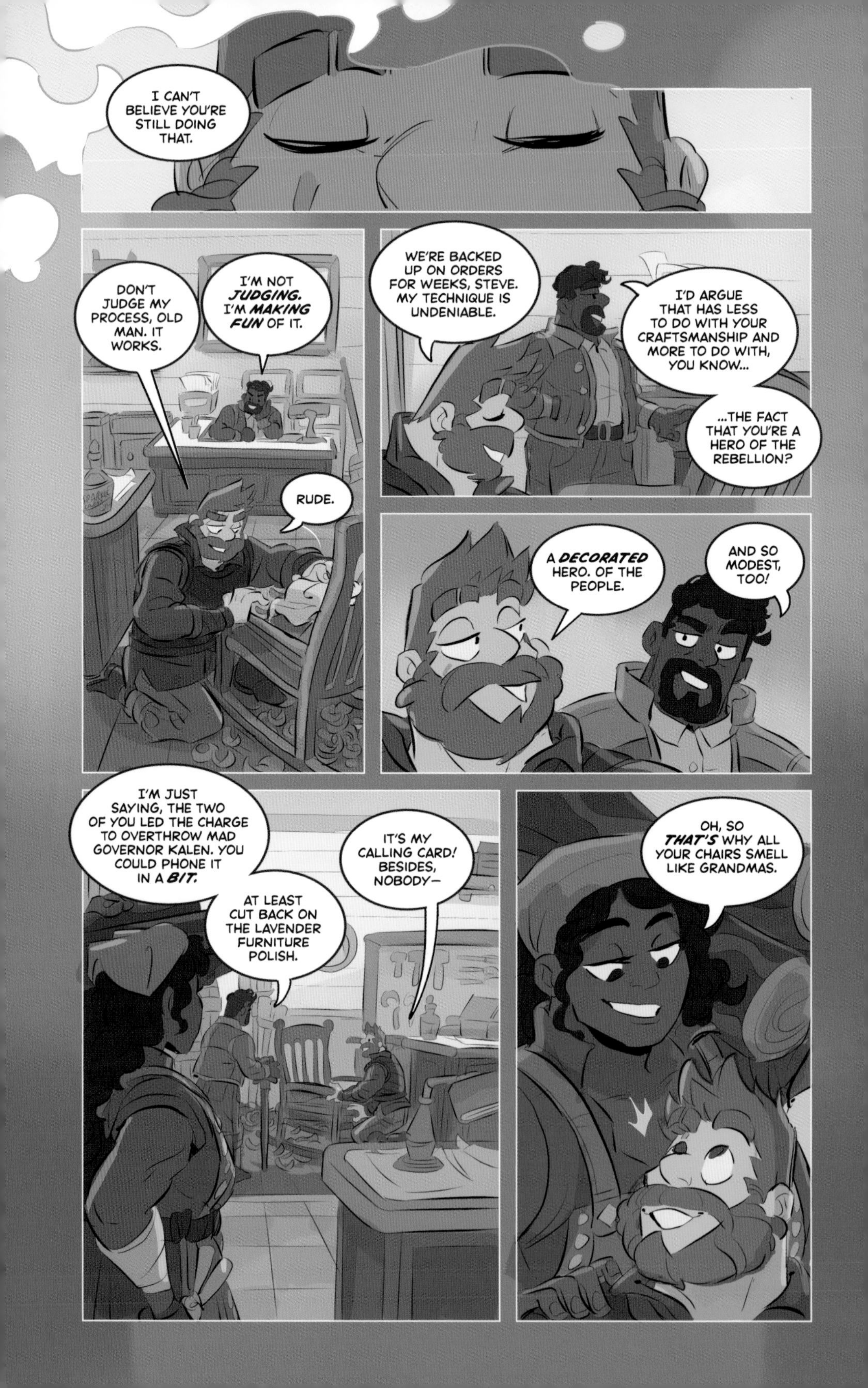
I CAN'T BELIEVE YOU'RE STILL DOING THAT.
DON'T JUDGE MY PROCESS, OLD MAN. IT WORKS.
I'M NOT JUDGING. I'M MAKING FUN OF IT.
RUDE.
WE'RE BACKED UP ON ORDERS FOR WEEKS, STEVE. MY TECHNIQUE IS UNDENIABLE.
I'D ARGUE THAT HAS LESS TO DO WITH YOUR CRAFTSMANSHIP AND MORE TO DO WITH, YOU KNOW...
...THE FACT THAT YOU'RE A HERO OF THE REBELLION?
A DECORATED HERO. OF THE PEOPLE.
AND SO MODEST, TOO!
I'M JUST SAYING, THE TWO OF YOU LED THE CHARGE TO OVERTHROW MAD GOVERNOR KALEN. YOU COULD PHONE IT IN A BIT.
AT LEAST CUT BACK ON THE LAVENDER FURNITURE POLISH.
IT'S MY CALLING CARD! BESIDES, NOBODY—
OH, SO THAT'S WHY ALL YOUR CHAIRS SMELL LIKE GRANDMAS.

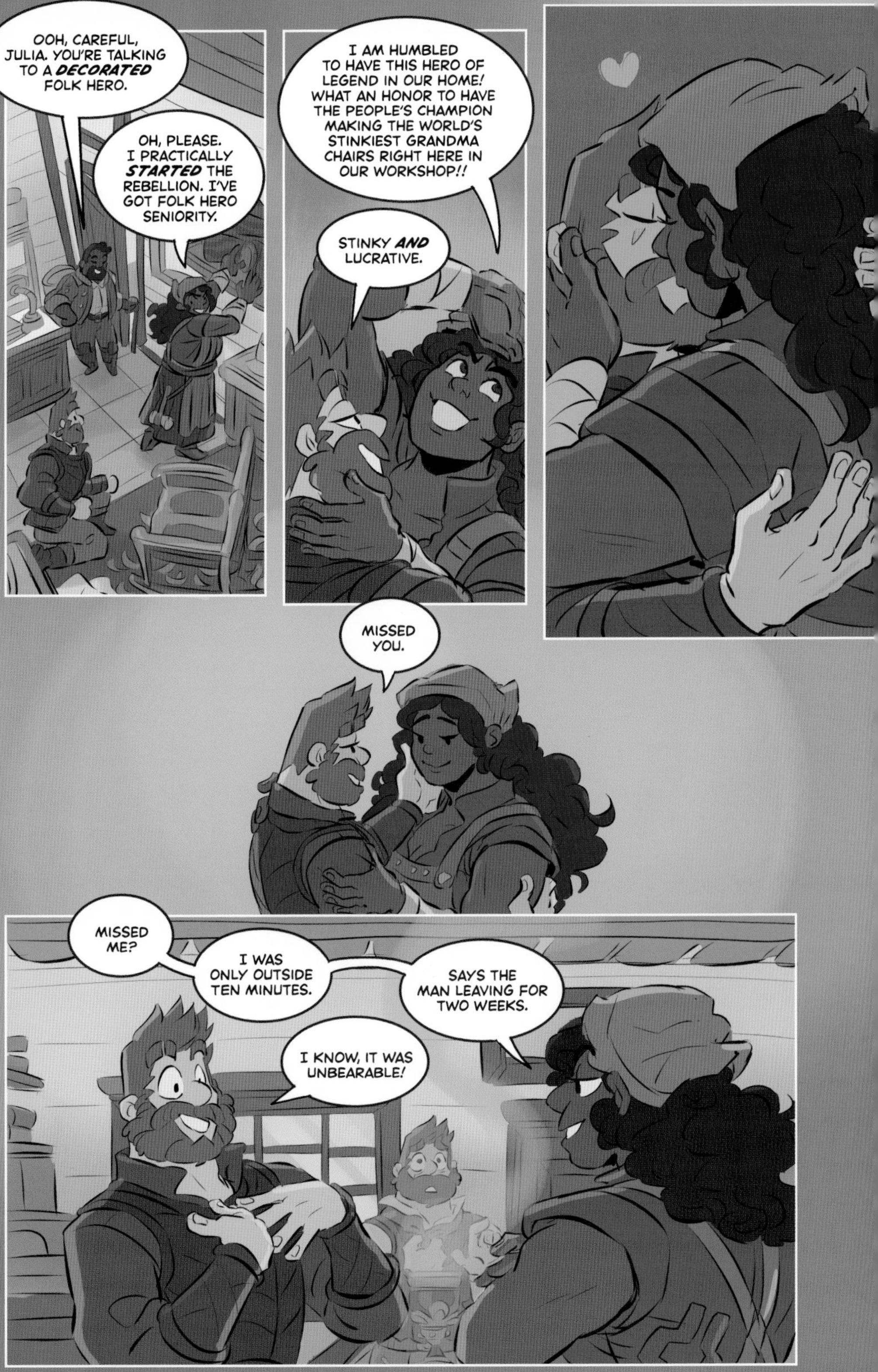
OOH, CAREFUL, JULIA. YOU'RE TALKING TO A *DECORATED* FOLK HERO.
OH, PLEASE. I PRACTICALLY *STARTED* THE REBELLION. I'VE GOT FOLK HERO SENIORITY.
I AM HUMBLED TO HAVE THIS HERO OF LEGEND IN OUR HOME! WHAT AN HONOR TO HAVE THE PEOPLE'S CHAMPION MAKING THE WORLD'S STINKIEST GRANDMA CHAIRS RIGHT HERE IN OUR WORKSHOP!!
STINKY *AND* LUCRATIVE.
MISSED YOU.
MISSED ME?
I WAS ONLY OUTSIDE TEN MINUTES.
SAYS THE MAN LEAVING FOR TWO WEEKS.
I KNOW, IT WAS UNBEARABLE!

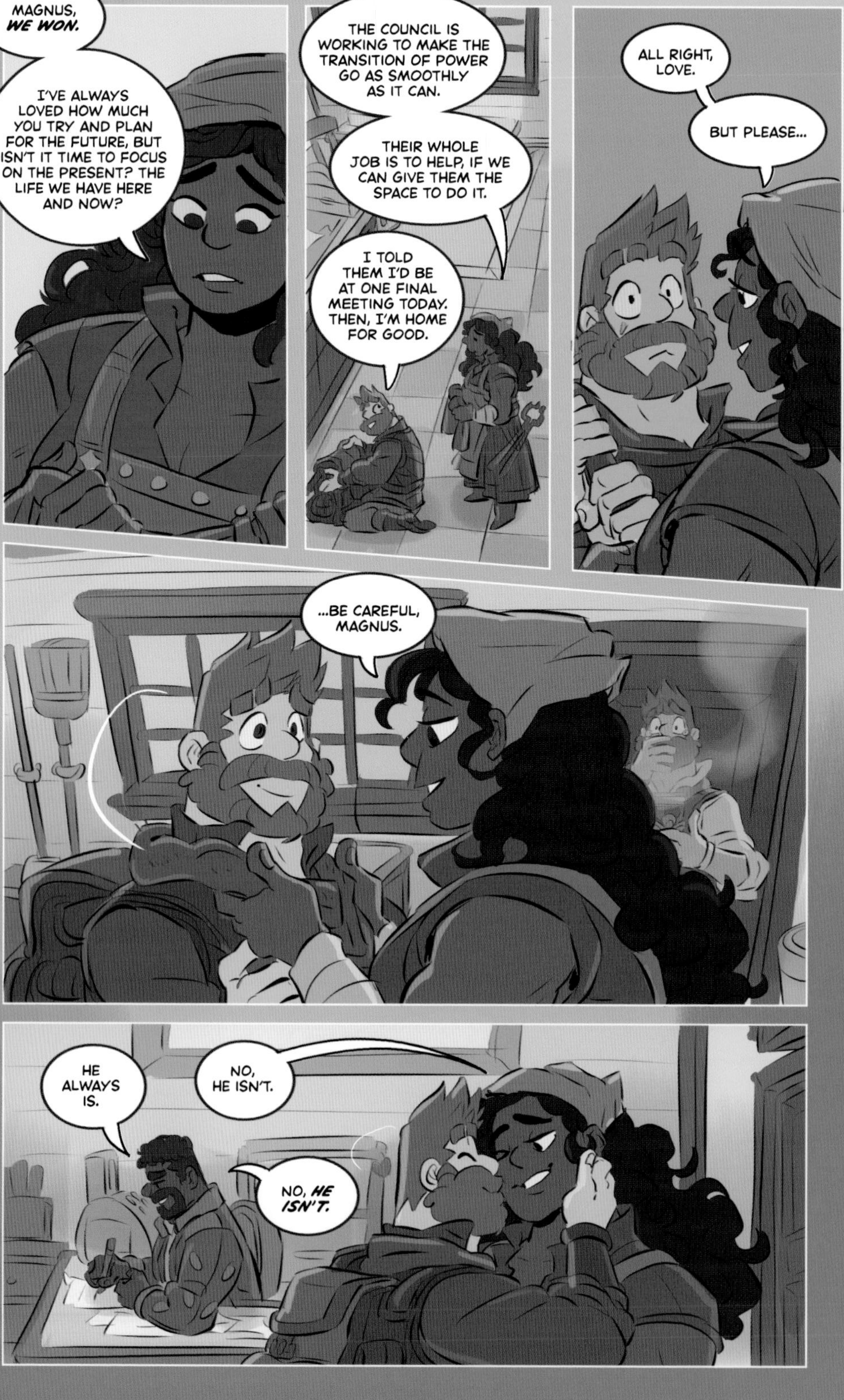
MAGNUS, ***WE WON.***
I'VE ALWAYS LOVED HOW MUCH YOU TRY AND PLAN FOR THE FUTURE, BUT ISN'T IT TIME TO FOCUS ON THE PRESENT? THE LIFE WE HAVE HERE AND NOW?
THE COUNCIL IS WORKING TO MAKE THE TRANSITION OF POWER GO AS SMOOTHLY AS IT CAN.
THEIR WHOLE JOB IS TO HELP, IF WE CAN GIVE THEM THE SPACE TO DO IT.
I TOLD THEM I'D BE AT ONE FINAL MEETING TODAY. THEN, I'M HOME FOR GOOD.
ALL RIGHT, LOVE.
BUT PLEASE...
...BE CAREFUL, MAGNUS.
HE ALWAYS IS.
NO, HE ISN'T.
NO, ***HE ISN'T.***

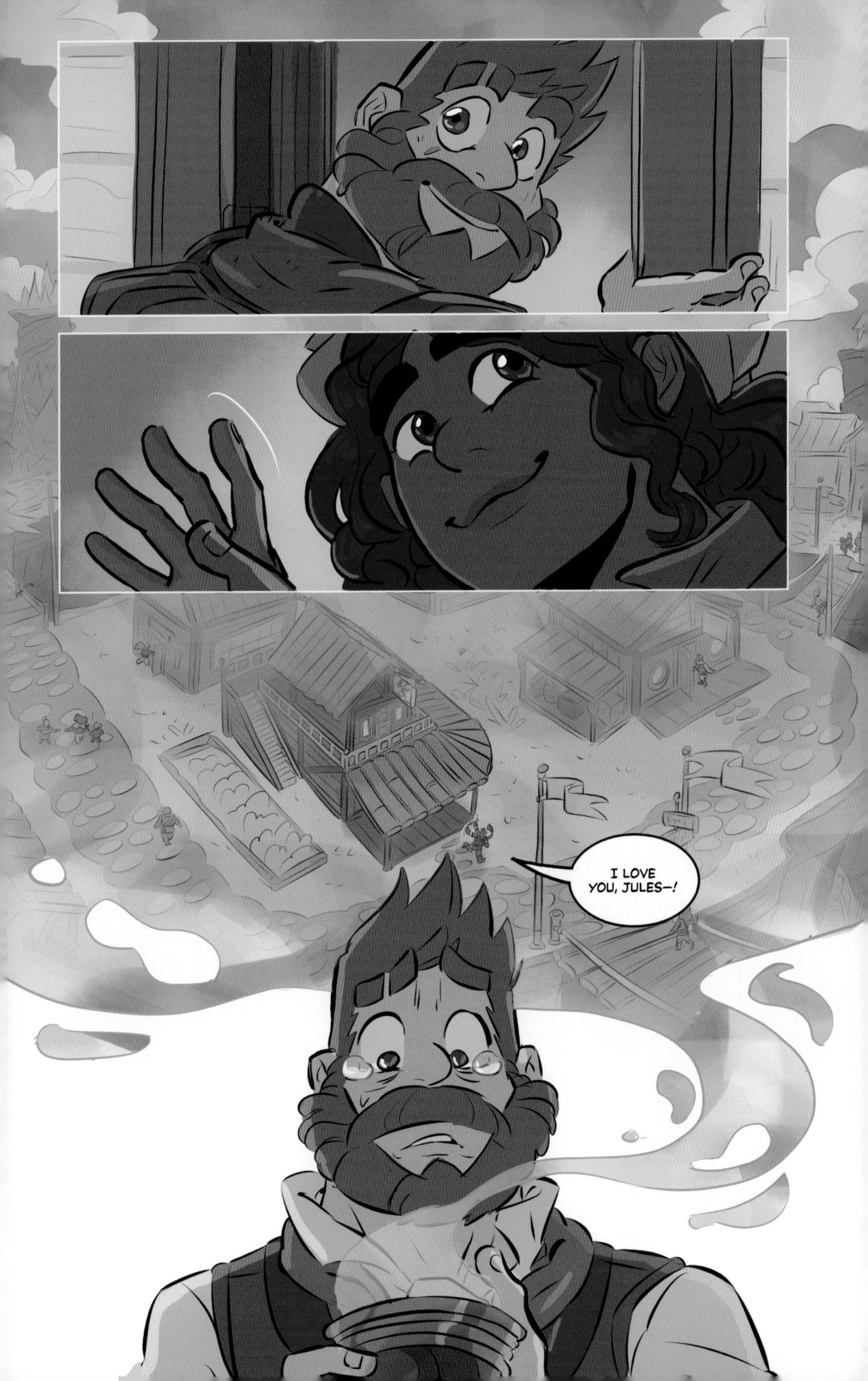
I LOVE YOU, JULES—!

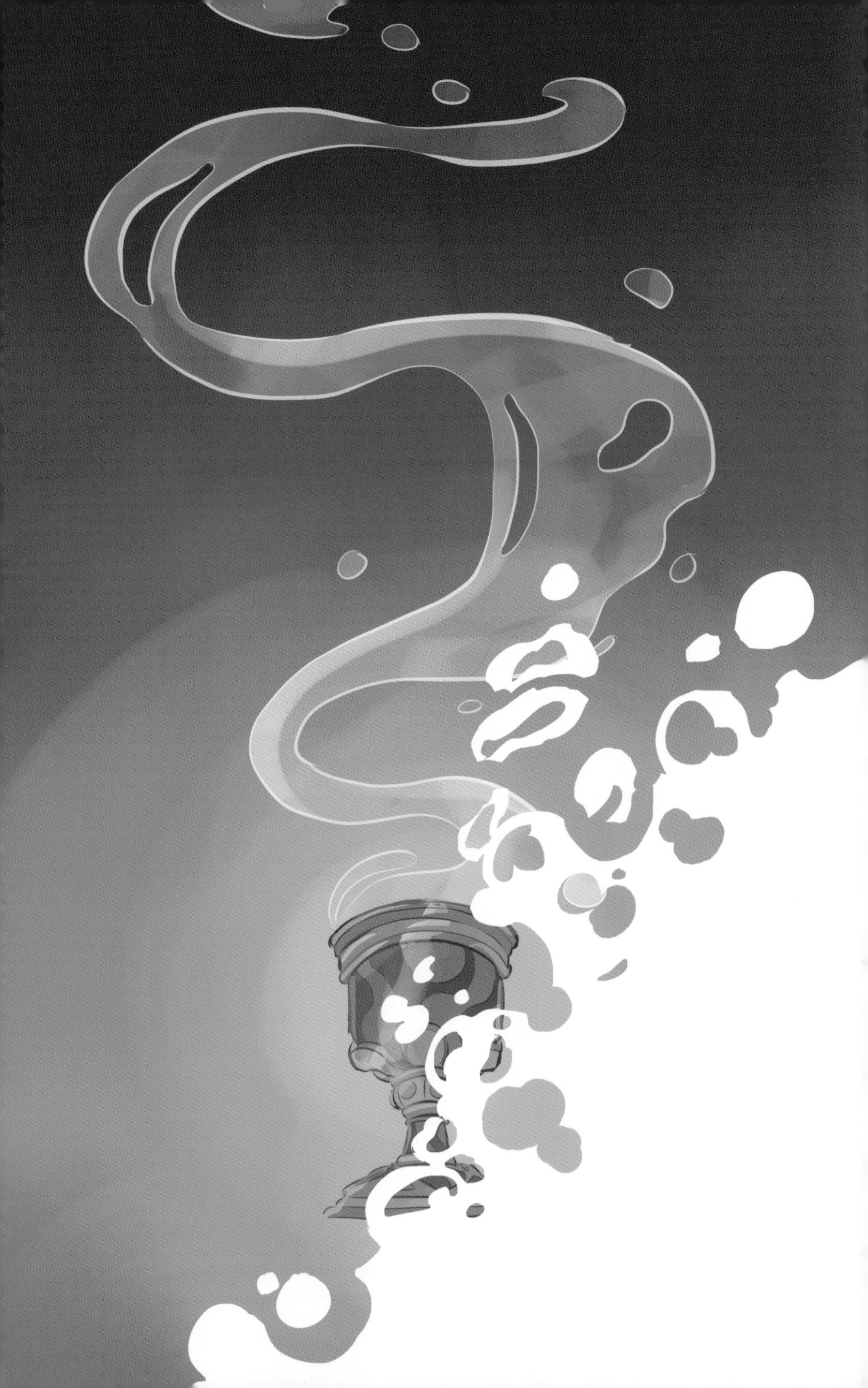

Chapter
113

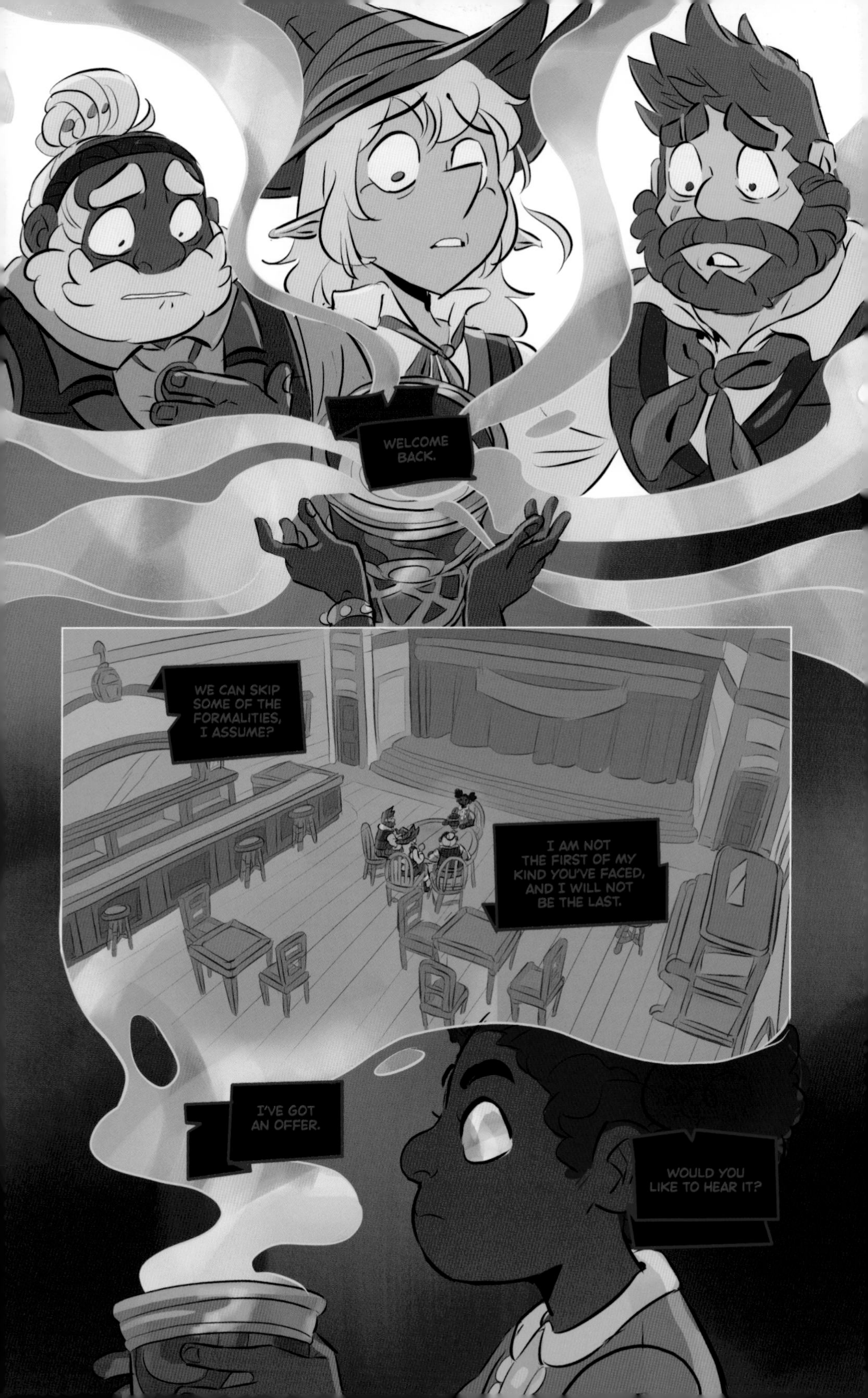
WELCOME BACK.
WE CAN SKIP SOME OF THE FORMALITIES, I ASSUME?
I AM NOT THE FIRST OF MY KIND YOU'VE FACED, AND I WILL NOT BE THE LAST.
I'VE GOT AN OFFER.
WOULD YOU LIKE TO HEAR IT?

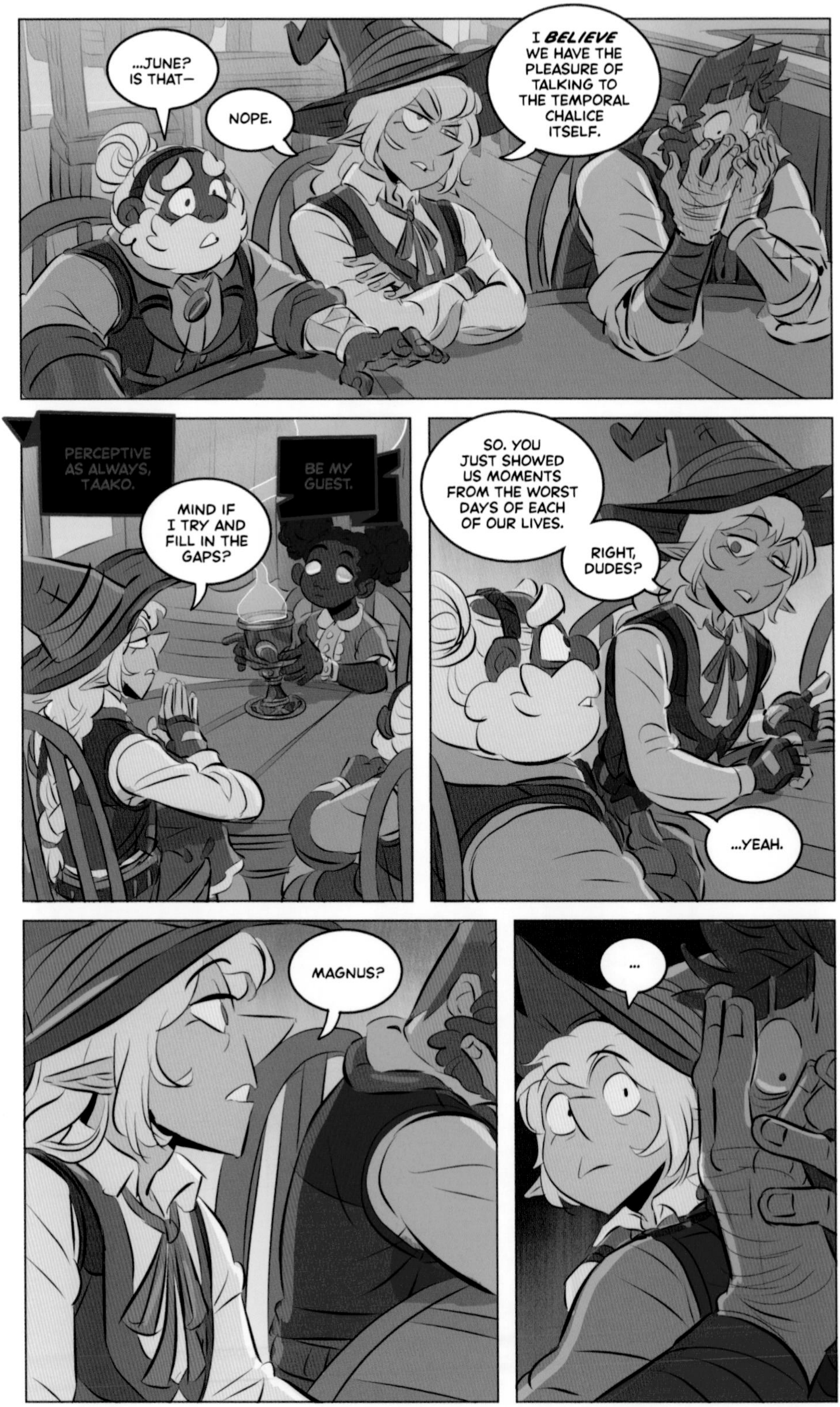
...JUNE? IS THAT—
NOPE.
I BELIEVE WE HAVE THE PLEASURE OF TALKING TO THE TEMPORAL CHALICE ITSELF.
PERCEPTIVE AS ALWAYS, TAAKO.
MIND IF I TRY AND FILL IN THE GAPS?
BE MY GUEST.
SO. YOU JUST SHOWED US MOMENTS FROM THE WORST DAYS OF EACH OF OUR LIVES.
RIGHT, DUDES?
...YEAH.
MAGNUS?
...

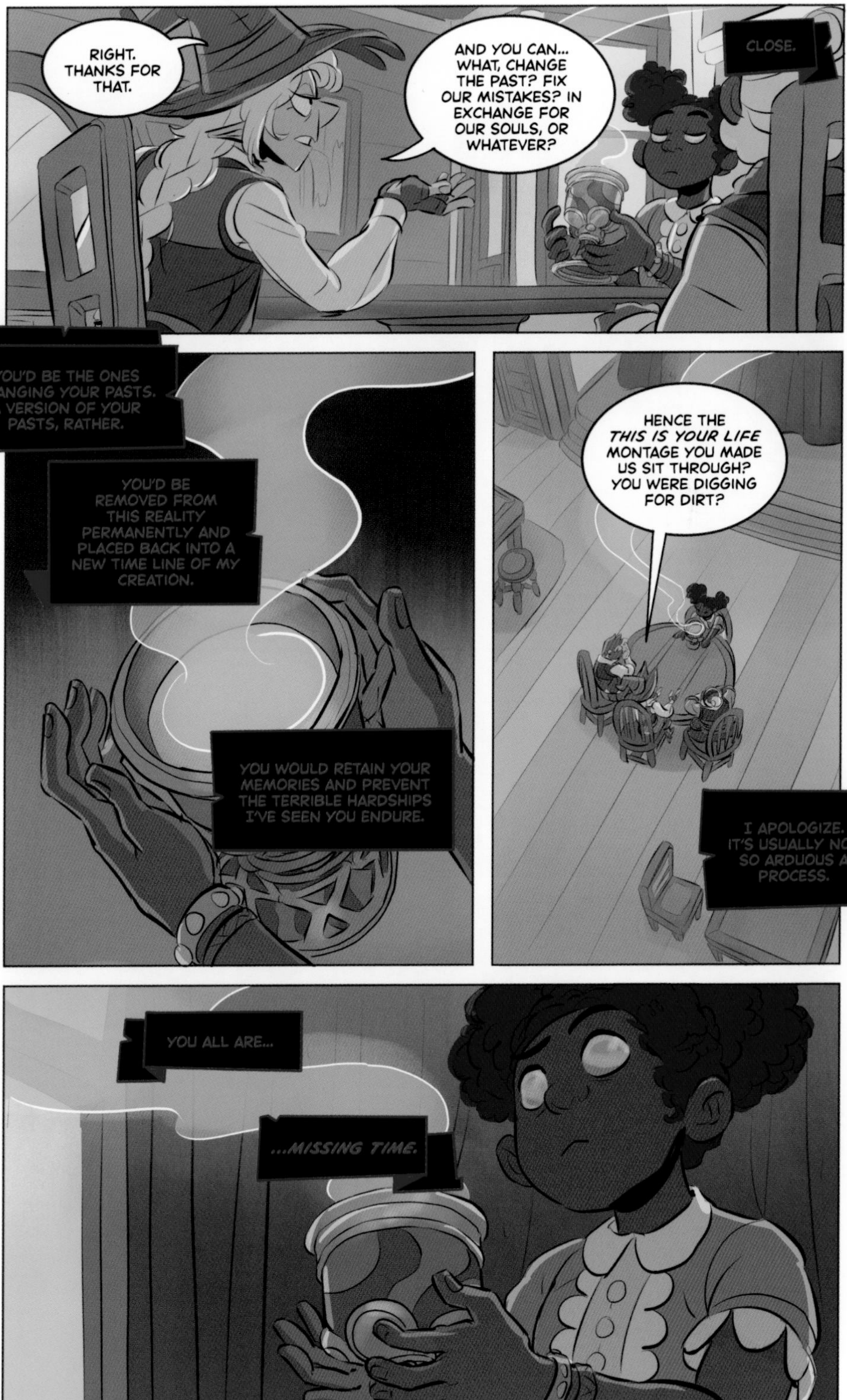
RIGHT. THANKS FOR THAT.
AND YOU CAN... WHAT, CHANGE THE PAST? FIX OUR MISTAKES? IN EXCHANGE FOR OUR SOULS, OR WHATEVER?
CLOSE.
YOU'D BE THE ONES CHANGING YOUR PASTS. A VERSION OF YOUR PASTS, RATHER.
YOU'D BE REMOVED FROM THIS REALITY PERMANENTLY AND PLACED BACK INTO A NEW TIME LINE OF MY CREATION.
YOU WOULD RETAIN YOUR MEMORIES AND PREVENT THE TERRIBLE HARDSHIPS I'VE SEEN YOU ENDURE.
HENCE THE *THIS IS YOUR LIFE* MONTAGE YOU MADE US SIT THROUGH? YOU WERE DIGGING FOR DIRT?
I APOLOGIZE. IT'S USUALLY NOT SO ARDUOUS A PROCESS.
YOU ALL ARE...
...MISSING TIME.

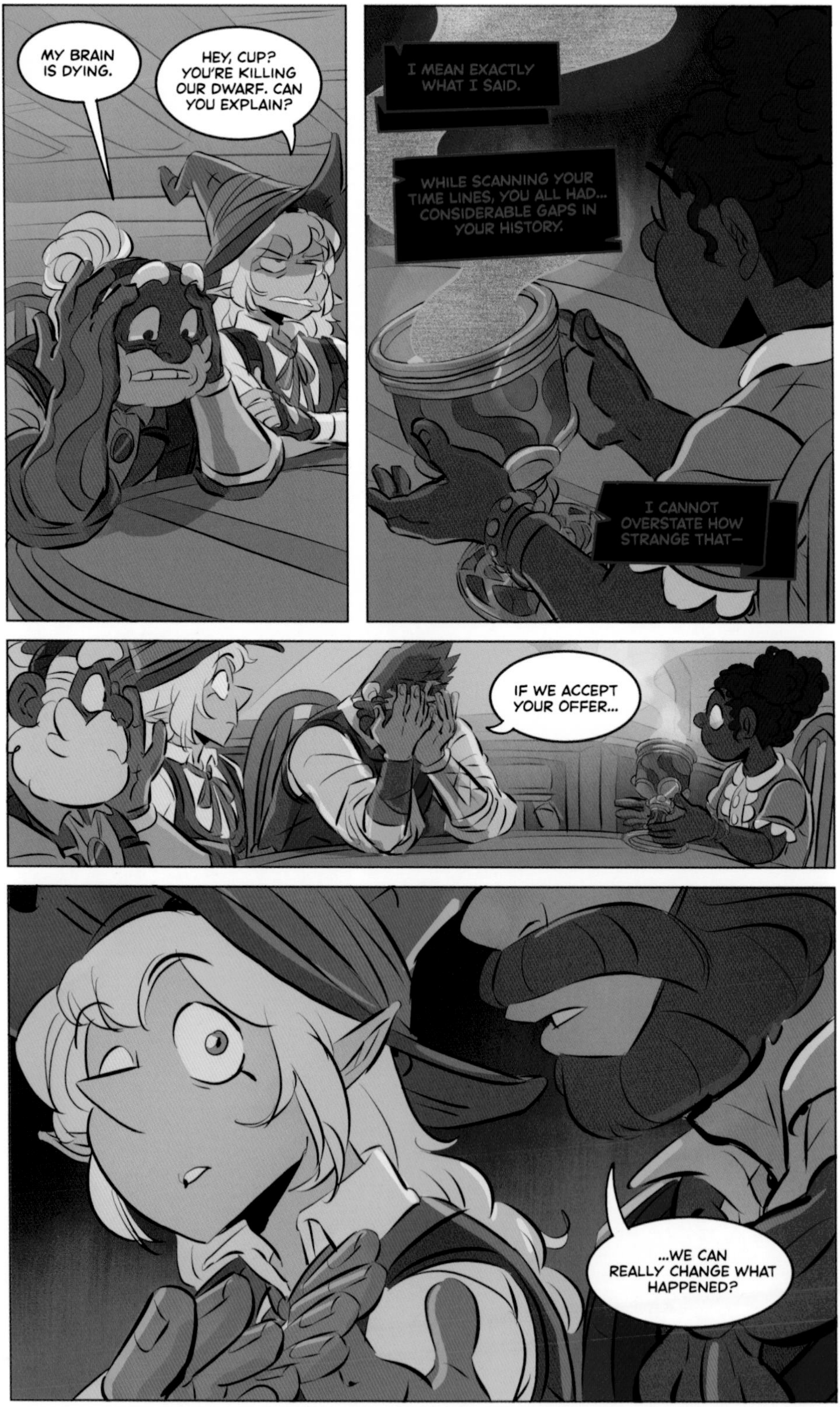
MY BRAIN IS DYING.
HEY, CUP? YOU'RE KILLING OUR DWARF. CAN YOU EXPLAIN?
I MEAN EXACTLY WHAT I SAID.
WHILE SCANNING YOUR TIME LINES, YOU ALL HAD... CONSIDERABLE GAPS IN YOUR HISTORY.
I CANNOT OVERSTATE HOW STRANGE THAT—
IF WE ACCEPT YOUR OFFER...
...WE CAN REALLY CHANGE WHAT HAPPENED?

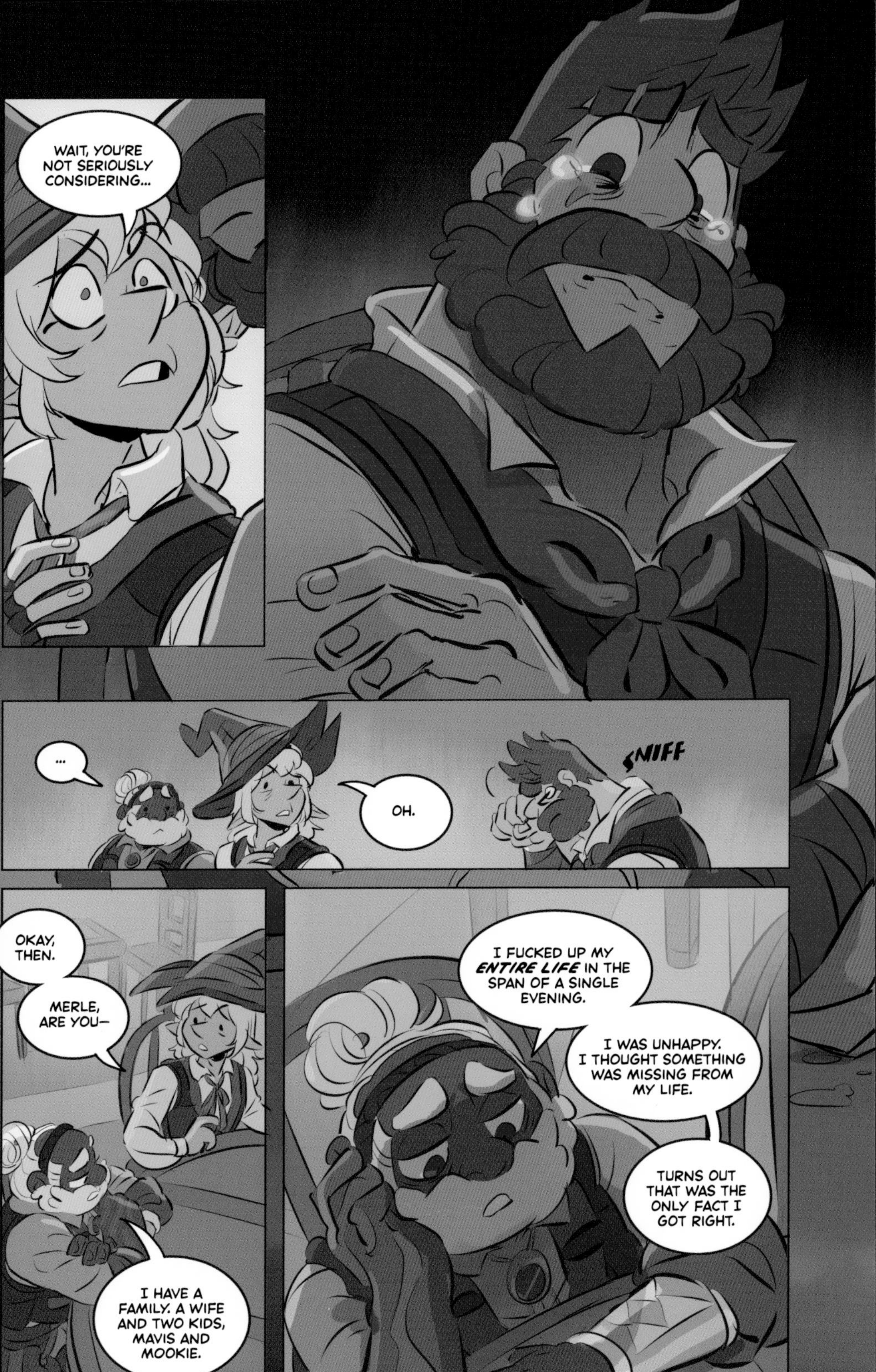
WAIT, YOU'RE NOT SERIOUSLY CONSIDERING...
...
OH.
SNIFF
OKAY, THEN.
MERLE, ARE YOU—
I HAVE A FAMILY. A WIFE AND TWO KIDS, MAVIS AND MOOKIE.
I FUCKED UP MY *ENTIRE LIFE* IN THE SPAN OF A SINGLE EVENING.
I WAS UNHAPPY. I THOUGHT SOMETHING WAS MISSING FROM MY LIFE.
TURNS OUT THAT WAS THE ONLY FACT I GOT RIGHT.

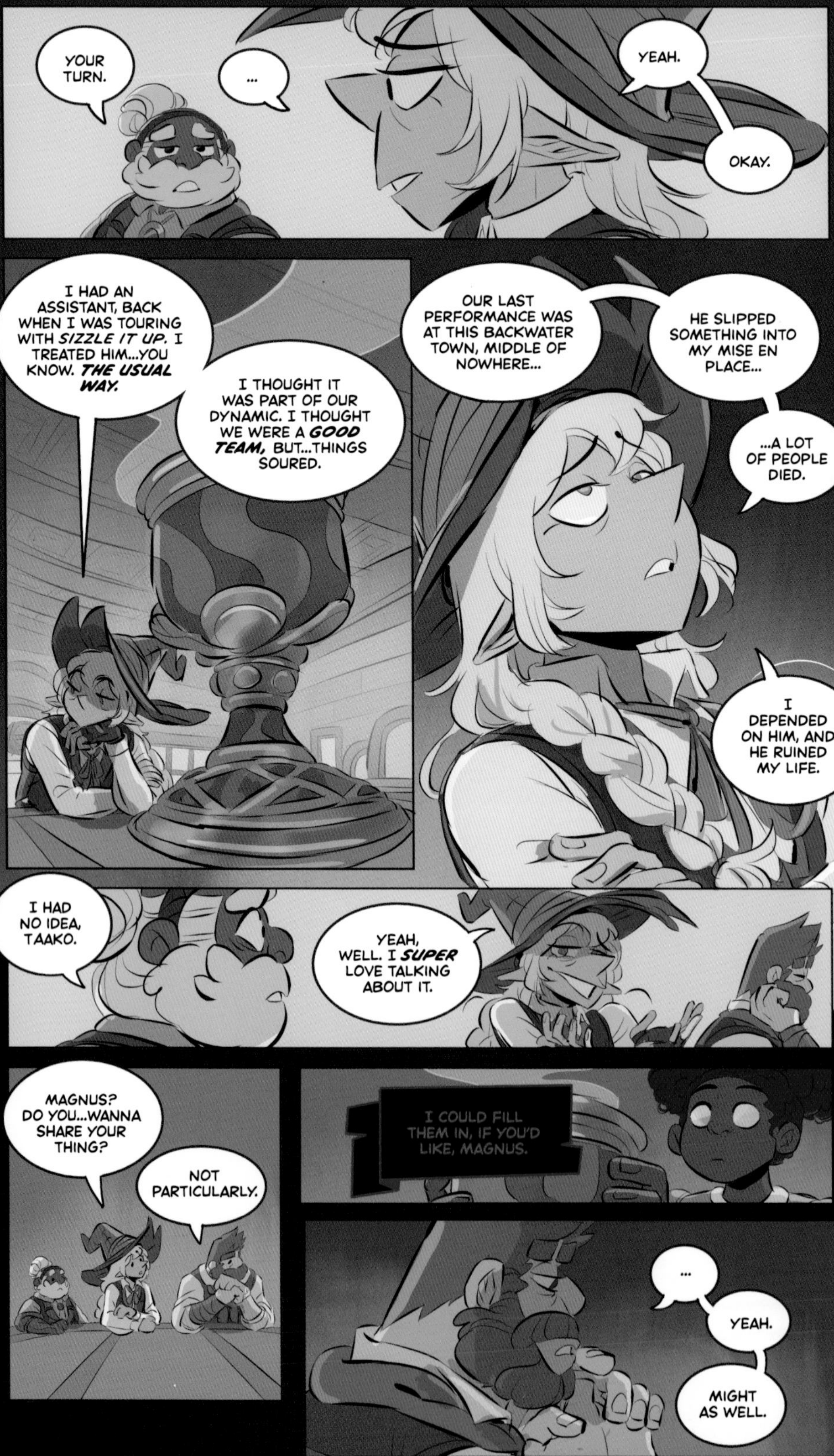
YOUR TURN.
...
YEAH.
OKAY.
I HAD AN ASSISTANT, BACK WHEN I WAS TOURING WITH *SIZZLE IT UP.* I TREATED HIM...YOU KNOW. ***THE USUAL WAY.***
I THOUGHT IT WAS PART OF OUR DYNAMIC. I THOUGHT WE WERE A ***GOOD TEAM,*** BUT...THINGS SOURED.
OUR LAST PERFORMANCE WAS AT THIS BACKWATER TOWN, MIDDLE OF NOWHERE...
HE SLIPPED SOMETHING INTO MY MISE EN PLACE...
...A LOT OF PEOPLE DIED.
I DEPENDED ON HIM, AND HE RUINED MY LIFE.
I HAD NO IDEA, TAAKO.
YEAH, WELL. I ***SUPER*** LOVE TALKING ABOUT IT.
MAGNUS? DO YOU...WANNA SHARE YOUR THING?
NOT PARTICULARLY.
I COULD FILL THEM IN, IF YOU'D LIKE, MAGNUS.
...
YEAH.
MIGHT AS WELL.

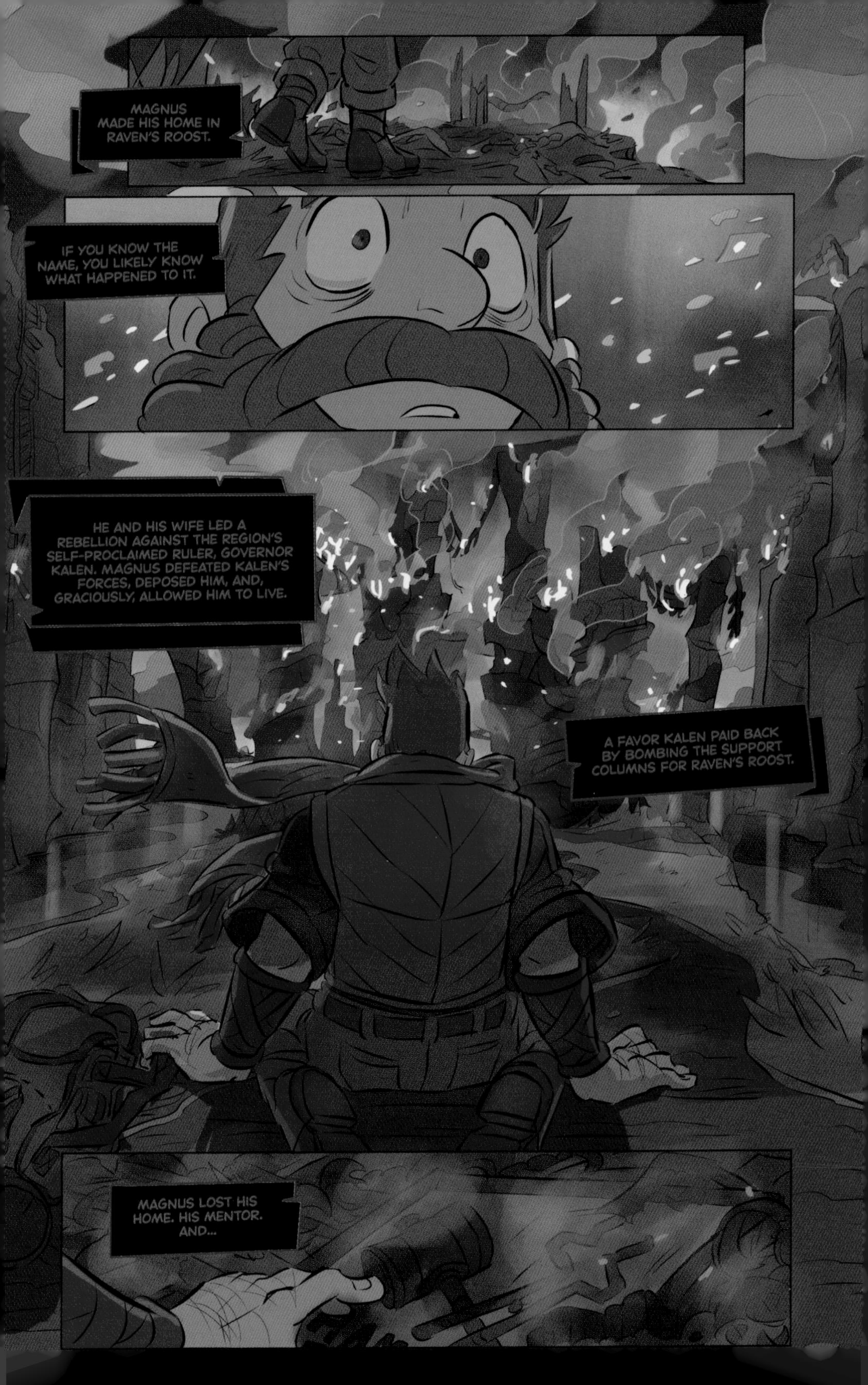
MAGNUS MADE HIS HOME IN RAVEN'S ROOST.
IF YOU KNOW THE NAME, YOU LIKELY KNOW WHAT HAPPENED TO IT.
HE AND HIS WIFE LED A REBELLION AGAINST THE REGION'S SELF-PROCLAIMED RULER, GOVERNOR KALEN. MAGNUS DEFEATED KALEN'S FORCES, DEPOSED HIM, AND, GRACIOUSLY, ALLOWED HIM TO LIVE.
A FAVOR KALEN PAID BACK BY BOMBING THE SUPPORT COLUMNS FOR RAVEN'S ROOST.
MAGNUS LOST HIS HOME. HIS MENTOR. AND...

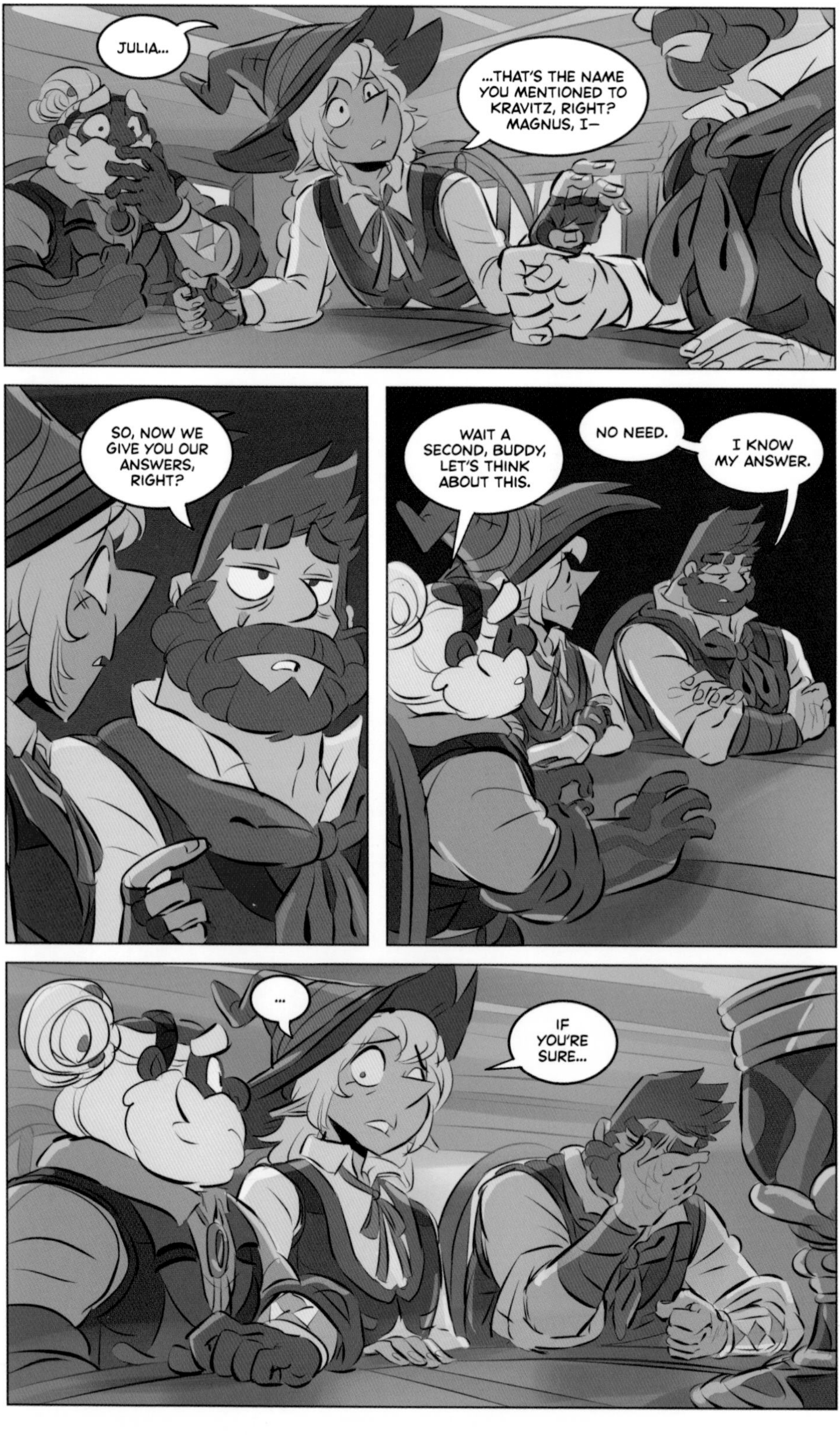
JULIA...
...THAT'S THE NAME YOU MENTIONED TO KRAVITZ, RIGHT? MAGNUS, I—
SO, NOW WE GIVE YOU OUR ANSWERS, RIGHT?
WAIT A SECOND, BUDDY, LET'S THINK ABOUT THIS.
NO NEED.
I KNOW MY ANSWER.
...
IF YOU'RE SURE...

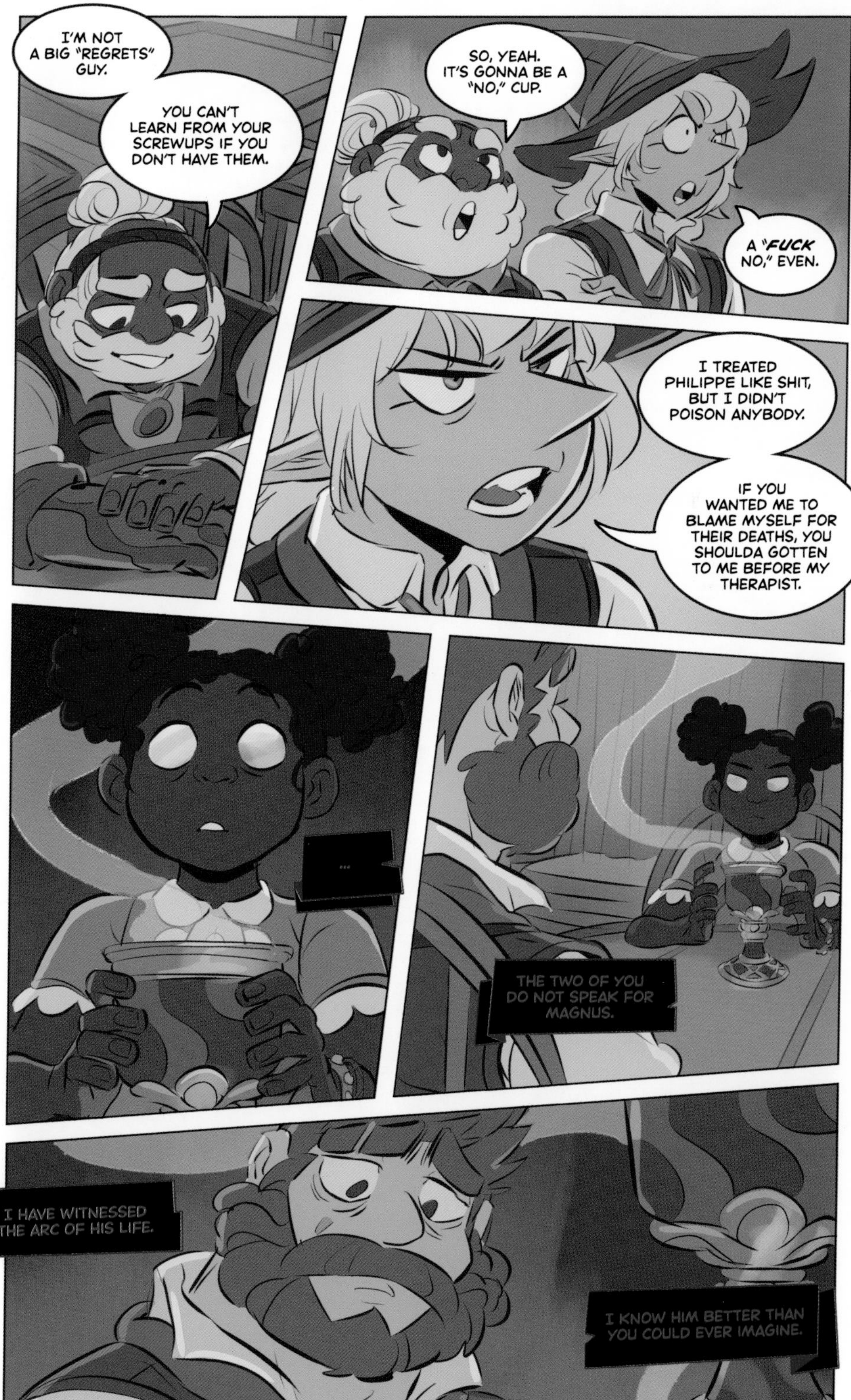

I'M NOT A BIG "REGRETS" GUY.
YOU CAN'T LEARN FROM YOUR SCREWUPS IF YOU DON'T HAVE THEM.
SO, YEAH. IT'S GONNA BE A "NO," CUP.
A "FUCK NO," EVEN.
I TREATED PHILIPPE LIKE SHIT, BUT I DIDN'T POISON ANYBODY.
IF YOU WANTED ME TO BLAME MYSELF FOR THEIR DEATHS, YOU SHOULDA GOTTEN TO ME BEFORE MY THERAPIST.
...
THE TWO OF YOU DO NOT SPEAK FOR MAGNUS.
I HAVE WITNESSED THE ARC OF HIS LIFE.
I KNOW HIM BETTER THAN YOU COULD EVER IMAGINE.

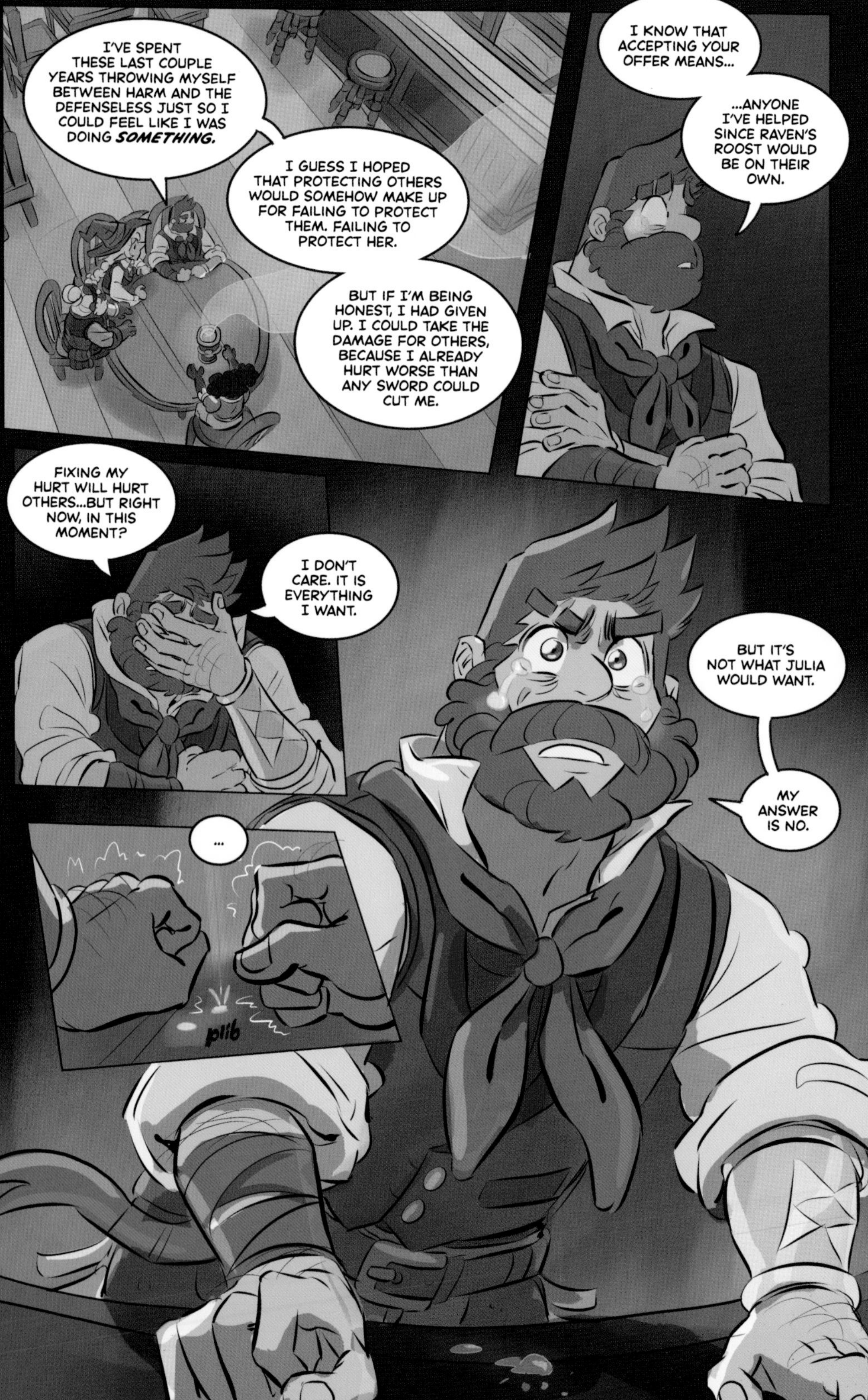

I'VE SPENT THESE LAST COUPLE YEARS THROWING MYSELF BETWEEN HARM AND THE DEFENSELESS JUST SO I COULD FEEL LIKE I WAS DOING *SOMETHING.*
I GUESS I HOPED THAT PROTECTING OTHERS WOULD SOMEHOW MAKE UP FOR FAILING TO PROTECT THEM. FAILING TO PROTECT HER.
BUT IF I'M BEING HONEST, I HAD GIVEN UP. I COULD TAKE THE DAMAGE FOR OTHERS, BECAUSE I ALREADY HURT WORSE THAN ANY SWORD COULD CUT ME.
I KNOW THAT ACCEPTING YOUR OFFER MEANS...
...ANYONE I'VE HELPED SINCE RAVEN'S ROOST WOULD BE ON THEIR OWN.
FIXING MY HURT WILL HURT OTHERS...BUT RIGHT NOW, IN THIS MOMENT?
I DON'T CARE. IT IS EVERYTHING I WANT.
BUT IT'S NOT WHAT JULIA WOULD WANT.
MY ANSWER IS NO.
...
plib

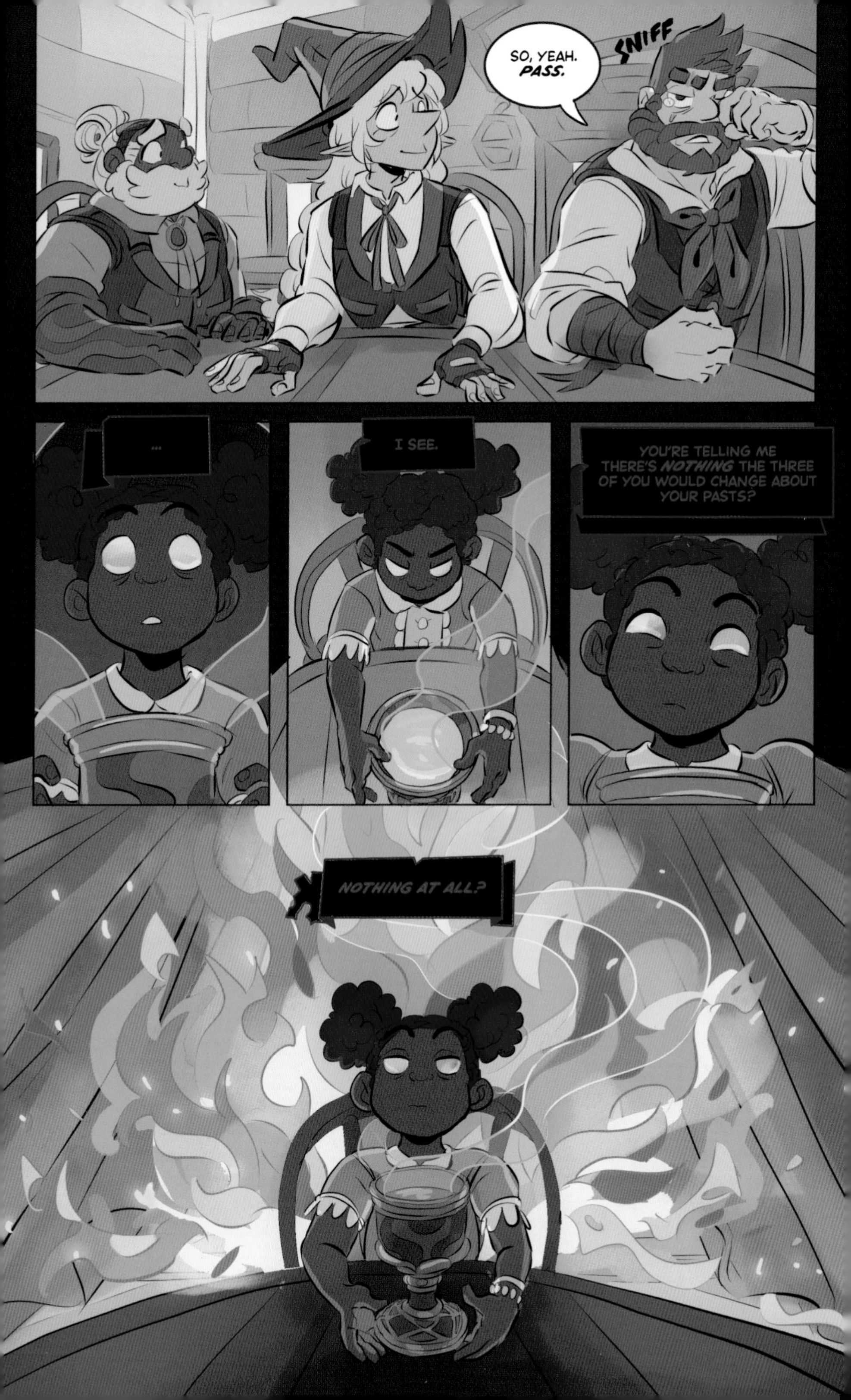
SO, YEAH.
PASS.
SNIFF
...
I SEE.
YOU'RE TELLING ME THERE'S ***NOTHING*** THE THREE OF YOU WOULD CHANGE ABOUT YOUR PASTS?
NOTHING AT ALL?

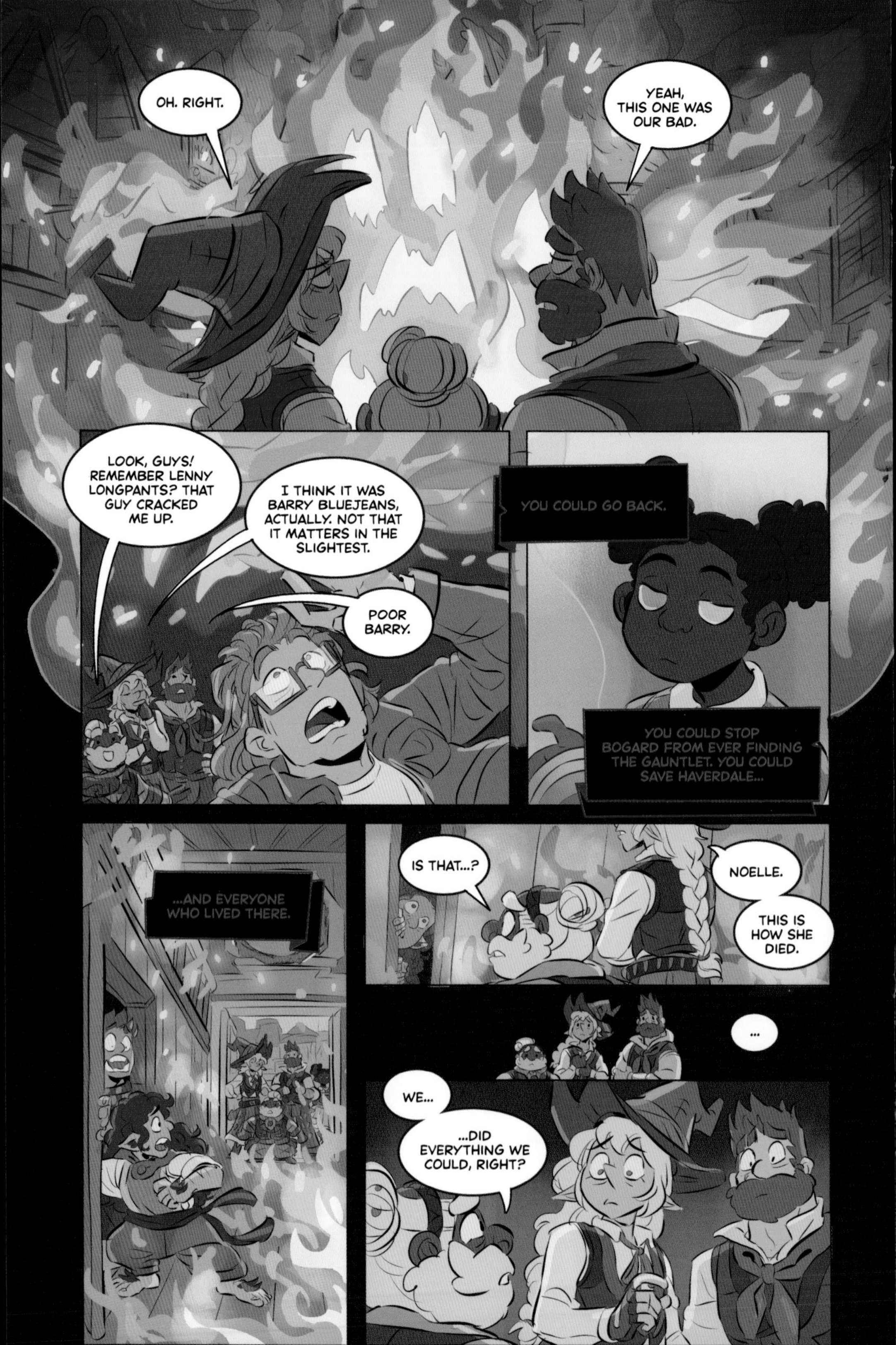
OH. RIGHT.
YEAH, THIS ONE WAS OUR BAD.
LOOK, GUYS! REMEMBER LENNY LONGPANTS? THAT GUY CRACKED ME UP.
I THINK IT WAS BARRY BLUEJEANS, ACTUALLY. NOT THAT IT MATTERS IN THE SLIGHTEST.
POOR BARRY.
YOU COULD GO BACK.
YOU COULD STOP BOGARD FROM EVER FINDING THE GAUNTLET. YOU COULD SAVE HAVERDALE...
...AND EVERYONE WHO LIVED THERE.
IS THAT...?
NOELLE.
THIS IS HOW SHE DIED.
...
WE...
...DID EVERYTHING WE COULD, RIGHT?

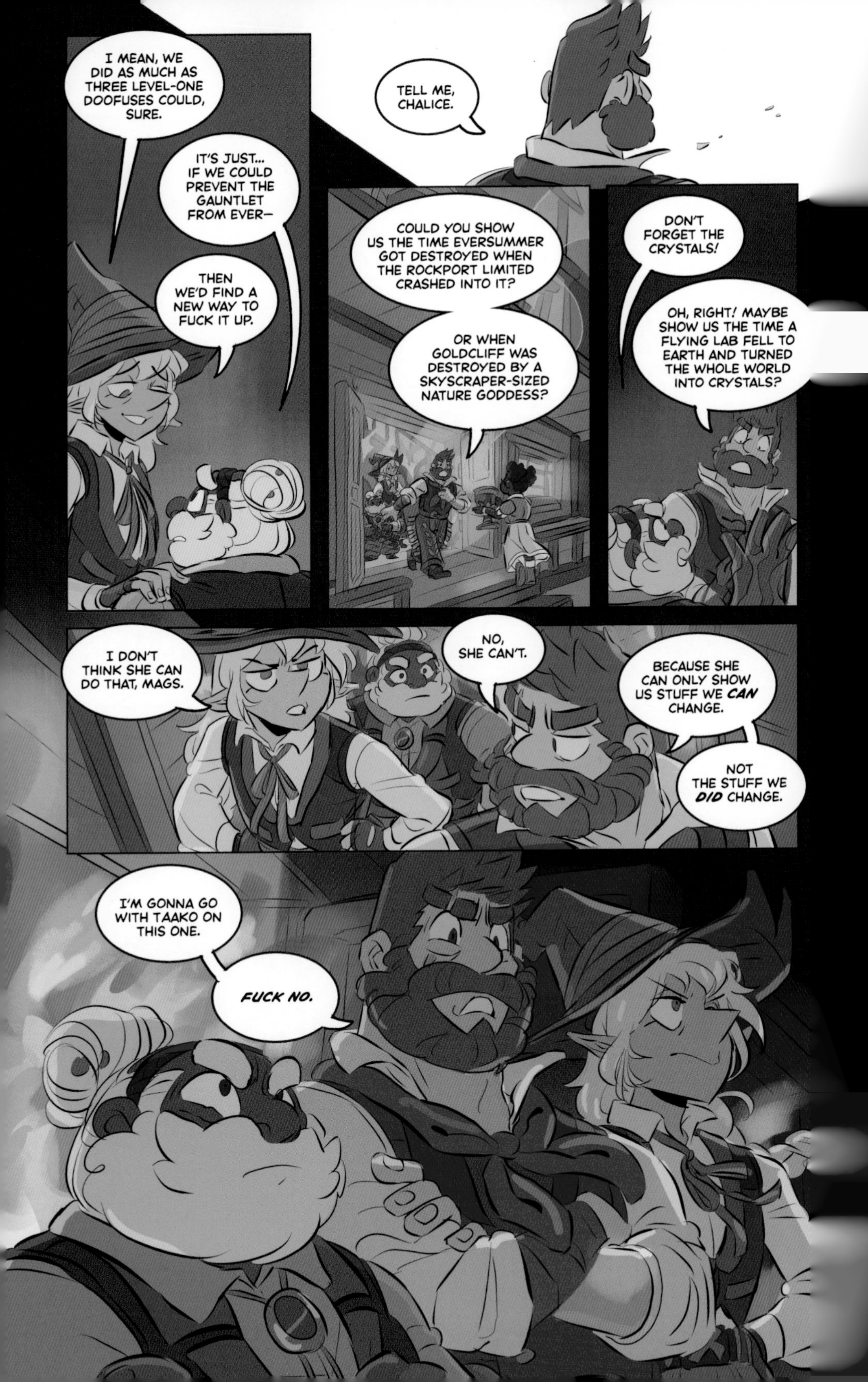
I MEAN, WE DID AS MUCH AS THREE LEVEL-ONE DOOFUSES COULD, SURE.
TELL ME, CHALICE.
IT'S JUST... IF WE COULD PREVENT THE GAUNTLET FROM EVER—
THEN WE'D FIND A NEW WAY TO FUCK IT UP.
COULD YOU SHOW US THE TIME EVERSUMMER GOT DESTROYED WHEN THE ROCKPORT LIMITED CRASHED INTO IT?
OR WHEN GOLDCLIFF WAS DESTROYED BY A SKYSCRAPER-SIZED NATURE GODDESS?
DON'T FORGET THE CRYSTALS!
OH, RIGHT! MAYBE SHOW US THE TIME A FLYING LAB FELL TO EARTH AND TURNED THE WHOLE WORLD INTO CRYSTALS?
I DON'T THINK SHE CAN DO THAT, MAGS.
NO, SHE CAN'T.
BECAUSE SHE CAN ONLY SHOW US STUFF WE *CAN* CHANGE.
NOT THE STUFF WE *DID* CHANGE.
I'M GONNA GO WITH TAAKO ON THIS ONE.
FUCK NO.

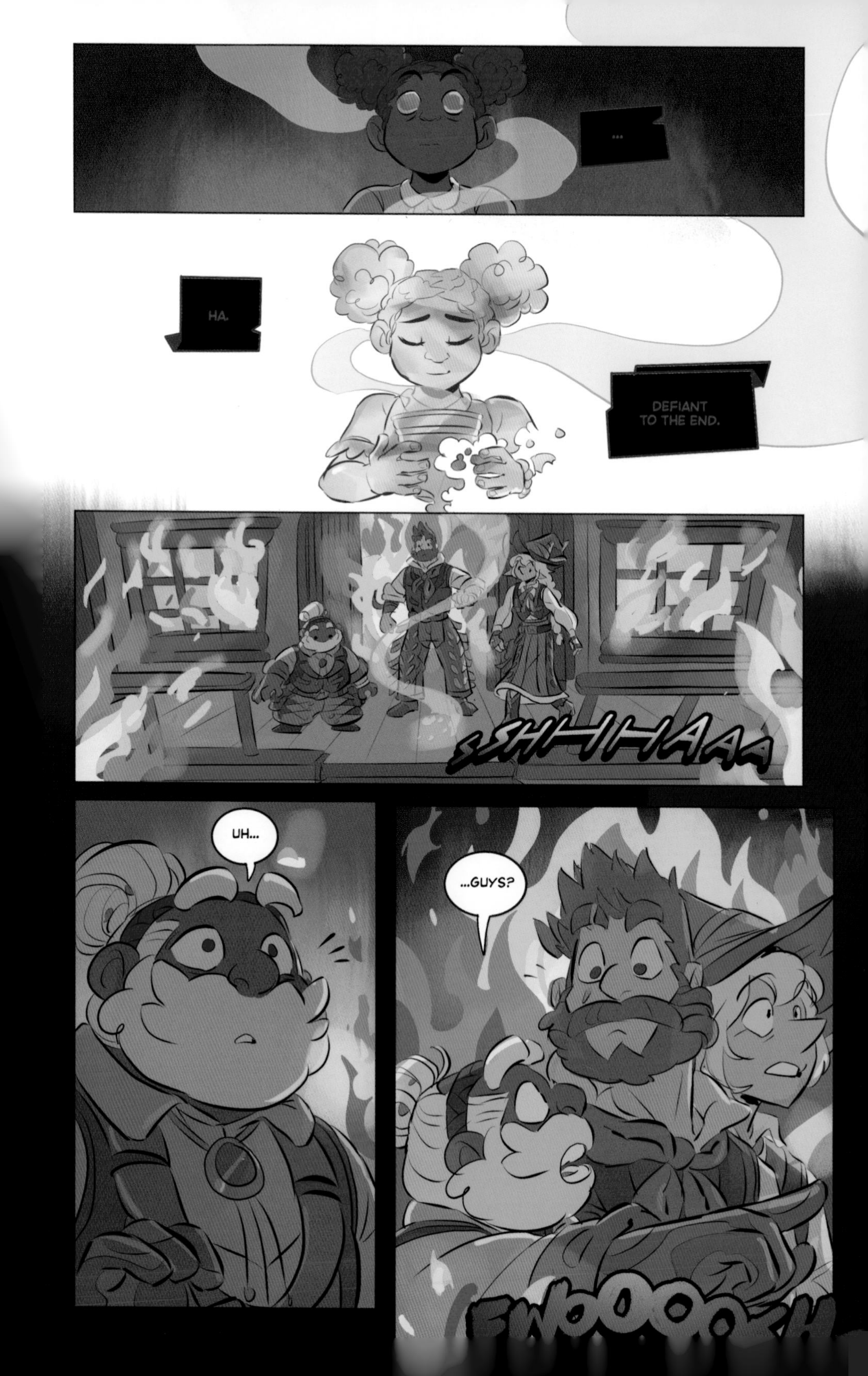
...
HA.
DEFIANT TO THE END.
SHHHHAAA
UH...
...GUYS?
FWOOOOSH

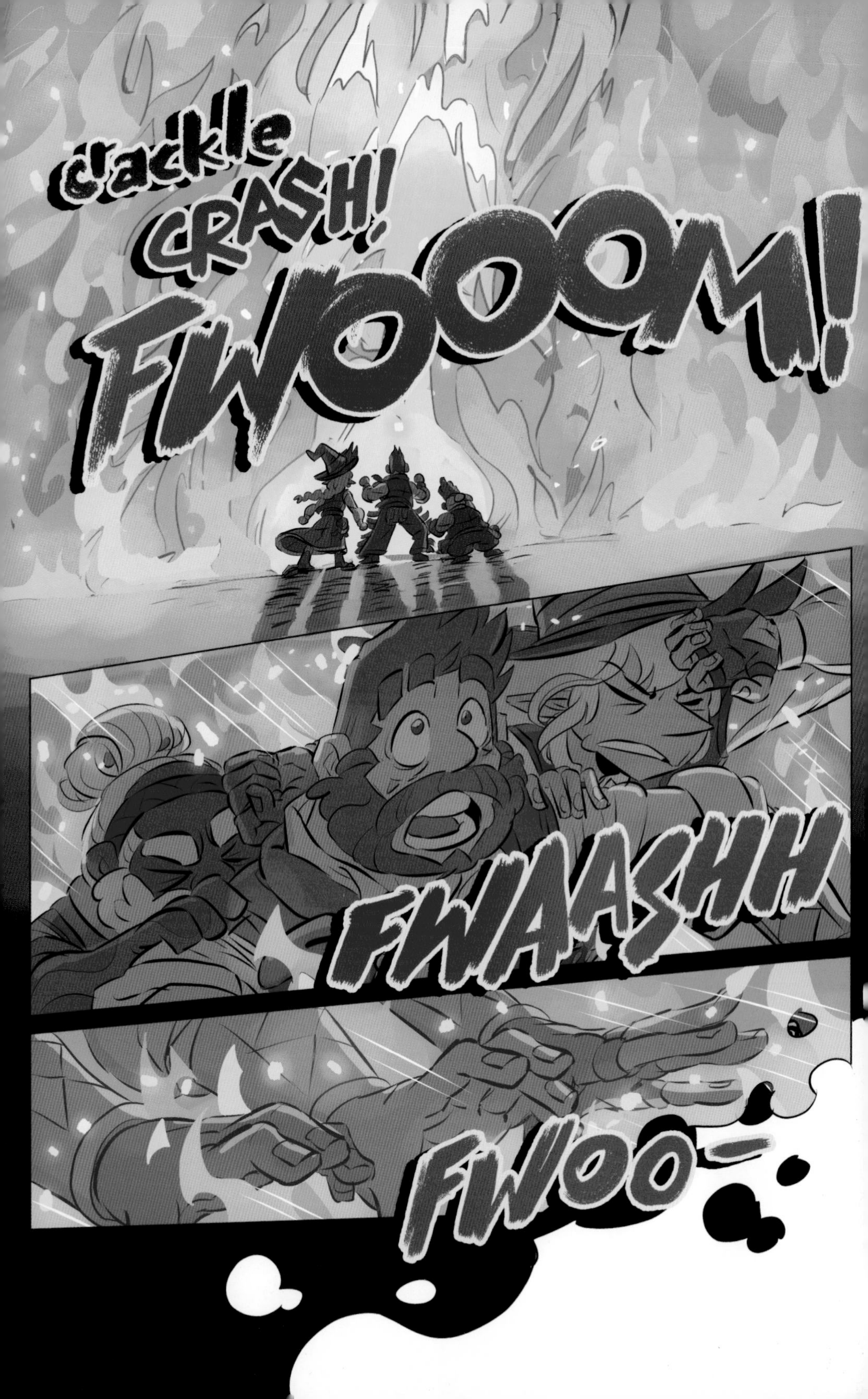
crackle
CRASH!
FWOOOM!
FWAASHH
FWOO-

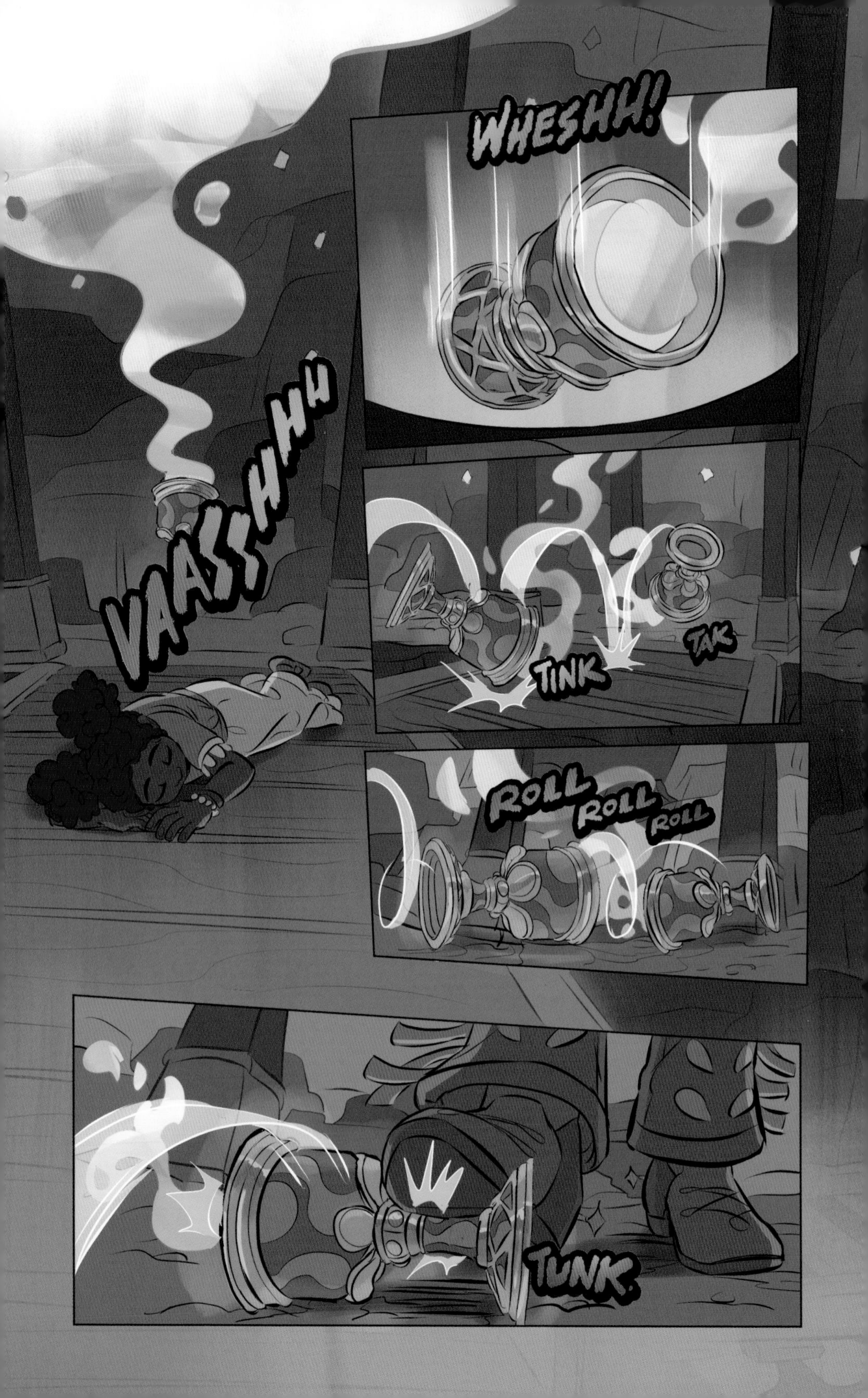
VAASHHH
WHESHH!
TINK
TAK
ROLL
ROLL
ROLL
TUNK

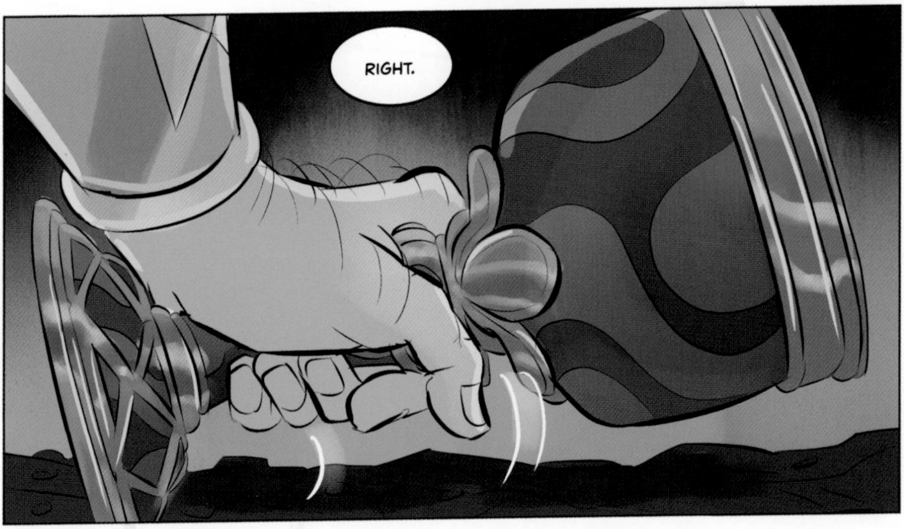
RIGHT.

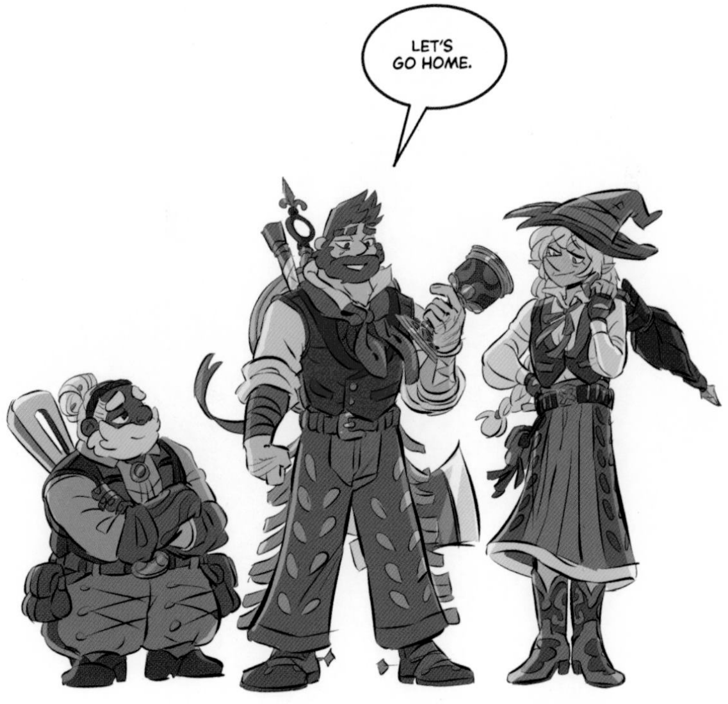
LET'S GO HOME.

Chapter
114

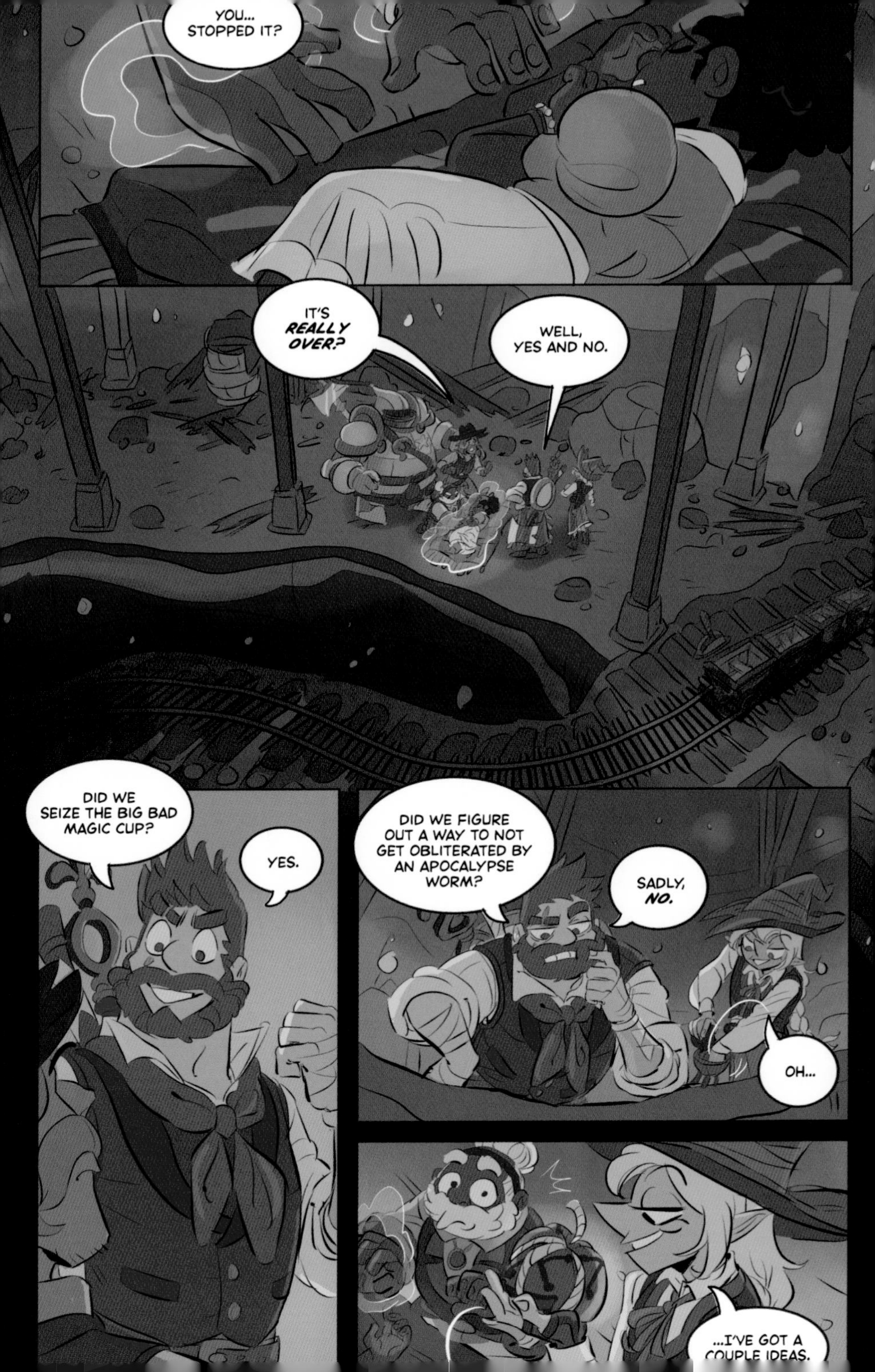
YOU... STOPPED IT?
IT'S *REALLY OVER?*
WELL, YES AND NO.
DID WE SEIZE THE BIG BAD MAGIC CUP?
YES.
DID WE FIGURE OUT A WAY TO NOT GET OBLITERATED BY AN APOCALYPSE WORM?
SADLY, *NO.*
OH...
...I'VE GOT A COUPLE IDEAS.

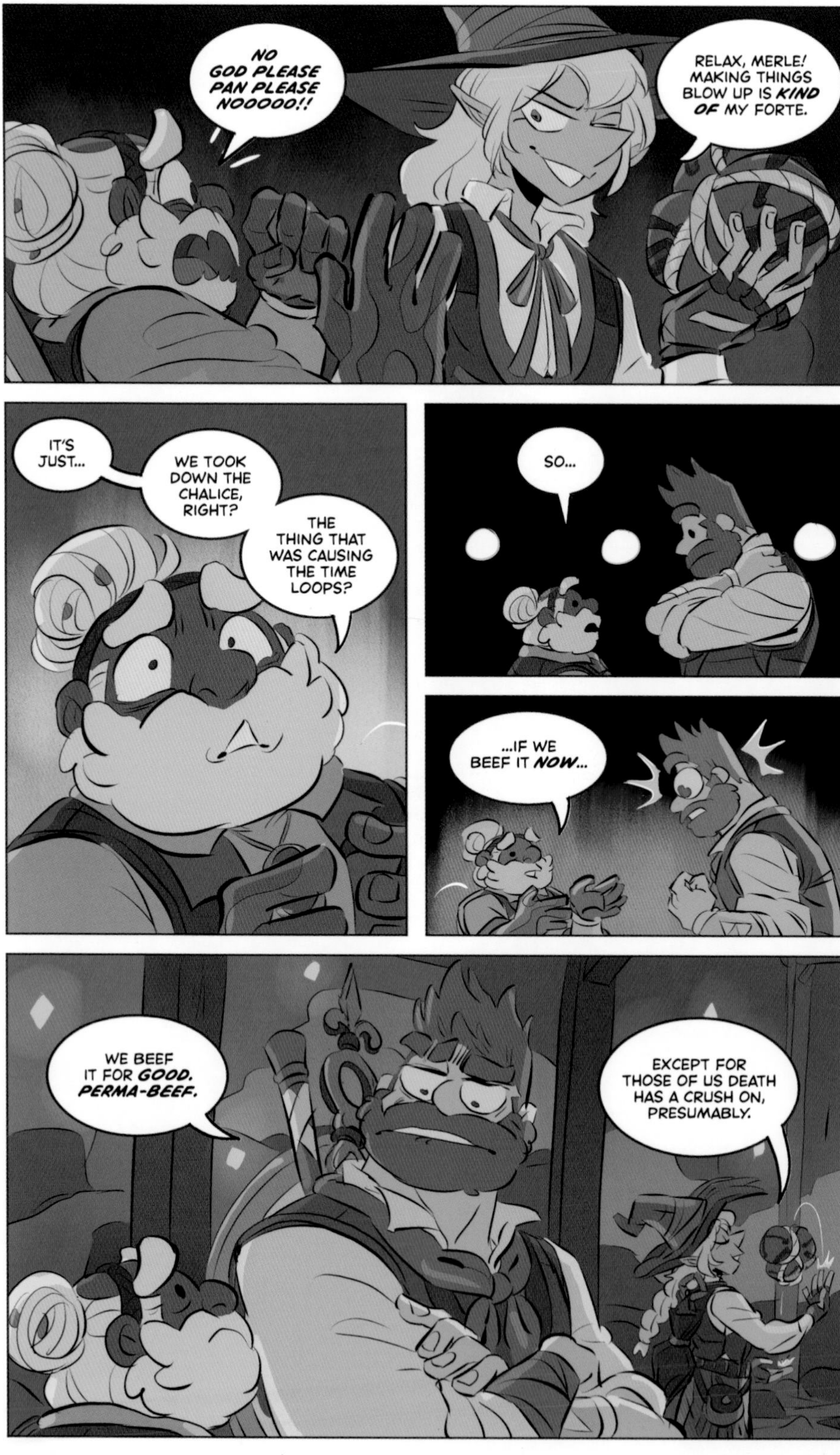
NO GOD PLEASE PAN PLEASE NOOOOO!!
RELAX, MERLE! MAKING THINGS BLOW UP IS *KIND OF* MY FORTE.
IT'S JUST...
WE TOOK DOWN THE CHALICE, RIGHT?
THE THING THAT WAS CAUSING THE TIME LOOPS?
SO...
...IF WE BEEF IT *NOW*...
WE BEEF IT FOR *GOOD. PERMA-BEEF.*
EXCEPT FOR THOSE OF US DEATH HAS A CRUSH ON, PRESUMABLY.

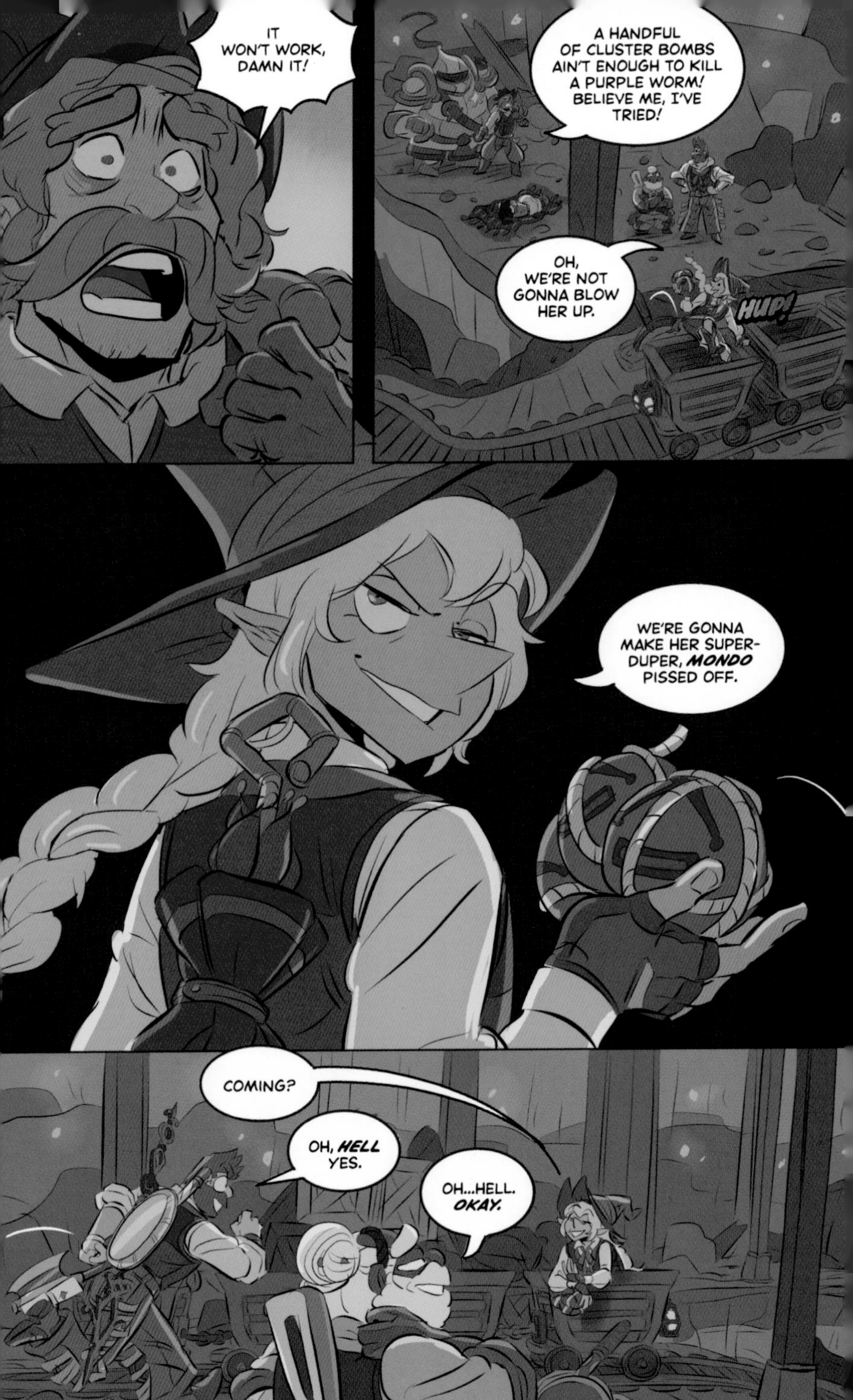
IT WON'T WORK, DAMN IT!
A HANDFUL OF CLUSTER BOMBS AIN'T ENOUGH TO KILL A PURPLE WORM! BELIEVE ME, I'VE TRIED!
OH, WE'RE NOT GONNA BLOW HER UP.
HUP!
WE'RE GONNA MAKE HER SUPER-DUPER, MONDO PISSED OFF.
COMING?
OH, HELL YES.
OH...HELL. OKAY.

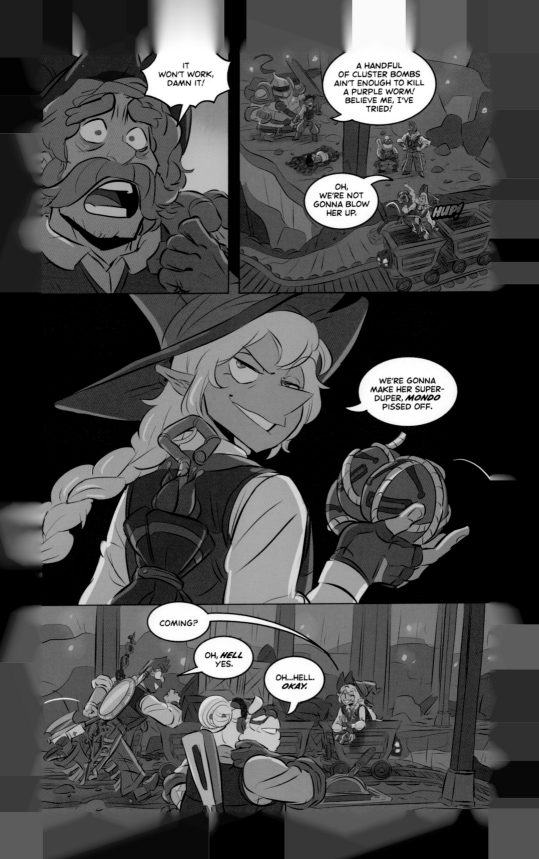

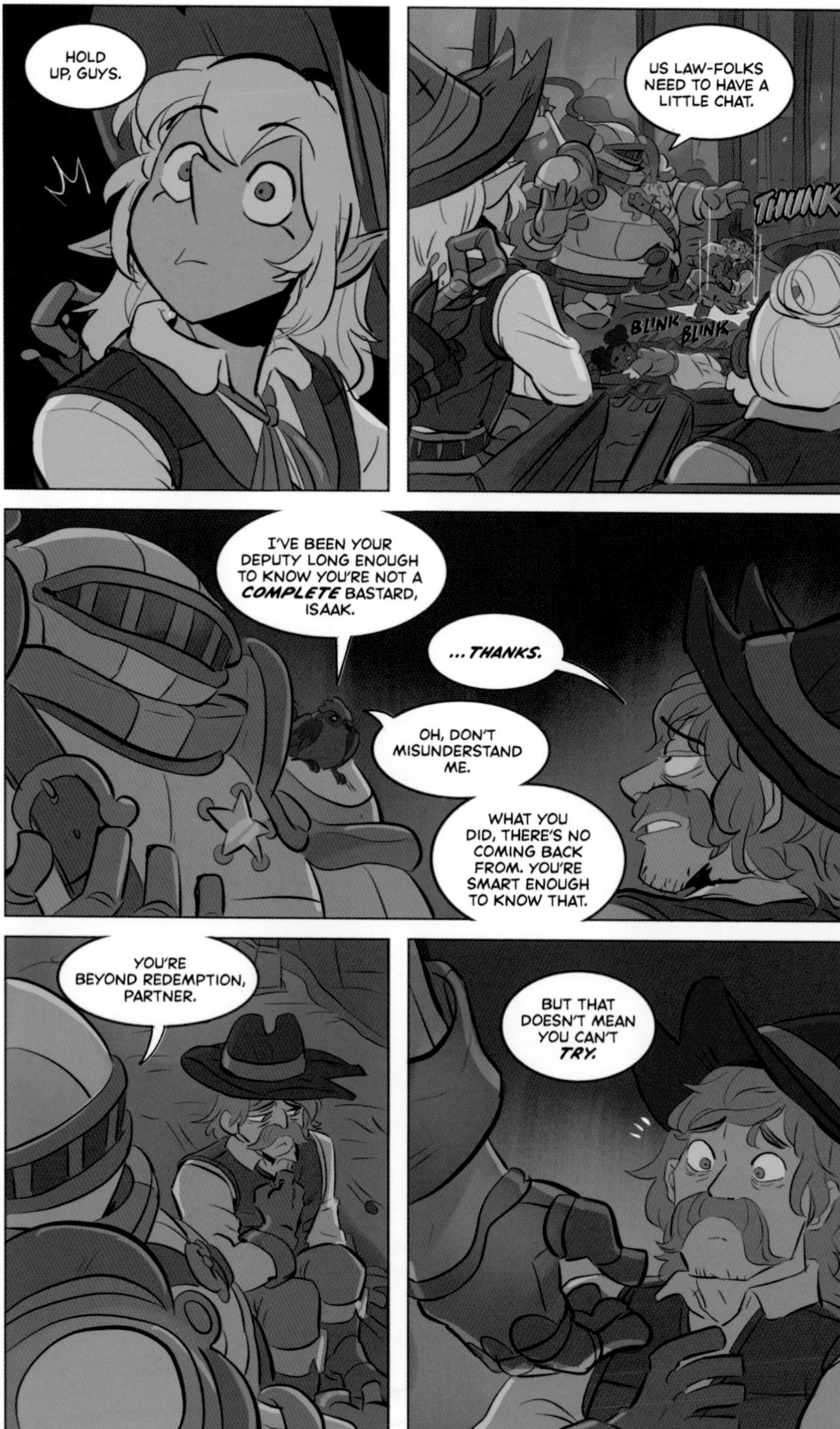
HOLD UP, GUYS.
US LAW-FOLKS NEED TO HAVE A LITTLE CHAT.
THUNK
BLINK
BLINK
I'VE BEEN YOUR DEPUTY LONG ENOUGH TO KNOW YOU'RE NOT A ***COMPLETE*** BASTARD, ISAAK.
...THANKS.
OH, DON'T MISUNDERSTAND ME.
WHAT YOU DID, THERE'S NO COMING BACK FROM. YOU'RE SMART ENOUGH TO KNOW THAT.
YOU'RE BEYOND REDEMPTION, PARTNER.
BUT THAT DOESN'T MEAN YOU CAN'T ***TRY.***

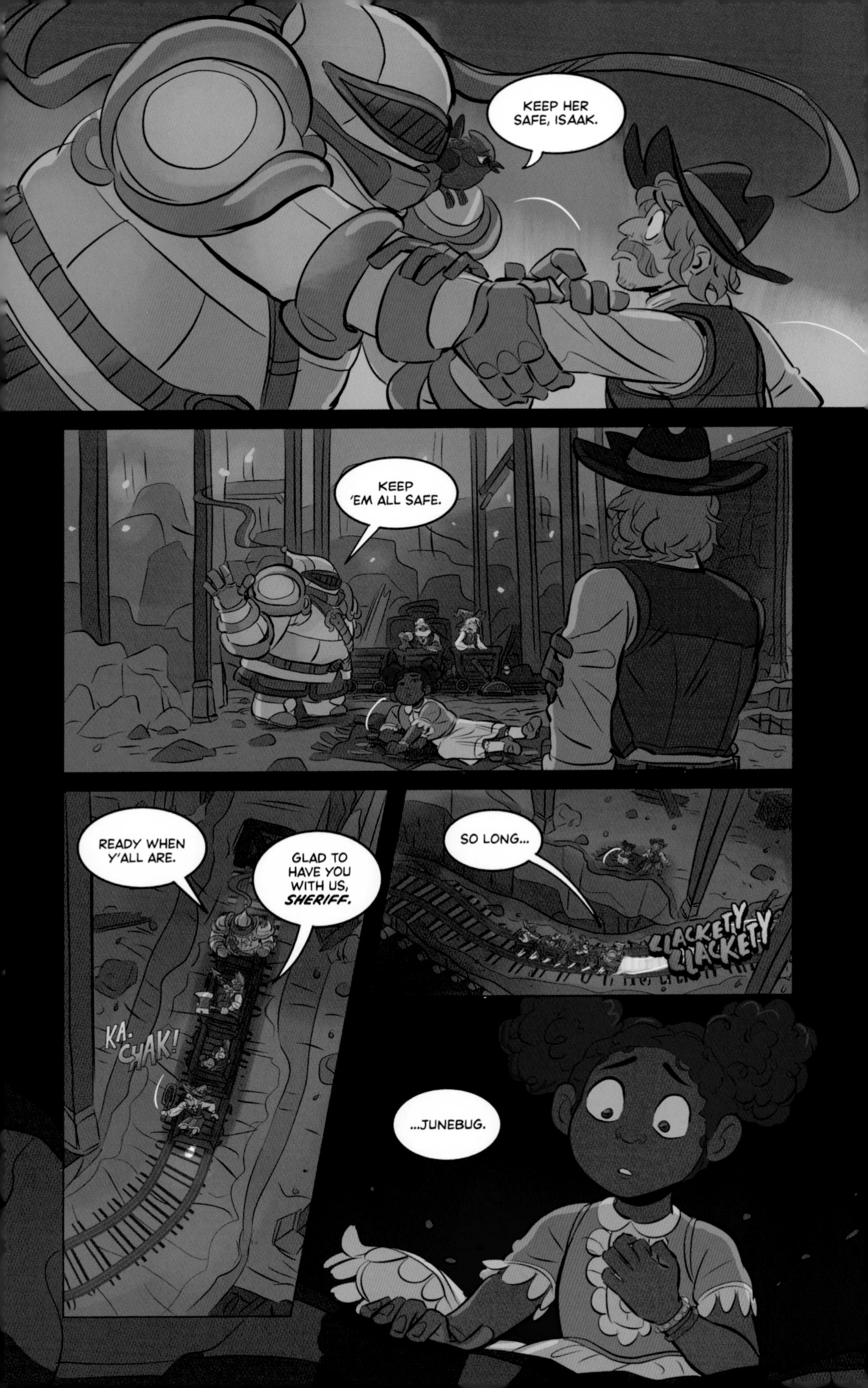
KEEP HER SAFE, ISAAK.
KEEP 'EM ALL SAFE.
READY WHEN Y'ALL ARE.
GLAD TO HAVE YOU WITH US, ***SHERIFF.***
KA-CHAK!
SO LONG...
CLACKETY-CLACKETY
...JUNEBUG.

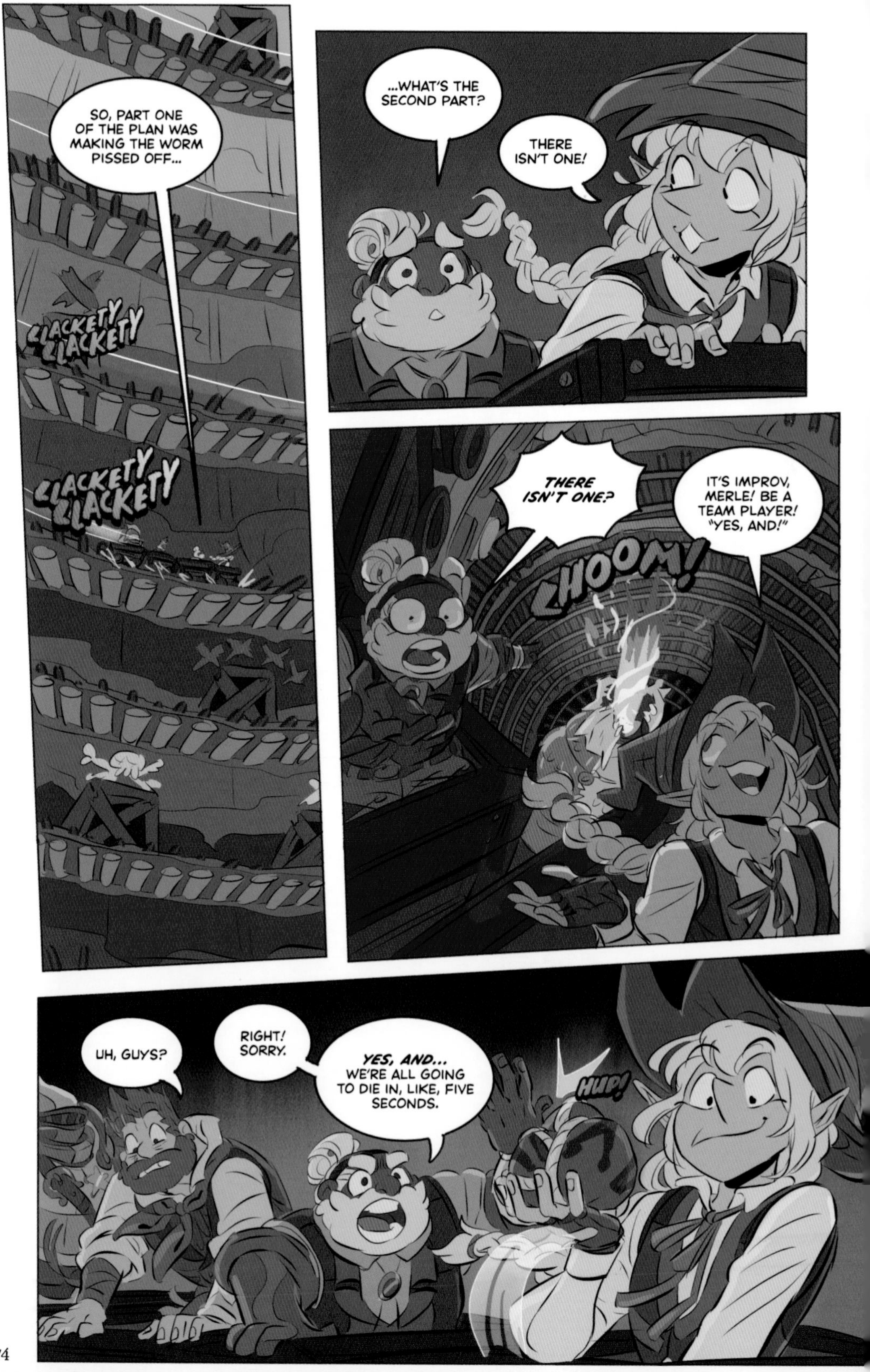
SO, PART ONE OF THE PLAN WAS MAKING THE WORM PISSED OFF...
CLACKETY CLACKETY
CLACKETY CLACKETY
...WHAT'S THE SECOND PART?
THERE ISN'T ONE!
THERE ISN'T ONE?
IT'S IMPROV, MERLE! BE A TEAM PLAYER! "YES, AND!"
CHOOM!
UH, GUYS?
RIGHT! SORRY.
YES, AND... WE'RE ALL GOING TO DIE IN, LIKE, FIVE SECONDS.
HUP!

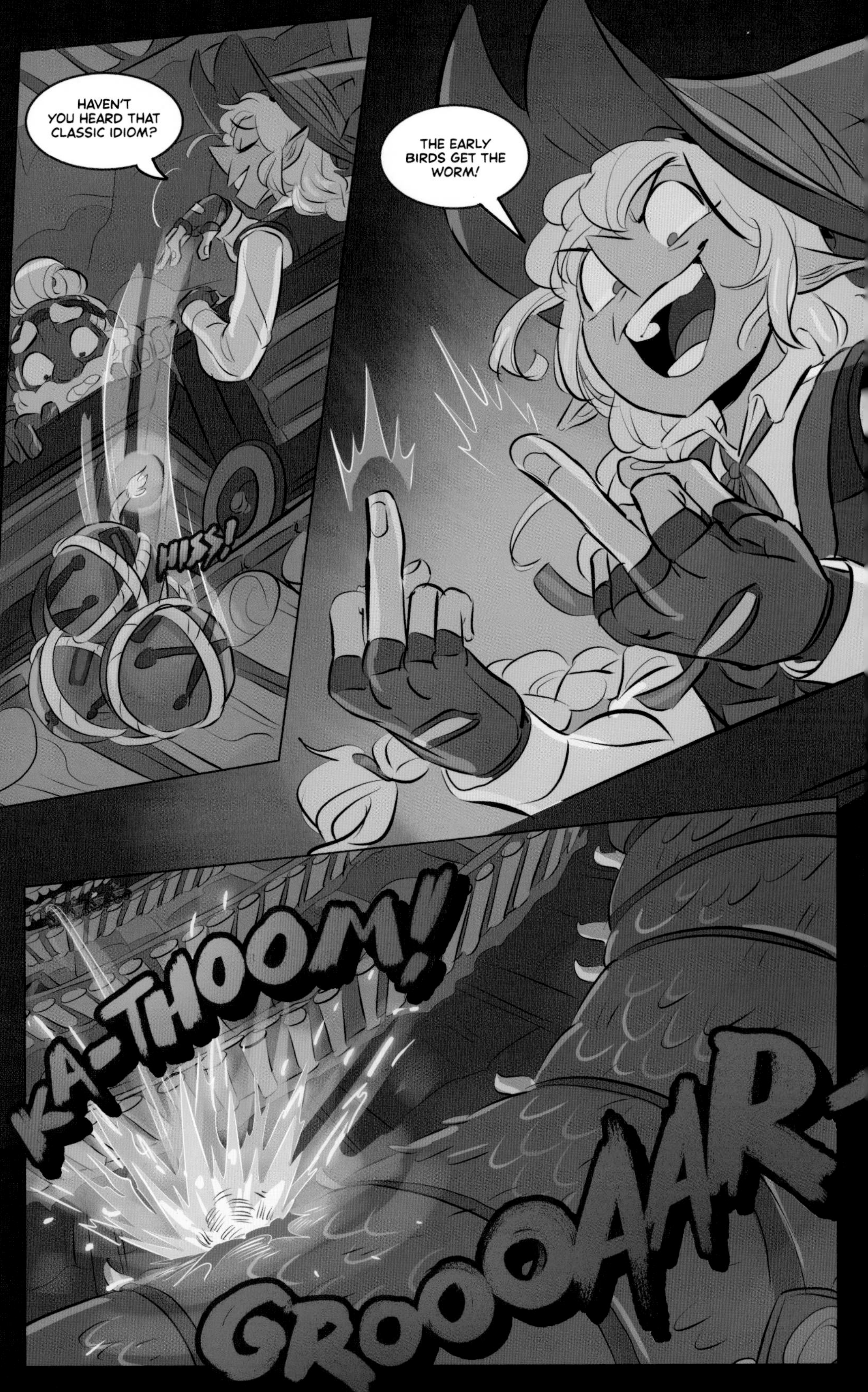
HAVEN'T YOU HEARD THAT CLASSIC IDIOM?
HISS!
THE EARLY BIRDS GET THE WORM!
KA-THOOM!
GROOOOAAR-

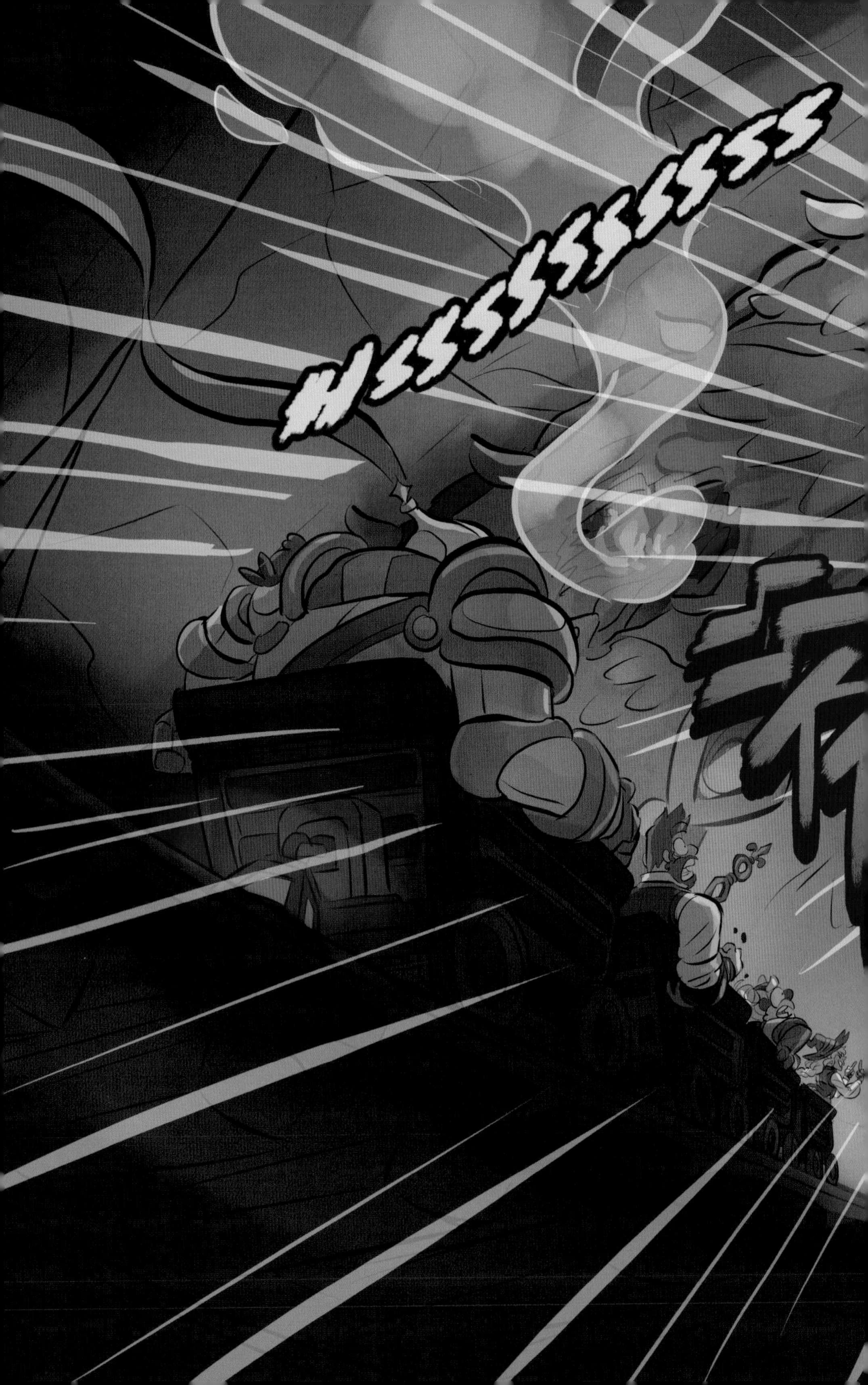
HSSSSSSSSSS

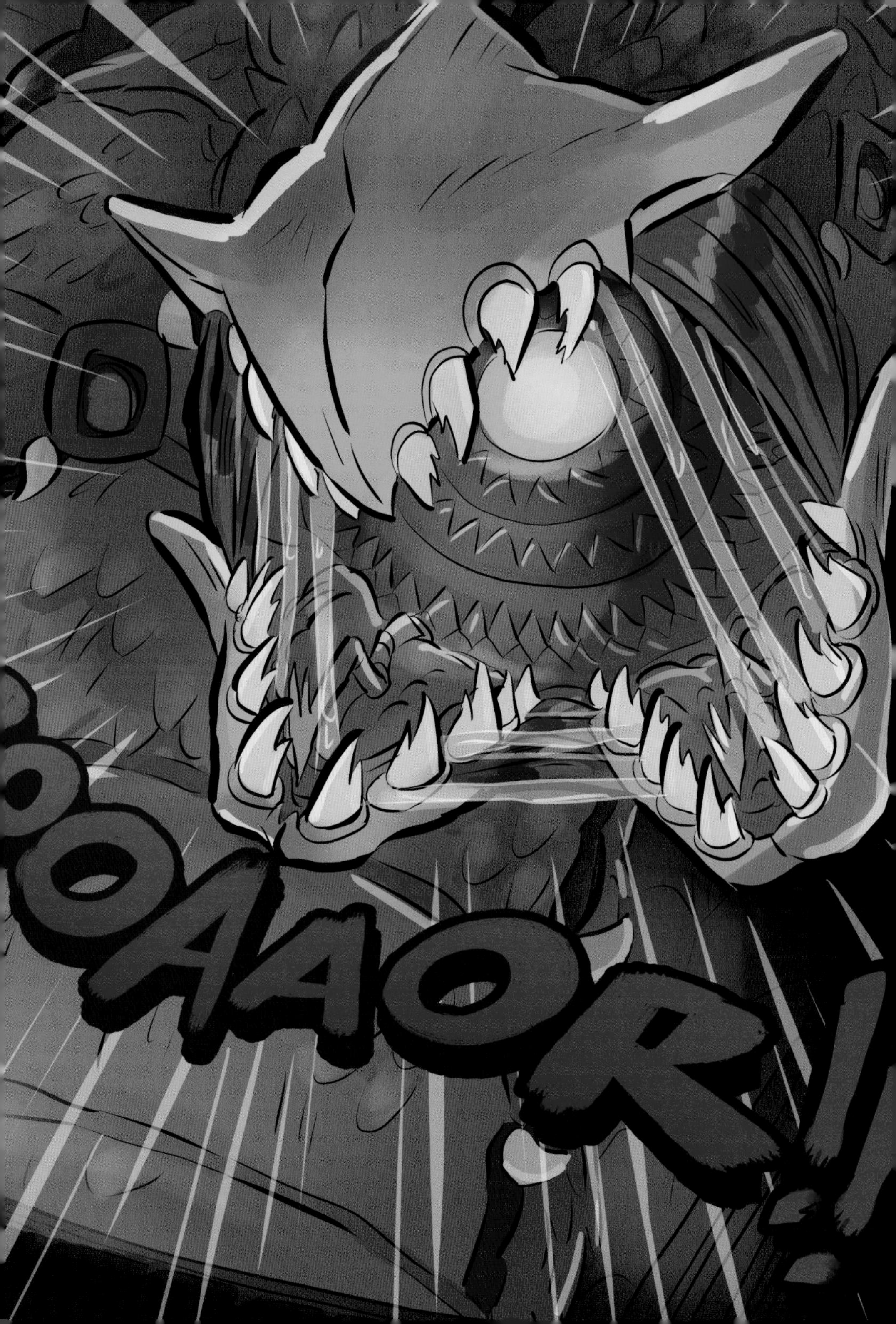
D
OOAAOR!

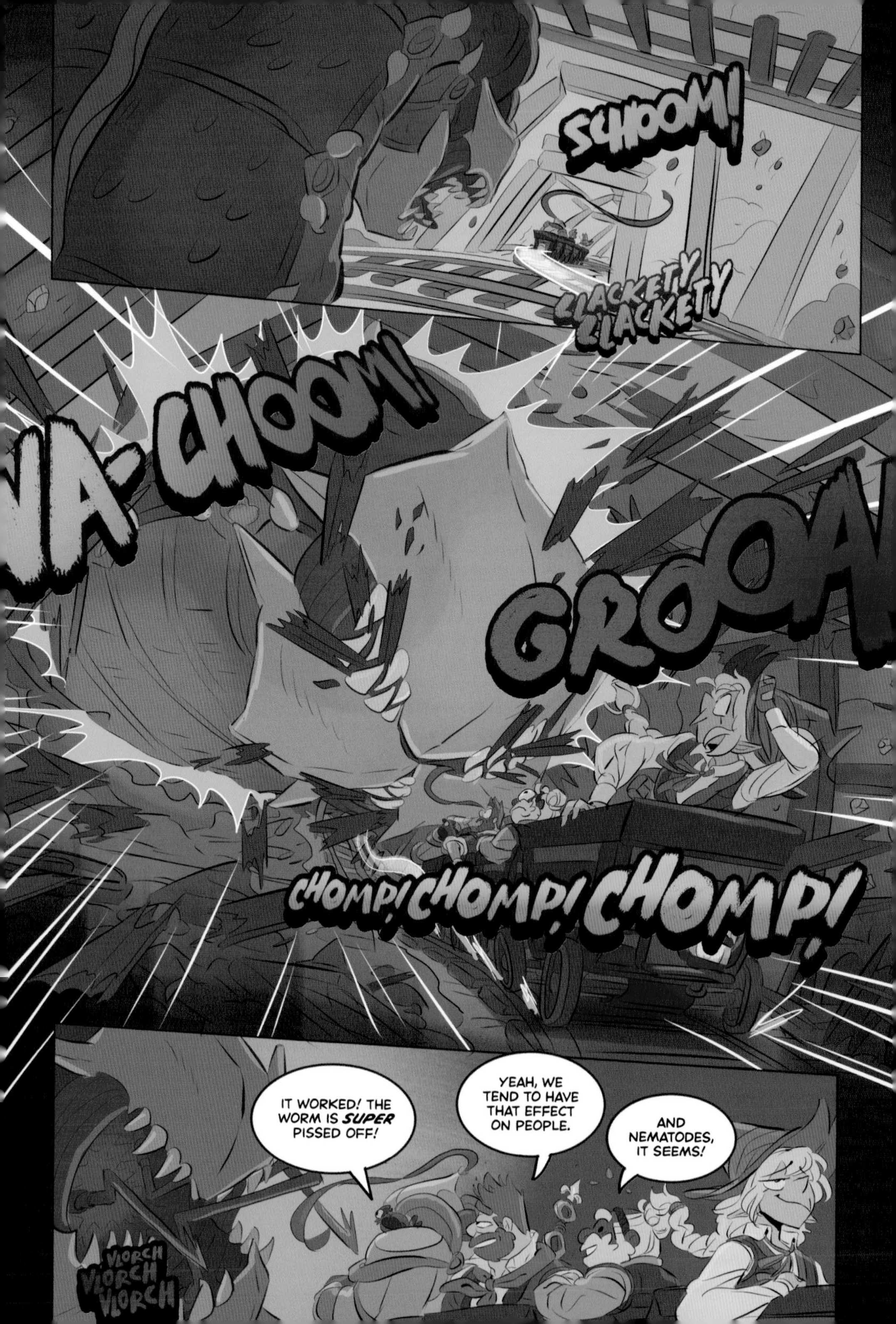
SCHOOM!
CLACKETY CLACKETY
-CHOOM!
GROOM
CHOMP! CHOMP! CHOMP!
IT WORKED! THE WORM IS *SUPER* PISSED OFF!
YEAH, WE TEND TO HAVE THAT EFFECT ON PEOPLE.
AND NEMATODES, IT SEEMS!
VLORCH VLORCH VLORCH

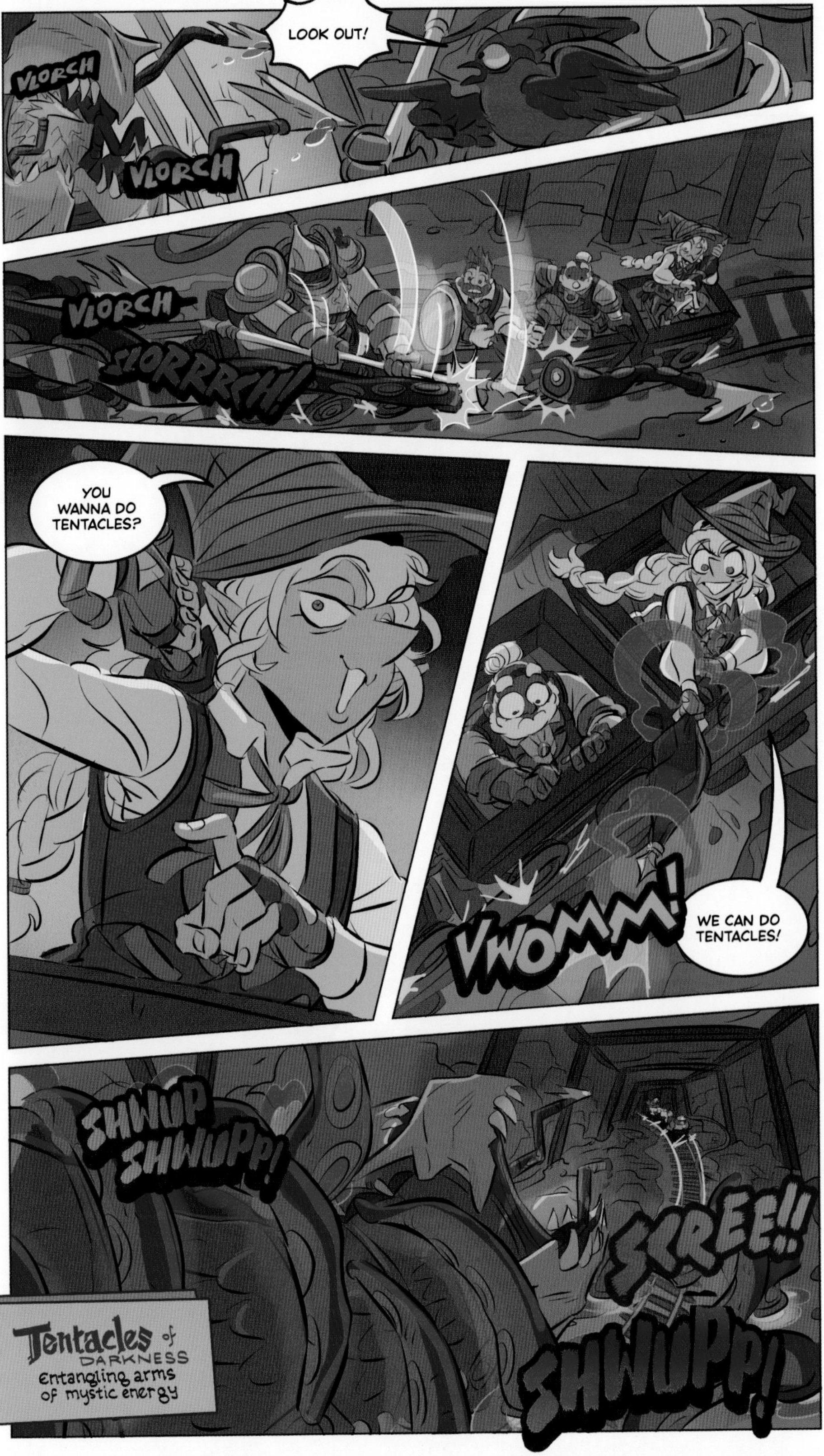
LOOK OUT!
VLORCH
VLORCH
VLORCH
SLORRRCH!
YOU WANNA DO TENTACLES?
VWOMM!
WE CAN DO TENTACLES!
SHWUP SHWUPP!
SCREE!!
Tentacles of DARKNESS
Entangling arms of mystic energy
SHWUPP!

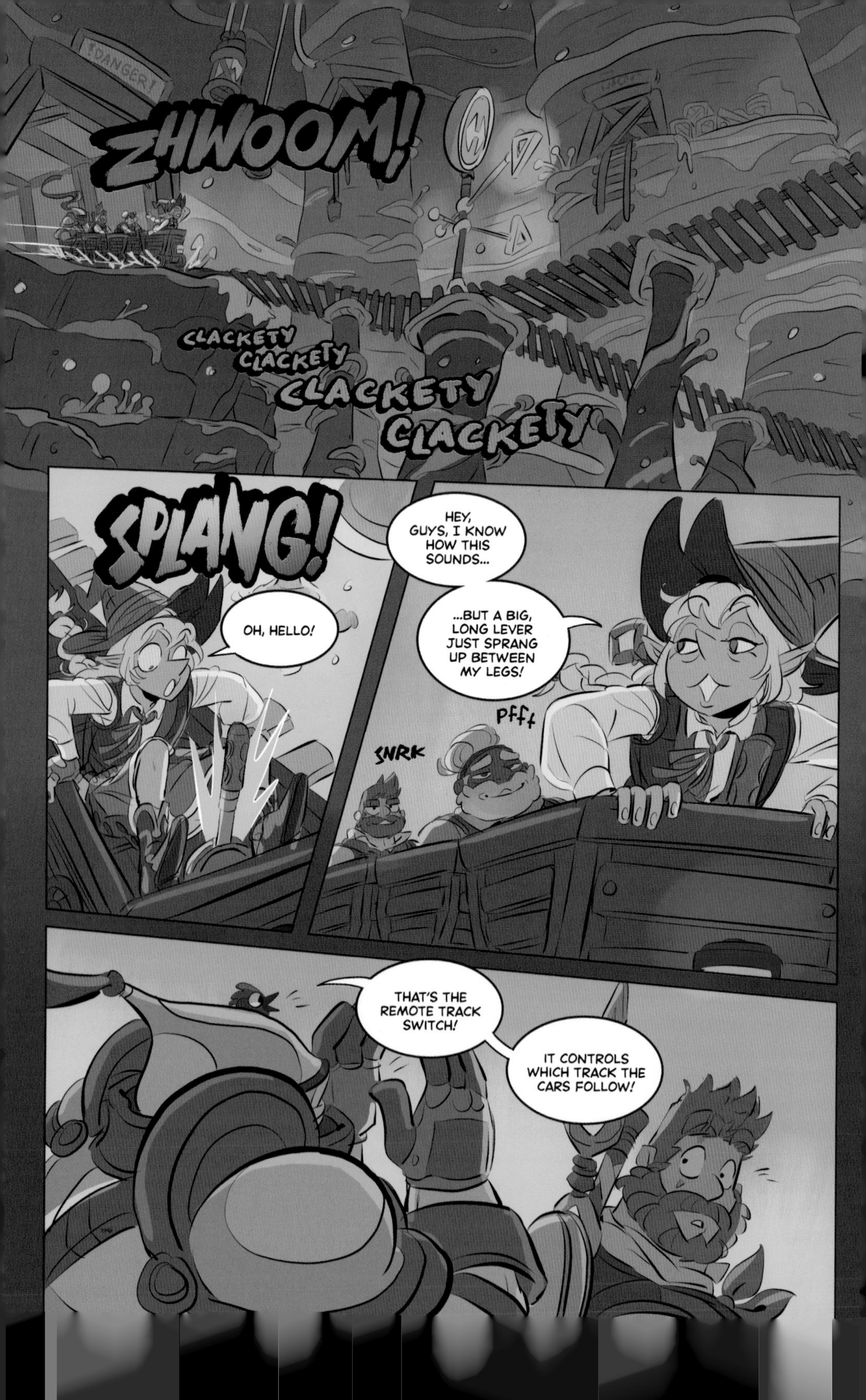

!DANGER!
ZHWOOM!
CLACKETY
CLACKETY
CLACKETY
CLACKETY
SPLANG!
OH, HELLO!
HEY, GUYS, I KNOW HOW THIS SOUNDS...
...BUT A BIG, LONG LEVER JUST SPRANG UP BETWEEN MY LEGS!
PFFT
SNRK
THAT'S THE REMOTE TRACK SWITCH!
IT CONTROLS WHICH TRACK THE CARS FOLLOW!

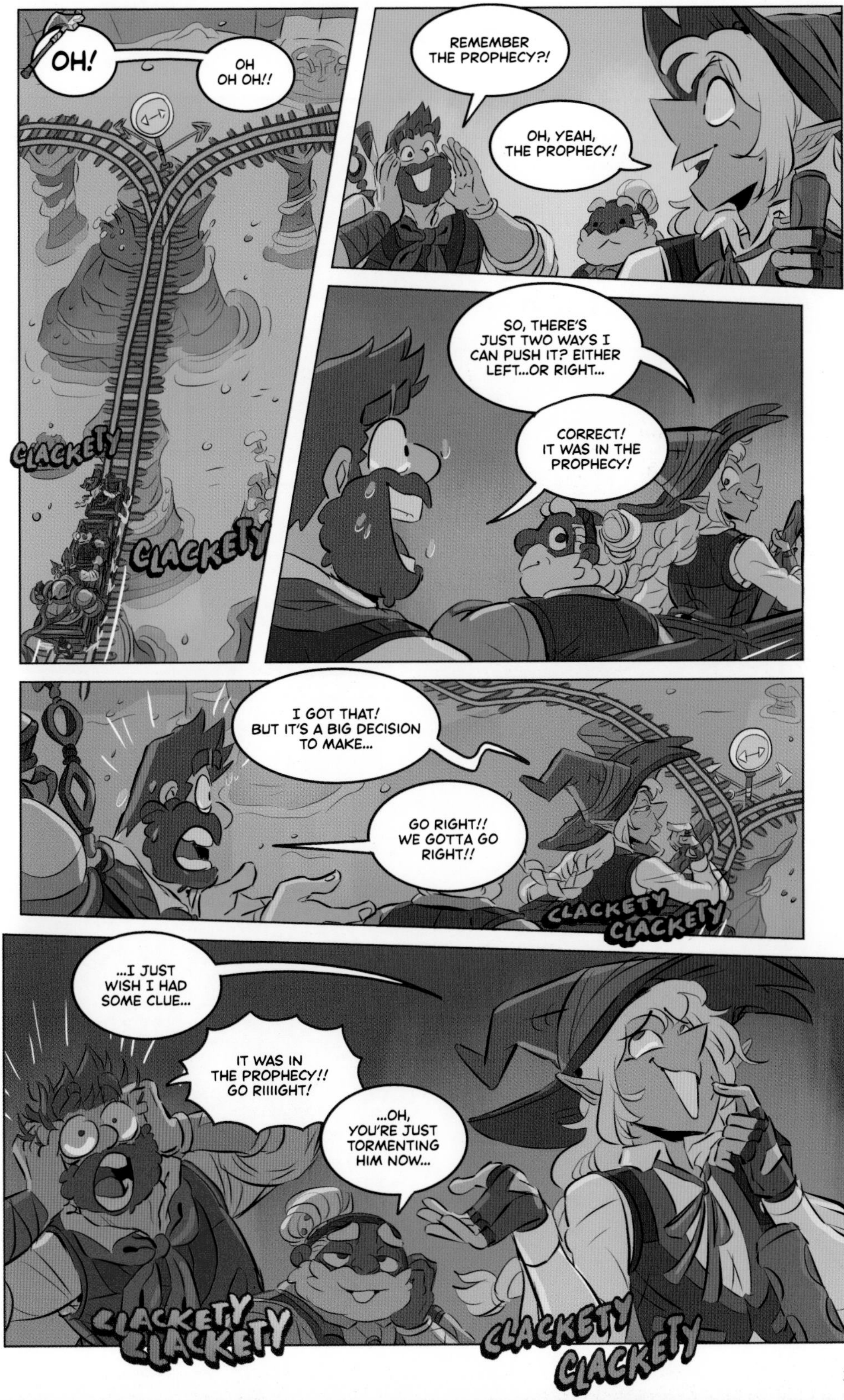
OH!
OH OH OH!!
CLACKETY
CLACKETY
REMEMBER THE PROPHECY?!
OH, YEAH, THE PROPHECY!
SO, THERE'S JUST TWO WAYS I CAN PUSH IT? EITHER LEFT...OR RIGHT...
CORRECT! IT WAS IN THE PROPHECY!
I GOT THAT! BUT IT'S A BIG DECISION TO MAKE...
GO RIGHT!! WE GOTTA GO RIGHT!!
CLACKETY CLACKETY
...I JUST WISH I HAD SOME CLUE...
IT WAS IN THE PROPHECY!! GO RIIIIGHT!
...OH, YOU'RE JUST TORMENTING HIM NOW...
CLACKETY CLACKETY
CLACKETY CLACKETY

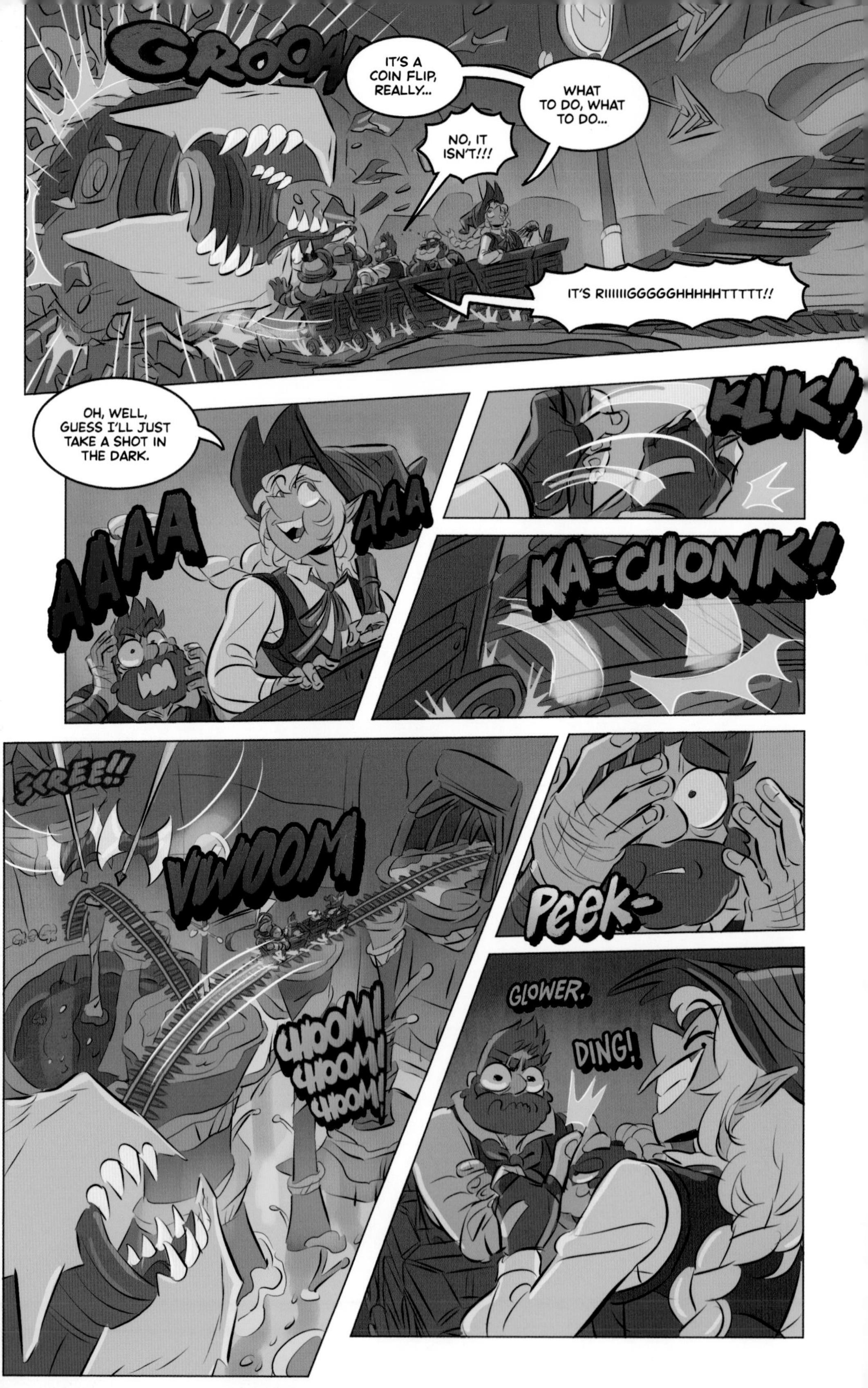
GROOA
IT'S A COIN FLIP, REALLY...
WHAT TO DO, WHAT TO DO...
NO, IT ISN'T!!!
IT'S RIIIIIIGGGGGHHHHHTTTTTT!!
OH, WELL, GUESS I'LL JUST TAKE A SHOT IN THE DARK.
AAAA AAA
KLIK!
KA-CHONK!
SCREE!!
VWOOM
CHOOM! CHOOM! CHOOM!
Peek-
GLOWER.
DING!

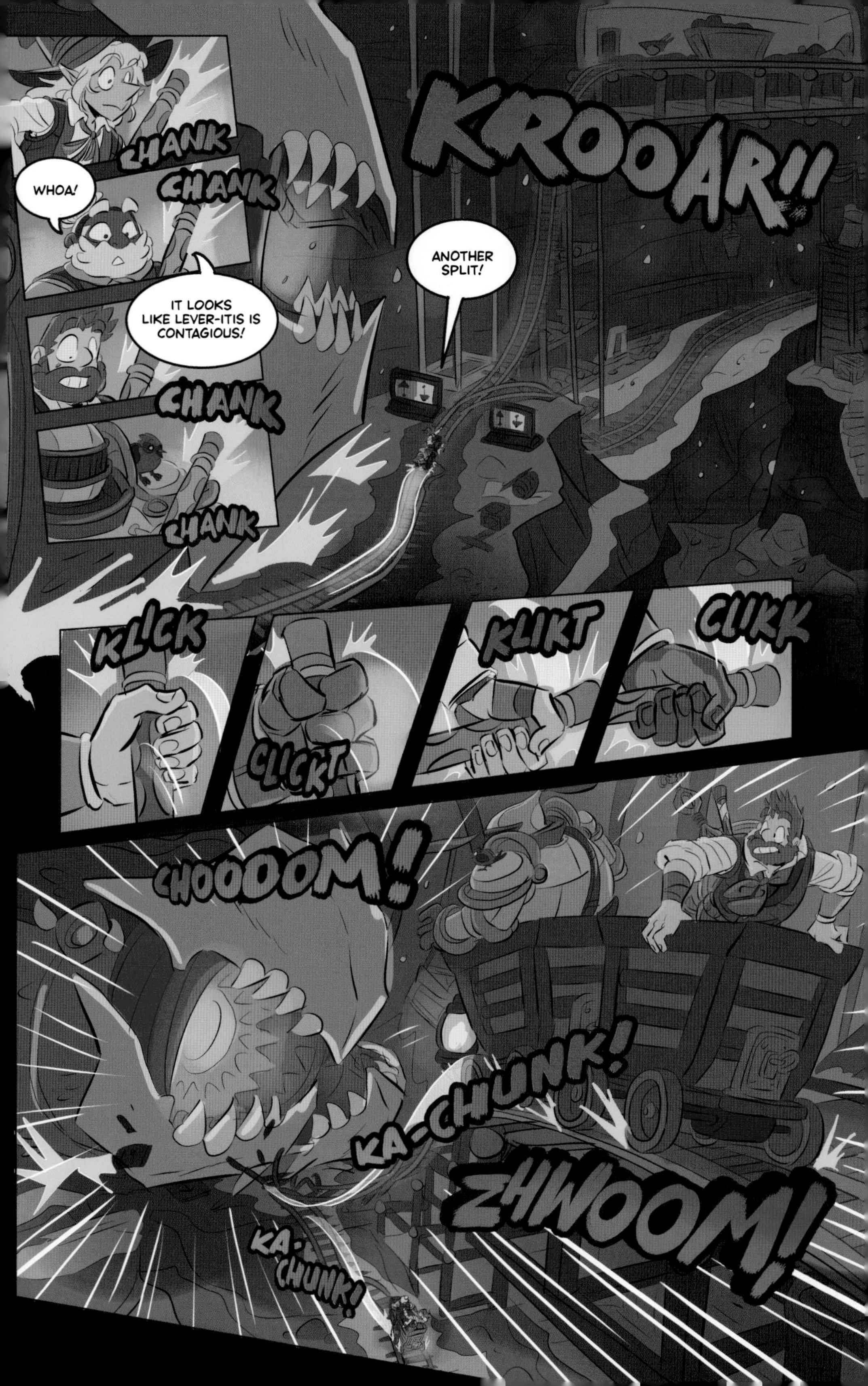

CHANK
WHOA!
CHANK
IT LOOKS LIKE LEVER-ITIS IS CONTAGIOUS!
CHANK
CHANK
KROOAR!!
ANOTHER SPLIT!
KLICK
CLICKT
KLIKT
CLIKK
CHOOOOM!
KA-CHUNK!
ZHWOOM!
KA-
CHUNK!

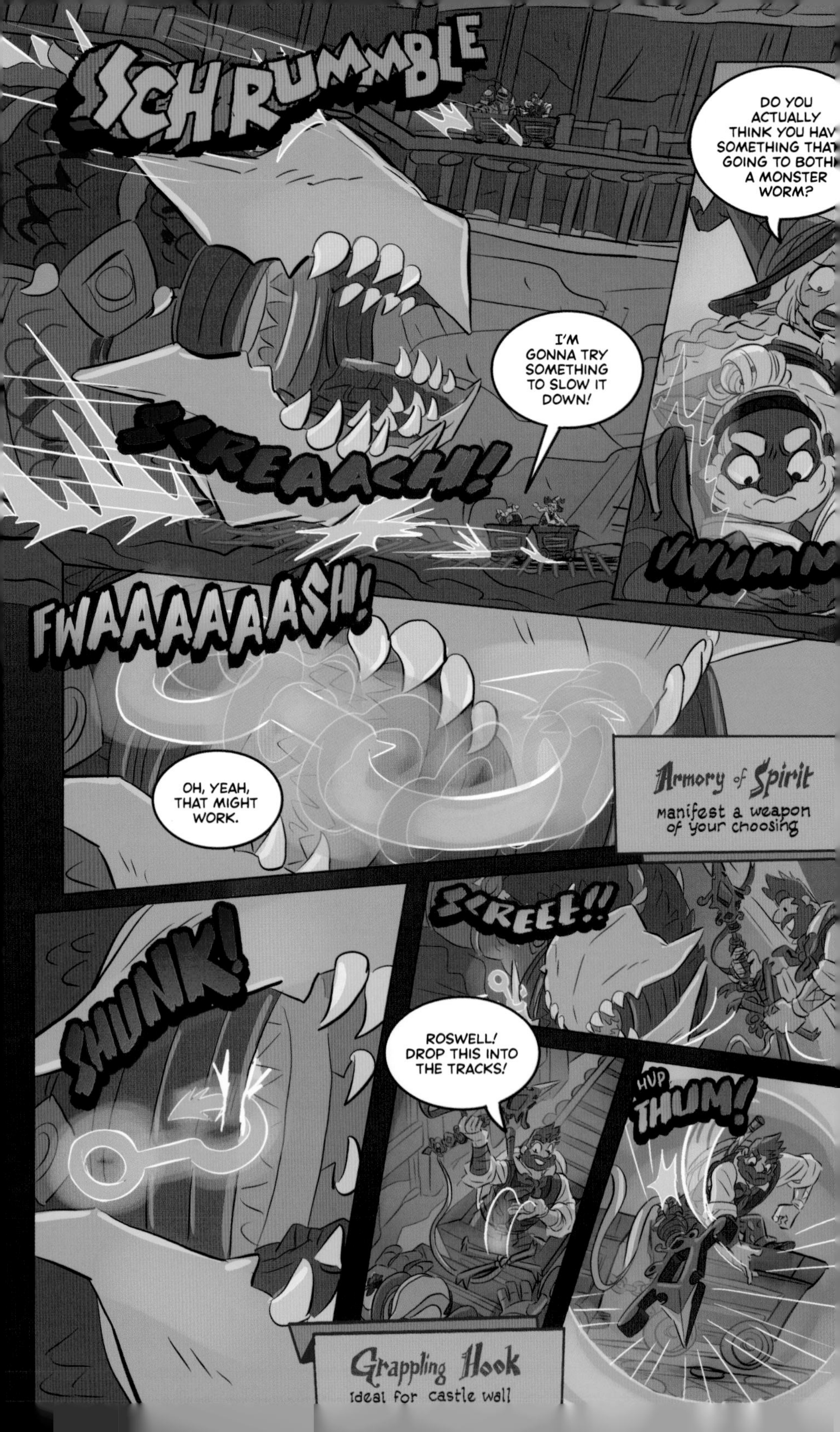
SCHRUMMBLE
DO YOU ACTUALLY THINK YOU HAV SOMETHING THAT GOING TO BOTH A MONSTER WORM?
I'M GONNA TRY SOMETHING TO SLOW IT DOWN!
SKREAACH!
VWUMM
FWAAAAAAASH!
OH, YEAH, THAT MIGHT WORK.
Armory of Spirit
manifest a weapon of your choosing
SHUNK!
SKREEE!!
ROSWELL! DROP THIS INTO THE TRACKS!
HUP
THUM!
Grappling Hook
Ideal for castle wall

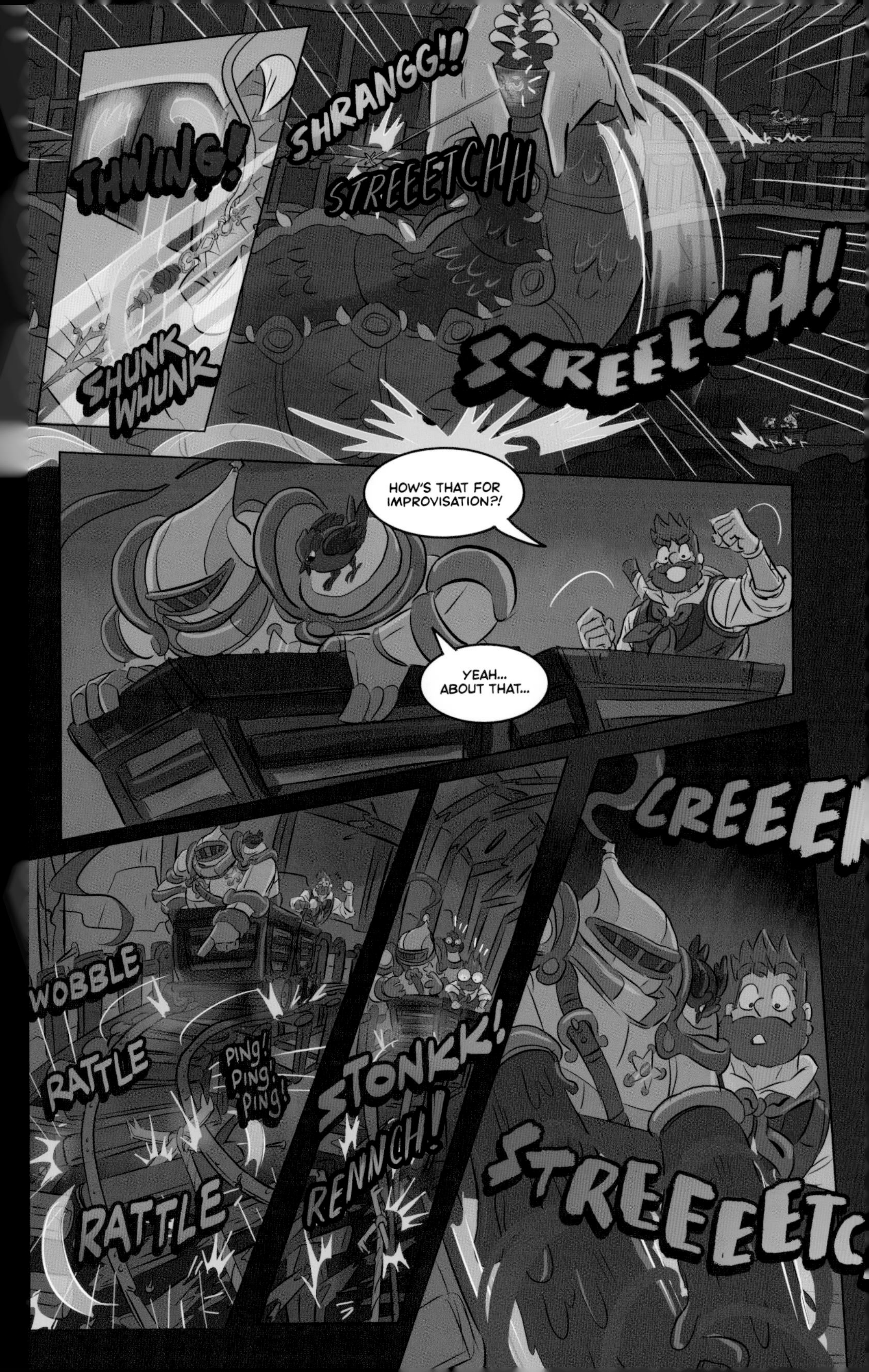
THWING!
SHRANGG!!
STREEETCHH
SHUNK WHUNK
SCREEECH!
HOW'S THAT FOR IMPROVISATION?!
YEAH... ABOUT THAT...
CREEEE
WOBBLE
RATTLE
PING! PING! PING!
RATTLE
STONKK!
RENNCH!
STREEEETC

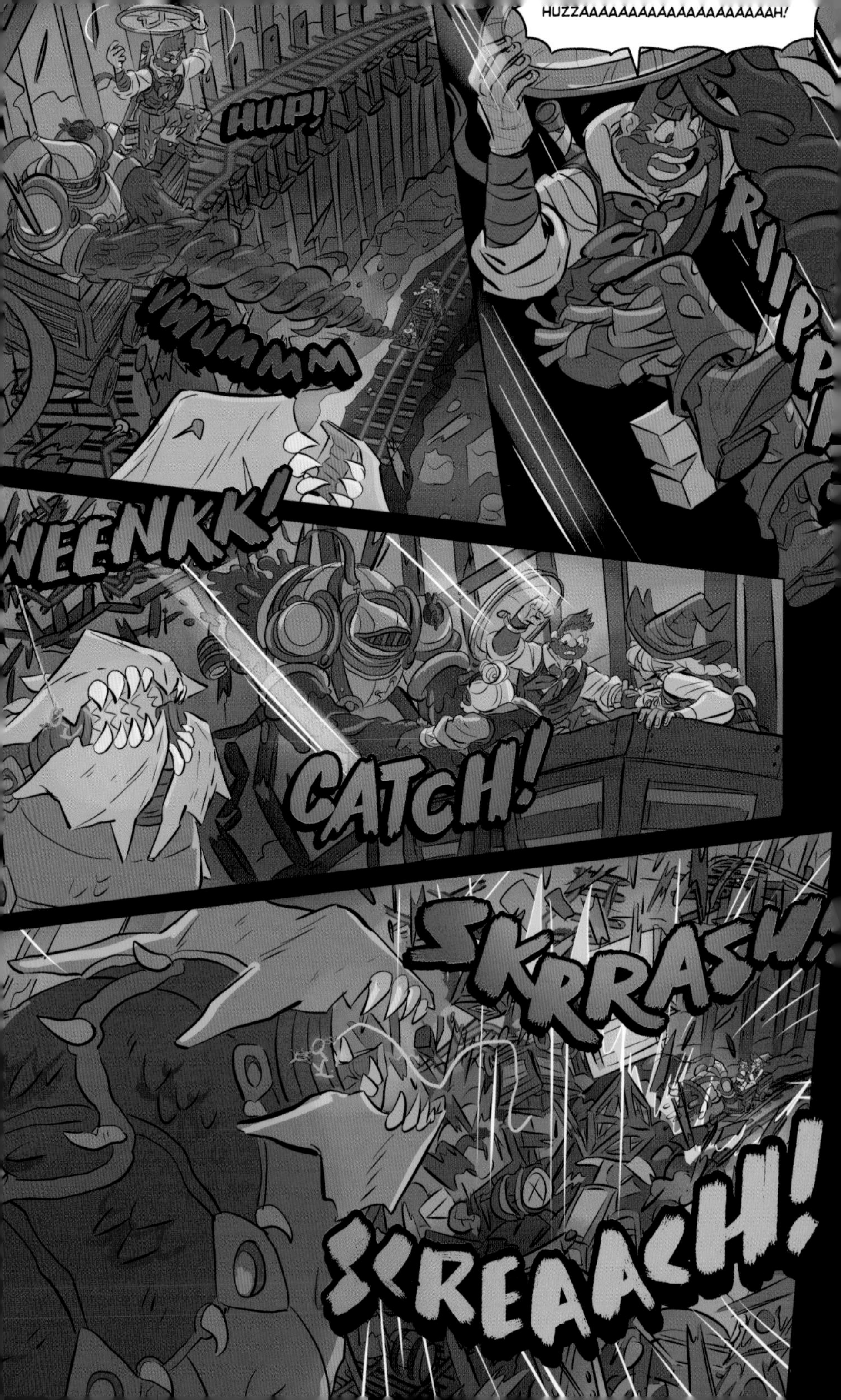
HUP!
VVUMMMM
HUZZAAAAAAAAAAAAAAAAAAAH!
RIPP
WEENKK!
CATCH!
SKRRASH
SCREAACH!

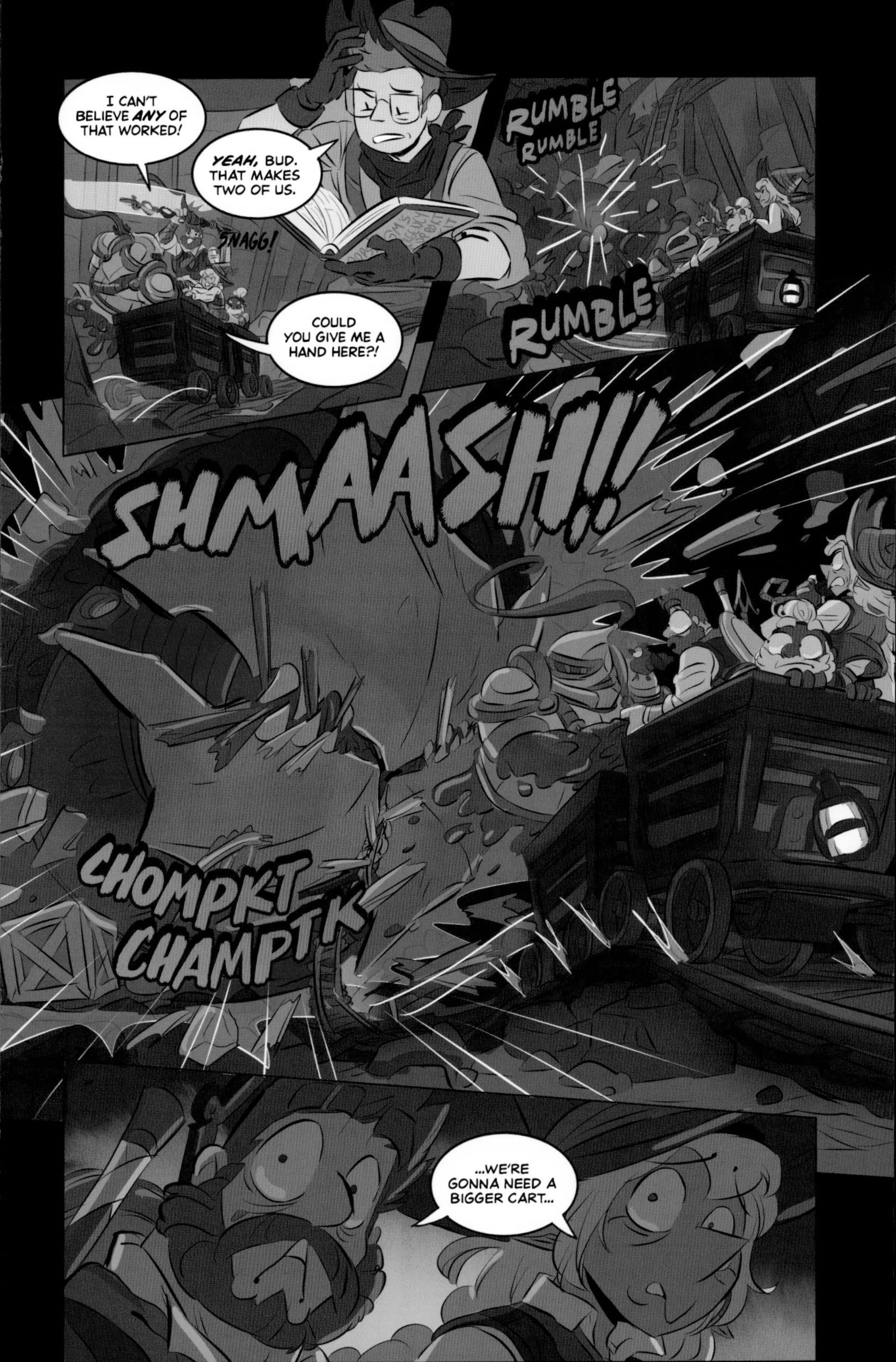
I CAN'T BELIEVE ANY OF THAT WORKED!
YEAH, BUD. THAT MAKES TWO OF US.
SNAGG!
COULD YOU GIVE ME A HAND HERE?!
RUMBLE RUMBLE
RUMBLE
SHMAASH!!
CHOMPKT CHAMPTK
...WE'RE GONNA NEED A BIGGER CART...

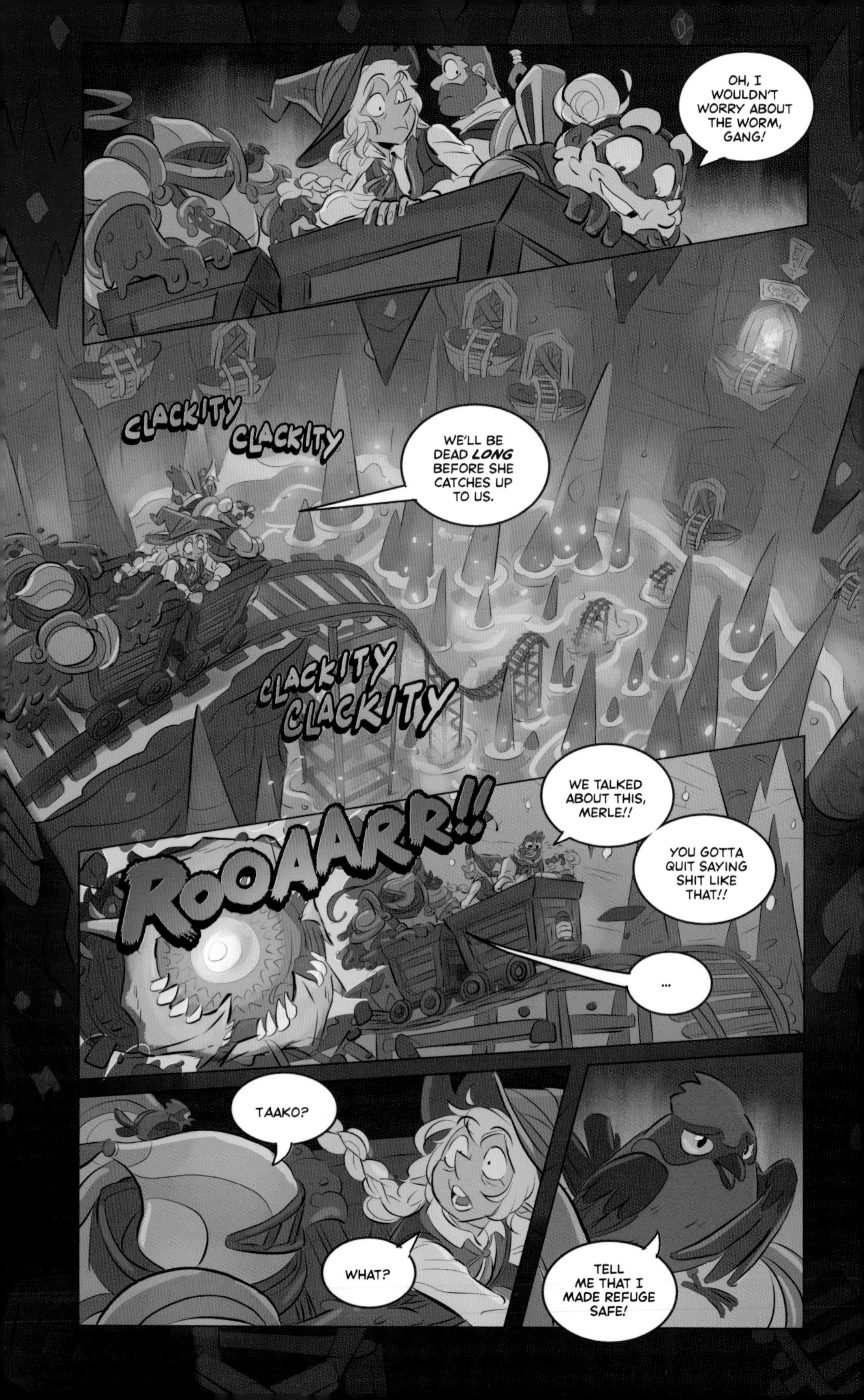

OH, I WOULDN'T WORRY ABOUT THE WORM, GANG!
CLACKITY CLACKITY
WE'LL BE DEAD LONG BEFORE SHE CATCHES UP TO US.
CLACKITY CLACKITY
ROOAARR!!
WE TALKED ABOUT THIS, MERLE!!
YOU GOTTA QUIT SAYING SHIT LIKE THAT!!
...
TAAKO?
WHAT?
TELL ME THAT I MADE REFUGE SAFE!

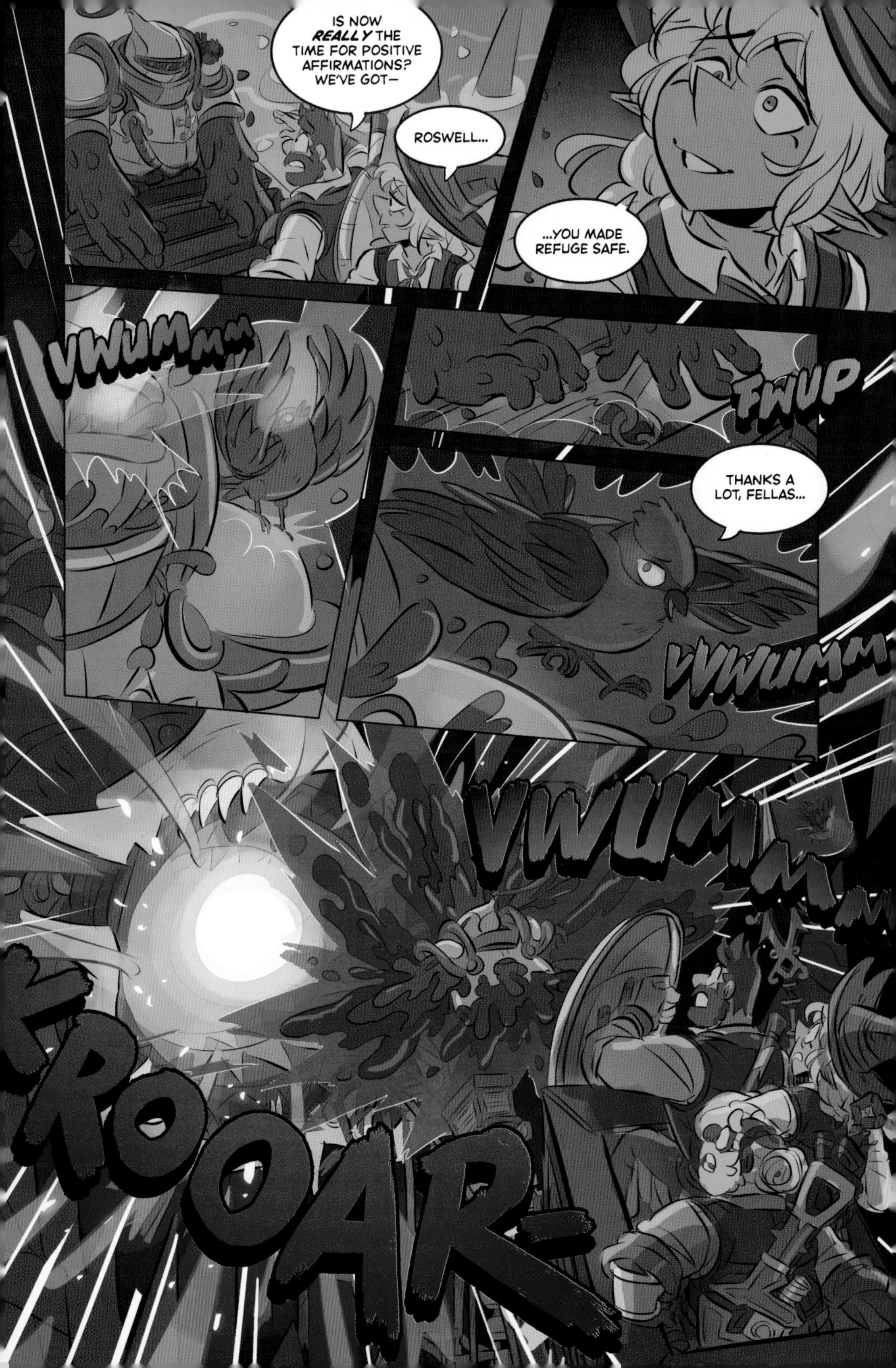
IS NOW *REALLY* THE TIME FOR POSITIVE AFFIRMATIONS? WE'VE GOT—
ROSWELL...
...YOU MADE REFUGE SAFE.
VWUMMM
FWUP
THANKS A LOT, FELLAS...
VVWUMMM
VWUMMMM
KROOAR-

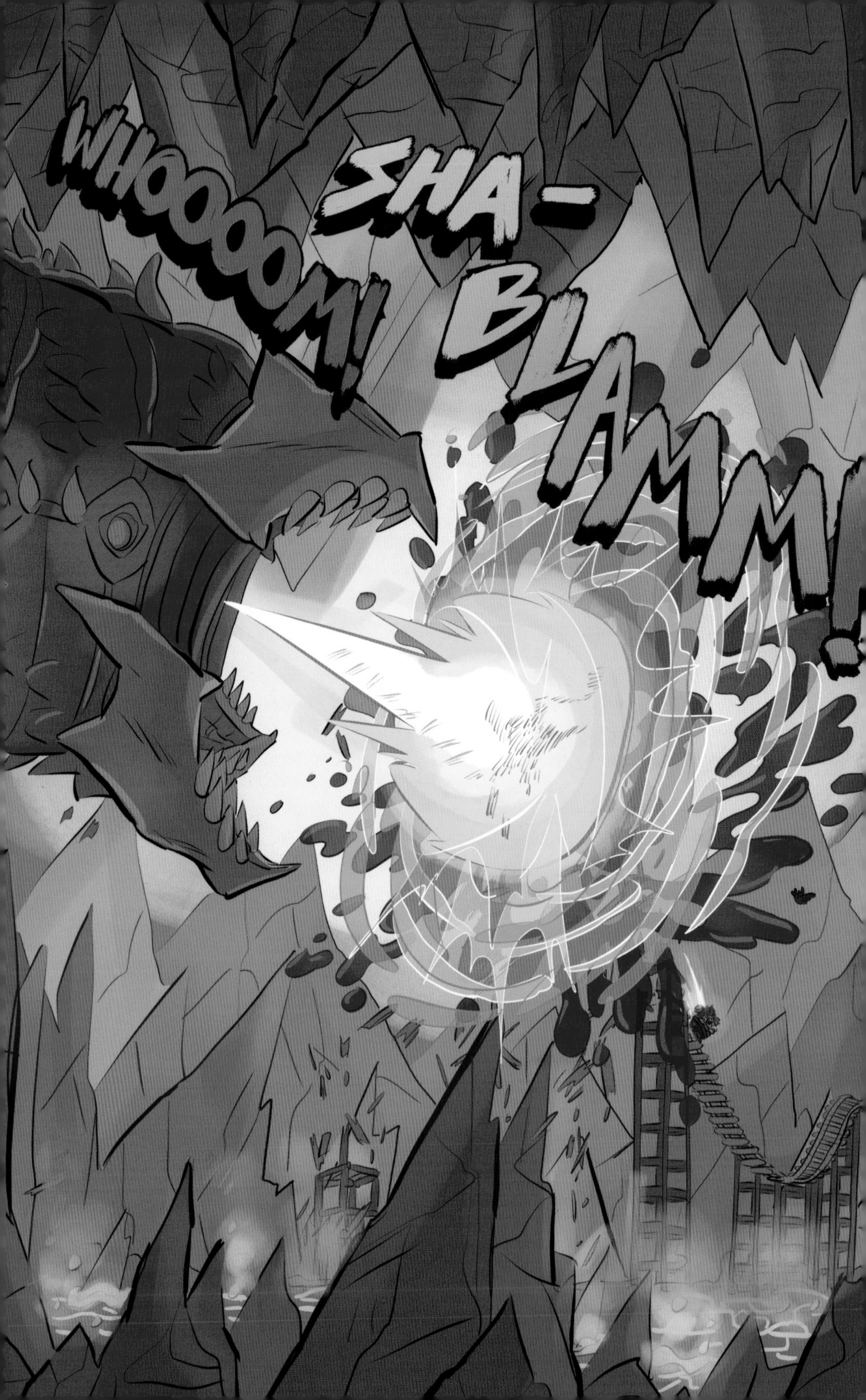
WHOOOOOM!
SHA-BLAMMM!

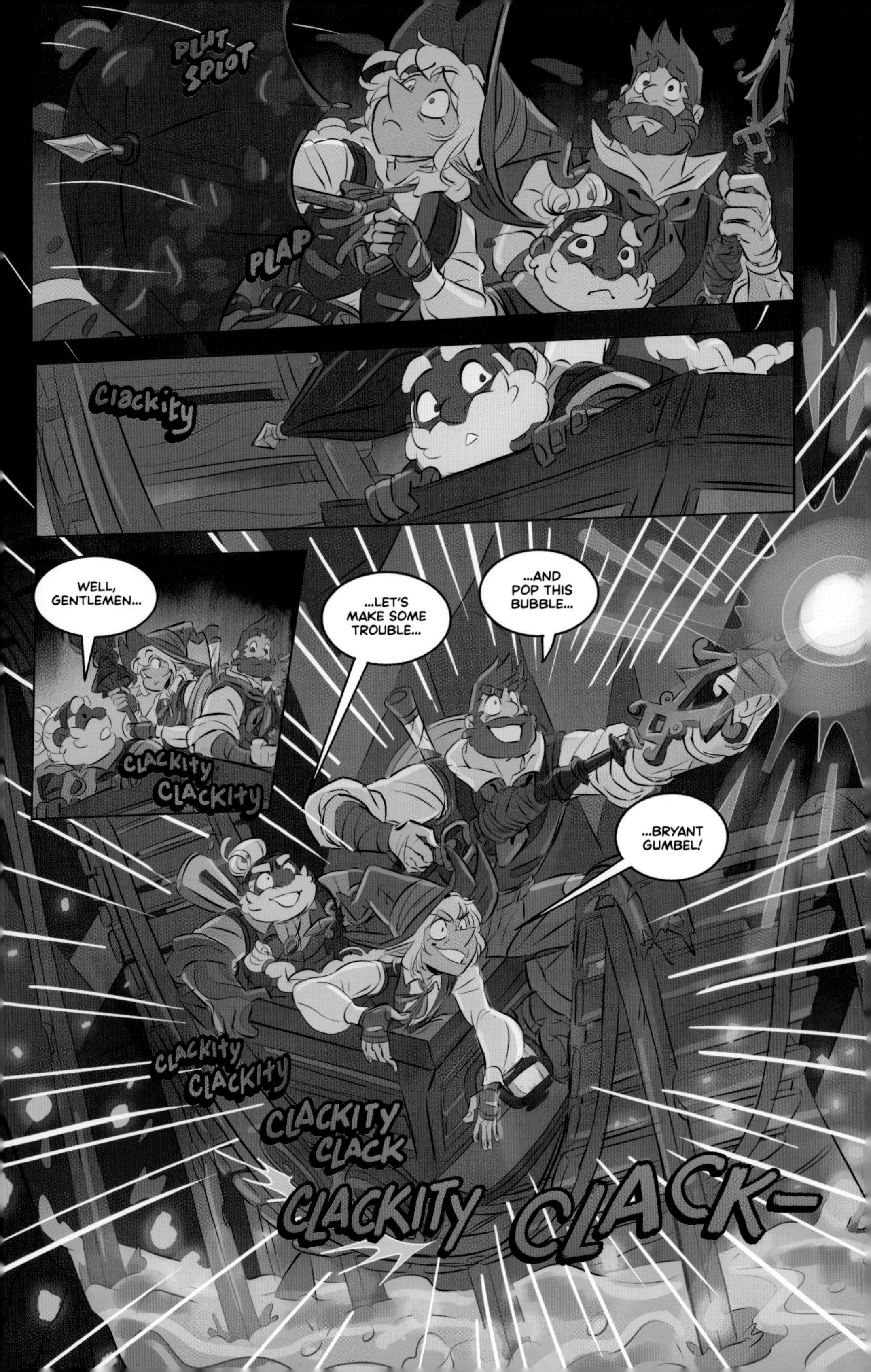
PLUT
SPLOT
PLAP
Clackity
WELL, GENTLEMEN...
CLACKity CLACKity
...LET'S MAKE SOME TROUBLE...
...AND POP THIS BUBBLE...
...BRYANT GUMBEL!
CLACKity CLACKity
CLACKITY CLACK
CLACKITY CLACK-

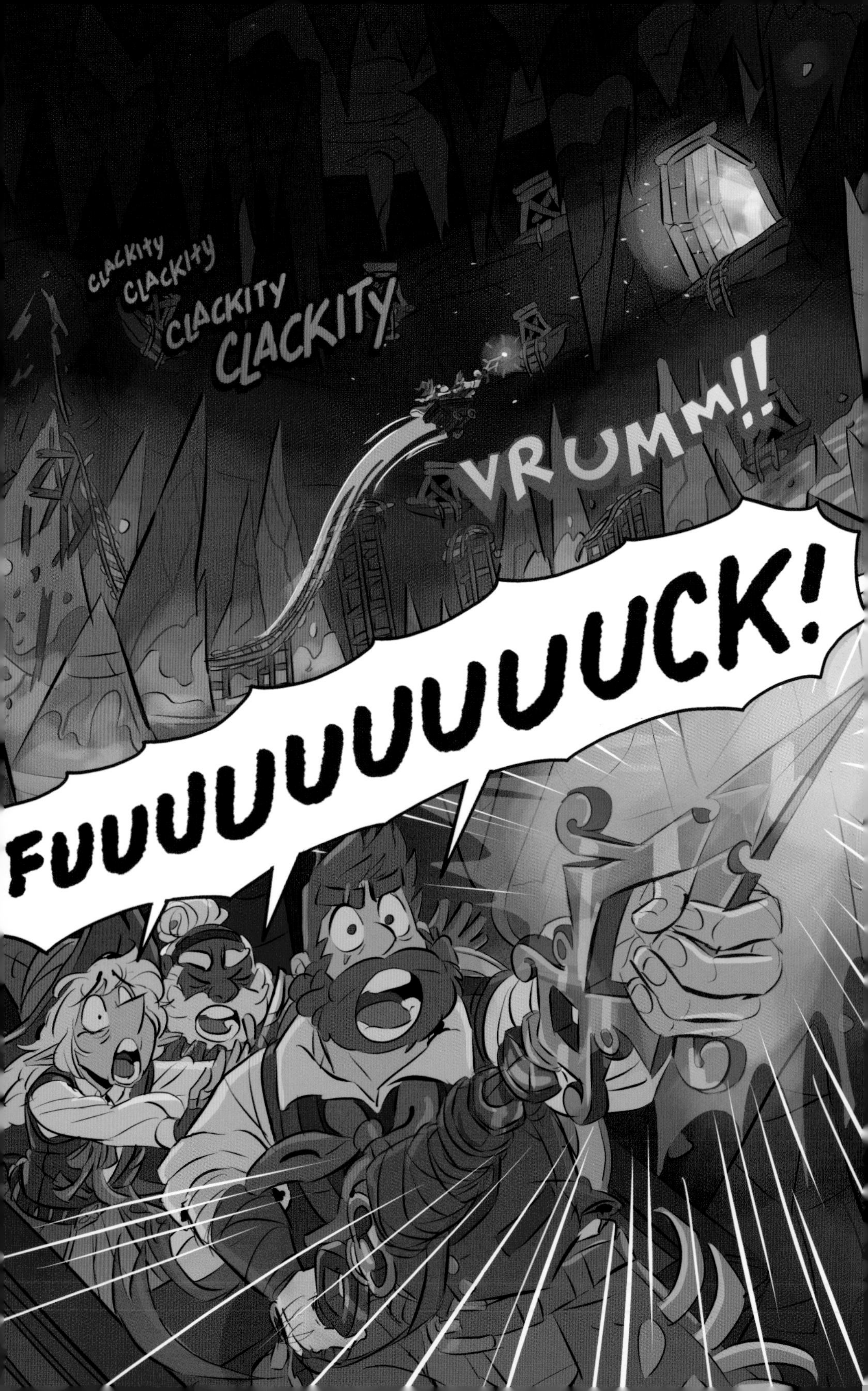
CLACKITY CLACKITY CLACKITY CLACKITY
VRUMM!!
FUUUUUUUUUCK!

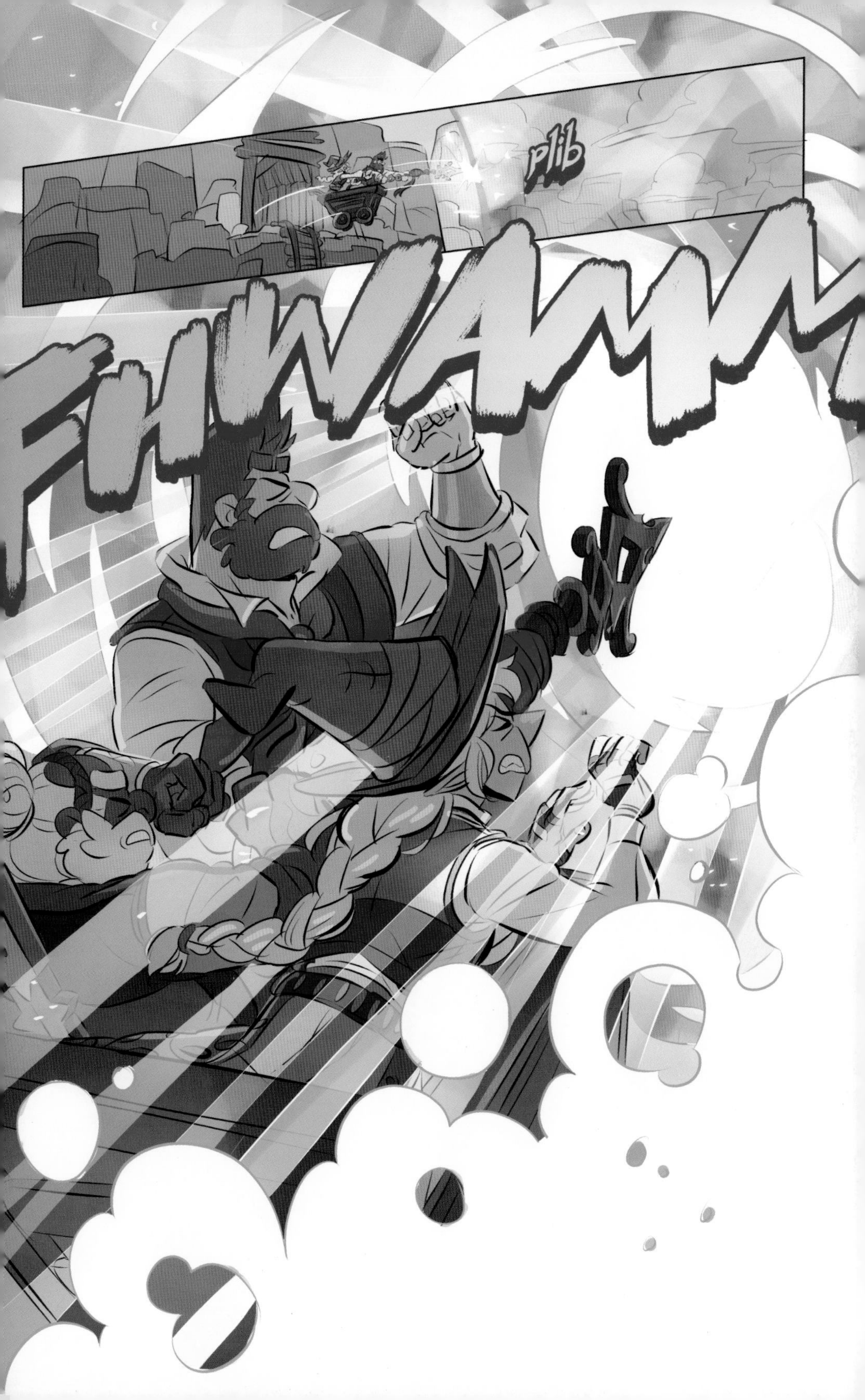
plib
FHWAM

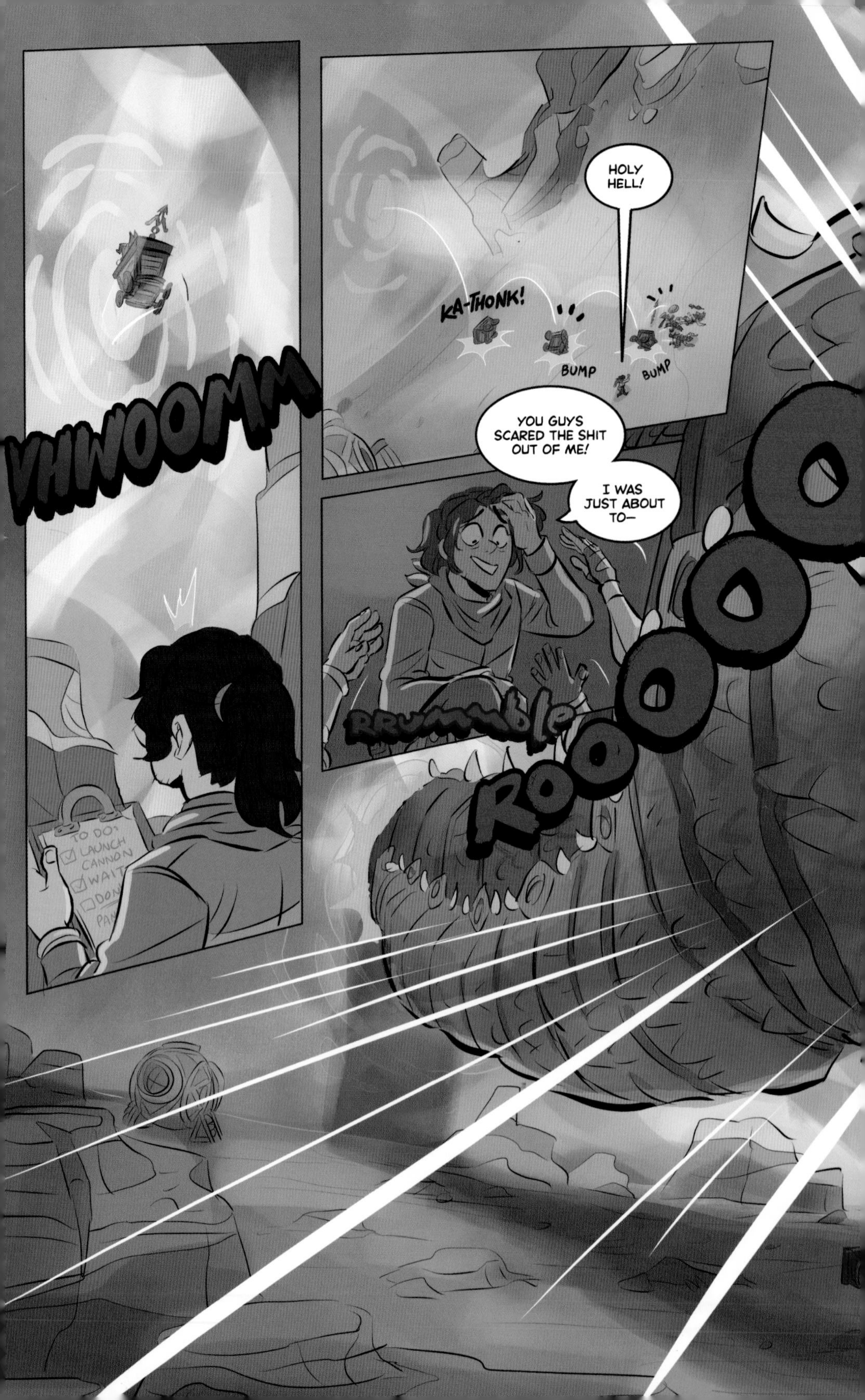
VHWOOMM
TO DO:
LAUNCH CANNON
WAIT
HOLY HELL!
KA-THONK!
BUMP
BUMP
YOU GUYS SCARED THE SHIT OUT OF ME!
I WAS JUST ABOUT TO—
RRUMMBLE
ROOOOOO

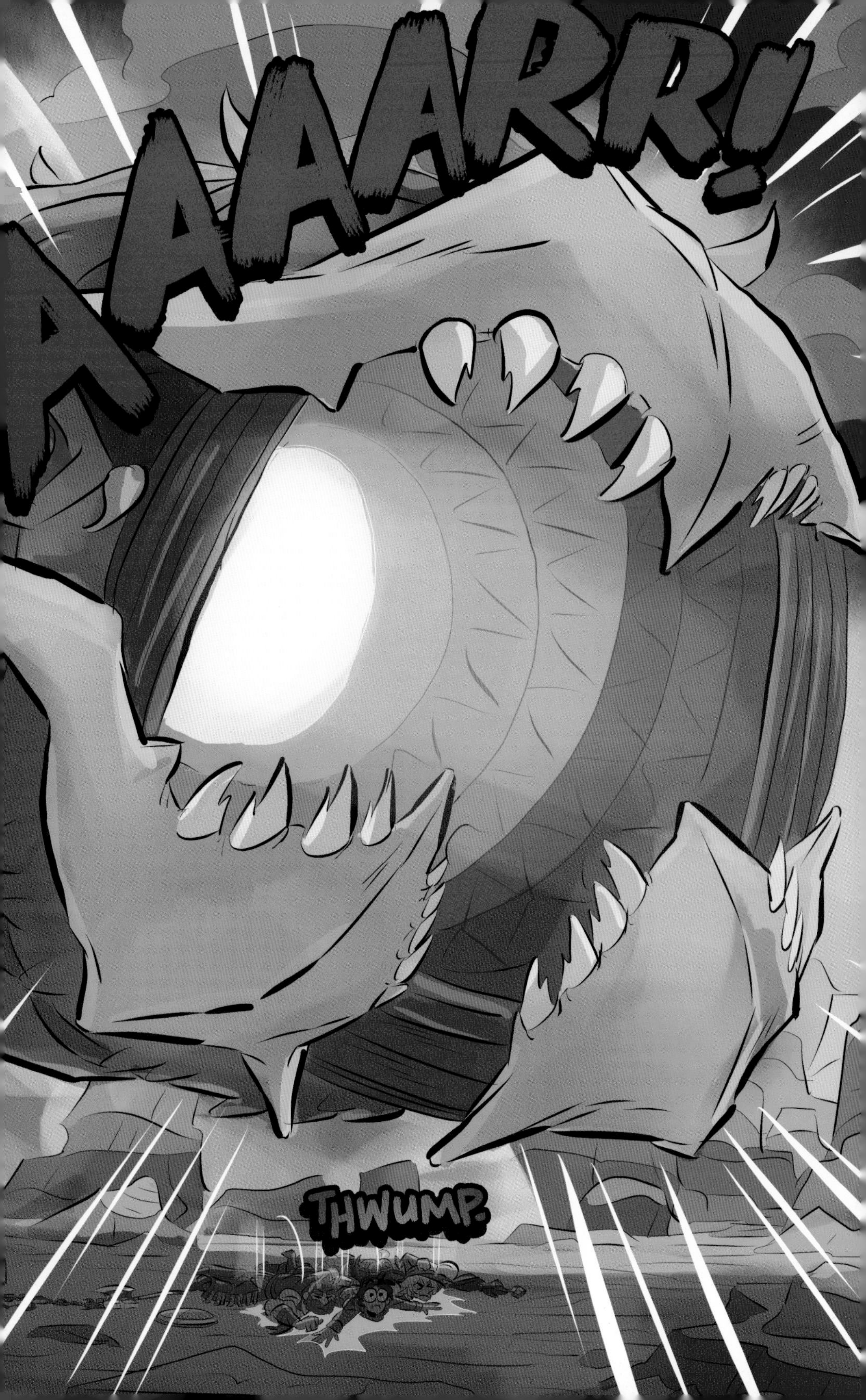
AAAARR!
THWUMP.

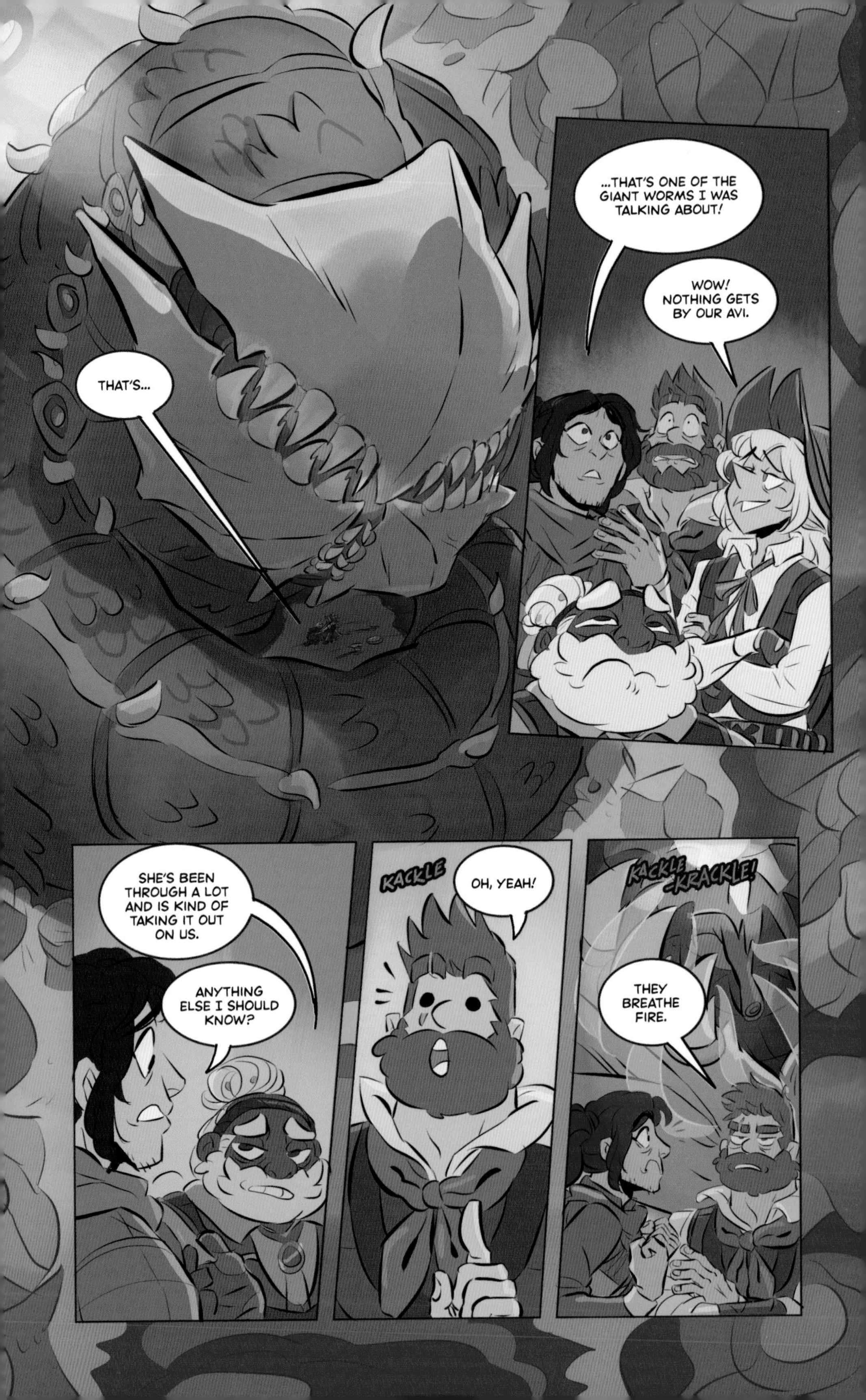
THAT'S...
...THAT'S ONE OF THE GIANT WORMS I WAS TALKING ABOUT!
WOW! NOTHING GETS BY OUR AVI.
SHE'S BEEN THROUGH A LOT AND IS KIND OF TAKING IT OUT ON US.
ANYTHING ELSE I SHOULD KNOW?
KACKLE
OH, YEAH!
KACKLE-KRACKLE!
THEY BREATHE FIRE.

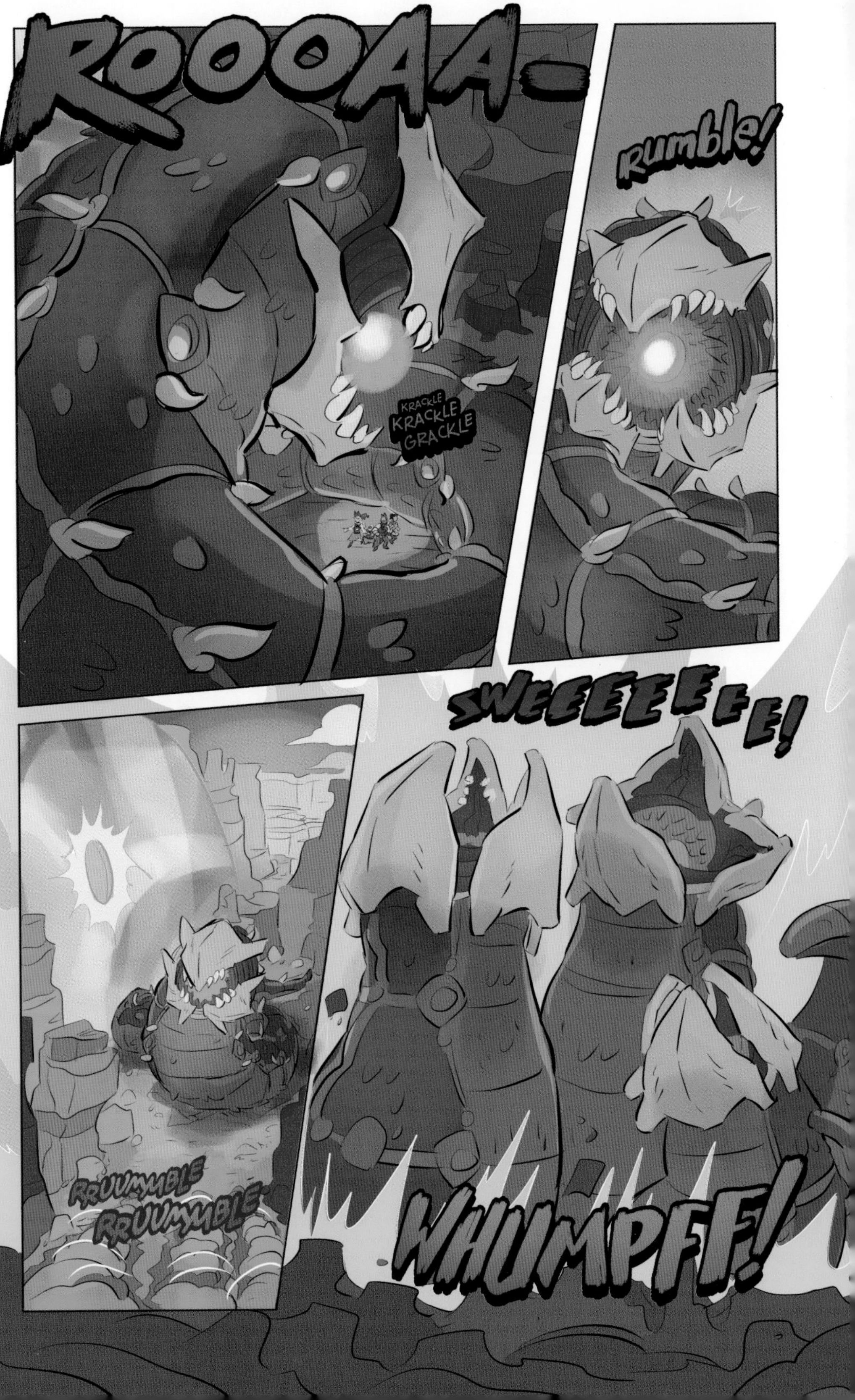
ROOOAA-
KRACKLE
KRACKLE
GRACKLE
rumble!
SWEEEEEEE!
RRUMMBLE
RRUMMBLE
WHUMPFF!

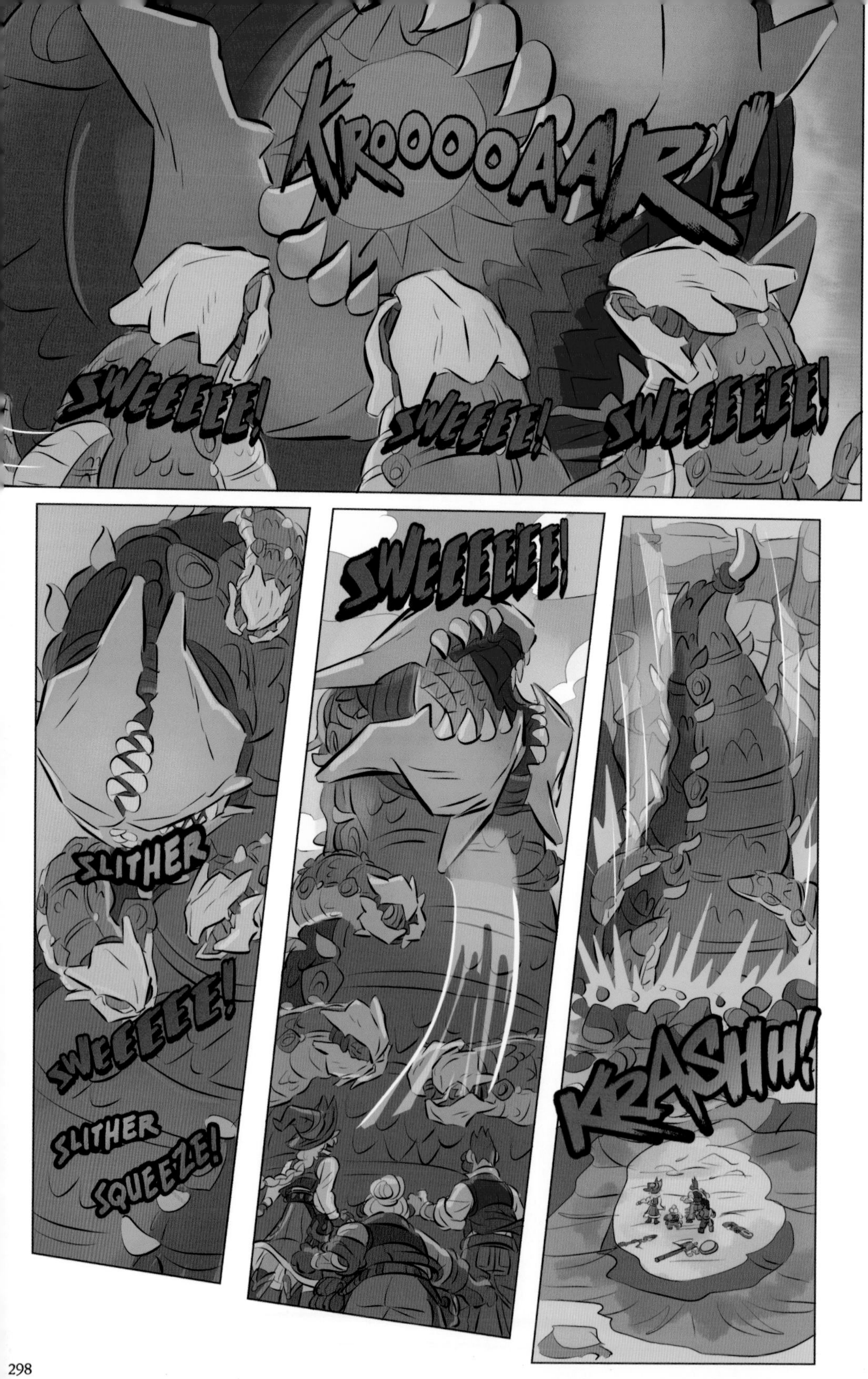
KROOOOAAR!
SWEEEEE!
SWEEEE!
SWEEEEEE!
SLITHER
SWEEEEE!
SLITHER
SQUEEZE!
SWEEEEEE!
KRASHH!

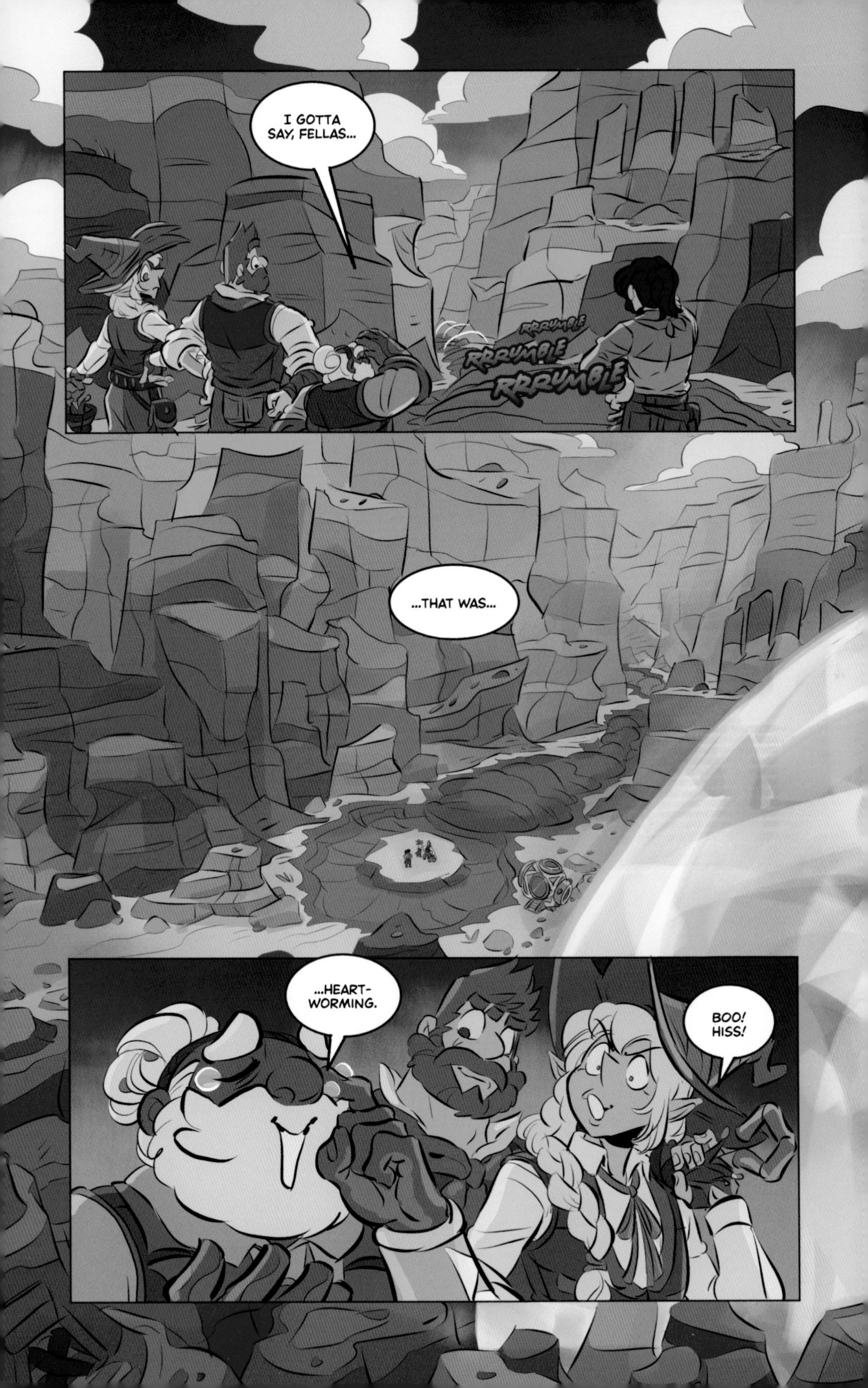
I GOTTA SAY, FELLAS...
RRRUMBLE
RRRUMBLE
RRRUMBLE
...THAT WAS...
...HEART-WORMING.
BOO! HISS!

Chapter
115

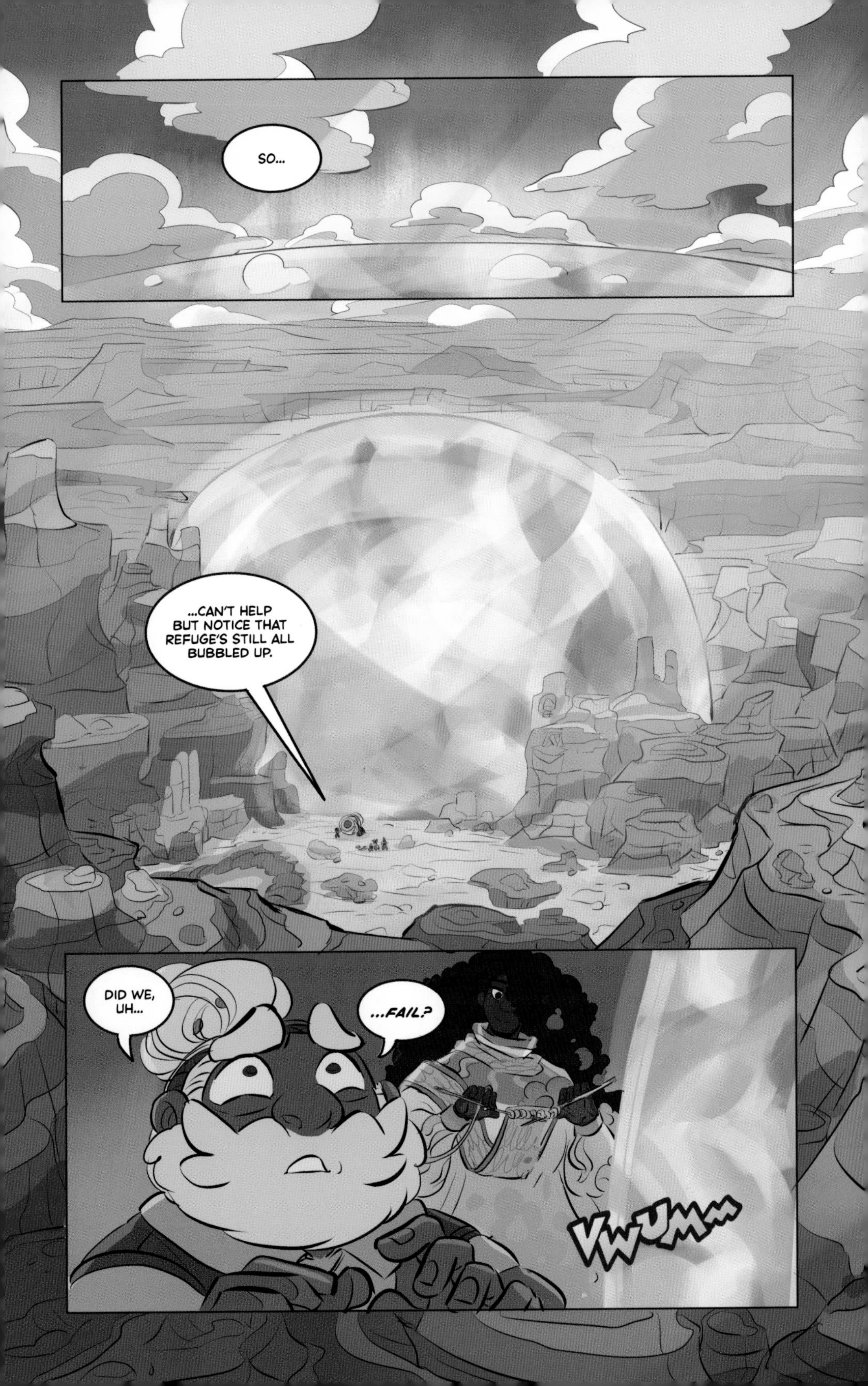
SO...
...CAN'T HELP BUT NOTICE THAT REFUGE'S STILL ALL BUBBLED UP.
DID WE, UH...
...FAIL?
VWUMM

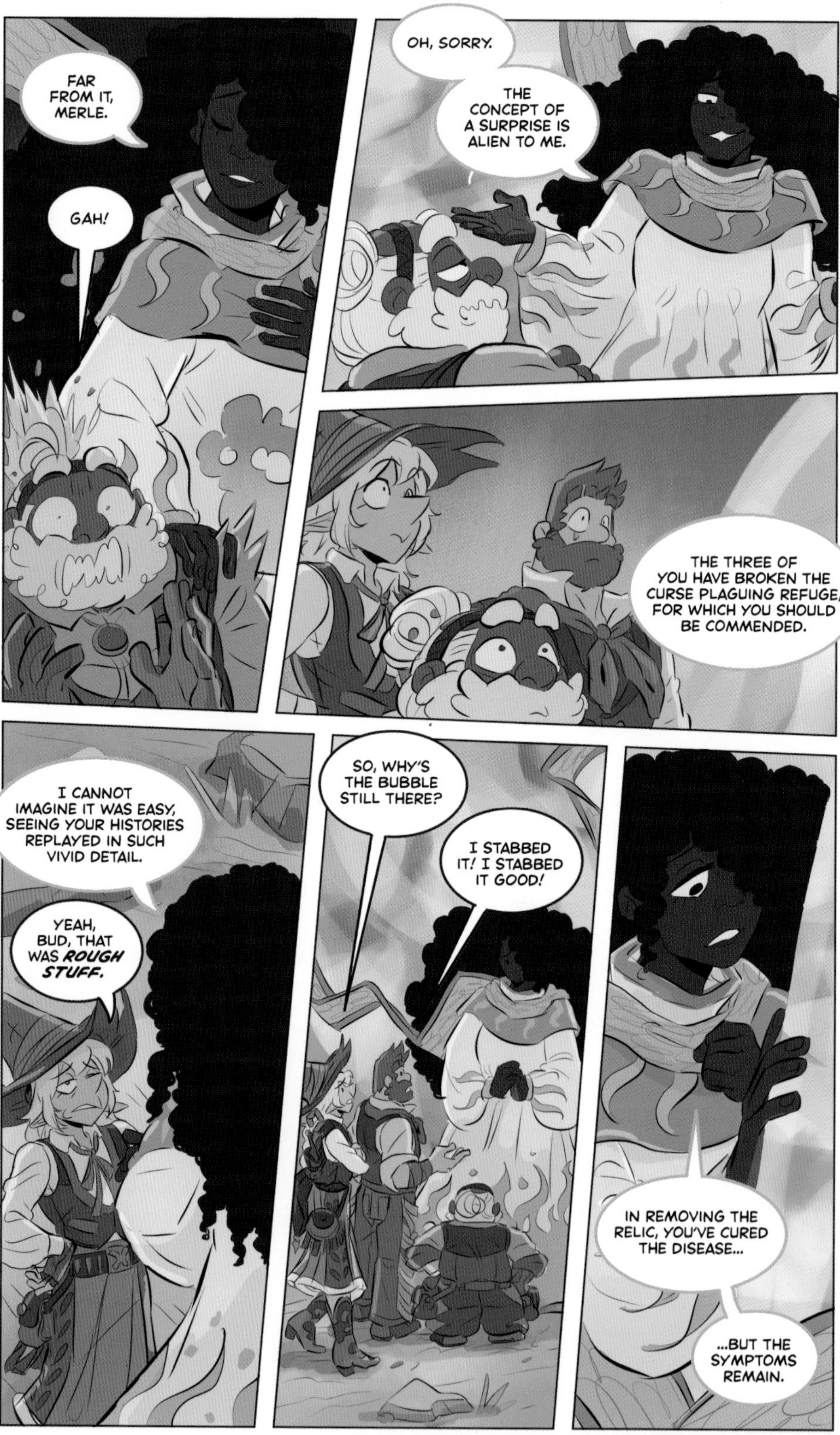
FAR FROM IT, MERLE.
GAH!
OH, SORRY.
THE CONCEPT OF A SURPRISE IS ALIEN TO ME.
THE THREE OF YOU HAVE BROKEN THE CURSE PLAGUING REFUGE, FOR WHICH YOU SHOULD BE COMMENDED.
I CANNOT IMAGINE IT WAS EASY, SEEING YOUR HISTORIES REPLAYED IN SUCH VIVID DETAIL.
YEAH, BUD, THAT WAS ROUGH STUFF.
SO, WHY'S THE BUBBLE STILL THERE?
I STABBED IT! I STABBED IT GOOD!
IN REMOVING THE RELIC, YOU'VE CURED THE DISEASE...
...BUT THE SYMPTOMS REMAIN.

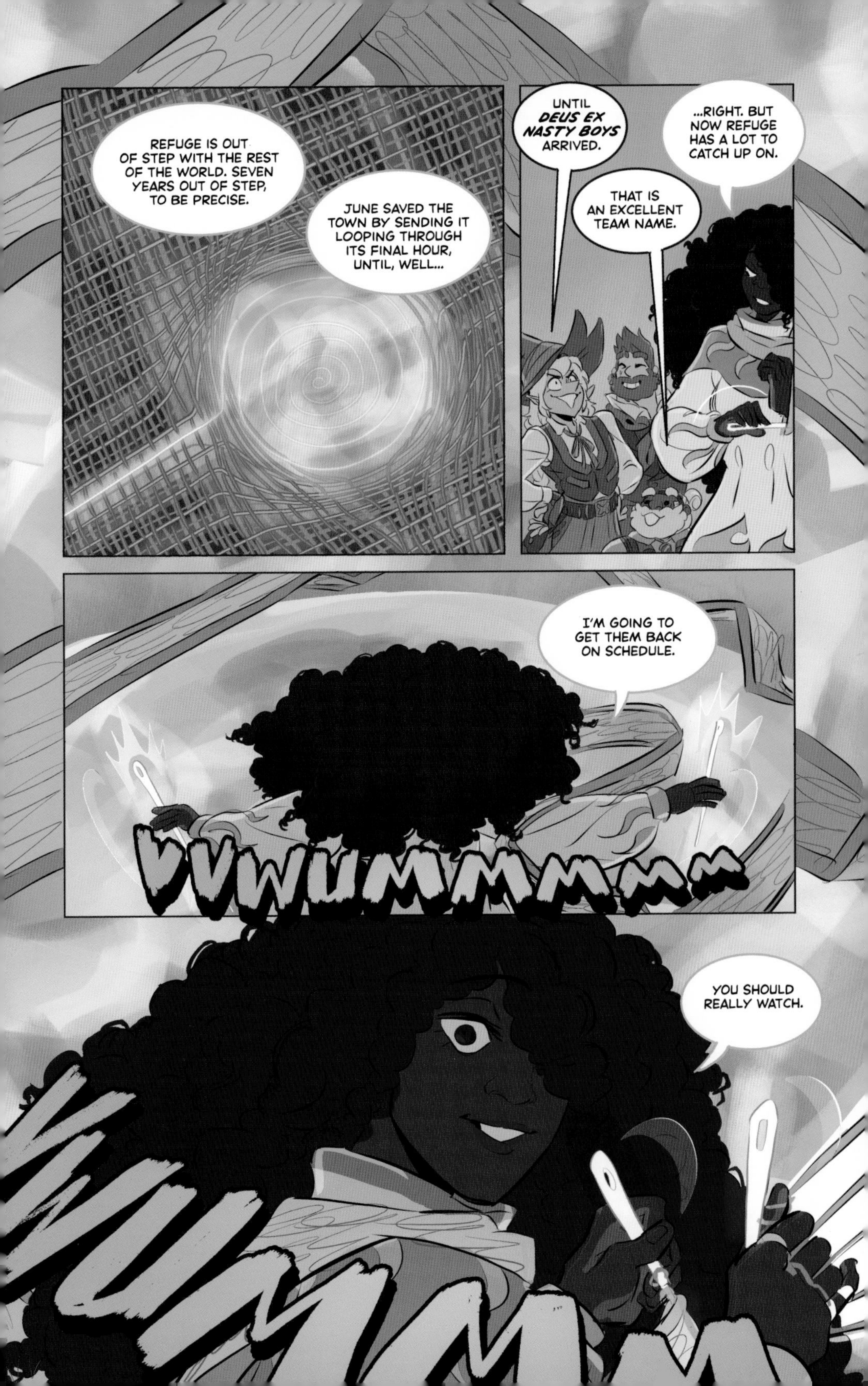
REFUGE IS OUT OF STEP WITH THE REST OF THE WORLD. SEVEN YEARS OUT OF STEP, TO BE PRECISE.
JUNE SAVED THE TOWN BY SENDING IT LOOPING THROUGH ITS FINAL HOUR, UNTIL, WELL...
UNTIL *DEUS EX NASTY BOYS* ARRIVED.
THAT IS AN EXCELLENT TEAM NAME.
...RIGHT. BUT NOW REFUGE HAS A LOT TO CATCH UP ON.
I'M GOING TO GET THEM BACK ON SCHEDULE.
VVWUMMMMM
YOU SHOULD REALLY WATCH.
WUMMM

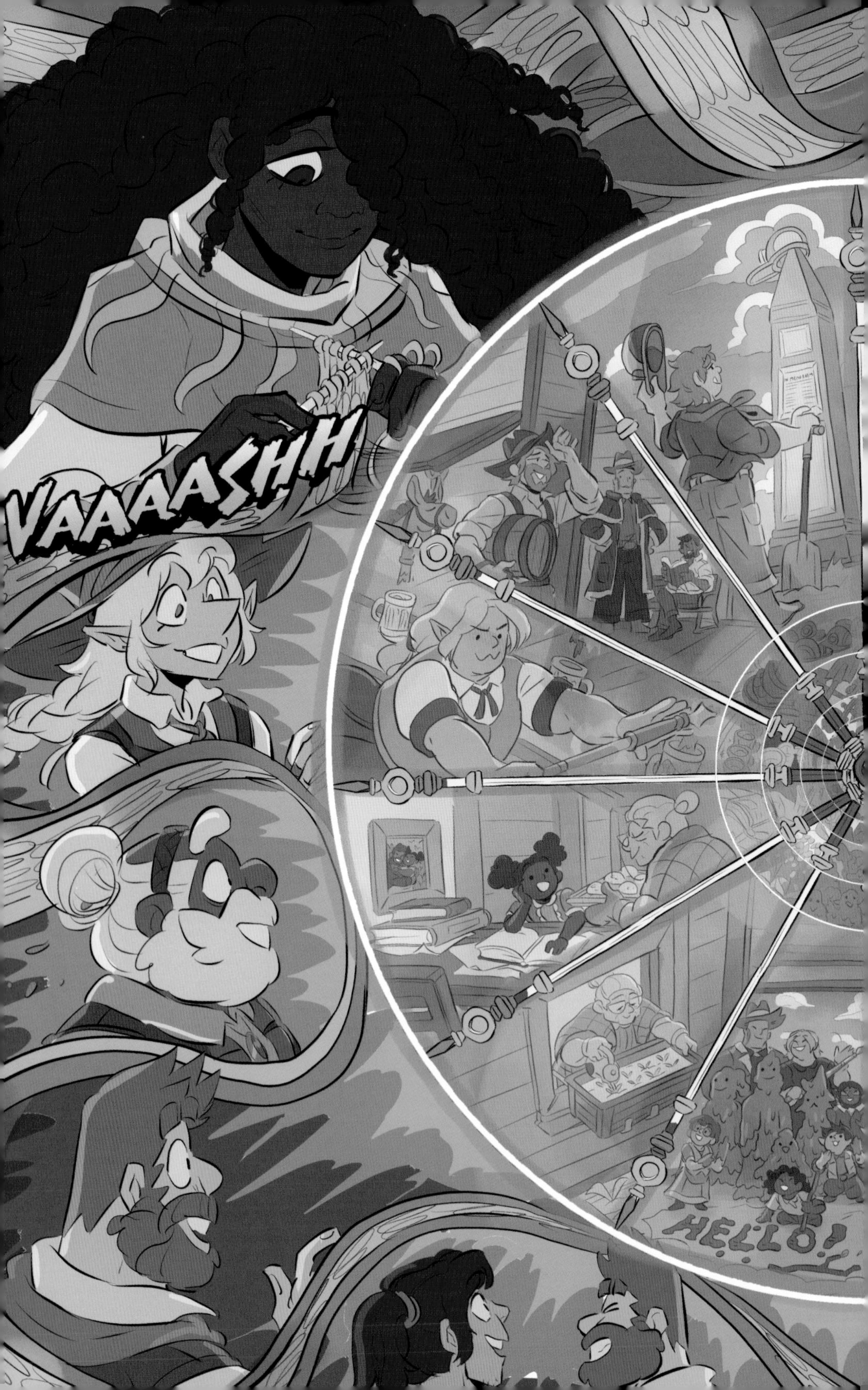

VAAAASHH
IN MEMORIAM
HELLO!

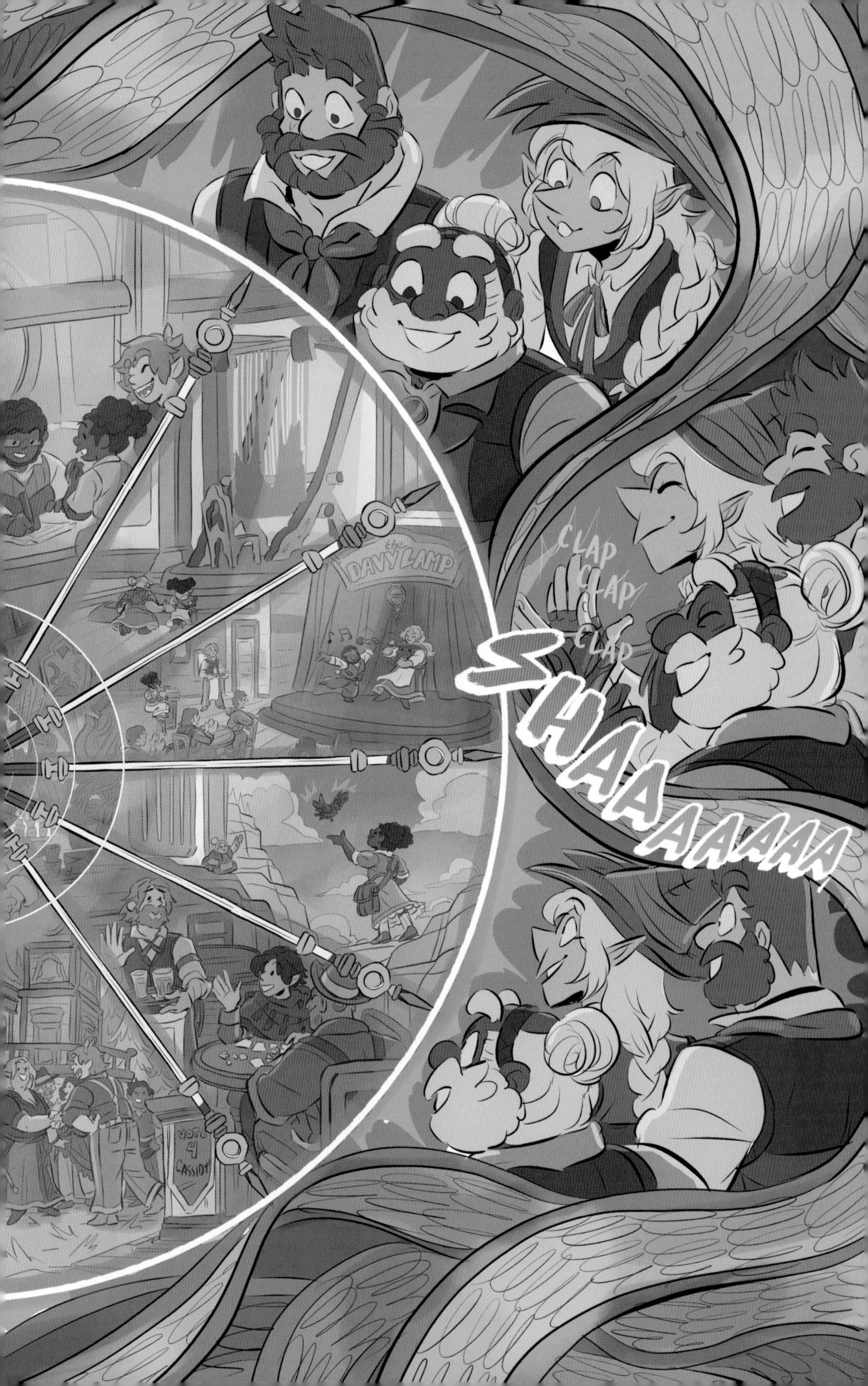
the DAVY LAMP
VOTE 4 CASSIDY
CLAP
CLAP
CLAP
CLAP
SHHAAAAAAAA

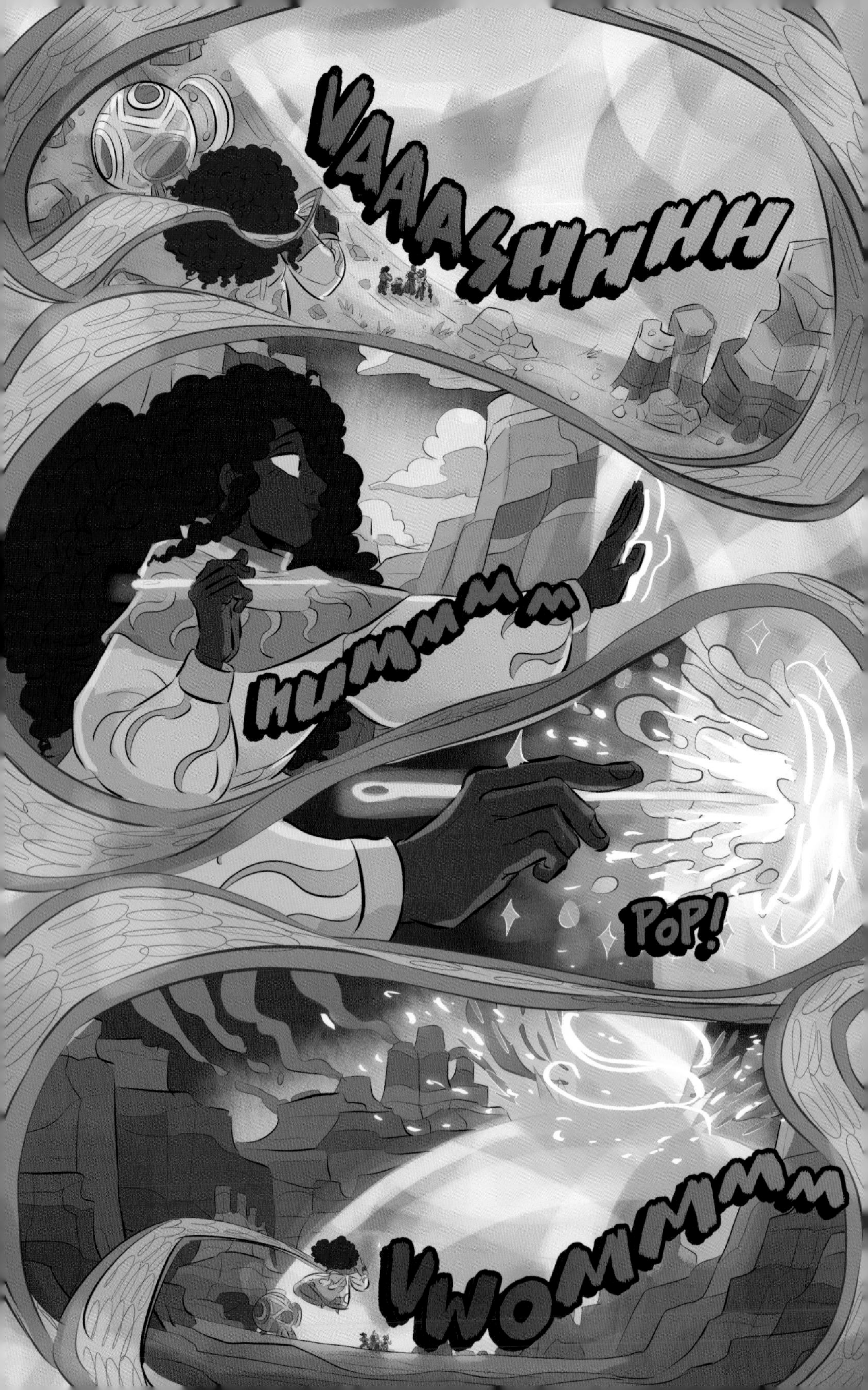
VAAASHHHH
HUMMMMM
POP!
VWOMMMMM

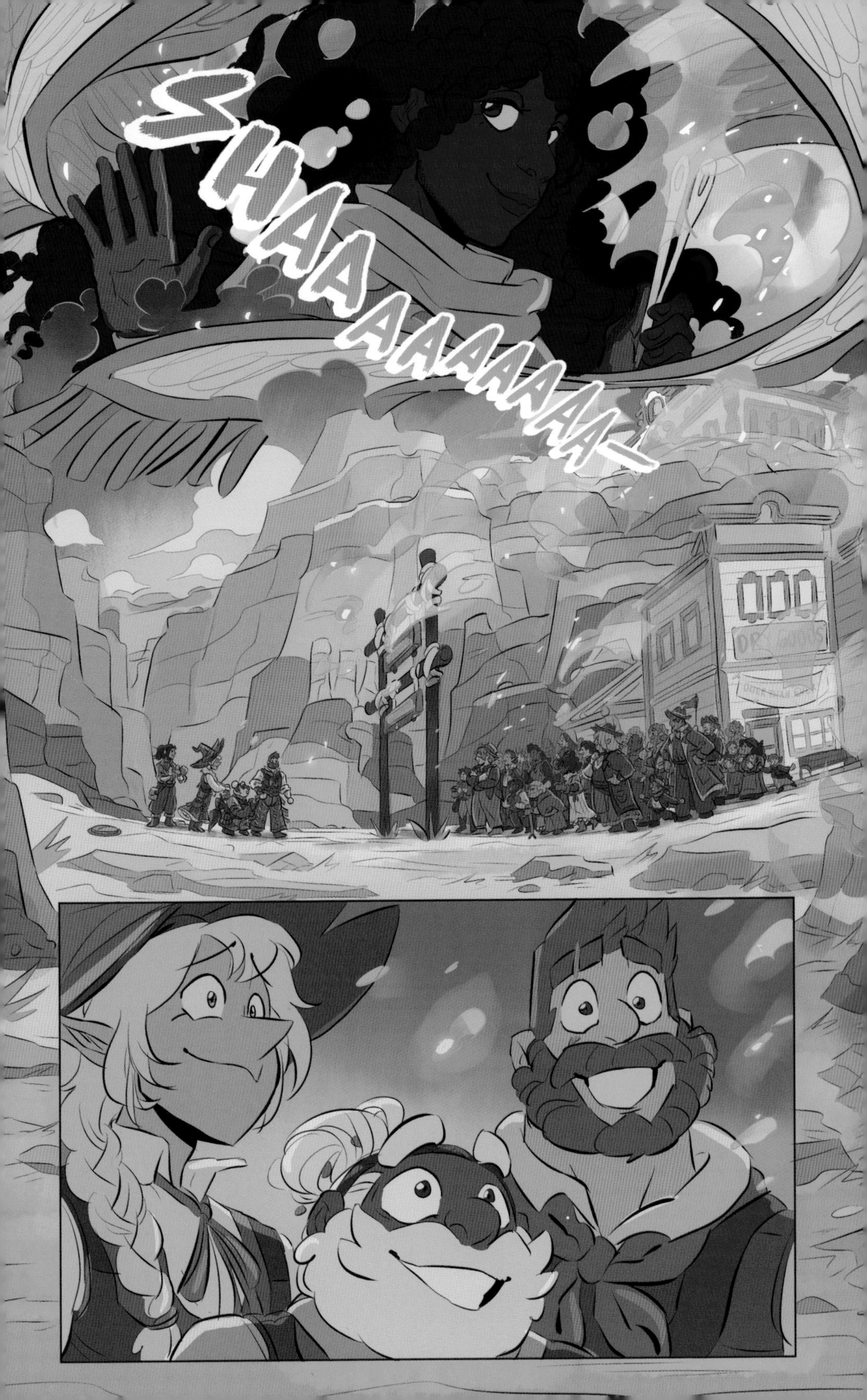
SHAAAAAAAA—

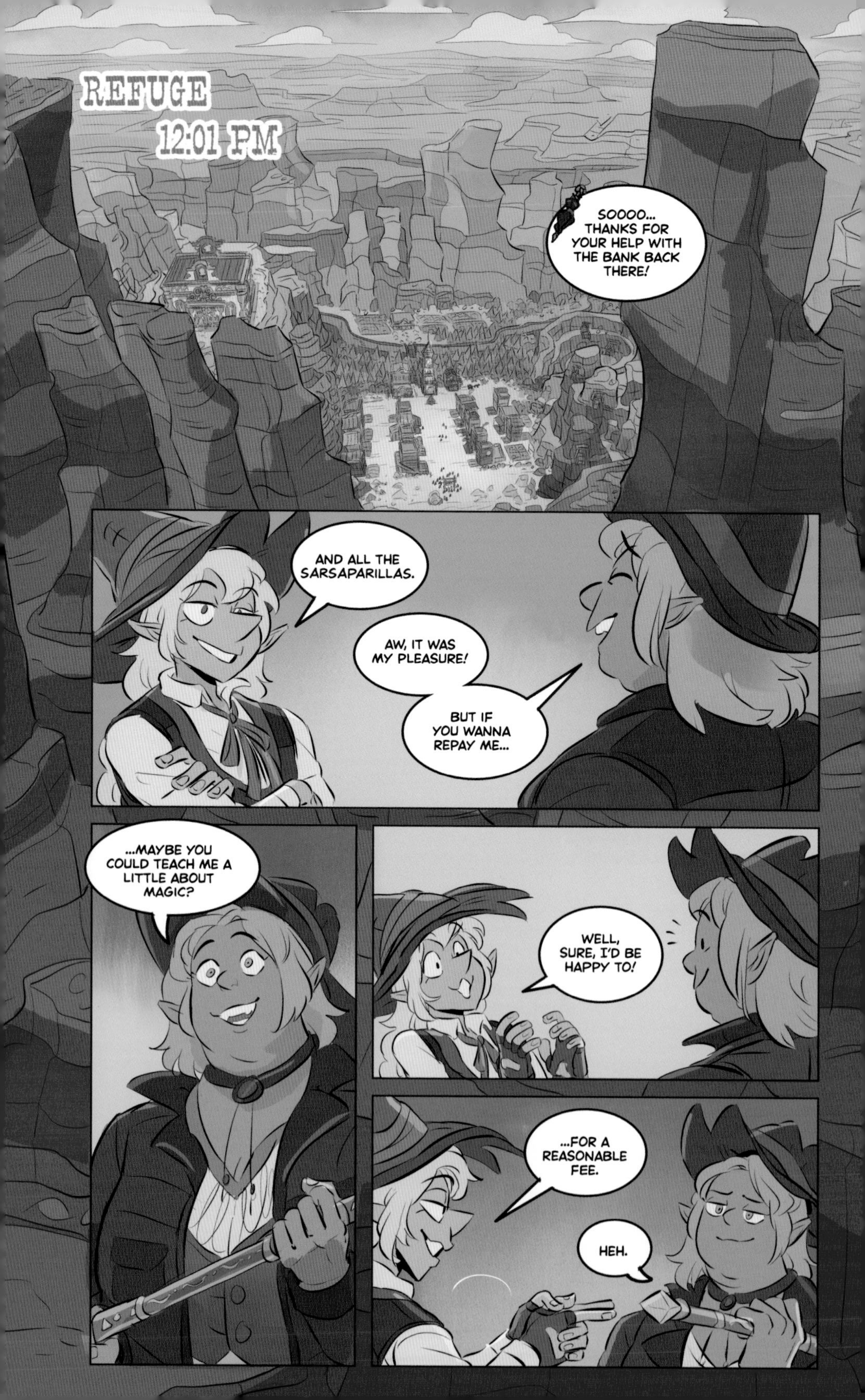
REFUGE
12:01 PM
SOOOO... THANKS FOR YOUR HELP WITH THE BANK BACK THERE!
AND ALL THE SARSAPARILLAS.
AW, IT WAS MY PLEASURE!
BUT IF YOU WANNA REPAY ME...
...MAYBE YOU COULD TEACH ME A LITTLE ABOUT MAGIC?
WELL, SURE, I'D BE HAPPY TO!
...FOR A REASONABLE FEE.
HEH.

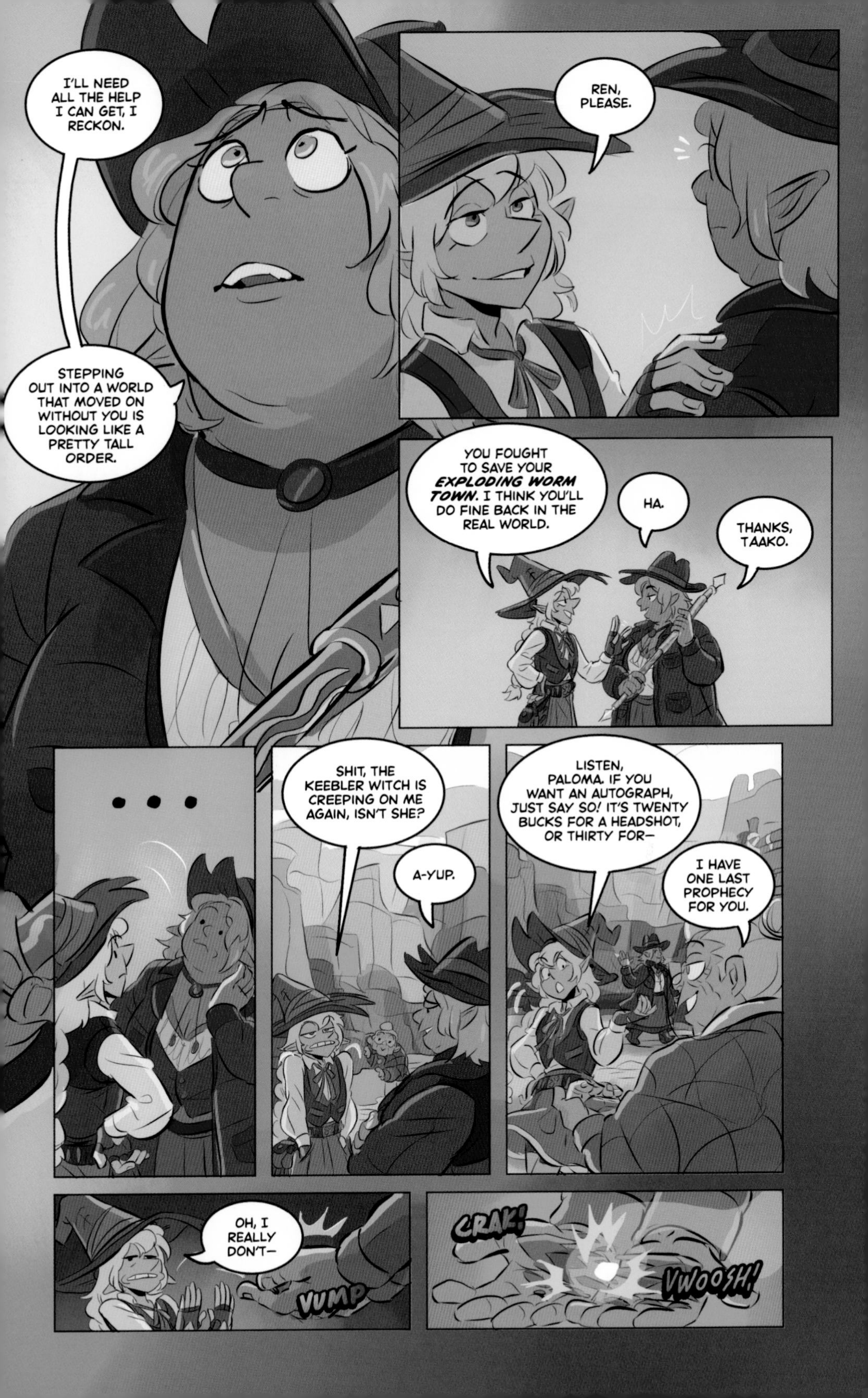
I'LL NEED ALL THE HELP I CAN GET, I RECKON.
STEPPING OUT INTO A WORLD THAT MOVED ON WITHOUT YOU IS LOOKING LIKE A PRETTY TALL ORDER.
REN, PLEASE.
YOU FOUGHT TO SAVE YOUR *EXPLODING WORM TOWN*. I THINK YOU'LL DO FINE BACK IN THE REAL WORLD.
HA.
THANKS, TAAKO.
...
SHIT, THE KEEBLER WITCH IS CREEPING ON ME AGAIN, ISN'T SHE?
A-YUP.
LISTEN, PALOMA. IF YOU WANT AN AUTOGRAPH, JUST SAY SO! IT'S TWENTY BUCKS FOR A HEADSHOT, OR THIRTY FOR—
I HAVE ONE LAST PROPHECY FOR YOU.
OH, I REALLY DON'T—
VUMP
CRAK!
VWOOSH!

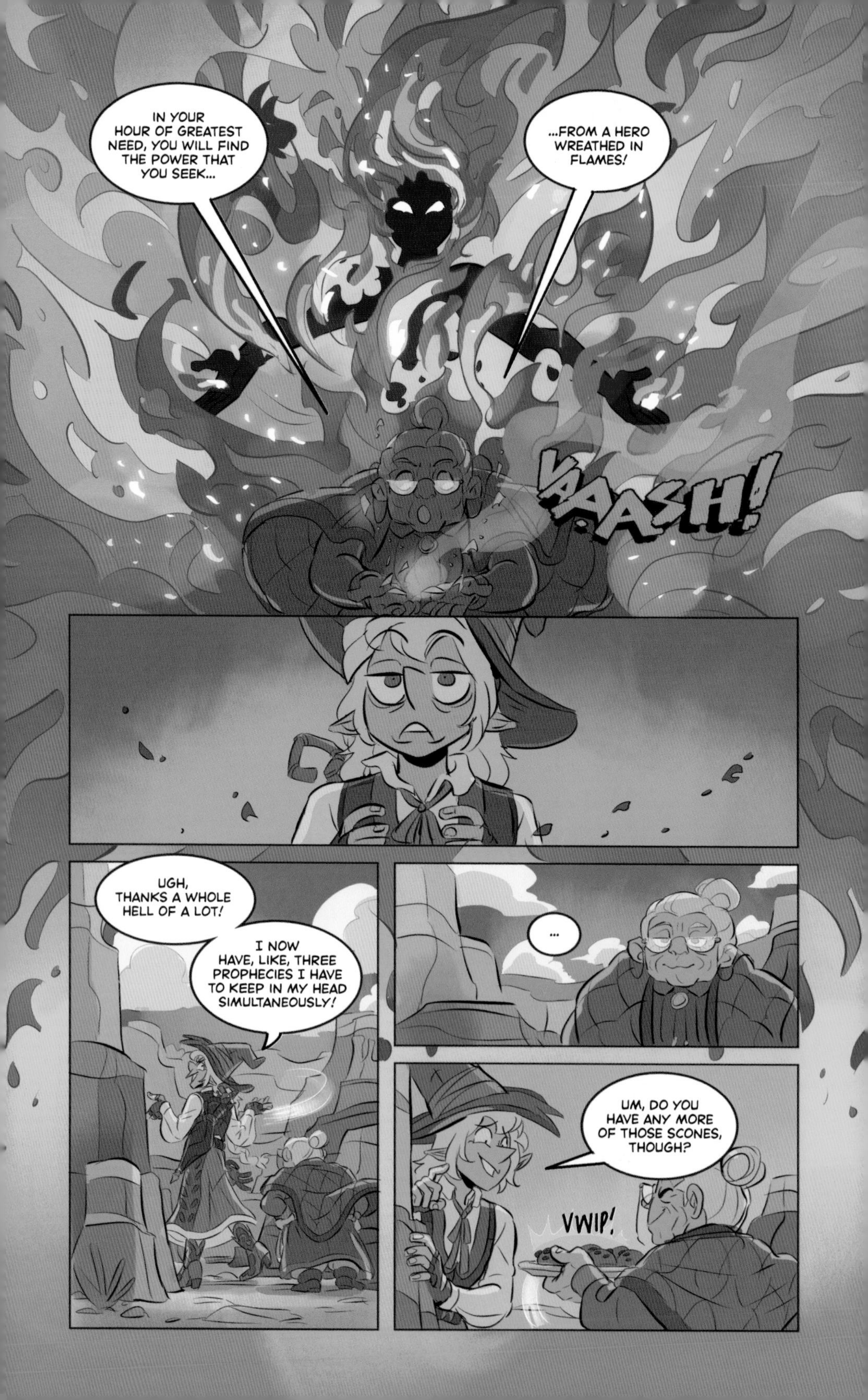
IN YOUR HOUR OF GREATEST NEED, YOU WILL FIND THE POWER THAT YOU SEEK...
...FROM A HERO WREATHED IN FLAMES!
VAASH!
UGH, THANKS A WHOLE HELL OF A LOT!
I NOW HAVE, LIKE, THREE PROPHECIES I HAVE TO KEEP IN MY HEAD SIMULTANEOUSLY!
...
UM, DO YOU HAVE ANY MORE OF THOSE SCONES, THOUGH?
VWIP!

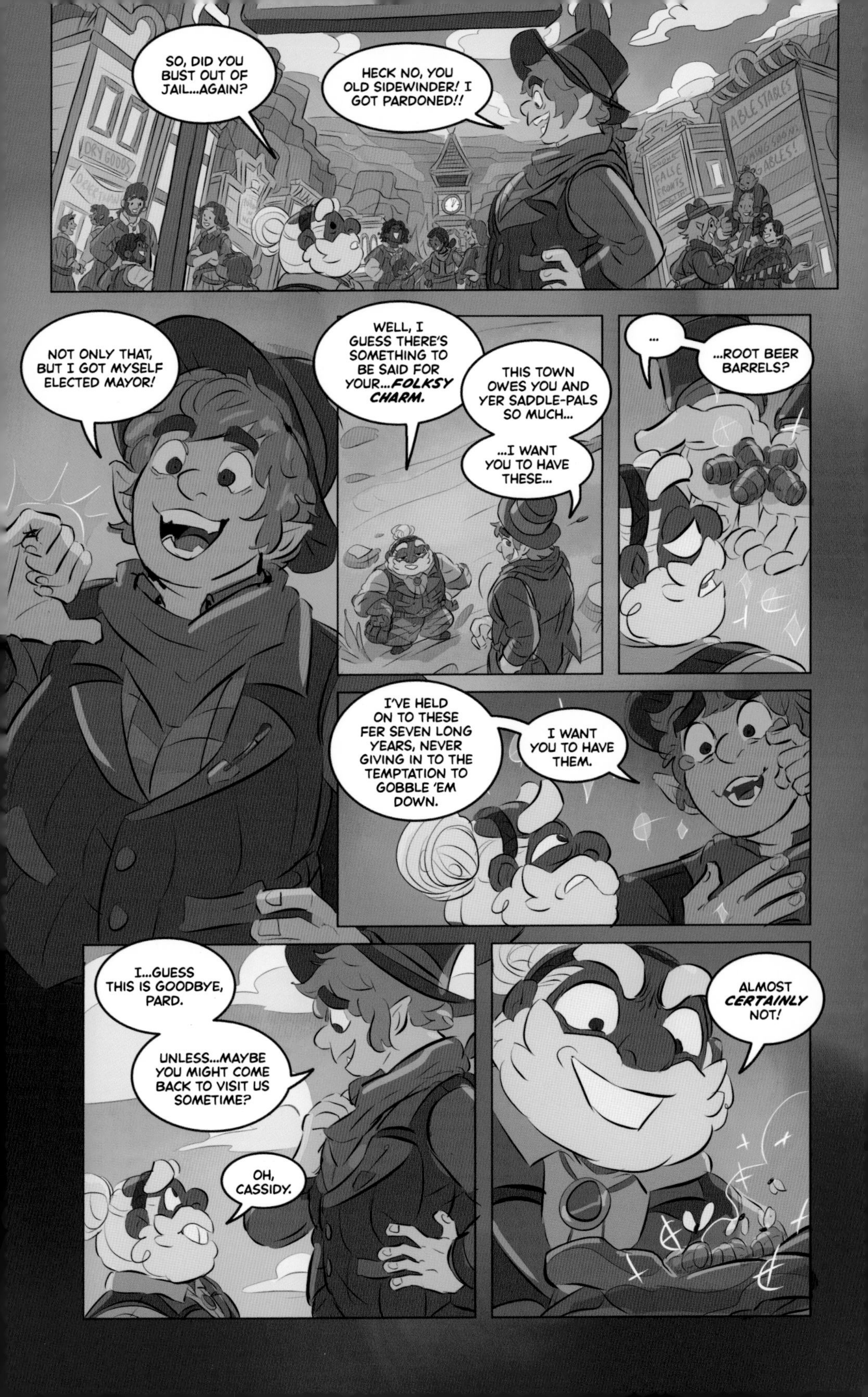
SO, DID YOU BUST OUT OF JAIL...AGAIN?
HECK NO, YOU OLD SIDEWINDER! I GOT PARDONED!!
NOT ONLY THAT, BUT I GOT MYSELF ELECTED MAYOR!
WELL, I GUESS THERE'S SOMETHING TO BE SAID FOR YOUR...*FOLKSY CHARM.*
THIS TOWN OWES YOU AND YER SADDLE-PALS SO MUCH...
...I WANT YOU TO HAVE THESE...
...
...ROOT BEER BARRELS?
I'VE HELD ON TO THESE FER SEVEN LONG YEARS, NEVER GIVING IN TO THE TEMPTATION TO GOBBLE 'EM DOWN.
I WANT YOU TO HAVE THEM.
I...GUESS THIS IS GOODBYE, PARD.
UNLESS...MAYBE YOU MIGHT COME BACK TO VISIT US SOMETIME?
OH, CASSIDY.
ALMOST *CERTAINLY* NOT!

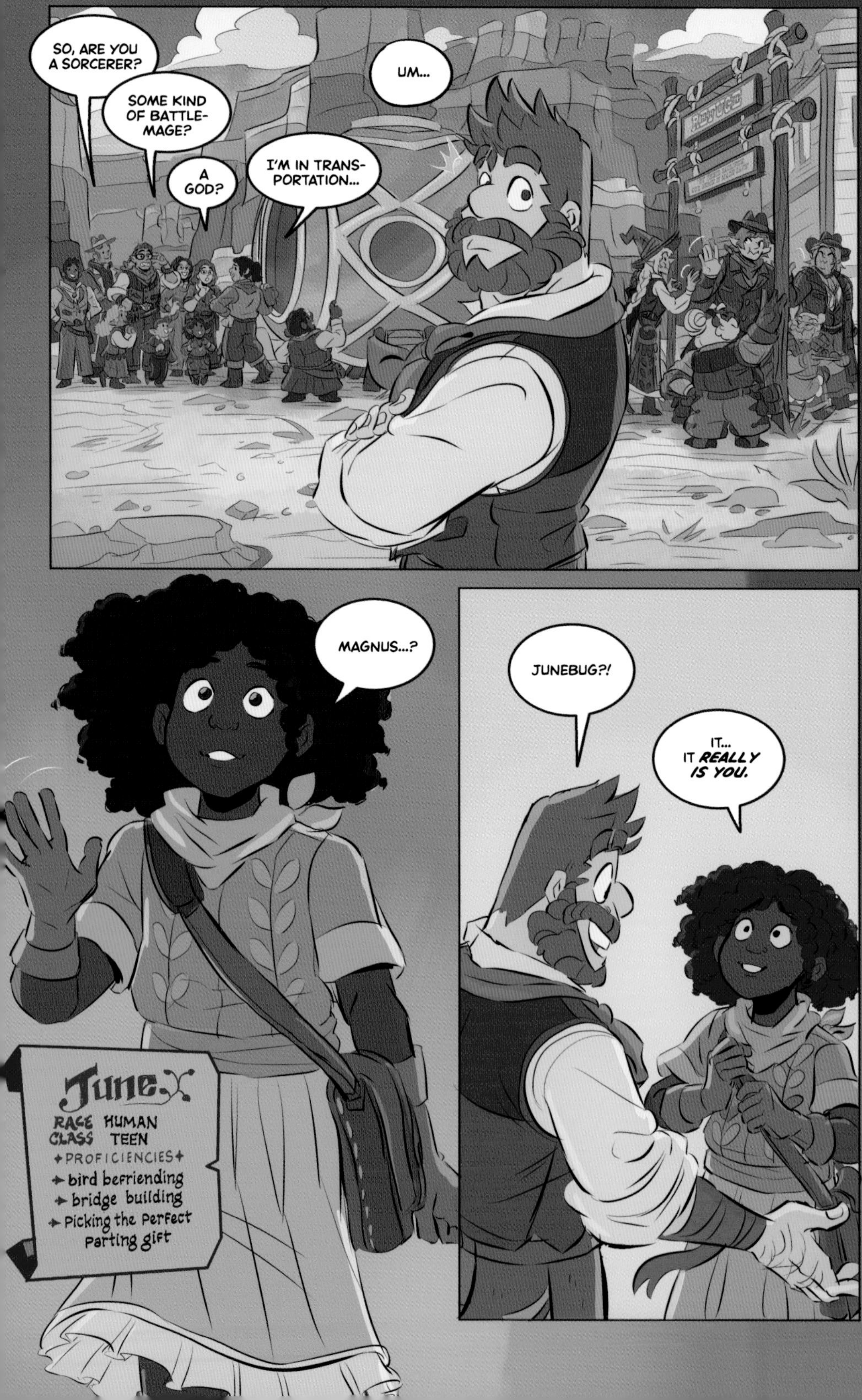
SO, ARE YOU A SORCERER?
SOME KIND OF BATTLE-MAGE?
A GOD?
UM...
I'M IN TRANS-PORTATION...
MAGNUS...?
June
RACE HUMAN
CLASS TEEN
PROFICIENCIES
bird befriending
bridge building
Picking the Perfect Parting gift
JUNEBUG?!
IT... IT *REALLY IS YOU.*

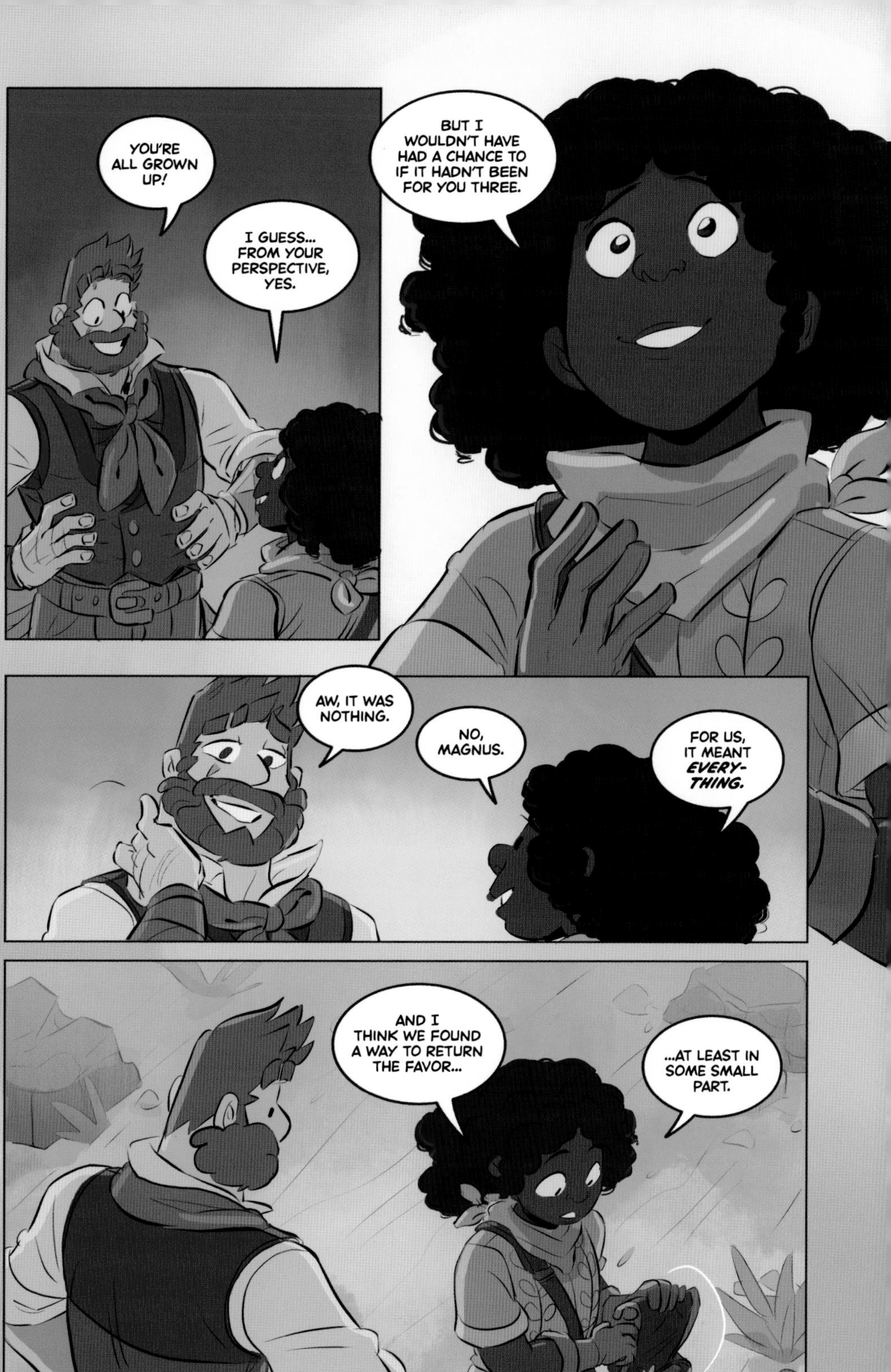

YOU'RE ALL GROWN UP!
I GUESS... FROM YOUR PERSPECTIVE, YES.
BUT I WOULDN'T HAVE HAD A CHANCE TO IF IT HADN'T BEEN FOR YOU THREE.
AW, IT WAS NOTHING.
NO, MAGNUS.
FOR US, IT MEANT *EVERY-THING.*
AND I THINK WE FOUND A WAY TO RETURN THE FAVOR...
...AT LEAST IN SOME SMALL PART.

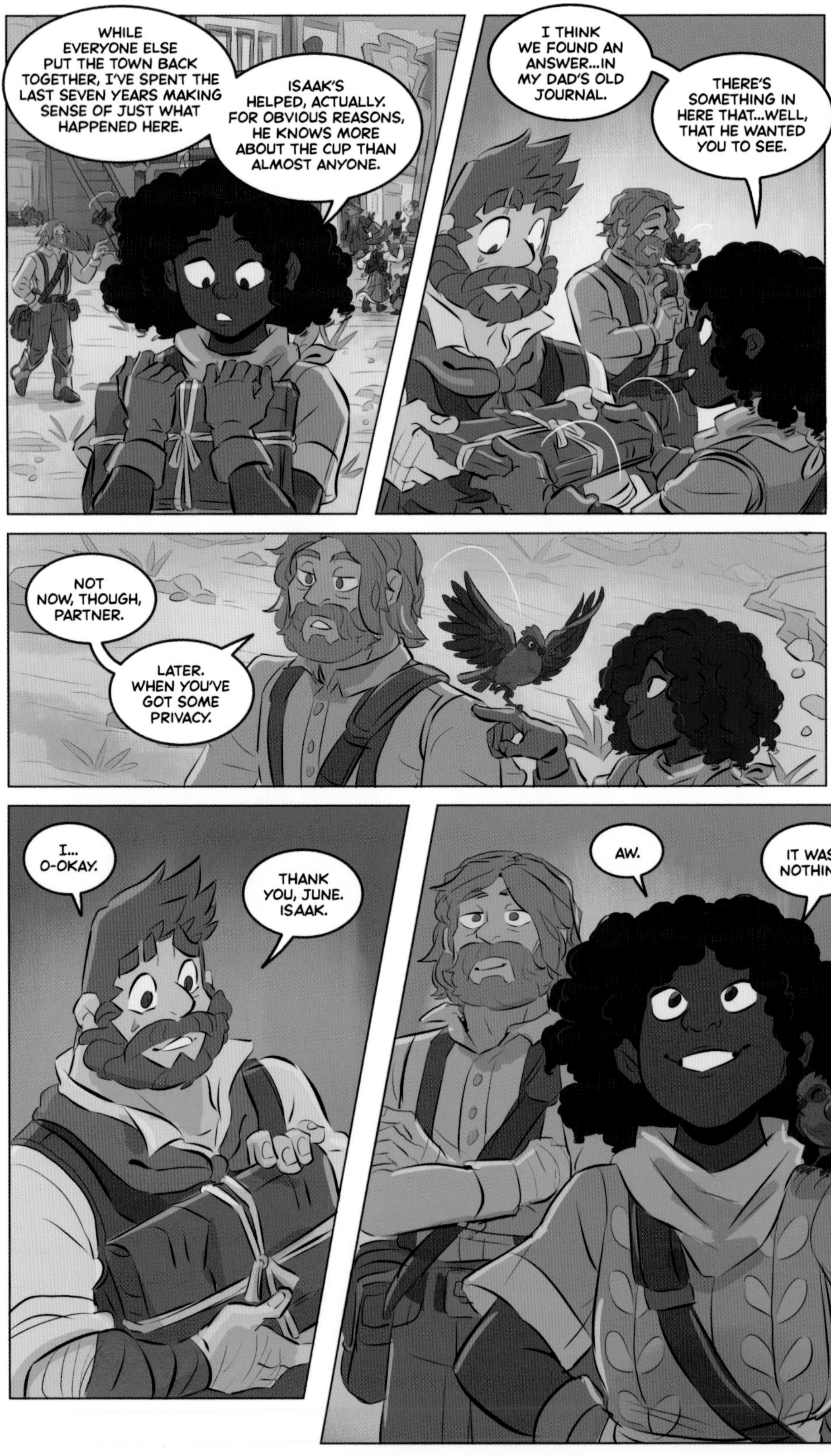
WHILE EVERYONE ELSE PUT THE TOWN BACK TOGETHER, I'VE SPENT THE LAST SEVEN YEARS MAKING SENSE OF JUST WHAT HAPPENED HERE.
ISAAK'S HELPED, ACTUALLY. FOR OBVIOUS REASONS, HE KNOWS MORE ABOUT THE CUP THAN ALMOST ANYONE.
I THINK WE FOUND AN ANSWER...IN MY DAD'S OLD JOURNAL.
THERE'S SOMETHING IN HERE THAT...WELL, THAT HE WANTED YOU TO SEE.
NOT NOW, THOUGH, PARTNER.
LATER. WHEN YOU'VE GOT SOME PRIVACY.
I... O-OKAY.
THANK YOU, JUNE. ISAAK.
AW.
IT WAS NOTHIN'.

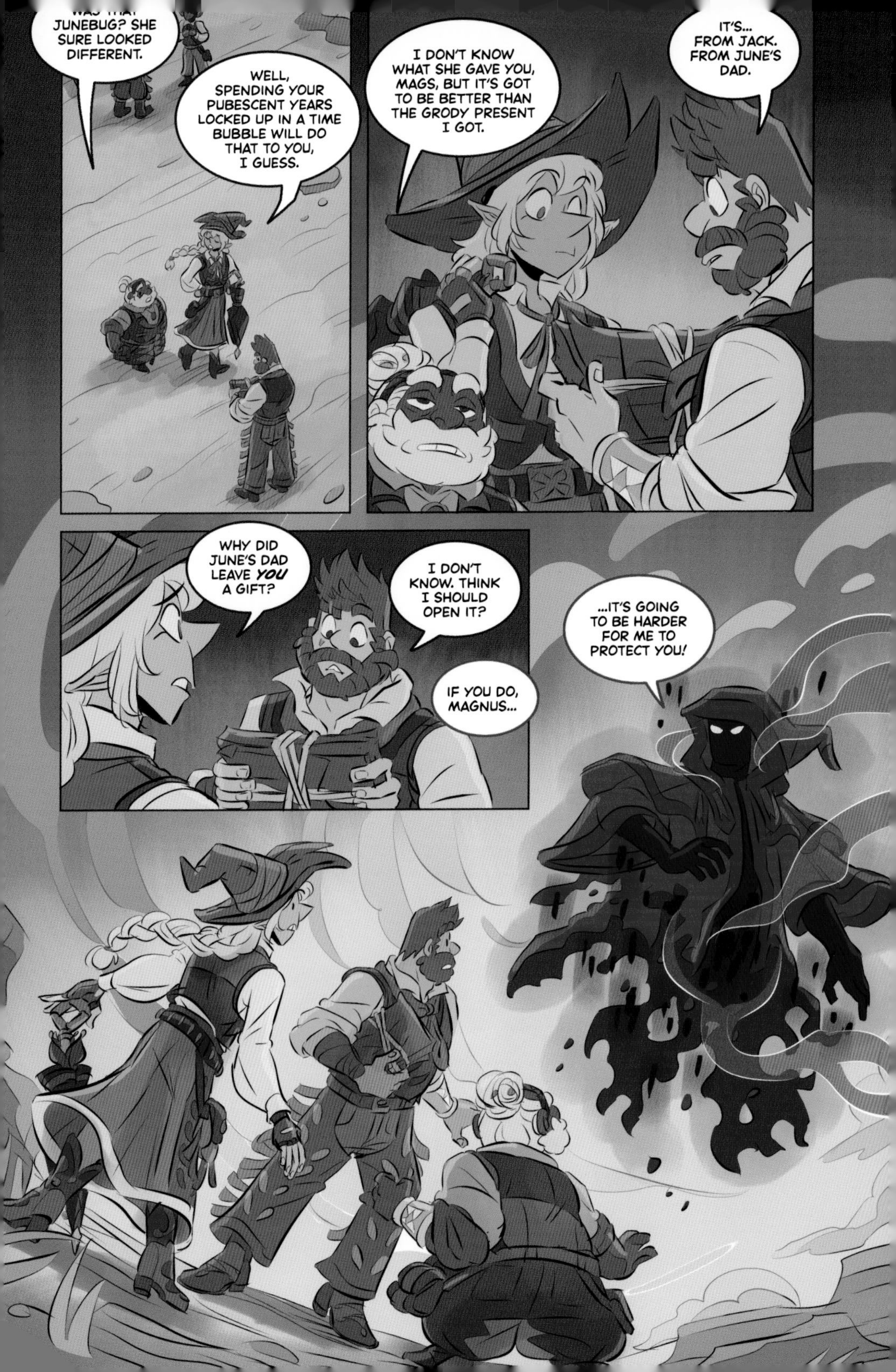

JUNEBUG? SHE SURE LOOKED DIFFERENT.
WELL, SPENDING YOUR PUBESCENT YEARS LOCKED UP IN A TIME BUBBLE WILL DO THAT TO YOU, I GUESS.
I DON'T KNOW WHAT SHE GAVE YOU, MAGS, BUT IT'S GOT TO BE BETTER THAN THE GRODY PRESENT I GOT.
IT'S... FROM JACK. FROM JUNE'S DAD.
WHY DID JUNE'S DAD LEAVE *YOU* A GIFT?
I DON'T KNOW. THINK I SHOULD OPEN IT?
IF YOU DO, MAGNUS...
...IT'S GOING TO BE HARDER FOR ME TO PROTECT YOU!

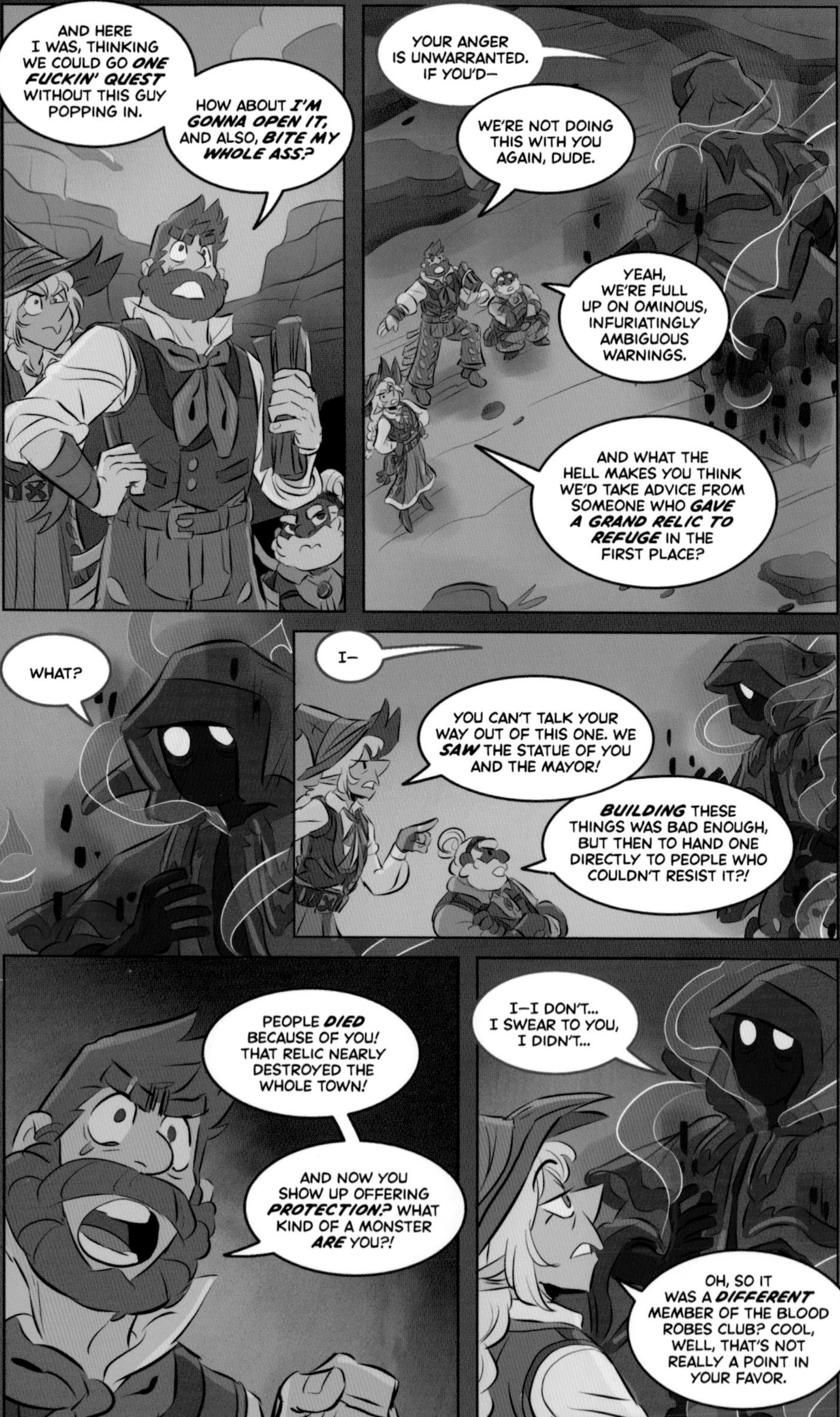
AND HERE I WAS, THINKING WE COULD GO ONE FUCKIN' QUEST WITHOUT THIS GUY POPPING IN.
HOW ABOUT I'M GONNA OPEN IT, AND ALSO, BITE MY WHOLE ASS?
YOUR ANGER IS UNWARRANTED. IF YOU'D—
WE'RE NOT DOING THIS WITH YOU AGAIN, DUDE.
YEAH, WE'RE FULL UP ON OMINOUS, INFURIATINGLY AMBIGUOUS WARNINGS.
AND WHAT THE HELL MAKES YOU THINK WE'D TAKE ADVICE FROM SOMEONE WHO GAVE A GRAND RELIC TO REFUGE IN THE FIRST PLACE?
WHAT?
I—
YOU CAN'T TALK YOUR WAY OUT OF THIS ONE. WE SAW THE STATUE OF YOU AND THE MAYOR!
BUILDING THESE THINGS WAS BAD ENOUGH, BUT THEN TO HAND ONE DIRECTLY TO PEOPLE WHO COULDN'T RESIST IT?!
PEOPLE DIED BECAUSE OF YOU! THAT RELIC NEARLY DESTROYED THE WHOLE TOWN!
AND NOW YOU SHOW UP OFFERING PROTECTION? WHAT KIND OF A MONSTER ARE YOU?!
I—I DON'T... I SWEAR TO YOU, I DIDN'T...
OH, SO IT WAS A DIFFERENT MEMBER OF THE BLOOD ROBES CLUB? COOL, WELL, THAT'S NOT REALLY A POINT IN YOUR FAVOR.

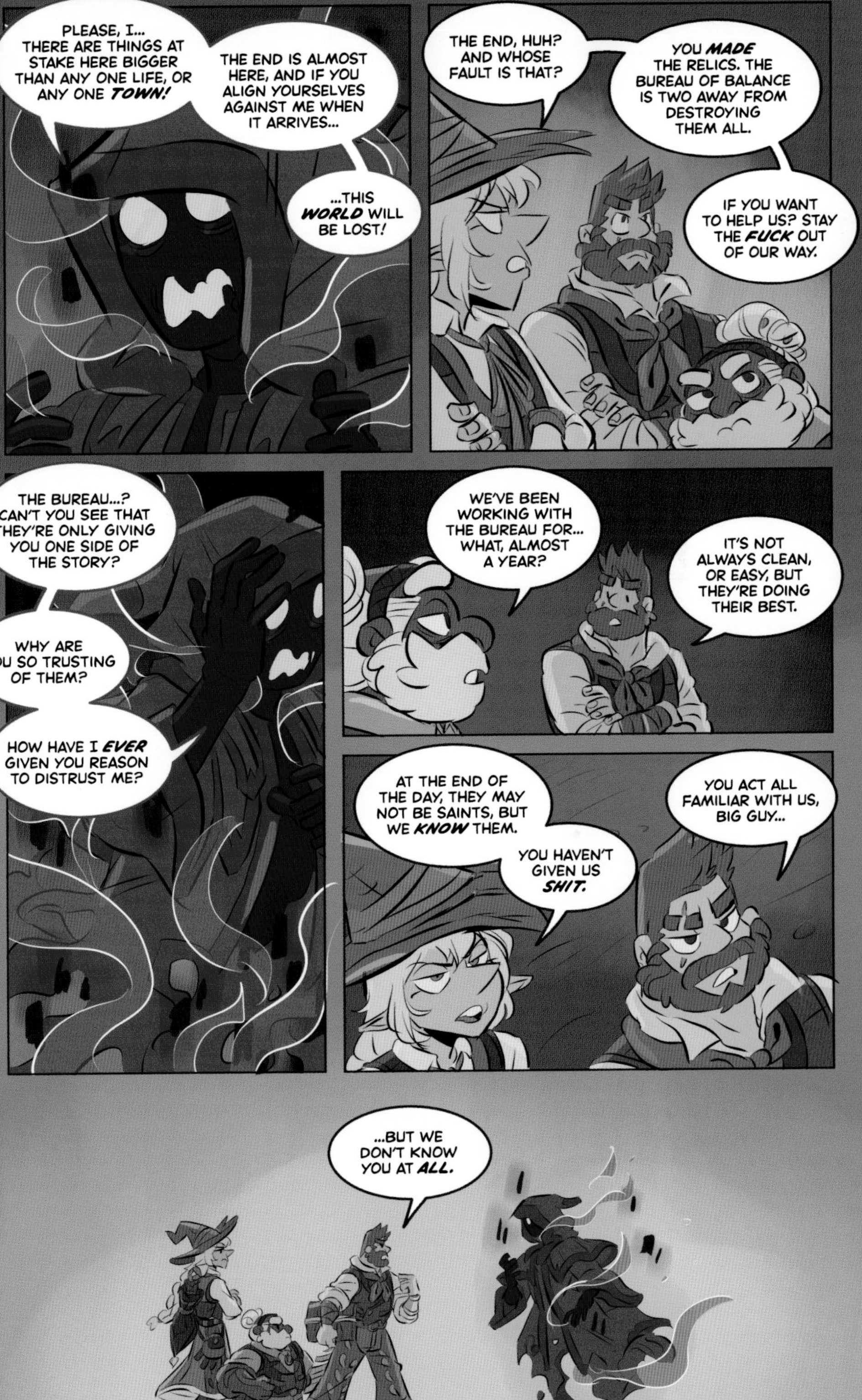
PLEASE, I... THERE ARE THINGS AT STAKE HERE BIGGER THAN ANY ONE LIFE, OR ANY ONE TOWN!
THE END IS ALMOST HERE, AND IF YOU ALIGN YOURSELVES AGAINST ME WHEN IT ARRIVES...
...THIS WORLD WILL BE LOST!
THE END, HUH? AND WHOSE FAULT IS THAT?
YOU MADE THE RELICS. THE BUREAU OF BALANCE IS TWO AWAY FROM DESTROYING THEM ALL.
IF YOU WANT TO HELP US? STAY THE FUCK OUT OF OUR WAY.
THE BUREAU...? CAN'T YOU SEE THAT THEY'RE ONLY GIVING YOU ONE SIDE OF THE STORY?
WHY ARE YOU SO TRUSTING OF THEM?
HOW HAVE I EVER GIVEN YOU REASON TO DISTRUST ME?
WE'VE BEEN WORKING WITH THE BUREAU FOR... WHAT, ALMOST A YEAR?
IT'S NOT ALWAYS CLEAN, OR EASY, BUT THEY'RE DOING THEIR BEST.
AT THE END OF THE DAY, THEY MAY NOT BE SAINTS, BUT WE KNOW THEM.
YOU HAVEN'T GIVEN US SHIT.
YOU ACT ALL FAMILIAR WITH US, BIG GUY...
...BUT WE DON'T KNOW YOU AT ALL.

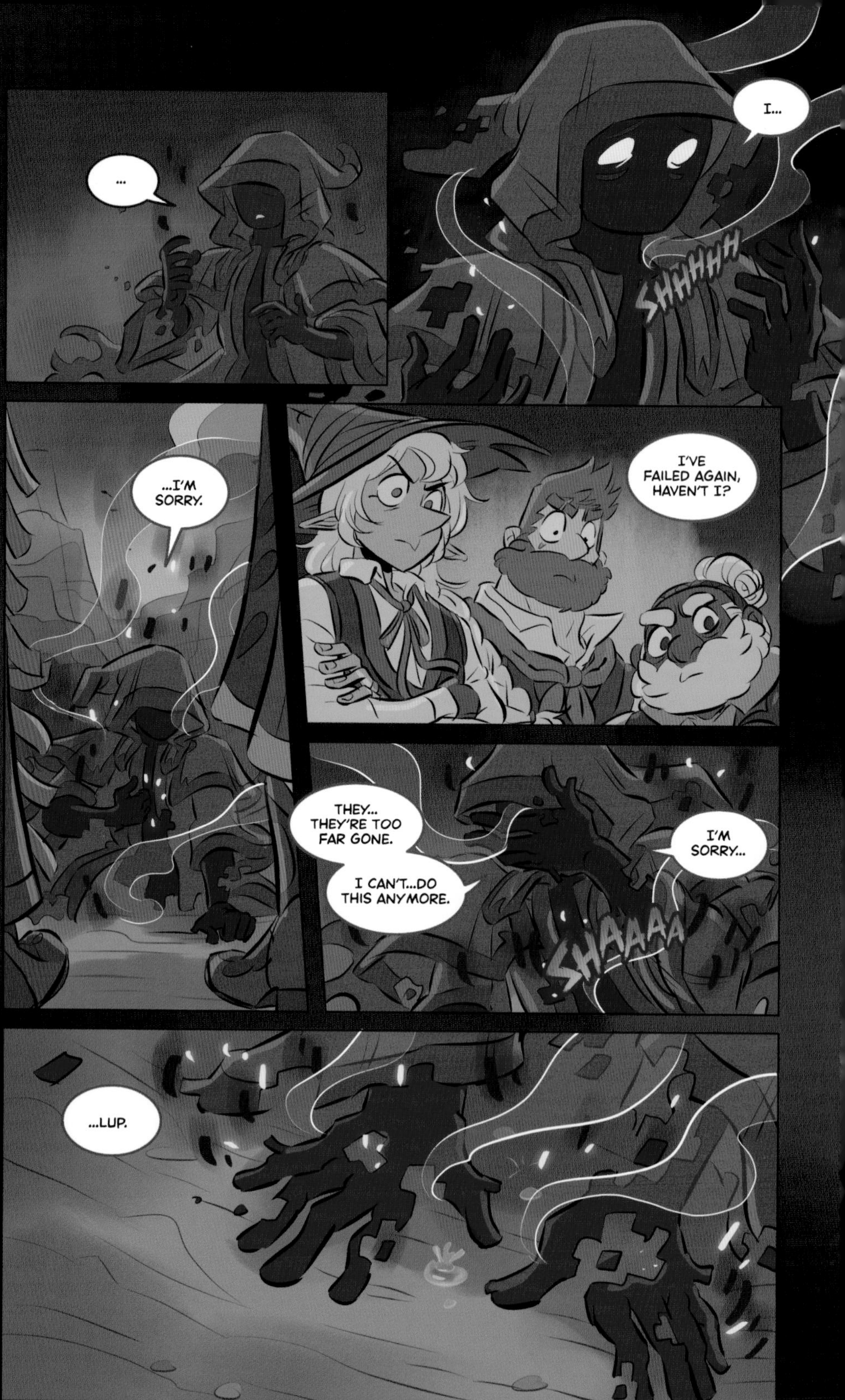
...
I...
SHHHHH
...I'M SORRY.
I'VE FAILED AGAIN, HAVEN'T I?
THEY... THEY'RE TOO FAR GONE.
I CAN'T...DO THIS ANYMORE.
I'M SORRY...
SHAAAA
...LUP.

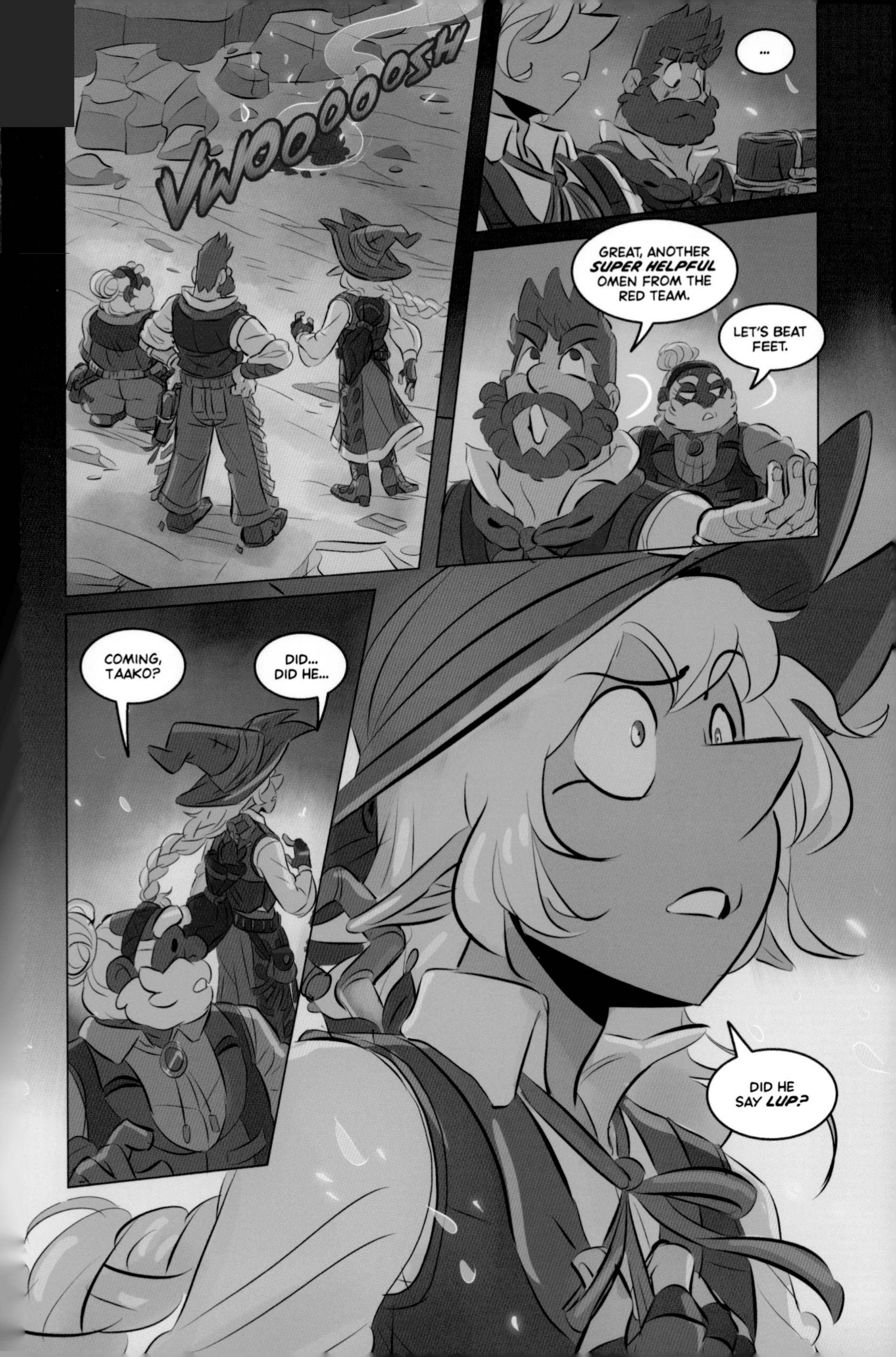
VWOOOOOOSH
...
GREAT, ANOTHER SUPER HELPFUL OMEN FROM THE RED TEAM.
LET'S BEAT FEET.
COMING, TAAKO?
DID... DID HE...
DID HE SAY LUP?

Chapter
116

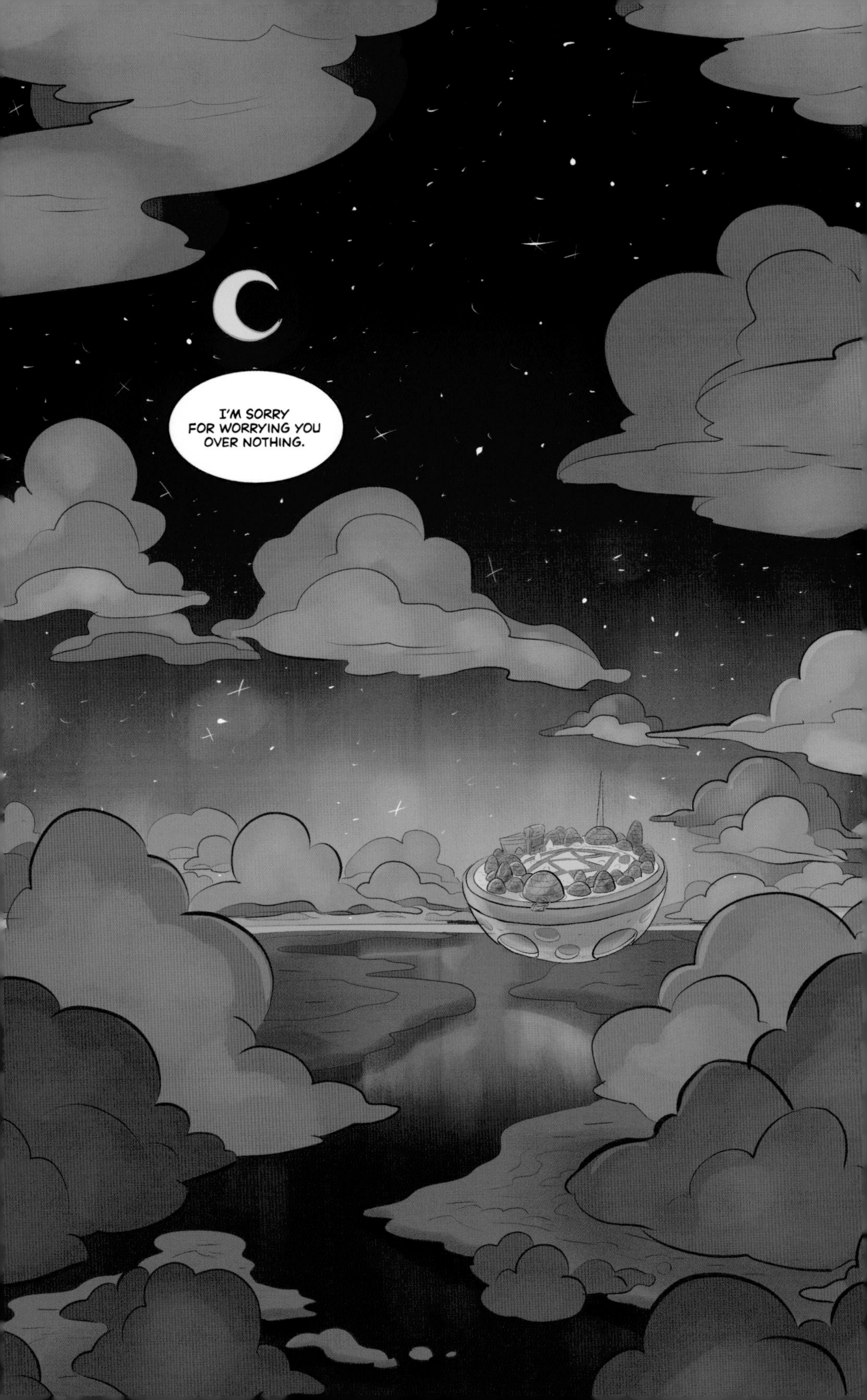
I'M SORRY FOR WORRYING YOU OVER NOTHING.

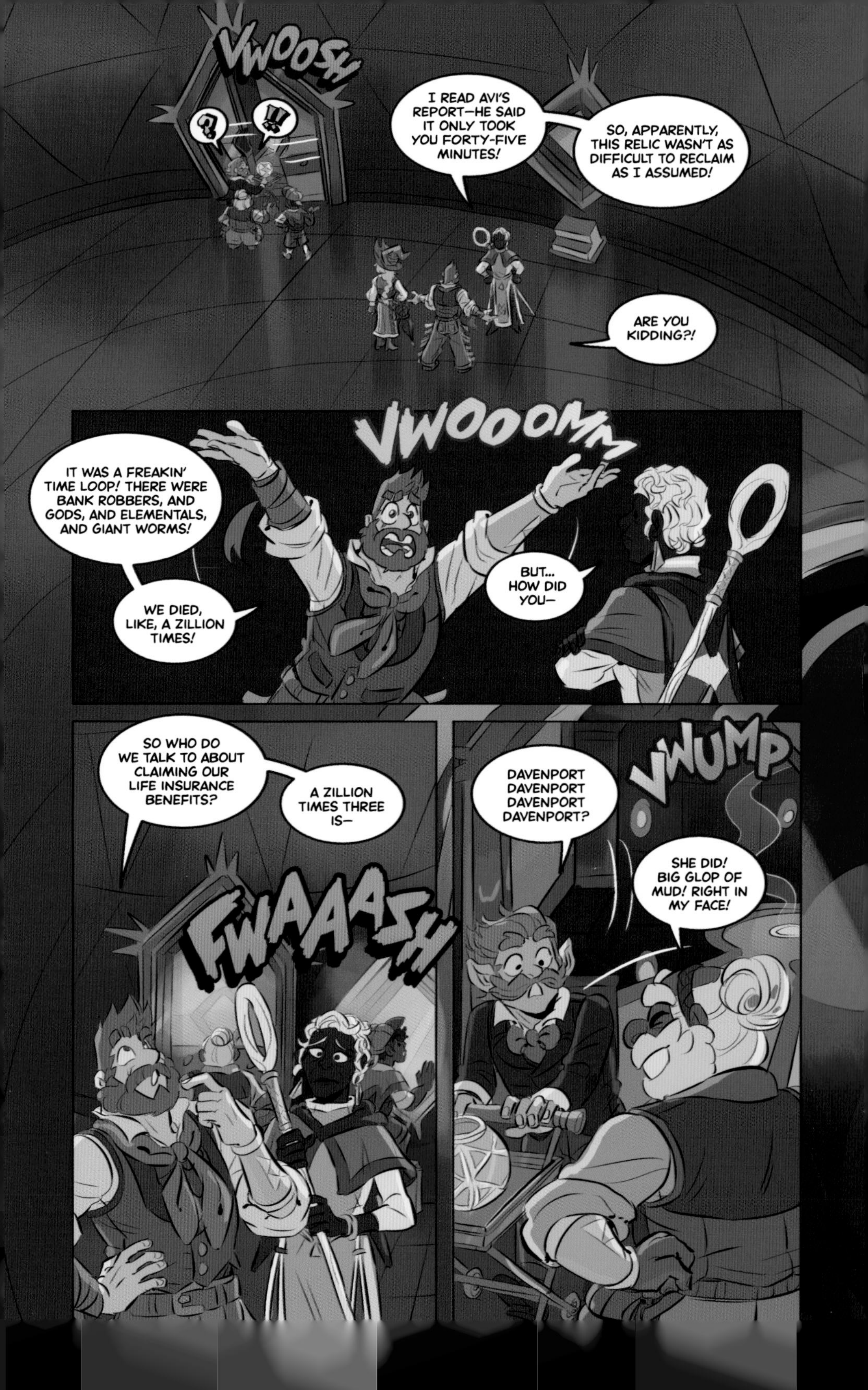
VWOOSH
I READ AVI'S REPORT—HE SAID IT ONLY TOOK YOU FORTY-FIVE MINUTES!
SO, APPARENTLY, THIS RELIC WASN'T AS DIFFICULT TO RECLAIM AS I ASSUMED!
ARE YOU KIDDING?!
VWOOOMM
IT WAS A FREAKIN' TIME LOOP! THERE WERE BANK ROBBERS, AND GODS, AND ELEMENTALS, AND GIANT WORMS!
WE DIED, LIKE, A ZILLION TIMES!
BUT... HOW DID YOU—
SO WHO DO WE TALK TO ABOUT CLAIMING OUR LIFE INSURANCE BENEFITS?
A ZILLION TIMES THREE IS—
FWAAASH
VWUMP
DAVENPORT DAVENPORT DAVENPORT DAVENPORT?
SHE DID! BIG GLOP OF MUD! RIGHT IN MY FACE!

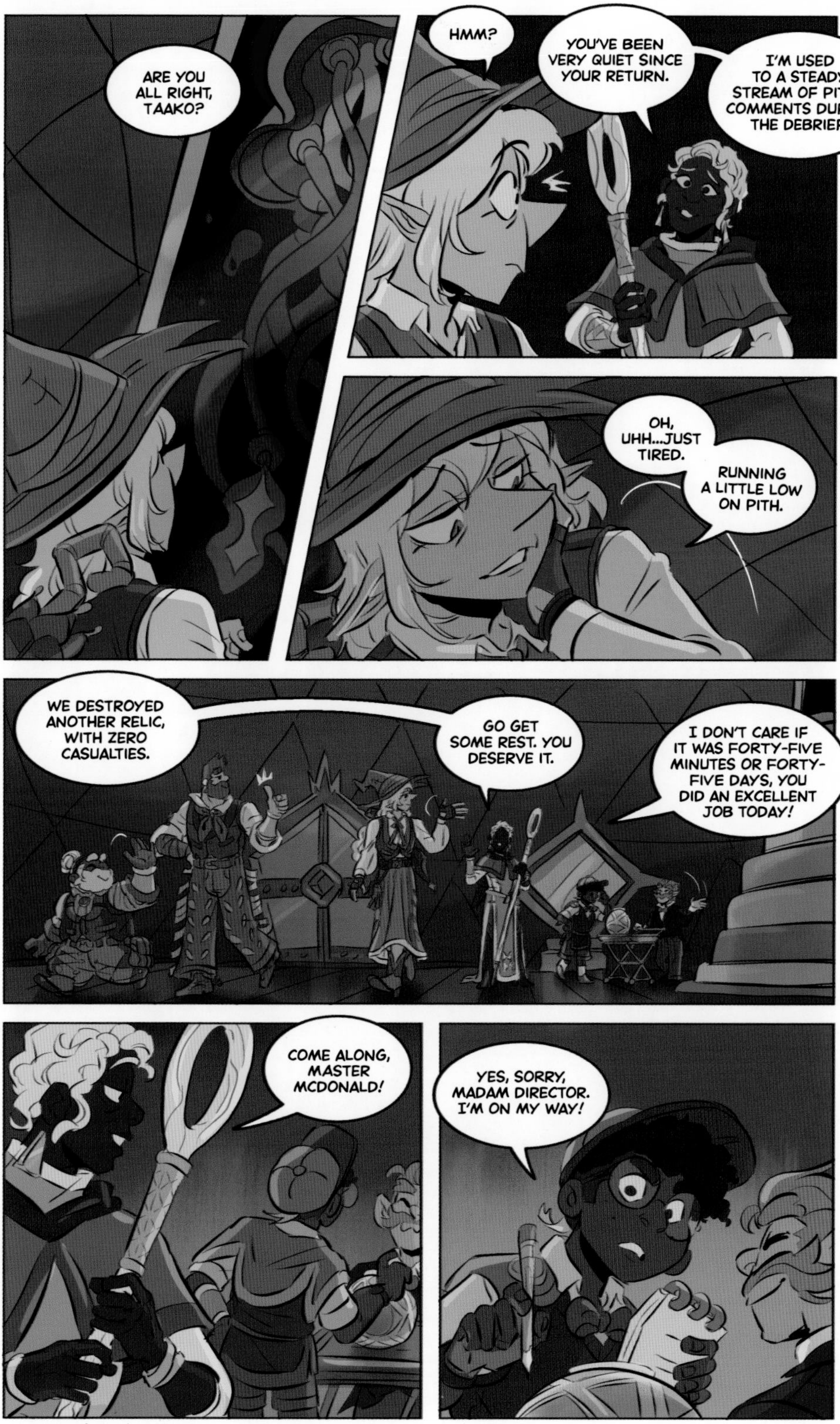
ARE YOU ALL RIGHT, TAAKO?
HMM?
YOU'VE BEEN VERY QUIET SINCE YOUR RETURN.
I'M USED TO A STEADY STREAM OF PITHY COMMENTS DURING THE DEBRIEF.
OH, UHH...JUST TIRED.
RUNNING A LITTLE LOW ON PITH.
WE DESTROYED ANOTHER RELIC, WITH ZERO CASUALTIES.
GO GET SOME REST. YOU DESERVE IT.
I DON'T CARE IF IT WAS FORTY-FIVE MINUTES OR FORTY-FIVE DAYS, YOU DID AN EXCELLENT JOB TODAY!
COME ALONG, MASTER MCDONALD!
YES, SORRY, MADAM DIRECTOR. I'M ON MY WAY!

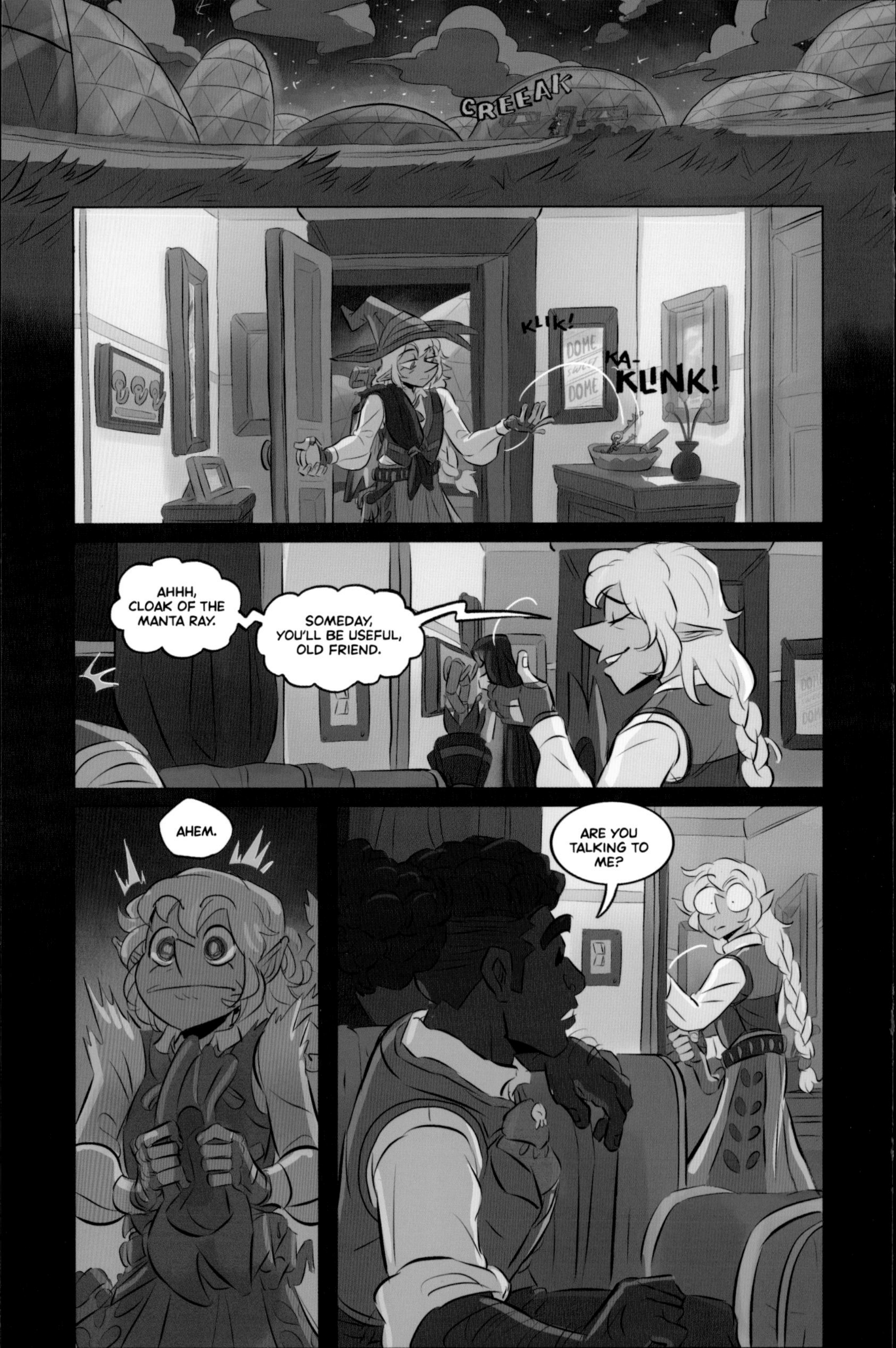
CREEAK
KLIK!
KA-KLINK!
DOME SWEET DOME
AHHH, CLOAK OF THE MANTA RAY.
SOMEDAY, YOU'LL BE USEFUL, OLD FRIEND.
AHEM.
ARE YOU TALKING TO ME?

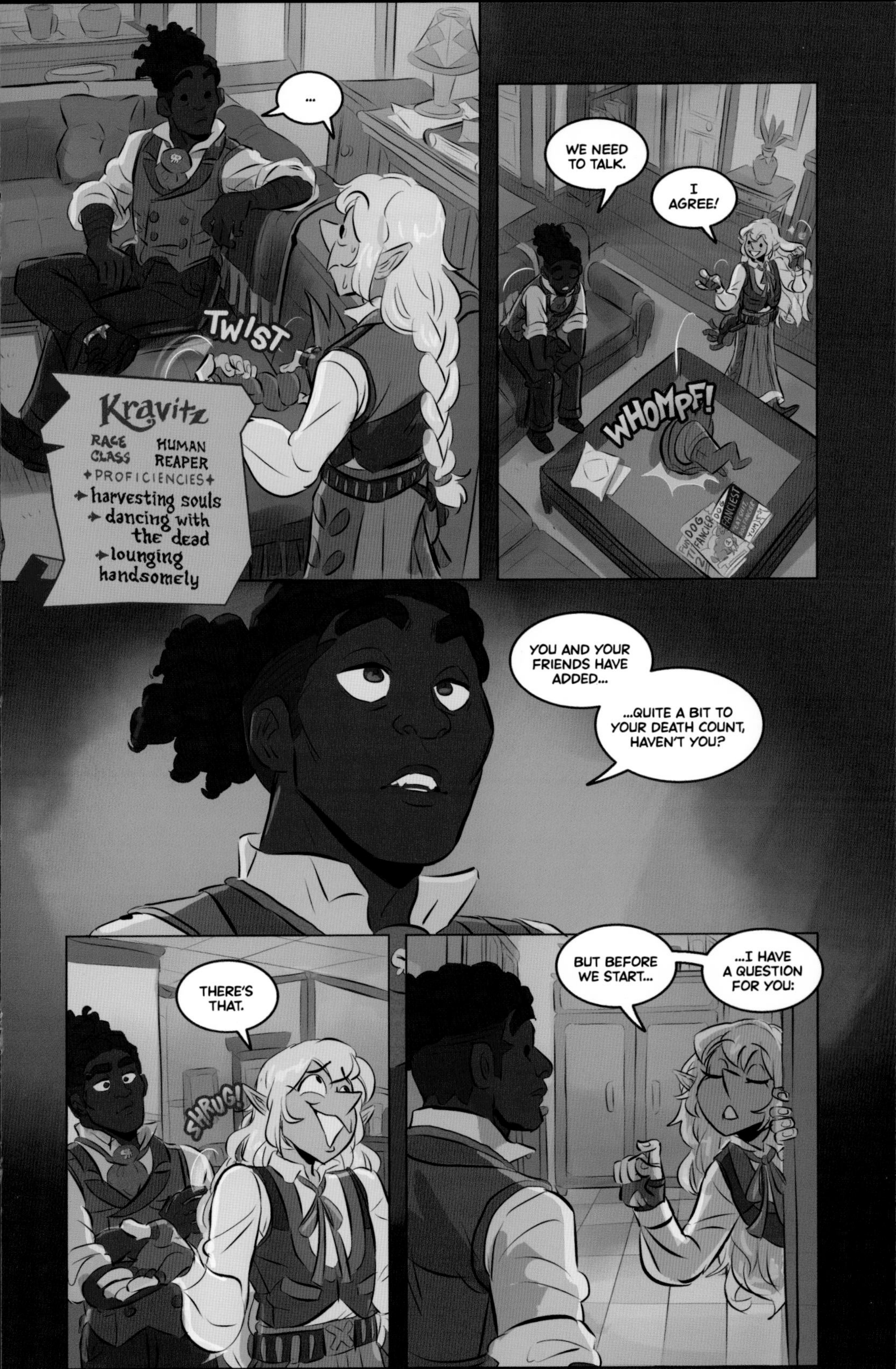
...
TWIST
Kravitz
RACE HUMAN
CLASS REAPER
PROFICIENCIES
harvesting souls
dancing with the dead
lounging handsomely
WE NEED TO TALK.
I AGREE!
WHOMPF!
YOU AND YOUR FRIENDS HAVE ADDED...
...QUITE A BIT TO YOUR DEATH COUNT, HAVEN'T YOU?
THERE'S THAT.
SHRUG!
BUT BEFORE WE START...
...I HAVE A QUESTION FOR YOU:

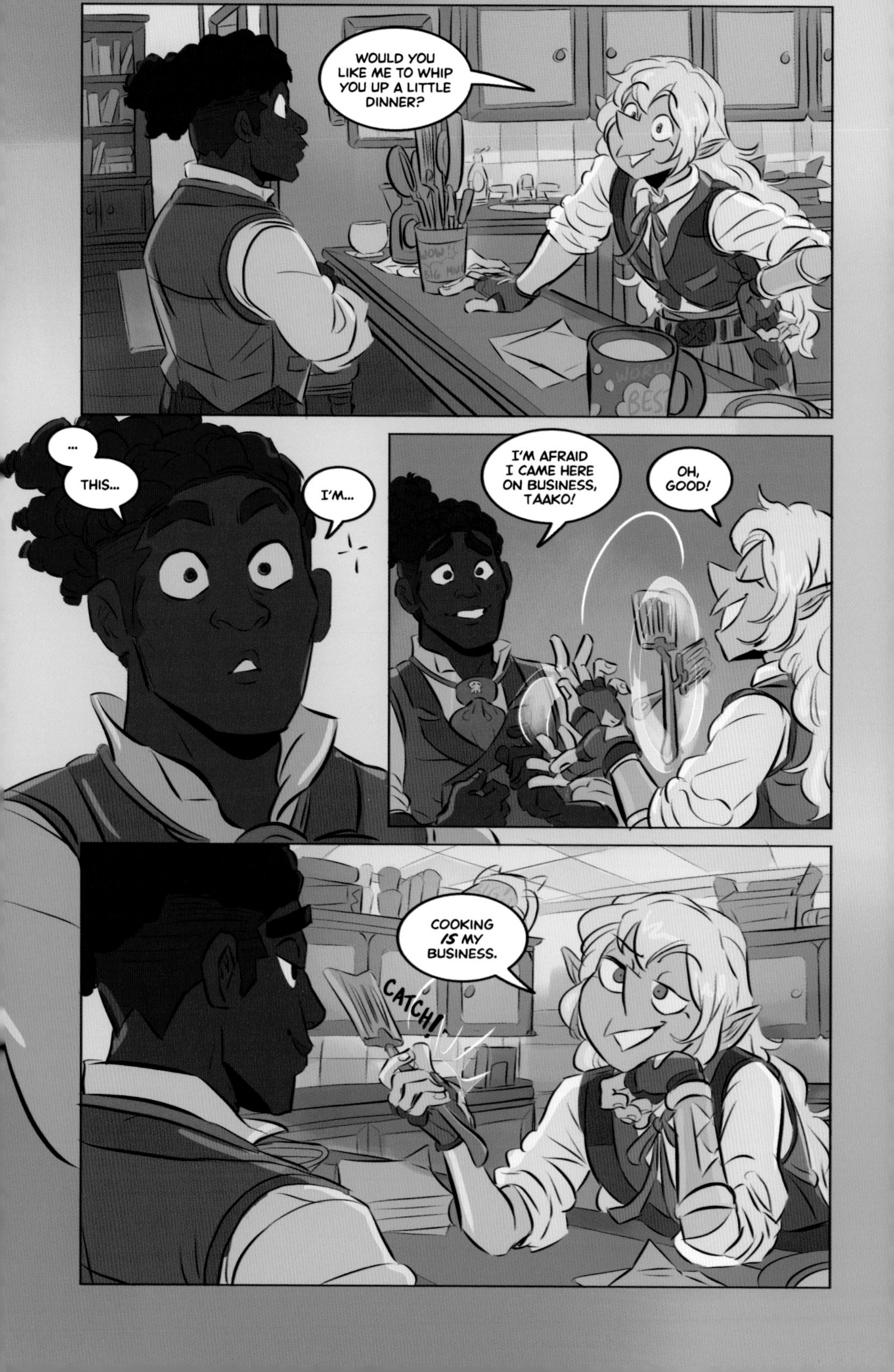
WOULD YOU LIKE ME TO WHIP YOU UP A LITTLE DINNER?
...
THIS...
I'M...
I'M AFRAID I CAME HERE ON BUSINESS, TAAKO!
OH, GOOD!
COOKING *IS* MY BUSINESS.
CATCH!

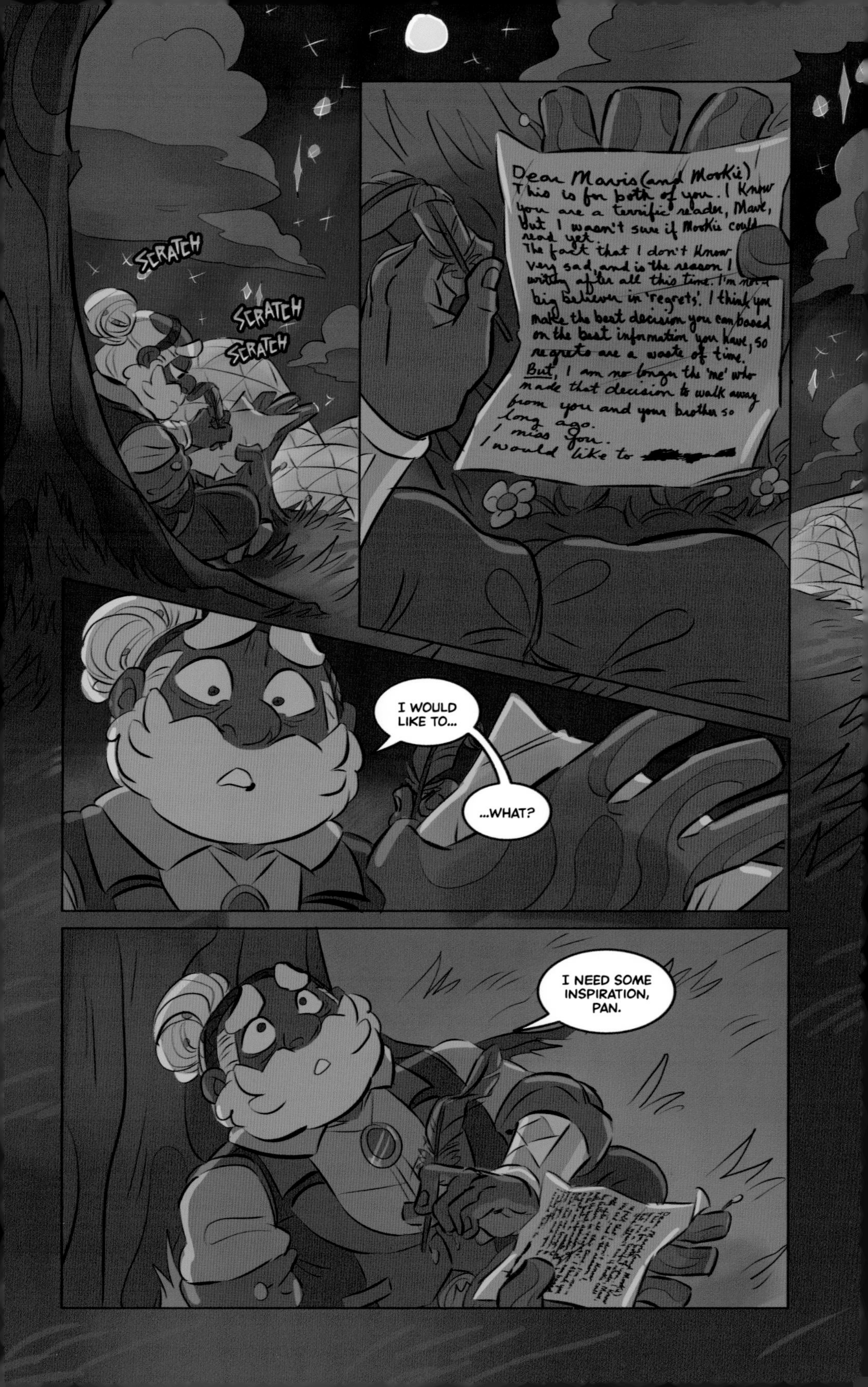

SCRATCH
SCRATCH
SCRATCH
Dear Mavis (and Mookie)
This is for both of you. I know you are a terrific reader, Mave, but I wasn't sure if Mookie could read yet.
The fact that I don't know very sad, and is the reason I writing after all this time. I'm not a big believer in 'regrets'. I think you make the best decision you can based on the best information you have, so regrets are a waste of time.
But, I am no longer the 'me' who made that decision to walk away from you and your brother so long ago.
I miss you.
I would like to
I WOULD LIKE TO...
...WHAT?
I NEED SOME INSPIRATION, PAN.

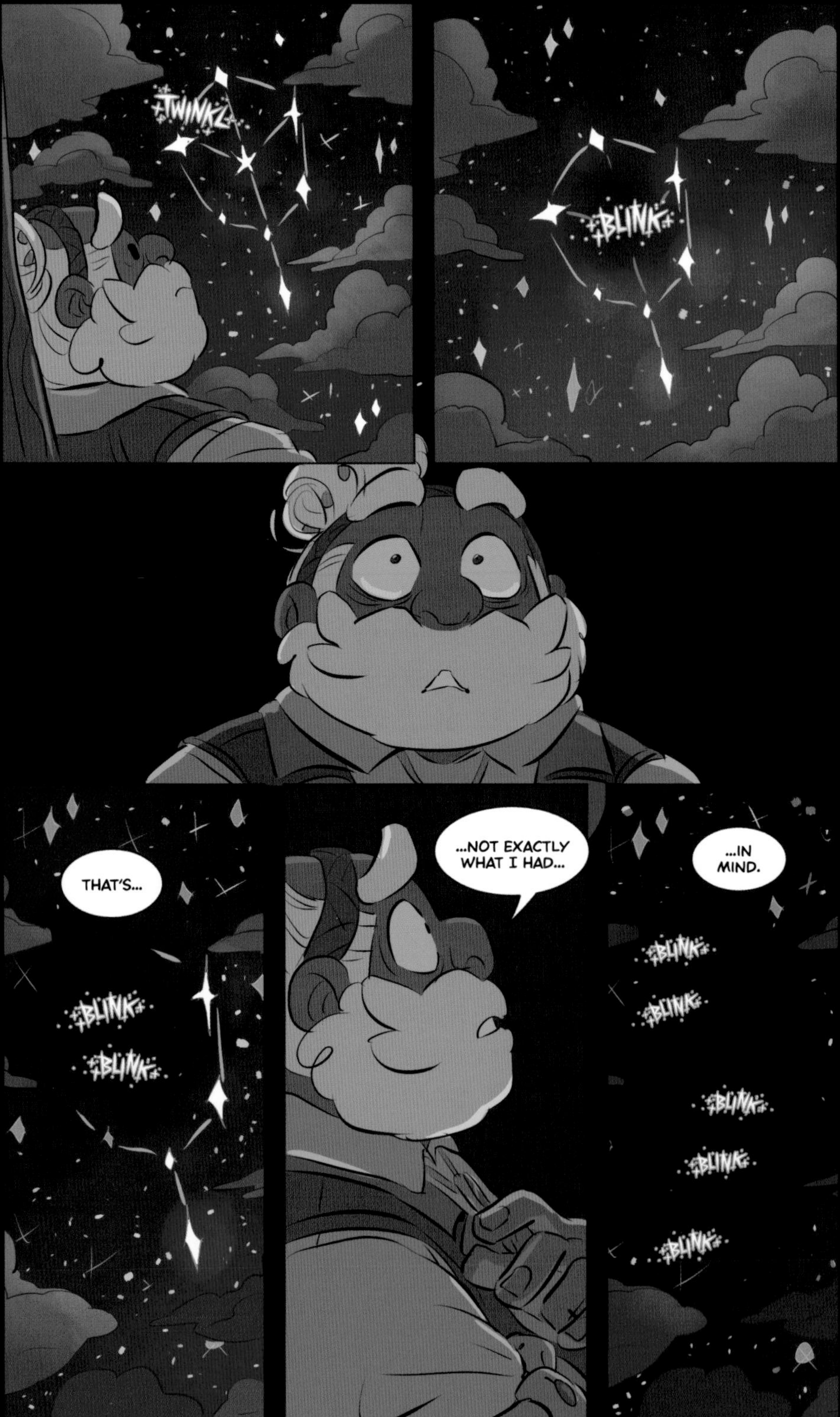
TWINKLE
BLINK
THAT'S...
BLINK
BLINK
...NOT EXACTLY WHAT I HAD...
...IN MIND.
BLINK
BLINK
BLINK
BLINK
BLINK

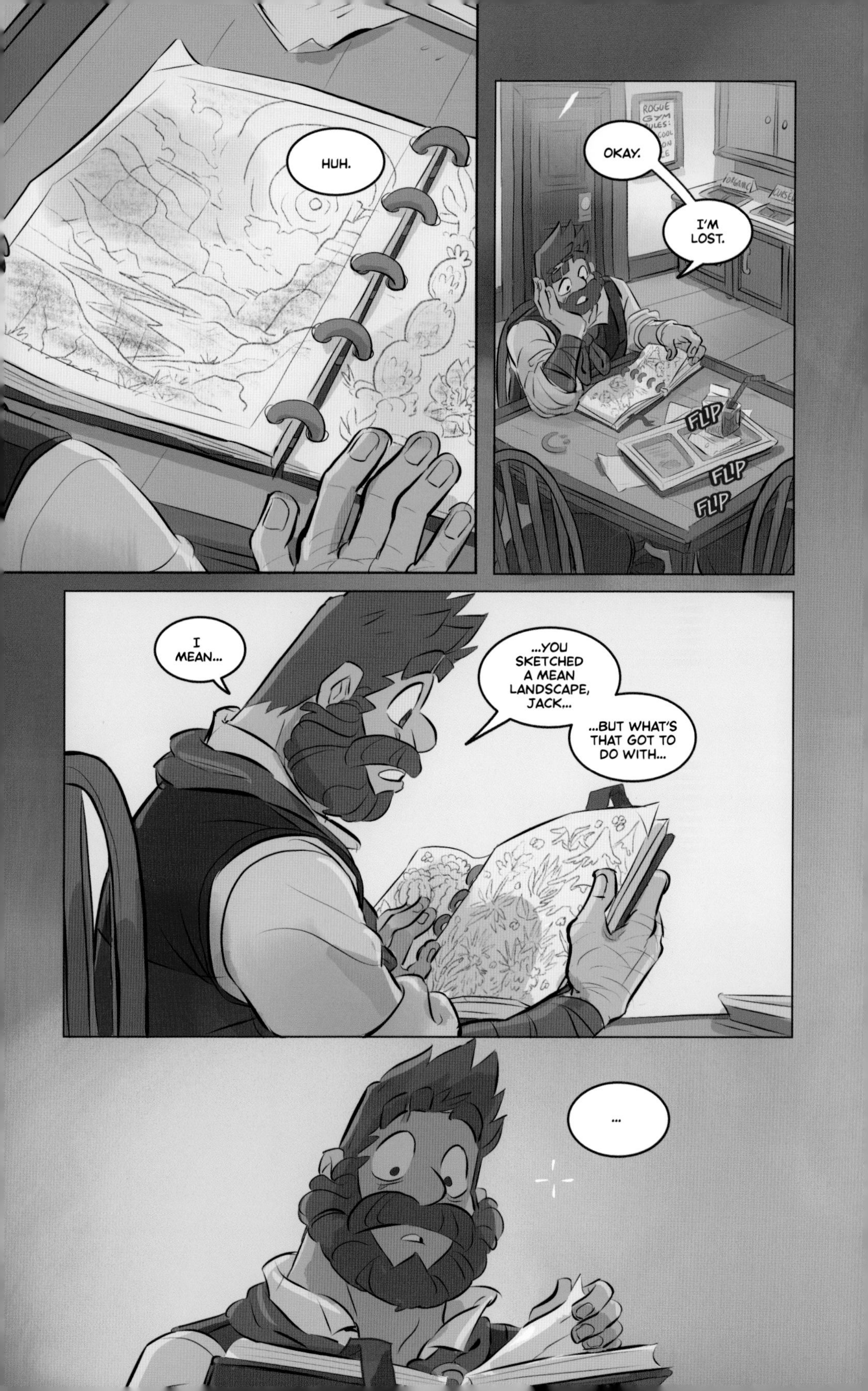
HUH.
ROGUE GYM RULES:
OKAY.
I'M LOST.
FLIP
FLIP
FLIP
I MEAN...
...YOU SKETCHED A MEAN LANDSCAPE, JACK...
...BUT WHAT'S THAT GOT TO DO WITH...
...

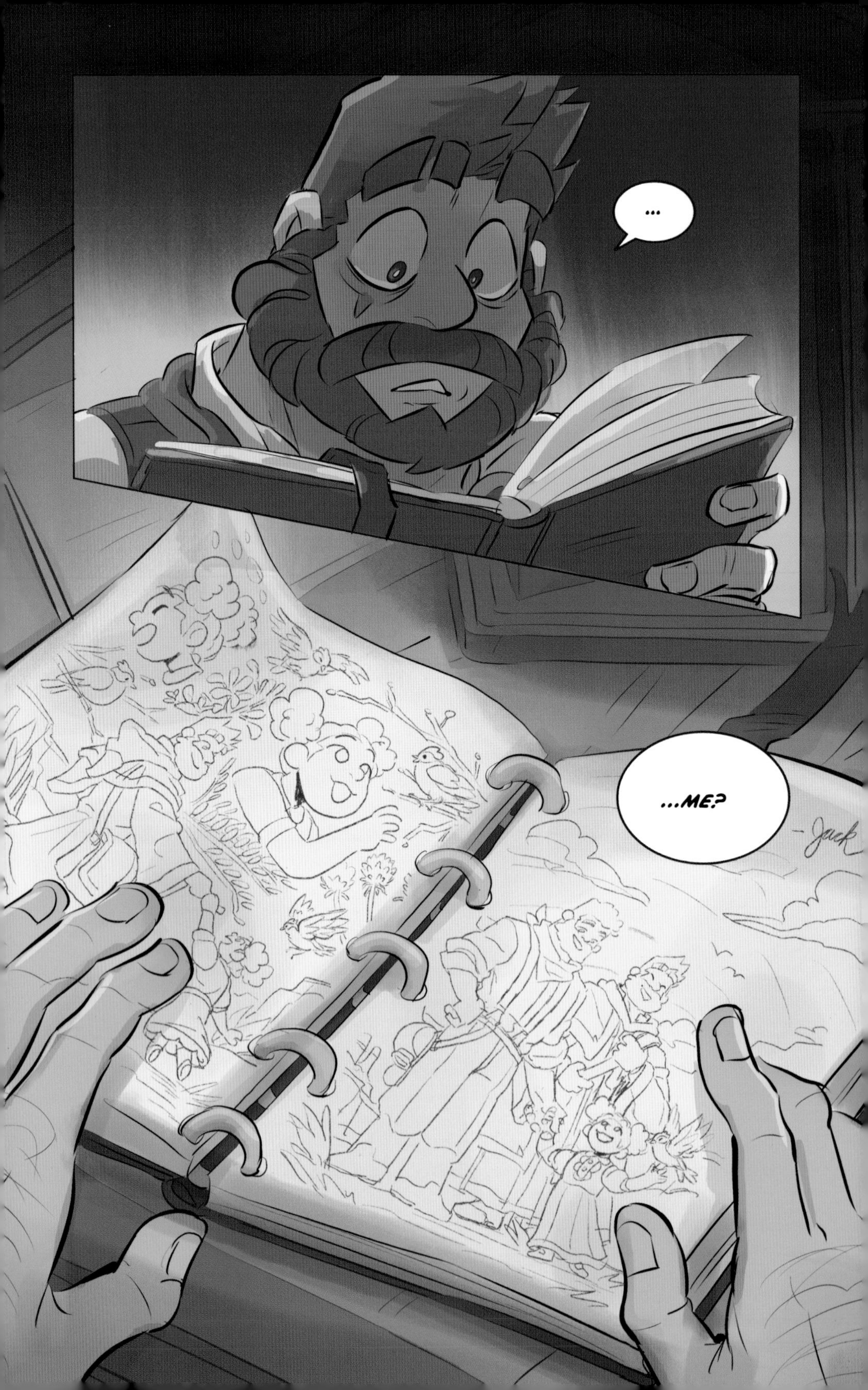
...
...ME?
-Jack

Design Roughs

I had a lot of fun with the designs for this book! Here's a peek at the tiny initial roughs we talked about and revised as a team at the very start of the process.

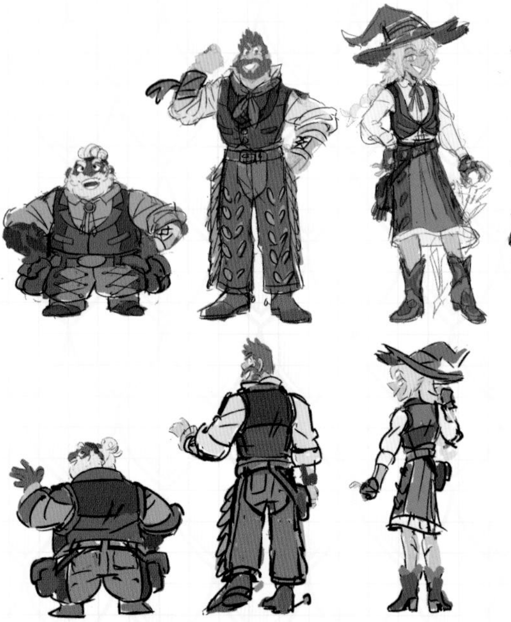

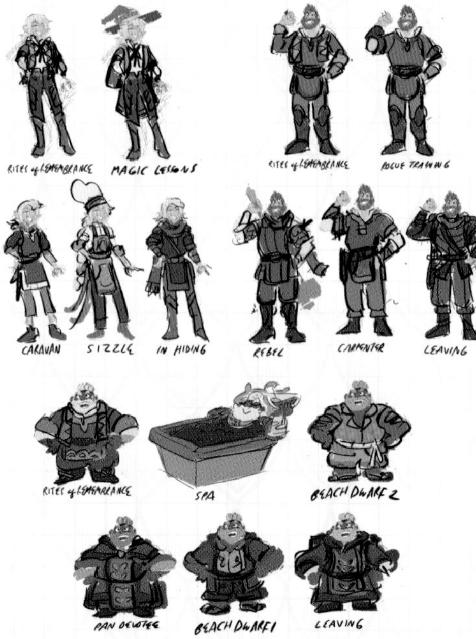
MAGIC LESSONS
CARAVAN
SIZZLE
IN HIDING
REBEL
LEAVING
SPA
BEACH DWARF 2
PAN DEVOTEE
BEACH DWARF 1
LEAVING

Main trio outfits: My favorite fun fact I learned working on research for this book—did you know that all chaps are, by definition, assless?

Flashbacks: I mixed up who got which spa package... Sorry you missed out on the giant pink drink, Merle.

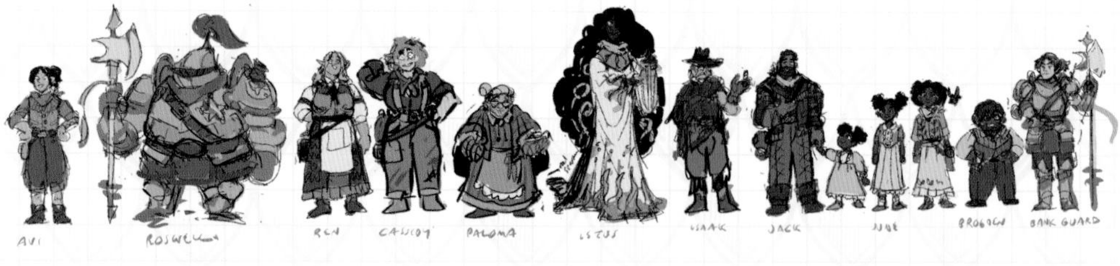
PALOMA
JACK
BANK GUARD

I think I ended up swapping teen June's little belt pouch for her dad's satchel in the final pages, but I want a bag like this one, it's cute.

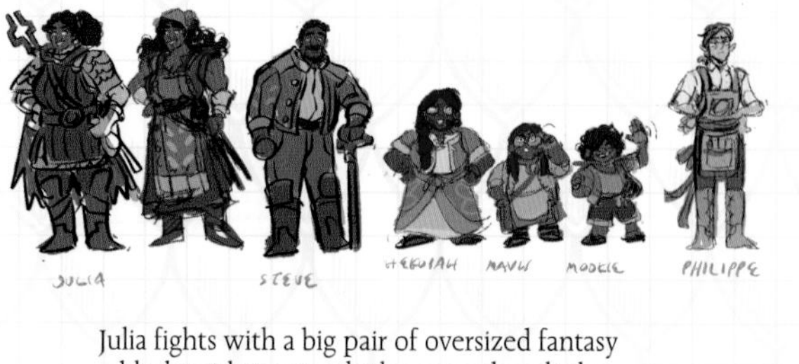
JULIA
STEVE
PHILIPPE

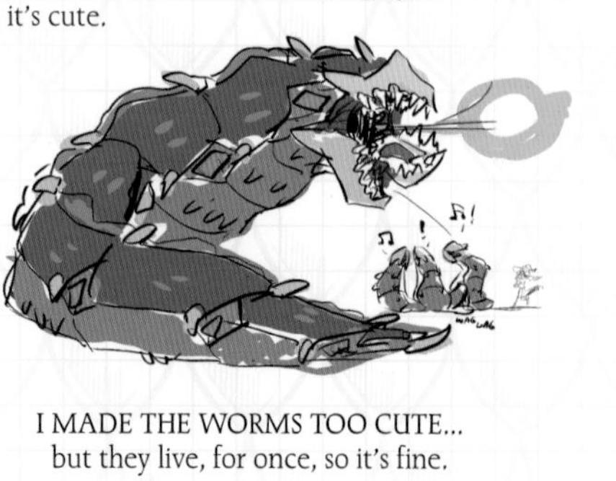

Julia fights with a big pair of oversized fantasy blacksmith tongs, which are maybe a little impractical...but they look very cool, and she's a professional.

I MADE THE WORMS TOO CUTE... but they live, for once, so it's fine.

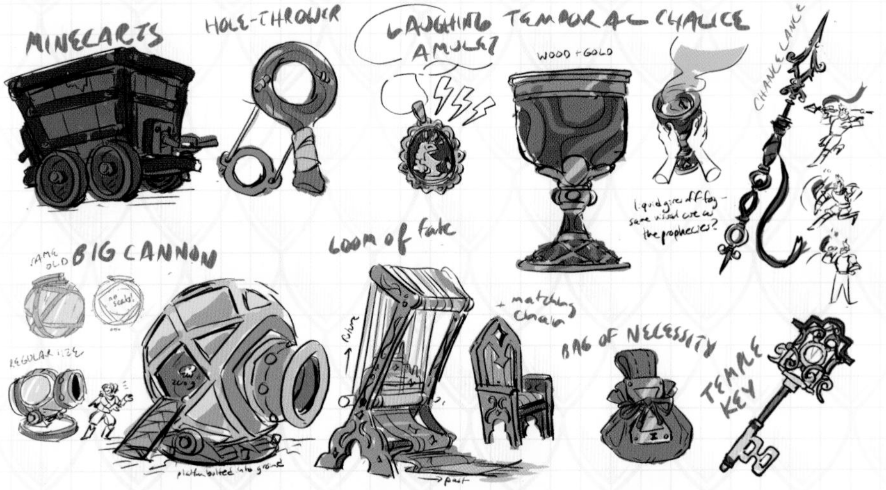
MINECARTS
HOLE-THROWER
LAUGHING AMULET
TEMPORAL CHALICE
WOOD + GOLD
CHANCE LANCE
SAME OLD
BIG CANNON
no scale!
REGULAR SIZE
platform bolted into ground
Loom of fate
future
past
+ matching chair
BAG OF NECESSITY
TEMPLE KEY

Cannon: Tiny Avi, for scale, convincing everyone that this is definitely going to work.

Loom of fate: It's a MAGIC loom, which is why it's missing several parts that would be key to the working of an actual standing handloom. Don't worry about it.

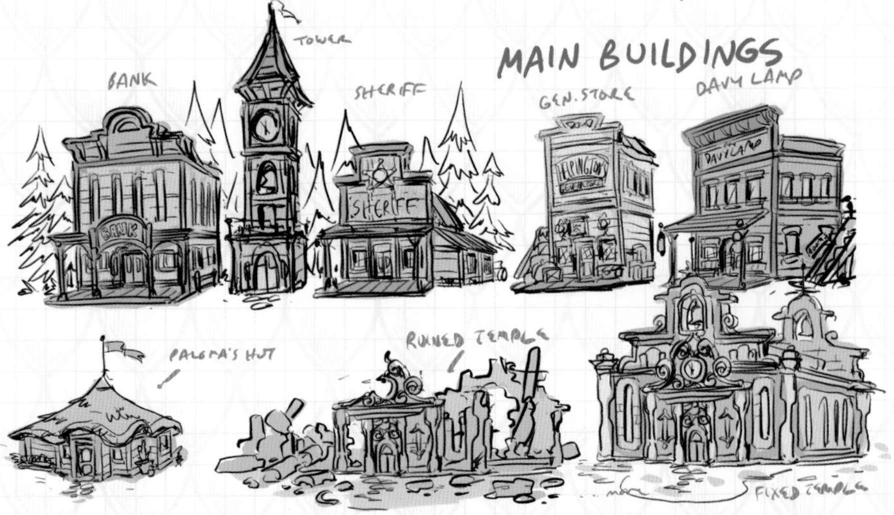
MAIN BUILDINGS
TOWER
BANK
SHERIFF
GEN. STORE
DAVY LAMP
BANK
SHERIFF
PALOMA'S HUT
RUINED TEMPLE
FIXED TEMPLE

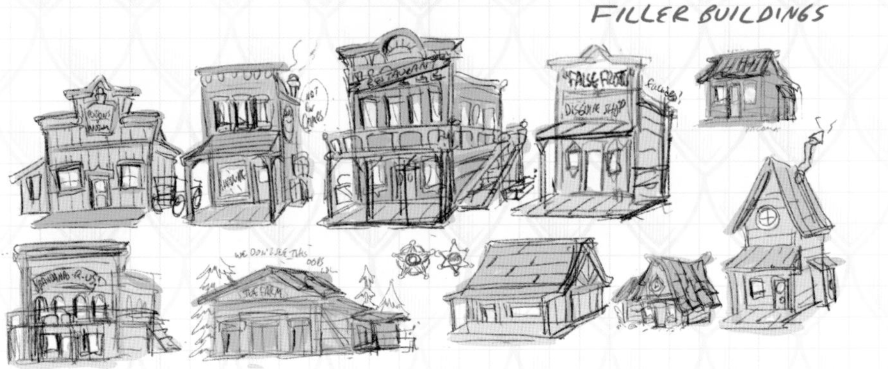
FILLER BUILDINGS
NOT for CHANGES
"FALSE FRONTS"
DISGUISE SHOP
THE FARM

I'm sorry I called you a filler building, False Fronts—you're number one in my heart!

Making Refuge

Everyone's comics process is different, but one of the hardest steps for me is visualizing and staging a physical space full of characters. Making little 2D set drawings has helped in the past, and I wanted to try making 3D models, too... So, for this book, I learned (very basic) Blender! It's FREE (take note, image editing–software giants!) and I highly recommend it. Grant Abbitt's low poly tutorials were a huge help.

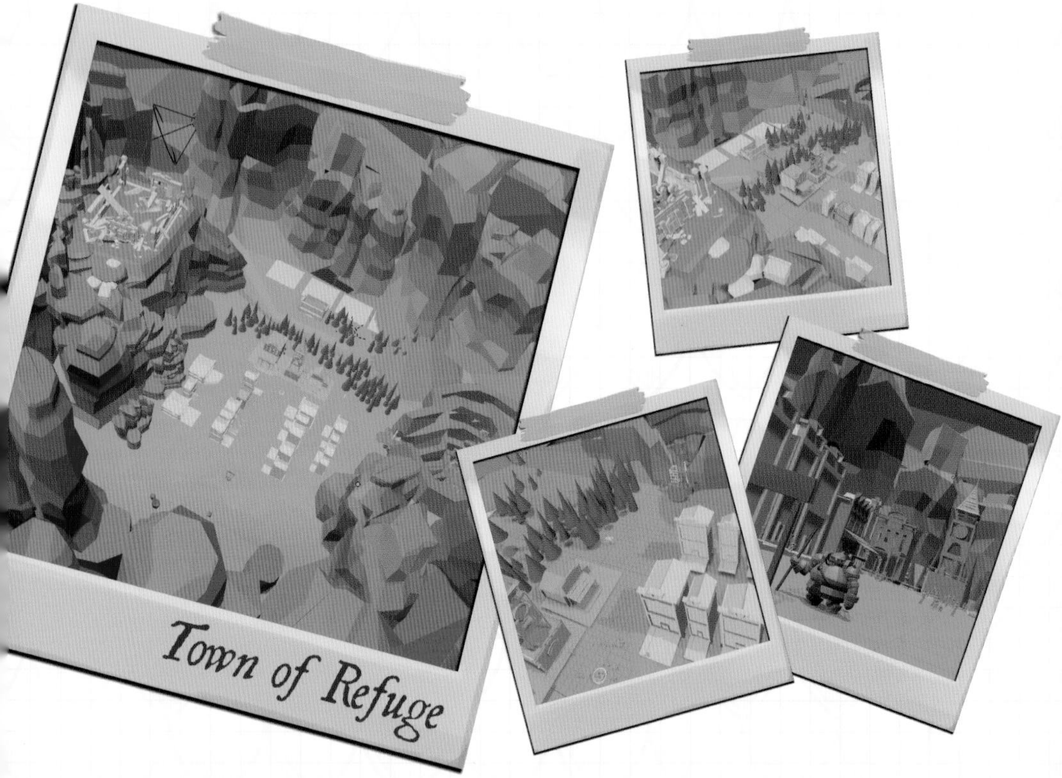
Town of Refuge

Here's a peek at some of the stuff I built. It's very simple, and VERY messy, but it really helped me think about moving characters in space! I had a fun time making it, and I hope this tiny town tour is fun, too.

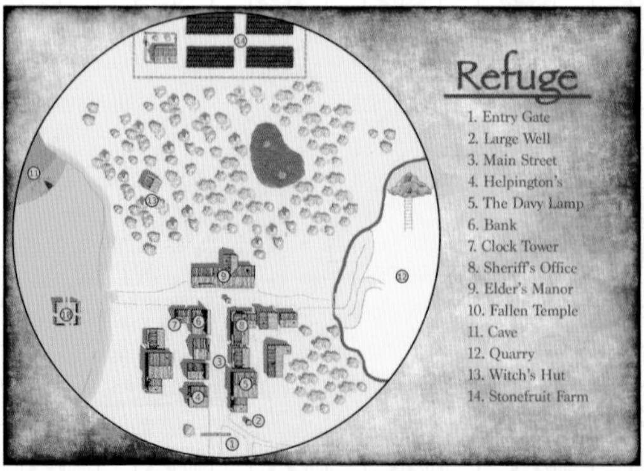
Refuge
1. Entry Gate
2. Large Well
3. Main Street
4. Helpington's
5. The Davy Lamp
6. Bank
7. Clock Tower
8. Sheriff's Office
9. Elder's Manor
10. Fallen Temple
11. Cave
12. Quarry
13. Witch's Hut
14. Stonefruit Farm

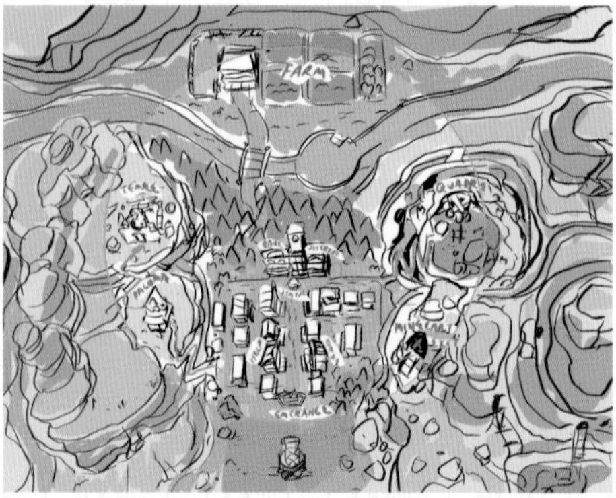
FARM

Refuge map: I love the map Griffin made for Refuge way back when the *Eleventh Hour* arc was first airing—seeing it felt like poring over the town maps in game manuals! We moved some stuff around for the graphic novel; the bank and sheriff's office frame the clock tower now. Getting to build on this foundation made the town design incredibly fun—and much easier! Initial layout plans are a TON of work.

Props: Building these was like making a teacher-sanctioned, handwritten cheat sheet to bring into a test...building something in 3D is a HUGE help in drawing it, because you have a way better understanding of its underlying forms. So, a lot of these, I didn't end up using much!

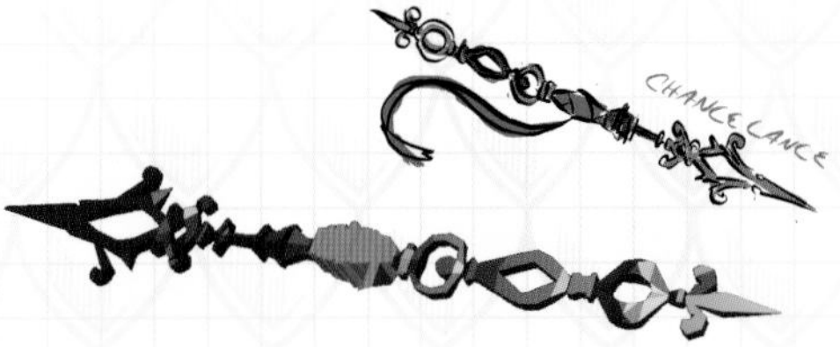
CHANCE LANCE

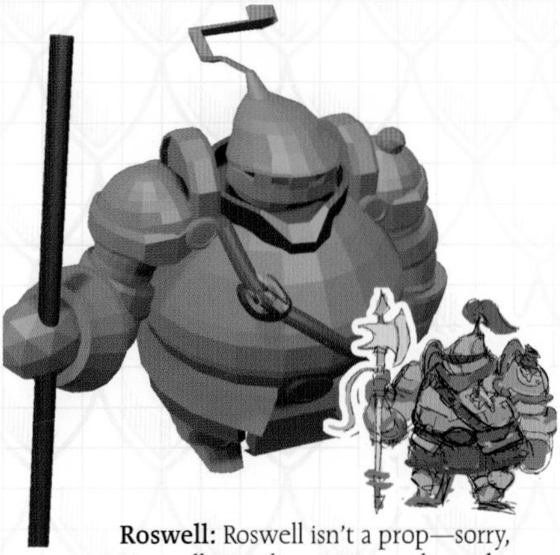

Chance lance: ...Except for the chance lance, which I designed, built, and then just dropped into pencils to ink right over. Have you seen how complicated this thing is??? Life is short, deadlines are tight, and wrist health is finite!

Roswell: Roswell isn't a prop—sorry, Roswell! But they ARE mostly made of inorganic materials, and it was helpful to build them out so I could get a handle on their particular orb arrangement.

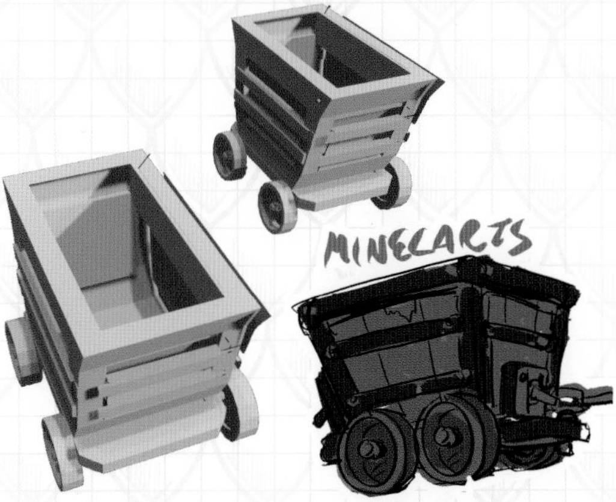
MINECARTS

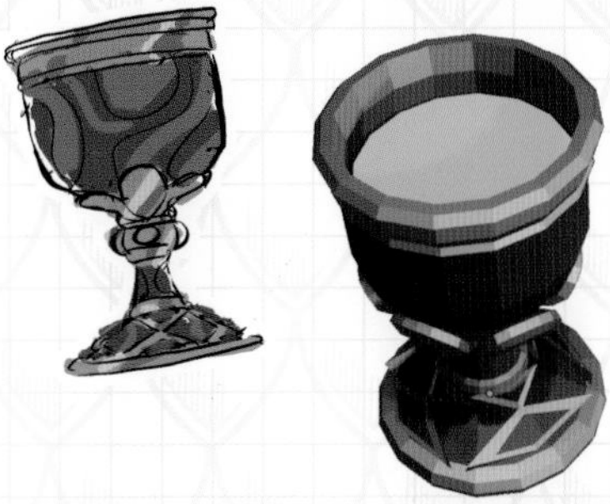

Minecarts: As I was building these, I received a psychic transmission from a version of myself in an alternate time line, where I learned Blender BEFORE drawing the battlewagon race in *Petals*. It went like this: LMFAOOOOO.

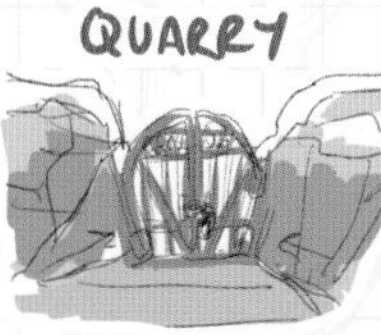
QUARRY

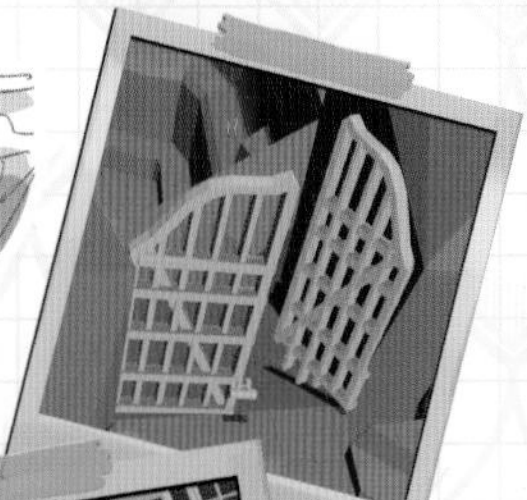

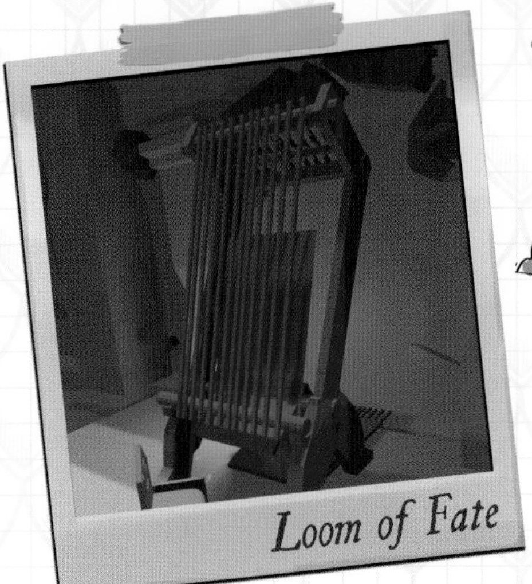
Loom of Fate

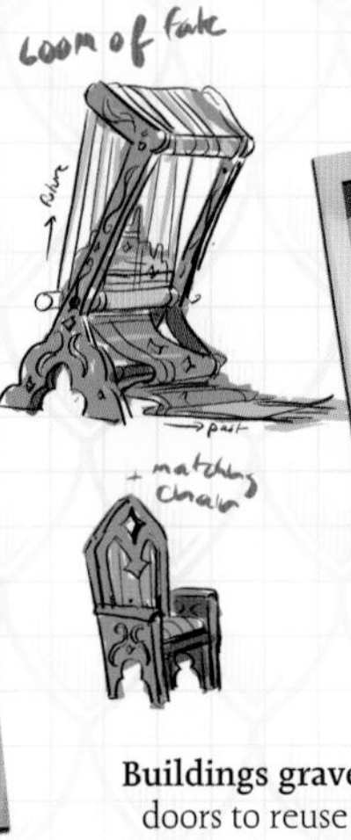
Loom of fate
+ matching chair

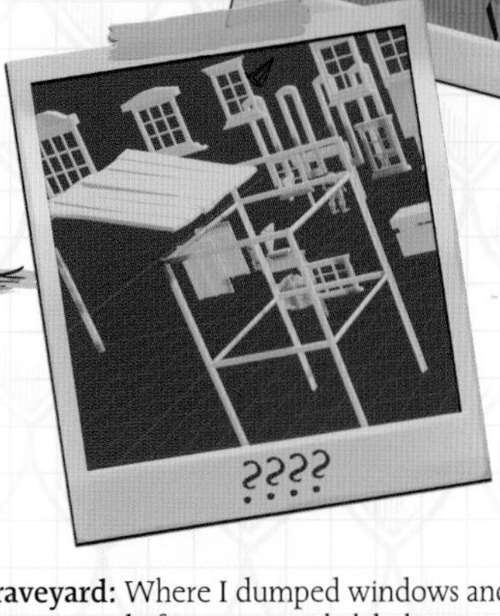
????

Buildings graveyard: Where I dumped windows and doors to reuse instead of just...properly labeling my objects. This is terrible file management. But it was fun!

Buildings

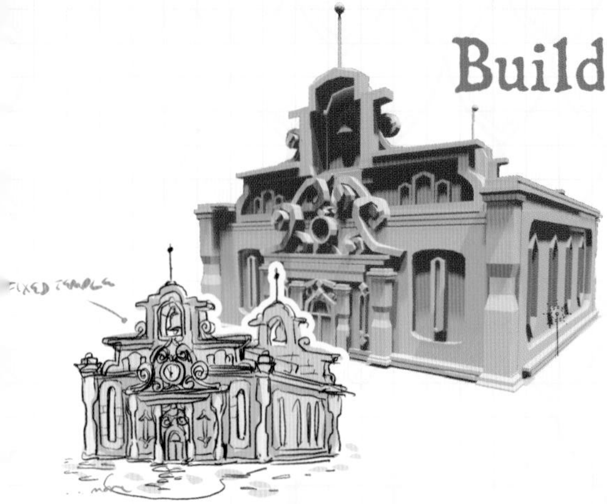
FIXED TEMPLE

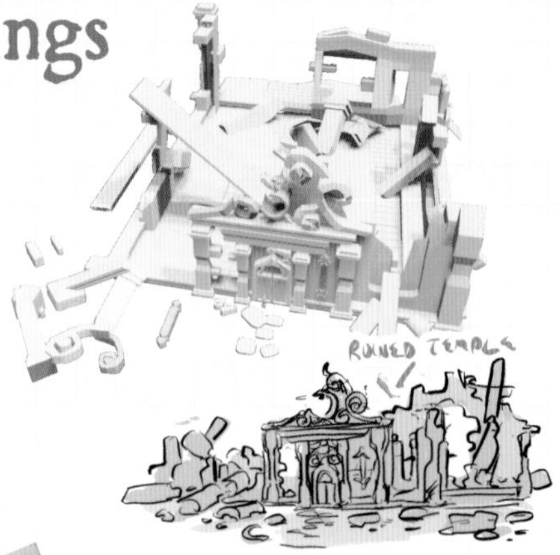
RUINED TEMPLE

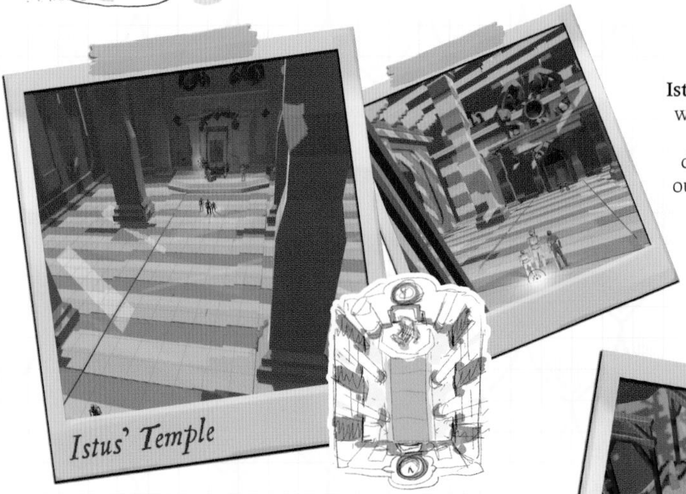
Istus' Temple

Istus' Temple: I had to come up with a lot more broken temple bits on the page, because it didn't look convincingly cast-out-of-time. It was fun to break the model, though!

Mineshaft: All those supports... If I was being kinder to myself, this would've been a flat-walled cylinder held up by, IDK, magic... But sometimes we have to suffer a LITTLE for art.

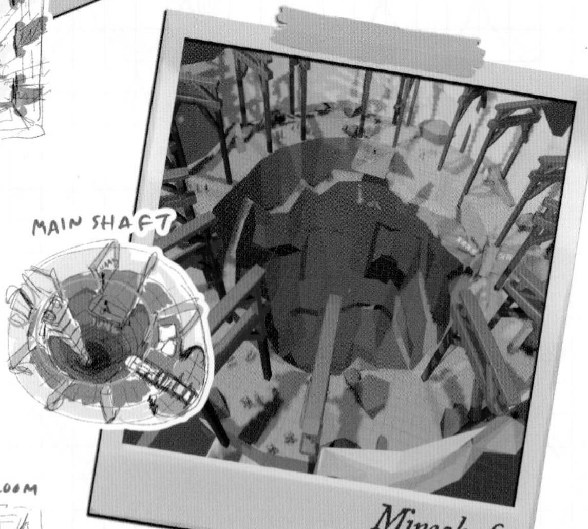
MAIN SHAFT
Mineshaft

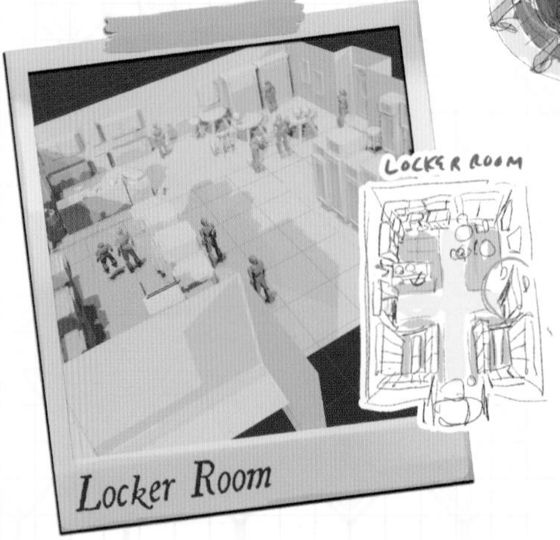
LOCKER ROOM
Locker Room

Locker room: I was originally going to build a whole alphabet's worth of tall lockers into this set, but it messed with the staging too much! Technically, all twenty-six are still in there, they're just...very small and obscured.

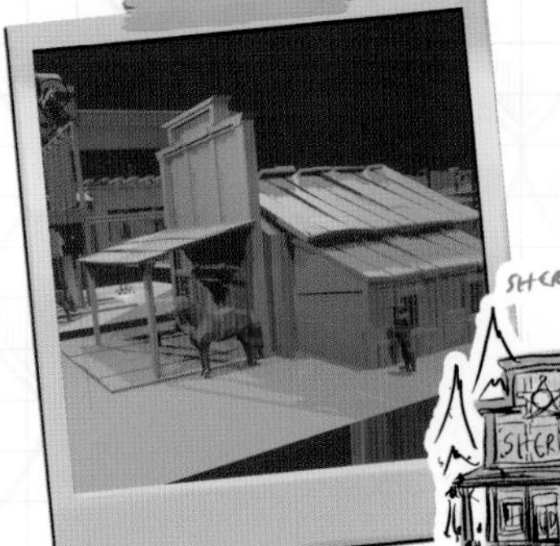

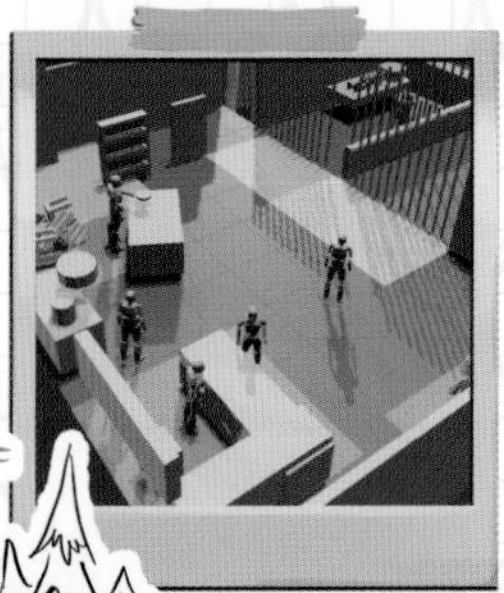

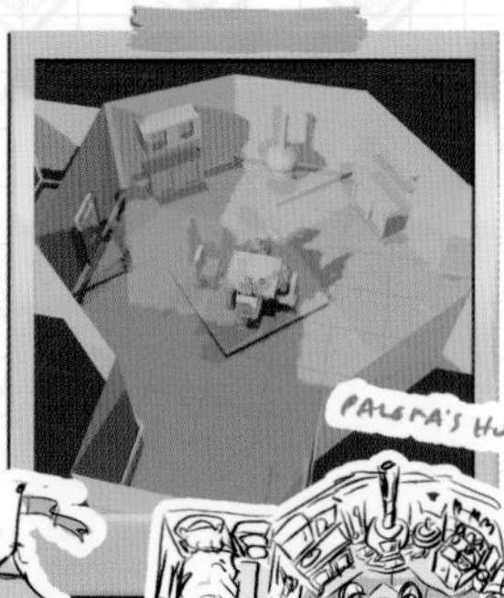

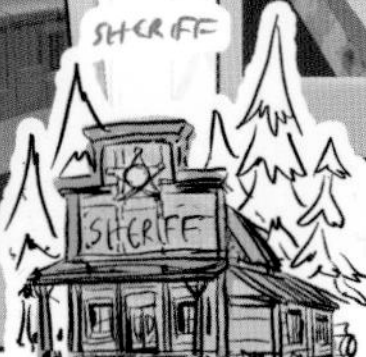
SHERIFF
SHERIFF

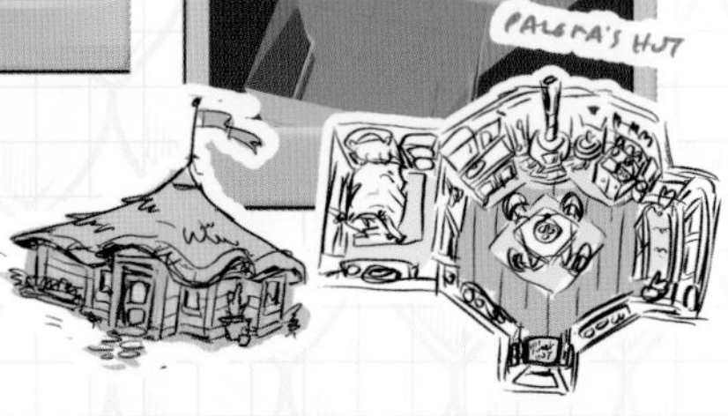

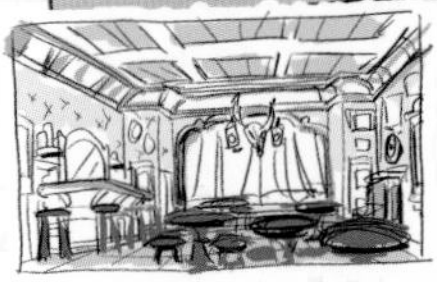

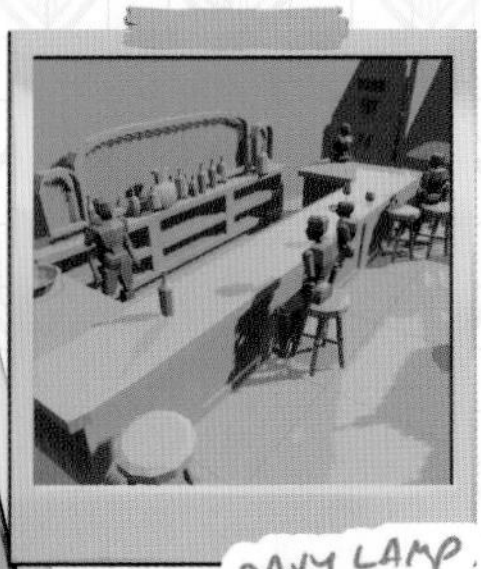

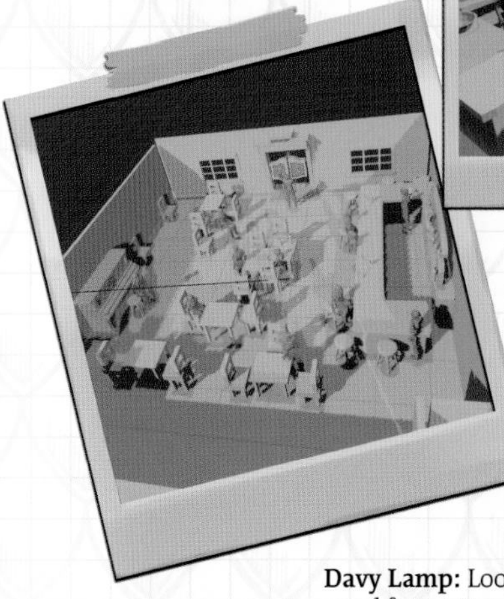

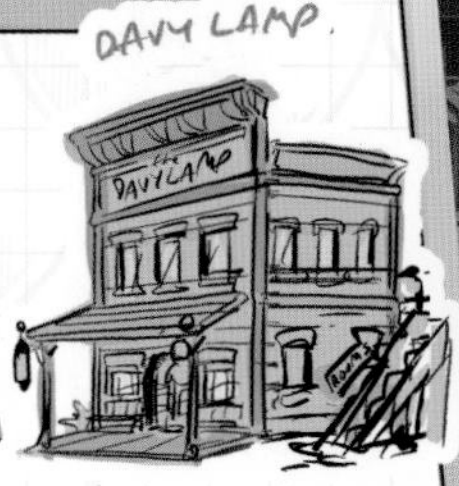
DAVY LAMP.
DAVY LAMP

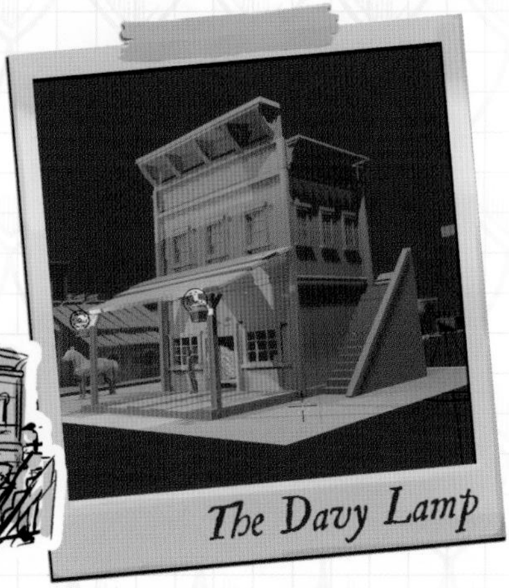
The Davy Lamp

Davy Lamp: Look at its cute exterior stair setup...that I forgot...to draw...in the book... and forgot I made...until this very moment... This is a secret only between me, who made it, and you, a person who read the whole book already. No take-backs.

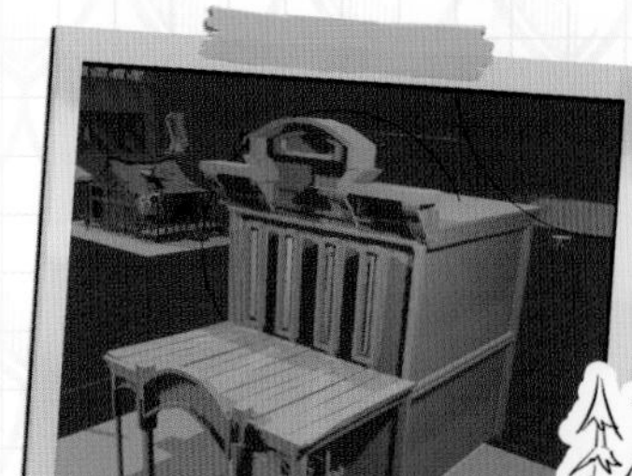
Refuge Savings and Loan

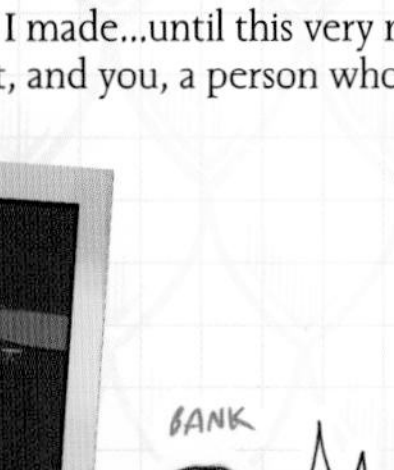
BANK
BANK

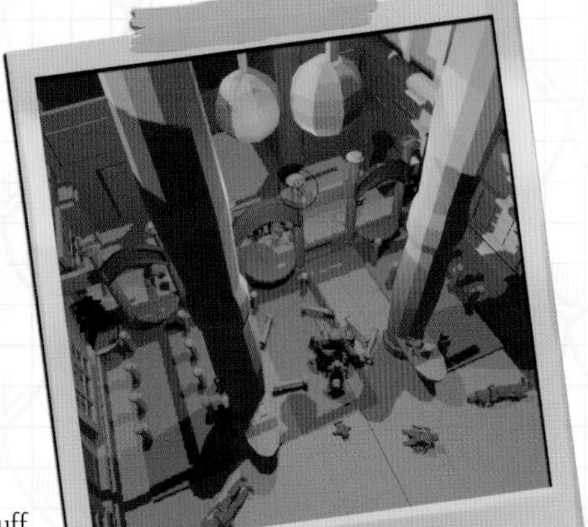

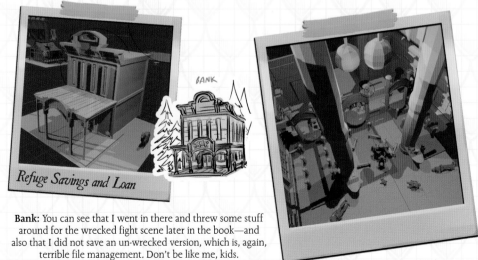

Bank: You can see that I went in there and threw some stuff around for the wrecked fight scene later in the book—and also that I did not save an un-wrecked version, which is, again, terrible file management. Don't be like me, kids.

Flashbacks

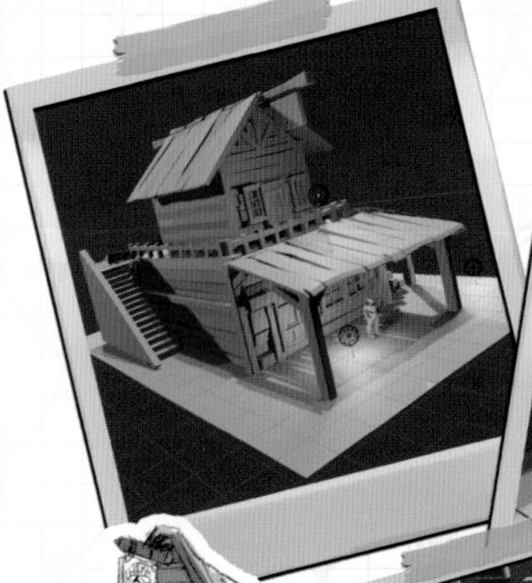

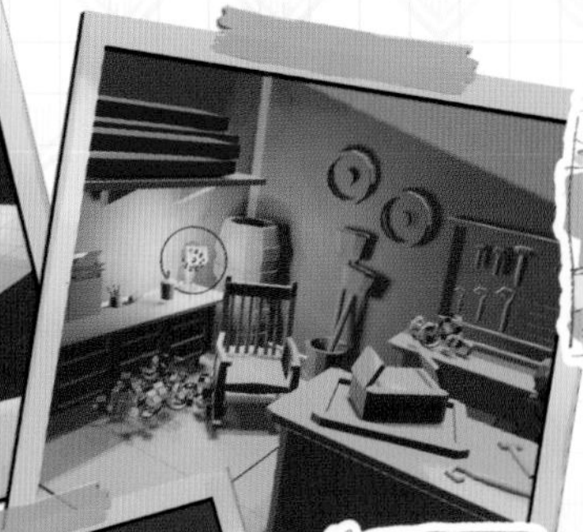

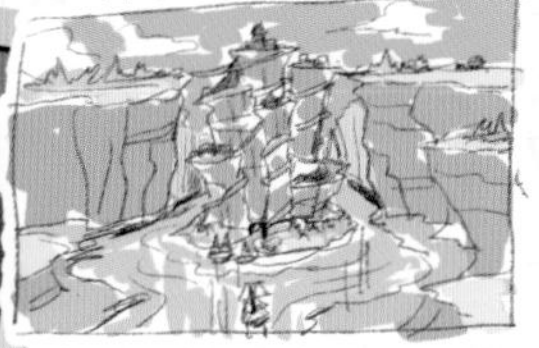
RAVEN'S ROOST

Hammer and Tongs: This is one of my favorite cute sets! I have very fond memories of making all those little wood shavings...as a way to procrastinate on thumbnails.

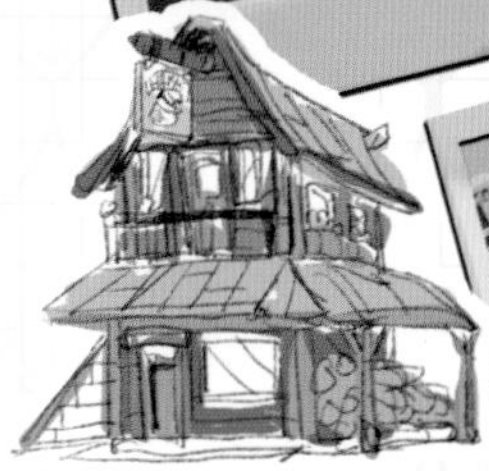
HAMMER + TONGS

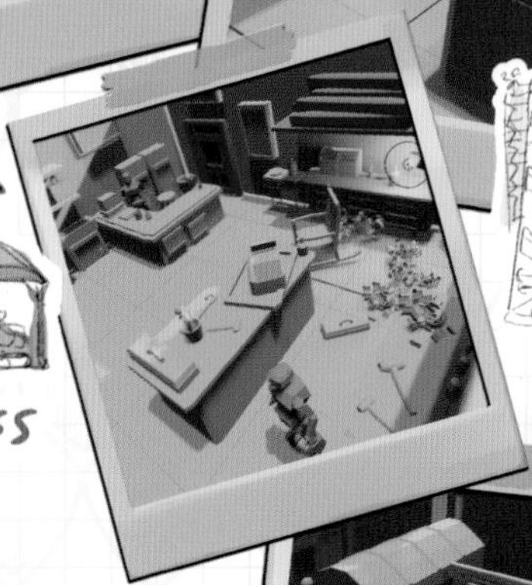

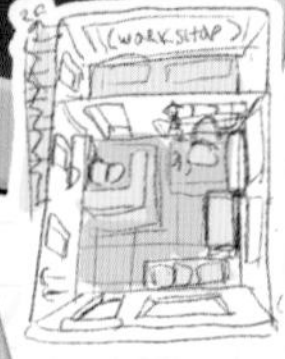
WORKSHOP

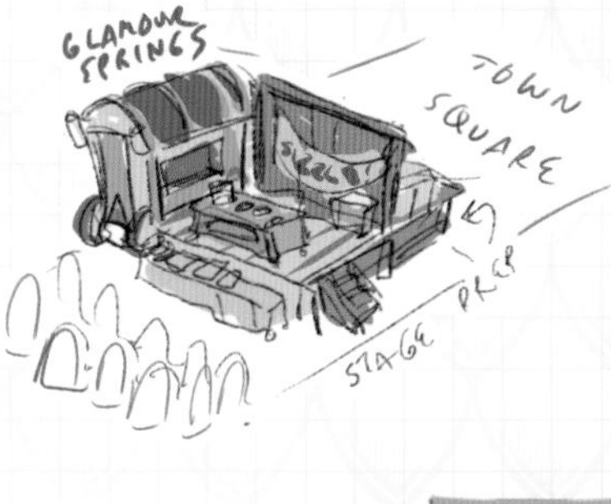
GLAMOUR SPRINGS
TOWN SQUARE
STAGE PREP

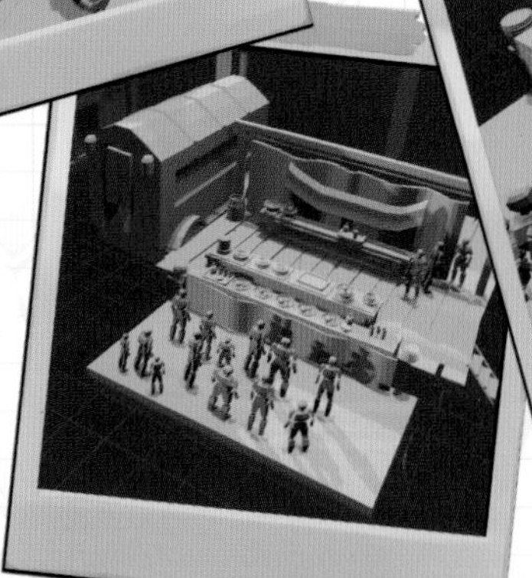

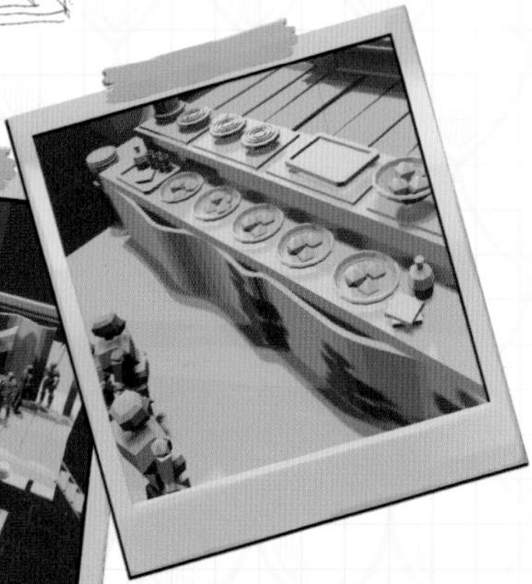

***Sizzle It Up* pageant wagon:** Wow, what's that dish everyone's enjoying...? Looks like a nice, tasty...pile of icospheres.

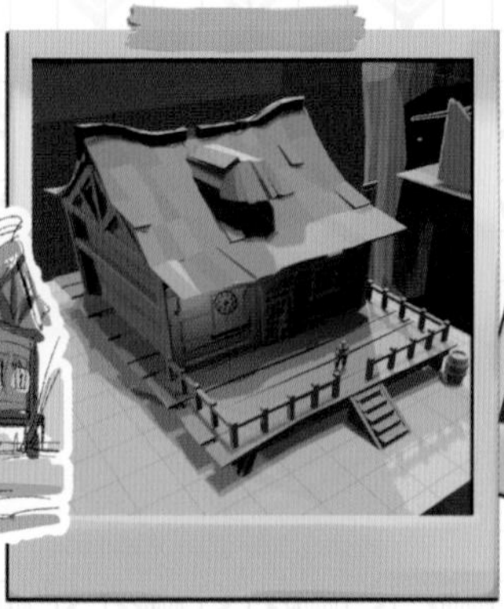
ON STILTS!

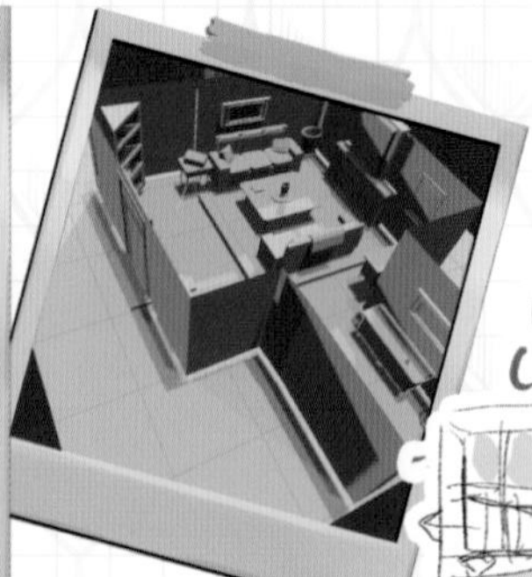

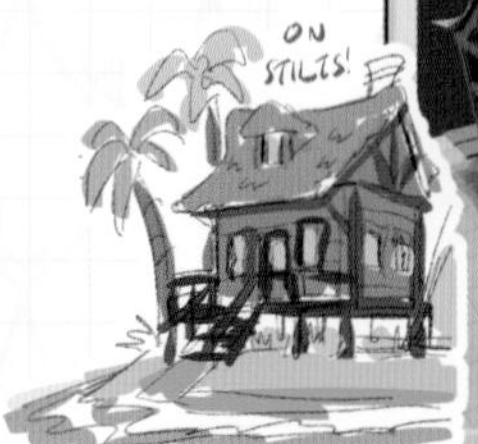

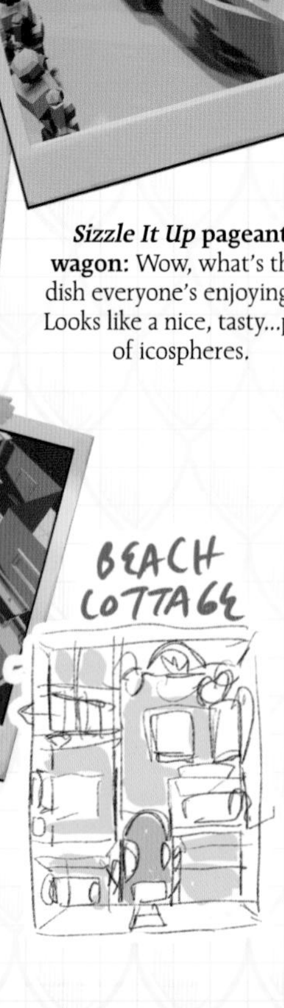
BEACH COTTAGE

Merle's beach cottage: This got a whole little interior set, even though we never see it! That's how you know I built it before March 2020, when I had spare brain space for frivolities.

B.O.B.

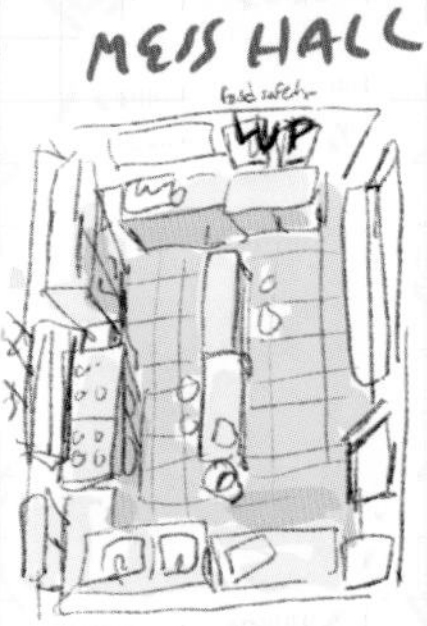
MESS HALL

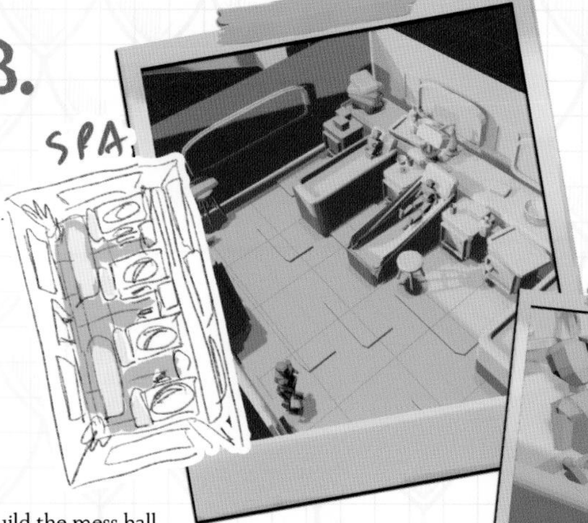
SPA

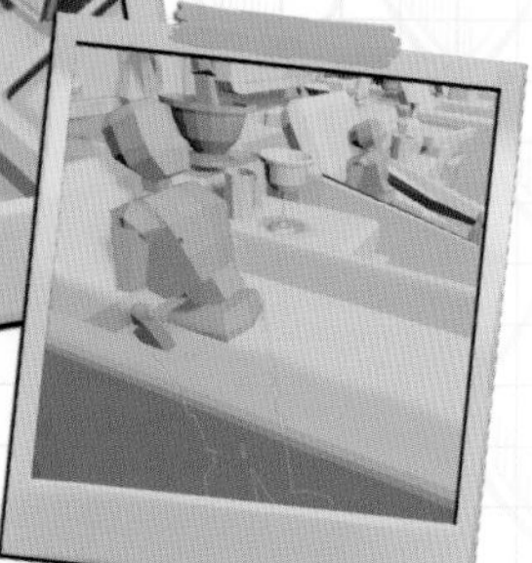

The spa: If you look a little too closely at this set, you can see that the models are a mess and are clipping straight through the too-tall bathtubs… Let's move on.

The mess hall: I didn't build the mess hall because it was March 2020. See Merle's beach cottage note.

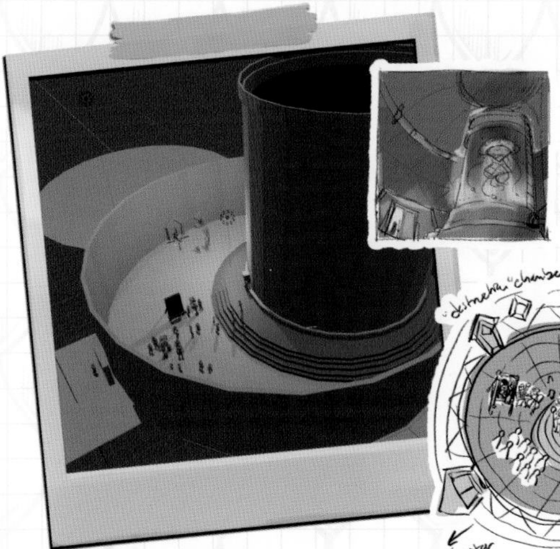

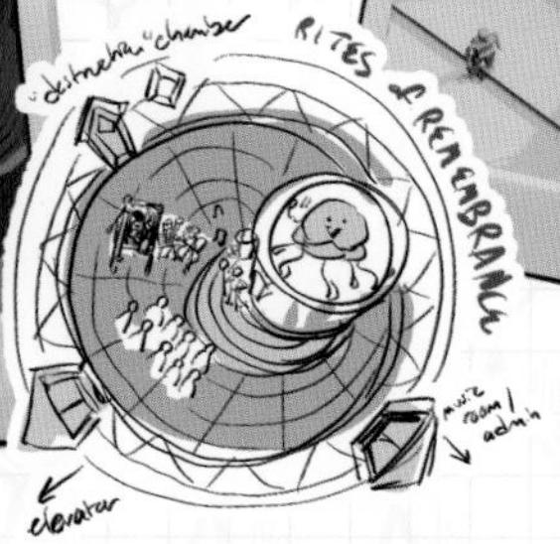
RITES of REMEMBRANCE
elevator

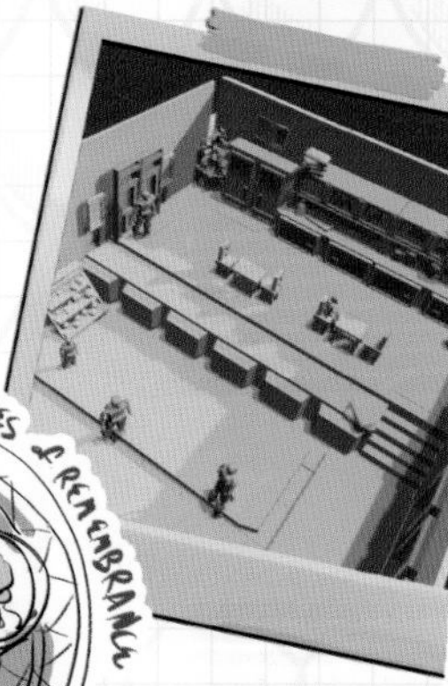

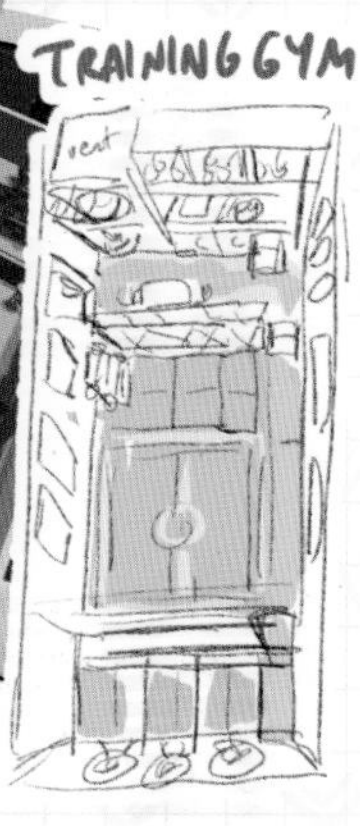
TRAINING GYM

New dorm: This is a GIANT apartment because I live in NYC, and I gotta experience the thrill of oversized living space SOMEhow.

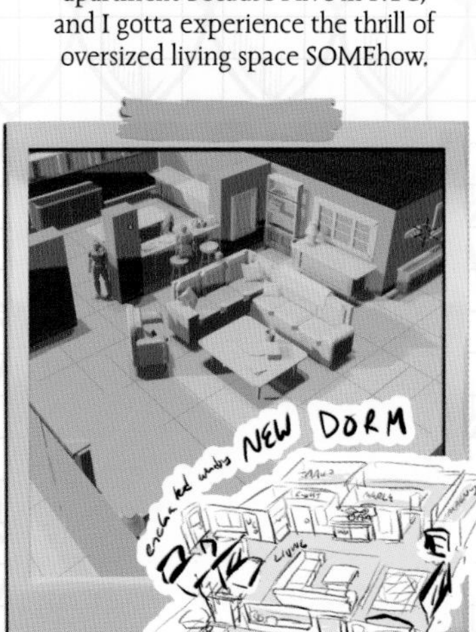

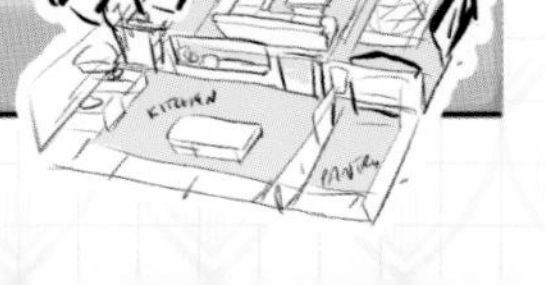
NEW DORM
KITCHEN

Building 3D sets can be a really cool part of making comics! There are lots of ways to do it—Roomstyler, Google SketchUp, paper dioramas, whatever works for you. Some big-brain geniuses, with WAY stronger willpower than me, even work in *Animal Crossing!* I'm excited to find ways to use Blender in my comics-making toolbox in the future…and to build more little virtual dollhouses, just for fun.

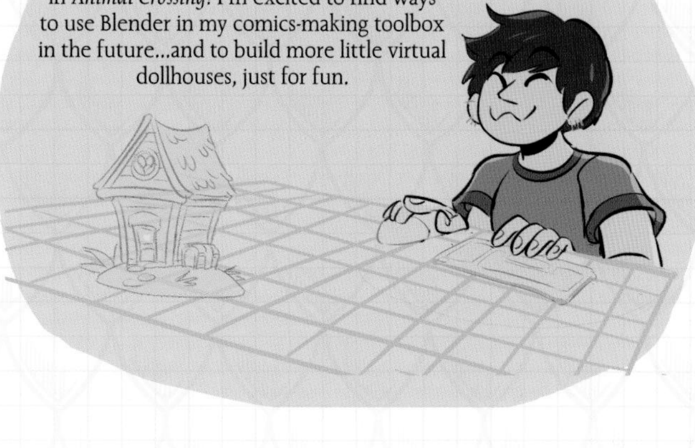

The ADVENTURE CONTINUES in

The Suffering
Game

Coming Soon!